Contributions to Management Science

Reza Zanjirani Farahani • Masoud Hekmatfar
Editors

Facility Location

Concepts, Models, Algorithms
and Case Studies

Physica-Verlag

Editors
Dr. Reza Zanjirani Farahani
Centre for Maritime Studies
National University of Singapore
Singapore
cmszfr@nus.edu.sg

Masoud Hekmatfar
Amirkabir University of Technology
Department of Industrial Engineering
Iran
hekmatfar@aut.ac.ir

ISSN 1431-1941
ISBN 978-3-7908-2150-5   e-ISBN 978-3-7908-2151-2
DOI 10.1007/978-3-7908-2151-2
Springer Dordrecht Heidelberg London New York

Library of Congress Control Number: 2009922331

© Springer-Verlag Berlin Heidelberg 2009
This work is subject to copyright. All rights are reserved, whether the whole or part of the material is concerned, specifically the rights of translation, reprinting, reuse of illustrations, recitation, broadcasting, reproduction on microfilm or in any other way, and storage in data banks. Duplication of this publication or parts thereof is permitted only under the provisions of the German Copyright Law of September 9, 1965, in its current version, and permission for use must always be obtained from Springer. Violations are liable to prosecution under the German Copyright Law.
The use of general descriptive names, registered names, trademarks, etc. in this publication does not imply, even in the absence of a specific statement, that such names are exempt from the relevant protective laws and regulations and therefore free for general use.

Cover design: WMXDesign GmbH, Heidelberg, Germany

Printed on acid-free paper

Physica-Verlag is a brand of Springer-Verlag Berlin Heidelberg
Springer-Verlag is part of Springer Science+Business Media (www.springer.com)

To
Professor Zvi Drezner,
to whom we are greatly indebted for his
generous scientific contribution in the area of
Facility Location

Contents

Introduction 1

1 Distance Functions in Location Problems 5
   Marzie Zarinbal

2 An Overview of Complexity Theory 19
   Milad Avazbeigi

3 Single Facility Location Problem 37
   Esmaeel Moradi and Morteza Bidkhori

4 Multifacility Location Problem 69
   Farzaneh Daneshzand and Razieh Shoeleh

5 Location Allocation Problem 93
   Zeinab Azarmand and Ensiyeh Neishabouri Jami

6 Quadratic Assignment Problem 111
   Masoumeh Bayat and Mahdieh Sedghi

7 Covering Problem 145
   Hamed Fallah, Ali NaimiSadigh, and Marjan Aslanzadeh

8 Median Location Problem 177
   Masoomeh Jamshidi

9 Center Problem 193
   Maryam Biazaran and Bahareh SeyediNezhad

10 Hierarchical Location Problem 219
   Sara Bastani and Narges Kazemzadeh

11	**Hub Location Problem**	243
	Masoud Hekmatfar and Mirsaman Pishvaee	
12	**Competitive Location Problem**	271
	Mohammad Javad Karimifar, Mohammad Khalighi Sikarudi, Esmaeel Moradi, and Morteza Bidkhori	
13	**Warehouse Location Problem**	295
	Zeinab Bagherpoor, Shaghayegh Parhizi, Mahtab Hoseininia, Nooshin Heidari, and Reza Ghasemi Yaghin	
14	**Obnoxious Facility Location**	315
	Sara Hosseini and Ameneh Moharerhaye Esfahani	
15	**Dynamic Facility Location Problem**	347
	Reza Zanjirani Farahani, Maryam Abedian, and Sara Sharahi	
16	**Multi-Criteria Location Problem**	373
	Masoud Hekmatfar and Maryam SteadieSeifi	
17	**Location-Routing Problem**	395
	Anahita Hassanzadeh, Leyla Mohseninezhad, Ali Tirdad, Faraz Dadgostari, and Hossein Zolfagharinia	
18	**Storage System Layout**	419
	Javad Behnamian and Babak Eghtedari	
19	**Location-Inventory Problem**	451
	Mohamadreza Kaviani	
20	**Facility Location in Supply Chain**	473
	Meysam Alizadeh	
21	**Classification of Location Models and Location Softwares**	505
	Sajedeh Tafazzoli and Marzieh Mozafari	
22	**Demand Point Aggregation Analysis for Location Models**	523
	Ali NaimiSadigh and Hamed Fallah	

Appendix: Metaheuristic Methods 535
Zohre Khoban and Saeed Ghadimi

Index 545

Introduction

The mathematical science of facility locating has attracted much attention in discrete and continuous optimization over nearly last four decades. Investigators have focused on both algorithms and formulations in diverse settings in both the private sectors (e.g., industrial plants, banks, retail facilities, etc.) and the public sectors (e.g., hospitals, post stations, etc.).

Facility location problems locate a set of facilities (resources) to minimize the cost of satisfying some set of demands (of the customers) with respect to some set of constraints. Facility location decisions are critical elements in strategic planning for a wide range of private and public firms. The branches of locating facilities are broad and long-lasting, influencing numerous operational and logistical decisions. High costs associated with property acquisition and facility construction make facility location or relocation projects long-term investments. Decision makers must select sites that will not only perform well according to the current system state, but also will continue to be profitable for the facility's lifetime, even as environmental factors change, populations shift, and market trends evolve. Finding robust facility locations is thus a difficult task, demanding decision makers to account for uncertain future events.

Location science is an area of analytical study that can be traced back to Pierre de Fermat, Evagelistica Torricelli (a student of Galileo), and Battista Cavallieri. Each one independently proposed (and some say solved) the basic Euclidean spatial median problem early in the seventeenth century.

The study of location theory started formally in 1909 when Alfred Weber considered how to locate a single warehouse in order to minimize the total distance between the warehouse and several customers. After that, location theory was driven by a few applications. Location theory gained researchers' interest again in 1964 with a publication by Hakimi (1964), who wanted to locate switching centers in a communications network and police stations in a highway system.

The term "location problem" refers to the modeling, formulation, and solution of a class of problems that can best be described as locating facilities in some given spaces. Deployment, positioning, and locating are frequently used as synonymous. There are differences between location and layout problems: the facilities in location problems are small relative to the space in which they are sited and the interaction among facilities may occur; but in layout problems, the facilities to be located are large relative to the space in which they are positioned, and the interaction among facilities is common.

There are four components that describe location problems: customers, who are assumed to be already located at points or on routes, facilities that will be located, a space in which customers and facilities are located, and a metric (standard) that indicates distances or time between customers and facilities.

Facility location models are used in a variety of applications. Some of them include locating warehouses within a supply chain to minimize the average time to market, locating noxious material to maximize their distances from the public, locating railroad stations to minimize the unpredictability of delivery schedules, locating automatic teller machines to serve bank customers better, etc. Facility location models can differ in their objective function, the distance metric applied, the number and size of the facilities to locate, and several other decision indices. Depending on the specific application, inclusion and consideration of these various indices in the problem formulation will lead to very different location models.

Facility location books are numerous. Francis et al. (1992) introduced some prevalent models such as single/multi facility location problems, quadratic assignment location problems (QAP) and covering problems. Mirchandani and Francis (1990) wrote about discrete location theory. The network based location theory book by Daskin (1995) focused on discrete location problems. Drezner (1995) represented some models and applications in location environments. Drezner and Hamacher (2002) published a book about the theory and applications of facility location. Nickel and Puerto (2005) extended a complete survey in the area of continuous and network based location models especially about median location problems.

In this book, most of the subjects are seen in an equal trend; classical models such as single facility location problem, multiple facility location problem, median problem, center problem and covering problem, contemporary models such as hierarchical facility location problem, hub location problem and competitive location problem and advanced models such as location in supply chain.

The arrangement of the chapters has a reasonable style in which the predecessors and successors have been regarded from concepts viewpoints; that is, to solve one of the P-center models, it has to be converted to some covering problems, therefore the covering chapter is followed by center chapter.

Most chapters have a similar trend to represent their concepts in which application and classification are included in part one, mathematical modeling, solution technique and some case studies in parts two, three and four, respectively.

Because of the importance of distances in objective functions of location problems, in Chap. 1 different kinds of distances in location problems are discussed. Chap. 2 introduces complexities employed in location problems.

Chapters 3–9 discuss some prevalent and classic concepts in location theory. Single facility and multiple facility location problems are treated in Chaps. 3 and 4, respectively, in which traditional concepts of location problems are introduced. Some prevalent models in both discrete and continuous spaces are introduced in these chapters.

Location area can be divided into three parts: location problems, allocation problems and location-allocation problems. We represent location-allocation problems in Chap. 5. In some cases of location problems, locating needs to consider distances and interactions between facilities, therefore we face quadratic assignment problems, which are discussed in Chap. 6. In covering problems, customers need to be with a specific distance through facilities which are servicing; these problems introduced different kinds of covering problems that are discussed in Chap. 7. Median problems are considered as the main topics in the location allocation problems. These problems try to find the median points among some candidate points to minimize the sum of costs, and most of their applications are in private areas. In Chap. 8, we study these kinds of problems as median problems. Public and emergency services need to be located to satisfy all customers, thus center problems have emerged to minimize the maximum distances between the facilities and the demand points (customers). In Chap. 9 we introduce these problems and their applications.

After Chap. 9, we will introduce some contemporary concepts in location problems. The first of them is the hierarchical facility location problem, which is discussed in Chap. 10. This chapter deals with different levels and categories of facilities, which have to be located with some relationships among them. In Chap. 11, hub location problems have been addressed. In some cases we want to eliminate some interactions between demand points (customers) and facilities to reduce the complexity of their networks, therefore we introduce some facilities as hub points and reduce these relations. This leads to minimizing the total cost of the network.

In Chap. 12, we cover some concepts about competitive areas not monopolized as competitive location problems. In these areas, facilities that have to be located need to compete with other facilities to gain a market share. In some areas facilities are warehouses and have to be located to satisfy customer demands, thus in Chap. 13 we will introduce warehouse location problems in which different kinds of siting and solution methods are discussed. In some cases, we need to locate some hazardous facilities that have to be far from public places. Their objectives minimize these kinds of facilities' exposure and, are introduced in a separate chapter as an obnoxious facility location problem (Chap. 14). The nature of facility location problems leads to considering future uncertainty. Thus in real world, we face problems which have no definite planning horizon. In Chap. 15, we treat these problems as dynamic facility location problems. In many real world cases, we face some incompatible objective functions, therefore a separate chapter is introduced as a multi criteria location problem, which deals with conflicted objectives and includes most facility location topics (Chap. 16).

In Chap. 17, we represent location routing problems which not only discuss locating some new facilities in some candidate points but also set routing between these facilities and demand points (customers). In this, we treat vehicle routing problems as a subordinate of the location routing problem. Inventory costs have a major effect on location problems and there is a close relationship between objective functions of delivery locating points and inventory costs, therefore it is better to consider inventory costs determining minimum costs in dealing with satisfying demand points (customers). Products need to be put into storage locations before they can be picked to fulfill customer orders, therefore the layout of storage will be an important matter which leads to better efficiency and delivery. This concept (different with warehouse location problem) which deals with siting of warehouses rather than their layouts in location areas as storage system layout is represented in Chap. 18. We represent location-inventory problems in a specific chapter (Chap. 19) which explains inventory concepts and their parameters in the siting of facilities. Nowadays, supply chains have been expanded in modern environments. In Chap. 20, two separate concepts are combined: supply chain and location. This chapter discusses relationships between supply chains and siting problems in modern areas named supply chain in location. The classification of facility location problems together with introducing some prevalent facility location softwares are covered in Chap. 21. Location problems often interest to find locations of new facilities that provide services of some kind to existing facilities. Sometimes finding all new facilities is not an economical task and an analysis is needed to aggregate the demand data by representing a collection of individuals as one demand point. In Chap. 22, this kind of analysis for demand point aggregation is represented. Finally, an appendix is introduced, and it contains meta-heuristic algorithms employed to determine and solve facility location models.

We express our appreciation for editorial who managed to edit successfully the manuscripts that were characterized by a great variety of individual preferences in style and layout, and to Dr. Werner A. Müller, Springer Executive Vice President in Business/Economics and Statistics, Dr. Niels Peter Thomas, Springer Editor in Business/Economics, Alice Blanck, Business/Economics and Statistics Editorial and also Indhu Arumugam, SPi Technologies India Private Ltd., project manager for their support.

References

Daskin MS (1995) Network and discrete location: Models, algorithms, and applications. Wiley, New York
Drezner Z (1995) Facility location: A survey of application and methods. Springer, Berlin
Drezner Z, Hamacher H (2002) Facility location: Applications and theory. Springer, Berlin
Francis RL, McGinnis LF, White JA (1992) Facility layout and location: An analytical approach. Prentice Hall, Englewood Cliffs, NJ
Hakimi SL (1964) Optimum locations of switching centers and the absolute centers and medians of a graph. Oper Res 12:450–459
Mirchandani PB, Francis RL (1990) Discrete location theory. Wiley, New York
Nickel S, Puerto J (2005) Location theory: A unified approach. Springer, Berlin

Chapter 1
Distance Functions in Location Problems

Marzie Zarinbal

Distance is a numerical description of how far apart objects are at any given moment in time. In physics or everyday discussion, distance may refer to a physical length, a period of time, or it is estimated based on other criteria.

While making location decisions, the distribution of travel distances among the service recipients (clients) is an important issue.

Most classical location studies focus on the minimization of the mean (or total) distance (the median concept) or the minimization of the maximum distance (the center concept) to the service facilities. (Ogryczak 2000) In these studies, the location modeling is divided into four broad categories:

1. *Analytic models*. These models are based on a large number of simplifying assumptions such as the fix cost of locating facility. The travel distances follow the Manhattan metric.
2. *Continuous models*. These models are the oldest location models, deal with geometrical representations of reality, and are based on the continuity of location area. The classic model in this area is the Weber problem. Distances in the Weber problem are often taken to be straight-line or Euclidean distances but almost all kind of the distance functions can be used here (Jiang and Xu 2006; Hamacher and Nickel 1998).

In the study of continuous location theory, it is generally assumed that the customers may be treated as points in space. This assumption is valid when the dimensions of the customers are small relative to the distances between the new facility and the customers. However, it is not always the case. Sometimes, we should not ignore the dimensions of the customers. Some researchers have treated the customers as demand regions representing the demand over a region.

Jiang and Xu (2006) discussed that some researchers such as Brimberg and Wesolowsky in 1997, 2000 and 2002 and Nickel et al. in 2003 used the distance between the facility and the closest point of a demand region; and in the others, the distance between the facility and a demand region may be calculated as some form of expected or average travel distance.

3. *Network models.* Network models are composed of links and nodes. Absolute 1-median, un-weighted 2-center and q-criteria L-median on a tree models are some well-known models in this area. Distances are measured with respect to the shortest path.
4. *Discrete models.* In these models, there are a discrete set of candidate locations. Discrete N-median, un-capacitated facility location, and coverage models are some well-known models in this area. Like the distances in continuous models, all kind of the distance functions can be used here but sometimes it could be specified exogenously (Hamacher and Nickel 1998; Fouard and Malandain 2005).

Distances and norms are usually defined on the finite space E^n and take real values. In discrete geometry, however, we sometimes need to have discrete distances defined on Z^n with their values in Z. Since Z^n is not a vector space, the notion of distances and norms had to be extended.

1.1 Distance and Norms Specifications

Assume $X = (x_1, y_1)$ and $Y = (x_2, y_2)$. Then $d(X, Y)$ is the distance function between points X and Y, and has these characteristics (Fouard and Malandain 2005).

$$d(X, Y) \geq 0 \quad \forall X, Y \quad \text{Possitivity,} \tag{1.1}$$

$$d(X, Y) = 0 \Leftrightarrow X = Y \quad \forall X, Y \quad \text{Definition,} \tag{1.2}$$

$$d(X, Y) = d(Y, X) \quad \forall X, Y \quad \text{Symmetry,} \tag{1.3}$$

$$d(X, Y) \leq d(X, R) + d(R, Y) \quad \forall X, Y \quad \text{Triangular Inequality.} \tag{1.4}$$

1.2 Distances Function

The distances function between points $X = (x_1, x_2, \ldots, x_n)$ and $Y = (y_1, y_2, \ldots, y_n)$ is called $d_{k,p}(X, Y)$ the Minkowski distance of order p, which defines as follows:

$$d_{K,p}(X, Y) = \left(\sum_{i=1}^{n} k_i |x_i - y_i|^p \right)^{\frac{1}{p}}. \tag{1.5}$$

- IF $k_1 = k_2 = \ldots = k_n = k_p$ then we have

$$d_{K,p}(X, Y) = K \left(\sum_{i=1}^{n} |x_i - y_i|^p \right)^{\frac{1}{p}}. \tag{1.6}$$

Equation (1.6) is called the weighted $d_{k,p}$-norm. (K is distance function's weight)

- IF $k_1 = k_2 = \ldots = k_n = 1$ then we have

$$d_{K,p}(X,Y) = \left(\sum_{i=1}^{n} |x_i - y_i|^p\right)^{\frac{1}{p}}. \tag{1.7}$$

The parameters k_1 and k_2 of the $d_{k,p}$-norm can be seen as unequal weights or non symmetric distance irregularities along the axis directions. An empirical work showed that the accuracy of distance estimations in the $d_{k,p}$-norm is better than the weighted $d_{k,p}$-norm. (Uster and Love 2003)

In the situation of (1.7), we can define some famous distance functions such as:

- IF $p = 1$ the 1-norm, rectilinear, Manhattan or right angle distances can be obtained: (1.8)

$$d_{K,p}(X,Y) = \sum_{i=1}^{n} |x_i - y_i|. \tag{1.8}$$

Rectilinear distances are applicable when travel is allowed only on two perpendicular directions such as North–South and East–West arteries. This distance is also popular among researchers because the analysis is usually simpler than employing other metrics (Drezner and Wesolowsky 2001).

The Rectilinear distance is also called Taxicab Norm distances; because it is the distance a car would drive in a city lay-out in square blocks (if there are no one-way streets).

- IF $p = 2$ the 2-Norm or Euclidean distances can be obtained by (1.9)

$$d_{K,p}(X,Y) = \left(\sum_{i=1}^{n} |x_i - y_i|^2\right)^{\frac{1}{2}}. \tag{1.9}$$

It is what would be obtained if the distance between two points were measured with a ruler: the "intuitive" idea of distance.

Air travel or travel over water can be exactly modeled by Euclidean distances (Drezner and Wesolowsky 2001).

- IF $p = \infty$ the Infinity Norm or Chebyshev distance can be obtained (1.10)

$$d_{\infty}(X,Y) = \lim_{p \to \infty} \left(\sum_{i=1}^{n} |x_i - y_i|^p\right)^{\frac{1}{p}} = \max(|x_1 - y_1|, \ldots, |x_n - y_n|). \tag{1.10}$$

d_1 and d_∞ are obviously discrete distances, but not d_2. The parameter d_2 is the most commonly used continuous distance, because of its rotation invariance.

1.3 Different Kinds of Distances

There are also other kinds of distances used in real problems. Some of them are as follows:

1.3.1 Aisle Distance

As mentioned above Rectilinear or Euclidean distance function are the most common methods used in models, however, these distance measures are not realistic for some applications such as material handling in plants. Figure 1.1 shows aisles in a plant.

The interdepartmental aisle travel distances can be found by formulating and finding the shortest path on a network problem and may be specified to provide the necessary distance between resources. This makes it possible to evaluate the actual aisle travel distance for each layout that is generated during the search process (Norman et al. 2001).

For calculating aisle distance, the strategies of handling systems must be considered. "The routing of a picker follows selective one-way traffic in that he traverses an entire length of the aisle containing the items to be picked and is not allowed to turn around or reverse but ends up on the opposite side of the aisle after picking the items. The optimal route in this strategy is to arrange the items within the batch such that the items found in the aisle nearest to Input/output station are collected first followed by the next nearest aisle. When the last item is picked, the picker will return to the I/O station". Chew and Tang (1999) is an example of these strategies.

1.3.2 Distance Matrix

Yu and Sarker (2003) indicated that Sarker in 1989 and Sarker et al. in 1994 and 1998 developed a number of amoebic properties of a distance matrix for equally

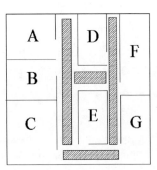

Fig. 1.1 Aisles in plant layout

spaced linear locations to generate different assignments of machines to locations that minimize the total unidirectional and/or bi-directional flows. The form of a distance matrix may vary as its corresponding location assignment changes.

$$d_{XY} = |X - Y| = \begin{cases} X - Y & \text{if } 1 \leq Y < X \leq L \\ Y - X & \text{if } 1 \leq X < Y \leq L \\ 0 & \text{if } 1 \leq Y = X \leq L \end{cases}. \quad (1.11)$$

Each location distance can be decomposed into two directional distances that are defined below.

- Backward: d^B is a backward distance matrix, with its element d_{XY}^B.

$$d_{XY}^B = \begin{cases} X - Y & \text{if } 1 \leq Y < X \leq L \\ 0 & \text{else} \end{cases}. \quad (1.12)$$

- Forward: d^F is a forward distance matrix, with its element d_{XY}^F (Yu and Sarker 2003)

$$d_{XY}^F = \begin{cases} Y - X & \text{if } 1 \leq X < Y \leq L \\ 0 & \text{else} \end{cases}. \quad (1.13)$$

1.3.3 Minimum Lengths Path

The distance between two points on P is the minimum length of any path between those points that lies on P. The "facility center", or "1-center", of the facility is the point of P that minimizes the maximum distance to a facility. There are some algorithms to find minimum lengths path (shortest path) such as Dijkstra Algorithm and the algorithm of Mitchell et al. which is a continuous version of Dijkstra Algorithm (Aronov et al. 2005).

1.3.4 Block Distance

Dearing et al. (2005) discussed that block distances are a special case of norm distances which were introduced to location models by Witzgall et al. in 1964, and Ward and Wendell in 1985. Block distances are used to model travel distance in applications where travel directions are restricted to the fundamental directions. Also it has a wide usage in barriers problems.

They can also be viewed as a generalization of distances in fixed orientations as introduced in 1987 by Widmayer et al. (Dearing et al. 2005) where it is assumed that all fundamental directions have unit length, that is

$$\|a_k\| = 1 \quad \forall k = 1, 2, \ldots, 2n, \quad (1.14)$$

where $\|a_k\|$ is the Euclidean norm of a_k.

The block distance between the points, X_1 and X_2 with respect to a given set of fundamental directions $a_1, a_2, \ldots, a_{2n}$ is denoted by $d_p(X_1, X_2)$ and is defined as

$$d_p(X_1, X_2) = \alpha_{12} + \beta_{12}, \tag{1.15}$$

where α_{12} and β_{12} are nonnegative scalars so that (Dearing et al. 2005)

$$X_2 - X_1 = \alpha_{12}a_k + \beta_{12}a_{k+1} \ \forall k = 1, 2, \ldots, 2n. \tag{1.16}$$

1.3.5 Gauges Measures

Most of the references in the literature concerning continuous location problems have considered distances induced by norms. There are also a number of papers that consider the use of gauges defined by the Minkowski functional of a compact convex set (not necessarily symmetric) containing the origin in its interior. These functions have been used in location theory to model situations where the symmetry property of a norm does not make sense.

There are also general models where the definiteness property of the gauge of a compact convex set is relaxed. Relaxing definiteness introduces the existence of zero-distance regions (Fig. 1.2).

Gauges of compact convex sets have a very interesting property: The distance between two points is the shortest path between them using only fundamental directions of the unit ball.

Let ψ be a closed convex set containing the origin. The function φ defined by

$$\phi(x) = \inf\{\alpha > 0 : x \in \alpha\psi\} \tag{1.17}$$

is called the gauge of π. The set π will be called the unit ball associated with φ. We define the distance from y to x by $\varphi(y - x)$.

If in addition π is symmetric with respect to the origin, φ is a norm and the symmetry property of a norm ($\varphi(y - x) = \varphi(x - y)$) added to $\varphi(y - x)$ properties. (Hinojosa and Puerto 2003).

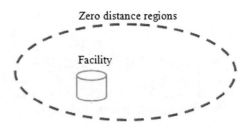

Fig. 1.2 Zero-Distance Region

1.3.6 Variance of Distances

The Variance of the Distances seeks locations that equalize distances from the demand points to the facility and thus seeks equitable location for all customers.

If the distance function is defines as Euclidean distance function, the variance of the distances between the clients (x) and the facility (y), $\delta^2(x, y)$ is

$$\delta^2(x, y) = \frac{\sum_{i=1}^{n} N_i d_i^2(x, y)}{\sum_{i=1}^{n} N_i} - \left(\frac{\sum_{i=1}^{n} N_i d_i(x, y)}{\sum_{i=1}^{n} N_i} \right)^2, \quad (1.18)$$

where "n" is the number of demand points and "N_i" the number of clients at demand point i ($i = 1, 2, \ldots, n$) (Drezner and Drezner 2007).

1.3.7 Hilbert Curve

Cantor was the first researcher to map the interval $[0, 1]$ into the square $[0, 1]^2$. Later the first space-filling curve, the Peano curve, was presented to construct a curve that passes through every entry of a two dimensional region. Afterwards, several different space-filling curves were presented and the Hilbert curve is the most well known (Chung et al. 2007).

Hilbert curve is a continuous curve that passes through each point in space exactly once. It enables one to continuously map an image onto a line and is an excellent 2D image to line mapping. The position of each pixel on the mapped line is called the Hilbert order of that pixel (Song and Roussopoulos 2002). Figure 1.3 shows a simple example of Hilbert curve.

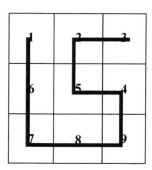

Fig. 1.3 The Hilbert Curve

1.3.8 Mahalanobis Distance

Mahalanobis distance is introduced by Mahalanobis in 1936 and widely used in cluster analysis and other classification techniques (De Maesschalck et al. 2000). It is closely related to Hotelling's T-Square Distribution used for multivariate statistical testing. Also, Mahalanobis distance and leverage are often used to detect outliers especially in the development of linear regression models.

Euclidean and Mahalanobis distance can be calculated both in the original variable space and in the principal component space.

The Euclidean is easy to compute and interpret, but this is less the case for the Mahalanobis. In the original variable space, the Mahalanobis takes into account the correlation in the data, since it is calculated using the inverse of the variance–covariance matrix of the data set of interest. However, the computation of the variance–covariance matrix can cause problems.

The (1.19) shows the original Mahalanobis distance x_i from the mean of data or the center of class ($d_M(x_i)$) and in the case of two variables, x_1 and, variance–covariance matrix is shown in (1.2) (κ) is the mean of data or the center of classes) (De Maesschalck et al., 2000).

$$d_M(x_i) = \sqrt{|x_i - \kappa| A^{-1} |x_i - \kappa|^T}, \qquad (1.19)$$

$$A = \begin{pmatrix} \sigma_1^2 & \rho_{12}\sigma_1\sigma_2 \\ \rho_{12}\sigma_1\sigma_2 & \sigma_2^2 \end{pmatrix}. \qquad (1.20)$$

1.3.9 Hamming Distance

The Hamming distance is introduced by Richard Hamming in 1950 and used in telecommunication to count the number of flipped bits in a fixed-length binary word as an estimate of error, and therefore is sometimes called the signal distance. Hamming weight analysis of bits is used in several disciplines including information theory, coding theory, and cryptography (Chae and Fromm 2005).

1.3.10 Levenshtein Distance

In 1965, Vladimir Levenshtein introduces the Levenshtein Distance (LD). In information theory and computer science, the Levenshtein distance is a string metric, which is one way to measure edit distance. The minimum number of operations needed to transform one string into the other, where an operation is an insertion, deletion, or substitution of a single character, gives the Levenshtein distance between two strings (Nickel and Puerto 2005). Thus,

LD ("IBM", "IBN") = 1, since one substitution is needed to transform IBM to IBN.

LD ("Success", "Successful") = 3, since three additions are needed to transform Success to Successful.

LD is robust to spelling errors and small local differences between the strings (Chae and Fromm 2005).

1.3.11 Hausdorff Distance

This kind of distance metric is used in continues models and is defines as follows:
If there are two compact sets, A and B, the Hausdorff distance between them is

$$d_H(A, B) = \max(\max_{x \in A} d_2(x, B), \max_{y \in B} d_2(y, A), \quad (1.21)$$

where (Nickel and Puerto 2005)

$$d_2(x, B) = \min_{y \in B} d_2(x, y). \quad (1.22)$$

Table 1.1 shows various kinds of locations problems, the distance Functions used to solve them and their developers.

Table 1.1 Distance functions used in location problems

Developed year	Problem	Distance	Developer	References
1909	Continues location problem	Euclidean distances	Weber	Hamacher and Nickel (1998)
1937	Multi facility location problem	Euclidean distances	Weiszfeld	Munoz-Perez and Saameno-Rodrõguez (1999)
1963	Multifacility location problem	Rectilinear distances in a network of aisles	Francis	Munoz-Perez and Saameno-Rodrõguez (1999)
1970	Private and public sector location models	Lp distance	ReVelle et al.	Munoz-Perez and Saameno-Rodrõguez (1999)
1973	Multifacility location problem	Euclidean & rectilinear distances (HAP procedure)	Eyster et al.	Munoz-Perez and Saameno-Rodrõguez (1999)

(continued)

Table 1.1 (continued)

Developed year	Problem	Distance	Developer	References
1977	Traveling salesman location problem	Rectilinear sistances	Chan, Hearn	Munoz-Perez and Saameno-Rodrõguez (1999)
1978	Fixed charge plant location problem (using LP)	Random and euclidean distances	Morris	Schilling et al. (2000)
1980	Unweighted 1-maximin problem in a bounded & convex polyhedron in Rk	Euclidean distances	Dasarathy, White	Chae and Fromm (2005)
1980	Weighted 1 maximin problem	Euclidean distances	Drezner, Wesolowsky	Chae and Fromm (2005)
1981	Generalized versions of 1-maximin models	Euclidean distances	Hansen et al.	Munoz-Perez and Saameno-Rodrõguez (1999)
1981	Location problem with barriers for median problem	Euclidean distances	Katz, Cooper	Plastria and Carrizosa (2004)
1982	Traveling salesman location problem	Rectilinear, euclidean, and Lp distance problems	Drezner, Wesolowsky	Munoz-Perez and Saameno-Rodrõguez (1999)
1983	Location problem with barriers for median problem	Rectilinear distances	Larson, Sadiq	Plastria and Carrizosa (2004)
1986	Location of an undesirable facility	Weighted inverse square distance	Melachrinoudis, Cullinane	Munoz-Perez and Saameno-Rodrõguez (1999)
1986	Location of an undesirable facility	Euclidean & rectilinear distances	Melachrinoudis, Cullinane	Munoz-Perez and Saameno-Rodrõguez (1999)
1986	Single facility location problem	Minimizing the variance of distances	Maimon	Chung et al. (2007)
1987	The median shortest path problem	Shortest path distance	Current et al.	Hamacher and Nickel (1998)
1989	Assigning machines to locations	Distance matrix	Sarker	Yu and Sarker (2003)
1992	Improved traveling salesman location problem	Rectilinear distances	Tamir	Munoz-Perez and Saameno-Rodrõguez (1999)

(continued)

Table 1.1 (continued)

Developed year	Problem	Distance	Developer	References
1994	Weber facility location in the presence of forbidden regions	Lp distance	Aneja, Palar	Hamacher and Nickel (1998)
1994	Competitive location model	Euclidean distances	T. Drezner	Plastria and Carrizosa (2004)
1995	Undesirable facility location by generalized cutting planes	Euclidean distances	Carrizosa, Plastria	Hamacher and Nickel (1998)
1995	Bi objective min quantile max covering problems	Euclidean distances	Carrizosa, Plastria	Munoz-Perez and Saameno-Rodrõguez (1999)
1996	Locating a point in a network	Shortest path distance	Drezner, Wesolowsky	Munoz-Perez and Saameno-Rodrõguez (1999)
1996	Location problem with barriers for median problem	Euclidean distances	Butt, Cavalier	Plastria and Carrizosa (2004)
1997	P-Median problem (new heuristic approach)	Euclidean distances	Dai, Cheung	Hamacher and Nickel (1998)
1998	Locating a new facility in a competitive environment	Euclidean distances with correction	Drezner T, Drezner Z	Drezner and Drezner (1998)
1999	A P-center grid positioning	Rectilinear distances	Rayco et al.	Hamacher and Nickel (1998)
2000	Designing distribution systems	Rectilinear distances	Erlebacher, Meller	Hamacher and Nickel (1998)
2000	Location problem with barriers for median problem	Lp distance	Hamacher, Klamroth	Hamacher and Nickel (1998)
2001	The K-centrum multi facility location problem	K largest distances in a graph	Tamir	Hamacher and Nickel (1998)
2002	Location problem with barriers for center problem	Rectilinear distances	Dearing et al.	Dearing et al. (2005)
2008	Quadratic assignment problem	Number of variables with different values in the population members (Ga)	Drezner Z	Drezner (2008)

1.4 Summary

The distance functions and its definition play an important role in facility location problems. As it is shown above, we have various kinds of distance function with different definitions. Each of them has its own domain, advantages, and disadvantages. For defining the distance function, one must consider the semantic of the problem, the distance characteristic, and its usage domain.

References

Aronov B, VanKreveld M, VanOostrum R, Varadarajan K (2005) Facility location on a polyhedral surface. Discrete Comput Geom 30:357–372
Chae A, Fromm H (2005) Supply chain management on demand. Springer, Berlin
Chew EP, Tang LC (1999) Travel time analysis for general item location assignment in a rectangular warehouse. Eur J Oper Res 112:582–597
Chung KL, Huang YL, Liu YW (2007) Efficient algorithms for coding Hilbert curve of arbitrary-sized image and application to window query. Inf Sci 177:2130–2151
Dearing PM, Klamroth K, Segars R Jr (2005) Planar location problems with block distance and barriers. Ann Oper Res 136:117–143
De Maesschalck R, Jouan-Rimbaud D, Massart DL (2000) The Mahalanobis distance. Chem Intell Lab Syst 50:1–18
Drezner Z (2008) Extensive experiments with hybrid genetic algorithms for the solution of the quadratic assignment problem. Comput Oper Res 35:717–736
Drezner T, Drezner Z (1998) Facility location in anticipation of future competition. Location Sci 6:155–173
Drezner T, Drezner Z (2007) Equity models in planar location. Comput Manage Sci 4:1–16
Drezner Z, Wesolowsky GO (2001) On the collection depots location problem. Eur J Oper Res 130:510–518
Fouard C, Malandain G (2005) 3-D chamfer distances and norms in anisotropic grids. Image Vision Comput 23:143–158
Hamacher HW, Nickel S (1998) Classification of location models. Location Sci 6:229–242
Hinojosa Y, Puerto J (2003) Single facility location problems with unbounded unit balls. Math Method Oper Res 58:87–104
Jiang J, Xu Y (2006) MiniSum location problem with farthest Euclidean distances. Math Methodol Oper Res 64:285–308
Munoz-Perez J, Saameno-Rodroguez JJ (1999) Location of an undesirable facility in a polygonal region with forbidden zones. Eur J Oper Res 114:372–379
Nickel S, Puerto J (2005) Location theory: A unified approach. Springer-Verlag, Berlin
Norman BA, Arapoglu R, Smith AE (2001) Integrated facilities design using a contour distance metric. IIE Trans 33:337–344
Ogryczak W (2000) Inequality measures and equitable approaches to location problems. Eur J Oper Res 122:347–391
Plastria F, Carrizosa E (2004) Optimal location and design of a competitive facility. Math Program 100:247–265
Schilling DA, Rosing KE, ReVelle CS (2000) Network distance characteristics that affect computational effort in p-median location problems. Eur J Oper Res 127:525–536

Song Z, Roussopoulos N (2002) Using Hilbert curve in image storing and retrieving. Inf Syst 27:523–536
Uster H, Love RF (2003) Formulation of confidence intervals for estimated actual distances. Eur J Oper Res 151:586–601
Yu J, Sarker BR (2003) Directional decomposition heuristic for a linear machine-cell location problem. Eur J Oper Res 149:142–184

Chapter 2
An Overview of Complexity Theory

Milad Avazbeigi

Computational complexity theory (Shortly: Complexity Theory) has been a central area of theoretical computer science since its early development in the mid-1960s. Its subsequent rapid development in the next three decades, has not only established it as a rich, exciting theory, but also has shown strong influence on many other related areas in computer science, mathematics, and operation research (Du and Ko 2000). However, the notions of algorithms and complexity are meaningful only when they are defined in terms of formal computation models (Du and Ko 2000).

Apparently, we need some models to base the foundation of complexity theory on them. In this chapter, we introduce only three basic models: deterministic turing machine (DTM), non-deterministic turing machine (NTM) and Oracle machine models. It should be noted there are also some other models (see Du and Ko 2000).

Using such models, allows us to separate the complexity notion from any physical machine. Hence, we can measure the time complexity of algorithms and hardness of problems independent from a specific machine which runs the algorithm(s). It should be noted that these are just abstract models; means, are defined mathematically (Sipser 1996).

The structure of this chapter is as follows. We first discuss why we actually need complexity theory. Then, we introduce three basic models of computation: DTM and NTM and Oracle model. Then we present a brief introduction about the concept of big O notation which is widely used in the complexity theory. In Sect. 2.5, the decision problems as a special form of problems are described. Following this section, the basic concepts of reduction are presented, which help us to make relationships between different classes of complexity and also provide a rich tool to identify the unknown complexity class of a new problem. Finally, we introduce the most popular classes of complexity: P, NP, NP-complete and NP-hard. In each class, also, some known problems are presented.

2.1 Advantage of Complexity Theory

As quoted in previous section, by using computation models, we try to generalize our results of algorithms runs to other problem instances, computers and implementations. However, without such computational models, and by just relying on physical machines, it would be difficult however to base a theory on the detailed specification of the physical objects and even if we could, the theory might not be very useful, because we would need to modify it for every different set of hardware (Martin 1996). In doing so, we attempt to define the execution time as a function of the size of the problem. Also Time is not measured in second, minutes or any another similar measures. Roughly speaking, we try to measure it as the number of steps that has to be taken to resolve an instance of the problem at hand which is apparently independent from any specific computer or machine.

2.1.1 Computational Complexity

1. Defines clearly what solving a problem "efficiently" means.
2. Categorizes problems into those that can be solved efficiently and those that cannot.
3. Estimates the amount of time (or memory) needed to solve problems (Daskin 1995).

These are main reasons underlying the use of "complexity theory". Using complexity theory, we can evaluate an algorithm in front of the problem at hand to understand whether the existing algorithm can resolve the given problem completely as the size of the problem grows or not. Also, we can compare algorithms in respect to the time and resources they need, to resolve a given problem. Recognition of the complexity class of a problem is another important help of this theory (2). Most of the time, the recognized complexity class of a problem, determines our future approach we choose to resolve the problem. For example, if we realize that the problem at hand is *NP*-complete (which is described in next sections), we shift our concentration from exact solutions to approximate and usually so called heuristic and meta-heuristic approaches.

2.2 Abstract Models of Computation: Abstract Machines

2.2.1 Preliminary Definitions

2.2.1.1 String

The basic data structure in complexity theory is usually considered as "String". All other data structure can be encoded and presented by strings. *A* string is a finite sequence of symbols. For instance, the word "string" is a string of over the symbols of English letters (Du and Ko 2000).

2.2.1.2 Language

If A is the set of strings that machine M accepts, we say that A is the language of machine M and write $L(M) = A$ (Sipser 1996); we say that M accepts A or M recognizes.

A machine may accept several strings, but it always accepts only one language. For convenience, we often work only on strings of the alphabet $\{0, 1\}$ (Du and Ko 2000). To show that this does not impose a serious restriction on the theory, we note that a simple method can be constructed of encoding strings over any finite alphabet into the strings over $\{0, 1\}$.

2.2.2 Turing Machine Models

The standard computer model in computability theory is the Turing machine, introduced by Alan Turing in 1936 (Turing 1936).

2.2.2.1 Deterministic Turing Machine (DTM) (Du and Ko 2000)

DTM consists of two basic units: the control unit and the memory unit. The control unit contains a finite number of states. The memory unit is a tape that extends infinitely to both ends. The tape is divided into an infinite number of tape squares (or tape cells). Each tape square stores one of a finite number of tape symbols. The communication between the control unit and the tape is through a read/write tape head that scans a tape square at a time. Figure 2.1 shows a simple single-tape DTM.

An important concept about Turing machine is the concept of configuration. A configuration of a TM is a record of all information of the computation of the machine at a specific moment, which includes the current state, the current symbols in the tape, and the current position of the tape head.

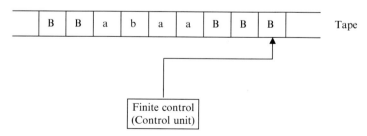

Fig. 2.1 Single-tape deterministic Turing Machine

2.2.2.2 Non-Deterministic Turing Machine (NTM) (Du and Ko 2000)

The Turing machine described in the previous section is a deterministic machine, because for each configuration of a machine there is at most one move to make, and hence there is at most one next configuration. If we allow more than one moves for some configurations, and hence those configurations have more than one next configuration, then the machine is called a nondeterministic Turing machine (NTM).

In complexity theory, we use the concept of Turing machines to model our computations and as described in Sect. 2.1, to make independent the computations from hardware of computer. To see examples about these models, see example of Du and Ko (2000) and Sipser (1997). Speaking in an imprecise manner, a computation changes the configuration of a machine and takes the machine from one configuration to a new configuration. Finally, a finite number of computations take us from an initial state of machine to target (desired) state of machine which can be considered as the answer to the problem to be resolved.

2.2.2.3 Oracle Turing Machine (Du and Ko 2000)

A function-oracle DTM is an ordinary DTM equipped with an extra tape, called the query tape, and two extra states, called the query state and the answer state. The oracle machine M works as follows: First, on input x and with oracle function f, it begins the computation at the initial state and behaves exactly like the ordinary TM when it is not in any of the special states.

The machine is allowed to enter the query state to make queries to the oracle, but it is not allowed to enter the answer state from any ordinary state. Before it enters the query state, machine M needs to prepare the query string y by writing the string y on the query tape and leaving the tape head of the query tape scanning the square to the right of the rightmost square of y. After the oracle machine M enters the query state, the computation is taken over by the "oracle" f, which will do the following for the machine: it reads the string y on query tape; it replaces y by the string $f(y)$; and it puts the tape head of the query tape back scanning the leftmost square of $f(y)$; it puts the tape head of the query tape back scanning the left most square of $f(y)$; and it puts the machine into answer state. Then the machine continues from the answer state as usual. The actions taken by the oracle count as only one unit of time.

2.3 Big-O Notation (Wood 1987)

The complexity of computational problems can be discussed by fixing a model of computation and then considering how much of the machines resources are required for the solutions. In order to make a meaningful comparison of the inherent complexity of two problems, it is necessary to look at instances over a range of sizes.

The most common approach is to compare the growth rates of the two runtimes, each viewed as a function of the instance size (Martin 1996).

We measure the time and space complexity of a problem or program by total function from N to N, since time and space are measured in positive integral units as is the size of input data. In order to compare time or space complexities of problems or programs we are usually interested only in their order, that is, multiplicative constants and lower-order terms are ignored. The big-O notation is used for this purpose.

Given the two functions $f, g: N \to N$, we write $f(n) = O(g(n))$, if there are positive integers c and d such that, for all $n \geq d$,

$$f(n) \leq cg(n), \tag{2.1}$$
$$cf(n) \leq g(n). \tag{2.2}$$

In this case f is said to be big-O of g.

Similarly, we write $f(n) = \Omega(g(n))$, if there are positive integers c and d such that, for all $n \geq d$,

In this case we say f is big-omega of g.

If $f(n) = O(g(n))$ and $f(n) = \Omega(g(n))$, then we write $f(n) = \Theta(g(n))$, that is, f is big-theta of g.

Whenever $f(n) = O(g(n))$, then $g(n)$ is an upper bound for $f(n)$ and whenever $f(n) = \Omega(g(n))$, $g(n)$ is a lower bound for $f(n)$.

Remember that the big-O notation compares only the rate of growth of functions rather than their values, so when $f(n) = \Theta(g(n))$, $f(n)$ and $g(n)$ have the same rates of growth, but can be very different in their values.

2.3.1 Example

Take the polynomials $f(x) = 6x^4 - 2x^3 + 5, g(x) = x^4$. We say $f(x)$ has order $O(g(x))$ or $O(x^4)$. From the definition of order, $|f(x)| \leq c|g(x)|$ for all $x > 1$, where c is a constant.

Proof.

$$|6x^4 - 2x^3 + 5| \leq 6x^4 + 2x^3 + 5 \text{ where } x.1, \tag{2.3}$$
$$|6x^4 - 2x^3 + 5| \leq 6x^4 + 2x^4 + 5x^4 \text{ because } x^3 < x^4, \text{ and so on}, \tag{2.4}$$
$$|6x^4 - 2x^3 + 5| \leq 13x^4. \tag{2.5}$$

So we can say:

$$f(x) \; is \; O(g(x)) \text{ as } x \to \infty. \tag{2.6}$$

2.4 Time Complexity

Now, using big-O notation, we can talk about complexity of algorithms in front of problems. As mentioned before, big-O notation gives us a tool to talk about complexity of algorithms in respect to steps (approximately) they take to resolve the problem at hand, so we make our models independent from a specific hardware configuration or implementation.

Also it is important to say in analysis of algorithms, we are interested in worst case analysis of algorithms; the longest time they take to resolve a problem.

2.4.1 Constant Time

In computational complexity theory, constant time, or $O(1)$ time, refers to the computation time of a problem when the time needed to solve that problem does not depend on the size of the data it is given as input.

For example accessing any single element in an array takes constant time as only one operation has to be made to locate it.

It can be noted, if the number of elements is known in advance and does not change, however, such an algorithm can still be said to run in constant time. For example, think about a problem as finding of an unknown chose square of a chess board. It is clear that, growth of board size changes the number of steps has to be taken to find the square. However, for any specific size of board, it is a constant predefined value. So our algorithm in front of this problem takes constant time.

2.4.2 Linear Time (Sipser 1996)

In computational complexity theory, an algorithm is said to take linear time, or $O(n)$ time, if the asymptotic upper bound for the time it requires is proportional to the size of the input, which is usually denoted n. Informally spoken, the running time increases linearly with the size of the input. For example, finding the minimal value in an unordered array takes $O(n)$ time because all the items in array have to be checked.

2.4.3 Polynomial Time (Papadimitriou 1994)

In computational complexity theory, polynomial time refers to the computation time of a problem where the run time, $m(n)$, is no greater than a polynomial function of the problem size, n. Written mathematically using big O notation, this states that $m(n) = O(n^k)$ where k is some constant that may depend on the problem.

Mathematicians sometimes use the notion of "polynomial time on the length of the input" as a definition of a "fast" or "feasible" computation, as opposed to "super-polynomial time", which is anything slower than that. Exponential time is one example of a super-polynomial time.

2.4.4 Exponential Time (Sipser 1996)

In complexity theory, exponential time is the computation time of a problem where the time to complete the computation, $m(n)$, is bounded by an exponential function of the problem size, n. In other words as the size of the problem increases linearly, the time to solve the problem increases exponentially.

Written mathematically, there exists $k > 1$ such that $m(n) = O(k^n)$ and there exists c such that $m(n) = O(c^n)$.

2.5 Decision Problems

In computability theory and computational complexity theory, a decision problem is a question in some formal system with a yes-or-no answer, depending on the values of some input parameters. For example, the problem "given two numbers x and y, does x evenly divide y?" is a decision problem. The answer can be either "yes" or "no", and depends upon the values of x and y.

A formal definition of decision problem is "A decision problem is any arbitrary yes-or-no question on an infinite set of inputs". Because of this, it is traditional to define the decision problem equivalently as: the set of inputs for which the problem returns yes (Martin 1996).

For every optimization problem, there is a Decision Problem version. Hence, we can convert an optimization problem into a decision problem which means a question with answer "yes" or "no". Satisfiability problem is a popular and classic example of decision problems which is described in Sect. 2.7.

2.6 Reduction

A reduction is a way of converting one problem into another problem in such a way that, if the second problem is solved, it can be used to solve the first problem (Sipser 1996).

For example, suppose you want to find your way around a new city. You know this would be easy if you had a map. This demonstrates reducibility. The problem of finding your way around the city is reducible to the problem of obtaining a map of the city (Sipser 1996).

Many examples also can be found in mathematics. For example the problem of solving a system of linear equations reduces to the problem of inverting matrix.

2.6.1 Linear Reduction

Linear reductions are used widely in complexity theory. Linear reduction in literature is defined as follows (Brassard and Bratley 1988):

Let A and B be two solvable problems. A is linearly reducible to B, denoted $A \leq^l B$, if the existence of an algorithm for B that works in a time in $O(t(n))$, for any function $t(n)$, implies that there exists an algorithm for A that also works in a time in $O(t(n))$. When $A \leq^l B$ and $B \leq^l A$ both hold. A and B are linearly equivalent, denoted $A \equiv^l B$.

2.6.2 Polynomial Reduction

Another important definition is polynomial reduction (Brassard and Bratley 1988):

Let X and Y be two problems. Problem X is polynomially reducible to problem Y in the sense of Turing, denoted $X \leq_T^v Y$, if there exists an algorithm for solving X in a time that would be polynomial if we took no account of the time needed to solve arbitrary instances of problem Y. In other words, the algorithm for solving problem X may make whatever use it chooses of an imaginary procedure that can somehow magically solve problem Y at no cost. When $X \leq_T^v Y$ and $Y \leq_T^v X$ simultaneously, then X and Y are equivalent in the sense of Turing, denoted $Y \equiv_T^\rho X$.

2.6.3 Polynomial Reduction: Many-One Polynomially Reducible

We introduced the decision problems as the problems in which we simply look for answer "yes" or "no". The restriction to decision problems allows us to introduce a simplified notion of polynomial reduction:

Let $X \subseteq I$ and $Y \subseteq J$ be two decision problems. Problem X is many-one reducible to problem Y, denoted by $X \leq_m^\rho Y$, if there exists a function $f : I \to J$ computable in polynomial time, known as the reduction function between X and Y, such that

When $X \leq_m^v Y$ and $Y \leq_m^v X$ both hold, then X and Y are many-one polynomially equivalent, denoted $X \equiv_m^\rho Y$ (Brassard and Bratley 1988).

2.7 Examples

In this section some classic problems that we would refer to them in Sect. 2.8, are presented. Here our aim is just explanation of problems. In Sect. 2.8, we analyze these problems from the view of complexity theory.

2.7.1 Traveling Salesman Optimization Problem

Given: A graph $G(N, A)$ with node set N and link set A. Associated with each link (i, j) in A is a nonnegative link length d_{ij}.

Find: circuit that visits all nodes and is of minimum total length (Daskin 1995).

As we said in Sect. 2.5, any optimization problem has a decision version. The corresponding decision problem to Traveling Salesman Problem (TSP) is: "Given a number n of cities, $n \geq 3$ integer, a non negative $n \times n$ distance matrix of integers $C = [c_{ij}]$, and a non negative integer L: Is there a closed tour passing from every city exactly once, with total length $\leq L$?".

This is the general form of TSP. By specifying the actual graph on which the traveling salesman problem is to be solved, we are specifying an instance of the problem.

When we speak of the size of an instance of a problem, we are referring to a way of characterizing how big the problem is (Daskin 1995).

In TSP the number of nodes and the number of links in a problem will constitute an adequate description of the size of a problem.

2.7.2 Satisfiability Problem

Given: A Boolean expression – a function of true/false variables.

Question: Is there an assignment of truth values (TRUE or FALSE) to the variables such that the expression is TRUE (Daskin 1995).

As the problem shows, satisfiability (SAT) problem is essentially expressed in the form of a decision problem. We just need to acquire the answer "yes" or "no".

A Boolean function is a function whose variable values and function value are all in {TRUE, FALSE}. We often denote TRUE by 1 and FALSE by 0 (Du and Ko 2000).

It can be shown that, given a general Boolean formula, we can construct an equivalent one in conjunctive normal form (CNF), that is a formula like:

"$C1$ AND $C2$ AND... AND Cm"

where Ci, $i = 1, \ldots, m$ are clauses consisting of disjunctions of Boolean variables, simple or negated.

$(x1$ OR $x2$ OR $x3)$ and $(x1$ OR $\neg x2)$ and $(x2$ OR $\neg x3)$ and $(x3$ OR $\neg x1)$ and $(\neg x1$ OR $\neg x2$ OR $\neg x3)$.

Now, the decision problem is:

Given a Boolean formula in conjunctive normal form (CNF), is it satisfiable? That is, is there a set of "true-false" values to be assigned to the various variables, such that the compound proposition is true?

2.7.3 Hamiltonian Cycle Problem

Given: A graph $G(N, A)$ where N is the set of nodes or vertices and A is the set of links.

Question: Does the graph contain a cycle that visits every vertex (i.e., a path that visits each node exactly once except the first node which is also visited at the last node on the path)? (Daskin 1995).

2.7.4 Clique Problem

Given: An undirected graph $G = (N, A)$ where N is the set of nodes or vertices and A is the set of links.

Question: A clique in G is a set of nodes $K \subseteq N$ such that $\{u, v\} \in A$ for every pair of nodes $u, v \in K$. Given a graph G and an integer k, the k-Clique problem consists of determining whether there exists a clique of k nodes in G (Brassard and Bratley 1988).

2.8 Complexity Classes

Now, after introduction of computation models (Turing machine models), big-O notation, different time complexities, decision problems and concepts of reduction, we are prepared to talk about complexity classes of problems.

First it is necessary to present a formal definition of complexity classes. Also it is necessary to note that there are some other classes, which are not presented here because this chapter aims to present an introduction to complexity theory. For more information about other complexity classes see references at the end of chapter.

In computational complexity theory, a complexity class is a set of problems of related complexity. A typical complexity class has a definition of the form: the set of problems that can be solved by abstract machine M using $O(f(n))$ of resource R (n is the size of the input) (Du and Ko 2000).

2.8.1 Class P

P is a class of languages that are decidable in a polynomial time on a deterministic single-tape Turing machine (Sipser 1996).

The class P plays a central role in our theory and is important because:

P is invariant for all models of computation that are polynomially equivalent to the deterministic single-tape Turing machine.

P roughly corresponds to the class of problems that are realistically solvable on a computer.

Item 1 indicates that problems in P class are not affected by the particulars of the model of computation that we are using.

Item 2 indicates whenever we prove a problem falls in Class P, an algorithm can be found which can solve the problem in polynomial time, means the run time, $m(n)$, is no greater than a polynomial function of the problem size, n. Written mathematically using big O notation, this states that $m(n) = O(n^k)$ where k is some constant that may depend on the problem.

We describe algorithms with numbered stages. The notion of stage of an algorithm is analogous to the step of a Turing machine, though of course, implementing one stage of an algorithm on a Turing machine, in general require many Turing machine steps (Sipser 1996).

To show an algorithm runs in polynomial time, we need to show two things. First, we have to give a polynomial upper bound (see Sect. 2.3 about big-O notation) of the stages that the algorithm uses when it runs on an input of length n. Then we have to examine the individual stages in the description of the algorithm to be sure each can be implemented in polynomial time on a reasonable deterministic model (Sipser 1996). In fact, the number of stages and running time of each stage both are bounded by polynomial functions. Kozen (2006) states that Cobham and Edmonds are "generally credited with the invention of the notion of polynomial time".

As quoted in Sect. 2.1, complexity theory helps us to determine whether an algorithm is efficient or not. Now we can define an efficient algorithm as: An algorithm is efficient (or polynomial-time) if there exists a polynomial $p(n)$ such that the algorithm can solve any instance of size n in a time in $O(p(n))$ (Brassard and Bratley 1988).

2.8.1.1 Example of Problems in P

P is known to contain many natural problems, including the decision versions of linear programming, calculating the greatest common divisor.

In 2002, it was shown that the problem of determining "if a number is prime" is in P (Agrawal et al. 2004). It is clear that this is a decision problem requires "yes" or "no" answer.

Sorting a set of integers also is another example of P class problems. This is because, an algorithm can be found capable of solving the problem in polynomial time. A classic known algorithm for sorting is select method.

2.8.2 Class NP

NP is the class of decision problems for which there exists a proof system such that the proofs are succinct and easy to check.

In fact, in order to prove a problem is in *NP*, we do not require that there should exists an efficient way to find a proof of x when $x \in X$, only there should exits an efficient way to check the validity of a proposed short proof (Brassard and Bratley 1988).

Equivalent to the verifier-based definition is the following characterization: *NP* is the set of decision problems solvable in polynomial time by a non-deterministic Turing machine.

The two definitions of *NP* as the class of problems solvable by a nondeterministic Turing machine (TM) in polynomial time and the class of problems verifiable by a deterministic Turing machine in polynomial time are equivalent (The proof is described by many textbooks, Sipser 1997, Sect. 2.7.3).

If we remember the definition of Class P, we immediately realize that all problems in P are in *NP* also. This is because we can verify all decision versions of problems in P in polynomial time.

2.8.2.1 Example of Problems in NP

For the class *NP*, we simply require that any "yes" answer is "easily" verifiable. In order to explain the verifier-based definition of *NP*, let us consider the subset sum problem:

Assume there is a set of integers. The task of deciding whether a subset with sum zero exists is called the subset sum problem.

Assume that we are given some integers, such as $\{-1, -2, 3, 9, 8\}$, and we wish to know whether some of these integers sum up to zero. In this example, the answer is "yes", since the subset of integers $\{-1, -2, 3\}$ corresponds to the sum $(-1) + (-2) + 3 = 0$. It is clear that evaluation of each possible answer with n member take $O(n)$ operation and hence can be verified in polynomial time.

Also the problem of Clique (described in Sect. 2.7) is in *NP*. The clique problem is to determine whether a graph contains a clique of a specified size. To prove clique is in *NP*, it is enough to generate a verifier which can check the correctness of an answer in polynomial time.

For example in the undirected graph in Fig. 2.2, we have a 4-clique:

The decision version of the traveling salesman problem is in *NP*. The problem is to determine if there is a route visiting all cities with total distance less than k. Again the proof arises directly from the fact that for any given possible answer, we can check whether the given circuit visits all nodes and is less than predetermined constant k or not.

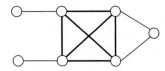

Fig. 2.2 A graph with 4-clique

2.8.3 Class NP-Complete

A decision problem X is NP-complete if: $X \in NP$; and for every problem $Y \in NP$, $Y \leq_T^p X$ (Brassard and Bratley 1988)

Item 1 indicates, first we need to prove the given problem belongs to class NP. From definition of class NP, we need to prove that a certificate exists which can be verified in polynomial time.

Item 2 indicates that all the other problems in NP, polynomially transform to it. The concepts of reductions presented in Sect. 2.6.

So if the problem X is NP-complete and the problem Z is in NP,
Z is NP-complete if and only if $X \leq_T^p Z$.
If $X \leq_m^p Z$ then Z is NP-complete (Brassard and Bratley 1988).

This is so important to us, because suppose we have a pool of problems that have already been shown to be NP-complete. To prove Z is NP-complete, we can choose an appropriate problem X from the pool and show X is polynomially reducible to Z (either many-one to in the sense of Turing). Several thousand problems have been enumerated in this way.

From a historical view, the concept of "NP-complete" was introduced by Stephen Cook in a paper entitled "The complexity of theorem-proving procedures" on pages 151–158 of the Proceedings of the 3rd Annual ACM Symposium on Theory of Computing in 1971.

2.8.3.1 Cooks Theorem

In the celebrated Cook–Levin theorem (independently proved by Leonid Levin), Cook proved that the Boolean satisfiability problem is NP-complete (See Gary and Johnson 1979 or Papadimitrious and Steiglits 1982 for proof). In 1972, Richard Karp proved that several other problems were also NP-complete (Karp 1972); thus there is a class of NP-complete problems (besides the Boolean satisfiability problem). Since Cook's original results, thousands of other problems have been shown to be NP-complete by reductions from other problems previously shown to be NP-complete; many of these problems are collected in Garey and Johnson's 1979 book Computers and Intractability: A Guide to NP-completeness.

From reduction concepts, a key characteristic of NP-complete problems is that if a polynomial time algorithm can be found for any such problem, then it will also solve all NP-complete problems in polynomial time. If we could find such an algorithm we would have shown that $P = NP$.

2.8.3.2 $P = NP$ Problem

An important aspect of the complexity theory is to categorize computational problems and algorithms into complexity classes. The most important open question of complexity theory is whether the complexity class P is the same as the complexity

Fig. 2.3 Open problem
$P = NP$

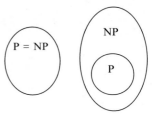

class *NP*, or is merely a subset as is generally believed (Fig. 2.3). Shortly after the question was first posed, it was realized that many important industry problems in the field of operations research are of an *NP* subclass called *NP*-complete. *NP*-complete problems have the property that solutions to these problems are quick to check, yet the current methods to find solutions are not "efficiently scalable". More importantly, if the *NP* class is larger than *P*, then no efficiently scalable solutions exist for these problems.

The openness of the *P*-*NP* problem prompts and justifies various research areas in the computational complexity theory, such as identification of efficiently solvable special cases of common computational problems, study of the computational complexity of finding approximate or heuristic solutions, as well as research into the hierarchies of complexity classes.

Nobody has yet been able to determine conclusively whether *NP*-complete problems are in fact solvable in polynomial time, making this one of the great unsolved problems of mathematics.

The point is, because of many known unresolved problems in *NP*-complete class, the trend is more toward $P \neq NP$.

2.8.3.3 The Importance of NP-completeness Phenomenon

The phenomenon of *NP*-completeness is important for both theoretical and practical reasons (Sipser 1996):

On the theoretical side, a researcher trying to show that *P* is unequal to *NP* only needs to look up to an *NP*-complete problem. If any problem in *NP* requires more than polynomial time, an *NP*-complete one does. Furthermore, a researcher attempting to prove that *P* equals *NP* only needs to find a polynomial time algorithm for an *NP*-complete problem to achieve this goal.

On the practical side, the phenomenon of *NP*-completeness may prevent wasting time searching for nonexistent polynomial time algorithm to solve a particular problem. Even though we may not have necessary mathematics prove that the problem is not polynomial time solvable ($P = NP$ problem), we believe that *P* is unequal to *NP*, so proving that a problem is *NP*-complete is strong evidence of its nonpolynomiality.

2.8.3.4 Example of Problems in NP-complete

Since the introduction of *NP*-complete class, many problems have been proved to be in *NP*-complete class. Here there is an in-complete list of problems (Du and Ko 2000):

- Boolean satisfiability problem (SAT)
- Knapsack problem
- Hamiltonian cycle problem
- Traveling salesman problem
- Sub graph isomorphism problem
- Subset sum problem
- Clique problem
- *N*-puzzle
- Vertex cover problem
- Independent set problem
- Graph coloring problem

Figure 2.4 shows a diagram of some of the problems and the reductions typically used to prove their *NP*-completeness. In this diagram, an arrow from one problem to another indicates the direction of the reduction. Note that this diagram is misleading

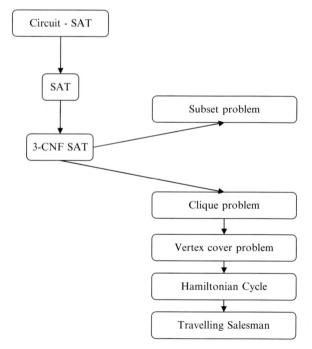

Fig. 2.4 Some *NP*-complete problems, indicating the reductions typically used to prove their *NP*-completeness (see http://en.wikipedia.org/wiki/*NP*-complete)

as a description of the mathematical relationship between these problems, as there exists a polynomial-time reduction between any two *NP*-complete problems; but it indicates where demonstrating this polynomial-time reduction has been easiest.

The Hamiltonian cycle problem was shown to be *NP*-complete by Karp (1972). As the Fig. 2.4 shows, TSP is also a *NP*-complete problem. To show that the TSP decision problem is *NP*-complete, we need to show two things: (a) that the TSP-decision problem is in class *NP* and (b) that a known *NP*-complete problem reduces to the TSP-decision problem (For this problem Hamiltonian cycle problem). To show (a), we note that, given any cycle, we can compute the cost of the cycle in polynomial time and therefore determine in polynomial time if the cycle has length less than or equal to B (in which case it would be a "yes" instance to the TSP-decision problem). Thus the TSP-decision problem is in class *NP*. To show (b), we construct a complete graph with the same vertex set as that found in the HCP. For each link in the new graph, if the corresponding link exits in the instance of the HCP, let the link length be 1; otherwise let the link length be 2. Clearly, the HCP has a solution if and only if the TSP on this complete graph has a solution with values less than or equal to n where n is the number of nodes in the vertex set (this proof is chose from Daskin 1995).

2.8.4 Class NP-Hard

NP-hard (nondeterministic polynomial-time hard), in computational complexity theory, is a class of problems informally "at least as hard as the hardest problems in *NP*." A problem H is *NP*-hard if and only if there is an *NP*-complete problem L that is polynomial time Turing reducible to H, i.e. $L \leq_T H$. In other words, L can be solved in polynomial time by an oracle machine with an oracle for H. Informally we can think of an algorithm that can call such an oracle machine as subroutine for solving H, and solves L in polynomial time if the subroutine call takes only one step to compute (Gary and Johnson 1979). *NP*-hard problems may be of any type: decision problems, search problems, optimization problems.

Such problems are ones such that an *NP*-complete problem polynomially reduces to the problem in question, but the problem under study is not provable in the class *NP*. Formally, the term *NP*-hard is also used to describe the optimization versions of the decision problems that are *NP*-complete (Daskin 1995).

2.8.4.1 Example of Problems in NP-Hard

An example of an *NP*-hard problem is the decision problem SUBSET-SUM. We already described this problem. The problem is, given a set of integers, does any non-empty subset of them add up to zero? That is a yes/no question, and happens to be *NP*-complete. Another example of an *NP*-hard problem is the optimization problem of finding the least-cost route through all nodes of a weighted graph or traveling salesman problem that we described it in Sect. 2.7.

There are also decision problems that are *NP*-hard but not *NP*-complete, for example the halting problem. This is the problem "given a program and its input, will it run forever?" That's a yes/no question and hence, a decision problem. It is easy to prove that the halting problem is *NP*-hard but not *NP*-complete. For example the Boolean satisfiability problem can be reduced to the halting problem by transforming it to the description of a Turing machine that tries all truth value assignments and when it finds one that satisfies the formula it halts and otherwise it goes into an infinite loop. It is also easy to see that the halting problem is not in *NP* since all problems in *NP* are decidable in a finite number of operations, while the halting problem, in general, is not (Garey and Johnson 1979).

2.9 Further Reading

Some classic books on complexity theory and network flows are Garey and Johnson (1979), Ahuja et al. (1993), Karp (1972), Papadimitriou and Steiglitz (1982), and Sahni and Horowitz (1978).

References

Agrawal M, Kayal N, Saxena N (2004) PRIMES is in P. Ann Math 160(2):781–793
Ahuja RK, Magnanti TL, Orlin JB (1993) Network flows: theory, algorithms, and applications. Prentice-Hall, Englewood Cliffs, NJ. ISBN: 013617549X
Brassard G, Bratley P (1988) Algorithmics theory and practice. Prentice-Hall, Englewood Cliffs, NJ
Cook S (1971) The complexity of theorem-proving procedures. Proceedings of the third annual ACM symposium on theory of Computing, pp 151–158
Daskin MS (1995) Network and discrete location models: Algorithms, and applications. Wiley, New York
Du D, Ko K (2000) Theory of computational complexity. Wiley, New York
Garey MR, Johnson DS (1979) Computers and intractability: A guide to the theory of *NP*-completeness. W.H. Freeman, San Francisco, CA
Karp RM (1972) Reducibility among combinational problems. In: Miller R, Thatcher J (eds) Complexity of computer computations. Plenum Press, New York, pp 86–103
Kozen DC (2006) Theory of computation. Springer-Verlag, Berlin
Martin JC (1996) Introduction to languages and the theory of computation. McGraw-Hill, New York
Papadimitriou CH (1994) Computational complexity. Addison-Wesley, Reading, MA
Papadimitrious CH, Steiglits K (1982) Combinatorial optimization: Algorithms and complexity. Prentice-Hall, Englewood Cliffs, NJ
Sahni S, Horowitz E (1978) Combinational problems: Reducibility and approximation. Oper Res 26:718–759

Sipser M (1996) Introduction to the theory of computation. Preliminary Edition. PWS Publishing
Sipser M (1997) Introduction to the theory of computation. PWS Publishing
Turing A (1936) On computable numbers with an application to the entscheidnungs problem. Proc Lond Math Soc ser 2, 42:230–265
Wood D (1987) Theory of computation. Wiley, New York

Chapter 3
Single Facility Location Problem

Esmaeel Moradi and Morteza Bidkhori

This chapter will focus on the simplest types of location problems, single facility location problem. These problems occur on a regular basis when working, layout problems (e.g., we may need to locate a machine in a shop, or items inside a warehouse). Also, on a larger scale, they can occur in, say, choosing the location of a warehouse to serve customers to whom goods must be delivered.

The models shall be studied as being "quick and dirty." They are "quick" in the sense that they can be used quickly and easily, and "dirty" in the send that they are approximate. The use of these models should be considered particularly when some location decision must be made quickly and with limited resource available for decision analysis.

When we wish to locate a single new facility in the plane, we often would like to minimize an objective function involving Euclidean or rectilinear distances between the new facility and a collection of existing facilities having known planar locations. The first objective function we consider is that of total travel distance, or total travel cost.

A number of interesting one-facility location problems exist and are amenable to the analysis presented in this chapter. Some typical examples of one-facility location problems are the location of:

1. New warehouse relative production facilities and customers.
2. Hospital, fire station or library in a metropolitan area.
3. New classroom building on a college campus.
4. New airfield to be used to provide supplies for a number of military bases.
5. Component in an electrical network.

In practice, many factors have an impact on location decisions. The relative importance of these factors depends on whether the scope of a particular location problem is international, national, statewide, or communitywide. For example, if we are trying to determine the location of a manufacturing facility in a foreign country, factors such as political stability, foreign exchange rates, business climate, duties, and taxes play a role. If the scope of the location problem is restricted to a few communities, then factors like community services, property tax incentive, local business climate, and local government regulations are more important.

It is often extremely difficult to find a single location that meets all these objectives at the desired level. For example, a location in the Midwest may offer a highly skilled labor pool, but construction and land costs may be too high.

This chapter is organized as follows. In Sect. 3.1, we consider a general problem formulation with rectilinear or square Euclidean or Euclidian or lp-norm distances, and Sect. 3.2, we consider solution techniques for discrete and continuous space. Continuous space is divided to MiniSum and MiniMax problem with various distances. MiniMax problem involving Euclidean distances is called the circle covering problem, which can be interpreted as the problem of covering all existing facility locations with a circle of minimum radius. MiniMax problems are more specialized than MiniSum problems and seem to be of interest, principally in cases where a worst case analysis is quite important. Finally, Sect. 3.3 represents one real world case studies briefly.

3.1 Problem Formulation

In this section, we represent a general problem formulation that is involving the distance traveled per trip with rectilinear or square Euclidean or Euclidian or lp-norm distances. In final section we discus about regional facilities.

3.1.1 A General Formulation of the Problem

3.1.1.1 Model Inputs

Model inputs of this model are as follows:

i: the index of existing facilities
n: the number of existing facilities

3.1.1.2 Model Outputs (Decision Variables)

Model outputs of this model are as follows:

$X = (x, y)$: coordinates of the location of new facility
$d(x_i, y_i)$: the distance between of new facility and existing facility i

3.1.1.3 Parameters

Parameters of this model are as follows:

$P_i = (a_i, b_i)$: coordinates of the location of existing facility i
w_i: weights of existing facility i

3.1.1.4 A General Formulation

A general formulation of the problem considered in this chapter may be given as follows:

$$f(X) = \sum_{t=1}^{m} w_i d(X, P_i). \quad (3.1)$$

The one-facility location problem is to determine the location of the new facility, say X^* that minimizes $f(X)$, the annual transportation cost.

3.1.2 Rectilinear Distance with Point Facilities

The rectilinear distance location problem combines the property of being a very appropriate distance measure for a large number of location problems and the property of being very simple to treat analytically.

Figure 3.1 illustrates that several different paths between x, p_i for each the rectilinear distance are the same. The number of such paths is, of course, infinite (Francis and White 1974).

The rectilinear distance location problem can be stated mathematically as

$$\text{Min } f(x, y) = \sum_{i=1}^{m} w_i \left(|x - a_i| + |y - b_i| \right). \quad (3.2)$$

From (2) it is seen that the problem can be equivalently stated as

$$\text{Min } f(x, y) = \text{Min} \sum_{i=1}^{m} w_i |x - a_i| + \sum_{i=1}^{m} w_i |y - b_i|. \quad (3.3)$$

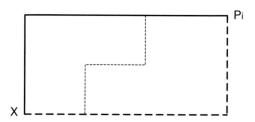

Fig. 3.1 Different rectilinear paths between X and P_i

where each quantity on the right-hand side can be treated as separate optimization problems:

$$\text{Min } f(x, y) = \sum_{i=1}^{m} w_i |x - a_i|, \quad (3.4)$$

$$\text{Min } f(x, y) = \sum_{i=1}^{m} w_i |y - b_i|. \quad (3.5)$$

3.1.3 Square Euclidean Distance with Point Facilities

In some facility location problems, cost is not a simple linear function of distance. As an example, the cost associated with the response of a fire truck to a fire is expected to be nonlinear with distance. Depending on the location problem, $f(X)$ can take on a number of different formulations. One nonlinear form of $f(X)$ treated in this chapter is the gravity problem. Suppose that cost is proportional to the square of the Euclidean distance between X and P_i. Thus, the function becomes

$$f(X) = \sum_{t=1}^{m} w_i \left[(x - a_i)^2 + (y - b_i)^2 \right]. \quad (3.6)$$

Location problem having the formulation given by (3.6) are referred to as gravity problems (Francis and White 1974).

3.1.4 Euclidean Distance with Point Facilities

The function of Euclidean distance is

$$f(X) = \sum_{t=1}^{m} w_i \left[(x - a_i)^2 + (y - b_i)^2 \right]^{0.5}. \quad (3.7)$$

Euclidian distance applies for some network location problems as well as some instances involving conveyors and air travel. Some electrical wiring problems and pipeline design problems are also examples of Euclidean distance problems (Francis and White 1974).

3.1.5 LP-Norm Distance with Point Facilities

Norms are usually employed as the basis for distance predicting functions in continuous location models. Since norms are convex functions, incorporating a norm in

3 Single Facility Location Problem

the objective function of a continuous location problem provides the useful property of convexity in the optimization model (Uster and Love 2001).

The l_p-norm distance between any two points $u = (u_1, u_2)$ and $v = (v_1, v_2)$ is given by

$$l_p(u, v) = \left[|u_1 - v_1|^p + |u_2 - v_2|^p\right]^{1/p}, \quad p \geq 1. \tag{3.8}$$

3.1.6 Regional Facilities Problem (Drezner 1986)

We consider the single-facility of the MiniSum type of location facilities on the plane. Both demand location and the facilities to be located are assumed to have circular shapes, and demand and service is assumed to have a uniform probability density inside each shape.

The problem reduces to the question of the effective distance d_e that should stand for distance between the demand area and the facility. d_e is actually the expected distance between the shapes with uniform probability distribution of demand and service. In Fig. 3.2, a circle of radius R representing a facility and a circle of radius r representing a demand area depicted. The distance between the circles center is d.

Let $d(x, y)$ be the distance between points X and Y (by any metric), F be the facility, and D be the demand. The probability that service and demand are generated at dF and dD, are $dF/\int x \in F\ dF$, and $dD/\int x \in F\ dD$, respectively. Therefore,

$$d_e = \frac{\int\limits_{x \in F} \int\limits_{y \in D} d(X, Y)\, dF\, dD}{\int\limits_{x \in F} dF \int\limits_{y \in D} dD}. \tag{3.9}$$

The MiniSum problem objective function is a sum of terms associated with pairs of facilities and demand points. d_e should represent the distance in the term associated with the facility F and the area demand D. This distance should be multiplied by the appropriate weight and the sum of all these terms should be minimized (Drezner 1986).

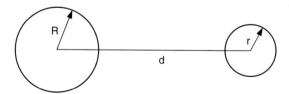

Fig. 3.2 Facility demand area

3.2 Solution Techniques

3.2.1 Techniques for Discrete Space Location Problems (Heragu 1997)

Our focus is primarily on the single-facility location problem. We provide both discrete space and continuous space models. The single facility for which we seek a location may be the only one that will serve all the customers, or it may be an addition to a network of existing facilities that are already serving customers.

3.2.1.1 Qualitative Analysis

The location scoring method is a very popular, subjective decision-making tool that is relatively easy to use. It consists of these steps:

- Step 1. List all the factors that are important-that have an impact on the location decision.
- Step 2. Assign an appropriate weight (typically between 0 and 1) to each factor based on the relative importance of each.
- Step 3. Assign a score (typically between 0 and 100) to each location with respect to each factor identified in step 1.
- Step 4. Compute the weighted score for each factor for each location by multiplying its weight by the corresponding score.
- Step 5. Compute the sum of the weighted scores for each location and choose a location based on these scores.

Although step 5 calls for the location decision to be made solely on the basis of the weighted scores, those scores were arrived at in a subjective manner, and hence a final location decision must also take into account objective measures such as transportation cost, loads, and operating costs (Heragu 1997).

3.2.1.2 Quantitative Analysis

Several quantitative techniques are available to solve the discrete space, single facility location problem. Each is appropriate for a specific set of objectives and constraints.

For example, the so-called MiniMax location model is appropriate for determining the location of an emergency service facility, where the objective is to minimize the maximum distance traveled between the facility and any customer.

The reader may be wondering: If the set of plants including their locations is given, where is the location problem? To answer this question, consider the following problem: We have m plants in a distribution network that serves n customers. Due to an increase in demand at one or more of these n customers, it has become necessary to open an additional plant the new plant could be located at p possible sites. To evaluate which of the p sites will minimize distribution (transportation) costs, we can set up p transportation models, each with n customers and $m + 1$ plants, where the $(m + 1)$ plant corresponds to the new location being evaluated. Solving the model will tell us not only the distribution of goods from the $m + 1$ plant (including the new one from the location being evaluated) but also the cost of the distribution. The location that yields the least overall distribution cost is the one where the new facility should be located (Heragu 1997).

3.2.1.3 Hybrid Analysis

A disadvantage of the qualitative method is that a location decision is made based entirely on a subjective evaluation. Although the quantitative method overcomes this disadvantage, it does not allow us to incorporate unquantifiable factors that have a major impact on the location decision. For example, the quantitative techniques can easily consider transportation and operational costs, but intangible factors, such as the attitude of a community toward businesses, potential labor unrest, and reliability of auxiliary service providers, though important in choosing a location, are difficult to capture. We need a method that incorporates subjective as well as quantifiable cost and other factors.

This model classifies the objective and subjective factors important to the specific location problem being addressed as:

- Critical;
- Objective;
- Subjective.

The meaning of the latter two factors is obvious, but the meaning of critical factors needs some discussion. In every location decision, at least one factor usually determines whether or not a location will be considered for further evaluation. For example, if water is used extensively in a manufacturing process (e.g., a brewery), then a site that does not have an adequate water supply now or in the future is automatically removed from consideration. This is an example of a critical factor. Some factors can be objective and critical or subjective and critical. For example, the adequacy of skilled labor may be a critical factor as well as a subjective factor.

After the factors are classified, they are assigned numeric values:

CF_{ij}: if location i satisfies critical factor j, 0 otherwise
OF_{ij}: cost of objective factor j at location i
SF_{ij}: numeric value assigned (on a scale of 0–1) to subjective factor j for location i.
W_j: weight assigned to subjective factor $J (0 \leq W_j \leq 1)$.

Assume that we have m candidate locations and p critical, q objective, and r subjective factors. We can determine the overall critical factor measure (CFM_j), objective factor measure (OFM_j) and subjective factor measure (CFM_j) for each location i with these equations:

$$CFM_i = CF_{i1}CF_{i2}\ldots CF_{iP} = \prod_{j=1}^{P} CF_{ij}, i = 1,\ldots,m, \qquad (3.10)$$

$$OFM_I = \frac{\max\left[\sum_{j=1}^{q} OF_{ij}\right] - \sum_{j=i}^{q} OF_{ij}}{\max\left[\sum_{j=1}^{q} OF_{ij}\right] - \min\left[\sum_{j=i}^{q} OF_{ij}\right]}, i = 1,\ldots,m, \qquad (3.11)$$

$$SFM_i = \sum_{j=1}^{R} w_j SF_{ij}, i = 1,\ldots,m. \qquad (3.12)$$

The location measure LM_j for each location is then calculated as:

$$LM_i = CFM[\alpha OFM_i + (1-\alpha)SFM_i], \qquad (3.13)$$

where is the weight assigned to the objective factor measure? Notice that even if one critical factor is not satisfied by a location i, then CFM_j and hence LM_j are equal to zero. The OFM_j values are calculated so that the location with the maximum $\sum OF_{ij}$ gets an OFM_j value of zero and the one with the smallest $\sum OF_{ij}$ value gets an OFM_j value of one. Equation (3.13) assumes that the objective factors are cost based. If any of these factors are profit based, then a negative sign has to be placed in front of each such objective factor and (3.13) can still be used. This works because maximizing a linear profit function z is the same as minimizing $-z$.

After LM_j is determined for each candidate location, the next step is to select the one with the greatest LM_j value. Because the a weight is subjectively assigned by the user, it may be a good idea for the user to evaluate the LM_j values for various appropriate a weights, analyze the trade off between objective and subjective measures, and choose a location based on this analysis (Heragu 1997).

3.2.2 Techniques for Continues Space Location Problems

3.2.2.1 MiniSum Problems for Rectilinear Distance

Median method with point facilities. As the name implies, the median method finds the median location (defined later) and assigns the new facility to it. This method is used for single-facility location problems with rectilinear distance. Consider m facilities in a distribution network. Due to marketplace reasons (e.g., increased customer demand), it is desired to add another facility to this network. The interaction between the new facility and existing ones is known. The problem is to locate the new facility to minimize the total interaction cost between each existing facility and the new one.

3 Single Facility Location Problem

We can rewrite expression (1) as follows:

$$\text{Min } f(X) = \sum_{i=1}^{m} w_i |x_i - \bar{x}| + \sum_{i=1}^{m} w_i |y_i - \bar{y}|. \tag{3.14}$$

Because the x and y terms can be separated, we can solve the optimal x and y coordinates independently. Here is the median method:

Median method's steps

- Step 1. List the existing facilities in no decreasing order of the x coordinates.
- Step 2. Find the jth x coordinate in the list (created in step 1) at which the cumulative weight equals or exceeds half the total weight for the first time;

$$\sum_{i=1}^{j-1} w_i < \sum_{i=1}^{m} \frac{w_i}{2} \text{ and } \sum_{i=1}^{j} w_i \geq \sum_{i=1}^{m} \frac{w_i}{2}. \tag{3.15}$$

- Step 3. List the existing facilities in no decreasing order of the y coordinate.
- Step 4. Find the kth y coordinate in the list (created in step 3) at which the cumulative weight equals or exceeds half the total weight for the first time:

$$\sum_{i=1}^{k-1} w_i < \sum_{i=1}^{m} \frac{w_i}{2} \text{ and } \sum_{i=1}^{k} w_i \geq \sum_{i=1}^{m} \frac{w_i}{2}. \tag{3.16}$$

The optimal location of the new facility is given by the jth x coordinate and the kth y coordinate identified in steps 2 and 4, respectively.

Programmed mathematical method with point facilities. Although the median method is the most efficient algorithm for the rectilinear distance, single facility location problem, we present programmed mathematical method for solving it. It involves transforming the nonlinear, unconstrained model given by (3.14) into an equivalent linear. Consider the following notation:

$$x_i^+ = \begin{cases} (x_i - \bar{x}) & \text{if } (x_i - \bar{x}) > 0 \\ 0 & \text{otherwise} \end{cases}, \tag{3.17}$$

$$x_i^- = \begin{cases} (x_i - \bar{x}) & \text{if } (x_i - \bar{x}) \leq 0 \\ 0 & \text{otherwise} \end{cases}. \tag{3.18}$$

We can observe that

$$|x_i - \bar{x}| = x_i^+ + x_i^-, \tag{3.19}$$

$$x_i + x^- = x_i^+ - x_i^-. \tag{3.20}$$

A similar definition of y_i^+, y_i^- yield

$$|y_i - \bar{y}| = y_i^+ + y_i^-, \tag{3.21}$$
$$y_i + \bar{y} = y_i^+ - y_i^-. \tag{3.22}$$

Thus the transformed linear model is:

$$\text{Min} \sum_{i=1}^{n} w_i (x_i^+ + x_i^- + y_i^+ + y_i^-). \tag{3.23}$$

Subject to

$$x_i + \bar{x} = x_i^+ + x_i^-, i = 1, \ldots, n, \tag{3.24}$$
$$y_i + \bar{y} = y_i^+ - y_i^-, i = 1, \ldots, n, \tag{3.25}$$
$$x_i^+, x_i^-, y_i^+, y_i^- \geq 0, i = 1, \ldots n, \tag{3.26}$$
$$\bar{x}, \bar{y} \text{ unrestricted in sign.} \tag{3.27}$$

For this model to be equivalent to (3.14), the solution must be such that either x_i^+ or x_i^-, but not both, is greater than zero. [If both are, then the values of x and x do not satisfy their definition in (3.17) and (3.18).] Similarly, only one of y_i^+, y_i^- must be greater than zero. Fortunately these conditions are automatically satisfied in the preceding linear model. This can be easily verified by contradiction. Assume that in the solution to the transformed model, x_i^+ and y_i^- take on values p and q, where $p, q > 0$. We can immediately observe that such a solution cannot be optimal because one can choose another set of values for, x_i^+, x_i^- as follows:

$$x_i^+ = p - \min\{p, q\}, x_i^- = q - \min\{p, q\}. \tag{3.28}$$

And obtain a feasible solution to the model that yields a lower objective value than before because the new x_i^+, x_i^- values are less than their previously assumed values. More over, at least one of the new values of x_i^+, x_i^- is zero according to the expression (3.28). This means that the original set of values for x_i^+, x_i^- could not have been optimal. Using a similar argument, we can show that either y^+ or y^- will take on a value of zero in the optimal solution.

The model described by expressions (3.19), (3.21), (3.23) and (3.27), can be simplified by noting that xi^+ can be substituted as $\bar{x} - x_i^- + x_i^+$ from equality (3.20) and the fact that x is unrestricted in sign. Also y may be substituted similarly, resulting in a model with $2n$ fewer constraints and variables.

Contour line method for point facilities. Contour lines are important because if the optimal location determined is infeasible, we can move along the contour line and choose a feasible point that will have a similar cost. Also, if subjective factors need to be incorporated, we can use contour lines to move away from the optimal location determined by the median method to another point that better satisfies the subjective criteria.

3 Single Facility Location Problem

We now provide an algorithm to construct contour lines, describe the steps, and illustrate with a numeric example. Algorithm for drawing contour lines is as follows:

- Step 1. Draw a vertical line through the x coordinate and a horizontal line through the y coordinate of each facility.
- Step 2. Label each vertical line v_i, $i = 1, 2, \ldots, p$, and horizontal line H_i, $i = 1, 2, \ldots, q$, where
- V_i = sum of weights of facilities whose x coordinates fall on vertical line i
- H_i = sum of weights of facilities whose y coordinates fall on horizontal line j
- Step 3. Set $i = j = 1$ and $N_0 = D_0 = -\sum_{i=1}^{m} w_i$.
- Step 4. Set $N_i = N_{i-1} + 2V_i$; and $D_i = D_{i-1} + 2H_i$. Increment $i = i+1$ and $j = j+1$.
  If $i \leq p$ or $j \leq q$, repeat 4. Otherwise, set $i = j = 0$.
- Steps 5. Determine S_{ij}, the slope of the contour lines through the region bounded by vertical lines i and $i+1$ and horizontal lines j and $j+1$ using the equation $S_i = -N_i/D_i$. Increment $i = i+1$ and $j = j+1$.
- Step 6. If $i \leq p$ or $j \leq q$, go to step 5. Otherwise, select any point (x, y) and draw a contour line with slope S_{ij} in the region $[i, j]$ in which (x, y) appears so that the line touches the boundary of this region. From one of the endpoints of this line, draw another contour line through the adjacent region with the corresponding slope. Repeat this until you get a contour line ending at point (x, y). You now have a region bounded by contour lines with (x, y) on the boundary of the region.

There are four points about this algorithm. First, the numbers of vertical and horizontal lines need not be equal. Two facilities may have the same x coordinate but not the same y coordinate, thereby requiring one horizontal line and two vertical lines. In fact, this is why the index i of V_i; ranges from one to p and that of H_i ranges from one to q.

Second, the N_i and D_i computed in steps 3 and 4 correspond to the numerator and denominator, respectively, of the slope equation of any contour line through the region bounded by the vertical lines i and $i+1$ and the horizontal lines j and $j+1$. To verify this, consider the objective function (14) when the new facility is located at some point (x, y) that is, $\overline{x} = x, \overline{y} = y$:

$$f(X) = \sum_{i=1}^{m} w_i |x_i - x| + \sum_{i=1}^{m} w_i |y_i - y|. \quad (3.29)$$

By noting that the $V_i's$ and $H_i's$ calculated in step 2 of the algorithm correspond to the sum of the weights of facilities whose x, y coordinates are equal to the x, y coordinates, respectively, of the i, j distinct lines and that we have p, q such coordinates or lines ($p \leq m$, $q \leq m$), we can rewrite (29) as follows:

$$f(X) = \sum_{i=1}^{m} V_i |x_i - x| + \sum_{i=1}^{m} H_i |y_i - y|. \quad (3.30)$$

Suppose that x is between the s and $(S+l)$, (distinct) x coordinates or vertical lines (since we have drawn vertical lines through these coordinates in step 1). Similarly, let y be between the t and $(t+l)$ vertical lines, then

$$f(X) = \sum_{i=1}^{S} V_i(x - x_i) + \sum_{i=S+1}^{P} V_i(x_i - x) + \sum_{i=1}^{t} H_i(y - y_i) + \sum_{i=t+1}^{q} H_i(y_i - y). \tag{3.31}$$

Rearranging the variable and constant terms and added and subtracted terms we can reach this equation (for details see Heragu 1997):

$$f(X) = \left[2\sum_{i=1}^{s} V_i - \sum_{i=1}^{m} w_i\right] x + \left[2\sum_{i=1}^{t} H_i - \sum_{i=1}^{m} w_i\right] y + c. \tag{3.32}$$

Equation (3.26) is $f(X) = N_s x + D_t y + c$, which can be rewritten as

$$y = -\frac{N_S}{D_t} x + (f(X) - c). \tag{3.33}$$

This expression for the total cost function at x, y or, in fact, any other point in the region $[s, t]$ has the form $y = mx + c$, where the slope $N = -N_s/D_t$. This is exactly how the slopes are computed in step 5 of the algorithm.

We have shown that the slope of any point x, y within a region $[s, t]$ bounded by vertical lines sand $s + 1$ and horizontal lines t and $t + 1$ can be easily computed. Thus the contour line (or is cost line) through x, y in region $[s, t]$ may be readily drawn. Proceeding from one line in one region to the next line in the adjacent region until we come back to the starting point (x, y) then gives us a region of points in which any point has a total cost less than or equal to that of (x, y).

Third, the lines V_0, V_{P+1} and H_0, H_{P+1} are required for defining the "exterior" regions. Although they are not included in the algorithm steps, the reader must take care to draw these lines.

Fourth, once we have determined the slopes of all the regions, the user may choose any point (x, y) other than a point that minimizes the objective function and draw a series of contour lines in order to get a region that contains points (i.e., facility locations) yielding as good or better objective function values than (x, y). Thus step 6 could be repeated for several points to yield several such regions. Beginning with the innermost region, if any point in it is feasible, we use it as the optimal location. If not, we can go to the next innermost region to identify a feasible point. We repeat this procedure until we get a feasible point (Heragu 1997).

3.2.2.2 MiniSum Square Euclidean Distance

Programmed mathematical method with point facilities. This problem can be formulated as follows:

3 Single Facility Location Problem

$$\text{Min } f(x,y) = \sum_{t=1}^{m} w_i \left[(x - a_i)^2 + (y - b_i)^2 \right]. \tag{3.34}$$

Any point (x^*, y^*) that minimizes (34) must satisfy the conditions

$$\left(\frac{\partial f(x^*, y^*)}{\partial x^*}, \frac{\partial f(x^*, y^*)}{\partial x^*} \right) = (0, 0). \tag{3.35}$$

Computing the partial derivatives of (3.34) with respect to x and y and then setting them to zero gives the following unique solution:

$$x^* = \frac{\sum_{i=1}^{m} w_i a_i}{\sum_{i=1}^{m} w_i}, \tag{3.36}$$

$$y^* = \frac{\sum_{i=1}^{m} w_i b_i}{\sum_{i=1}^{m} w_i}. \tag{3.37}$$

The coordinates x^* and y^* of the new facility may thus be interpreted as weighted averages of the x and y coordinates of the existing facilities, and are, in fact, the coordinates that minimize (3.34). Conditions (3.35) can be shown to be both necessary and sufficient for a minimum. Thus, the gravity problem has a simple solution. The solution is sometimes referred to as the cancroids or center of gravity solution.

Contour line method for point facilities. Contour lines for this problem can be obtained quite easily. We have two cases; in the first case there exists a single facility. In the second case there is equal item movement between the new facility and each of the two existing facilities. Consequently, it is easy to imagine that the contour lines will be concentric circles centered on the optimum location.

Now, what do you think the contour lines will look like when we have any number of existing facilities with unequal item movement? If you suspect the contour lines will still be concentric circles centered on the optimum location, your intuition is remarkable, for that is the case. To see why this is true, notice that from (3.34) we want to determine the set of all points (x, y) such that

$$k = \sum_{i=1}^{m} w_i \left[(x - a_i)^2 + (y - b_i)^2 \right]. \tag{3.38}$$

In this section k is a constant value. Consequently, on expanding the squared terms we find that

$$k = x^2 \sum_{i=1}^{m} w_i - 2x \sum_{i=1}^{m} w_i a_i + \sum_{i=1}^{m} w_i a_i^2 + y^2 \sum_{i=1}^{m} w_i - 2y \sum_{i=1}^{m} w_i b_i + w_i b_i^2. \tag{3.39}$$

If we let

$$W = \sum_{i=1}^{m} w_i. \qquad (3.40)$$

Divide (3.40) b_i W, and employ the relations (3.36) and (3.37), we find that

$$\frac{k}{W} = x^2 - 2xx^* + \sum_{i=1}^{m} \frac{w_i a_i^2}{W} + y^2 - 2yy^* + \sum_{i=1}^{m} \frac{w_i b_i^2}{W}. \qquad (3.41)$$

On adding $(X^*)^2$ and $(y^*)^2$ to both sides of (3.41) and simplifying, we obtain the equation for a circle,

$$r^2 = (x - x^*)^2 + (y - y^*)^2. \qquad (3.42)$$

Centered on the point (x^*, y^*) with radius

$$r = \left[\frac{k}{W} + (x^*)^2 + (y^*)^2 - \sum_{i=1}^{m} \frac{w_i (a_i^2 + b_i^2)}{W} \right]^{0.5}. \qquad (3.43)$$

This is an interesting and, to us, a nonnutritive result. Based on this result, if you are unable to locate the new facility at the optimum location (x^*, y^*) and must evaluate alternative sites, you should always choose the one that has the smallest straight-line distance to the point (x^*, y^*) (Francis and White 1974).

Solution method for regional facilities. For simplicity of notation, the effective distance is denoted in the square Euclidean case by De^2. Polar coordinates are used. A point inside the facility circle is (x, θ), and a point inside the demand circle is (y, θ) (where the origin is the center of that circle). Note that the denominator of (3.9) is the product of the areas of the two circles. It follows from (3.9) that

$$D_e^2 = \frac{\int_0^{2\pi} \int_0^r \int_0^{2\pi} \int_0^R [(d + y \cos\phi - x \cos\theta)^2 + (y \sin\phi - x \sin\theta)^2] x.dx.d\theta.y.dy.d\phi}{\pi R^2 \pi r^2}. \qquad (3.44)$$

Straightforward calculations lead to

$$D_e^2 = d^2 \frac{R^2 + r^2}{2}. \qquad (3.45)$$

Formula (3.45) leads to the following simple theorem:

When demand points and/or facilities have a circular area, then the squared-Euclidean MiniSum problem has the same optimal locations of facilities as the problem defined whit point at the center of the circles.

By (3.45), the objective function consists of two parts. The first (the weighted sum of d^2) is identical to that of the problem defined with points. The second part [the weighted sum of $(R^2 + r^2)/2$] is a constant for given weights and radii of circles. The theorem clearly follows.

Note that even though the optimal locations of the facilities are the same, the minimal cost increase by the constant value of the second term of the objective function (Drezner 1986).

3.2.2.3 MiniSum Euclidean Distance

Weisfeld method with point facilities. The approach that immediately comes to mind in solving the Euclidean distance problem is again to compute the partial derivative of (3.7) and set them to zero. Assuming $(x, y) \neq (a_i, b_i), i = 1, 2, \ldots, m$, the partial derivatives are

$$\frac{\partial f(x, y)}{\partial x} = \sum_{i=1}^{m} \frac{w_i(x - a_i)}{\left[(x - a_i)^2 + (y - b_i)^2\right]^{0.5}}, \quad (3.46)$$

$$\frac{\partial f(x, y)}{\partial y} = \sum_{i=1}^{m} \frac{w_i(y - b_i)}{\left[(x - a_i)^2 + (y - b_i)^2\right]^{0.5}}. \quad (3.47)$$

Notice that If, for any $i, (x, y) = (a_i, b_i)$, then (3.46) and (3.47) are undefined. Consequently, we see that difficulties arise when the location for the new facility coincides (mathematically) with the location of some existing facility. If there were some guarantee that any optimum location of the new facility would never be the same as the location of an existing facility, then (3.46) and (3.47) would still give necessary and sufficient conditions for a least cost location of the new facility. Unfortunately, there is no such guarantee available. Consequently, a modification of the partial derivative approach is required. The modification is based on the two-tupelo $R(x, y)$, which is defined as follows, if $(x, y) \neq (a_i, b_i)$, $i = 1, \ldots, m$:

$$R(x, y) = \left(\frac{\partial f(x, y)}{\partial x}, \frac{\partial f(x, y)}{\partial y}\right). \quad (3.48)$$

And if $(x, y) = (a_k, b_k)$, $k = 1, 2, \ldots, m$,

$$R(x, y) = R(a_k, b_k) = \begin{cases} (0, 0), & \text{if } u_k \leq w_k \\ \left(\frac{u_k - w_k}{u_k} s_k, \frac{u_k - w_k}{u_k} t_k\right), & \text{if } u_k > w_k \end{cases} \quad (3.49)$$

where

$$s_k = \sum_{\substack{i=1 \\ \neq k}}^{m} \frac{w_i(a_k - a_i)}{\left[(a_k - a_i)^2 + (b_k - b_i)^2\right]^{0.5}}. \quad (3.50)$$

$$t_k = \sum_{\substack{i=1 \\ \neq k}}^{m} \frac{w_i(b_k - b_i)}{\left[(a_k - a_i)^2 + (b_k - b_i)^2\right]^{0.5}}. \quad (3.51)$$

The two-tuple $R(x, y)$ is defined for all points in the plane. A necessary and sufficient condition for (x^*, y^*) is established to be a least-cost new facility location is that $R(x^*, y^*) = (0, 0)$, Consequently, the location of some existing facility (a_k, a_k), will be the optimum location for the new facility if and only if $u_k < w_k$ Thus, one should compute the value of u_k and compare it with the value of Wk if it is suspected that the optimum new facility location coincides with the location of existing facility k.

Although we have available necessary and sufficient conditions for an optimum solution to the Euclidean problem, we still do not have a way of determining (x^*, y^*). The two-tuple $R(x, y)$, referred to subsequently as Kuhn's modified gradient, can also be manipulated to provide the basis for a computational procedure for finding the location (x^*, y^*). Notice that, on setting (3.46) equal to zero, we obtain the expression

$$x \sum_{i=1}^{m} \frac{w_i}{\left[(x-a_i)^2 + (y-b_i)^2\right]^{0.5}} = \sum_{i=1}^{m} \frac{w_i a_i}{\left[(x-a_i)^2 + (y-b_i)^2\right]^{0.5}}, \quad (3.52)$$

If we let

$$g_i(x, y) = \frac{w_i}{\left[(x-a_i)^2 + (y-b_i)^2\right]^{0.5}}. \quad (3.53)$$

Then (3.53) can be given as

$$x = \frac{\sum_{i=1}^{m} a_i g_i(x, y)}{g_i(x, y)}. \quad (3.54)$$

Likewise, from (3.47) we obtain

$$y = \frac{\sum_{i=1}^{m} b_i g_i(x, y)}{g_i(x, y)}. \quad (3.55)$$

So long as $g(x, y)$ is defined, we can employ the following iterative procedure:

$$x^k = \frac{\sum_{i=1}^{m} a_i g_i(x^{(k-1)}, y^{(k-1)})}{\sum_{i=1}^{m} g_i(x^{(k-1)}, y^{(k-1)})}, \quad (3.56)$$

$$y^k = \frac{\sum_{i=1}^{m} b_i g_i(x^{(k-1)}, y^{(k-1)})}{\sum_{i=1}^{m} g_i(x^{(k-1)}, y^{(k-1)})}. \quad (3.57)$$

3 Single Facility Location Problem

The superscripts denote the iteration number. Thus, a starting value (x^0, y^0) is required to determine. The value of (x^1, y^1) is used to determine the value of (x^2, y^2), and so forth. The iterative procedure continues until no appreciable improvement occurs in the estimate of the optimum location for the new facility, or until a location is found that satisfies Kuhn's modified gradient condition.

HAP method with point facilities. An alternative iterative solution procedure can be employed to solve the Euclidean problem without employing Kuhn's modified gradient procedure. The procedure is almost identical to that given by (3.56) and (3.57). With the exception that $g_i(X, y)$ is defined as

$$g_i(x, y) = \frac{w_i}{\left[(x - a_i)^2 + (y - b_i)^2 + \epsilon\right]^{0.5}}; i = 1, 2, \ldots, m, \quad (3.58)$$

where ε is an arbitrarily small, it is positive valued constant. Notice that (3.58) is always defined. Furthermore, as the value of ε approaches zero, the new function approaches the original function. We have found that the use of (3.58) in (3.56) and (3.57) produce a very efficient solution procedure for the Euclidean problem.

Contour line method for point facilities. Unfortunately, exact methods for constructing contour lines are not available for the Euclidean problem, except for the simplest cases where there are one or two existing facilities. As illustrated in Fig. 3.3. The contour lines for case (a) are for a single existing facility and for case (b) are for two existing facilities, each having equal item movement with the new facility.

It is relatively simple to obtain approximate contour lines by evaluating the cost function over, say, a rectangular grid of points covering the ranges of (x, y) values of interest. The contour lines can then be drawn by interpolating between grid points. Alternatively, one can assign a given value k to $f(x, y)$ in (7), pick a value of x, and search over y for the two values that yield the value k. The process is continued for successive values of x until a family of points is obtained for the contour line having value k (Francis and White 1974).

Solution method for regional facilities. For similarity of notation, the expression for d_e in this case is similar to that of (3.44). The change is that the integrand in (3.44) is put under a square root. This small change turns the four-dimensional integration into a real challenge.

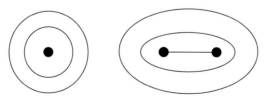

Fig. 3.3 Contour lines for two simple Euclidean location problems (Francis and White 1974)

First calculate an approximation for d^2 for a large d, i.e., $d \gg R$, R. let I be the integrand. Then

$$I^2 = (d + y \cos \phi - x \cos \theta)^2 + (y \sin \phi - x \sin \theta)^2. \tag{3.59}$$

With appropriate integrand, we have

$$d_e^2 \cong d^2 + \frac{R^2 + r^2}{4} + \frac{(R^2 + r^2)^2}{64d^2}. \tag{3.60}$$

And if the last term is ignored (since d is large), then (3.60) is similar to (3.45).
Therefore, for a large d,

$$\overline{d_e} \cong \sqrt{d^2 + (R^2 + r^2)/4}. \tag{3.61}$$

Is a good approximation of d_e. Note that the approximation (3.60) is not defined for $d = 0$ and tat it is far off for a small d, while $\overline{d_e}$ turns out to be quite accurate for small d, also.

The exact calculation of d_e is long and tedious. You can see the summarized of exact calculation of d_e in Drezner (1986).

The goodness of the approximation of $\overline{d_e}$ to d_e was checked in Drezner (1986), the ratio between the two was calculated. The ratio $\overline{d_e}/d_e$ was found to be between 0.75 (for $r = d = 0$) and 1 (for large d and any r).

Finally, it was checked the goodness of the approximation:

$$d_A = \sqrt{d^2 + \frac{4}{9}(R^2 + r^2)}. \tag{3.62}$$

The number 4/9 was chosen so that $d_A = d_e$ for $r = d = 0$. It was found that $d_e \leq d_A \leq 1.07 d_e$, which is a better approximation than $\overline{d_e}$.

The point facilities location problem in two regions with different norms. Suppose the plane is divided by a straight line into two regions with different norms. We find the location of a single new facility such that the sum of the distances from the existing facilities to this point is minimized. This is a non-convex optimization problem. We have the optimal solution lies in the rectangular hull of the existing points.

Suppose the plane, R^2, is divided by a straight line, $y = mx$, into two region, π_1, with an l_{P1}, and π_2 with an $lP2$ norm ($p_1, p_2 \geq 1$). Suppose also that there are respectively, n_1 and n_2 points on each side. The problem is to find the location of a new point such that the sum of the weighted distances from the existing $n_1 + n_2$ points to this is minimized. Mathematically the problem can be stated as

$$p_1 : \min_x \left\{ \sum_{p_i \in \pi_1} w_i \, d(x, p_i) + \sum_{p_i \in \pi_2} w_i \, d(x, p_i) \right\}, \tag{3.63}$$

3 Single Facility Location Problem

where $d(x, p_i)$ is the shortest distance, induced by the norms, between the existing point $p_i = (a_i, b_i)$, and the new point $x = (x, y)$; w_i's > 0 are given weights assigned to the p_i's. when x and p_i are both on the same side of the dividing line, then the problem reduces to a single norm problem; for the l_1 and l_2, $d(x, p_i)$ is the rectilinear or Euclidean distances between them. The difficulty arises when x and p_i are on different sides of the boundary line.

We consider the special case of l_1 and l_2 with the boundary line $y = mx$. Note that without loss of generality we assume that the line passes through the origin. There are also make the more realistic assumption that for the points on the π_1 side, the shortest distance may involve passing through the boundary.

Model properties. There are some properties of the problem for the special case of l_1 and l_2 norms. We have a fixed point $p \in \pi_2$, an $x \in \pi_1$, and a fixed (straight) line segment L of any orientation. Let

$$d(x, p) = \min_{z \in l} \{k_1(x, z) + k_2(z, p)\}, \qquad (3.64)$$

where k_1 and k_2 are arbitrary norms. Then d is a convex function of X.

There is a characterization of the crossing (gate) points on the boundary line and the shortest path connecting two points on different sides of the line.

Suppose R^2 is divided by a straight line, $y = mx$, into two regions, π_1 and π_2, whit l_1, and l_2 norms, respectively. Assume, without loss of generality, that $m > 0$. Then for any pair of given points $p_1 = (a_1, b_1) \in \pi_1$ and $p_2 = (a_1, b_1) \in \pi_2$ the shortest path form p_1 to p_2 passes through the line segment connecting points $(a_1, m\,a_1)$ and $(b_1/m, b_1)$ on the boundary line.

The intersection of the shortest path connecting points $p_1 \in \pi_1$ and $p_2 \in \pi_2$ whit the boundary line $y = mx$ $(m > 0)$ is either one of the points (a_1, ma_1) and $(b_1/m, b_1)$, or the point $(\bar{x}, m\bar{x})$, with $\bar{x}$ given above, if $a_1 \leq \bar{x} \leq b_1/m$.

There is optimal solution to the overall problem in the rectangular hull of the existing points. The rectangular hull of a set of points is defined as the smallest rectangle with sides parallel to the (x and y) axes) containing the set.

Solution procedure. Big square small square (BSSS) method is a geometrical branch and bound algorithm.

The procedure start with the rectangular hull, R, of the existing points, it contains the optimal solution then we partition R into four rectangles by drawing vertical and horizontal lines through the middle of its sides. At partitioning level k, denote these rectangles by R_{k1}, R_{k2}, R_{K3}, and, R_{k4}. We take the points at the center of each rectangle and evaluate the objective at these points. The best solution provides an upper bound for the overall problem.

The distance between points inside a rectangle is taken to be zero. The distance between a point p_i outside a rectangle R and the point inside that rectangle is taken to be the distance between p_i and the closest point to it on the boundary of R which could either be a corner point of R, or the projection of p_i onto R. note that since R is closed and convex, such a point indeed exists.

A sub-square for which the lower bound exceeds the value of the best known solution is fathomed. The process continues until the larger side of the sub-rectangle is less than a given tolerance, ε. The steps of the algorithm are outlined below. The input to the algorithm is a set of existing points, and the termination tolerance ε. The output is the optimal location of the new facility, X_b, and the optimal objective value, f_b.

Algorithm

1. Find the rectangular hull of existing facilities, R; set $L = 0$, $f_b = \infty$; and let $d^* = \max \{x^-_{max}\ x_{min},\ y^-_{max}\ y_{min}\}$;
2. Set $l = l+1$, and partition R into four equal sub-rectangles $R_{l,1}$, $R_{l,2}$, $R_{l,3}$, $R_{l,4}$. Calculate the objective value flr at the midpoint of each sub-rectangle. If minr{flr} $< f_b$, update f_b to this value.
3. For each demand point p_i find the minimum distance dir from p_i to $R_{l,r}$, $r = 1, \ldots, 4$, $l_{bl,r} = \sum i\ w_i$ dir. If $l_{bL,r} > f_b$, fathom $R_{L,r}$ and set $l_{bL,r} = \infty$.
4. Set $l'_b = \text{minr}\{l_{bL,r}\}$ and $r' = \text{argminr}\{l_{bL,r}\}$. If $l'_b = \infty$, go to step(6); else, if $(0.5)L\ d^* < \varepsilon$ go to step (5); else, set $R = R_{L,r'}$: fathom $R_{L,r'}$ and set $R_{L,r'} = \infty$, and go to step (2).
5. If $lb' < f_b$, set $f_b = l'_b$, define Xb as the center of sub-rectangle $R_{L,r'}$, and fathom this rectangle.
6. Set $L = L - 1$; if $L = 0$ go to step (7); else, if unfathomed sub-rectangles at level L are found, choose the one with the most favorable l_b; donet it as R, and return to step (2); else, repeat step (6).
7. Terminate the algorithm with optimal new facility location X_b having the objective function value f_b (Zaferanieh et al. 2008).

3.2.2.4 MiniSum LP-Norm Distance (Francis et al. 1992)

Weiszfeld procedures. The Weiszfeld procedure depends upon the convexity of the Euclidean metric, and thus, utilizes the first order necessary and sufficient conditions. Since it is impossible to express the unknown variables x_1 and x_2 in closed form equations, the first order derivatives cannot be solved directly. Instead, an iteration function is obtained by using these derivatives. In order to eliminate the obvious difficulty caused by the discontinuities in the derivatives, we use an approximation of the l_p-norm in the objective function. We employ the following hyperbolic approximation of the l_p-norm.

$$\bar{l}_p(u,v) = \left[\left((u_1-v_1)^2 + \epsilon\right)^{p/2} + \left((u_2-v_2)^2 + \epsilon\right)^{p/2}\right]^{1/p}, \text{ where } p \geq 0, \epsilon > 0. \tag{3.65}$$

We use the notation $\tilde{s}(X)$ to denote the objective functions of the approximated l_p-norm for single facility location problem.

3 Single Facility Location Problem

$$x_t^{k+1} = \frac{\sum_{j=1}^{n} w_j \left((x_t^k - a_{jt})^2 + \epsilon\right)^{(p/2)-1} \left(\bar{l}_p(x^k, a_j)\right)^{1-p} a_{jt}}{\sum_{j=1}^{n} w_j \left((x_t^k - a_{jt})^2 + \epsilon\right)^{(p/2)-1} \left(\bar{l}_p(x^k, a_j)\right)^{1-p}}, \quad t = 1, 2. \quad (3.66)$$

It should be noted that in order to deal with a well-formulated problem, we assume that all new facilities are chained. New facility i is chained if there exists a positive w_{1ij} where j is any existing facility or if there exists a positive w_{1ij} where r is any *chained* new facility (Uster and Love 2001).

In addition, the convergence of the Weiszfeld algorithm is discussed in Uster and Love (2000).

Bounding method. The Weiszfeld procedure is basically an iterative steepest-descent algorithm with a predetermined step size. Therefore, to terminate the iterative procedure, a stopping rule or a bound for the best objective function value is required. The rectangular bound at iteration is obtained by solving a rectangular distance location problem. The bound problem involves locating the same number of facilities in the original problem with respect to the existing facility locations with newly created weights. At iterations, the percent difference between the optimum objective function value of the rectangular bound problem and the current objective function value of the original problem is calculated. If this difference is smaller than a termination value that prespecified by the user, the procedure is terminated (Uster and Love 2001). A rectangular bound for the iterative can be obtained by using the Holder inequality given by

$$\sum_{i=1}^{N} |\alpha_i \beta_i| \leq \left(\sum_{i=1}^{N} |\alpha_i|^p\right)^{1/p} \left(\sum_{i=1}^{N} |\beta_i|^q\right)^{1/q}, \quad (3.67)$$

where α and β are N-dimensional vectors, $p > 1$ and $1/p + 1/q = 1$. Taking $N = 2$ for the planar location model and letting

$$\alpha_1 = \left((x_1 - a_{j1})^2 + \epsilon\right)^{1/2}, \quad (3.68)$$

$$\beta_1 = \left((x_1^k - a_{j1})^2 + \epsilon\right)^{(p-1)/2}, \quad (3.69)$$

$$\alpha_2 = \left((x_2 - a_{j2})^2 + \epsilon\right)^{1/2}, \quad (3.70)$$

$$\beta_2 = \left((x_2^k - a_{j2})^2 + \epsilon\right)^{(p-1)/2}. \quad (3.71)$$

We obtain

$$\alpha_1 \beta_1 + \alpha_2 \beta_2 \leq ((\alpha_1)^p + (\alpha_2)^p)^{1/p} \times ((\beta_1)^q + (\beta_2)^q)^{1/q}. \quad (3.72)$$

Rearranging terms, we have

$$\bar{l}_p(x,a_j)\left(\left((x_1^k - a_{j1})^2 + \epsilon\right)^{p/2} + \left((x_2^k - a_{j2})^2 + \epsilon\right)^{p/2}\right)^{1/q} \geq \alpha_1\beta_1 + \alpha_2\beta_2. \tag{3.73}$$

Rewriting the second term on the left-hand side, we obtain

$$\bar{l}_p(x,a_j)\left(\bar{l}_p(x^k,a_j)\right)^{p-1} \geq \alpha_1\beta_1 + \alpha_2\beta_2. \tag{3.74}$$

In order to obtain the cost function of the minimum model, we multiply both sides by w_j and sum for $j = 1,\ldots,n$. Thus, we have

$$\overline{S}(X) = \sum_{j=1}^n w_j \bar{l}_p(x,a_j) \geq \sum_{j=1}^n w_i \frac{\alpha_1\beta_1}{(\bar{l}_p(x^k,a_i))^{p-1}} + \sum_{j=1}^n w_i \frac{\alpha_2\beta_2}{(\bar{l}_p(x^k,a_i))^{p-1}}. \tag{3.75}$$

Minimizing both sides of the inequality over x gives

$$\overline{S}(x^*) \geq \min_x \left\{ \sum_{j=1}^n w_i \frac{\alpha_1\beta_1}{(\bar{l}_p(x^k,a_i))^{p-1}} + \sum_{j=1}^n w_i \frac{\alpha_2\beta_2}{(\bar{l}_p(x^k,a_i))^{p-1}} \right\}. \tag{3.76}$$

Without changing the direction of the inequality, the terms α_1 and α_2 can be simplified as $|x_1 - \alpha_{j1}|$ and $|x_2 - \alpha_{j2}|$, respectively. Thus, the bound as a rectangular distance problem, $\tilde{S} B^K(X)$, is found as

$$\tilde{S} B^K(x^R) = \min_{x_2^R} \sum_{j=1}^n u_j \left|x_1^R - a_{j1}\right| + \min_{x_2^R} \sum_{j=1}^n u_j \left|x_1^R - a_{j1}\right|, \tag{3.77}$$

where

$$u_j = w_j \frac{\beta_1}{(\tilde{l}_p(x^k,a_j))^{p-1}} \quad \text{and} \quad v_j = w_j \frac{\beta_2}{(\tilde{l}_p(x^k,a_j))^{p-1}}, \quad j = 1,\ldots,n. \tag{3.78}$$

For notational convenience, we denote the solution of a rectangular distance location problem by x^R, and thus, the bound at an iteration k is given by $\tilde{S} B^K(x^{R*})$. Let $\tilde{s}_j(X)$, $j = 1,\ldots,n$, denote the terms in $\tilde{s}(X)$. Then the first derivatives of $\tilde{s}_j(X)$ with respect to x_1 and x_2 are

$$\frac{\partial \tilde{s}_j(x)}{\partial x_1} = w_j \frac{\left((x_1 - a_{j1})^2 + \epsilon\right)^{(p-1)/2}}{(\tilde{l}_p(x^k,a_j))^{p-1}} \left(\frac{(x_1 - a_{j1})}{\alpha_1}\right). \tag{3.79}$$

And

$$\frac{\partial \tilde{S}_j(x)}{\partial x_2} = w_j \frac{\left((x_2 - a_{j2})^2 + \epsilon\right)^{(p-1)/2}}{(\tilde{l}_p(x^k, a_j))^{p-1}} \left(\frac{(x_2 - a_{j2})}{\alpha_2}\right), \quad j = 1, \ldots, n. \tag{3.80}$$

By letting $e \to 0$ and using the equality $(x_t - \alpha_{jt}) = \text{sign}(x_t - \alpha_{jt})|x_t - \alpha_{jt}|$, for $t = 1, 2$, we can simplify the last terms and obtain

$$\frac{\partial \tilde{S}_j(x)}{\partial x_1} = w_j \frac{\left((x_1 - a_{j1})^2 + \epsilon\right)^{(p-1)/2}}{(\tilde{l}_p(x^k, a_j))^{p-1}} \text{sign}(x_1 - a_{j1}), \tag{3.81}$$

And

$$\frac{\partial \tilde{S}_j(x)}{\partial x_2} = w_j \frac{\left((x_2 - a_{j2})^2 + \epsilon\right)^{(p-1)/2}}{(\tilde{l}_p(x^k, a_j))^{p-1}} \text{sign}(x_2 - a_{j2}), \quad j = 1, \ldots, n. \tag{3.82}$$

Thus, u_j and v_j can be rewritten as

$$u_j = \left|\frac{\partial \tilde{S}_j(x^k)}{\partial x_1}\right| \quad \text{and} \quad v_j = \left|\frac{\partial \tilde{S}_j(x^k)}{\partial x_2}\right|, \quad j = 1, \ldots, n. \tag{3.83}$$

3.2.2.5 MiniMax Problems

There is another class of single facility location problems that we should mention, called MiniMax problems. One of the best known such problems, called the circle covering problem, involves enclosing m known points in the plane within a circle of minimum radius. The circle covering problem is equivalent to the problem of locating a new facility with respect to m existing facilities so as to minimize the maximum Euclidean distance from the new facility to the existing facilities. The circle covering problem may be of interest in locating a transmitter of some kind, or a receiver, so as to "cover" m stations with as strong signal strength as possible. Also, the problem of stationing a helicopter so as to minimize the maximum time for it to respond to an emergency at anyone of m sites is closely related to the circle covering problem. Contrary to what one might think, the circle covering problem cannot be solved by inspection (or at least no one has yet been able to do so). There are, however, very efficient and relatively simple algorithms for solving the problem.

If we draw a circle about each of the m points of radius r. The intersection of the m circles. Consists of all points whose maximum Euclidean distance to the m given points is r or less. If we imagine reducing r until the intersection of the circles is a single point, we obtain the solution to the circle covering problem. Such an approach is now quite feasible when one has a computer terminal with the facility for displaying circles, provided that m is not too large.

Another problem, which we might term the diamond covering problem, occur when we replace the Euclidean distances of the circle covering problem by rectilinear distances. Here by "diamond" we mean a square with each edge making an angle of $\pm 45°$ with an axis; the radius of the diamond is half the length of the line segment joining opposite vertices. The diamond covering problem is easy to solve by applying a $45°$ rotation we obtain an equivalent square covering problem which we solve by constructing a smallest enclosing rectangle. If the rectangle is square, its center is a MiniMax location. Otherwise, we extend the shortest of a pair of edges to have the same length as the longer pair, and take the center of a square so constructed as a MiniMax location. Of course, we must apply a revel $45°$ rotation to translate our answer back to a solution of the original problem in some cases there will be more than one smallest enclosing diamond, resulting in alternative optimum locations. As with the circle covering problem, it is easy construct contour sets. The set of all points such that the maximum rectilinear distance between the points and the m existing facilities is at most r consists of t intersection of m diamonds, with diamond i having a center at point i and a radius of r, for $i = 1, \ldots, m$. Much the same comments apply to these contour sets as made above for the circle covering problem.

Circle covering problem. In this section we consider two approaches for solving the circle covering problem. The first approach is basically geometrical in nature and is particularly well suited for planar circle covering problems. The second approach is more general, in the sense that it can be used not only for planar problems but for analogous problems in three or more dimensions. For the first approach we present an algorithm. For the second approach we show how to convert the problem into an equivalent quadratic programming problem. Most available algorithms for solving quadratic programming can then be applied to solve the equivalent problem. Let, first state the problem of interest precisely. We wish to minimize the function $g(x, y)$ defined by

$$g(x, y) = \max\{[(x - a_i)^2 + (y - b_i)^2]^{1/2} : 1 \leq i \leq m\}. \tag{3.84}$$

Here, as usual, the points (a_i, b_i) are m existing facility locations, and (x, y) is a new facility to be located in such a way as to minimize $g(x, y)$. A problem equivalent to minimizing $g(x, y)$ is as follows:

$$\text{Min } Z \tag{3.85}$$

Subject to

$$[(x - a_i)^2 + (y - b_i)^2]^{1/2} \leq Z, \quad 1 \leq i \leq m. \tag{3.86}$$

The equivalent problem has the following geometrical interpretation. The constraints state that each existing facility location must lie in a circle with center (x, y) and radius z, so that the geometrical problem is to find a smallest circles that encloses all the existing facility locations.

3 Single Facility Location Problem

We now consider briefly an algebraic approach to the circle covering problem which is valid in any number of dimensions. With X and P_i denoting the location of the new facility and existing facility i, respectively, the Euclidean distance between the two locations is the square root of the following term (where the superscript denotes the transpose operation):

$$(x - p_i)^T (x - p_i). \tag{3.87}$$

Hence an equitant version of the circle covering problem is as follows:

$$\text{Min } u \tag{3.88}$$

Subject to

$$(x - p_i)^T (x - p_i) \le u, \quad i = 1, \ldots, m. \tag{3.89}$$

Because

$$(x - p_i)^T (x - p_i) = x^T x - 2 p_i^T X + P_I^T p_i. \tag{3.90}$$

An equivalent way to write the constraints is as follows:

$$x^T x - 2 p_i^T X + P_I^T p_i \le u, \quad i = 1, \ldots, m. \tag{3.91}$$

But now if we make the following change of variables,

$$v = x^T x - u. \tag{3.92}$$

We obtain the following equivalent version of the problem:

$$\text{Min } x^T x - u. \tag{3.93}$$

Subject to

$$2 p_i^T x - v \ge p_i^T P_I, \quad i = 1, \ldots, m \tag{3.94}$$

The latter problem is a quadratic programming problem with a convex objective function and linear constraints, and thus is solvable by most quadratic programming algorithms.

MiniMax location problems with rectilinear distances. The problem we consider now is one of finding a new facility location that will minimize the following function:

$$g(x, y) = \max\{W_i[|x - a_i| + |y - b_i|] + h_i : 1 \le i \le m\}. \tag{3.95}$$

As a possible example of the problem, suppose that (x, y) is the location of a "convenience" center and that "users" of the center are located at the existing' facility locations, the points (a_i, b_i) through (a_m, b_m). User i require a time of h_i to prepare to go to the center and then travels to the center at a time per unit distance of w_i, so that $w_i[|x - a_i| + |y - b_i|] + h_i$ is the total time to prepare to go to the center and then go there. The center is to be located so that the maximum such time for any user will be minimized.

An alternative but equivalent formulation of the problem of minimizing $g(x, y)$ is the following one:

$$\text{Min } z \tag{3.96}$$

Subject to

$$W_I[|x - a_i| + |y - b_i|] + h_i \leq z, \quad i = 1, \ldots, m. \tag{3.97}$$

Because all the weights are positive, we can also write the problem as follows:

$$\text{Min } z \tag{3.98}$$

Subject to

$$|x - a_i| + |y - b_i| \leq \frac{z - h_i}{w_i}, \quad i = 1, \ldots, m \tag{3.99}$$

The constraints of the latter formulation state that the existing facility location (a_i, b_i) is to be in a diamond with center (x, y) and radius $(z - h_i)/w_i$ for $i = 1, \ldots, m$. Let us denote the problem with all unit weights and all zero addends by UP, which represents "unweighed problem." Similarly, we let WPA denote the weighted problem with some nonzero addends, and we let UPA denote the unweighed problem with some nonzero addends. For UP, the simplest problem, we conclude that the problem is one of finding a diamond of minimum radius that will contain all the existing facility locations. We now give an approach to solve the more general problem UPA. This approach is based on the fact inequality.

$$|x - a_i| + |y - b_i| \leq r_i \equiv z - h_i. \tag{3.100}$$

Equivalent is to the following four inequalities:

$$x - a_i + y - b_i \leq r_i, \tag{3.101}$$
$$x - a_i - y + b_i \leq r_i, \tag{3.102}$$
$$-x + a_i - y + b_i \leq r_i, \tag{3.103}$$
$$-x + a_i + y - b_i \leq r_i. \tag{3.104}$$

We can use this fact to transform UPA to a linear program which can be solved as follows. Compute the following numbers:

$$c_1 = \min\{a_i + b_i - h_i : i = 1, \ldots, m\}, \tag{3.105}$$
$$c_2 = \min\{a_i + b_i + h_i : i = 1, \ldots, m\}, \tag{3.106}$$
$$c_3 = \min\{-a_i + b_i - h_i : i = 1, \ldots, m\}, \tag{3.107}$$
$$c_4 = \min\{-a_i + b_i + h_i : i = 1, \ldots, m\}, \tag{3.108}$$
$$c_5 = \min\{c_2 - c_1, c_4 - c_3\}. \tag{3.109}$$

3 Single Facility Location Problem

The minimum objective function value is $c_5/2$, and the MiniMax locations are the locations on the line segment L joining the following two points:

$$(x_1^*, y_1^*) = \frac{1}{2}(c_1 - c_3, c_1 + c_3 + c_5), \tag{3.110}$$

$$(x_2^*, y_2^*) = \frac{1}{2}(c_2 - c_4, c_2 + c_4 - c_5). \tag{3.111}$$

Consider the construction of level lines for the function $g(x, y)$ of the problem WPA. To construct level lines we construct level sets; the boundaries of the level sets are the level lines. Level lines are of interest for exactly the same reasons we discussed earlier for the MiniSum problems; they allow us to evaluate easily location other than the optimal locations [those that minimize the function $g(x, y)$]. Let us denote a level set of $g(x, y)$ of boundary value Z by $S(z)$, so that $S(z) = \{(x, y) : g(x, y) \leq z\}$. We construct $S(z)$ as follows. Given a value of Z of interest, we first compute the following numbers:

$$c_1(z) = \min\left\{a_i + b_i + \frac{z - h_i}{w_i} : i = 1, \ldots, m\right\}, \tag{3.112}$$

$$c_2(z) = \min\left\{a_i + b_i + \frac{-z + h_i}{w_i} : i = 1, \ldots, m\right\}, \tag{3.113}$$

$$c_3(z) = \min\left\{-a_i + b_i + \frac{z - h_i}{w_i} : i = 1, \ldots, m\right\}, \tag{3.114}$$

$$c_4(z) = \min\left\{-a_i + b_i + \frac{-z + h_i}{w_i} : i = 1, \ldots, m\right\}. \tag{3.115}$$

The level $S(z)$ is then as follows:

$$S(z) = \{(x, y) : c_2(z) \leq x + y \leq c_1(z), c_4(z) \leq -x + y \leq c_3(z)\}. \tag{3.116}$$

If at least one of the inequalities $c_2(z) \leq c_1(z), c_4(z) \leq c_3(z)$ does not hold, you have chosen a value of Z that is smaller than the minimum value of $g(x, y)$ and the level set will be empty; thus you mast pick another value of Z which is large enough so that both of inequalities hold. Supposing the level set to be nonempty, you should be able to see that the level set is a rectangle, with two parallel sides making $a + 45°$ angle with the x axis and the other two parallel sides making $a - 45°$ angle with the x axis. The vertices of the level set, starting at the top corner and proceeding clockwise, are as follows:

$$v_1(z) = \frac{1}{2}(c_1(z) - c_3(z), c_1(z) + c_3(z)), \tag{3.117}$$

$$v_2(z) = \frac{1}{2}(c_1(z) - c_4(z), c_1(z) + c_4(z)), \tag{3.118}$$

$$v_3(z) = \frac{1}{2}(c_2(z) - c_4(z), c_2(z) + c_4(z)), \qquad (3.119)$$

$$v_4(z) = \frac{1}{2}(c_2(z) - c_3(z), c_2(z) + c_3(z)). \qquad (3.120)$$

Hence you can plot a level set of value Z by first choosing Z, computing $c_1(z)$ through $c_1(z)$, checking to be sure that the inequalities $c_2(z) \leq c_1(z)$, $c_4(z) \leq c_3(z)$, are satisfied by the Z you have chosen, computing $v_1(z)$ through $v_4(z)$ and plotting the four points, and then constructing lines joining $v_1(z)$ and $v_2(z)$, $v_2(z)$ and $v_3(z)$, $v_3(z)$ and $v_4(z)$, $v_4(z)$ and $v_1(z)$. The rectangle the lines enclose is the level set of value Z, and its boundary is the level lines of value Z.

MiniMax problems with Tchebychev and rectilinear distances. In Sect. 3.2.2.4 we saw that the diamond covering problem could be interpreted, given a 45° rotation, as a square covering problem, and that this interpretation led to a simple solution procedure for the diamond covering problem. What we do now is to exploit this discovery in a systematic way. As a result, we will obtain an efficient means of solving WAP, the MiniMax weighted rectilinear distance problem with addends.

Consider two points X and Y in the plane. Suppose that X and Y are the endpoints of the hypotenuse H of a right triangle, with the other two sides of the triangle, denoted by A and B, being parallel to the horizontal and vertical axes, respectively. We have seen earlier that the length of the hypotenuse H is the Euclidean distance between X and Y, while the sum of the lengths of sides A and B is the rectilinear distance between X and Y. We now introduce a new distance, called the Tchebychev distance between X and Y, defined to be the maximum of the lengths of sides A and B. In other words, if A is longer than B, then A is the Tchebychev distance between X and Y, while if A is not longer than B, then B is the Tchebychev distance between X and Y. We denote the Tchebychev distance between X and Y by $t(X, V)$. Thus if $X = (X_1, X_2)$, and $Y = (Y_1, Y_2)$, then

$$t(X, Y) = \max\{|x_1 - y_1|, |x_2 - y_2|\}. \qquad (3.121)$$

What does a contour set of Tchebychev distance look like? Consider the set of all points X whose Tchebychev distance from the origin is at most 1, that is, the 1 set of all points $X = (X_1, X_2)$ satisfying $t(x, 0) \leq 1$, or, equivalently, satisfying $\max\{|X_1||X_2|\} \leq 1$. The latter inequality is equivalent to $|X_1| \leq 1$ and $|X_2| \leq 1$. But these last two inequalities are in turn equivalent to

$$-1 \leq x_1 \leq 1 \text{ and } -1 \leq x_2 \leq 1. \qquad (3.122)$$

Hence the set of all points X whose Tchebychev distance from the origin is at most 1 is a square with its center at the origin and each side of length 2. This square is the Tchebychev analog of a circle with center at the origin and radius 1 and the Tchebychev analog (for rectilinear distance) of a diamond with center at the origin and radius 1. Of course, if we rotate a diamond by 45°, we obtain a square, a result that should give you a good clue about the relationship between Tchebychev, and rectilinear distances.

3 Single Facility Location Problem

Let us now explore the relationship between Tchebychev and rectilinear distances. It is convenient to introduce the following linear transformation, which we denote by $Q(X, Y)$:

$$Q(x, y) = (x, y) \begin{bmatrix} 1 & -1 \\ 1 & 1 \end{bmatrix} = (x + y, -x + y). \tag{3.123}$$

You should be able to verify that the inverse transformation, denoted by $Q^{-1}(u, v)$, is given by

$$Q(u, v) = (u, v) \begin{bmatrix} \frac{1}{2} & \frac{1}{2} \\ -\frac{1}{2} & \frac{1}{2} \end{bmatrix} = \frac{1}{2}(u - v, u + v). \tag{3.124}$$

Another aspect is that the rectilinear distance between any two vertices of D, namely 2, is the same as the Tchebychev distance between the corresponding transformed points, the vertices of the square S. This result is no coincidence. Given any points X and Y in the plane, let $r(x, y)$ denote the rectilinear distance between X and Y, if we compute points X' and Y' using the equations $x' = Q(X)$ and $Y' = Q(X)$, it is known that

$$r(X, Y) = t(X', Y'). \tag{3.125}$$

That is, the rectilinear distance between X and Y is the same as the Tchebychev distance between the transformed points X' and Y'. Equivalently, given any points X' and Y' in the plane, if we compute points X and Y using the equations.

$$X = Q^{-1}(X') \text{ and } Y = Q^{-1}(Y). \tag{3.126}$$

We conclude that

$$t(X', Y') = r(X, Y). \tag{3.127}$$

The consequence of the two equations above is that we can transform a planar location problem involving rectilinear distances into an equivalent problem involving Tchebychev distances, and vice versa. Hence we obtain equivalence between planar location problems involving Tchebychev and rectilinear distances. This equivalence is useful since it is often the case that one problem is easier to analyze than the other.

Let us consider converting the general MiniMax problem with rectilinear distance, denoted by WPA, into an equivalent problem with Tchebychev distances. Recall that WPA is the problem of minimizing the function $g(x, y)$, where

$$g(x, y) = \max\{W_I[|x - a_i| + |y - b_i|] + h_i : 1 \leq i \leq m\}. \tag{3.128}$$

Let (u, v) be the result of applying the transformation Q to the point (x, y), and let (α_i, β_i) be the result of applying the transformation Q to the point $(\alpha i, \beta i)$. We know that

$$W_I[|x - a_i| + |y - b_i|] + h_i = w_i \max[|u - \alpha_i|, |v - \beta_i|] + h_i = \\ \max[w_i |u - \alpha_i| + h_i, w_i |v - \beta_i| + h_i] \tag{3.129}$$

We can thus conclude that

$$g(x, y) = \max\{\max[w_I[|u - \alpha_i| + h_i, w_i + |v - \beta_i|] + h_i] : i = 1, \ldots, m\}. \quad (3.130)$$

Suppose that we know define the function $g_1(u)$ and $g_2(u)$ as follows:

$$g_1(u) = \max\{w_I |u - \alpha_i| + h_i : i = 1, \ldots, m\}, \quad (3.131)$$
$$g_2(u) = \max\{w_I |v - \beta_i| + h_i : i = 1, \ldots, m\}. \quad (3.132)$$

It then follows that

$$\max\{\max[w_I |u - \alpha_i| + h_i, w_i |v - \beta_i| + h_i] : i = 1, \ldots, m\} = \max\{g_1(u), g_2(u)\}. \quad (3.133)$$

The reason for the latter equality is that regardless of the order in which we compute the maximum of a collection of numbers, we obtain the same result.

If you examine the latter equation, you can see that the term on the left is the same as the term on the right in our most recent equation for $g(x, y)$; hence we obtain a very useful result as follows: Given

$$(u, v) = Q(x, y). \quad (3.134)$$

We have

$$g(x, y) = \max\{g_1(u), g_2(u)\}. \quad (3.135)$$

The consequence of our result is that we can minimize $g(x, y)$ by solving two independent minimization problems as follows:

1. We minimize $g_1(u)$ and obtain a minimizing point, say u.
2. Next, we minimize $g_2(u)$ and obtain a minimizing point, say v.
3. We can then apply the inverse transformation to (u^*, v^*) to obtain a point, say (x^*, y^*), and conclude that (x^*, y^*) minimizes $g(x, y)$.
4. Further, the minimum value of $g(x, y)$ is equal to max $\{g_1(u^*), g_2(u^*)\}$ (Francis et al. 1992).

3.3 Case Study (Heragu 1997)

We now present a relocation project undertaken by a small facility. A small manufacturing company currently located in a university "tech park" has witnessed major growth since introducing an innovative technology into the marketplace. Its owner now wants to find a new location and build a bigger facility. In January she hired senior industrial and management engineering (IME) students at the university to investigate several potential locations and select the one that best suits her needs.

3 Single Facility Location Problem

The student group adopted the following five step approach, which is based on the hybrid analysis discussed earlier.

- Step 1. *Determination of requirements*: The students conducted interviews with the owner and facility manager to determine these company specific requirements for the new facility:

    - The company will relocate in New York or Vermont.
    - At least 15,000 ft of space is required.
    - A power source of three phase, 440 W, and 200 A electrical service is mandatory to power the atomizers used in the manufacturing process.
    - The current rent is $7.50 per square foot per year; the company wants to pay between $3.50 and $4.50 per square foot.
    - The company wants to move within the next 8 months.
    - All suppliers and vendors should be within 100 miles of the facility.
    - A lease of 1–2 years is preferred.
    - There should be adequate room for expansion.
    - An industrial park or shared facility is preferred.
    - The facility should be located close to major highways and airports.
    - A loading bay is required; easy access to the bay is desired.
    - The new facility should be built to suit.
    - The facility maintenance costs should be low or the owner of the building must pay the maintenance and related expenses.
    - The general condition of the building should be good.
    - The building should not be considered high risk by insurance companies.
    - It is desirable to have secretarial services available nearby.
    - The local and state taxes must be reasonable.

- Step 2. *Classification of location factors*: Based on the interview with the owner, the IME students classified the requirements into three categories:

Critical factors

- Minimum space requirement
- Three phase, $440\ W$, $200\ A$ electrical service
- Support service providers and vendors within 100 miles

Objective factors

- Rent
- Space rented or leased
- Maintenance and insurance costs and taxes

Subjective factors

- Shared facility
- Build to suit
- Condition of loading bay
- Proximity to airport and major highways
- Lease length

- Secretarial support
- Condition of building

- Step 3. *Data collection*: This step requires the most time, but it is very important and should be done carefully. Information on potential sites and locations was obtained from sources such as these:
  - Chamber of Commerce
  - Economic Development Council
  - Real estate brokers
  - Facility owners

- Step 4. *Elimination of sites not meeting critical objectives and development of a rating chart*: From the ten sites for which data were collected, four did not satisfy the first or the second critical requirement. For the remaining six sites, machine shops and other support service providers as well as vendors were within 100 miles. The IME student group devised a chart showing the weights of the objective and subjective factor.
- Step 5. Site visits and site evaluation: The students visited all six sites. Data and rated collected for the sites.

After careful evaluation, the six sites were rated on this evaluation; the Cohoes, New York, site appears to be the best location, with Bennington, Vermont, as a (close) second best location (Heragu 1997).

References

Drezner Z (1986) Location of regional facilities. Naval Res Logist Quart 33:523–529
Francis Rl, White JA (1974) Facility layout and location: An analytical approach. Prentice Hall, Englewood Cliffs, NJ
Francis Rl, McGinnis LF, White JA (1992) Facility layout and location: An analytical approach. Prentice Hall, Englewood Cliffs, NJ
Heragu SS (1997) Facilities design. PWS publishing company, a division of International Thomson Publishing Inc. Boston
Uster H, Love RF (2000) The convergence of the Weiszfeld algorithm. Management Science/Information Systems Area
Uster H, Love RF (2001) A generalization of the rectangular bounding method for continuous location models. Comput Math Appl 44:181–191
Zaferanieh M, Taghizadeh KH, Brimberg J, Wesolowsky GO (2008) A BSSS algorithm for the single facility location problem in two regions with different norms. Eur J Oper Res 190(1):79–89

Chapter 4
Multifacility Location Problem

Farzaneh Daneshzand and Razieh Shoeleh

In the previous chapter, we studied the case of a single new facility to be located relative to a number of existing facilities. In this chapter we consider the problem of optimally locating more than one new facilities with respect to locations of a number of existing facilities (demand points), the locations of which are known.

While the problems are natural extension of those of single facility location, there are two important conditions:

1. At least two facilities are to be located
2. Each new facility is linked to at least one other new facility

If the first condition contracted, this problem is considered as a single facility location problem (SFLP) and if the second condition contracted, we can consider the problem as some of independent single facility location problems. Thus the SFLP can be considered as a spatial case of the multifacility location problem (MFLP).

4.1 Applications and Classifications

As it is expected, applications of MFLPs occur in the same contexts as discussed in the chapter "Single Facility Location Problem" by Esmaeel Moradi and Morteza Bidkhori, this volume for SFLP. Ostresh (1977) represented some applications of the MFLP as follows:

1. A system of warehouses is to be established to serve a set of predetermined regions.
2. Industrial and commercial establishments tend to be more concentrated than expected on the basis of minimizing transport costs alone.
3. In large organizations (such as the Federal government) face to face communication must take place between adjacent (usually) levels of the hierarchy.

A classification of different types of MFLP and their properties is shown in the following statement:

- Area solution: discrete, continual
- The space in which facilities are located: planer location, sphere location
- Objective function: MiniMax, MiniSum
- Type of the distance: rectangular distance, Euclidean distance, squared Euclidean distance, l_p distance
- Parameters: stochastic, deterministic
- How facilities are assumed: point, region

Researchers have worked on a variety of MFLPs. However no research has been conducted on many types of MFLPs resulted from multiplying the above items.

4.2 Models

In this section we introduce MFLP models represented and developed as mathematical models.

4.2.1 MiniSum

The MiniSum multifacility location problem consisting of finding locations of new facilities which will minimize a total cost function consists of a sum of costs directly proportional to the distances between the new facilities, and costs directly proportional to the distances between new and existing facilities.

The general-model for this problem can be stated as follows:

4.2.1.1 Model Assumptions

The assumptions of this model are as follows:

- The area solution is continual
- The space in which facilities are located is planer
- The objective function is MiniSum
- Type of the distance can be either rectangular, Euclidean, squared Euclidean or l_p distance
- Parameters are deterministic
- Facilities are assumed as points

4 Multifacility Location Problem

4.2.1.2 Model Inputs

Model inputs of this model are:

n: Number of new facilities
m: Number of existing facilities
w_{ij}: Nonnegative weight between new facility i and existing facility j by a unit distance
v_{ik}: Nonnegative weight between new facilities i and k by a unit distance
$d(X_j, P_i)$: Distance between the location of new facility j and existing facility i
$d(X_j, X_k)$: Distance between the location of new facilities j and k
$P_j : (a_j, b_j)$ The location coordinates of existing facility j

4.2.1.3 Model Output (Decision Variable)

Model output of this model is:

$X_i : (x_i, y_i)$ The location coordinates of new facility i

4.2.1.4 Objective Function

$$\text{Min} \sum_{1 \leq j < k \leq n} v_{jk}.d(X_j, X_k) + \sum_{j=1}^{n}\sum_{i=1}^{m} w_{ji}.d(X_j, P_i). \tag{4.1}$$

Thus each of the m new facilities is to be located with respect to the n existing facilities and also with respect to the other new facilities. The location of X_j may depend on the location of some point X_k because of the terms involving v_{jk}. For convenience in the presentation, we assume all the w_{ji} and all the v_{jk} are positive.

Notice that it is the cost proportional to the distance between new facilities which distinguish the MFLP from SFLP. In fact, when terms v_{ji} are zero then (4.1) may be written as

$$\text{Min} \sum_{j=1}^{n}\sum_{i=1}^{m} w_{ji}.d(X_j, P_i). \tag{4.2}$$

And (4.2) just defines a one-facility total cost expression. So that (4.2) is the sum of n different one-facility cost expression and may be written as

$$\text{Min} \sum_{j=1}^{n} \left(\text{Min} \sum_{i=1}^{m} w_{ji}.d(X_j, P_i) \right). \tag{4.3}$$

Since the location of one new facility has no effect upon the cost of locating other new facilities for the special case where all v_{ij} are zero, locations of new facilities may be found by solving n SFLP independently.

4.2.1.5 Rectangular Distance MiniSum Location Problem

In this section, we consider MFLP when we have rectangular distance. The objective of this problem is minimization of the weighted sum of the rectangular distance between the locations of new facilities and new and existing facilities. For formulation of this problem if in (4.1) we replace the $d(X_j, P_i)$ and $d(X_j, X_k)$ by (4.4) and (4.5) The Rectangular MFLP problem can be formulated as (4.6) this problem is of added interest since it will be shown that its optimal solution can be used to compute both a lower and an upper bound for the value of the optimal solution to the Euclidean problem.

$$d(X_j, X_k) = |x_j - x_k| + |y_j - y_k|, \quad (4.4)$$

$$d(X_j, P_i) = |x_j - a_i| + |y_j - b_i|, \quad (4.5)$$

$$\text{Min} \sum_{1 \leq j < k \leq n} v_{jk} \left(|x_j - x_k| + |y_j - y_k| \right)$$

$$+ \sum_{j=1}^{n} \sum_{i=1}^{m} w_{ji} \left(|x_j - a_i| + |y_j - b_i| \right). \quad (4.6)$$

The objective function is converted into two minimum problems:

$$\text{Min } f = \text{Min } f_1(x) + \text{Min } f_2(x). \quad (4.7)$$

where:

$$f_1(X) = \sum_{1 \leq j < k \leq n} v_{jk} |x_j - x_k| + \sum_{j=1}^{n} \sum_{i=1}^{m} w_{ji} |x_j - a_i|, \quad (4.8)$$

$$f_2(Y) = \sum_{1 \leq j < k \leq n} v_{jk} |y_j - y_k| + \sum_{j=1}^{n} \sum_{i=1}^{m} w_{ji} |y_j - b_i|. \quad (4.9)$$

Just like single facility location case in the chapter "Single Facility Location Problem" by Esmaeel Moradi and Morteza Bidkhori, this volume, optimum x coordinate of new facilities can be found independent from optimum y coordinates. As you see the objective function is nonlinear and we should make it linear. The method of linearization is very similar to the method we used in single facility location in the chapter "Single Facility Location Problem" by Esmaeel Moradi and Morteza Bidkhori, this volume.

Linearization

Given numbers a, b, p and q,
   If

$$a - b - p + q = 0,$$
$$p.q = 0,$$
$$p \geq 0, \ q \geq 0.$$

Then
$$|a - b| = p + q.$$
So minimizing the objective function is equivalent to the following problem:

$$\text{Min} \sum_{1 \le j < k \le n} v_{jk}(p_{jk} + q_{jk}) + \sum_{j=1}^{n}\sum_{i=1}^{m} w_{ji}(r_{ji} + s_{ji}), \quad (4.10)$$

Subject to

$$x_j - x_k - p_{jk} + q_{jk} = 0 \quad 1 \le j < k \le n, \quad (4.11)$$

$$x_j - r_{ji} + s_{ji} = a_i \quad i = 1, \ldots, m, j = 1, \ldots, n, \quad (4.12)$$

$$p_{jk}, q_{jk} \ge 0 \quad 1 \le j < k \le n, \quad (4.13)$$

$$r_{ji}, s_{ji} \ge 0 \quad i = 1, \ldots, m, j = 1, \ldots, n, \quad (4.14)$$

$$p_{jk}q_{jk} = 0 \quad 1 \le j < k \le n, \quad (4.15)$$

$$r_{ji}.s_{ji} = 0 \quad i = 1, \ldots, m, j = 1, \ldots, n, \quad (4.16)$$

$$x_j \text{ unrestricted,} \quad j = 1, 2, \ldots, n. \quad (4.17)$$

As in the single facility location for any basic feasible solution, if p_{jk} is in the basic feasible solution, q_{jk} will not be and vice versa. Likewise, if r_{ji} is in the basic feasible solution, s_{ji} will not be and vice versa. Since variables not in the basic feasible solution are zero, the multiplicative constraints will be therefore satisfied for every feasible solution. Minimizing f_2 is the same as what was done for f_1.

4.2.1.6 Squared Euclidean Distance MiniSum Location Problem

In this section, we consider MFLP when we have squared Euclidean distance. The objective of this problem is minimization of the weighted sum of the square of the Euclidean distance between the locations of new facilities and new and existing facilities. The problem considered in this section is also referred to as a "quadratic facility location problem" and the "gravity problem".

Although there aren't too many situations where there are physical reasons for using squared Euclidean distance, there are at least two reasons for the gravity problem. First, in some cases the solution to the gravity problem can be used to approximate the solution to the location problem where costs increase linearly with Euclidean distance. Second, there exist location problems where costs increase quadratically with the Euclidean distance between facilities.

For formulation of this problem if in (4.1) we replace the $d(X_j, P_i)$ and $d(X_j, X_k)$ by (4.18) and (4.19) the squared Euclidean MFLP problem can formulate as (4.20)

$$d(X_j, X_k) = (x_j - x_k)^2 + (y_j - y_k)^2, \quad (4.18)$$

$$d(X_j, X_i) = (x_j - a_i)^2 + (y_j - b_i)^2, \qquad (4.19)$$

$$\text{Min } f = \sum_{1 \leq j < k \leq n} v_{jk} \cdot \left[(x_j - x_k)^2 + (y_j - y_k)^2 \right]$$

$$+ \sum_{j=1}^{n} \sum_{i=1}^{m} w_{ji} \cdot \left[(x_j - a_i)^2 + (y_j - b_i)^2 \right]. \qquad (4.20)$$

4.2.1.7 Contour Lines for Squared Euclidean MFLP

In MFLP construction of contour lines is possible expect for certain special case when $n = 2$. In this section we want to observe the property of contour lines for squared Euclidean MFLP

Let $f(x, y)$ given in (4.20) be written as $f(x, y) = f(x) + f(y)$ where

$$f(x) = \sum_{1 \leq j < k \leq n} v_{jk}(x_j - x_k)^2 + \sum_{j=1}^{n} \sum_{i=1}^{m} w_{ji}(x_j - a_i)^2. \qquad (4.21)$$

And

$$f(y) = \sum_{1 \leq j < k \leq n} v_{jk}(y_j - y_k)^2 + \sum_{j=1}^{n} \sum_{i=1}^{m} w_{ji}(y_j - b_i)^2. \qquad (4.22)$$

If $n = 2$, contour lines for $f(x)$ are concentric ellipses centered on (x^*, y^*) and contour lines for $f(y)$ are concentric ellipses centered on (x^*, y^*)

Because of the squared Euclidean MFLP is separable and symmetric in x and y, only $f(x)$ is considered and contour line is defined as the set of all points (x_1, x_2) for which

$$k = v_{12}(x_1 - x_2) + \sum_{i=1}^{m} w_{1i}(x_1 - a_i)^2 + \sum_{i=1}^{m} w_{1i}(x_2 - a_i)^2. \qquad (4.23)$$

And k is a constant denoting the value of the contour line. By expanding and collecting terms it is seen that (4.23) can be expressed in the form of a general conic section:

$$Ax_1^2 + Bx_1x_2 + Cx_2^2 + Dx_1 + Ex_2 + F = 0, \qquad (4.24)$$

where

$$A = v_{12} + \sum_{i=1}^{m} w_{1i},$$

$$B = -2v_{12},$$

$$C = v_{12} + \sum_{i=1}^{m} w_{2i},$$

4 Multifacility Location Problem

$$D = -2 \sum_{i=1}^{m} w_{1i} a_i,$$

$$E = -2 \sum_{i=1}^{m} w_{2i} a_i,$$

$$D = \sum_{i=1}^{m} w_{1i} a_i^2 + \sum_{i=1}^{m} w_{2i} a_i^2 - k.$$

A sufficient condition given by Thomas (1968) for (4.24) to be an ellipse is for the discriminate, $B^2 - 4AC$, to be negative. Direct substitution gives

$$B^2 - 4AC = 4v_{12}^2 - 4v_{12}^2 - 4v_{12}\left(\sum_{i=1}^{m} w_{1i} + \sum_{i=1}^{m} w_{2i}\right) - 4\left(\sum_{i=1}^{m} w_{1i}\right)\left(\sum_{i=1}^{m} w_{2i}\right) < 0. \tag{4.25}$$

Assuming the problem is well formulated (4.24) is the equation for a rotated ellipse as noted by the presence of the $x_1 x_2$ term. Due to symmetry a similar result is found for the y variables. Furthermore, by definition of a contour line since k achieves its smallest value at (x_1^*, x_2^*) the contour line is centered on the optimum location with respect to the nonrotated axes (Eyster and White 1973).

4.2.1.8 Euclidean Distance MiniSum Location Problem

The Euclidean multifacility location problem often assumes that the transportation costs from the new facility to a demand point are proportional to the Euclidean distance between these points, with the factor of proportionality (weight) depending on the demand point.

Here, this problem is mathematically formulated:

$$\text{Min} \sum_{1 \leq j < k \leq n} v_{jk} \cdot \left[(x_j - x_k)^2 + (y_j - y_k)^2\right]^{1/2} \tag{4.26}$$
$$+ \sum_{j=1}^{n} \sum_{i=1}^{m} w_{ji} \cdot \left[(x_j - a_i)^2 + (y_j - b_i)^2\right]^{1/2}.$$

It is interesting to note that when all the existing facility locations are collinear, that is, all lie on a single line, the Euclidean model essentially includes the rectilinear distance model.

4.2.2 MiniMax

Minimization of a sum of weighted distances that was introduced in Sect. 4.1.1 may not be a proper goal when the facilities to be located must provide services of an urgent nature. Therefore in this section we introduce some multifacility location problems with MiniMax objective function and by different type of distances.

4.2.2.1 Model Assumptions

Model assumptions of this model are as follows:

- The area solution is continual
- The space in which facilities are located is planer
- The objective function is MiniMax
- Type of the distance can be either rectangular, Euclidean, squared Euclidean or l_p distance
- Parameters are deterministic
- Facilities are assumed as points

4.2.2.2 Model Inputs

We have all the inputs in previous model.

4.2.2.3 Model Outputs (Decision Variables)

The outputs of this model are similar to the previous model.

4.2.2.4 Objective Function

$$\text{Min } f = \text{Max}\{v_{jk}.d(X_j, X_k), w_{ji}.d(X_j, P_i)\}. \tag{4.27}$$

4.2.2.5 Rectangular Distance MiniMax Location Problem

The problem considered is that of locating n new facilities among m existing facilities with the objective of minimizing the maximum weighed Rectangular distance among all facilities.

$$\begin{aligned}\text{Min } f = \text{Max } \{&w_{ji}\left|x_j - a_i\right| + \left|y_j - b_i\right| \mid j = 1,\ldots,n, \ i = 1,\ldots,m; \\ &v_{jk}\left|x_j - x_k\right| + \left|y_j - y_k\right| \mid 1 \le j < k < n\}.\end{aligned} \tag{4.28}$$

4.2.2.6 Euclidean Distance MiniMax Location Problem

The problem considered is that of locating n new facilities among m existing facilities with the objective of minimizing the maximum weighed Euclidean distance among all facilities.

Elzinga et al. formulated this problem in 1976:

$$\text{Min } f = \text{Max} \left\{ w_{ji}[(x_j - a_i)^2 + (y_j - b_i)^2]^{1/2} \; j = 1, \ldots, n, i = 1, \ldots, m; \right.$$
$$\left. v_{jk}[(x_j - x_k)^2 + (y_j - y_k)^2]^{1/2} 1 \leq j < k < n \right\}. \tag{4.29}$$

4.2.3 Other Models

4.2.3.1 Rectangular Multi Product Multifacility Location Problem

This model considers multi products in MFLP. Sherali and Shetty (1978) formulated the rectangular multi product MFLP.

4.2.3.2 Model Assumptions

Model assumptions of this model are as follows:

- The area solution is continual
- The space in which facilities are located is planer
- The objective function is MiniSum
- The distances are rectangular
- Parameters are deterministic
- Facilities are assumed as points

4.2.3.3 Model Inputs and Outputs (Decision Variables)

Model inputs and outputs of this model are as follows:

c_{ijk}: The cost per unit of product k to be transported from a new facility i to a new or existing facility j

u_{ijk}: The known amount of product k to be transported from a new facility i to a new or existing facility j at a cost of c_{ijk} per unit of the product, per unit distance.

(x_j, y_i): decision variables for $i = 1, 2, \ldots, n$ and are fixed and known for each facility $n + i$, $i = 1, 2, \ldots, m'$.

4.2.3.4 Objective Function

The objective function of this model and its related constraints are as follows:

$$\text{Min} \sum_{k=1}^{p} \sum_{i=1}^{n} \sum_{j=1}^{n+m'} c_{ijk} u_{ijk} \{|x_i - x_j| + |y_i - y_j|\}. \tag{4.30}$$

The objective function may be written as:

$$\text{Min} \sum_{k=1}^{p} \sum_{i=1}^{n} w_{ij} \{|x_i - x_j| + |y_i - y_j|\}, \tag{4.31}$$

$$w_{ij} = \sum_{k=1}^{p} (c_{ijk} u_{ijk} + c_{jik} u_{jik}) \quad j = n+1, \ldots, n+m'. \tag{4.32}$$

4.2.3.5 Multifacility Location Problem on Sphere

As it is known, one of the assumptions when locating facilities is concerned with the size of the area covering the destinations (or the demand points). If the area covering the demand points is sufficiently small, then this part of the earth's surface can be approximated by a plane. When the destination points are widely separated, the area covering these points can no longer be approximated by a plane and the formulations we discussed so far is not suitable.

Problems concerning location of international headquarters, distribution/marketing centers, detection station placement, and placement of radio transmitters for long range communication may fall into this category.

The location problem on a sphere is more complicated than its counterpart on the plane, because unlike on plane the solution space is not convex on sphere.

Dhar and Rao (1982) formulated this problem. Any point on the sphere can be defined by its latitude $-\pi/2 \leq \Phi \leq \pi/2$ and longitude $-\pi \leq \theta \leq \pi$ and d_{ij} is the shortest distance between points i and j.

4.2.3.6 Model Assumptions

Model assumptions of this model are as follows:

- The area solution is continual
- The space in which facilities are located is on sphere
- The objective function is MiniSum
- Parameters are deterministic
- Facilities are assumed as points
- The distance is defined as

$$d_{ij} = \text{Arc} \cos[\cos \Phi_i \cos \Phi_j \cos(\theta_i - \theta_j) + \sin \Phi_i \sin \Phi_j]. \tag{4.33}$$

4 Multifacility Location Problem

4.2.3.7 Model Inputs

We have all the inputs in MiniSum models.

4.2.3.8 Model Outputs (Decision Variables)

The outputs of this model are similar to the MiniSum models.

4.2.3.9 Objective Function

The objective function of this model and its constraints are as follows:

$$\text{Min}_{\Phi_j \theta_j} \sum_{1 \leq j < k \leq n} v_{jk}(d_{jk}) + \sum_{j=1}^{n} \sum_{i=1}^{m} w_{ji}(d_{ji}). \tag{4.34}$$

Subject to

$$-\pi/2 \leq \Phi_j \leq \pi/2, \tag{4.35}$$

$$-\pi \leq \theta \leq \pi. \tag{4.36}$$

4.2.3.10 Multifacility Location Problem with Rectangular Regions

So far we assumed each existing and new facility as a point. Wesolowsky and Love applied the concept of Rectangular regions to MFLP in 1971a, b. They stated that in many different contexts it is proper to treat the destination to be served as a region, rather than a point such as in the location of a library or emergency services or other public service facility designed to serve either a neighborhood or a densely populated urban area.

Even when the users of the new facility are discretely distributed, the number of users may become so large that it may be infeasible in terms of data collection and computational efficiency to represent each customer by a point. In this situation it is necessary to assume regional destinations in order to solve the problem.

4.2.3.11 Model Assumptions

Model assumptions of this model are as follows:

- The area solution is continual
- The space in which facilities are located is planer
- The objective function is MiniSum
- The distances are rectangular

- Parameters are deterministic
- Facilities are assumed as regions

4.2.3.12 Model Inputs

We have all the inputs in MiniSum models in addition to the following inputs:
$R_i = [a_{i_1}, a_{i_2}]$ Rectangular region i, where $a_{i_1} < a_{i_2}$ and $b_{i_1} < b_{i_2}$
A_i: The area of R_i

4.2.3.13 Model Outputs (Decision Variables)

The outputs of this model are similar to MiniSum models.

4.2.3.14 Objective Function

The objective function of this model and its constraints are as follows:

$$\text{Min} \sum_{j=1}^{n} \sum_{i=1}^{m} \frac{w_{ij}}{A_i} \int\int_{R_i} (|x_j - a_i| + |y_j - b_i|) da_i db_i \\ + \sum_{i \leq j < k \leq n} v_{jk} (|x_j - x_k| + |y_j - y_k|). \quad (4.37)$$

4.2.3.15 Stochastic Multifacility Location Problem

In many cases the parameters of the model are not deterministic. This model is represented and solved by Seppalla (1975). In order to define a stochastic decision model, we should first determine the stochastic parameters, how they are distributed, whether they are correlated, and which decision criterion will be used in industrial applications. The set of stochastic elements of planning models are often restricted to consist only of demands for products, while other parameters or variables, such as unit costs, capacities and locations, are considered to be fixed.

4.2.3.16 Model Assumptions

Model assumptions of this model are as follows:

- The area solution is continual
- The space in which facilities are located is planer
- The objective function is MiniSum
- The distances are Euclidean

4 Multifacility Location Problem

- Parameters are stochastic
- Facilities are assumed as points
- The weights v_{jk}, w_{ji} for all i, j and k are normally distributed random variables

4.2.3.17 Model Inputs

The inputs of this model are similar to the MiniSum model in addition to the following:

α: is a predetermined probability
δ: is an assisting
$P\{.\}$: is a probability operator

4.2.3.18 Model Outputs (Decision Variables)

The output of this model is similar to the MiniSum model.

4.2.3.19 Objective Function

The objective function of this model and its constraints are as follows:

$$\text{Min } \delta. \tag{4.38}$$

Subject to

$$P\left\{ \sum_{1 \leq j < k \leq n} v_{jk} \cdot \left[(x_j - x_k)^2 + (y_j - y_k)^2\right]^{1/2} \right. \\ \left. + \sum_{j=1}^{n}\sum_{i=1}^{m} w_{ji} \cdot \left[(x_j - a_i)^2 + (y_j - b_i)^2\right]^{1/2} \leq \delta \right\} \geq \alpha. \tag{4.39}$$

4.3 Solution Techniques

4.3.1 MiniSum

4.3.1.1 Rectangular Distance MiniSum Location Problem

The rectangular distance multifacility location problem always has a minimum cost solution where the x coordinate of each new facility is equal to the x coordinate of some existing facility and the same is true for y coordinate (Francis et al. 1992).

If we call p_1 the linear programming problem obtained in (4.10) a straight forward linear programming of p_1 can be time consuming when a large number of new and existing facilities are involved.

Depending on the characteristics of a particular multifacility Rectangular location problem, the optimum solution can be sometimes obtained in an iterative mode by solving some single facility location problems. Also, a dual formulation of the linear programming problem (p_1) can provide more efficient solution to the rectangular MFLP (Francis et al. 1992).

- Francis (1964) solved a special case of the MFLP, with rectilinear distance when the weights are equal.
- Cabot et al. (1970) decomposed the location problem into two independent subproblems, each of which is equivalent to a linear programming problem which is essentially the dual of a minimal cost network flow problem. The dual variables in each of the optimum tableaus to the two flow problems give the x and y coordinates respectively of the optimum locations of the new facilities.
- Pritsker and Ghare (1970) suggested a gradient technique for this problem. The basic contribution of them was a derivation of necessary conditions for an optimal solution and an algorithm for obtaining optimal solutions to the decomposed problems.
- Rao (1973) considered a direct search approach to the RMFLP in detail, however he demonstrated that the gradient technique was basically a primal simplex-based linear programming approach, and in the presence of degeneracy, the optimality conditions were not sufficient. A necessary condition for optimality to be sufficient in special cases and the main difficulties associated with the direct search approach were discussed.
- Wesolowsky and Love (1971a, b) and Morris (1975) showed that the problem with linear locational constraints could be solved by linear programming.
- A thorough set of necessary and sufficient optimality conditions were developed by Juel and Love (1976).
- Idrissi et al. (1989) developed a dual problem for the constrained multifacility minisum location problems involving mixed norms. General optimality conditions were obtained providing new algorithms which are decomposition methods based on the concept of partial inverse of a multifunction.
- A nonlinear approximation method was developed by Wesolowsky and Love (1972), where any number of linear and (or) nonlinear constraints defining a convex feasible region can be included.
- The hyperboloid approximation procedure for solving the perturbed rectilinear distance MFLP was also proposed by Eyster et al. (1973).
- Morris (1975) used the dual problem of Rectangular MFLP and then reduced it to a problem with substantially fewer variables and constraints. He stated that linear and pairwise constraints limiting distances between new points and between new and existing points can be imposed to restrict the location of new points.
- Picard and Ratliff (1978) solved the problem via at most ($m - 1$) minimum cut problems on derived networks containing at most ($n - 2$) vertices. They showed

that the optimum location of new facilities is dependent on the relative orderings of old facilities but not on the distances between them.
- Subsequently, Kolen (1981) exhibited the equivalence of the method of Sherali and Shetty and Picard and Ratliff. The main difference between these two procedures was principally in the computational implementation. Moreover, this type of approach is known to be the most effective way of solving the rectilinear distance MFLP.
- A modified version of the method of Picard and Ratliff (1978) was proposed by Cheung (1980).
- Dax (1986) presented a new method that, as he stated, handles efficiently the rectilinear distance Problem MFLP having large clusters, i.e. where several new facilities are located together at one point. This paper states and proves a new necessary and sufficient optimality condition. This condition transforms the problem of computing a descent direction into a constrained linear least-squares problem. The latter problem is solved by a relaxation method that takes advantage of its special structure. The new technique is incorporated into the direct search method.
- As an alternative to linear programming, a simple approach which sometimes finds optimal locations was presented by (Francis et al. 1992) as coordinate descent. By deleting the term that shows the relationship between new facilities in objective function, the problem is converted to some single facility location problems to which we can apply median conditions. The first coordinate we choose is the first variable and the second coordinate is the second variable, and so on. It is continued until we obtain the same vector by coordinate descent that we have obtained previously by coordinate descent, at which point we stop.
- Allen (1995) developed a dual-based lower bound to the multifacility ℓp distance location problem and he stated that the bound is as good or better than other bounds.

4.3.1.2 Squared Euclidean Distance MiniSum Location Problem

In this problem, it is obvious that the function that is to be minimized is strictly convex, and unlike the Euclidean distance case, it has continuous first partial derivatives with respect to x and y.

Consequently the optimal solution is unique and the approach to finding optimal solution is the same for the SFLP; partial derivation of (4.20) with respect to each variable are computed and set to equal to zero.

The result of the partial derivation computation is two sets of line equation on involving the x coordinate (and y coordinate) of the new facilities.

To compute the partial derivations, it is convenient to define a new quantity $\hat{v}_{ik}$ where

$$\hat{v}_{ik} = \begin{cases} v_{ij} & k > j \\ v_{kj} & k \leq j \end{cases}. \tag{4.40}$$

Computing the partial derivation of (4.21) with respect to x_i and (4.22) with respect to y_i gives, for $j = 1, \ldots, n$,

$$\frac{\partial f}{\partial x_j} = 2\sum_{k=1}^{n} \hat{v}_{ik}(x_j - x_k) + 2\sum_{i=1}^{m} w_{ji}(x_j - a_i). \tag{4.41}$$

And

$$\frac{\partial f}{\partial y_j} = 2\sum_{k=1}^{n} \hat{v}_{ik}(y_j - y_k) + 2\sum_{i=1}^{m} w_{ji}(y_j - b_i). \tag{4.42}$$

If we set the (4.41) and (4.42) to zero and solve it, the optimum values of the x and y coordinates for the new facilities are related by the following expressions:

$$x_j = \frac{\sum_{k=1}^{n} \hat{v}_{ik} x_k + \sum_{i=1}^{m} w_{ji} a_i}{\sum_{k=1}^{n} \hat{v}_{ik} + \sum_{i=1}^{m} w_{ji}}. \tag{4.43}$$

And

$$y_j = \frac{\sum_{k=1}^{n} \hat{v}_{ik} y_k + \sum_{i=1}^{m} w_{ji} b_i}{\sum_{k=1}^{n} \hat{v}_{ik} + \sum_{i=1}^{m} w_{ji}}. \tag{4.44}$$

Furthermore, White (1971) established that the optimum solution to the multifacility problem is given by

$$x^* = A^{-1}Wa. \tag{4.45}$$

and

$$y^* = A^{-1}Wb, \tag{4.46}$$

where x^* and y^* are $n \times 1$ column vectors giving the optimum coordinate locations for the new facilities, a and b are $m \times 1$ column vectors giving the x and y coordinate locations, respectively, for the existing facilities W is an $n \times m$ matrix containing the weights w_{ij}, and A is an $n \times n$ nonsingular matrix given as follows:

$$A = \begin{bmatrix} \sum_{k=1}^{n} \hat{v}_{1k} + \sum_{i} w_{1i} & -\hat{v}_{12} & \cdots & -\hat{v}_{1n} \\ -\hat{v}_{21} & \sum_{k=1}^{n} \hat{v}_{2k} + \sum_{i} w_{2i} & \cdots & -\hat{v}_{2n} \\ \cdot & \cdot & \cdot & \cdot \\ \cdot & \cdot & \cdot & \cdot \\ -\hat{v}_{n1} & -\hat{v}_{n2} & \cdots & \sum_{k=1}^{n} \hat{v}_{nk} + \sum_{i} w_{ni} \end{bmatrix}. \tag{4.47}$$

The matrix A is strictly diagonally dominant, allowing (4.45) and (4.46) to be solved using the method of simultaneous displacements, an iterative solution procedure based on (4.43) and (4.44) (Eyster and White 1973).

It is interesting to note that the solution of the squared Euclidean distance problem has been used to obtain a good starting solution for the corresponding Euclidean MFLP (Francis et al. 1992).

4.3.1.3 Euclidean Distance MiniSum Location Problem

The objective function of Euclidean MFLP is convex, since it is the sum of norms that are convex functions and Francis and Cabot (1972) have proven that a necessary and sufficient condition for the objective function to be strictly convex is that for each new facility i, the set $S_i = \{j : w_{ij} > 0\}$ is nonempty and that the location of the points in S_i are non-collinear. As it is known, the optimal solution of Euclidean MFLP problem exists and lies in the convex hull of the existing facilities, and therefore, this optimal solution can be expressed as the convex combination of the existing facilities (Francis et al. 1983).

In the previous treatment of the rectilinear distance problem and the squared Euclidean distance problem; we found that multifacility problems were not substantially more difficult to solve than the corresponding single facility version. Such is not the case for Euclidean distance problem. The main difficulty with the Euclidean SFLP arises because its objective function is not differentiable at the points $a_1, \ldots, a_n$. For Euclidean MFLP the function f is nondifferentiable not only at a set of isolated points, but also on linear subspaces $X_i = X_k$.

Eyster et al. (1973) used an extension of the Weiszfeld algorithm. In this procedure, in order to avoid difficulties of the partial derivatives of the distance function not existing at points P_i and at points where other new facilities have been located

$$d(X_j, X_k) = [(x_j - x_k)^2 + (y_j - y_k)^2 + \varepsilon]^{1/2}, \qquad (4.48)$$
$$d(X_j, X_i) = [(x_j - a_i)^2 + (y_j - b_i)^2 + \varepsilon]^{1/2}. \qquad (4.49)$$

This procedure is labeled the hyperboloid approximation procedure (HAP) and is probably the most common procedure for solving the multifacility location problem, using Euclidean distances or even rectilinear distances. Rosen and Xue (1993) proved the global convergence of HAP when applied to the problems MFLP. Hap comes from computing partial derivatives of the function f, setting them to zero, and solving for new facility locations.

To simplify, we define terms $\alpha_t(X_1, \ldots, X_n), \beta_t(X_1, \ldots, X_n), \Gamma_t(X_1, \ldots, X_n)$, and for $t = 1, \ldots, n$ as follows:

$$\alpha_t(X_1, \ldots, X_n) = \sum_{j=1}^{n} v_{tj} \frac{x_j}{[(x_t - x_j)^2 + (y_t - y_j)^2 + \varepsilon]^{1/2}}$$
$$+ \sum_{i=1}^{m} w_{ti} \frac{a_i}{[(x_t - a_i)^2 + (y_t - b_i)^2 + \varepsilon]^{1/2}} \quad t = 1, \ldots, n, \qquad (4.50)$$

$$\beta_t(X_1,\ldots,X_n) = \sum_{j=1}^{n} v_{tj} \frac{y_j}{[(x_t - x_j)^2 + (y_t - y_j)^2 + \varepsilon]^{1/2}}$$

$$+ \sum_{i=1}^{m} w_{ti} \frac{b_i}{[(x_t - a_i)^2 + (y_t - b_i)^2 + \varepsilon]^{1/2}} \quad t = 1,\ldots,n, \quad (4.51)$$

$$\Gamma_t(X_1,\ldots,X_n) = \sum_{j=1}^{n} \frac{v_{ij}}{[(x_t - x_j)^2 + (y_t - y_j)^2 + \varepsilon]^{1/2}}$$

$$+ \sum_{i=1}^{m} \frac{w_{ti}}{[(x_t - a_i)^2 + (y_t - b_i)^2 + \varepsilon]^{1/2}} \quad t = 1,\ldots,n. \quad (4.52)$$

Then it may be shown that the partial derivatives of f with respect to x_t and y_t is as follows:

$$\frac{\partial f}{\partial x_t} = \Gamma_t(X_1,\ldots,X_n)x_t - \alpha_t(X_1,\ldots,X_n) \quad t = 1,\ldots,n, \quad (4.53)$$

and

$$\frac{\partial f}{\partial y_t} = \Gamma_t(X_1,\ldots,X_n)y_t - \beta_t(X_1,\ldots,X_n) \quad t = 1,\ldots,n. \quad (4.54)$$

By setting the partial derivatives to zero for x_1 and y_1 we have:

$$x_t = \frac{1}{\Gamma_t(X_1,\ldots,X_n)} \alpha_t(X_1,\ldots,X_n) \quad t = 1,\ldots,n. \quad (4.55)$$

And

$$y_t = \frac{1}{\Gamma_t(X_1,\ldots,X_n)} \beta_t(X_1,\ldots,X_n) \quad t = 1,\ldots,n. \quad (4.56)$$

The iteration procedure determines x^{k+1} and y^{k+1} in terms of x^k and y^k using the following:

$$x_t^{k+1} = \frac{1}{\Gamma_t(X_1^k,\ldots,X_n^k)} \alpha_t(X_1^k,\ldots,X_n^k) \quad t = 1,\ldots,n, \quad (4.57)$$

$$y_t^{k+1} = \frac{1}{\Gamma_t(X_1^k,\ldots,X_n^k)} \beta_t(X_1^k,\ldots,X_n^k) \quad t = 1,\ldots,n. \quad (4.58)$$

By making an initial choice of new facility locations, say $\alpha_t(X_1^{(0)},\ldots,X_n^{(0)})$, use the algorithm to compute new answers for new facility locations. In using HAP to solve multifacility location problems, it has been observed that the larger the value of ε the faster the convergences to optimum value of approximating function. However, the accuracy of approximation decrease with increasing values of ε consequently, in solving location problem using HAP a large value of ε is used initially; the solution obtained used as starting solution, using a smaller value of ε; and the process is continued by successively reducing the value of ε until no signification decrease in the value of either (x_i, x_j). interestingly, HAP can be used to solve the rectangular location problem and can also be used to handle situation involving a mixture of recliner and Euclidean distance (Eyster et al. (1973).

4.3.1.4 Some other Kinds of Algorithms in Euclidean MFLP

- Eyster et al. (1973) used an extension of the Weiszfeld algorithm.
- Calamai and Conn (1980) have proposed a pseudo-gradient technique that classifies the new facilities into distinct categories based on their coincidence with other facilities in order to derive a descent method for solving Euclidean MFLP.
- Chatelon (1978) have also approached Euclidean MFLP by using a general e-subgradient method in which search directions are generated based on the subdifferential of the objective function over a neighborhood of the current iterate.
- Sequential unconstrained minimization techniques used by Love (1969) and the Weiszfeld fixed-point iterative method as utilized by Rado (1988), are also among other efforts to solve Euclidean MFLP.
- Several second-order methods have also been designed to solve the Euclidean MFLP. Calamai and Conn (1980) were the first to propose a projected gradient-based algorithm.
- Various quadratic convergence approaches have also been developed by Calamai and Conn (1982, 1987), in which specialized line-searches are used in conjunction with projected second-order techniques.
- Rosen and Xue (1992) developed an algorithm which, from any initial point, generates a sequence of points that converges to the closed convex set of optimal solutions to the Problem Euclidean MFLP.
- For the multifacility location problem with no constraints on the location of the new facilities, Juel and Love (1980) derived some sufficient conditions for the coincidence of facilities that are valid in a general symmetric metric.
- The results of Juel and Love (1980) were later extended by Lefebvere et al. (1991) to be applicable to some location problems having certain locational constraints.
- Mazzerella and Pesamosca (1996) have used the optimality conditions of Euclidean MFLP as a tool for obtaining both stopping rules for some computational algorithms such as the projected Newton procedure of Calamai and Conn (1987), and the analytical solution of many simple problems.
- Love (1969) applied convex programming to the problem in three dimensions.
- Carrizosa et al. (1993) derived the geometrical characterizations for the set of efficient, weakly efficient and properly efficient solutions of the Euclidean MFLP when it includes certain convex locational constraints.
- Love and Yoeng (1981), Elzinga and Hearn (1983), Juel (1984), and Love and Dowling (1989) explored the bounding method that continuously updates a lower

bound on the optimal objective function value during each iteration. This method is based on the idea that the convex hull and the current value of the gradient determine an upper bound on the objective function's improvement.
- Wendell and Petersen (1984) have derived a lower bound from the dual to Euclidean MFLP.
- Love (1974) developed the dual problem corresponding to a hyperbolic approximation of the constrained multifacility location problem with l_p distances.
- White (1976) gave a Varignon frame interpretation of the dual problem.
- Sinha (1966) have used duality results involving general quadratic forms.
- Francis (1972) derived a differentiable, convex quadratically constrained dual optimization problem, and achieved several useful relationships between the dual and Euclidean MFLP.
- Xue et al. (1996) have suggested the use of polynomial-time interior point algorithm to solve this dual problem based on this idea, they presented a procedure in which an approximate optimum to Euclidean MFLP can be recovered by solving a sequence of linear equations, each associated with an iterate of the interior point algorithm used to solve the dual problem.
- Love and Kraemer (1973) gave a dual decomposition method for solving the constrained Euclidean MFLP.
- Love (1974) developed the dual problem corresponding to a hyperbolic approximation of the objective function for the constrained MFLP with l_p distance.

4.3.2 MiniMax

4.3.2.1 Rectangular Distance MiniMax Location Problem

Some procedures for solving rectangular MiniMax MFLP are shown here:

- Wesolowsky (1972) converted the rectangular MiniMax MFLP into a parametric linear programming problem with $5mn + 5/2n(n-1)$ constraints and $2mn + n(n-1) + 2n$ variables in addition to the parameters.
- Elzinga and Hearn (1973) recognized some simplifications in linear program presented by Wesolowsky.
- Dearing and Francis (1974) showed that the problem can be decomposed into two sub problems that have identical structures and that may be solved independently each of which had $2mn + n(n-1)$ constraints and $n+1$ variables. Each problem is solved efficiently by converting it into an equivalent network flow problem.
- Morris (1973) has introduced this problem with linear constraints which (a) limit the new facilities location and (b) enforce upper bounds on the distances between new and existing facilities and between new facilities. He uses dual variables that provide information about the complete range of new facility locations which satisfies the MiniMax criterion.

- Drezner and Wesolowsky (1978) presented a method involved the numerical integration of ordinary differential equations and was computationally superior to methods using nonlinear programming.

4.3.2.2 Euclidean Distance MiniMax Location Problem

The application of nonlinear duality theory shows Euclidean minimax MFLP can always be solved by maximizing a continuously differentiable concave objective subject to a small number of linear constraints. This leads to a solution procedure which produces very good numerical results. Love et al. (1973) presented a nonlinear programming method for computing the solution to MFLPs using Euclidean distances when the MiniMax criterion is to be satisfied.

4.3.3 Solution Techniques for other Models

In this section we introduce some solution techniques for the models shown in Sect. 1.3

- A specialized simplex based-algorithm was derived by Sherali and Shetty (1978) for solving rectangular multiproduct MFLP.
- Dhar and Rao (1982) presented an iterative solution for MFLP on sphere. The procedure involved the approximation of the domain of objective function which in the limit approaches to that of the original objective function. Aykin and Babu (1987) considered Euclidean, squared Euclidean and the great circle distances. They formulated an algorithm and investigated its convergence properties.
- Wesolowsky and Love (1971a, b) considered the problem of MFLP with rectangular regions for the cases $n = 1$ or 2. They used a simple gradient reduction technique to solve the single facility problem. As they stated, the procedure becomes very complex when $n > 2$. Aly and Marucheck (1982) stated that if there is interfacility interaction among the new facilities, a gradient-free nonlinear search algorithm is utilized. Computational experience suggests that this algorithm is expedient even in the solution of large problems.
- Seppalla (1975) stated that in order to be able to solve the stochastic MFLP, we must transform it into the deterministic equivalent forms.

4.3.4 Some Heuristic and Metaheuristic Methods

There are a few heuristics methods for solving MFLP:
- Vergin and Rogers (1967) introduced a simple heuristic for solving MFLP with Euclidean distance. This procedure locates each of new facilities in a temporary

location at each step and locates the next new facility according to the facilities located so far. After all n new facilities are located in this manner the process is repeated and the readjustment process is continued until no further movements occur during a complete round of adjustment evaluations.
- Davoud Pour and Nosraty (2006) solved the MFLP with ant-colony optimization metaheuristic when the distances are rectangular and Euclidian. This algorithm produces optimal solutions for problem instances of up to 20 new facilities.

4.4 Case Study

Smallwood (1965) introduced a model for the placement of n detection stations so as to maximize the probability that at least one of them will detect any enemy event occurring within the area. This research was done within boundaries of USA and USSR. The model is based on five assumptions that one of them is the assumption of plane area that was made in order to allow the use of the relatively convenient Cartesian coordinate system. Each of these assumptions can be relaxed to reduce the error of the model.

References

Allen WR (1995) An improved bound for the multifacility location model. Oper Res Lett 17(4):175–180
Aly AA, Marucheck AS (1982) Generalized Weber problem with rectangular regions. J Oper Res Soc 33(11):983–989
Aykin T, Babu AJG (1987) Multifacility location problems on a sphere. Int J Math Math Sci 10(3):583–596
Cabot AV, Francis RL, Stary MA (1970) A network flow solution to a rectilinear distance facility location problem. AIIE Trans 2(2):132–141
Calamai PH, Charalambous C (1980) Solving multifacility location problem involving euclidean distances. Naval Res Logist Quart 27:609–620
Calamai PH, Conn AR (1980) A stable algorithm for solving the multifacility location problem involving euclidean distances. SIAM J Sci Stat Comput 1:512–525
Calamai PH, Conn AR (1982) A Second-order method for moving the continuous multifacility location problem. In: Watson GA (ed) Numerical analysis: proceeding of the ninth biennial conference, Dundee, Scotland, Lecture Notes in Mathematics, vol 912. Springer, Berlin, pp 1–25
Calamai PH, Conn AR (1987) A projected Newton method for L_p norm location problems. Math Program 38:75–109
Carrizosa E, Conde E, Fernandez FR, Puerto J (1993) Efficiency in euclidean constrained location problems. Oper Res Lett 14:291–295
Chatelon JA (1978) A subgradient algorithm for certain minimax and minisum Problems. Math Program 15:130–145
Cheung To-Yat (1980) Multifacility location problem with rectilinear distance by the minimum-Cut approach. ACM Trans Math Softw 6(3):387–390

Davoud Pour H, Nosraty M (2006) Solving the facility and layout and location problem by ant-colony optimization-metaheuristic. Int J Prod Res 44(23):5187–5196

Dax A (1986) An efficient algorithm for solving the rectilinear multifacility location problem. IMA J Numer Anal 6:343–355

Dearing PM, Francis RL (1974) A network flow solution to a multifacility minimax location problem involving rectangular distances. Transport Sci 9:126–141

Dhar UR, Rao JR (1982) domain approximation method for solving multifacility location problems on a sphere. J Oper Res Soc 33(7):639–645

Drezner Z, Wesolowsky GO (1978) A trajectory method for the optimization of the multifacility location problem with distances. Manage Sci 24(14):1507–1514

Elzinga DJ, Hearn DW (1973) A note on a minimax location problem. Transport Sci 7:100–103.

Elzinga DJ, Hearn DW (1983) On stopping rules for facilities location algorithm. AIIE Trans 15:81–82

Elzinga DJ, Hearn DW, Randolph WR (1976) Minimax multifacility location with euclidean distances. Transport Sci 10(4):321–336

Eyster JW, White JA (1973) Some properties of the squared euclidean distance location problem. AIIE Trans 5(3):275–280

Eyster JW, White JA, Wierwille WW (1973) On solving multifacility location problems using a hyperboloid approximation procedure. AIIE Trans 5:1–6

Francis RL (1964) On the location of multiple new facilities with respect to existing facilities. J Ind Eng 15(2):106–107

Francis RL, Cabot AV (1972) Properties of a multifacility location problem involving euclidean distances. Naval Res Logist Quart 19:335–353

Francis RL, McGinnis LF, White JA (1983) Locational analysis. Eur J Oper Res 12:220–252

Francis RL, McGinnis LF, White JA (1992) Facility layout and location: an analytical approach, 2nd edn. Prentice Hall, Englewood Cliffs, NJ

Idrissi HO, Lefebvre, Michelot (1989) Duality constrained multifacility location problems with mixed norms and applications. Ann Oper Res 18:71–92

Juel H (1984) On a rational stopping rule for facilities location algorithms. Naval Res Logist Quart 31:9–11

Juel H, Love RF (1976) An efficient computational procedure for solving the multifacility rectilinear facilities location problem. Oper Res Quart 27(3):697–703

Juel H, Love RF (1980) Sufficient conditions for optimal facility location to coincide. Transport Sci 14:125–129

Kolen A (1981) Equivalence between the direct search approach and the cut approach to the rectilinear distance location problem. Oper Res 29(3):616–620

Lefebvere O, Michelot C, Plastria F (1991) Sufficient conditions for coincidence in minisum multifacility location problem with a general metric. Oper Res 39(3):437–442

Love RF (1969) Locating facilities in three-dimensional space by convex programming. Naval Res Logist Quart 16(4):503–516

Love RF (1972) A computational procedure for optimally locating a facility with respect to several rectangular regions. J Region Sci 12(2):233–242

Love RF (1974) The dual of a hyperbolic approximation to the generalized constrained multifacility location problem with lp distances. Manage Sci 21:22–33

Love RF, Dowling PD (1989) A generalized bounding method for multifacility location models. Oper Res 37(4):653–657

Love RF, Kraemer S (1973) A dual decomposition method for minimizing transportation costs in multifacility location problems. Transport Sci 7(4):297–316

Love RF, Yoeng WY (1981) A stopping rule for facilities location algorithms. AIIE Trans 13:357–362

Love RF, Wesolowsky GO, Kraemer SA (1973) A multifacility minimax location method for euclidean distances. Int J Prod Res 11(1):37–45

Mazzerella F, Pesamosca G (1996) The analytical solution of some EMFL minisum problems. Isolde VII, June 25–July 3

Morris JG (1973) A linear programming approach to the solution of constrained multifacility minimax location problems where distances are rectangular. Oper Res Quart 24:419–435

Morris JG (1975) Linear programming solution to the generalized rectangular distance weber problem. Naval Res Logist Quart 22:155–164

Ostresh LM (1977) The multifacility location problem: applications and descent theorems. J Region Sci 17:409–419

Picard J, Ratliff HD (1978) A cut approach to the rectilinear distance facility location problem. Oper Res 26(3):422–433

Pritsker AAB, Ghare PM (1970) locating new facilities with respect to existing facilities. AIIE Trans 2(4):290–297

Rado F (1988) The euclidean multifacility location Problem. Oper Res 36(3):485–492

Rao MR (1973) On the direct search approach to the rectilinear facilities location problem. AIIE Trans 5(3):256–264

Rosen JB, Xue GL (1992) A globally convergent algorithm for solving the euclidean multifacility location problem. Acta Math Appl Sin 8(4):357–366

Rosen JB, Xue GL (1993) On the Convergence of a hyperboloid approximation procedure for the perturbed euclidean multifacility location problem. Oper Res 41(6):1164–1171

Seppalla Y (1975) On a Stochastic multifacility location problem. AIIE Trans 7(1):56–62

Sherali HD, Shetty CM (1978) A primal simplex based solution procedure for the rectilinear distance multifacility location problem. J Oper Res Soc 29(4):373–381

Sinha SM (1966) A duality theorem for nonlinear programming. Manage Sci 12:385–390

Smallwood RD (1965) Minimal detection station placement. Oper Res 13(4):632–646

Thomas GB (1968) Chlculus and analytic geometry. AddisonWesley, Reading, MA

Vergin RC, Rogers JD (1967) An algorithm and computational procedure for locating economic facilities. Manage Sci 3(6):240–254

Wendell RE, Petersen EL (1984) A dual approach for obtaining lower bounds to the weber problem. J Region Sci 24:219–228

Wesolowsky GO (1972) Rectangular distance location under minimax optimality criterion. Transport Sci 6:103–113

Wesolowsky GO, Love RF (1971a) Location of facilities with rectangular distances among point and area destinations. Naval Res Logist Quart 18:83–90

Wesolowsky GO, Love RF (1971b) The optimal location of new facilities using rectangular distances. Oper Res 19(1):124–130

Wesolowsky GO, Love RF (1972) A nonlinear approximation method for solving a generalized rectangular distance weber problem. Manage Sci 18(11):656–663

Wesolowsky GO, Truscott GW (1976) Dynamic location of multiple facilities for a class of continuous problems. AIIE Trans 8(1):76–83

White DJ (1976) An analogue derivation of the dual of the general fermat problem. Manage Sci 23:92–94

White JA (1971) A quadratic facility location problem. AIIE Trans 3(2):156–157

Xue GL, Rosen JB, Pardalos PM (1996) A polynomial time dual algorithm for the euclidean multifacility location problem. Oper Res Lett 18:201–204

Chapter 5
Location Allocation Problem

Zeinab Azarmand and Ensiyeh Neishabouri Jami

Location-allocation (LA) problem is to locate a set of new facilities such that the transportation cost from facilities to customers is minimized and an optimal number of facilities have to be placed in an area of interest in order to satisfy the customer demand.

This problem occurs in many practical settings where facilities provide homogeneous services such as the determination and location of warehouses, distribution centers, communication centers and production facilities.

Since LA problem was proposed by Cooper (1963) and spread to a weighted network by Hakimi (1964), network LA problem and many models were presented by Badri (1999).

For solving these models, numerous algorithms have been designed, involving branch-and-bound algorithms (Kuenne and Soland 1972), simulated annealing (Murray and Church 1996) and Tabu search (Brimberg and Mladenovic 1996; Ohlemüller 1997) and P-Median plus Weber (Hansen et al. 1998). Some hybrid algorithms have been also suggested, such as the one based on simulated annealing and random descent method (Ernst and Krishnamoorthy 1999) and the one utilizing the Lagrange relaxation method and genetic algorithm (Gong et al. 1997). Brimberg et al. (2000) improved present algorithms and proposed variable neighborhood search, which is proved to obtain the best results when the number of facilities to locate is large.

5.1 Classification of Location-Allocation Problem

The basic components of location-allocation problems can be thought to consist of facilities, locations, and customers. The definitions and properties of these basic components will be discussed in this part along with some different types of location-allocation models. The presentation provided in this part has been influenced by the paper of Scaparra and Scutellà (2001) which proposes a unified framework for characterizing the different aspects of location problems.

5.1.1 Classifications of Facilities

The facilities are usually characterized by, among other things, their number, type, and costs. Other facility-connected properties can include for instance profit, capacity, attraction range (within which the customers are drawn to the facility), and the type of service provided.

One of the properties characterizing is the number of new facilities, the simplest case is the single-facility problem in which only one new facility is to be established. The more general case is called the multi-facility problem in which the aim is to locate simultaneously more than one facility.

The type of a facility is another important property, in the simplest case, all the facilities are supposed to be identical with respect to their size and the kind of service they offer. However, it is often necessary to locate facilities that differ from one another, for instance hospitals and smaller health care units. Location-allocation models can also be differentiated into single-service and multi-service types, based on whether the facilities can provide only one or many services.

It can also be taken into consideration whether the facilities can supply an infinite demand or whether their production and supply capacity is limited. In this respect, the problems are often classified into uncapacitated and capacitated.

5.1.2 Classified on the Physical Space or Locations

The set of eligible locations has three possible representations: discrete, continuous, and network.

Continuous space models are sometimes referred to as site-generation models since the generation of appropriate sites is left to the model at hand.

Discrete space models are sometimes referred to as site-selection models since we have a priori knowledge of the site candidates.

The network-based model is the third type of location models that can be distinguished with respect to the locations. Problems defined on networks can be either continuous or discrete depending on whether the links of the network are considered as a continuous set of candidate locations or whether only the nodes are eligible for the placement of new facilities.

5.1.3 Classifications of the Demand

The demands of customer are deterministic or probabilistic:

5.2 Models

The models of location-allocation problem are divided into two main parts: the general models which are discussed in Sect. 5.2.1 and developed models which are discussed in Sects. 5.2.2 and 5.2.4.

For modeling these problems we use operation research, to minimize the total cost. The LA model has some variables as follows:

- Facilities' number
- Facilities' location
- Amount of allocation of the facilities to customers
- Capacity of each facility

5.2.1 General LA Model (Cooper 1963)

Cooper (1963) introduced and solved a general model of LA with two new facilities and seven demand's points for the first time.

5.2.1.1 Model Assumptions

Model assumptions are as follows (The problem is also known as the multisource Weber problem):

- The solution space is continuous
- Each customer's demand can supply by several facilities ignoring the opening cost of new facility
- Facilities are uncapacitated
- Parameters are deterministic supplying all the demand
- No relationship between new facilities

5.2.1.2 Model Inputs

Model inputs are as follows:

n: number of customer (existing facilities)
r: customer's demand $j = 1, 2 \ldots, n$
a_j: the coordinates of the customers $j = 1, 2 \ldots, n$

5.2.1.3 Model Outputs (Decision Variables)

Model outputs of this model are as follows:

φ: Total cost for transportation the goods\services between facilities and customer
m: Number of facilities
x_i: The coordinates of the new facilities $i = 1, 2 \ldots, m$
w_{ij}: Quantity supplied to customer j by facility i
$d(x_i, a_j)$: The distance between a customer j and new facility i

5.2.1.4 Objective Function and its Constraints

The objective function of this model and its related constraints are as follows:

$$\text{Min } \varphi = \sum_{i=1}^{m} \sum_{j=1}^{n} w_{ij} d(x_i, a_j). \tag{5.1}$$

Subject to

$$\sum_{i=1}^{m} w_{ij} = r_j, \ j = 1, 2, \ldots n, \tag{5.2}$$

$$w_{ij} \geq 0, \quad \begin{matrix} i = 1, 2, \ldots, m \\ j = 1, 2, \ldots, n \end{matrix}. \tag{5.3}$$

Equation (5.1) minimizes the total transportation cost. Equation (5.2) ensures that all customer demand is satisfied. Because there are no capacity constraints on the facilities, an optimal solution will have the demand at each customer served by the facility that is closest to it. Equation (5.3) is standard constraints.

As you see there are some assumptions in the general model, if we change some of these, then the model will be converted to a developed LA model. We can see the importance of modeling in such problems.

5.2.2 LA Model Each Customer Covered by Only One Facility

5.2.2.1 Model Assumptions

In this model the second assumption in general model changes so that, each customer can use only one facility. The other assumptions of this model are similar to the general model.

5　Location Allocation Problem

5.2.2.2　Model Inputs

The inputs of this model are similar to the general model.

5.2.2.3　Model Outputs (Decision Variables)

We have all the outputs in general model in addition to the following output:

$z_{ij} = 1$ if an customer j is assigned to a new facility i;
0 otherwise;
And w_{ij} = demand of each customer so we don't have w_{ij} in this model

5.2.2.4　Objective Function and its Constraints

The objective function of this model and its related constraints are as follows:

$$\text{Min } \phi = \sum_{i=1}^{m} \sum_{j=1}^{n} z_{ij} r_j d(x_i, a_j). \tag{5.4}$$

Subject to

$$\sum_{i=1}^{m} z_{ij} = 1, \ j = 1, 2, \ldots n, \tag{5.5}$$

$$z_{ij} \in \{0, 1\}, \quad \begin{array}{l} i = 1, 2, \ldots, m \\ j = 1, 2, \ldots, n \end{array}. \tag{5.6}$$

Equation (5.4) minimizes the total transportation cost. Equation (5.5) ensures that all customer demand is satisfied. Equation (5.6) is standard constraints

In this form, the LA problem may involve the determination of z, the allocation matrix.

5.2.3　LA Model with Facility's Opening Cost

5.2.3.1　Model Assumptions

In this model, the third assumption in general model changes to, spot the facility's opening cost. The other assumptions of this model are similar to the general model.

5.2.3.2 Model Inputs

We have all the inputs in general model in addition to the following input:

$f(x_i)$ = facility's opening cost.

5.2.3.3 Model Outputs (Decision Variables)

The outputs of this model are similar to the general model.

5.2.3.4 Objective Function and its Constraints

The differences between the objective function of this model and general model are as follows:

Equation (5.1) is eliminated and the following term is added to the objective function:

$$\sum_{i=1}^{m} f(x_i). \tag{5.7}$$

The constraints of this model are similar to the general model.

If we assume that the opening cost is independent of facility location and m is known, the problem reduces to the well-known multi source Weber problem since the sum of opening costs is now constant and may be deleted from the objective function.

5.2.4 Capacitated LA Model with Stochastic Demands (Zhou and Liu 2003)

This model was proposed by Zhou and Liu (2003).

5.2.4.1 Model Assumptions

In this model, the fourth and fifth assumption in general model changes so that, facilities are capacitated and demand of customer are probabilistic. The other assumptions of this model are similar to the general model.

5.2.4.2 Model Inputs

We have all the inputs in general model in addition to the following input:

ξ_j: stochastic demand of customer j
$\xi_j(\omega)$: a realization of stochastic vector j
s_i: capacity of facility i

5.2.4.3 Model Outputs (Decision Variables)

The outputs of this model are similar to the general model. But in a deterministic LA problem, the allocation w is a decision variable which is fixed all the time. However, in a stochastic LA problem, the decision w will be made every period after the demands of customers are realized.

5.2.4.4 Objective Function and its Constraints

The objective of this model is similar to general model:

$$\text{Min } \phi = \sum_{i=1}^{m} \sum_{j=1}^{n} w_{ij} d(x_i, a_j). \tag{5.8}$$

Subject to

$$\sum_{i=1}^{m} w_{ij} = \xi_j(\omega), \quad j = 1, 2, \ldots n, \tag{5.9}$$

$$\sum_{j=1}^{m} w_{ij} \leq S, \tag{5.10}$$

$$w_{ij} \geq 0, \quad \begin{matrix} i = 1, 2, \ldots, m \\ j = 1, 2, \ldots, n \end{matrix}. \tag{5.11}$$

Equations (5.9) and (5.10) ensure that w is feasible. Equations (5.11) are standard constraints.

If we don't find the feasible point for w; then demands of some customers are impossible to be met, and the right-hand side of (5.8) becomes meaningless. As a penalty, we define:

$$\text{Min } \phi = \sum_{i=1}^{m} \sum_{j=1}^{n} \xi_j(\omega) d(x_i, a_j). \tag{5.12}$$

5.3 Solution Techniques

The calculation aspects of solving certain classes of LA problems are, exact equations, heuristic methods and meta-heuristic methods that are presented for solving these problems.

5.3.1 Exact Solutions (Cooper 1963)

In order to find the set of (x_i, y_i) that will minimize φ we differentiate (13) with respect to x_i and y_i solve the equations resulting from setting the derivatives (into (xx_i, yx_i)) equal to zero. Thus:

$$\phi = \sum_{i=1}^{m} \sum_{j=1}^{n} Z_{ij} W_i d_{ij}, \tag{5.13}$$

$$\frac{\partial \phi}{\partial X_{x_i}} = \sum_{j=1}^{n} Z_{ij} W \left[\frac{\partial d_{ij}}{\partial X_{x_i}} \right] = 0; i = 1, \ldots, m, \tag{5.14}$$

$$\frac{\partial \phi}{\partial Y_{x_i}} = \sum_{j=1}^{n} Z_{ij} W \left[\frac{\partial d_{ij}}{\partial Y_{x_i}} \right] = 0; i = 1, \ldots, m. \tag{5.15}$$

Solving (5.14) and (5.15) will yield the $2m$ values of (x_i, y_i) which will cause φ to be a minimum, for some particular set of Z_{ij}.

It is well to consider the amount of computation that may be involved. For m sources and n destinations there are $S(n,m)$ possible assignments of n destinations to m sources is given by:

$$S(n, m) = \frac{1}{m!} \sum_{k=0}^{m} \binom{m}{k} (-1)^K (m-k)^m. \tag{5.16}$$

For very large n, these Stirling numbers can be formidably large. Equation (5.14) and (5.15) would have to be solved $S(n, m)$ times to find which particular allocation of sources to destinations, among this minimum set, is the absolute minimum we seek.

For small-scale problems this is feasible using a digital computer. However, for large-scale problems of industrial importance the amount of computation is prohibitive.

Suppose it is desired to minimize Euclidean distance between sources and destinations, under the assumption that cost is proportional to distance. For this case we have:

$$\phi = \sum_{i=1}^{m} \sum_{j=1}^{n} Z_{ij} W_i \left[(X_{x_i} - X_{a_j})^2 + (Y_{x_i} - Y_{a_j})^2 \right]^{1/2}. \tag{5.17}$$

Differentiating to find the minimum yields:

$$\sum_{j=1}^{n} \left\{ \frac{Z_{ij} W_i (X_{x_i} - X_{a_j})}{\left[(X_{x_i} - X_{a_j})^2 + (Y_{x_i} - Y_{a_j})^2 \right]^{1/2}} \right\} = 0; i = 1, \ldots, m, \tag{5.18}$$

$$\sum_{j=1}^{n}\left\{\frac{Z_{ij}W_i\left(Y_{x_i}-Y_{a_j}\right)}{\left[\left(X_{x_i}-X_{a_j}\right)^2+\left(Y_{x_i}-Y_{a_j}\right)^{1/2}\right]}\right\}=0; i=1,\ldots,m. \quad (5.19)$$

Cooper (1963) has found from experience that, of several methods tried, the following "method of iteration" works best.

These equations are solved iteratively. Let the superscript indicate the iteration parameter. The iteration equations for x_i and y_i are simply:

$$X_{x_i}^{k+1}=\sum_{j=1}^{n}\left[\frac{\frac{Z_{ij}W_i X_{a_j}}{D_{ij}^k}}{\sum_{j=1}^{n}\frac{Z_{ij}W_i}{D_{ij}^k}}\right], \quad (5.20)$$

$$Y_{x_i}^{k+1}=\sum_{j=1}^{n}\left[\frac{\frac{Z_{ij}W_i Y_{a_j}}{D_{ij}^k}}{\sum_{j=1}^{n}\frac{Z_{ij}W_i}{D_{ij}^k}}\right]. \quad (5.21)$$

A set of convenient starting values that always yields a convergent algorithm is simply the weighted mean coordinates:

$$X_{x_i}^0=\sum_{j=1}^{n}\left[\frac{Z_{ij}W_i X_{a_j}}{\sum_{j=1}^{n}Z_{ij}}\right]; i=1,\ldots,m, \quad (5.22)$$

$$Y_{x_i}^0=\sum_{j=1}^{n}\left[\frac{Z_{ij}W_i Y_{a_j}}{\sum_{j=1}^{n}Z_{ij}}\right]; i=1,\ldots,m. \quad (5.23)$$

For large numbers of destinations (>10) the method is not computationally attractive.

5.3.2 Heuristic Methods

Many heuristics have been proposed for classic location-allocation, as well as a few exact algorithms. Heuristics are needed to quickly solve large problems and to provide good initial solutions for exact algorithms. The first heuristics is the well-known iterative location-allocation algorithm of Cooper (1964).

Cooper's heuristic generates p subset of fixed points and then solved each one using the exact method for solving a single-facility location problem. The fixed points' set is divided into p subsets. For each of these p subsets, using an initial facility location, the exact location method is applied to find the optimal single facility location. Each fixed point is then reallocated to the nearest facility. After all fixed points have been completely reallocated, the exact location method is applied again to improve the location of those facilities where the set of customers assigned has changed. This process, alternating between the location and the allocation phases, is repeated until no further improvement can be made. The solution found by the alternate algorithm is a local minimum. Eilon et al. (1971) showed that for a problem with $p = 5$ and $n = 50$, using 200 randomly generated starting solution, 61 local optima were found, and the worst solution deviates from the best one by 40.9%. In order to have the closest local minimum to the optimal one, the method is repeated several times using different starting locations at random.

Cooper (1963) proved that the objective function is neither concave nor convex, and may contain several local minima. Hence, the classic location-allocation falls in the realm of global optimization problem (Henrik and Robert 1982).

If two points in K dimensional space are given by $q = (q_1, \ldots, q_k)$ and $s = (s_1, \ldots, s_k)$ then the l_p distance between q and s is given by

$$l_q(q,s) = \|q - s\|_p = \left[\sum_{i=1}^{k} |q_i - s_i|^p\right]^{1/p}. \tag{5.24}$$

The location-allocation problem with l_p distances in two dimensions is given by:

$$\text{Min} \sum_{i=1}^{m} \sum_{j=1}^{n} w_{ij} \|x_i - a_j\|_p. \tag{5.25}$$

Subject to

$$\sum_{i=1}^{m} w_{ij} = r_j; j = 1, \ldots, m, \tag{5.26}$$

$$w_{ij} = 0; i = 1, \ldots, m; j = 1, \ldots, n. \tag{5.27}$$

If we consider the w_{ij} to be given constants, then the dual of the objective function of (5.27) for $p > 1$ is given by Love as:

$$\text{Max } g(u) = -\sum_{i=1}^{m} \sum_{j=1}^{n} a_j U'_{ij}. \tag{5.28}$$

5 Location Allocation Problem

Subject to

$$\sum_{j=1}^{n} U'_{ij} = 0, i = 1, \ldots, m, \tag{5.29}$$

$$\|U_{ij}\| \le w_{ij}, i = 1, \ldots, m; j = 1, \ldots, n, \tag{5.30}$$

$$q = p/(p-1), U_{ij} = (u_{ij1}, u_{ij2}). \tag{5.31}$$

And a prime denotes transpose. The U_{ij} are the dual variables.

This is a nonlinear programming problem with a linear objective function and constraints that are either linear or well-behaved in the sense that the feasible constraint set is convex. This latter property is ensured since $\|U\|_q$ is convex in U. we next state a theorem about nonlinear programming problems.

We may state the location-allocation problem given by (5.27) as a concave minimization problem. The vector w be defined as

$$w = (0, \ldots, 0, w_{11}, w_{12}, \ldots, w_{1m}, w_{21}, \ldots, w_{mn}). \tag{5.32}$$

Then, using the dual formulation of the location problem given by (5.28), let

$$G^*(w) = \max .g(u) = -\sum_{i=1}^{m}\sum_{j=1}^{n} a_j u'_{ij} \tag{5.33}$$

Subject to

$$\sum_{j=1}^{n} U_{ij} = 0, i = 1, \ldots, m, \tag{5.34}$$

$$\|U_{ij}\|_q \le w_{ij}, i = 1, \ldots, m, j = 1, \ldots, n. \tag{5.35}$$

We may write the location-allocation problem as

$$\text{Min} G^*(w). \tag{5.36}$$

Subject to

$$\sum_{i=1}^{m} w_{ij} = r_j; j = 1, \ldots, m, \tag{5.37}$$

$$w_{ij} = 0, i = 1, \ldots, m; j = 1, \ldots, n. \tag{5.38}$$

$G^*(w)$ is concave and this is a concave minimization problem.

A small number of computational algorithms for concave minimization problems are available. Each of these was considered but proved to be computationally inefficient for the problem at hand. It was decided, therefore, to test a set of algorithm which exploits the properties of the location-allocation problem. It which follows from the concavity of $G^*(w)$ and which was previously given by Cooper, is that the optimal solution must lie at an extreme point of the constraint set of (5.31). The formulation given by (5.31) presents the location-allocation problem as a concave minimization problem subject to linear constraints. An algorithm which proceeds only to adjacent extreme points is not guaranteed to reach optimality for concave minimization problem in general. A more elaborate scheme is to test pairs of new variables for entry into the basis at each iteration in addition to investigating adjacent extreme points. Procedures are analogous in linear programming to testing all possible pairs of non-basic variables for entry into the solution at each step of the simplex method in addition to testing all single non-basic variables for entry to the solution. For minimization programming problems with linear or convex objective functions, the examination of pairs of variables for entry is not required, since single variable entry methods converge to optimality. However, since the location-allocation problem may have many local minima, testing pairs of variables for possible entry to the solution at each iteration enables the algorithm to "step over" a local minimum, thus greatly increasing the algorithm's chance of the globally minimum point. As an example, two procedures are as follows:

Procedure 1

Step 1: Locate the new facilities arbitrarily.
Step 2: Given the locations, find the optimal allocation.
Step 3: Given the allocations, find the optimal locations.
Step 4: If the locations find in step 3 differ from the locations previously tried, go to step 2; Otherwise, the current local minimum has been found, its cost is computed, and the perturbation scheme can be started.
Step 5: Set $i = 0$.
Step 6: Set $i = i + 1$; if $i > m$ stop.
Step 7: Set $j = 0$.
Step 8: Set $j = j + 1$; if $j > m$ go to step 6.
Step 9: If existing facility j is allocated to new facility i in the current local minimum, go to step 8; otherwise, tentatively allocate existing facility j to new facility i.

From this tentative solution, a new local minimum is found by alternative locating and allocating.

Step 10: If the cost of the new local minimum exceeds the lowest cost found so far, go to step 8; otherwise, update the current local minimum and restart the perturbation scheme.

Procedure 2

Step 1: Locate the new facilities arbitrarily.
Step 2: Given the locations, find the optimal allocations.
Step 3: Given the allocations, find the optimal locations.
Step 4: If the locations find in step 3 differ from the locations previously tried, go to step 2; Otherwise, the current local minimum has been found, its cost is computed, and the perturbation scheme can be started.
Step 5: Set $i = 0$.
Step 6: Set $i = i + 1$; if $i > m$ stop.
Step 7: Set $j = 0$.
Step 8: Set $j = j + 1$; if $j > m$ go to step 6.
Step 9: If existing facility j_1 is allocated to new facility i in the current local minimum, go to step 11.
Step 10: Set $j_2 = j_1$.
Step 11: Set $j_2 = j_2 + 1$; if $j_2 > n$ go to step 8.
Step 12: If existing facility j_2 is allocated to new facility i in the current local minimum, go to step 11; otherwise, tentatively allocate existing facility j_1 and j_2 to new facility i.

From this tentative solution, a new local minimum is found by alternative locating and allocating.

Step 13: If the cost of the new local minimum exceeds the lowest cost found so far, go to step 11; otherwise, update the current local minimum and restart the perturbation scheme.

In 102 test problems for which the optimal solutions are known, two of algorithms achieved the exact optimum solutions in all cases.

5.3.3 Metaheuristic Methods (Salhi and Gamal 2003)

Location-allocation problem is NP-hard problem, metaheuristic methods have been shown to the best way to tackle larger NP-hard problems. Meta-heuristic such as simulated annealing, Tabu search, genetic algorithm (GA), variable neighborhood search, and ant systems increase the chance of avoiding local optimally.

5.4 Case Study

In this section we will introduce some real-world case studies related to location-allocation problems.

5.4.1 A Facility Location Allocation Model for Reusing Carpet Materials (Louwers et al. 1999)

Each year tons of carpets are disposed. In Western Europe alone, 1.6 million tons were deposed in 1996. At the moment, almost all this "waste" is disposed in landfills, using up a lot of space, whereas most of this "waste" can be reused as a material or fuel. Therefore, it is not surprising that in more countries, including Germany and The Netherlands, the legislation concerning the disposal of carpet waste has become more stringent.

This article focuses on the design of the logistic structure of the above network, i.e. the physical locations where the different activities should take place, the capacities of the facilities at these locations for storing and preprocessing the carpets that are disposed, the allocation of disposed carpet waste flows to these locations and facilities, as well as the transportation modes to be used.

The first activity concerns the collection of carpets that are no longer desired by their owners. There are many different sources, including households and companies, collecting used pieces of carpet from houses, offices, cars, etc.

The above suggests that identifying, sorting, separating and compressing carpet waste should take place at the same location. In the rest of this paper the centers where this takes place are denoted by RPC (regional preprocessing center).

Carpets are disposed in many different ways, varying from rolls up to very small irregular shaped pieces. The quality of these carpets varies from new, unused to used-up, and contaminated.

There are different types of carpets, containing different materials like wool and synthetic fibers that are interesting for different parties. This requires that carpet waste is identified and sorted.

In order to determine the economically optimal logistic structure of the carpet waste reuse network, the number and capacities of the RPCs for which the calculations are to be done have been calculated. As mentioned before, at an RPC only certain preprocessing capacities can be installed. For the two applications of Europe and the USA, only three possibilities existed denoted by PC_1, PC_2 and PC_3, where $PC_1 < PC_2 < PC_3$.

The optimal locations and capacities of the RPCs are resulted from the calculations for one of the scenarios for Germany and the Benelux. In order to have a readable figure, the flows to and from the RPCs have not been indicated in Fig. 5.1. So for this scenario four RPCs should be opened, three of them with a capacity of 150 kt/yr and one with a capacity of 50 kt/yr.

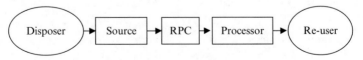

Fig. 5.1 The main activities in the context of reusing carpet waste

5.4.2 A New Organ Transplantation Location-Allocation Policy (Bruni et al. 2006)

In this part they propose a location model for the optimal organization of transplant system. Instead of simulation approach, which is typical when facing many health care applications, their approach is distinctively based on a mathematical programming formulation of the relevant problem. The allocation of transplantable organs across regions with the objective of attaining regional equity in health care is the aim of this part.

The allocation of scarce donated organs is both an increasingly complex clinical and social problem, as well as a challenging example of mathematical programming problem formulation. The process leading to donor identification, consent, organ procurement and allocation continue to dominate debates and efforts in the field of transplantation. A huge storage of donors remains while the number of patients needing organ transplantation increases.

The problem of long waiting times for transplant candidates and the continual growth in waiting list size underscores a simple reality: supply of organs does not meet the need. This evidence has produced substantial debate about the mechanisms for allocation of organs to potential recipients, with issues of fairness, efficiency and regional versus national interests.

The following discussion focuses on the key issues that are most relevant for the purposes of their study:

- The factors considered in the development of an organ allocation policy
- The design of an equitable transplant system

As far as the design of the transplant system is concerned, we have to take into account the spatial distribution of some organizations (referred as OPO – Organ Procurement Organization), that play a crucial role in the design of a fair and equitable transplant system.

The transplantation is performed on condition that the recipients reach the transplant hospital in the reasonable time. Therefore, once the organ is allocated, the access of the transplant service can be measured in terms of distance to the nearest or time taken to travel to the health facility. The probability of the waiting list in which the patient is registered, this size is influenced by the location of the OPOs within the national area.

Our contribution is placed in this respect. In particular, we propose a mixed integer linear programming model to face the problem of transplant system organization. The proposed model can be used to analyze simultaneously:

- The location problem of OPOs and referring donor hospital and transplant centers
- The districting problem
- The waiting lists balancing problem

These issues have a crucial role for the fairness and the equity of the transplant in the transplant system.

The goal of an efficient and fair transplant system is to allocate organs in an equitable and timely fashion. A fair and efficient transplant system should guarantee the greatest survival rate, for patients and for organs used.

When donor organs become available after an individual dies, an organ procurement organization (OPO) takes the organs into custody. The OPO then matches the donor organs with the appropriate transplant patients, by gathering information about the donor organs.

The elapsed time between removal and implantation is critical for the organ because they cannot be used if they have been waiting more than an upper bound time known to clinician as "cold-ischemia time". The time spent in the transplant process has two components.

For the organ, the first segment of travel time is between the explanation and the arrival to the transplant center. The second segment of waiting refers to the time spent by the potential host traveling to the transplant center.

They design and formulate transplant location allocation model (TRALOC model for short); TRALOC is clearly not able to fully capture the complexity of the transplant system. Nevertheless, the assumptions they made are quite general and allow an elegant and easy formulation. They make clear that the objective of their study is to make the appropriate simplifications that lead to a tractable model.

With the aim to asses and validate TRALOC model. They applied it to the Italy transplant network. The national area is divided into 20 regions and 105 provinces. In particular each province represents a demand node and, therefore, the problem is a 105 node network.

To solve this model different values of p are being tested based on the minimum required amount, where p is the number of OPOs that should be established. By determining the number of new facilities, the NP-hard problem changes to NP-complete problem, then Lingo 6 is applied to solve it. Finally decision makers and policy makers were offered the results in order to choose the optimum form according to their own point of view.

References

Badri MA (1999) Combining the analytic hierarchy process and goal programming for global facility location-allocation problem. Int J Prod Econ 62:237–248

Brimberg J, Mladenovic N (1996) Solving the continuous Location-Allocation problem with tabu search. Stud Locational Ann 8:23–32

Brimberg J, Hansen P, Mladenovic N, Taillard ED (2000) Improvements and comparison of heuristics for solving the uncapacitated multi source Weber problem. Oper Res 48:444–460

Bruni M, Conforti D, Sicilia N, Trotta S (2006) A new organ transplantation Location-Allocation policy: A case study of Italy. Health Care Manage Sci 9:125–142

Cooper L (1963) Location-Allocation problems. Oper Res 11(3):331–343

Cooper L (1964) Heuristic methods for location-allocation problems. SIAM Rev 6(1):37–53

Eilon S, Watson-Gandy CDT, Christofides N (1971) Distribution Management. New York, Hafner

Ernst AT, Krishnamoorthy M (1999) Solution algorithms for the capacitated single allocation hub location problem. Ann Oper Res 86:141–159

Gong D, Gen M, Yamazaki G, Xu W (1997) Hybrid evolutionary method for capacitated location-allocation problem. Comput Ind Eng 33:577–580

Hakimi S (1964) Optimum distribution of switching centers in a communication network and some related graph theoretic problems. Oper Res 13:462–475

Hansen P, Jaumard B, Taillard E (1998) Heuristic solution of the multi source Weber problem as a p-median problem. Oper Res Lett 22:55–62

Henrik J, Robert FL (1982) Properties and solution methods for large location-allocation problems. J Oper Res Soc 33(5):443–452

Kuenne RE, Soland RM (1972) Exact and approximate solutions to the multi source Weber problem. Math Program 3:193–209

Louwers D, Kip BJ, Peters E, Souren F, Flapper SDP (1999) A facility location-allocation model for reusing carpet materials. Comput Ind Eng 36:855–869

Murray AT, Church RL (1996) Applying simulated annealing to location-planning models. J Heuristics 2:31–53

Ohlemüller M (1997) Tabu search for large location-allocation problems. J Oper Res Soc 48(7):745–750

Scaparra MP, Scutellà MG (2001) Facilities, locations, customers: Building blocks of location models: A survey. Technical report TR-01-18, Computer Science Department, University of Pisa, Italy

Salhi S, Gamal MDH (2003) A Genetic algorithm based approach for the uncapacitated continuous location–allocation problem. Ann Oper Res 123:203–222

Zhou J, Liu B (2003) New stochastic models for capacitated location-allocation problem. Comput Ind Eng 45:111–125

Chapter 6
Quadratic Assignment Problem

Masoumeh Bayat and Mahdieh Sedghi

The quadratic assignment problem (QAP) in location Theory is the problem of locating facilities the cost of placing a facility depends on the distances from other facilities and also the interaction with other facilities. QAP was introduced by Koopmans and Beckman in 1957 who were trying to model a facilities location problem.

It is possible to formulate some classic problems of combinatorial optimization, such as the traveling salesman, maximum clique and graph partitioning problems as a QAP. The QAP belongs to the class of NP-complete problems and is considered one of the most difficult combinatorial optimization problems. Exact solution strategies for the QAP have been unsuccessful for large problem (approximately $N \leq 25$).

In Fig. 6.1 the QAP search trends and tendencies in about 50 years is shown (Hahn et al. 2007). Figure 6.1 shows the distribution of QAP publications with respect to the categories: applications, theory and algorithms.

Figure 6.2 distributes the number of articles by 5-year periods since 1957, for each period, the work is also classified according to the same categories of Fig. 6.1. Figure 6.2 shows that an explosion of interest in theory and algorithm development occurred in the period from 1992 to the present.

Figure 6.3 shows a steady increase in interest in the QAP in recent years.

Figure 6.4, which covers the recent years, shows that the interest in algorithms continues to be very strong, with a cyclical trend in theoretical developments. Applications continue to be of interest, but to a lesser extent. It is noteworthy that there is recently a growing interest in applications to communication link design and to the optimization of communications networks.

As a first example for introducing the problem we describe the problem of assigning facilities to locations in an office. Let have four facilities that each facility is designated to exactly one location and vice-versa. Our problem is to find a minimum cost allocation of facilities into locations taking the costs as the sum of all possible distance-flow products. For example in Fig. 6.5 an assignment $\pi = (3, 2, 4, 1)$ is shown:

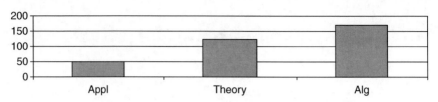

Fig. 6.1 Publications classification according to their contents (Hahn et al. 2007)

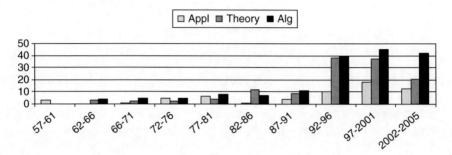

Fig. 6.2 Number of publications in 50 years according to their content (Hahn et al. 2007)

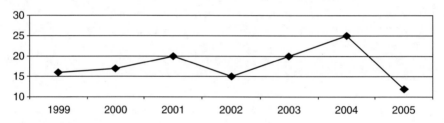

Fig. 6.3 Number of QAP papers published in recent years (Hahn et al. 2007)

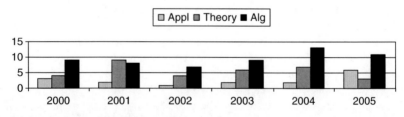

Fig. 6.4 Recent advances. (Hahn et al. 2007)

For this assignment, the objective function value is the product of matrix D, the distance matrix describing the distance between two facilities, and matrix F, the flow matrix corresponding with this assignment. For this example, given D and F as follows:

6 Quadratic Assignment Problem

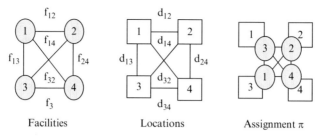

Fig. 6.5 Assignment $\pi = (3, 2, 4, 1)$

Table 6.1 QAP's application in different science

Authors	Subject	Publication years
Koopmans & Beckmann	Proposed the QAP as a mathematical model	1957
Steinberg	Minimize the number of connections in a backboard wiring with QAP	1961
Heffley	Applied QAP to economic problems	1972
White & Francis	For assigning a new facility	1974
Geoffrion & Graves	Scheduling problems	1976
Krarup & Pruzan	Applied QAP to archeology	1978
Hubert	Applied QAP in statistical analysis	1987
Forsberg	Used QAP in the analysis of reaction chemistry	1994
Brusco & Stahl	In numerical analysis	2000
Ben-David & Malah	Error control in communications	2005
Wess and Zeitlhofer	The problem of memory layout optimization in signal processors	2004

$$D = \begin{pmatrix} 0 & 10 & 20 & 30 \\ 10 & 0 & 15 & 18 \\ 20 & 15 & 0 & 11 \\ 30 & 18 & 11 & 0 \end{pmatrix}, \quad F = \begin{pmatrix} 0 & 2 & 3 & 2 \\ 2 & 0 & 7 & 1 \\ 3 & 7 & 0 & 5 \\ 2 & 1 & 5 & 0 \end{pmatrix}.$$

$D\pi$ represents the distance matrix corresponding to assignment π.

$$D^{\pi} = \begin{pmatrix} 20 & 10 & 30 & 0 \\ 15 & 0 & 18 & 10 \\ 0 & 15 & 11 & 20 \\ 11 & 18 & 0 & 30 \end{pmatrix}, \quad F = \begin{pmatrix} 0 & 2 & 3 & 2 \\ 2 & 0 & 7 & 1 \\ 3 & 7 & 0 & 5 \\ 2 & 1 & 5 & 0 \end{pmatrix}.$$

Then, the total cost for this assignment is $D\pi F = 2,117$ and our object is minimizing total cost by permutation of matrix D columns. Any assignment π will result in a feasible solution, therefore, there are $N!$ feasible solutions.

Since its first formulation, the QAP has been applied in many problems in different sciences. In Table 6.1 its application in different sciences and in Table 6.2. its application in location problems has been indicated.

Table 6.2 QAP's applications in location problem

Authors	Subject	Publication years
Hopkins & Dickney	Assignment of buildings in a University campus	1972
Pollatschek	Design of typewriter keyboards and control panels	1976
Elshafei	In a hospital planning	1977
Bos	Forest management	1993
Beenjaafar	In facilities layout for minimizing work-in-process (WIP)	2002
Miranda	Placement of electronic components	2005

In Sect. 6.1 we describe QAP's formulations that are represented in literature. In Sect. 6.2 we point out some problems that are related to QAP. In Sect. 6.3 QAP's lower bounds and solution methods are discussed and in Sect. 6.4 some case studies are presented.

6.1 Formulations of QAP

In this section we introduce QAP formulations represented in literature.

6.1.1 Integer Programming Formulations (ILP)

6.1.1.1 Model Assumptions

The objective function is MiniSum.
Each facility is designated to exactly one location and vice-versa
The solution space is discrete and finite.
The number of location and facilities is known (exogenous).
All decision variables of the model are binary (0–1) variables.

6.1.1.2 Model Inputs

$F = [f_{ij}]$: flow matrix between facility i and j
$D = [d_{kp}]$: distances matrix between locations k and p
$B = [b_{ik}]$: allocation costs of facility i to location k

6.1.1.3 Model Outputs (Decision Variables)

$$x_{ik} = \begin{cases} 1, & \text{if facility } i \text{ assigned in location } k \\ 0, & \text{otherwise} \end{cases}$$

6 Quadratic Assignment Problem

6.1.1.4 Koopman and Beckman (1957) Formulation

This formulation is the first mathematical formulation of QAP. Koopman and Beckman (1957) represented this formulation. Let $N = \{1,\ldots,n\}$, our objective is finding permutation Φ of set N to minimize the objective function.

6.1.1.5 Objective Function and its Constraint

$$\text{Min} \sum_{i=1}^{n} b_{i\varphi(i)} + \sum_{j=1}^{n}\sum_{i=1}^{n} f_{ij} d_{\varphi(i)\varphi(j)}, \tag{6.1}$$

Subject to

$$\sum_{i=1}^{n} x_{ij} = 1 \quad \forall j = 1,\ldots,n, \tag{6.2}$$

$$\sum_{j=1}^{n} x_{ij} = 1 \quad \forall i = 1,\ldots,n, \tag{6.3}$$

$$\begin{array}{l} x_{ij} \in \{0,1\} \quad \forall i,j = 1,\ldots,n \\ i,j,k,p = 1,\ldots,n \end{array} \tag{6.4}$$

Equation (6.1) assures that to each location assigned only one facility and (6.3) assure that each facility assigned only to one location.

6.1.1.6 Lawler (1963) Formulation

Lawler (1963) represented a general model of QAP that Koopman and Beckman introduced. He proposed c_{ijkp} coefficient that have the special form:

$$C_{ijkp} = d_{kp} f_{ij}.$$

6.1.1.7 Objective Function and its Constraint

$$\text{Min} \sum_{j=1}^{n}\sum_{i=1}^{n} C_{ijkp} x_{ik} x_{jp}, \tag{6.5}$$

Subject to

$$\sum_{i=1}^{n} x_{ij} = 1 \quad \forall j = 1,\ldots,n, \tag{6.6}$$

$$\sum_{j=1}^{n} x_{ij} = 1 \quad \forall i = 1,\ldots,n, \tag{6.7}$$

$$\begin{aligned} x_{ij} \in \{0,1\} \quad &\forall i, j = 1,\ldots,n \\ i, j, k, p = 1,\ldots,n & \end{aligned} \tag{6.8}$$

6.1.1.8 Linearization

For linearization of the model Lawler (1963) proposed to replace the product $x_{ij}x_{kp}$ by n^4 new binary variables y_{ijkp}:

$$y_{ijkp} = x_{ij}x_{kp},$$

and showed that the QAP is equivalent to a linear integer program with $O(n^4)$ variables and constraints.

Theorem 6.1. *The QAP is equivalent to the integer linear program of the form:*

$$\text{Min} \sum_{j=1}^{n} \sum_{i=1}^{n} C_{ijkp} y_{ijkp}, \tag{6.9}$$

Subject to

$$\sum_{i=1}^{n} \sum_{j=1}^{n} \sum_{k=1}^{n} \sum_{p=1}^{n} y_{ijkp} = n^2, \tag{6.10}$$

$$x_{ij} + x_{kp} - 2y_{ijkp} \geq 0 \quad \forall i, j, k, p = 1,\ldots,n, \tag{6.11}$$

$$\sum_{i=1}^{n} x_{ij} = 1 \quad \forall j = 1,\ldots,n, \tag{6.12}$$

$$\sum_{j=1}^{n} x_{ij} = 1 \quad \forall i = 1,\ldots,n, \tag{6.13}$$

$$\begin{aligned} x_{ij} \in \{0,1\} \quad &\forall i, j = 1,\ldots,n \\ i, j, k, p = 1,\ldots,n & \end{aligned} \tag{6.14}$$

6.1.2 Mixed Integer Programming Formulations (MILP)

The linearization of the problem is inconvenient, because of the large additional amount of variables and constraint. Finding linearization with fewer variable and constraint is proper.

6.1.2.1 Kaufman and Broeckx (1978) MILP Formulation

Kaufman and Broeckx (1978) developed another linearization by mixed integer programming. They used Glover's linearization technique which is extremely favorable in this type of problems, where one only has positive cost-coefficients. They have shown that the MILP formulation and QAP are equivalent. Z rewrite as:

$$z = \sum_i \sum_k x_{ik} \left(\sum_j \sum_p f_{ij} d_{kp} x_{jp} \right). \qquad (6.15)$$

And continuous variable introduce as:

$$w_{ik} = x_{ik} \sum_{k=1}^{n} \sum_{p=1}^{n} f_{ij} d_{kp} x_{jp}. \qquad (6.16)$$

There are n^2 such new continuous variables, and the new objective is to minimize:

$$z = \sum_i \sum_k w_{ik}. \qquad (6.17)$$

6.1.2.2 Objective Function and Constraints

$$\text{Min } z = \sum_{j=1}^{n} \sum_{i=1}^{n} w_{ij}, \qquad (6.18)$$

Subject to

$$\sum_{i=1}^{n} x_{ij} = 1 \quad \forall j = 1, \ldots, n, \qquad (6.19)$$

$$\sum_{j=1}^{n} x_{ij} = 1 \quad \forall i = 1, \ldots, n, \qquad (6.20)$$

$$h_{ij} x_{ij} + \sum_{k=1}^{n} \sum_{p=1}^{n} c_{ijkp} x_{kp} - w_{ij} \leq h_{ij} \quad \forall i, j = 1, \ldots, n, \qquad (6.21)$$

$$x_{ij} \in \{0, 1\}, w_{ij} \geq 0 \quad \forall i, j = 1, \ldots, n, \qquad (6.22)$$

where $h_{ij} = \sum_{k=1}^{n} \sum_{p=1}^{n} C_{ijkp}. \qquad (6.23)$

6.1.2.3 Frieze and Yadegar (1983) MILP Formulation

Frieze and Yadegar (1983) proposed a mixed integer linear programming model to discuss the relationship between Gilmore-Lawler lower bounds with decomposition for the quadratic assignment problem and a Lagrangian relaxation of a particular integer programming formulation. Their model has n^4 real variables, n^2 Boolean variables and $n^4 + 4n^3 + n^2 + 2n$ constraints. Frieze and Yadegar have shown that this MILP model and QAP are equivalent.

6.1.2.4 Objective Function and Constraints

$$\text{Min} \sum_{i=1}^{n}\sum_{j=}^{n}\sum_{k=1}^{n}\sum_{p=1}^{n} f_{ij}d_{kp}y_{ijkp}, \quad (6.24)$$

Subject to

$$\sum_{i=1}^{n} x_{ik} = 1 \quad \forall k = 1,\ldots,n, \quad (6.25)$$

$$\sum_{k=1}^{n} x_{ik} = 1 \quad \forall i = 1,\ldots,n, \quad (6.26)$$

$$\sum_{i=1}^{n} y_{ijkp} = x_{jp} \quad \forall i,j,k,p = 1,\ldots,n, \quad (6.27)$$

$$\sum_{j=1}^{n} y_{ijlp} = x_{jp} \quad \forall i,j,k,p = 1,\ldots,n, \quad (6.28)$$

$$\sum_{k=1}^{n} y_{ijlp} = x_{jp} \quad \forall i,j,k,p = 1,\ldots,n, \quad (6.29)$$

$$\sum_{p=1}^{n} y_{ijlp} = x_{jp} \quad \forall i,j,k,p = 1,\ldots,n, \quad (6.30)$$

$$y_{ikik} = x_{ik} \quad \forall i,k = 1,\ldots,n, \quad (6.31)$$

$$\begin{aligned} x_{ik} \in \{0,1\} & \quad \forall i,k = 1,\ldots,n \\ 0 \leq y_{ijkp} \leq 1 & \quad \forall i,j,k,p = 1,\ldots,n, \end{aligned} \quad (6.32)$$

6.1.3 Formulation by Permutations

Let S_n be the set of all permutations with n elements and $\pi \in s_n$ consider f_{ij} the flows between facilities i and j and $d_{\pi(i)\pi(j)}$ the distances between locations $\pi(i)$ and $\pi(j)$. Each permutation represents an allocation of facilities to locations.

$$X_{ij} = \begin{cases} 1 & \text{if } \pi(i) = j \\ 0 & \text{if } \pi(i) \neq j. \end{cases}$$

6.1.3.1 Objective Function and Constraint

$$\underset{\pi \in s_n}{\text{Min}} \sum_{i=1}^{n} \sum_{j=1}^{n} f_{ij} d_{\varphi(i)\varphi(j)}. \quad (6.33)$$

Has the same (6.1)–(6.4).

6.1.4 Trace Formulation

Trace formulation is supported by linear algebra and use the trace function to determine QAP lower bound for the cost. This approach allows for the application of spectral theory, which makes possible the use of semi-definite programming to the QAP (Hahn et al. 2007).

$$\text{Trace}(A) = \sum_{i=1}^{n} a_{ii}$$

6.1.4.1 Edwards (1980) Formulation

Objective function and constraint

$$\underset{x \in s_n}{\text{Min}} \; tr(F.X.D.X^t), \quad (6.34)$$

Subject to

$$X \in \pi, \quad (6.35)$$

where F and D are $n \times n$ matrices, tr denotes the trace of a matrix and π is the set of $n \times n$ permutation matrices.

6.1.5 Graph Formulation

The QAP can be defined in terms of graphs in the following way.

6.1.5.1 Models Inputs

$G^f = (V^f, E^f)$: an undirected flow graph,
$V^f = \{v_i;\ i = 1,\ldots, n\}$: vertices that represent facilities,
$(v_i, v_j) \in E^f$: the edges that represent the existence of a flow between facilities i and j,
$f_{ij} =$ The cost of edge (v_i, v_j),
$G^d = (V^d, E^d)$ be a distance graph,
$V^d = \{v_i;\ i = 1,\ldots, n\}$ vertices that represent locations $d_{\Phi(i)\Phi(j)}$.

The edge costs are the distances between the corresponding locations.

6.1.5.2 Objective Function and Constraints

$$\underset{\rho \in s_n}{\text{Min}} \sum_{(v_i,v_j) \in E^f} f_{ij}\, d_{\varphi(i)\varphi(j)} \quad (6.36)$$

Has the same (6.1)–(6.4).

6.2 QAP Related Problems

6.2.1 The Quadratic Bottleneck Assignment Problem (QBAP)

Steinberg (1961) proposed QBAP for minimizing the maximum-wire-length norms in backboard wiring problem. The QBAP general program is obtained from the QAP formulation by changing its minisum objective function with minimax, which suggests the term bottleneck function.

6.2.1.1 Objective Function

$$\text{Min Max}\, \{f_{ij} d_{\pi(i)\pi(j)};\ 1 \le i, j \le n\}. \quad (6.37)$$

6.2.2 The Biquadratic Assignment Problem (BiQAP)

The biquadratic assignment problem (BiQAP) is a generalization of the quadratic assignment problem (QAP). The problem was first introduced and studied by Burkard et al. (1994). It is a nonlinear integer programming problem where the objective function is a fourth degree multivariable polynomial and the feasible domain is the assignment polytope. BiQAP motivated by a practical problem arising in VLSI synthesis.

6.2.2.1 Objective Function and its Constraints

$$\text{Min} \sum_{i=1}^{n}\sum_{j=1}^{n}\sum_{k=1}^{n}\sum_{l=1}^{n}\sum_{m=1}^{n}\sum_{p=1}^{n}\sum_{s=1}^{n}\sum_{r=1}^{n} f_{ijkl} d_{mpst} x_{im} x_{jp} x_{ks} x_{lt}. \tag{6.38}$$

Has the same (6.1)–(6.4)

6.2.3 The Quadratic Semi-Assignment Problem (QSAP)

This is a special case used to model clustering and partitioning problems by Hansen and Lih (1992). This problem belongs to the class of the NP-hard problems some task-assignment problems in distributed systems can be easily formulated as quadratic semi-assignment problems.

6.2.3.1 Objective Function and Constraints

$$\text{Min} \sum_{k=1}^{m}\sum_{i,j=1}^{n} C_{ij} x_{ik} x_{jk}. \tag{6.39}$$

Subject to

$$\sum_{k=1}^{m} x_{ik} = 1 \quad 1 \leq i \leq n, \\ x_{ij} \in \{0,1\} \quad 1 \leq i, j \leq n. \tag{6.40}$$

6.2.4 The Multiobjective QAP (MQAP)

6.2.4.1 Knowles and Corne Formulation

Knowles and Corne (2003) introduced the multiobjective QAP (mQAP), with multiple flow matrices that naturally models any facility layout problem where we are concerned with the flow of more than one type of item or agent. This problem has different flow matrices but it always keeps the same distance matrix.

6.2.4.2 Objective Function and its Constraints

$$\min_{\pi \in s_n} \overline{C}(\pi) = \{C^1(\pi), \ldots, C^m(\pi)\}, \tag{6.41}$$

$$\text{where} \quad C^k(\pi) = \sum \sum f_{ij} d_{\pi(i)\pi(j)}, \forall k = 1, \ldots, m. \tag{6.42}$$

Has the same (6.1)–(6.4).

6.2.4.3 Hamacher Formulation

Hamacher et al. (2003) introduced a different formulation of a multiobjective QAP that considers different matrices of flows and distances for modeling problems found in facility layout for social institutions.

$$\min \begin{pmatrix} \sum_{i,j,k,l=1}^{n} f_{ik} d_{jl} x_{ij} x_{kl} \\ \vdots \\ \sum_{i,j,k,l=1}^{n} f_{ik}^Q d_{kl}^Q x_{ij} x_{kl} \end{pmatrix}, \tag{6.43}$$

where the problem is to find assignment x as:

$$x_{ij} = \begin{cases} 1, & \text{if facility } i \text{ assigned in location } j \\ 0, & \text{otherwise} \end{cases}.$$

Has the same (6.1)–(6.4).

6.2.5 The Quadratic Three-Dimensional Assignment Problem (Q3AP)

Pierskalla (1967a, b) introduced the quadratic three-dimensional assignment problem (Q3AP) in a technical memorandum. The Q3AP is an extension of the QAP that can be represented as a three-dimensional assignment problem.

6.2.5.1 Objective Function and Constraints

Where I, J and P are disjoint sets of constraints

$$\text{Min} \left\{ \sum_{i=1}^{n}\sum_{j=1}^{n}\sum_{p=1}^{n} b_{ijp}x_{ijp} + \sum_{i=1}^{n}\sum_{j=1}^{n}\sum_{p=1}^{n} \sum_{\substack{k=1 \\ k \neq i}}^{n} \sum_{\substack{n=1 \\ n \neq j}}^{n} \sum_{\substack{q=1 \\ q \neq p}}^{n} C_{ijpknq} x_{ijp} x_{knq} \right\},$$

(6.44)

where $x \in I \cap J \cap P$, x binary

$$I = \left\{ x \geq 0 : \sum_{j=1}^{n}\sum_{p=1}^{n} x_{ijp} = 1 \quad \text{for } i = 1, \ldots, n \right\}, \tag{6.45}$$

$$J = \left\{ x \geq 0 : \sum_{i=1}^{n}\sum_{p=1}^{n} x_{ijp} = 1 \quad \text{for } j = 1, \ldots, n \right\}, \tag{6.46}$$

$$P = \left\{ x \geq 0 : \sum_{i=1}^{n}\sum_{j=1}^{n} x_{ijp} = 1 \quad \text{for } p = 1, \ldots, n \right\}. \tag{6.47}$$

6.2.6 The Generalized Quadratic Assignment Problem (GQAP)

Lee and Ma (2004) indicated that the GQAP had been proposed by them in 1991 which is a generalized problem of the QAP in that there is no restriction that one location can accommodate only single equipment. This problem arises in many real world applications such as facility location problem and logistics network design.

6.2.6.1 Model Inputs

M: a set of equipments ($= \{1, 2, \ldots, m\}$),
N: a set of locations ($= \{1, 2, \ldots, n\}$),
s_i: space requirement of equipment i,
S_k: total available space at location k,
c_{ik}: the cost of installing equipment i at location k,
q_{ij}: the flow volume from equipment i to j in the planning horizon,
d_{kh}: the distance between location k and h ($= d_{hk}$),
v: the travel cost per unit distance and per unit flow volume.

6.2.6.2 Model Outputs (Decision Variables)

$$x_{ik} = \begin{cases} 1, & \text{if equipment } i \text{ is assigned to location } k, \\ 0, & \text{otherwise.} \end{cases}$$

6.2.6.3 Assumptions

Just to avoid trivial cases, we will assume:

(a) There is no single location that is big enough to hold all the equipments or:

$$\sum_{i \in M} s_i > S_k \quad \forall k \in N.$$

(b) There is no equipment which is too big to be assigned to any location or:

$$S_k \geq \max_i s_i, \quad \forall k \in N$$

(c) All the locations are distinctive or:

$$d_{ij} \neq 0, \; \forall j \neq h \in N$$

(d) The distance between locations is symmetric.

6.2.6.4 Objective Function and its Constraints

$$\text{Min} \sum_{j=1}^{m} \sum_{k=1}^{n} c_{ik} x_{ik} + v \sum_{i=1}^{m} \sum_{j=1}^{m} \sum_{k=1}^{n} \sum_{h=1}^{n} q_{ij} d_{kh} x_{ik} x_{jh}, \tag{6.48}$$

Subject to

$$\sum_{k=1}^{n} x_{ik} = 1, \quad \forall i \in \{1, \ldots, m\}, \tag{6.49}$$

$$\sum_{i=1}^{m} s_i x_{ik} \leq S_k, \quad \forall k \in \{1, \ldots, n\}, \tag{6.50}$$

$$x_{ik} \in \{0, 1\}, \quad \forall i, k. \tag{6.51}$$

6.2.7 Stochastic QAP (SQAP)

SQAP is basically a network design problem, whenever there is a need to assign activities to the nodes of a network in order to minimize congestion; the SQAP is an appropriate model of the problem. In SQAP we have distance matrix and P matrix that is the probability of having interaction between facility i and j (Smith and Li 2001).

6.3 Solution Techniques

The methods used in combinatorial optimization problems can be either exact, heuristic or metaheuristic shown in Fig. 6.6. The most frequently used strategies are branch-and-bound or dynamic programming general methods and also there are a number of heuristic techniques using different conceptions. In what follows, we discuss about computational complexity and both approaches and bring their most important references.

6.3.1 Computational Complexity

In fact, the QAP belongs to the class of computationally hard problems known as *NP* complete. The proof that the QAP is indeed *NP*-complete was first shown by Sahni and Gonzales (1976) and they also proved that any routine that finds even an ε-approximate solution is also *NP*-complete, thus making the QAP among the "hardest of the hard" of all combinatorial optimization problems. Belonging to this class of problems suggests that an algorithm which solves the problem to optimality in polynomial time is unlikely to exist. Therefore, to practically solve the QAP one has to apply heuristic algorithms which find very high quality solutions in short computation time.

6.3.2 Lower Bounds

Lower bounds are useful for measuring heuristic search worst-case solutions quality, and are an essential component in the construction of Branch and Bound (B&B) methods for achieving optimal solutions. We are trying to derive bound that is not being hard to compute, can easily be evaluated for subsets of the problem which occur after some branching, and finally is tight. There are many different proposals for deriving bounds. In the following we briefly survey bounds for QAP problem.

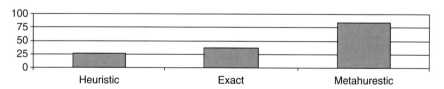

Fig. 6.6 Publications: solution techniques (Hahn et al. 2007)

6.3.2.1 The Gilmore and Lawler Lower Bound (GLB)

The Gilmore–Lawler bound (GLB) which was proposed by Gilmore (1962) and Lawler (1963) is one of the best-known lower bounds for the small QAP's problem. It is easy to compute, but it deteriorates fast by increasing in the size of the problem.

$$\text{GLB} = \text{LAP}(F) \leq \text{QAP}.$$

This bounding technique is combinatorial in nature and requires the solution of a LAP for a Koopman–Beckmann problem that can be computed in $O(n^3)$ time (Anstreicher 2003). Several authors proposed different approaches to improve the GLB, Frieze and Yadegar (1983) proposed GLB with decomposition, Assad and Xu (1985) proposed the AX bound that is obtained iteratively, where $n^2 + 1$ assignment of size n are solved in each iteration. Hence, the running time to compute is $O(kn^5)$ where k is the number of iterations.

6.3.2.2 Bounds Based on LP and Dual-LP

Frieze and Yadegar (1983), discuss the relationship between GLB with decomposition and a Lagrangian relaxation of a mixed integer programming formulation (6.24)–(6.32).

Drezner (1995) proved that the optimal solution for a MILP-formulation is a lower bound for the corresponding QAP that is at least as good as the classical Gilmore-Lawler lower bound. Adams and Johnson (1994) develop a dual ascent procedure for approximating the dual of the MILP relaxation and proved that each dual solution of the linear programming is also a lower bound for the QAP. These bounds are quite expensive to compute and can only be applied to problems of dimension $n \leq 30$.

6.3.2.3 Eigenvalue Related Bounds (EVB)

Finke et al. (1987) proposed Eigenvalue bounds which are based on the trace formulation of QAP. The basic idea to derive this bound consists in minimizing objective function of trace formulation over orthogonal rather than just permutation matrices.

Let $\lambda_1, \lambda_2, \ldots, \lambda_n$ be the eigenvalues of the symmetric matrix F and let $\mu_1, \mu_2, \ldots, \mu_n$ be the eigenvalue of the symmetric matrix D. since F and D are symmetric, the eigenvalues are real and we can assume the ordering

$$\lambda_1 \leq \lambda_2 \leq \ldots \leq \lambda_n \text{ and } \mu_1 \geq \mu_2 \geq \ldots \mu_n.$$

For all permutation Φ

$$\sum_{i=1}^{n} \lambda_i \mu_i \leq \sum_{i=1}^{n} \sum_{j=1}^{n} f_{ij} d_{\varphi(i)\varphi(j)} \leq \sum_{i=1}^{n} \lambda_i \mu_{n-i}. \quad (6.52)$$

Hadley et al. (1992a) consider also the case of non-symmetric QAPs and develop for them eigenvalue bounds by means of Hermitian matrices. These bounds have good quality in comparison to Gilmore–Lawler-like bounds; however, they are expensive in terms of computation time and deteriorate quickly when lower levels of a branch and bound tree are searched. The simple EVB is too weak to be computationally useful, but several schemes for improving the bound have been considered. Hadley et al. (1992b) proposed improved eigenvalue bound which have been derived from the projected QAP (PD). EVD and PD both require $O(n^3)$ computing time.

6.3.2.4 Bounds Based on Reformulations

Reformulation linearization technique (RLT) is designed to generate a hierarchy of linear programming (LP) relaxations leading from the ordinary continuous relaxation to the convex hull representation for mixed-integer 0–1 programming problems (Sherali and Adams 1990). Sherali et al. (2000) proposed reduced reformulation linearization technique to improve RLT. Adams et al. (2007) calculate bounds using a level-2 reformulation linearization technique (2-RLT) that provides sharp and tight lower bounds.

6.3.2.5 Variance Reduction Bounds

Initially proposed by Li et al. (1994a), these bounds are based on reduction schemes and are defined from the variance of F and D matrices. These bounds, when used in a branch-and-bound algorithm, take less computational time and generally obtain better performance than GLB. They show more efficiency when the flow and distance matrices have high variances (Hahn et al. 2007).

6.3.2.6 Semi-Definite Programming and Reformulation–Linearization Bounds

Semi-definite programming (SDP) has proven to be very successful in providing tight relaxations for hard combinatorial problems. SDP relaxations for the quadratic assignment problem (QAP) are derived using the dual of the (homogenized) Lagrangian dual of appropriate equivalent representations of QAP (Zhao et al. 1998).

Anstreicher (2001) compares SDP relaxations and eigenvalue bounds; Anstreicher and Brixius (2001) describe a new convex quadratic programming bound for the QAP. The new bound dominates the well-known projected eigenvalue bound, and appears to be competitive with existing bounds in the trade-off between bound quality and computational effort.

Burer and Vandenbussche (2006) applied Lagrangian relaxation on a lift-and-project QAP relaxation, following the ideas in Lova'sz and Schrijver (1991), thus obtaining very tight SDP bounds. A report, by Rendl and Sotirov (2003), discusses a very good semi-definite programming (SDP) lower bound for the QAP. In 2003, when the report was written, it reported the tightest lower bounds for a large number of QAPLIB instances.

Hahn et al. (2007) indicated that according to the research of Povh and Rendl in 2006, the strongest relaxation (R3) from Rendl and Sotirov (2003) and the relaxation from Burer and Vandenbussche (2006) are actually the same The differing lower bound values in the two papers are due to the fact that Rendl and Sotirov use the bundle method, which gives only underestimates of the true bound, while Burer and Vandenbussche are able to compute this bound more accurately (Hahn et al. 2007).

6.3.3 Exact Algorithms

The different methods used to achieve a global optimum for the QAP include branch-and-bound, cutting planes or combinations of these methods, like branch-and-cut and dynamic programming. These algorithms are time consuming for large scale problem.

6.3.3.1 Branch-and-Bound

Among all three methods Branch-and-bound are the most known and used algorithms. There are several references concerning QAP branch-and-bound algorithms:

The first two branches and bound algorithms were developed by Gilmore (1962) and Lawler (1963) which assign single facilities to single locations. The main difference between two algorithms is in computing the lower bounds. Land (1963) and Gavett and Plyter (1966) proposed a algorithm which assign pairs of facilities to pairs of locations. Graves and Whinston (1970) and Lawler (1963) developed procedure which assign one unassigned facility to vacant location. Bazaraa and Kirca (1983) proposed the algorithm eliminates "mirror image" branches, thus reducing the search space. Mans et al. (1995) applied a parallel depth first search branch and bound algorithm for the quadratic assignment problem. Hahn and Grant (1998) presented a new branch-and-bound algorithm for solving the quadratic assignment problem (QAP). The algorithm is based on a dual procedure (DP) similar to the Hungarian method for solving the linear assignment problem. Hahn et al. (1998) applied a branch-and-bound algorithm for the quadratic assignment problem based on the Hungarian method.

6.3.3.2 Cutting Plane

Cutting plane methods introduced by Bazaraa and Sherali (1980), initially, did not present satisfactory results. The employed technique is not widely used so far, but good quality solutions for QAP cases are being presented. The slow convergence of this method makes it proper only for small instances. There are some references presented as follows:

Burkard and Bonniger (1983) which improved a cutting plane method to solve the QAP, Kaufman and Broeckx (1978), Bazaraa and Sherali (1982), Miranda et al. (2005).

6.3.3.3 Branch-and-Cut

The branch-and-cut technique, a variation proposed by Padberg and Rinaldi (1991), appears to be an alternative cutting strategy that exploits the polytope defined by the feasible solutions of the problem. Its main advantage over cutting planes is that the cuts are associated with the polypore's facets. Cuts associated with facets are more effective than the ones produced by cutting planes, so the convergence to an optimal solution is accelerated. The dearth of knowledge about the QAP polytope is the reason why polyhedral cutting planes are not widely used for this problem, and also Padberg and Rinaldi (1991), Kaibel (1998), Jünger and Kaibel (2000, 2001a, b), Blanchard et al. (2003).

6.3.3.4 Dynamic Programming

Dynamic programming is a technique used for QAP special cases where the flow matrix is the adjacency matrix of a tree.

Christofides and Benavent (1989) studied this case using a MILP approach to the relaxed problem. It was then solved with a dynamic programming algorithm, taking advantage of the polynomial complexity of the instances.

6.3.4 *Heuristic Algorithms*

Heuristic algorithms do not guarantee optimality of the best solution obtained and is a procedure dedicated to search good quality solutions. So, all approximate methods are included in this category.

Heuristic procedures include the following categories: constructive, limited enumeration, improvement methods and simulated approach.

6.3.4.1 Constructive Method

Gilmore (1962) introduced a constructive method that completes a permutation (i.e., feasible solution) at each iteration of the algorithm. There are some references in this field: Armour and Buffa (1963), Buffa et al. (1964), Tansel and Bilen (1998), Burkard et al. (1991), Arkin et al. (2001), Gutin and Yeo (2002), Yu and Sarker (2003).

6.3.4.2 Enumerative Methods

Enumeration can guarantee that the obtained solution is optimum only if they can go to the end of the enumerative process. Nissen and Paul (1995) applied the threshold accepting technique to the QAP. Burkard and Bonniger (1983), West (1983).

6.3.4.3 Improvement Methods

Improvement methods correspond to local search algorithms. Most of the QAP heuristics are in this category. White (1993) proposed a new approach, where the actual data are relaxed by embedding them in a data space that satisfies an extension of the metric triangle property. Arora et al. (2002) proposed a randomized procedure for rounding fractional perfect assignments to integral assignments and a also Heider (1973), Mirchandani and Obata (1979), Bruijs (1984), Pardalos et al. (1993), Burkard and Cela (1995), Li and Smith (1995), Anderson (1996), Talbi et al. (1998a), Deineko and Woeginger (2000), Misevicius (2000a), Mills et al. (2003).

6.3.5 Metaheuristic Algorithms

They are characterized by the definition of a priori strategies adapted to the problem structure. Several of these techniques are based on some form of simulation of a natural process studied within another field of knowledge (metaphors) so they have two important categories "metaheuristics based on natural process metaphors" and "metaheuristics based directly on theoretical and experimental considerations".

6.3.5.1 Metaheuristics Based on Natural Process Metaphors

This kind of algorithm; categorizes to simulated annealing, genetic algorithm, scatter search algorithm, ant colony optimization (ACO) and neural networks and Markov chains.

6.3.5.2 Simulated Annealing Algorithm

Burkard and Rendl (1984) proposed one of the first applications of simulated annealing to the QAP and Wilhelm and Ward (1987) presented the new equilibrium components for it. Yip and Pao (1994) applied the new technique, called guided evolutionary simulated annealing (GESA) to QAP, there is also Bos (1993a, b).

6 Quadratic Assignment Problem

A metaheuristic closely related to SA, was also applied to QAP by Nissen and Paul (1995). Abreu et al. (1999) applied the technique by trying to reduce the number of inversions associated to the problem solution, together with the cost reduction. Misevicius (2000b, 2003) propose a modified simulated annealing algorithm for the QAP-M-SA-QAP and tested the algorithm on a number of instances from the library of the QAP instances (QAPLIB) and also Bos (1993a, b), Burkard and Cela (1995), Peng et al. (1996), Mavridou and Pardalos (1997), Chiang and Chiang (1998), Tian et al. (1996 and 1999), Siu and Chang (2002), Baykasoglu (2004).

6.3.5.3 Genetic Algorithm

The GA can be good in order to find a "quite" good but non-optimal solution in a fast way. However since we are not sure of the convergence of the algorithm toward a defined value, this algorithm is not usable.

Drezner (2005a) presented a two-phase genetic algorithm and also Tavakkoli-Moghaddain and Shayan (1998), Gong et al. (1999), Drezner and Marcoulides (2003), El-Baz (2004), Wang and Okazaki (2005).

6.3.5.4 Scatter Search Algorithm

Glover (1977) introduced in a heuristic study of integer linear programming problems. Application of scatter search to the QAP can be found in Cung et al. (1997).

6.3.5.5 Ant Colony Optimization (ACO)

Maniezzo and Colorni (1999) first applied the ACO to the QAP. Stützle and Dorigo (1999) proposed a simple "2-opt" local search with ACO for QAP. Gambardella et al. (1999) show ant colony as a competitive meta heuristic, mainly for instances that have few good solutions close to each other. Middendorf et al. (2002) proposed a new ACO algorithm called s-m-p-Ant and experimented it on instances of the QAP. Solimanpur et al. (2004) solved the inter-cell layout problem and flow between the cells which is modeled as a quadratic assignment problem (QAP), by ACO, there are some more references Colorni et al. (1996), Stützle and Holgez (2000), Talbi et al. (2001), Ying and Liao (2004), Acan (2005).

6.3.5.6 Neural Networks and Markov Chains

This algorithm is structurally different from metaheuristics, they are also based on a nature metaphor and they have been applied to the QAP by: Ishii and Sato (1998) applied constrained neural approaches to QAP.

Tsuchiya et al. (1996) applied proposed algorithm to QAPLIB.

Bousonocalzon and Manning (1995) proposed the Hopfield neural network as a method for solving the QAP. Uwate et al. (2004) performance of chaos and burst noises injected on the Hopfield neural network for quadratic assignment problems, and there are some more references listed below: Obuchi et al. (1996), Rossin et al. (1999), Nishiyama et al. (2001), Hasegawa et al. (2002).

6.3.5.7 Metaheuristics Based Directly on Theoretical and Experimental Considerations

This kind of algorithm; categorizes to Tabu search, GRASP, VNS and hybrid algorithms.

6.3.5.8 Tabu Search

Tabu search is a local search algorithm that was introduced by Glover (1989a, b) to find good quality solutions for integer programming problems.

Despite the inconvenience of depending on the size of the tabu list and the way this list is managed, the performances of those algorithms show them as being very efficient strategies for the QAP, as analyzed by Taillard (1991) and Battiti and Tecchiolli (1994). In Skorin-Kapov (1990) a TS application is used to solve QAPs. The method, called Tabu-navigation, uses swap moves (i.e., the exchange in the location of two objects) to search the solution space. Taillard (1991) applied robust tabu search for the quadratic assignment problem and also Taillard (1991) developed a TS procedure with less complexity for QAP with incorporates a quick update for the moves in the candidate list at every iteration, this procedure allows the complete evaluation of the swap neighborhood.

Chakrapani and Skorin-Kapov (1993) applied a dynamically changing tabu list sizes, aspiration criterion and long term memory, tabu search for QAP, Skorin-Kapov (1994) also implemented dynamic tabu list sizes for their algorithm. Drezner (2005b) extended concentric tabu for the quadratic assignment problem.

6.3.5.9 GRASP

Li et al. (1994b) presented a GRASP for QAPLIB. Mavridou et al. (1998) proposed GRASP for the biquadratic assignment problem. Pitsoulis (2001) presented GRASPs for solving the following NP-hard nonlinear QAP and also biquadratic assignment problem (BiQAP). Fleurent and Glover (1999) indicate that memory based medications improve the solution quality of GRASP for solving the QAP. Rangel et al. (2000) introduced new GRASP uses a criterion to accept or reject a given initial solution, thus trying to avoid potentially fruitless searches. Oliveira et al. (2004) built a GRASP using the path-relinking strategy, which looks for improvements along the paths joining pairs of good solutions.

6.3.5.10 VNS

This method was introduced by Mladenovic and Hansen (1997). In Gambardella et al. (1999), three VNS strategies are proposed for the QAP. One of them is a search over variable neighborhood, according to the basic paradigm. The other two are hybrids in combination with some of the previously described methods.

6.3.5.11 Hybrid Algorithms

Usually, there are combinations of two or more metaheuristic algorithm. Most of the time hybrid algorithm produces better solution for the same problem than single algorithm. Some references are listed below:

Fleurent and Ferland (1994) applied a new hybrid procedure that combines genetic operators to existing heuristic, local search and tabu search to solve the quadratic assignment problem (QAP). Li et al. (1994a, b) proposed genetic algorithm for the QAP which incorporates the construction phase of the GRASP to generate the initial population. Battiti and Tecchiolli (1994), Bland and Dawson (1994), Chiang and Chiang (1998) use tabu search with simulated annealing.

Bölte and Thonemann (1996) presented a combination of simulated annealing and genetic algorithm. Dorigo et al. (1997) presented HAS-QAP, an hybrid ant colony system coupled with a local search, applied to the quadratic assignment problem. HAS-QAP is compared with some of the best heuristics available for the QAP: two taboo search versions, that is, robust and reactive taboo search, a hybrid genetic algorithm, and simulated annealing. Ahuja et al. (2000), Drezner (2003) introduced a genetic algorithm incorporates many greedy principles in its design and, hence refer to it as a greedy genetic algorithm. Youssef et al. (2003) use tabu search, simulated annealing and fuzzy logic together. Balakrishnan et al. (2003) used GATS, a hybrid algorithm that considers a possible planning horizon, which combines genetic with tabu search and is designed to obtain all global optima.

Misevicius (2003) propose a modified simulated annealing algorithm for the QAP-M-SA-QAP combined with a tabu search. Misevicius (2004) introduced new results for the quadratic assignment problem used an improved hybrid genetic procedure. Dunker et al. (2004) combined dynamic programming with evolutionary computation for solving a dynamic facility layout problem.Tseng and Liang propose (2005) a hybrid metaheuristic called ANGEL to solve QAP. ANGEL combines the ant colony optimization (ACO), the genetic algorithm (GA) and a local search method (LS).

6.3.6 Comparing QAP Algorithms

From the computational results which were gathered out of many papers, it is clear that hybrid algorithms almost perform better than single heuristic or metaheuristic algorithms. And from the frequency of resolution methods (Fig. 6.7) we understand that, although heuristic and metaheuristic algorithm do not guarantee the optimal solution, because of their lower computational time than exact algorithms, they apply further. There are some results with their reference that bring below:

Battiti and Tecchiolli (1994) compared simulated annealing (SA) and Tabu search (TS) on the quadratic assignment problem. A recent work on the same benchmark suite argued that SA could achieve a reasonable solution quality with fewer function evaluations than TS.

Orhan and Cigdem (2001) applied a fuzzy tabu on various sized QAPs. The developed algorithm is different from the tabu search approaches. The obtained results show that fuzzy tabu search algorithms is more dominant than other algorithms in terms of the quality of the solutions found and the number of the points searched in solution space (and tabu search appears to be the most effective local search approach to the QAP and also for many QAP instances of QAPLIB (Bullnheimer 1998).

Ahuja et al. (2000) test greedy genetic algorithm on all the benchmark instances of QAPLIB, a well-known library of QAP instances. Out of the 132 total instances in QAPLIB of varied sizes, the greedy genetic algorithm obtained the best known solution for 103 instances, and for the remaining instances (except one) found solutions within 1% of the best known solutions.

Misevicius (2003) proposed a modified simulated annealing algorithm for the QAP-M-SA-QAP combined with a tabu search We tested our algorithm on a number of instances from the library of the QAP instances – QAPLIB. The results obtained from the experiments show that the proposed algorithm appears to be superior to earlier versions of the simulated annealing for the QAP. The power of M-SA-QAP is also corroborated by the fact that the new best known solution was found for the one of the largest QAP instances.

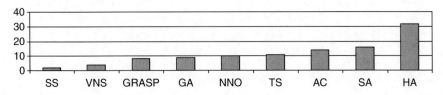

Fig. 6.7 Publications: metaheuristics used to the QAP (Hahn 2007)

Tseng and Liang (2005) applied hybrid metaheuristic called ANGEL combines the ant colony optimization (ACO), the genetic algorithm (GA) and a local search method (LS) to QAP. Over a hundred instances of QAP benchmarks were tested and the results show that ANGEL is able to obtain the optimal solution with a high success rate of 90%.

Gambardella et al. (1999), in this paper presents HAS-QAP, an hybrid ant colony system coupled with a local search, applied to the quadratic assignment problem. HAS-QAP is compared with some of the best heuristics available for the QAP: two tabu search versions, that is, robust and reactive tabu search, an hybrid genetic algorithm, and simulated annealing. Experimental results show that HAS-QAP and the hybrid genetic algorithm are the best performing on real world, irregular and structured problems.

Merz and Freisleben (1999) investigated Memetic algorithm (MA) on a set of problem instances containing between 25 and 100 facilities/locations. The results indicate that the proposed MA is able to produce high quality solutions quickly. A comparison of the MA with some of the currently best alternative approaches- reactive tabu search, robust tabu search and the fast ant colony system-demonstrates that the MA outperforms its competitors on all studied problem instances of practical interest.

Tsutsui (2007) applied the cunning ant system (CAS) and ACO to QAP, the result showed promising performance of CAS on QAP.

6.4 Case Study

In this section we introduce some case study in real world concerning with QAP.

6.4.1 Hospital Layout as a Quadratic Assignment Problem (Elshafei 1977)

The problem of locating hospital departments so as to minimize the total distance traveled by patients can be formulated as a quadratic assignment problem. The hospital concerned (the Ahmed Maher Hospital) is located in a rather densely populated part of Cairo. It is composed of six major departments: out-patient, in-patient, dental research, accident and emergency, physiotherapy and housekeeping and maintenance, each department occupying a separate building. The out-patient department is more overcrowded with the average daily number of patients now exceeding 700 people and patients having to move among the 17 clinics in the department. The locations of the clinics relative to each other has been criticized for causing too much traveling for patients and for causing bottlenecks and serious delays. It was therefore decided to improvement in the layout of the department to reduce the total distance traveled by patients and hence in the frequency of bottlenecks and congestions.

The cost of the original layout is 13,973,298 the cost of the best solution obtained is 11,281,887, so we obtain approximately the total 19.2% decreasing in distance. The full solution required 136 seconds CPU time on an IBM 360140, the initial solution being obtained after 44 s CPU time so the remaining 92 s being taken by part B. The initial solution was 16.4% better than the original layout, a further 2.8% improvement being obtained from part B.

6.4.2 Backboard Wiring Problem (Steinberg 1961)

In 1961, Leon Steinberg's paper described a backboard wiring problem (SWP) that concerns the placement of computer components so as to minimize the total amount of wiring required to connect them. In the particular instance considered by Steinberg 34 components with a total of 2,625 interconnections are to be placed on a backboard with 36 open positions. To formulate the wiring problem mathematically it is convenient to add two Dummy components_ with no connections to any others_ so that the numbers of components and locations are both $n = 36$ so for showing the answer he considered a 6×6 rectangle that each pieces shows the location of the components. After solving the problem with branch- and bound algorithm the result shows that PB and the related QPB perform very poorly and the performance of GLB is reasonable, and although the dual_ LP and polyhedral bounds are better the computational cost of these bounds is many orders of magnitude higher than that of GLB. The computation to obtain TDB is also much greater than that required for PB or GLB.

6.4.3 Minimizing WIP Inventories (Benjaafar 2002)

Benjaaafar (2002) use the model to introduce a formulation of the facility layout design problem where the objective is to minimize work-in-process (WIP) they show that layouts obtained using a WIP-based formulation can be very different from those obtained using the conventional quadratic assignment problem (QAP) formulation. For example, a QAP-optimal layout can be WIP-infeasible. In general, they show that WIP is not monotonic in material-handling travel distances so it is possible to reduce overall distances between departments but increase WIP, Furthermore, they find that the relative desirability of a layout can be affected by changes in material-handling capacity even when travel distances remain the same. After solving this problem with branch- and bound algorithm layout that minimize p_f (probability of full handling), does not necessarily minimize p_e (probability of empty handling) and we can have a layout with similar p_f but different p_e so QAP model does not guarantee to be feasible.

6.4.4 Zoning in Forest (Bos 1993)

Bos (1993), proposed Zoning the Waterbloem a national forest in southern of Netherlands, where less than 10% covered by forest, and formulate as QAP so it can take apart of land quality, management goals and interaction between environment of the forest for assigning a particular grid to particular use. Waterbloem is presented by 84 grids and its environment is 80 grids and four utility identify:

1. Timber production
2. Nature conservation
3. Recreation
4. Timber production & dispersed recreation

Other area is assign as 5 – residential area, 6 – forest, 7 – agriculture or 8 – road.

QAP model solved using simulated annealing method with different weighted the table of interaction between uses and the results of problem are available in the referenced article.

6.4.5 Computer Motherboard Design Problem (Miranda 2005)

The model have N electronic components and N location and the goal is minimize the distance between components so to control the temperature put all heat resource component together and call it hot – spot and determine the optimal placement. Miranda for solving the electronic motherboard design problem described it as a quadratic assignment problem with additional linear costs and solves it by Bender decomposition heuristic algorithm. At the end they find that QAP model design produce lower temperature (there are some picture in the reference article).

References

Abreu NMM, Querido TM, Boaventura-Netto PO (1999) RedInv- SA: A simulated annealing for the quadratic assignment problem. RAIRO Oper Res 33(3):249–273

Acan A (2005) An external partial permutations memory for ant colony optimization. Lect Notes Comput Sci 3448:1–11

Adams WP, Johnson TA (1994) Improved linear programming-based lower bounds for the quadratic assignment problem. In: Pardalos PM, Wolkowicz H (eds) Quadratic assignment and related problems, DIMACS Series in Discrete Math Theor Comput Sci, AMS, Rhode Island 16:43–75

Adams WP, Guignard M, Hahn PM, Hightower WL (2007) A level-2 reformulation-linearization technique bound for the quadratic assignment problem. Eur J Oper Res 180(3):983–996

Ahuja R, Orlin JB, Tiwari A (2000) A greedy genetic algorithm for the quadratic assignment problem. Comput Oper Res 27(10):917–934

Anderson EJ (1996) Theory and methodology: Mechanisms for local search. Eur J Oper Res 88:139–151

Anstreicher KM (2001) Eigenvalue bounds versus semidefinite relaxations for the quadratic assignment problem. SIAM J Optimiz 11(1):254–265

Anstreicher KM (2003) Recent advances in the solution of quadratic assignment problems. Math Program 97(1–2):27–42

Anstreicher KM, Brixius NW (2001) A new bound for the quadratic assignment problem based on convex quadratic programming. Math Program 89(3):341–357

Arkin EM, Hassin R, Sviridenko M (2001) Approximating the maximum quadratic assignment problem. Inf Process Lett 77(1):13–16

Armour GC, Buffa ES (1963) Heuristic algorithm and simulation approach to relative location of facilities. Manage Sci 9(2):294–309

Arora S, Frieze A, Kaplan H (2002) A new rounding procedure for the assignment problem with applications to dense graph arrangement problems. Math Program 92(1):1–36

Assad AA, Xu W (1985) On lower bounds for a class of quadratic {0,1} programs. Oper Res Lett 4(4):175–180

Balakrishnan J, Cheng CH, Conway DG, Lau CM (2003) A hybrid genetic algorithm for the dynamic plant layout problem. Int J Prod Econ 86(2):107–120

Battiti R, Tecchiolli G (1994) Simulated annealing and tabu search in the long run: A comparison on QAP tasks. Comput Math Appl 28(6):1–8

Baykasoglu A (2004) A metaheuristic algorithm to solve quadratic assignment formulations of cell formation problems without presetting number of cells. J Intell Manuf 15(6):753–759

Bazaraa MS, Sherali HD (1980) Benders' partitioning scheme applied to a new formulation of the quadratic assignment problem. Naval Res Logist Quart 27:29–41

Bazaraa MS, Sherali HD (1982) On the use of exact and heuristic cutting plane methods for the quadratic assignment problem. J Oper Res Soc 33:991–1003

Bazaraa MS, Kirca O (1983) A branch- and -bound based heuristic for solving the quadratic assignment problem. Naval Res Logist Quart 30:287–304

Ben-David G, Malah D (2005) Bounds on the performance of vector-quantizers under channel errors. IEEE Trans Inf Theor 51(6):2227–2235

Benjaafar S (2002) Modeling and analysis of congestion in the design of facility layouts. Manage Sci 48(5):679–704

Blanchard A, Elloumi S, Faye A, Wicker N (2003) A cutting algorithm of the quadratic assignment problem. INFO 41(1):35–49

Bland JA, Dawson GP (1994) Large- scale layout of facilities using a heuristic hybrid algorithm. Appl Math Model 18(9):500–503

Bölte A, Thonemann UW (1996) Optimizing simulated annealing schedules with genetic programming. Eur J Oper Res 92(2):402–416

Bos J (1993a) A quadratic assignment problem solved by simulated annealing. J Environ Manage 37(2):127–145

Bos J (1993b) Zoning in forest management: a quadratic assignment problem solved by simulated annealing. J Environ Manage 37:127–145

Bousonocalzon C, Manning MRW (1995) The Hopfield neural-network applied to the quadratic assignment problem. Neural Comput Appl 3(2):64–72

Bruijs PA (1984) On the quality of heuristic solutions to a 19 · 19 quadratic assignment problem. Eur J Oper Res 17:21–30

Brusco MJ, Stahl S (2000) Using quadratic assignment methods to generate initial permutations for least-squares unidimensional scaling of symmetric proximity matrices. J Classification 17-(2):197–223

Buffa ES, Armour GC, Vollmann TE (1964) Allocating facilities with CRAFT. Harvard Bus Rev 42(2):136–158

Bullnheimer B (1998) An examination – scheduling model to maximize students' study time. Lect Notes Comput Sci 1408:78–91

Burer S, Vandenbussche D (2006) Solving lift-and-project relaxations of binary integer programs. SIAM J Optimiz 16:726–750

Burkard RE, Bonniger T (1983) A heuristic for quadratic Boolean programs with applications to quadratic assignment problems. Eur J Oper Res 13:374–386

Burkard RE, Rendl F (1984) A thermodynamically motivated simulation procedure for combinatorial optimization problems. Eur J Oper Res 17(2):169–174

Burkard RE, Cela E (1995) Heuristics for biquadratic assignment problems and their computational comparison. Eur J Oper Res 83(2):283–300

Burkard RE, Karisch S, Rendl F (1991) QAPLIB – A quadratic assignment problem library. Eur J Oper Res 55:115–119

Burkard RE, Cela E, Klinz B (1994) On the biquadratic assignment problem. In: Pardalos PM, Wolkowicz H (eds) Quadratic assignment and related problems, DIMACS series on discrete mathematics and theoretical computer science, vol 16, AMS, Providence, RI, pp 117–146

Chakrapani J, Skorin-Kapov J (1993) Massively parallel tabu search for the quadratic assignment problem. Ann Oper Res 41(1–4):327–342

Chiang WC, Chiang C (1998) Intelligent local search strategies for solving facility layout problems with the quadratic assignment problem formulation. Eur J Oper Res 106(2–3):457–488

Christofides N, Benavent E (1989) An exact algorithm for the quadratic assignment problem. Oper Res 37(5):760–768

Colorni A, Dorigo M, Maffioli F, Maniezzo V, Righini G, Trubian M (1996) Heuristics from nature for hard combinatorial optimization problems. Int Trans Oper Res 3(1):1–21

Cung VD, Mautor T, Michelon P, Tavares A (1997) A scatter search based approach for the quadratic assignment problem. In: Proceedings of IEEE International Conference on Evolutionary Computation, pp 165–169

Deineko VG, Woeginger GJ (2000) A study of exponential neighborhoods for the traveling salesma problem and for the quadratic assignment problem. Math Program, Ser A 78:519–542

Dorigo M, Gambardella LM, Tailard ED (1997) Ant colonies for Q A P, Technical Report, IDSIA, 4

Drezner Z (1995) Lower bounds based on linear programming for the quadratic assignment problem. Computat Optimiz Appl 4(2):159–165

Drezner Z (2005a) Compounded genetic algorithms for the quadratic assignment problem. Oper Res Lett 33(5):475–480

Drezner Z (2005b) The extended concentric tabu for the quadratic assignment problem. Eur J Oper Res 160:416–422

Drezner Z, Marcoulides GA (2003) A distance-based selection of parents in genetic algorithms. In: Resende MGC, de Sousa JP (eds). Metaheuristics: Computer decision-making, combinatorial optimization book series. Kluwer, Dordecht, pp 257–278

Dunker T, Radons G, Westkämper E (2004) Combining evolutionary computation and dynamic programming for solving a dynamic facility layout problem. Eur J Oper Res 165(1):55–69

Edwards CS (1980) A branch and bound algorithm for the Koopmans–Beckmann quadratic assignment problem. Math Program Study 13:35–52

El-Baz MA (2004) A genetic algorithm for facility layout problems of different manufacturing environments. Comput Ind Eng 47(2–3):233–246

Elshafei A (1977) Hospital layout as a quadratic assignment problem. Oper Res Quart 28(1):167–179

Finke G, Burkard RE, Rendl F (1987) Quadratic assignment problems. Ann Discrete Math 31:61–82

Fleurent C, Ferland JA (1994) Genetic hybrids for the quadratic assignment problem. In: Pardalos PMM, Wolkowicz H (eds). Quadratic assignment and related problems. DIMACS Series in Discrete Math Theor Comput Sci, vol. 16. AMS, Rhode Island, pp 173–187

Fleurent C, Glover F (1999) Improved constructive multistart strategies of quadratic assignment problem using adaptive memory. INFORMS J Comput 11:189–203

Forsberg JH, Delaney RM, Zhao Q, Harakas G, Chandran R (1994) Analyzing lanthanide-included shifts in the NMR spectra of lanthanide (III) complexes derived from 1,4,7,10-tetrakis (N,N-diethylacetamido)-1,4,7,10-tetraazacyclododecane. Inorg Chem 34:3705–3715

Francis RL, White JA (1974) Facility layout and location: An analytical approach. Prentice-Hall, Englewood Cliffs, NJ

Frieze A.M, Yadegar J (1983) On the quadratic assignment problem. Discrete Appl Math 5:89–98
Gambardella LM, Taillard D, Dorigo M (1999) Ant colonies for the QAP. J Oper Res Soc 50:167–176
Gavett JW, Plyter NV (1966) The optimal assignment of facilities to locations by branch- and-bound. Oper Res 14:210–232
Geoffrion AM, Graves GW (1976) Scheduling parallel production lines with changeover costs: Practical applications of a quadratic assignment/LP approach. Oper Res 24:595–610
Gilmore PC (1962) Optimal and suboptimal algorithms for the quadratic assignment problem. SIAM J Appl Math 10:305–313
Glover F (1977) Heuristics for integer programming using surrogate constraints. Decis Sci 8:156–166
Glover F (1989a) Tabu search – Part I. ORSA J Comput 1:190–206
Glover F (1989b) Tabu search – Part II. ORSA J Comput 2:4–32
Gong D, Yamazaki G, Gen M, Xu W (1999) A genetic algorithm method for one-dimensional machine location problems. Int J Prod Econ 60–61:337–342
Graves GW, Whinston AB (1970) An algorithm for the quadratic assignment problem. Manage Sci 17(7):453–471
Gutin G, Yeo A (2002) Polynomial approximation algorithms for TSP and QAP with a factorial domination number. Discrete Appl Math 119(1–2):107–116
Hadley SW, Rendl F, Wolkowicz H (1992a) Nonsymmetric quadratic assignment problems and the Hoffman–Wielandt inequality. Linear Algebra Appl 58:109–124
Hadley SW, Rendl F, Wolkowicz H (1992b) A new lower bound via projection for the quadratic assignment problem. Math Oper Res 17:727–739
Hahn P, Grant T (1998) Lower bounds for the quadratic assignment problem based upon a dual formulation. Oper Res 46(6):912–922
Hahn P, Grant T, Hall N (1998) A branch-and-bound algorithm for the quadratic assignment problem based on the Hungarian method. Eur J Oper Res 108:629–640
Hahn P, Loiola EM, de Abreu NMM, Boaventura-Netto PO, Querido T (2007) A survey for the quadratic assignment problem. Eur J Oper Res 176:657–690
Hamacher H, Nickel S, Tenfelde-Podehl D (2003) Facilities layout for social institutions. In: Operation Research Proceedings 2001, Selected papers of the international conference on operations research (OR2001). Springer-Verlag, Berlin, pp 229–236
Hansen P, Lih KW (1992) Improved algorithms for partitioning problems in parallel, pipelined, and distributed computing. IEEE Trans Comput 41(6):769–771
Hasegawa M, Ikeguchi T, Aihara K, Itoh K (2002) A nove chaotic search for quadratic assignment problems. Eur J Oper Res 139(3):543–556
Heffley DR (1972) The quadratic assignment problem: A note. Econometrica 40(6):1155–1163
Heider CH (1973) An N- step, 2- variable search algorithm for the component placement problem. Naval Res Logist Quart 20:699–724
Hubert L (1987) Assignment methods in combinatorial data analysis. Statistics: textbooks and monographs series, vol 73. Marcel Dekker, New York
Ishii S, Sato M (1998) Constrained neural approaches to quadratic assignment problems. Neural Netw 11(6):1073–1082
Jünger M, Kaibel V (2000) On the SQAP-polytope. SIAM J Optimiz 11(2):444–463
Jünger M, Kaibel V (2001a) The QAP-polytope and the star transformation. Discrete Appl Math 111(3):283–306
Jünger M, Kaibel V (2001b) Box- inequalities for quadratic assignment polytopes. Math Program 91:75–97
Kaibel V (1998) Polyhedral combinatorics of quadratic assignment problems with less objects than locations. Lecture Notes Comput Sci 1412:409–422
Kaufman L, Broeckx F (1978)An algorithm for the quadratic assignment problem using Benders'decomposition, Eur J Oper Res 2:204–211

Knowles J, Corne DW (2003) Instance generators and test suites for the multiobjective quadratic assignment problem. In: Evolutionary multi-criterion optimization (EMO 2003) Second International Conference, Portugal, Proceedings. Berlin, Springer-Verlag, LNCS, pp 295–310

Koopmans TC, Beckmann MJ (1957) Assignment problems and the location of economic activities. Econometrica 25:53–76

Krarup J, Pruzan PM (1978) Computer-aided layout design. Math Program Study 9:75–94

Land AM (1963) A problem of assignment with interrelated costs. Oper Res Quart 14:185–198

Lawler EL (1963) The quadratic assignment problem. Manage Sci 9:586–599

Lee CG, Ma Z (2004) The generalized quadratic assignment problem. Research Report, Department of mechanical and industrial engineering, University of Toronto, Canada

Li WJ, Smith JM (1995) An algorithm for quadratic assignment problems. Eur J Oper Res 81:205–216

Li Y, Pardalos PM, Ramakrishnan KG, Resende MGC (1994a) Lower bounds for the quadratic assignment problem. Oper Res 50:387–410

Li Y, Pardalos PM, Resende, MGC (1994b) A greedy randomized adaptive search procedure for the quadratic assignment problem. In: Pardalos PM, Wolkowicz H (eds), Quadratic assignment and related problems, DIMACS series in Discrete Math Theor Comput Sci, vol. 16. AMS, Rhode Island, pp 237–261

Lova'sz L, Schrijver A (1991) Cones of matrices and set-functions, and 0–1 optimization. SIAM J Optimiz 1:166–190

Maniezzo V, Colorni A (1999) The ant system applied to the quadratic assign ment problem. Knowl Data Eng 11(5):769–778

Mans B, Mautor T, Roucairol C (1995) A parallel depth first search branch and bound algorithm for the quadratic assignment problem. Eur J Oper Res 81:617–628

Mavridou T, Pardalos PM (1997) Simulated annealing and genetic algorithms for the facility layout problem: A survey. Computat Optimiz Appl 7:111–126

Mavridou T, Pardalos PM, Pitsoulis LS, Resende MGC (1998) A GRASP for the biquadratic assignment problem. Eur J Oper Res 105(3):613–621

Merz P, Freisleben B (1999) A comparison of mimetic algorithms, tabu search, and ant colonies for the quadratic assignment problem. In: Proceedings of the 1999 International Congress of Evolutionary Computation (CEC'99). IEEE Press, New York, pp 2063–2070

Middendorf M, Reischle F, Schmeck H (2002) Multi colony ant algorithms. J Heuristics 8(3):305–320

Mills P, Tsang E, Ford J (2003) Applying an extended guided local search to the quadratic assignment problem. Ann Oper Res 118(1–4):121–135

Miranda G, Luna HPL, Mateus GR, Ferreira RPM (2005) A performance guarantees heuristic for electronic components placement problems including thermal effects. Comput Oper Res 32:2937–2957

Mirchandani PB, Obata T (1979) Algorithms for a class of quadratic assignment problems. Presented at the Joint ORSA/TIMS National Meeting, New Orleans

Misevicius A (2000a) An intensive search algorithm for the quadratic assignment problem. Informatica 11:145–162

Misevicius A (2000b) A new improved simulated annealing algorithm for the quadratic assignment problem. Inf Technol Contr 17:29–38

Misevicius A (2003) A modified simulated annealing algorithm for the quadratic assignment problem. Informatica 14(4):497–514

Misevicius A (2004) An improved hybrid genetic algorithm: New results for the quadratic assignment problem. Knowl-Based Syst 17(2–4):65–73

Mladenovic N, Hansen P (1997) Variable neighborhood search. Comput Oper Res 24:1097–1100

Nishiyama T, Tsuchiya K, Tsujita K (2001) A Markov chain Monte Carlo algorithm for the quadratic assignment problem based on replicator equations. Lecture Notes Comput Sci 2130:148–155

Nissen V, Paul H (1995) A modification of threshold accepting and its application to the quadratic assignment problem. OR Spektrum 17(2–3):205–210

Obuchi Y, Masui H, Ohki M (1996) Weighted parallel problem solving by optimization networks. Neural Netw 9(2):357–366

Oliveira CAS, Pardalos MP, Resende MGG (2004) GRASP with path relinking for the quadratic assignment problem. In: Experimental and efficient algorithms, Third International Workshop (WEA 2004), Brazil, LNCS 3059. Springer, Berlin, pp 356–368

Orhan T, Cigdem A (2001) A fuzzy Tabu search approach for the plant layout problem

Padberg MW, Rinaldi G (1991) A branch-and-cut algorithm for the resolution of large-scale symmetric traveling salesman problems. SIAM Rev 33:60–100

Pardalos P M, Murthy K A, Harrison TP (1993) A computational comparison of local search heuristics for solving quadratic assignment problems. Information 4(1–2):172–187

Peng T, Huanchen W, Dongme Z (1996) Simulated annealing for the quadratic assignment problem: A further study. Comput Ind Eng 31(3–4):925–928

Pierskalla WP (1967a) The tri-substitution method for the three-multidimensional assignment problem. Can Oper Res Soc J 5(2):71–81

Pierskalla WF (1967b) The multi-dimensional assignment problem. Technical Memorandum No. 93, Operations Research Department, CASE Institute of Technology, Available on line at: http://www.anderson.ucla.edu/faculty/william.pierskalla/Chronological_Bank/Research_and_Publication_Chro.html#Mathematical, State September 1967

Pitsoulis LS, Pardalos PM, Hearn DW (2001) Approximate solutions to the turbine balancing problem. Eur J Oper Res 130m(1):147–155

Pollatschek MA, Gershoni N, Radday YT (1976) Optimization of the typewriter keyboard by simulation. Angewandte Informatik 17:438–439

Rangel M C, Abreu NMM, Boaventura-Netto PO (2000) GRASP in the QAP: an acceptance bound for initial solutions (in Portuguese). Pesquisa Operacional 20(1):45–58

Rendl F, Sotirov R (2003) Bounds for the quadratic assignment problem using the bundle method. Accepted for publication in Math. Program. B, and will appear in the special issue dedicated to Jos Sturm, First available in 2003 as a Technical Report, Department of Mathematics, University of Klagenfurt

Rossin DF, Springer MC, Klein BD (1999) New complexity measures for the facility layout problem: An empirical stud using traditional and neural network analysis. Comput Ind Eng 36(3):585–602

Sahni S, Gonzales T (1976) P-complete approximation problems. J Assoc Comput Mach 23: 555–565

Siu F, Chang RKC (2002) Effectiveness of optimal node assignments in wavelength division multiplexing networks with fixed regular virtual topogies. Comput Netw 38(1):61–74

Sherali HD, Adams WP (1990) A hierarchy of relaxations between the continuous and convex hull representations for zero-one programming problems. SIAM J Disc Math 3:411–430

Sherali HD, Adams WP, Smith JC (2000) Reduced first-level representations via the reformulation-linearization technique: results, counterexamples, and computations. Discrete Appl Math 101:247–267

Skorin-Kapov J (1990) Tabu search applied to the quadratic assignment problem. ORSA J Comput 2(1):33–45

Skorin-Kapov J (1994) Extensions of a tabu search adaptation to the quadratic assignment problem. J Comput Oper Res 21(8):855–865

Smith M, Li W (2001) Quadratic assignment problems and M/G/C/C/ state dependent network flows. J Comb Optimiz 5:421–443

Solimanpur M, Vrat P, Shankaz R (2004) Ant colony optimization algorithm to the inter- cell layout problem in cellular manufacturing. Eur J Oper Res 157(3):592–606

Steinberg L (1961) The backboard wiring problem: a placement algorithm. SIAM Rev 3:37–50

Stützle T, Dorigo M (1999) ACO algorithms for the quadratic assignment problem. In: Corne D, Dorigo M, Glover F (eds). New Ideas Optimiz. McGraw-Hill, New York, pp 33–55

Stützle T, Holgez H (2000) Max-Min ant system. Future Gener Comput Syst 16(8):889–914

Taillard E (1991) Robust taboo search for the quadratic assignment problem. Parallel Comput 17:443–455

Talbi EG, Hafidi Z, Kebbal D, Geib JM (1998a) A fault-tolerant parallel heuristic for assignment problems. Future Generation Comput Syst 14(5–6):425–438

Talbi EG, Roux O, Fonlupt C, Robillard D (2001) Parallel ant colonies for the quadratic assignment problem. Future Generation Comput Syst 17(4):441–449

Tansel BC, Bilen C (1998) Move based heuristics for the unidirectional loop network layout problem. Eur J Oper Res 108(1):36–48

Tavakkoli-Moghaddain R, Shayan E (1998) Facilities layout design by genetic algorithms. Comput Ind Eng 35(3–4):527–530

Tian P, Wang HC, Zhang DM (1996) Simulated annealing for the quadratic assignment problem: A further study. Comput Ind Eng 31(3–4):925–928

Tian P, Ma J, Zhang DM (1999) Application of the simulated annealing algorithm to the combinatorial optimization problem with permutation property: An investigation of generation mechanism. Eur J Oper Res 118(1):81–94

Tseng LY, Liang SC (2005) A hybrid metaheuristic for the quadratic assignment problem. Comput Optimiz Appl 34:85–113

Tsuchiya K, Bharitkar S, Takefuji Y (1996) A neural network approach to facility layout problems. Eur J Oper Res 89(3):556–563

Tsutsui S (2007) Cunning ant system for quadratic assignment problem with local search and parallelization. Lecture Notes Comput Sci. Springer, Berlin, pp 269–278

Uwate Y, Nishio Y, Ushida A (2004) Markov chain modeling of intermittency chaos and its application to Hopfield NN. IEICE Trans Fundam Electron Commun Comput Sci E87A(4):774–779

Wang RL, Okazaki K (2005) Solving facility layout problem using an improved genetic algorithm. IEICE Trans Fundam Electron Commun Comput Sci E88A(2):606–610

Wess B, Zeitlhofer T (2004) On the phase coupling problem between data memory layout generation and address pointer assignment. Lecture Notes Comput Sci 3199:152–166

West DH (1983) Algorithm 608: Approximate solution of the quadratic assignment problem. ACM Trans Math Softw 9:461–466

White DJ (1993) A parametric-based heuristic program for the quadratic assignment problem. Nava Res Logist 40(4):553–568

Wilhelm MR, Ward TL (1987) Solving quadratic assignment problems by simulated annealing. IEEE Trans 19:107–119

Ying KC, Liao CJ (2004) An ant colony system for permutation flow- shop sequencing. Comput Oper Res 31(5):791–801

Yip PPC, Pao YH (1994) A guided evolutionary simulated annealing approach to the quadratic assignment problem. IEEE Trans Syst Man Cybernet 24(9):1383–1387

Youssef H, Sait SM, Ali H (2003) Fuzzy simulated evolution algorithm for VLSI cell placement. Comput Ind Eng 44(2):227–247

Yu J, Sarker BR (2003) Directional decomposition heuristic for a linear machine – cell location problem. Eur J Oper Res 149(1):142–184

Zhao Q, Karisch SE, Rendl F, Wolkowicz H (1998) Semidefinite programming relaxations for the quadratic assignment problem. J Comb Optimiz 2:71–109

Chapter 7
Covering Problem

Hamed Fallah, Ali NaimiSadigh, and Marjan Aslanzadeh

In many covering problems, services that customers receive by facilities depend on the distance between the customer and facilities. In a covering problem the customer can receive service by each facility if the distance between the customer and facility is equal or less than a predefined number. This critical value is called coverage distance or coverage radius and shown by Dc.

Church and ReVelle (1974) modeled the maximization covering problem. Covering problems are divided into two branches; tree networks and general networks, according to their graph. In addition, these problems are divided into two problems: Total covering and partial covering problems, based on covering all or some demand points.

The total covering problem is modeled by Toregas (1971). Up to the present time many developments have occurred about total covering and partial covering problems in solution technique and assumptions.

Covering problem has many applications such as: designing of switching circuits, data retrieving, assembly line balancing, air line staff scheduling, locating defend networks (at war), distributing products, warehouse locating, location emergency service facility (Francis et al. 1992).

Let us first introduce the concept of covering a demand point with an example. Consider the tree network Fig. 7.1:

Demand points in this problem are A, B, C and D. The distance between each two demand points, is shown on their connecting arc. Consider that we want the demand of point A to be covered. Coverage distance is supposed to be 5. Thus in order to cover point A, we should locate at least one facility on the network (feasible space of problem), in a way that it's distance from point A is equal or less than 5. Therefore, the demand point A will be covered if at least one facility is located on one of thick lines, in Fig. 7.2:

Consider three candidate locating sites I, II and III (that III is conformed on demand point D). Among these three places only II can cover point A; it means that one facility is located in place II, the demand point A will be covered.

Note that the coverage distance (Dc) can be a kind of time or cost. For example, if the walking time from a residential region to a store is equal or less than 5 min the demand of that region will be covered.

Fig. 7.1 Covering a demand point

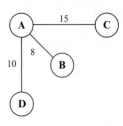

Fig. 7.2 The space that can cover A

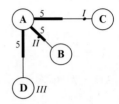

7.1 Problem Formulation

The covering problem is one of well known problems of binary programming. Feasible solution space of this problem is a network (graph).

In all problems of this chapter, the capacity of facilities is considered to be unlimited. In addition, facilities are desirable; therefore, the nearness of them to the demand points is interesting.

We want to cover all demand points with minimum possible cost. The general parameters of the problem are as follow:

$i = 1, 2, \ldots, m$	Index of demand points
M	The number of demand point
$j = 1, 2, \ldots, n$	Index of candidate locating points
n	The number of candidate locating point
f_j	The cost of locating a facility on candidate locating point j

a_{ij}: is 1 if candidate locating point j can cover the demand point i, otherwise is 0.

For perception of the concept of a_{ij} consider Fig. 7.3:

The demand points are A and B and the distance between them is 15 km. Assume than coverage distance is $Dc = 5\,km$, thus the reduced feasible solution space is containing of points A, B and two intersection points shown by Fig. 7.4.

As an instance since candidate locating point 2 cannot cover the demand of B, $a_{B2} = 0$ and since candidate locating point 1 can cover the demand of A, $a_{A1} = 1$; thus:

Fig. 7.3 An example for perception of the concept of a_{ij}

Fig. 7.4 The reduced solution space

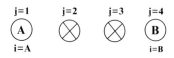

$$\begin{cases} a_{A1} = 1 \\ a_{A2} = 1 \\ a_{B1} = 0 \\ a_{B2} = 0 \end{cases} \quad \begin{cases} a_{A3} = 0 \\ a_{A4} = 0 \\ a_{B3} = 1 \\ a_{B4} = 1 \end{cases}$$

Decision variable of model:

X_j: is 1 if a facility be located on place j, otherwise is 0

Thus the total covering problem model is as follows:

$$\text{Min} \sum_{j=1}^{n} f_j X_j, \tag{7.1}$$

Subject to

$$\sum_{j=1}^{n} a_{ij} X_j \geq 1; \forall i, \tag{7.2}$$

$$X_j = 0, 1; \forall j. \tag{7.3}$$

Equation (7.1) minimized total locating costs and (7.2) ensures that all demand points will be covered. Note that the (7.2) illustrates the number of located facilities that can cover demand of i. In other words (7.2) explains that for each demand point i. We should locate at least one facility in one of places that can cover that demand point.

7.2 Total Covering Problem

The total covering problem is divided into two branches: Tree network and general network (cyclic network), there is a simple solution for tree networks because of no cycle and it will be described in Sect. 7.2.1.

Fig. 7.5 Example of general network

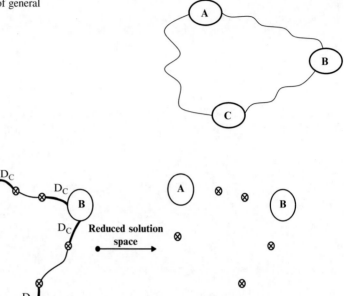

Fig. 7.6 Reducing solution space from continuous space to set points (Daskin 1995)

The general networks (Cyclic networks), are networks that there are more than one rout between some or all of their nodes.

These networks have a closed loop as their name implies. Consider network below:

In Fig. 7.5 the demand points are *A, B, C*, the coverage distance is *Dc* and the feasible solution space of this problem is the set of points of network.

It seems very difficult to determine the location of facilities and to enter them to the mathematical model as quantities. It is proved that instead of all points of network (Daskin 1995) we can consider a reduced solution space including demand points and intersection points. Intersection points are points that their distance from at least one of demand points is exactly equal to coverage distance. As we can see in Fig. 7.6 the solution space is reduced from a continuous space to a set of nine candidate locating points.

Thus all of covering problems have finite candidate locating points (that are always demand points) or we can reduce their space to discreet solution space, so in this chapter we consider the solution space to be discreet.

If the cost of locating is equal in different places, we have

$$f_j = 1; \qquad j = 1, \ldots, n, \tag{7.4}$$

7 Covering Problem

So the objective function of the model will be the minimization of number of required facilities covering all demand points.

$$\text{Min} \sum_j X_j. \tag{7.5}$$

The problem above is known as classical total covering problem.

The covering problem often has alternative optimal solutions, so we can add more objectives to the total covering problem.

7.2.1 Maximizing the Number of Points Covered More than Once

Consider a state that we want to locate the facilities such that the number of demand points covered two times, is maximized, in addition to cover all demand points with minimum number of facilities, so that, if a facility is not able to service, another facility works as a supplementary.

We define:

M = the number of demand points.
S_i: is 1 if demand points i is covered at least two times, otherwise is 0

The model of this problem is as follows:

$$\text{Min}(M+1) \sum_j X_j - \sum_i S_i, \tag{7.6}$$

Subject to

$$\sum_j a_{ij} X_j - S_i \geq 1, \tag{7.7}$$

$$X_j = 0, 1; \quad \forall j, \tag{7.8}$$

$$S_j = 0, 1; \quad \forall i. \tag{7.9}$$

Equation (7.7) ensures that S_i is 1 if $\sum a_{ij} X_j$ is greater than or equal 2. Moreover, since the coefficient S_i in the objective function is -1, the variable S_i will be 1 to satisfy the optimal solution. The weight $(M+1)$ in the objective function ensures that the number of required facilities is not more than primary model of total covering problem.

7.2.2 Multiple Total Covering Problems (Mirchandani et al. 1990)

Classical total covering problem is indeed a special kind of multiple total covering problem. In this problem we want to cover each demand point bi times, based on it's importance (that $i = 1, \ldots, m$ and $b = 1, 2, \ldots$). In addition at each candidate locating maximum U_j facilities can be located. ($U_j = 1, 2, \ldots; j = 1, \ldots, n$).

The model of this problem is as follows:

$$\text{Min} \sum_{j=1}^{n} f_j X_j, \qquad (7.10)$$

Subject to

$$\sum_{j=1}^{n} a_{ij} X_j \geq b_i, \quad i = 1, \ldots, m, \qquad (7.11)$$

$$0 \leq X_j \leq u_j; \quad X_j \text{ integer}; j = 1, \ldots, n. \qquad (7.12)$$

It is obvious that this problem has feasible solution if:

$$\sum_{j=1}^{n} a_{ij} u_j \geq b_i; \quad i = 1, \ldots, n. \qquad (7.13)$$

In this model for some point it isn't sufficient to facilities be available and the demand value or importance of demand of each point specifies the number of needed facilities (Mirchandani and Francis 1990).

7.2.3 Total Covering Problem with the Preference of Selecting Location of Existing Facilities (Daskin 1995)

We want to select solutions including points of existing facilities among optimal solutions of total covering problems.

So we can define:

J_e: Set of locations of existing facilities
J_n: Set of new candidate locating points
ε: an infinitesimal

The model of the problems is as follows:

$$\text{Min} \sum_{j \in J_e} X_j + (1+\varepsilon) \sum_{j \in J_n} X_j, \qquad (7.14)$$

Subject to

$$\sum_{j \in J_e} a_{ij} X_j + \sum_{j \in J_n} a_{ij} X_j \geq 1; \quad \forall i, \qquad (7.15)$$

$$X_j = 0, 1; \quad j \in \{J_e \cup J_n\}. \qquad (7.16)$$

In order to number of facilities not be greater than the optimal solution of initial total covering model (classical model), it is necessary to have $\varepsilon < 1/|J_n|$. The large value for coefficient $X_j \mid j \in J_n$ in objective function causes the model to tend more to selecting locations having available facilities (Daskin 1995).

7.2.4 Total Edge Covering Problem (Daskin 1995)

All problems studied in this chapter yet, discussed about covering or not covering demand points (nodes of network).

There are problems in practice that we should cover edges of graph.

For example in locating police stations.

Edge covering problem similar to covering nodes of graph, can be discussed with different objectives and constraints. In this chapter we consider total edge covering problem with objective minimizing cost of locating.

As before we can reduce feasible solution space to set of demand points and intersection points. To simplify the problem we assume that each edge should be totally covered only by one node and we can not cover a part of an edge by a node and cover other part of it by another node.

But to have feasible solution for the problem, we should have:

(Length of longest edge) – (coverage distance) ≤ (coverage distance).

To prove this claim, consider Fig. 7.7.

If we can cover the longest edge of above network by one facility, we can certainly cover all shorter edges.

In Fig. 7.7, *AB* is the longest edge. If we can not cover an edge by any of candidate locating points on it, certainly we can not cover it totally by out of that edge. Thus to have feasible solution X_1 (or X_2) should cover total edge *AB*, therefore the distance between X_1 and B (or between X_1 and A) should be less than or equal to coverage distance.

To solve the problem of lack of any feasible solution on edges violating the above condition, we consider one (or more) artificial edge(s) and thus decompose each edge to two or more edges in a way that above condition be satisfied. These artificial nodes will be added to the set of candidate locating points.

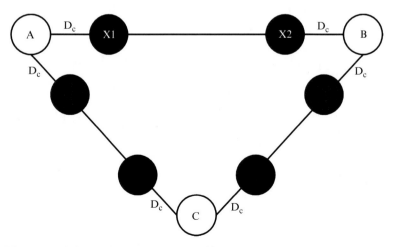

Fig. 7.7 A network for proving relation (Daskin 1995)

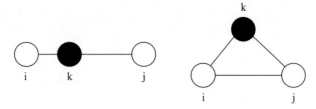

Fig. 7.8 Example (Daskin 1995)

Parameters of problem:

$G(V, E)$	The graph of problem
V	Set of nodes
E	Set of edges
$i = 1, \ldots, m$	indices of nodes of network
$ij \in E(i < j)$	indices of edges of network
d_{ij}	Distance of nodes i and j
$K = 1, \ldots, n$	indices of candidate locating points
F_k	Cost of locating at candidate locating point k
D_c	Coverage distance

a_{ijk}: is 1 if candidate locating point k can cover edge k completely, otherwise is 0.

Parameter a_{ijk} nodes more explain. Consider Fig. 7.8, in part a candidate locating point k is on the edge ij. Here the point k can cover all of edge ij if it can cover both i and j.

It means:
$$a_{ijk} = a_{ik} . a_{jk}$$

But in part (b) point k can cover all of edge ij if:

$$\text{Max}\{\circ, D_C - d_{ki}\} + \text{Max}\{\circ, D_C - d_{kj}\} \geq d_{ij}. \qquad (7.17)$$

The statement above ($D_C - d_{ki}$) shows a part of edge ij that can be covered by node k by node i and ($D_C - d_{kj}$) shows a part of edge ij that can be covered by node k by node j. Obviously, whole of edge ij will be covered if sum of these two parts is greater than or equal to the length of edge ij. Decision variable of problem:

X_k: is 1 if a facility is located of candidate point k, otherwise is 0

The model of this problem is as follows:

$$\text{Min} \sum_{k=1}^{n} f_k X_k, \qquad (7.18)$$

7 Covering Problem

Subject to

$$\sum_{k=1}^{n} a_{ijk} X_j \geq 1; \forall ij \in E; i < j, \quad (7.19)$$

$$X_j = 0, 1. \quad (7.20)$$

As we can see, the model is similar to the total covering model and the only difference is in computing coefficients of coverage matrix (a_{ijk}) (Daskin 1995).

7.2.5 Notes on Total Covering Problems

7.2.5.1 Total Covering Problem with Fuzzy Matrix of Coverage Coefficients (Chiang et al. 2005)

There are problems in practice that we can not exactly talk about covering a demand point by a candidate locating location.

In other words, the possibility of covering demand point i by facility j, that is shown by $\mu_j(i)$ has a value which belongs to interval [0,1].

The objective is that with minimum cost of locating facilities the possibility of covering each demand point is greater than or equal to a predefined value α.

Thus the primary model of the problem is as follows:

$$\text{Min} \sum_{j=1}^{n} C_j X_j, \quad (7.21)$$

Subject to

$$1 - \prod_{j=1}^{n} (1 - \mu_j(i) X_j) \geq \alpha; \quad i = 1, \ldots, m, \quad (7.22)$$

$$X_j \in \{0, 1\}. \quad (7.23)$$

That C_j is the cost of locating a facility at point $j : (j = 1, 2 \ldots n)$.

Chiang et al. (2005) proved that we can transform the (7.21) of above model to the following linear model:

Subject to

$$\sum_{j=1}^{n} \left[-\ln(1 - \mu_j(i))\right] X_j \geq -\ln(1 - \alpha); \quad i = 1, \ldots, m, \quad (7.24)$$

Note that in this model we don't consider $\alpha = 1$ and $\circ < \alpha < 1$ (Chiang et al. 2005).

7.2.5.2 Symmetrical Total Covering Problem (The Lottery Problem) (Jans and Degraeve 2008)

In a lottery game, n numbers are randomly drawn from a set of m numbers. On a lottery ticket, we fill out n number hoping that they will match the n numbers selected. We want to know the minimum number of tickets we have to fill out in order to ensure that there is at least one ticket which has p or more matching numbers. We call this a (m, n, p)-lottery problem, with $m \geq n \geq p$. Of course, we also want to know which specific numbers we have to fill out. We will show how this problem can be formulated as an integer linear programming (*ILP*) problem, more specifically a set-covering problem.

Define S as the set of all possible tickets. This same set S also defines all possible draws, as a selection of n numbers out of m defines both a possible draw and a possible ticket. For the *IP* formulation, we define a variable for each possible ticket: $x_j = 1$ if ticket j is filled out, 0 otherwise, $\forall j \in S$. Further, define S_i as the set of all tickets which have at least p out of n numbers in common with draw i. Due to the equivalence between a ticket and a draw, S_i is also the set of all draws which have at least p out of n numbers in common with ticket i. Finally, we define the parameters of the coefficient matrix as follows: $a_{ij} = 1$ if ticket $j \in S_i$, $= 0$ otherwise.

The objective is to minimize the number of tickets that we have to fill out (7.24). There is only one set of constraints imposing that for each possible outcome, there must be at least one ticket filled out which has at least p numbers in common with that outcome (7.25). The variables for the tickets must be binary (7.26). The resulting formulation is a set covering problem:

$$\text{Min} \sum_{j \in S} x_j, \tag{7.25}$$

Subject to

$$\sum_{j \in S} a_{ij} x_j \geq 1 \ \forall i \in S, \tag{7.26}$$

$$x_j \in \{0, 1\}. \tag{7.27}$$

We characterize the cardinality of the sets for a general *(m, n, p)*-lottery. The total number of variables equals the number of combinations of n elements out of m (Jans and Degraeve 2008):

$$|S| = \binom{m}{n}.$$

7.2.5.3 Stochastic Total Covering Problem for Destructive and Constructive Cases (Hwang 2004)

In all works done yet there was the assumption that the value of inventory always remains constant.

Special cases of stochastic total covering location are studied for destructive and constructive instances. This problem can be formulated using stochastic total covering that is solvable with binary programming.

Objective: minimizing the number of storing facilities in a set of discreet points.
Constraint: probability of covering each point should not be less than a critical value.

Presumptions:

- Passing time causes improvement or decay in inventory
- Distances can be of any type

Decision variable: X_j

X_j: is 1 if a facility is located at point j, otherwise is 0

Parameter:

F_{ij}: Sum of transportation costs in each period and costs of constructive or destructive

A_i: Service level needed for demand point i

r_i: Critical value of probability of covering demand point i

The small model is as follows (Hwang 2004):

$$\text{Min} \sum_{j=1}^{n} x_j, \tag{7.28}$$

Subject to

$$\sum_{j=1}^{n} a_{ij} x_j \geq 1 \quad \forall i = 1, \ldots, m, \tag{7.29}$$

$$x_j = \{0, 1\} \quad \forall j = 1, \ldots, n, \tag{7.30}$$

$$a_{ij} = \begin{cases} 1 & \text{if } p(F_{ij} \leq A_i) \geq r_i \\ 0 & \text{Otherwise} \end{cases}. \tag{7.31}$$

7.3 Partial Covering Problem

Total covering problem can not cover all location problems in real world, because in many problems budget constraints and other constraints do not let us cover all points. For example, consider that we need four facilities to cover all demand points but budget constraint does not let us locate more than three facilities, thus covering problem doesn't have feasible solution.

On the other hand, the total covering problem considers all demand points similarly regardless of their demand. For example in a total covering problem, satisfying a demand point that has 10 units demand, has the same importance with satisfying a demand point that has 1,000 units demand.

To confront such problems, another covering problem is proposed that called partial covering problem. In this part we will introduce some samples of it.

7.3.1 Minimizing Costs Arisen from Not Covering Demand Points (Mirchandani and Francis 1990)

In this problem, maximum number of facilities is limited and equal to P. In other words the problem is exogenous and P_i is penalty cost of not covering demand point i. In addition consider the number of demand points is m and the number of candidate locating points is n.

Decision variables of problem are:

X_j: is 1 if a facility is located at j, otherwise is 0
Z_i: is 1 if the demand point i is not satisfied, otherwise is 0

The model of this problem is as follows:

$$\text{Min} \sum_{i=1}^{m} p_i Z_i, \tag{7.32}$$

Subject to

$$\sum_{j=1}^{n} a_{ij} X_j + Z_i \geq 1 \; ; \; i = 1, \ldots, m, \tag{7.33}$$

$$\sum_{j=1}^{n} X_j \leq P, \tag{7.34}$$

$$X_j \in \{0, 1\}; j = 1, \ldots, n, \tag{7.35}$$

$$Z_i \in \{0, 1\} \; ; \; i = 1, \ldots, m. \tag{7.36}$$

Assumption above the objective of this model is to minimize total penalty costs of points that their demand is not satisfied. Equation (7.32) ensures that Z_i is 1 if $\sum a_{ij} X_j$ is zero; it means that their demand is not satisfied. Equation (7.33) ensures that the number of facilities can not be more than P.

If costs of locating facilities at different points are different, it means we have

F_j = the cost of locating a facility at candidate point j.

We can replace constraint of the number of facilities represented by (7.33) with capital constraint as follows:

$$\sum_{j=1}^{n} F_j X_j \leq C. \tag{7.37}$$

C is minimum capital to locate facilities (Mirchandani and Francis 1990).

7.3.2 Minimizing Costs of Locating Facilities and Costs Arisen from Not Covering Demand Points

In this condition, there is no limitation to number of facilities (or maximum budget of locating facilities), in other words the problem is endogenous.

The objective is to minimize sum of locating costs and penalty costs arisen from not covering demand points.

Model of this problem is as follows:

$$\text{Min} \sum_{j=1}^{n} F_j X_j + \sum_{i=1}^{m} p_i Z_i, \tag{7.38}$$

Subject to

$$\sum_{j=1}^{n} a_{ij} X_j + Z_i \geq 1 \,;\, i = 1, \ldots, m, \tag{7.39}$$

$$X_j \in \{0, 1\}; \quad j = 1, \ldots, n, \tag{7.40}$$

$$Z_i \in \{0, 1\}; \quad j = 1, \ldots, m. \tag{7.41}$$

F_j is cost of locating a facility at point j and Pi is penalty of not covering demand point i in (7.37). Equation (7.38) ensures that Z_i is 1 if $\sum a_{ij} X_j$ is zero, it means that demand point i is not covered.

7.3.3 Maximum Covering Location Problems (Berman et al. 2003)

One of most famous partial covering problem is maximum covering location problem.

This problem proposed by Church and ReVelle (1974), they limited candidate locating points to the nodes in network (Berman et al. 2003).

The objective of this problem is to maximize total satisfied demands. In this problem, maximum number of facilities is limited (the problem is exogenous).

The model is as follows:

$$\text{Max} \sum_{i} h_i Z_i, \tag{7.42}$$

Subject to

$$Z_i \leq \sum_j a_{ij} X_j; \, \forall i, \tag{7.43}$$

$$\sum_j X_j \leq P, \tag{7.44}$$

$$X_j = 0, 1; \, \forall j, \tag{7.45}$$

$$Z_i = 0, 1; \quad \forall i. \tag{7.46}$$

Equation (7.42) states that we want to minimize total demands of satisfied demand points. h_i is demand point i and Z_i is one if demand of point i is covered.

This model similar to the classic covering problem, we can reduce the size of problem using (column deletion rule) but we can not use any of (row deletion rules) (see Sect. 7.2.1).

7.3.4 Expected Maximum Covering Problem (Daskin 1995)

So far, we assumed that in order to cover each demand point, it is enough that each facility be located in a distance lower than or equal to coverage distance from that demand point. This assumption is valid if the capacity of facilities is assumed to be unlimited. Now consider a simple network in Fig. 7.9. Assume that $Dc = 8$.

The amount of demands and distance of demand points are shown in the picture. The reduced feasible solution space of this problem is including of points A and B and two intersection points shown by Fig. 7.10.

For example if we locate a facility at point $j = 2$ and assuming that the capacity is unlimited, total demand of network (maximum demand) will be covered.

Now assume that the facility can service only one of demand points each time. In this condition if demand points A and B need this facility simultaneously the facility can service one of demand points in practice and the other point will not be covered.

Thus if the capacity of the facilities is limited, they must be available in addition to cover demand points. But since availability or unavailability of facilities is not precisely predictable each time, the objective of this problem is to maximize expected coverage by available facilities.

$$q = \frac{\text{Sum of hours that facilities worked in a period}}{\text{Number of facilities used}}.$$

Assume that the probability of being unavailable for each facility at any moment is similar and equal to q. the amount of q can be estimated using past data. A way to estimate amount of q is as follows:

Assume that the number of facilities that can cover point i is n_i. Thus probability of covering demand point i is equal to probability that at least one of facilities be available

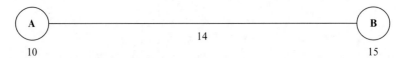

Fig. 7.9 The network with $Dc = 8$ (Daskin 1995)

Fig. 7.10 The reduced network (Daskin 1995)

Then we have:
$$1 - q^{n_i}. \qquad (7.47)$$

Thus expected value of covered demand is:
$$\sum_{i=1}^{m} h_i (1 - q^{n_i}). \qquad (7.48)$$

Above statement is not linear, but using (7.48) and property of objective function, it can be easily transformed to linear form.

$$1 - q^{n_i} = (1 - q)(1 + q + q^2 + \ldots + q^{n_i - 1}). \qquad (7.49)$$

Z_{ik}: is 1 If the demand point i is covered at least k times, otherwise is 0

P = Maximum number of facilities
X_j = number of located facilities at candidate locating point j

Note that X_j is not necessarily zero or one. Indeed the more number of facilities at a candidate locating point, the more probability of availability of at least one facility for covered demand points by that point. Now we place instead of $1 - q^n i$

$$(1 - q)(Z_{i1} + q Z_{i2} + \ldots + q^{p-1} Z_{ip}). \qquad (7.50)$$

And we have the constraint below:

$$\sum_{k=1}^{p} Z_{ik} = \sum_j a_{ij} X_j. \qquad (7.51)$$

It means the number of Z_{ik} that is one, is exactly equal to the number of facilities that can cover demand point i.

Consider graph in Fig. 7.11:
Assume that the coverage distance is 8 and two facilities are located at A and B. Thus right hand side of equality (7.52) for demand point A is 1 and we have:

$$Z_{A,1} + Z_{A,2} = 1. \qquad (7.52)$$

Now we should prove that optimal solution is necessarily $Z_{A,1} = 1$, $Z_{A,2} = 0$ and Solution $Z_{A,1} = 0$ and $Z_{A,2} = 1$ is not candidate of optimality. Since the objective function is max and coefficient Z_{ik} decreases with increasing k, the model prefers to

Fig. 7.11 Graph of covered demand (Daskin 1995)

Z_{ik} with smaller k be one and thus for example in this problem, solution $Z_{A,1} = 0$ and $Z_{A,2} = 1$ is not candidate of optimality.

The model of expected maximum covering problem is as follows (Daskin 1995):

$$\text{Max} \sum_i h_i \sum_{k=1}^{P} (1-q)(q^{k-1} Z_{ik}), \tag{7.53}$$

Subject to

$$\sum_{k=1}^{P} Z_{ix} = \sum_{j=1}^{n} a_{ij} X_j ; \forall i \tag{7.54}$$

$$\sum_{j=1}^{P} X_j \leq P, \tag{7.55}$$

$$X_j \geq 0 \quad and \quad \text{integer;} \forall j, \tag{7.56}$$

$$Z_{i,k} = 0, 1; \forall i, k. \tag{7.57}$$

7.3.5 Maximum Covering Problem Considering Non-Ascending Coverage Function (Berman et al. 2003)

One of presumptions of covering problem is that demand points in a critical distance are covered and they will not be covered out of this distance.

For example in fire station location problem assume that the coverage distance is 3 miles. Thus if the distance of a residential region from the fire station is 2.9 miles, in classic view of covering problem any amount of demand can not be covered by that station. This point of view seems unreal in practice. Berman et al. (2003) developed a kind of covering problem that two coverage bounds replaced with coverage distance.

As we can see in Fig. 7.12 if the distance between demand point and candidate locating point as less than lower bound of coverage (l) this point can be covered totally. If their distance is more than upper bound (u), the demand point will not be covered and if their distance is between two critical bounds a proportion of its demand will be covered (f).

Berman et al. (2003) also proved that if the function f is convex the solution space of problem will be reduced to a set of demand points and intersection points. But here intersection points are points that their distances from at least one of demand points are equal to coverage lower bound or coverage upper bound.

We assume that function f is a linear function and define:

$$f(d(i,j)) = \frac{u - d(i,j)}{u - l}; \quad i = 1, \ldots, m; \quad j = 1, \ldots, n. \tag{7.58}$$

7 Covering Problem

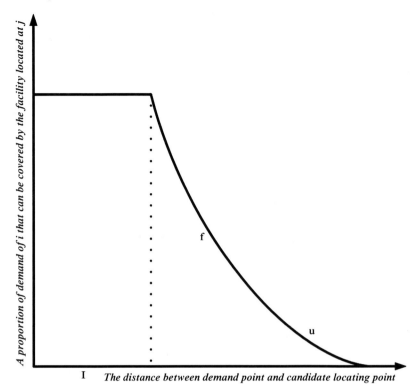

Fig. 7.12 Relationship of D_c with demand will be covered (Berman et al. 2003)

Thus the proportion of demand of point i that can be covered by candidate locating point j is equal to:

$$C(i,j) = \begin{cases} 1 & ; \quad if\ d(i,j) \leq l \\ \frac{u-d(i,j)}{u-l} & ; \quad if\ l < d(i,j) \leq u \\ 0 & ; \quad if\ d(i,j) > l \end{cases}.$$

$C(i,j)$s are parameters of problem and should be determined before solving it.

Assume that h_i is the demand of point i and P is maximum number of facilities. The model of this problem is as follows:

$$\text{Max} \sum_{i=1}^{m} h_j \, \underset{j}{Max} \{C(i,j)X_j\}. \tag{7.59}$$

Subject to

$$\sum_{j=1}^{n} X_j \leq P, \tag{7.60}$$

$$X_j = 0, 1; \quad j = 1, \ldots, n. \tag{7.61}$$

Equation (7.59) for each demand point i, choose a point among candidate locating points j, nearer to demand point i and have more $C(i, j)$.

This value is indeed maximum coverage that demand point i receives from different facilities. As we can see the objective function of problem states sum of covered demands.

Equation (7.60) limits maximum number of facilities to P.

Note that the above model can be transformed easily to linear model below (Berman et al. 2003):

$$\text{Max} \sum_i h_i Y_i, \tag{7.62}$$

Subject to

$$\sum_{j=1}^{n} X_j \le P \tag{7.63}$$

$$Y_i = \sum_{j=1}^{n} C(i, j) Z_{ij}, \tag{7.64}$$

$$\sum_{j=1}^{n} Z_{ij} = 1, \tag{7.65}$$

$$Z_{ij} \le X_j, \tag{7.66}$$

$$Y_i \ge 0 \qquad i = 1, 2, \ldots, m, \tag{7.67}$$

$$X_j = 0, 1 \qquad j = 1, 2, \ldots, n, \tag{7.68}$$

$$Z_{ij} = 0, 1 \qquad i = 1, 2, \ldots, m \ \& \ j = 1, 2, \ldots, n. \tag{7.69}$$

7.4 The Bi-Objective Covering Tour Problem (Jozefowieza et al. 2007)

The aim is to investigate the solution of a multi-objective routing problem, namely the bi-objective covering tour problem (*BOCTP*), by means of a cooperative strategy involving a multi-objective evolutionary algorithm and a single-objective branch-and-cut algorithm.

The BOCTP aims to determine a minimal length tour for a subset of nodes while also minimizing the greatest distance between the nodes of another set and the nearest visited node. The BOCTP can be formally described as follows: let $G = (V \cup W, E)$ be an undirected graph, where $V \cup W$ is the vertex set, and $E = \{(v_i, v_j) | v_i, v_j \in V \cup W, i < j\}$ is the edge set. Vertex v_1 is a depot is the set of vertices that can be visited $\subseteq V$ is the set of vertices that must be visited ($v \in T$), and W is the set of vertices that must be covered. A distance matrix $C = (c_{ij})$, satisfying triangle inequality, is defined for E. The BOCTP consists of define a tour for a subset of V, which contains all the vertices from T, while at the same time optimizing the following two objectives: (a) the minimization of the tour length and (b) the minimization of the cover. The cover of a solution is defined as the greatest distance between a node $w \in W$, and the nearest visited node $v \in V$.

One generic application of the CTP involves designing a tour in a network whose vertices represent.

Points that can be visited, and from which the places that are not on the tour can be easily reached.

For instance, Toregas et al. (1971) have used the CTP to model the determination of a tour for a mobile.

Medical facility in an area of Ghana, where every village cannot be reached (Jozefowieza et al. 2007).

7.5 A Fuzzy Multi Objective Covering Based Vehicle Location Model for Emergency Services (Araz et al. 2007)

Timeliness is one of the most important objectives that reflect the quality of emergency services such as ambulance and firefighting systems. To provide timeliness, system administrators may increase the number of service vehicles available. Unfortunately, increasing the number of vehicles is generally impossible due to capital constraints. In such a case, the efficient deployment of emergency service vehicles becomes a crucial issue. The objectives considered in the model are maximization of the population covered by one vehicle, maximization of the population with backup coverage and increasing the service level by minimizing the total travel distance from locations at a distance bigger than a pre specified distance standard for all zones.

The model addresses the issue of determining the best base locations for a limited number of vehicles so that the service level objectives are optimized. Three of the important surrogates that reflect the quality of emergency service systems are considered as objectives in the model:

- Maximization of the population covered by one vehicle
- Maximization of the population with backup coverage and
- Minimization of the total travel distance from locations at a distance bigger than a pre specified distance standard for all zones.

The proposed model allows the incorporation of decision maker's imprecise aspiration levels for the goals by means of FGP approach.

Timeliness can be measured in many ways such as:

- Minimization of the total or average time to serve all emergency calls;
- Minimization of the maximum travel time to any single call;
- Maximization of area coverage (ensures that as many zones in the area as possible is covered within S minutes of travel)
- Maximization of call coverage (ensures that as many calls in the area as possible is covered within minutes of travel).

A new model, formed by considering maximal backup coverage model of Hogan and ReVelle (1986) and capacitated maximal covering model of Pirkul and Schilling (1991) as the base, is introduced in this section. The proposed model formulation is stated to allocate a fixed number of emergency service vehicles to previously defined locations so that three important service level objectives can be achieved.

$$a_{ij} = \begin{cases} 1 & \text{If } d_{ij} \leq S \\ 0 & \text{If } d_{ij} > S \end{cases} \qquad e_{ij} = \begin{cases} 1 & \text{If } d_{ij} > S \\ 0 & \text{If } d_{ij} \leq S \end{cases}$$

$$Y_i = \begin{cases} 1 & \text{If demand node i is covered once} \\ 0 & \text{Otherwise} \end{cases}.$$

where U_i is the fraction of population in zone i covered by more than one vehicle, h_i is the population in zone i, P_{ij} is the fraction of population in zone i served by a facility/facilities located in zone j, d_{ij} is the travel distance or time from j to i, S is the distance or time standard, C is the number of vehicles to be located, and k_j is the workload capacity for a vehicle located in zone j. The mathematical statement of the proposed model is as follows:

$$\text{Max } Z_1 = \sum h_i Y_i, \qquad (7.70)$$

$$\text{Max } Z_2 = \sum_i h_i U_i, \qquad (7.71)$$

$$\text{Min } Z_3 = \sum_i \sum_j e_{ij} h_i d_{ij} P_{ij}, \qquad (7.72)$$

Subject to

$$\sum_j a_{ij} P_{ij} - Y_i - U_i \geq 0 \; \forall i \in I, \qquad (7.73)$$

$$U_i - Y_i \leq 0 \; \forall i \in I, \qquad (7.74)$$

$$\sum_j P_{ij} \geq 1 \; \forall i \in I, \qquad (7.75)$$

$$\sum_i h_i P_{ij} \leq K_j X_j \; \forall j \in J, \qquad (7.76)$$

$$\sum_j X_j \leq C, \qquad (7.77)$$

$$U_i \leq 1 \; \forall i \in I, \qquad (7.78)$$

$$X_j \geq 1 \; \& \text{ integer } \forall j \in J, \qquad (7.79)$$

$$Y_j = [0, 1] \; \forall j \in J, \qquad (7.80)$$

$$P_{ij} \leq 1 \; \forall (i, j). \qquad (7.81)$$

In this model, first and second objectives maximize the population covered by at least one vehicle and the population with backup coverage, respectively. Third objective provides the maximization of the service level by minimizing the total travel distance from locations at a distance bigger than S for all zones. Populations of the zones are included as weights in the third objective. The first two constraints; determine which zones receive backup coverage. The first constraint set determine the number of facilities within the coverage distance of a zone. The second constraint ensures that backup coverage can only be provided if first coverage already exists. Equation (7.75) provides that the entire population at each zone will be assigned to some facility. Equation (7.76) ensures that the total population assigned to a facility does not exceed the capacity of that facility. This constraint also ensures that population will only be assigned to facility sites which have facilities actually located at them. Equation (7.77) limits the total number of facilities to be located. In (7.78), U_i, is considered as a continuous variable to allow fractional backup coverage for a zone. We restrict the value of U_i in the range of [0, 1] so that as much zone as possible can take the advantage of having backup coverage. As can be seen, locating more than one vehicle in a zone is allowed with (7.79). In contrast to the basic location covering models it is no longer assumed that the entire population in a zone will be served by its nearest facility. In this formulation it is also assumed that the entire population in a zone does not have to be assigned to the same vehicle and that some portion of the population in a zone may be covered and the rest of it not covered. It is provided by using the continuous form of the assignment variable, p_{ij}.

7.6 Solving Methods

7.6.1 Exact Methods

7.6.1.1 Solving Total Covering Problem in Tree Networks (Francis et al. 1992)

In total covering problem we want to cover total demand by minimum number of facilities. We assume that each demand point has its own coverage distance.

As we mentioned before a demand point is covered if at least one facility is located at its coverage distance. Thus in this problem it should be located at least one facility at coverage distance of each demand point.

In the following we explain the optimal solution algorithm of this problem by an example.

Consider tree network shown by Fig. 7.13 (Francis et al. 1992), we want to cover all demand points. The distances between demand points are shown on the edges of network.

We suppose that the wavy lines emanating from vertices 1 through 5 are strings whose lengths are the coverage distances. For example the coverage distance of node 1, is 10.

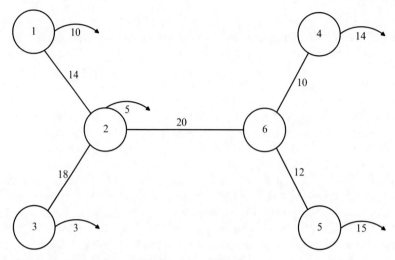

Fig. 7.13 The covering of tree network (Francis et al. 1992)

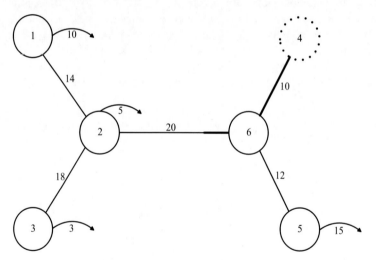

Fig. 7.14 Coverage distance of node 4 (Francis et al. 1992)

1 Suppose that we can locate a facility at any points on the network. The algorithm begins from an end node of network and continues its string. As we can see in Fig. 7.14 this string passing node 6 continues 4 units (the weighted line).

Now we eliminate node 4 and consider the remained part of string as a new string and connect it to node 6 shown by Fig. 7.15.

We do the same for node 5 shown by Fig. 7.16:

Now node 6 acts as an end node, we consider shortest string connected to this node. Since this string doesn't reach to the adjacent node (node 2) we locate the first facility at the end of this string and then eliminate node 6 shown by Fig. 7.17.

7 Covering Problem

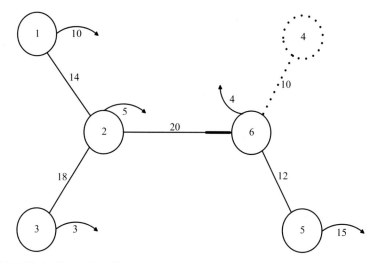

Fig. 7.15 Eliminating node 4 (Francis et al. 1992)

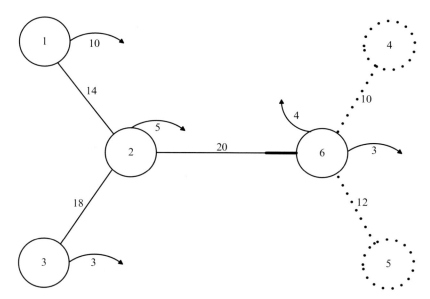

Fig. 7.16 Eliminating node 5 (Francis et al. 1992)

With locating the first facility at $X1$ node 4, 5 and 6 are covered. Now we begin from one of end nodes again. For example we continue the string connected to node 1 on the arc between 2 and 3. Since the end of this string does not reach to node 2, we locate the second facility at the end of this string and eliminate node 1 shown by Fig. 7.18.

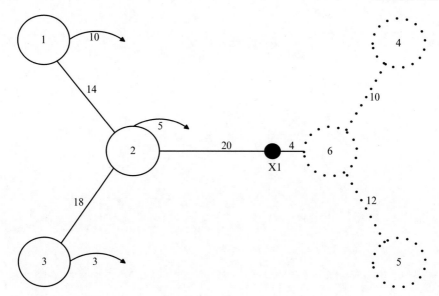

Fig. 7.17 Cating the first facility (Francis et al. 1992)

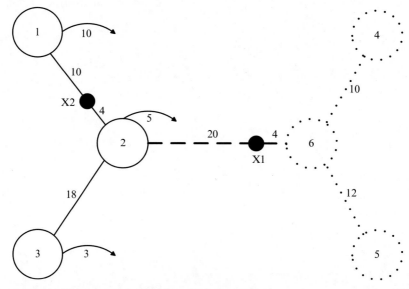

Fig. 7.18 Locating the second facility (Francis et al. 1992)

Since the end of string connected to node 2, reaches $X2$, thus the second facility can cover demand of point 2 and we can eliminate this node too shown by Fig. 7.19.

Now we continue the string connected to node 3 toward node 2. Since the end of this string does not reach to node 2 we can locate the third facility at the end of this

7 Covering Problem

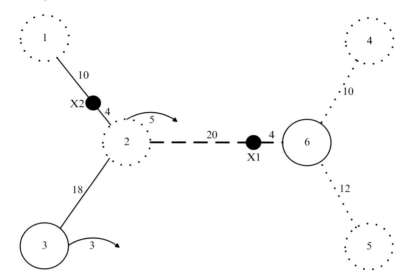

Fig. 7.19 Eliminating node 2 (Francis et al. 1992)

string and then all demand points of network are covered by minimum number of facilities (3 facilities).

The steps of algorithm are as follows:

- A: Continue strings connected to the end points toward the common node connected to them.
- B: Locate a facility at the end of strings that is not reached to the adjacent node and consider the remained part of it as a new string and eliminate the end nodes.
- C: Continue the shortest string connected to the common node toward its adjacent node if this string passed the adjacent node, consider the remained part of it as a new string, otherwise locate a facility at the end of it and eliminate that common node.
- D: Do these steps until all demand points be covered.

2. Consider that we can locate only at nodes of network. With a simple revision in algorithm, we can reach to optimal solution of this problem. For this aim, for nodes that the end of their string does not reach to adjacent node we locate a facility at the end of string, and for nodes that their string passes the adjacent node locate a facility at the adjacent node.

7.6.1.2 Reduction Rules in Classic Total Covering Problem (Daskin 1995)

When all of the fixed costs are equal (i.e., $f_j = 1$), we can often reduce the size of the problem using a variety of reduction rules.

Fig. 7.20 An example (Daskin 1995)

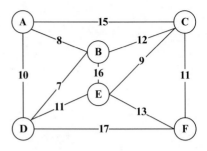

Consider network shown by Fig. 7.20 (Daskin 1995), the coverage distance is $Dc = 11$:

We begin with a column reduction rule. Consider two columns j and k. If $a_{ij} \leq a_{ik}$ for all demand nodes i and $a_{ij} < a_{ik}$ for at least one demand node i, then location k covers all demands covered by location j. We say that location k dominates location j. In this case, column j may be eliminated, since, if we were to locate at node j, we could always do at least as well by locating at node k. In addition, we can then set $X_j = 0$. For example, in the problem above, candidate site D dominates nodes A and B (since a facility located at D will cover nodes A, B, D, and E, while a facility located at A will only cover nodes A, B, and D, and a facility at B will only cover nodes A, B, and D). Thus, we can set $X_A = X_B = 0$. Similarly, candidate site C dominates site F (since a facility located at C covers demand nodes C, E, and F, while a facility at $-F$ covers only nodes C and F). We therefore set $X_F = 0$. (Note that we can also eliminate all but one of a set of equivalent sites, where sites j and k are said to be equivalent if $a_{ij} = a_{ik}$ for all demand nodes i.) After the column reductions described above, the problem becomes

$$\text{Min } X_C + X_D + X_E, \tag{7.82}$$

Subject to

$$X_D \geq 1, \tag{7.83}$$
$$X_D \geq 1, \tag{7.84}$$
$$X_D + X_E \geq 1, \tag{7.85}$$
$$X_D + X_E \geq 1, \tag{7.86}$$
$$X_C + X_D + X_E \geq 1, \tag{7.87}$$
$$X_C \geq 1, \tag{7.88}$$
$$X_C, X_D, X_E = 0, 1. \tag{7.89}$$

We now consider row reduction techniques which allow us to eliminate rows from the problem. Consider row i. If $\sum_j a_{ij} = 1$, then there is only one facility site that

7 Covering Problem

can cover node i. In that case, we find the location j^* such that $a_{ij}^* = 1$ and set $X_j^* = 1$. We can then eliminate any row in which X_j^* appears, since, with $X_j^* = 1$, those constraints will be satisfied (i.e., those nodes will be covered by the facility at location j^*). For example, in the problem above, there is only one nonzero coefficient in the first constraint. Therefore, we know that X_D must equal 1. We set $X_D = 1$ and then eliminate the constraint corresponding to rows A, B, D, and E, since these demand nodes will all be covered by the facility at location D. Similarly, the constraint for node F has only one nonzero coefficient. Thus, we can set $Xc = 1$ and remove the rows corresponding to nodes C and F. At this point, there are no remaining rows, and the problem becomes the trivial problem of minimizing X_E subject to the integrality constraint that X_E equals either 0 or 1. Clearly, we *set* $X_E = 0$. At this point, we know the optimal value of all of the decision variables and the problem is solved.

Note that despite the fact that this is an NP-complete problem whose optimal solution is technically difficult to obtain, we have been able to solve the problem without resorting to any formal optimization technique (such as linear programming).

The row and column reduction rules outlined above may be used iteratively until neither rule allows us to eliminate a column or a row. Often, application of these rules will allow us to solve the problem completely. This is not always the case, however, as the following example shows. This example also allows us to introduce an additional row reduction rule. In this example, we consider the network shown in Fig. 7.20, but now use a coverage distance of 18 (*i.e.*, $Dc = 18$).

After using the column reduction rule outlined above, we can eliminate the columns corresponding to candidate sites A and F (and set $X_A = X_F = 0$).

Since no row has only a single element, we cannot use, the row reduction rule outlined above to eliminate any rows. However, we can use a second row reduction rule. Consider two rows m and n. If $a_{mj} \leq a_{nj}$ for all candidate sites j and $a_{mj} < a_{nj}$ for at least one candidate site j. then we can eliminate row n. This is so because the requirement that demand node m be covered will guarantee that node n is also covered. (Any facility site that covers demand node m also covers demand node n). This rule allows us to eliminate the rows corresponding to nodes B and E, since any facility that covers node A (i.e., a facility located at node B, C, or D) will also cover nodes B and E. (As before, we can eliminate all but one of a set of equivalent demand nodes, where demand nodes m and n are said to be equivalent if $a_{mj} = a_{nj}$ for all candidate sites j.).

Unfortunately, we cannot reduce the size of this problem any further. Repeated application of the column reduction rule and the two row reduction rules to this problem will not eliminate any more rows or columns. Thus, we must find some other way to solve this problem. One way of doing so is to ignore the integrality constraint and replace it by a nonnegative constraint.

If we solve the resulting linear programming problem, we find $X_B = X_c = X_D = X_E = 1/3$. The objective function is 4/3. Clearly, this is not an all-integer solution; it does not solve the original set covering problem.

7.6.1.3 The Branch and Bound Method (Daskin 1995)

To ensure that we obtain an all-integer solution, additional techniques will generally be required. One approach is to use branch and bound.

After reducing the problem size using above rules, we can solve the model using optimal solving methods such as branch and bound or Balas algorithm (Daskin 1995).

7.6.2 Heuristic Methods

7.6.2.1 The Greedy Adding Algorithm (Daskin 1995)

This algorithm and its variants may be used to solve (at least approximately) a large number of other location problems. The algorithm is known as a greedy algorithm since it does what is best at each step of the algorithm without looking ahead to see how the current decisions will impact on later decisions and alternatives.

If we were to locate only one facility (*i.e.*, $P = 1$), we could solve the problem optimally by simply evaluating how many demands each candidate site covers (candidate site j covers $\sum_i a_{ij} h_i$ demands) and selecting the site that covers the most demands (Daskin 1995).

7.6.2.2 Lagrangian Relaxation (Daskin 1995)

Lagrangian relaxation is an approach to solving difficult problems (such as integer programming problems). The approach outlined below is cast in terms of solving a maximization problem. The approach involves the following general steps:

1. Relax one or more constraints by multiplying the constraint(s) by Lagrange multiplier(s) and bringing the constraint(s) into the objective function.
2. Solve the resulting relaxed problem to find the optimal values of the original decision variables (in the relaxed problem)
3. (Optional) Use the resulting decision variables from the solution to the relaxed problem found in step 2 to find a feasible solution to the original problem.
4. Use the solution obtained in step 2 to compute an upper bound on the best value of the objective function.
5. Examine the solution obtained in step 2 and determine which of the relaxed constraints are violated. Use some method to modify the Lagrange multipliers in such a way that the violated constraints are less likely to be violated on the subsequent iteration. After new Lagrange multipliers have been identified, return to step 2 (Daskin 1995).

7.6.3 Metaheuristic Methods

7.6.3.1 Grasp Algorithm (Bautista and Pereira 2006)

The *GRASP* metaheuristic is a random iterative optimization procedure. This metaheuristic has been used to solve diverse problems of optimization, including scheduling, route design, logic, location, graphs, assignment, manufacturing, transport, and telecommunications problems, among others.

Each iteration in the metaheuristic is made up of two phases: a constructive and a local search phase. During the constructive phase, the algorithm uses a randomized greedy heuristic to obtain an initial solution to the problem. This is based on modified greedy procedures, where the greedy rule is substituted by a random selection among a limited list of candidates showing the best values for the greedy selection rule.

On the other hand, the local search phase permits exploration of the generated solution neighborhood in an attempt to find higher-quality solutions. After local search, the best solution found during this phase is compared to the best-known solution, and substitutes it if the objective value is better than the previously known. Once a stopping criterion is met, the best solution obtained during the procedure is returned.

In order to solve an optimization problem by means of a *GRASP* procedure, it is necessary to define at least the following elements integrated in the heuristics:

- The randomized constructive procedure used during this procedure,
- The neighborhood of the solution and the procedure to investigate it,
- The stopping criterion usually associated to a maximum number of iterations.

One of the major advantages of the *GRASP* metaheuristic is how easy this general scheme may be adapted to the solution of particular problems. GRASP requires few parameters, basically the stopping criterion, associated to the maximum number of iterations, and a rule to construct the restricted candidate list (*RCL*) during the constructive phase (Bautista and Pereira 2006).

7.7 Case Study

7.7.1 Combination of MCDM and Covering Techniques (Farahani and Asgari 2007)

In this paper, locating some warehouses as distribution centers (DCs) in a real-world military logistics system will be Investigated. There are two objectives: finding the least number of DCs and locating them in the best possible locations. The first objective implies the minimum cost of locating the facilities and the latter expresses the quality of the DCs locations, which is evaluated by studying the value of appropriate attributes affecting the quality of a location. Quality of a location depends on a number of attributes; so the value of each location is determined by using multi attribute decision making models, by considering the feasible alternatives, the related attributes and their weights according to decision maker's (DM) point of view. Then, regarding the obtained values and the minimum number of DCs, the two objective functions are formed. Constraints imposed on these two objectives cover all centers, which must be supported by the DCs. Using multiple objective decision making techniques, the locations of DCs are determined. In the final phase, we use a simple set partitioning model to assign each supported center to only one of the located DCs.

The supply chain is composed of three types of facilities:

- Origins;
- Supportive centers;
- Supported centers.

The objective functions and the constraints of the problem are as follows:

Objective function 1: Maximizing the utility of the selected locations. Utility of a potential point depends on 23 attributes that will be explained later.
Objective function 2: Minimizing the number of supportive centers.
Constraint 1: All of the supported centers must be covered (coverage criteria will be presented later) by supportive centers.
Constraint 2: Each of the supported centers must be supported by one and only one of the located supportive centers.
Phase 1. Determining all attributes that influence the utility of a location.
Phase 2. In this phase, we use all possible alternatives as initial inputs of our process.
Phase 3. Using *MADM* techniques to assess the quality of the locations Normally.
Phase 4. Using a multiple objective set covering model to find the best locations. Covering problems hold a central place in location theory. In these problems, we are given a set of demand points and a set of potential sites for locating facilities. A demand point is said to be covered by a facility if it lies within a pre-specified distance of that facility.

Set covering model is as follows (Francis et al. 1992; Daskin 1995; Mirchandani and Francis 1990):

$$\text{Min } Z = \sum_{i=1}^{m} X_i, \tag{7.90}$$

Subject to

$$\sum_{i=1}^{m} a_{ik} X_i \geq 1; k = 1, 2, \ldots, n, \tag{7.91}$$

$$X_i \in \{0, 1\} ; i = 1, 2, \ldots, m, \tag{7.92}$$

7 Covering Problem

x_i is a binary variable that is equal to one if the feasible alternative $_i$ (a potential location for supportive centers) is suitable for locating supportive centers; otherwise it is equal to 0. Equation (7.90) ensures that the minimum number of supportive centers are located. Equation (7.90) ensures that all of the supported centers are covered. In this expression $A = [a_{ki}]$ is called covering matrix; a_{ki} is equal to 1 if a potential supportive center located in location i ($x_i = 1$) is able to cover the supported center located in location k. Generating a covering matrix $A = [a_{ki}]$ is based on a factor called critical distance. Critical distance is the maximum time or distance that a supportive center can serve. Covering models focus on the worst-case behavior of the system (*Daskin 1995*). In our problem, we have used critical distances equal to 8, 12 or 24 h. Here, there are a number of 233 supported centers. We have designed a modified set covering model with two objective functions as follows (Model 0):

$$\text{Min } Z_1 = \sum_{i=1}^{33} x_i, \qquad (7.93)$$

$$\text{Max } Z_2 = \sum_{i=1}^{33} c_i x_i, \qquad (7.94)$$

Subject to

$$\sum_{i=1}^{33} a_{ki} x_i \geq 1; k = 1, \ldots, 233 \qquad (7.95)$$

$$x_i \in \{0, 1\} \, i = 1, \ldots, 33, \qquad (7.96)$$

where c_i has been already defined as output of Phase 3. Equation (7.93) is similar to (7.90). Equation (7.94) maximizes the quality of the selected facilities. Equation (7.95) is similar to (7.90). In this problem, it can be considered three scenarios as follows:

Scenario 0 (Model 0): The problem is solved for the first time and no supportive center already exists. In this case, the model is the same as Model 0.

Scenario 1 (Model 1): There already exist some active supportive centers (existing facilities) and all of these supportive centers must carry on operating. In this case, we treat the location of these existing facilities as new locations. But in Phase 4 we use Model 1 instead of
Model 0 in which we have added the following constraints:
$x_i = 1$
$\forall i \in \{\text{set of existing facilities }\}$

Scenario 2 (Model 2): There already exist some active supportive centers (existing facilities) and we try to keep them active if possible. In this case, we consider the location of these existing facilities as new locations. However, in Phase 4 we use Model 2 instead of Model 0 in which we have used the following objective function instead of (7.93):

Where $n1$ shows the number of existing supportive centers and $(n - n_1)$ shows the number of new supportive centers. ε is a parameter that tries to increase the coefficient of binary variables of the new facilities; this forces the objective function to use existing facilities as much as possible. Our computational results and sensitivity analysis show that $\varepsilon = 2/n$ is an appropriate value in this case.

References

Araz C, Hasan S, Irem O (2007) A fuzzy multi objective covering-based vehicle location model for emergency services. Comput Oper Res 34:705–726

Bautista J, Pereira J (2006) A GRASP algorithm to solve the unicost set covering problem. Comput Oper Res 34(10):3162–3173

Berman O, Krass D, Drezner Z (2003) The gradual covering decay location problem on a network. Eur J Oper Res 151(3):474–480

Chiang CI, Hwang MJ, Liu YH (2005) An alternative formulation for certain fuzzy set-covering problems. Math Comput Model 42:363–365

Church R, ReVelle C (1974) the maximal covering location problem. Papers Region Sci Assoc 32:101–118

Daskin MS (1995) Network and discrete location: Models, algorithms, and applications. Wiley, New York

Farahani R, Asgari N (2007) Combination of MCDM and covering techniques in a hierarchical model for facility location: A case study. Eur J Oper Res 176(3):1839–1858

Francis RL, McGinnis LF, White JA (1992) Facility layout and location: An analytical approach. Prentice Hall, Englewood Cliffs, NJ

Hogan K, ReVelle C (1986) Concepts and applications of backup coverage. Manage Sci 32:1434–1444

Hwang HS (2004) A stochastic set-covering location model for both ameliorating and deteriorating items. Comput Ind Eng 46:313–319

Jans R, Degraeve Z (2008) A note on a symmetrical set covering problem: the lottery problem. Eur J Oper Res 186(1):104–110

Jozefowieza N, Semetb F, Talbia EG (2007) The bi-objective covering tour problem. Comput Oper Res 34:1929–1942

Mirchandani PB, Francis RL (1990) Discrete location theory. Wiley, New York

Pirkul H, Schilling DA (1991) The maximal covering location problem with capacities on total workload. Manage Sci 37:233–248.

Toregas C, Swain R, ReVelle C, Bergman L (1971) The location of emergency service facilities. Oper Res 19:1363–1373

Chapter 8
Median Location Problem

Masoomeh Jamshidi

The median problem is considered as the main problems identified with the location-allocation problems (see Chap. 5). These problems are intended to find the median points among the candidate points, so that the sum of costs can be minimized through this target function. These kinds of problems include the establishment of the public services including schools, hospitals, firefighting, Ambulance, technical audit stations of cars, and etc. The target function in the median problems is of the minisum kind. In fact in these problems we try to quantify the sum of distances (costs).

We call the first algorithm to be considered the Chinese algorithm. Apparently, the problem that motivated the development of the Chinese algorithm was the location of a threshing floor, used to separate the wheat from the chaff after a wheat harvest. In this case the tree network represents a road network, with the vertices being the location of wheat fields. The weight for each vertex represents the amount of wheat to be transported to and from the field and the threshing floor. Locating the threshing floor at the 1-median causes the total cost of transporting the wheat to and from the threshing floor to be minimized (Francis et al. 1992).

In median problems, there is the location finding in the kind of network or graph. The discussion of median problems is focused on graph theory and cannot be beyond the network or graph.

Fermat (seventeenth century) proposed one problem in order to minimize the sum of distances. In this problem, one rectangular was considered (three points on the plane) and the aim was to find a point among three points, so that the sum of distances among the chosen point could be minimized through three angles of the rectangular. The problem was developed by Alfred Weber and again was introduced in twentieth century. In this problem, Weber called them as the clients demand through applying the weight on the angles points of rectangular, and called the median point as the servicing point. He defined the servicing point among three pointof clients demand, so that the sum of distances can be minimized. This problem is called as the first problem of the location-Allocation (see Chap. 5). Later the problem proposed by Weber was introduced for multiple servicing states (multiple facilities) and developed more than three points. The problem introduced by Weber was connection problem. N can be achieved through choosing the median points on apexes points of the graph or the nodes of network. This problem was quite similar to the candidate of the correlated problem proposed by Weber. Again the problem was developed by Hakimi (1964), and through application of the weight on the graph, he began to find the P point on it in order to minimize the sum of the weighted distance from the points.

8.1 Classification

8.1.1 1-Median

The median problems are intended to find the location of one facility on the network, so that the total cost can be minimum.

8.1.2 P-Median

The P-median problems it is a disconnected problem and we can choose the candidate points through it.

8.1.3 An Example

Now, with an example, we want showing that how we can change continues problem to discrete problem and find feasible solution. Assume in the city we want to find some location for change store. This problem is a continuous problem. For changing this problem into a discrete problem, we can divide the city into smaller regions. These regions can be municipal regions or any other region. In every region, we determine the demand for chain stores. If we divide the city into five regions, the continuous map of city with its demands will be changed into a problem with five demand points. Determining the center of every region and putting whole of the demand on that point, the problem changes into network. For determining the center of every region we can use the weight of every region, for example the center of region can be in the east or west of region of course the location of facility is only on nodes. Consequently, we face with discrete network. Figure 8.1 is the schematic representation of this network.

In this network, the nodes are considered among two points of supply. The supply can be in one of the following forms:

- *Static demand.* That is the demand defined in a fixed or definite form
- *Probable demand.* The demand which involves a variable with a gravity function
- *Dynamic demand.* The demand of network (defined in a function of time.

8 Median Location Problem

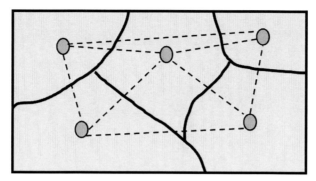

Fig. 8.1 Distance–cost relationship in three conditions

Since in modeling design, the demand of network in real problems depends on the population, we can argue that the dynamic demand is more correct and true than any other kind of demands. These suggestions can lead us to the proper answers.

8.2 Mathematical Models

8.2.1 Classic Model

The median problems are intended to find the location of P facility on the network, so that the total cost can be at minisum. The cost means the cost of providing services from node i to the nearest node established there. This cost depends on factors like distance between the node of i and servicing node and volume of demands of in node. The Classic Median Problem has some assumption as follows:

- Linear relationship between cost and distance
- Good facilitated
- Infinite time horizon
- Infinite facility capacity
- Don't have an initial setup cost
- Exogenous problem
- Same facilities
- Stationary facilities
- Constant node's demand
- Discrete problem

In this problem;

X_{ij}: is equal to 1 if the demand of node i is covered by the facility that has been setup at node j, otherwise is 0

Y_j: is equal to 1 if a facility is setup at node j, otherwise is 0

d_{ij}: The distance between the node of i demand and candidate node to establish facility j (d_{ij} is zero if $i = j$).

P: The number of facilities to be established
h_i: Demand of i node
n: Number of nodes

This model was proposed by ReVelle and Swain (1970);

$$\text{Min} \sum_i \sum_j h_i d_{ij} X_{ij} \qquad i, j = 1, 2, \ldots, n. \tag{8.1}$$

Subject to

$$\sum_j X_{ij} = 1 \qquad \forall i, \tag{8.2}$$

$$\sum_j Y_j = P, \tag{8.3}$$

$$X_{ij} \leq Y_j \qquad \forall i, j, \tag{8.4}$$

$$X_{ij}, Y_j \in \{0, 1\} \qquad \forall i, j. \tag{8.5}$$

In this problem, the aim is to minimize the total cost needed to satisfy the needs of nodes (to minimize sum of demand-distance). Equation (8.2) states that all demands should and each node is serviced by just one facility (demand limitation). Equation (8.3) states that there is an endogenous problem and proves the exact P establishment. Equations (8.4) states that open facilities can meet the demands. Thus the demand of i node can be provided with facility established in j node ($X_{ij} = 1$) through one facility in j node ($Y_j = 1$).

8.2.2 Capacitated Plant Location Problem Model (CPLPM)

In this part, we introduce the capacitated plant location problem (CPLP) with multiple facilities in the same site (CPLPM), a special case of the classical CPLP where several facilities can be opened in the same site. Applications of the CPLPM arise in a number of contexts, such as the location of polling stations. Although the CPLPM can be modeled and solved as a standard CPLP, this approach usually performs very poorly. CPLP is a classical combinatorial optimization problem (Bramel et al. 1998). This location problem is of utmost importance for many public and private organizations and its aim is determining a set of capacitated facilities (warehouses, plants, polling stations, etc.) in such a way that the sum of facility construction costs and transportation costs is minimized. Unlike other problem we allow multiple facilities in the same site. The CPLP is strongly NP-hard (Mirchandani and Francis 1990) and has been extensively studied in clustering and location theory. As a result, an overabundance of solution approaches has been proposed in the past decades. Exact algorithms have been developed, among others, by Christo Edes and Beasley (1983), Leung and Magnanti (1989), whereas heuristics have been investigated by

Van Roy (1985), Beasley (1988), ChristoEdes and Beasley (1983), GeoIrion and McBride (1978), Guinard and Kim (1987), Jacobsen (1983), Khumawala (1974). A systematic comparison of heuristics and relaxations for the capacitated plant location problem is provided by Cornuejols et al. (1991) Based on both a theoretical analysis and extensive computational results; they suggest the use of a Lagrangian heuristic to solve large instances of the CPLP.

In this problem;

U: The set of potential facilities,
V: The set of customers,
d_j: The demand of customer j ($j \in V$), where $d_j > 0$,
q_i: The capacity of facility i ($i \in U$), where $q_i > 0$,
c_{ij}: The cost of supplying all the demand of customer j ($j \in V$) from facility i ($i \in U$),
f_i: The fixed cost associated with opening facility i ($i \in U$), where $f_i > 0$,
p: The desired number of open facilities (also referred to as medians),
y_i: A binary decision variable, which takes the value 1, if facility i ($i \in U$) is open, 0 otherwise,
x_{ij}: A continuous decision variable, corresponding to the fraction of the demand of customer j ($j \in V$) supplied from facility i ($i \in U$).

Then CPLP can be formulated as a mixed integer linear programming problem as follows:

$$\text{(CPLP) Min} \sum_{i \in U} \sum_{j \in V} c_{ij} x_i + \sum_{i \in U} f_i y_i. \tag{8.6}$$

Subject to

$$\sum_{i \in U} x_{ij} = 1, \quad i \in V, \tag{8.7}$$

$$\sum_{j \in V} d_j x_{ij} \leq q_i y_i, \quad i \in U, \tag{8.8}$$

$$\sum_{i \in U} y_i = p, \tag{8.9}$$

$$x_{ij} \geq 0, \quad i \in U, j \in V, \tag{8.10}$$

$$y_i \in \{0, 1\}, \quad i \in U. \tag{8.11}$$

The objective function (8.6) expresses the minimization of the total costs. Equations (8.7) ensure that the demand of each customer is satisfied. Equations (8.8) establish the connection between (x_{ij}) and (y_i) variables. They state that no customer can be supplied from a closed facility and the total demand supplied from each open facility does not exceed the capacity of the facility. Equation (8.9) establishes that the number of open facilities is p. Equations (8.10) provide lower bounds on the (x_{ij}) variables. It is worth noting that (8.7)–(8.10) imply $x_{ij} \leq 1$ ($i \in U; j \in V$). Finally, (8.11) are the integrality constraints.

In the CPLPM, U represents a set of areas where facilities can be located. Such set is partitioned into n nonempty $U_1 `\ldots ` U_n$, each corresponding to a site where one or more areas are available. Consequently $f_i = f'_i$, if i; $i \in U_K$ ($k \in \{1, \ldots, n\}$), and $C_{ij} = C'_{ij}$ if $i \in U_K$ ($k \in \{1, \ldots, n\}$) and j, $j' \in V$.

8.2.3 Capacitated P-median Problem (Lorenaa 2004)

If no fixed costs are associated to the potential facilities, then the CPLP is called the capacitated p-median problem (CPMP).

Where $N = \{1, \ldots, n\}$ is the index set of entities to allocate and also of possible medians with $x_{ij} = 1$ if entity i is allocated to median j, and $x_{ij} = 0$, otherwise; $x_{jj} = 1$ if median j is selected and $x_{jj} = 0$, otherwise.

The CPMP model can be formulated in two ways. The first is the following binary integer-programming problem (P):

$$\text{Min} \sum_{i \in N} \sum_{j \in N} c_{ij} x_{ij}. \tag{8.12}$$

Subject to

$$\sum_{i \in N} x_{ij} = 1, \quad i \in N, \tag{8.13}$$

$$\sum_{j \in N} x_{jj} = P, \tag{8.14}$$

$$\sum_{i \in N} d_i x_{jj} \leq q_i x_{jj}, \quad j \in N, \tag{8.15}$$

$$x_{ij} \in \{0, 1\}, \quad i \in N, j \in N. \tag{8.16}$$

Equations (8.13)–(8.14) impose that each entity is allocated to only one median. Equations (8.15) imposes that a total median capacity must be respected, and (8.16) provide the integer conditions.

The CPMP problem can also be modeled as the following set partitioning problem with a cardinality constraint (SPP).This is the formulation found in Minoux. The same formulation can be obtained from the problem P by applying the Dantzig–Wolfe decomposition.

Where $S = \{S_1, S_2, \ldots, S_m\}$, is a set of subsets of N;
$A = [a_{ik}]_{n \times m}$, is a matrix with

$$a_{ik} = \begin{cases} 1 & \text{if } i \in S_{K'} \\ 0 & \text{otherwise.} \end{cases}$$

$$\text{(SPP) Min} \sum_{k=1}^{m} c_k x_k. \tag{8.17}$$

Subject to

$$\sum_{k=1}^{m} A_k x_k = 1, \tag{8.18}$$

$$\sum_{k=1}^{m} x_k = P, \tag{8.19}$$

$$x_{ij} \in \{0, 1\}. \tag{8.20}$$

Equations (8.12)–(8.13) are conserved and respectively updated to (18) and (20), according the Dantzig–Wolfe decomposition process.

If S is the set of all subsets of N, the formulation can give an optimal solution to the CPMP. However, the number of subsets may be huge, and a partial set of columns can be considered instead.

The SPP defined above is also known as the restricted master problem in the column generation context.

8.3 Solution Techniques

Some kinds of solution for solving the p-median problems are as follows:

- Exact methods
- Heuristic algorithm
- Metaheuristic algorithm

The complete accounting, heuristic and met heuristic algorithm are one of the first technique that are used them for solving the median problem.

Teitz and Bart (1968) proposed two innovated algorithm to solve the P-median problems through studying the complete number algorithm of Hakimi. This algorithm is based on choosing a primary series of nodes and then exchanging its members with other nodes of the network in order to improve the target function. Jarvinen et al. (1972) proposed a branch and bound algorithm to solve P-median problem. Meanwhile, Egbo, Samelson and colleagues proposed a branch and bound algorithm used to determine its limit through method of logerangean reparation (Narula et al. 1968). Neebe (1978) defined the transportation P-median problem in which the number of supply points was limited to P. Also he proposed a branch and bound algorithm for this problem in which the logerangean reparation method was used to determine its limit. Kariv and Hakimi (1979) proved to find the P-median in a network was to find NP-Hard, and to determine 1-median for a tree was possible in $O(n^2)$ stage. Galvao (1980) determined the dual form of P-median problem, and obtained a low limit for the problem using the solution by an innovative method. This limit has been used in a branch and bound algorithm and applied to solve the problems with 30 nodes and desirable P numbers.

8.3.1 Lemma

The Weber's problem was developed by Hakimi (1964), and through application of the weight on the graph, he began to find the P point on it in order to minimize the sum of the weighted distance from the points. To solve the problem, there was no limitation far the places of the points, and they could be placed in any points of the graph. Though the points were not located exactly on the apexes in the resulted solutions, Hakimi (1964) showed that there could be always a series apexes P to minimize the target functions. Thus, through the constraint of finding the solution just on the apexes, again Hakimi (1964) considered this disconnected problem as the candidate of Weber's problem. In the median problems, the solution consisting of the apexed P is called the P-median. Also, these problems are to be studied and defined just over the graph or networks. Hakimi (1964) generalized the concept of 1-median to multi-median. He used the concept to determine how to distribute the switching centers in the Tele-communication network. Later the P-median problems were considered as the inseparable part of the location theory and were called as a main problem.

8.3.2 Solving 1-Median Problem Algorithm on Tree (Goldman 1971)

- Put for all nodes $\hat{h}_i = h_i$
- Choice one node beside the i if it is $\hat{h}_i \geq \frac{\sum h_i}{2}$, put the facility in the node and go to step 3.
- Otherwise add W_i to w_k. k is the only node that it has intersection with inside i node.
- Calculate the objective function.

In the algorithm, time of solving the algorithm increases by developing the number of nodes linearly, because any node will consider its application just one time $O(n^2 p^2)$. Kariv and Hakimi (1979) submitted one algorithm for finding the place of facility P on a tree networks with (n)nodes.

According to previous, without considering the type of network that can be a tree network or general, if at least half of the application of all network appear on a node, we can get at least one best solution by putting facility on that node. In tree network, we will lead to getting place of best facility through using the node on top of the tree and mixing those with other connected nodes. This subject is not possible in general networks. For better understanding of this subject consider Fig. 8.2. These different conditions that all tree nodes can be placed on best settlement are changed according to the length of relating vectors.

8 Median Location Problem

Fig. 8.2 Instance of general network

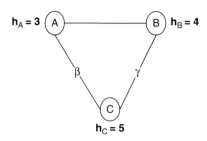

8.3.3 Exact Methods

In solving median problem, mathematic models are used by applying the integer programs. For solving this model of linear integer program, some ways are submitted that will solve based on relieving model of original model and by the dual theory and relieving Lagrangian method.

8.3.3.1 Complete Accounting (Teitz and Bart 1968)

First, for solving the median problem, we should consider a condition that a facility may be put on a network. In this method, by counting all conditions we will simply get the best result simply. Especially, we know this characteristic of median problems that one best result is obtained by putting the facilities on nodes. In order to calculate the amount of objective function, we can use this condition:

$$Z_j = \sum_j h_i d_{ij}. \tag{8.21}$$

When we put the facility on j node, we can calculate the amount of Z_j for all nodes and choose the least one for the best result. In this phrase, just one facility has located from p-facility that should be located and is left p-1 facilities.

The number of forward solution is calculated with this equation:

$$\binom{N}{P} = \frac{N!}{P!(N-P)!}. \tag{8.22}$$

8.3.4 Heuristic Algorithms

Just as mentioned, solving the median problem in time dimension imitate just one polynomial, but it had been shown by Kariv and Hakimi (1979) that if this subject be in a general network, it is a NP-complete. So some struggles have drawn for finding heuristic solutions for solving these problems. The important facts about these facility algorithms are that how much these are good or possible answers.

Although these algorithms result in real world problems very well, they don not guarantee achieving the optimum or approximating it. In solving some problems, these solutions may be optimum or near the best. In other cases, these solution may be very far. The first Heuristic algorithm for solving the median problems:

- Greedy-adding algorithm
- Alternate algorithm
- Vertex substitutions algorithm

According to these tree algorithms, innumerable algorithms and new techniques are made for solving the median problems that are based on those three algorithms. From these three basic algorithms, the vertex substitution algorithm is more general in comparison to the other two algorithms and up to the present time, it was one of the mostly used algorithms for solving median problems. Another heuristic algorithm is the branch and bound algorithm. (Heuristic branch and bound algorithm is not the same as one of the linear-program problems techniques named branch and bound.)

According to a classification, algorithms are classified into two groups of reply maker algorithms and recovering reply algorithms.

Myopic algorithm is one of the reply maker algorithms. This algorithm tries to get one primary and possible solution for median problems. The algorithm is similar to Greedy adding algorithm that is applied for maximum covering problems.

Both exchange and neighborhood search algorithms are kinds of recovering reply algorithm. These algorithms are not able to get the primary reply for problems, but they use them to improve reply that how got from maker algorithms. Two algorithms are similar to both Greedy adding and maximum heuristic algorithms for maximum covering and substitution problems. When Lagrangian discounting method is used besides one or more heuristic algorithm that will be introduced this section, they will get the best or near the best reply.

8.3.5 Metaheuristic Algorithms

Meta heuristic algorithms for solving the median problem:

- Genetic algorithm
- Concentration algorithm
- Neural network
- Tabu search algorithm
- Simulated annealing

In recent decades metaheuristic algorithms are submitted for solving these kinds of problems. Among these algorithms we can mention the genetic algorithm, neighborhood search algorithm, tabu search algorithm, concentration algorithm, simulated annealing algorithm and neural network. Also there are some other algorithms for obtaining one reply with acceptable quality.

Metaheuristic methods are usually used for too many nodes (100, 200, 300, 400, 500, 600, 700, 800 and 900).

8.4 Comparison of Methods

In this section, all achieved results that have been concluded from a 12-nodes network are mentioned. Here there is no solution way and just we consider their comparisons results.

- The solutions that have been achieved by using the myopic algorithms, in the most cases, appears almost in 30% error of amount of Lagrange objective function.
- In each stage, all solution that has been achieved from exchange algorithms method is always for the each number of facilities better than solution by using the neighborhood search algorithms.
- It is better in some situations that neighborhood search algorithms applied after setting each facility at network in each stage, and in some other situations, it is better to apply the neighborhood search algorithms after setting all facilities.
- We should consider that when the number of settled facilities will be average figure, the differences between all achieved results differ from various algorithms together and with Lagrange algorithm method.
- When the number of the settled facilities is few, it seams that all algorithms work better. For instance, when the number of the settled facilities is more, all results that have been achieved from algorithms are so good and algorithms work so well. But when the number of the settled facilities is neither few nor more, the problem is so difficult.
- Exchange algorithm is the best method for this network, considering that exchanging appears after putting all facilities by using the myopic algorithm.

8.5 Studying Statically the Methods for Solutions of Median Problem (Reese 2005)

The aim here is to study the methods used to solve the median problems and the years of proposing them which were classified for 1963–2005 periods. The following factors were selected among other sources:

- Those focused directly on median problems,
- Those involved minisum target function,
- Those which define median problems on the graph or network,
- Sum of answers limited to searching on nodes,
- Those that did not have primary cost of establishment,
- Those belonging to median problems with limited capacity or unlimited facilities.

Also we avoided the resources with one of the following conditions:

- They had minimax target function,
- Study establishment of median problems in a connected space,
- There was a probable state demand or cost,
- There was a multi-purpose target function,
- Considering dislocation of facilities in a time horizon.

The following classification obtained considering the proposed solutions.

8.5.1 Classification of Solving Methods by Period

The number of presented paper in this area before 1970 were 7, between 1970 and 1974 were 9, between 1975 and 1979 were 12, between 1980 and 1984 were 9, between 1985 and 1989 were 6, between 1990 and 1994 were 11, between 1995 and 1999 were 24 and between 2000 and 2005 the number of paper have the remarkable growth so that it reaches 42 paper.

It should also be noted that the methods obtained and used in the last 10 years are so higher than the methods used in 1963–1994.

8.5.2 Classification of Different Solving Methods

According to the researches between 1965 and 2005 the LP Relaxation was used more than other methods, after that respectively Vertex substitution, approximation algorithm, genetic algorithm (GA), IP formulation were used, graph theory and surrogate relaxation are in the same level, and other methods were assigned less than five cases.

8.6 Case Study

In this section we will introduce some real-world case studies related to p-median problem:

8.6.1 Post Center Locations (Alba and Dominquez 2006)

In Australia in order to determine ten post centers among 200 centers, 10-median problem formulated and finally ten cities including Sidney, Melborn and Adlid, etc. were selected as post centers.

8.6.2 Entrance Exam Facilities (Correa et al. 2004)

PARANA State University (UFPR) in Curitiba in Brazil used the median P model to determine the location of facilities concerning M.A entrance exam in 2001. The aim was to appropriate 19,710 candidate students to the facilities located nearer to their homes as possible.

It was determined that 26 facilities needed to meet the demands of 19,710 students among 43 candidate facilities. Finally the number of candidate solutions should be 421 billion.

$$\binom{43}{26} = 421,171,648,758.$$

The problem was solved by a genetic algorithm.

8.6.3 Polling Station Location (Ghiani et al. 2002)

Polling station location problem in Italy: Number of polling stations was determined according to the number of resident voters in five Italian municipalities (data: November 2000).

This study of the CPLPM was motivated by a polling station location problem in an Italian municipality. In Italy, the following binding obligations must be taken into account:

- The number of polling stations is fixed for each municipality and calculated according to the number of resident voters the number of voters assigned to each polling station may not exceed given lower and upper bounds;
- The suitability of the potential sites is established by specific safety measures on the accessibility and typology of the buildings (for example, in some countries, only public buildings, such as schools, are eligible).

8.6.3.1 Formulating the Problem as a CPLPM

U: The set of areas where polling stations can be located.
P: Number of polling stations to be activated.
V: The set of streets having at least one resident voter
d_j: The number of voters in street j ($j \in V$), where $d_j > 0$.
q_i: The upper limit on the total number of voters assigned to a polling station located in area i ($i \in U$); q_i may be the same for all areas, i.e.

$$q_i = q = \sum_{j \in V} \frac{d_j}{p}; i \in U. \tag{8.23}$$

c_{ij}: The transportation cost incurred if all voters resident in street j ($j \in V$) are assigned to a polling station in area i ($i \in U$); c_{ij} can be chosen, for simplicity, equal to $d_j{}^*S_{ij}$ j, where S_{ij} is the walking distance between area i and the "centre of gravity" of street j; $f_i = f$, for all areas. Consequently, the contribution of the fixed costs to the objective function (6) can be excluded.

8.6.3.2 Computational Results

As far as the experimental phase is concerned, we have solved first the problem of the optimal location of polling stations in the municipality of Castrovillari. Town located in Southern Italy with a population, dated back to November 2000, of 15,709 voters, located in 351 different streets spread in a wide area. The solution actually adopted by the local government is based on the assignment of all voters resident in the same street to the same polling station, chosen among the nearest ones. As a result, the walking distance covered by all voters is about 10,731 km, and the number of voters for each polling station was reported. It was observed that, with respect to the ideal capacity, the fourth polling station has 18% of voters less, whereas the 18th polling station has 21% of voters more. The feasible solution found by the heuristic is well balanced and has a cost 37.6% less than that of the solution currently adopted by the municipality of Castrovillari. Computational results show that the average deviation of the heuristic solution over the lower bound is less than 2%.

References

Alba E, Dominquez E (2006) Comparative analysis of modern optimization tools for the p-median problem. Stat Comput 16:251–260
Beasley JE (1988) An algorithm for solving large capacitated warehouse location problems Eur J Oper Res 33:314–325
Bramel J, Simchi-Levi D (1998) The logic of logistics. Springer-Verlag, New York
ChristoEdes N, Beasley JE (1983) Extensions to a lagrangian relaxation approach for the capacitate warehouse location problem Eur J Oper Res 12:19–28
Cornuejols G, Sridharan R, Thizy JM (1991) A comparison of heuristics and relaxations for the capacitated plant location problem Eur J Oper Res 50:280–297
Correa ES, Steiner MTA, Freitas AA, Carnieri C (2004) Genetic algorithm for solving a capacitated p-median problem. Numer Algorithms 35:373–388
Francis RL, McGinnis LF, White JA (1992) Facility layout and location: An analytical approach. Prentice Hall, Englewood Cliffs, NJ
Galvao RD (1980) A dual-bounded algorithm for the p-median problem. J Oper Res 28(5): 1112–1121
Geolrion AM, McBride R (1978) Lagrangian relaxation applied to capacitated facility location problem AIIE Trans 1:40–47
Ghiani G, Guerriero F, Musmanno R (2002) The capacitated plant location problem with multipli facilities in the same site. Eur J Oper Res 29:1903–1912
Goldman AJ (1971) Optimal center location in simple networks. Trans Sci 5:212–221
Guinard M, Kim S (1987) A strong lagrangian relaxation for capacitated plant location problems Math Program 39:215–528

Hakimi SL (1964) Optimum locations of switching centers and the absolute centers and Medians of a graph. Eur J Oper Res 12(3):450–459

Hakimi SL (1965) Optimum distribution of switching centers in a communication network and some related graph theoretic problems. Eur J Oper Res 13(3):462–475

Jacobsen SK (1983) Heuristics for the capacitated plant location model Eur J Oper Res 12:253–261

Jarvinen P, Rajala J, Sinervo V (1972) A branch-and-bound algorithm for seeking the p median. Eur J Oper Res 20(1):173–178

Kariv O, Hakimi SL (1979) An algorithmic approach to network location problems. II. The p-medians. SIAM J Appl Math 37(3):539–560

Khumawala BM (1974) An efficient heuristic procedure for the capacitated warehouse location problem Nav Res Logist Quart 21:609–623

Leung JM, Magnanti TL (1989) Valid inequalities and facets of the capacitated plan location problem Math Program 44:271–291

Lorenaa L, Senneb E (2004) A column generation approach to capacitated p-median problems Oper Res 31:863–876

Mirchandani PB, Francis RL (1990) Discrete location theory. Wiley, New York

Narula SC, Ogbu UI, Samuelsson HM (1968) An algorithm for the p-Median problem. Eur J Oper Res 16(5):955–961

Neebe AW (1978) A branch and bound algorithm for the p-median transportation problem. J Oper Res Soc 29:989–995

Reese J (2005) Methods for solving the p-median problem: An annotated bibliography. Technical report, Department of Mathematics, Trinity University

ReVelle C, Swain R (1970) Central facilities location. Geograph Anal 2:30–42

Teitz MB, Bart P (1968) Heuristic methods for estimating the generalized vertex median of a weighted graph. Eur J Oper Res 16(5):955–961

Van Roy TJ (1985) A cross decomposition algorithm for capacitated facility location. Eur J Oper Res 34:145–63

Chapter 9
Center Problem

Maryam Biazaran and Bahareh SeyediNezhad

In the covering problems, the attempt is to determine the location of the minimum number of facilities necessary to cover all demand nodes. In this type of problems, the coverage distance is an exogenous data. But sometimes the number of facilities needed to cover all demand nodes with a predefined coverage distance may be quite large. In order to overcome this, the maximum covering location problem has been discussed. In this model, the objective is to maximize the number of covered demand nodes with a fixed number of facilities. In other words, we relaxed the total coverage requirement (Daskin 1995).

A different strategy is discussed in this chapter. Now, instead of asking the model to minimize the number of facilities with a given coverage distance, we will ask the model to minimize the coverage distance with a given number of facilities, while maintaining the coverage of all demand nodes. This model is introduced under the title of p-center problem which is in fact a minimax problem. In this model, the objective is to find locations of p facilities so that all demands are covered and the maximum distance between a demand node and the nearest facility (coverage distance) is minimized. It can be said that we have relaxed the coverage distance (Daskin 1995).

In the p-center model, each demand point has a weight. These weights may have different interpretations such as time per unit distance, cost per unit distance or loss per unit distance (Daskin 1995). So the problem would be seeking a center to minimize a maximum time, cost or loss. In other words, the concern is about the worst case and we want to make it as good as possible (Francis et al. 1992).

For example, assume that we need to establish a number of fire stations in a town. If the time to reach the scene from facility j to demand node i is d_{ij}, then this amount must not be greater than minutes. Therefore, we are looking to provide $d_{ij} <$ for each node i and a closest facility j. If we are to cover all the points, we need certain number of facilities. To evaluate the number of facilities needed, one needs to solve a set covering problem. Now assume that there is a budget constraint and we can not establish enough fire stations, then there are two ways of approaching the problem. One is to cover maximum points; in this case you are facing a maximum covering problem. The second approach is to cover all of demand nodes, but through increasing the radius of coverage distance. Evaluation of the minimum increase in

Fig. 9.1 Example network illustrating suboptimality of nodal locations (Daskin 1995)

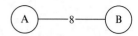

the coverage distance with respect to the given number of facilities can be done with a p-center model.

One should recognize the difference between problems in which new facilities can be established anywhere on the network (on the nodes and on the links of the network) and problems in which the new facilities can only be established on the nodes of the network. These problems are called absolute center problem and vertex center problem respectively. It can easily be shown that the solution to the absolute center problem may be better than the solution to the vertex one. Consider the sample network in Fig. 9.1. If one new facility ($p = 1$) can be located only on the nodes, each node can be the optimum answer and the maximum distance between the facility and the other node is equal to 8. But if we can locate the new facility anywhere on the network, the optimum place would be the midway between A and B and the coverage distance can be reduced to 4 (Daskin 1995).

This chapter is organized as follows. In Sect. 9.1, we will discuss applications and classifications of p-center problems. In Sect. 9.2 mathematical models are presented. Some of the exact solution algorithms for center problems are discussed in Sect. 9.3 and a number of approximate solution approaches are introduced in Sect. 9.4. Finally in Sect. 9.5 a short summary of a real-world case study is given.

9.1 Applications and Classifications

Some of the potential applications of the p-center model would be in:

- Quick services (hospital emergency services, fire stations, police stations,...)
- Computer network services (location of the data files)
- Distribution (warehouses, garages,...)
- Military purpose
- Government and general (parks, hotels,...)
- Location-allocation for post boxes and bus stops

Since we have a minimax objective function for the p-center model, it seems that it would be most applicable to emergency cases. Thus, Pacheco and Casado (2005) applied the p-center model to find the best locations in which to place special health resources.

The literature on p-center problem has grown rapidly after Hakimi (1964) published a paper on the absolute center and median problems. The p-center problem was defined and formulated by Hakimi (1964, 1965). Many papers have been published since 1960s. The emphasis of papers was on suggesting solution procedures.

The following is a classification of different types of p-center models and their properties:

- Solution area: *plane, network*
- In case of network: *tree network, general graph*
- Facility capacity: *limited, unlimited*
- Number of centers: *one center, more than one center*
- Demand type: *only on nodes, on links and nodes (continuous)*
- Weights of demand points: *equal (unweighted), positive (frienly facilities), negative (obnoxious facilities* (see Chap. 14)), *mixed (pos/neg)*
- Possible facility locations: *anywhere on the network (absolute), only on nodes (vertex)*

The following are a number of generalized p-center problems:

9.1.1 K-Network P-Center Problem

The problem of locating p centers on k underlying networks corresponding to k periods (Hochbaum and Pathria 1998). There is one network for each period of time. It is required to locate *permanent* facilities and the objective is to minimize the maximum distance over all k periods.

9.1.2 P-Facility λ-Centdian Problem

The problem consists of finding the p points that minimize a convex combination of the p-center and p-median objective function (Pérez-Brito et al. 1998). For example, locating a local branch bank may call for the minimization of the average distance traveled by all prospective customers without being located too far away from any customer.

9.1.3 K-Centrum Multi-Facility Problem

This problem generalizes and unifies the p-center problem and p-median problem (Tamir 2001). The objective of this unifying model is to minimize the sum of the k largest service distances. The p-center and the p-median problems correspond to the cases where $k = 1$ and n, respectively.

9.1.4 P-Center Problem with Pos/Neg Weights

Burkard and Dollani (2003) was the first to introduce this model. The model is a *p*-center problem in which nodes can have positive or negative weights, which indicate friendly and obnoxious facilities (see Chap. 14).

9.1.5 Anti P-Center Problem

This problem was introduced for the first time by Klein and Kincaid (1994). Instead of minimizing the maximum weighted distance between a demand node and its nearest facility, in *anti-p*-center, the objective is to maximize the minimum weighted distance between demand nodes and the nearest facility. In other words, we are locating *p* obnoxious facilities (see Chap. 14). All weights are negative in this model.

9.1.6 Continuous P-Center Problem

In the case where each point in the network is a demand point, as opposed only to vertices, the problem will be referred to as the continuous *p*-center problem (Tansel et al. 1983). Tamir (1987) discussed this problem in his paper.

9.1.7 Asymmetric P-Center Problem

The problem is said to be asymmetric when for each pair of nodes i and j in the network, we have $d_{ij} \neq d_{ji}$. Panigrahy and Vishwanathan (1998) were the first to introduce this type of *p*-center problem.

9.2 Models

In this section, we introduce mathematical models of *p*-center.

9.2.1 Vertex P-Center Problem

The vertex *p*-center problem was formulated by Hakimi (1965) and we present it as follows:

9.2.1.1 Model Assumptions

The assumptions of this model are as follows:
- The facilities can only be located on the nodes of the network (*vertex*)
- The capacities of the facilities are *unlimited*
- There are p facilities to be located
- Demand points are on the nodes of the network
- Demand nodes are *unweighted*

9.2.1.2 Model Inputs

The inputs of this model are as follows:

d_{ij}: length of the shortest path between demand node i to candidate facility site j
p: number of facilities to locate

9.2.1.3 Model Outputs (Decision Variables)

The outputs of this model are as follows:

$X_j = 1$ if a facility is located at candidate site j and 0 otherwise
$Y_{ij} = 1$ if demand node i is assigned to facility at candidate node j and 0 otherwise
$z =$ maximum distance between a demand node and the nearest facility

9.2.1.4 Objective Function and its Constraints

$$\text{Min } z. \tag{9.1}$$

Subject to

$$\sum_j Y_{ij} = 1 \ \forall i, \tag{9.2}$$

$$\sum_j X_j = p, \tag{9.3}$$

$$Y_{ij} \leq X_j \ \forall i, j, \tag{9.4}$$

$$z \geq \sum_j d_{ij} Y_{ij} \ \forall i, \tag{9.5}$$

$$X_j \in \{0, 1\} \ \forall j, \tag{9.6}$$

$$Y \in \{0, 1\} \ \forall i, j, \tag{9.7}$$

Equation (9.1) in conjunction with (9.5) minimizes the maximum distance between a demand node and its nearest facility. Equations (9.2) state that all of a demand at node i must be assigned to a facility at some node j for all nodes i. Equation (9.3) guarantees that p facilities are located. Equations (9.4) ensure that assignments can only be made to open facilities. Equations (9.6)–(9.7) are the integrality constraints.

9.2.2 Vertex P-Center Problem with Demand-Weighted Distance

In some cases, we want to consider the demand-weighted distance (Daskin 1995).

9.2.2.1 Model Assumptions

Model assumptions are similar to the ones of vertex p-center model except that demand nodes are weighted.

9.2.2.2 Model Inputs

We have all inputs in previous model in addition to the following inputs:

h_i: demand at node i

9.2.2.3 Model Outputs (Decision Variables)

The outputs of this model are similar to the previous model.

9.2.2.4 Objective Function and its Constraints

The objective function and constraints are similar to the previous model except that (9.5) must be replaced by:

$$z \geq h_i \sum_j d_{ij} Y_{ij} \ \forall i. \tag{9.8}$$

9.2.3 Capacitated Vertex P-Center Problem

Ozsoy and Pinar (2006) represented the capacitated vertex p-center model. We introduce it as follows:

9.2.3.1 Model Assumptions

Model assumptions are similar to the vertex p-center model except that the capacities of the facilities are limited.

9.2.3.2 Model Inputs

We have all inputs in previous model in addition to the following inputs:

Q_j: service capacity of facility site j

9.2.3.3 Model Outputs (Decision Variables)

Model outputs are similar to the previous model.

9.2.3.4 Objective Function and its Constraints

The objective function and constraints are similar to the vertex p-center model in addition to the following constraints:

$$\sum_i h_i Y_{ij} \leq Q_j \; \forall j. \tag{9.9}$$

With (9.9), capacity restrictions of the facilities are incorporated into the vertex p-center model.

9.3 Exact Solution Approaches

Kariv and Hakimi (1979) showed that the p-center problem on a general graph is NP-hard. However, when the network is a tree, the optimal solution can be found in polynomial time. Hence, the first part of this section is dedicated to center problems on tree networks and in the second part, center problems on general graphs are discussed.

9.3.1 Center Problems on a Tree Network

9.3.1.1 Vertex 1-Center on a Tree Network (Daskin 1995)

A vertex center in a tree network is a node that has the minimum distance to its farthest node. Hakimi (1964) presented an algorithm to find this node. First we need

Fig. 9.2 An example of a tree network

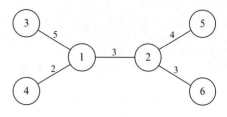

to compute the square matrix $D = (d_{ij})$ of order n:

$$d_{ij} = \begin{cases} d(v_i, v_j), & \text{for } i, j = 1, 2, \ldots, n \text{ and } i \neq j \\ d(v_i, v_j) = 0, & \text{for } i = j, i = 1, 2, \ldots, n \end{cases}. \quad (9.10)$$

Let d_i^m be the maximum entry in the ith column of D. v_c is a vertex center if:

$$d_c^m = \min(d_1^m, d_2^m, \ldots, d_n^m). \quad (9.11)$$

For example, consider the tree network in Fig. 9.2. It is easily determined that v_1 is the center of this tree with $d_1^m = 7$.

$$D(d_{ij}) = \begin{bmatrix} 0 & 3 & 5 & 2 & 7 & 6 \\ 3 & 0 & 8 & 5 & 4 & 3 \\ 5 & 8 & 0 & 7 & 12 & 11 \\ 2 & 5 & 7 & 0 & 9 & 8 \\ 7 & 4 & 12 & 9 & 0 & 7 \\ 6 & 3 & 11 & 8 & 7 & 0 \end{bmatrix},$$

$$d_c^m = \min(d_1^m, d_2^m, \ldots, d_n^m) = 7.$$

If we have a tree with weighted demand nodes, the procedure is similar to above except that each row of $D(d_{ij})$ must be multiplied by its respective node's demand weight h_i.

9.3.1.2 Absolute 1-Center on an Unweighted Tree Network (Daskin 1995)

For the unweighted case, Handler (1973) presented an especially elegant algorithm. Handler's method finds any longest path in the tree and locates the absolute center at the midpoint of the path. The steps are as follows:

1. Pick any vertex on the tree and find the farthest vertex from it. Call this vertex v_s.
2. Find a vertex that is farthest from v_s and call it v_t.
3. This path is the longest path and its midpoint is the unique absolute center of the tree.

We can illustrate this algorithm using Fig. 9.3.

9 Center Problem

Fig. 9.3 An example of a tree network

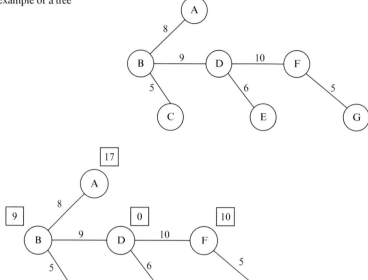

Fig. 9.4 Calculated distances from node D

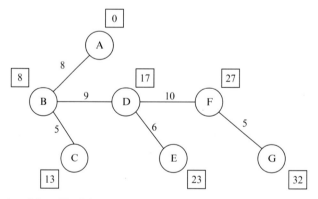

Fig. 9.5 Continued form Fig. 9.4

We begin by picking a vertex, for example D. We then find the distance between node D and all vertices on the tree. Figure 9.4 shows the result of this calculation.

Node A is the farthest node from D, so we let node A be v_s. Figure 9.5 shows the distances from node A.

Since G is the farthest node from A, we call it v_t. the absolute 1-center is at the point midway between A and G on the unique path from node A to node G, or 1 unit from node D on the edge between D and B, as shown in Fig. 9.6. The objective function equals 16.

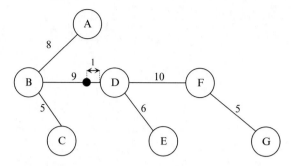

Fig. 9.6 Location of the absolute 1-center in the network of Fig. 9.3

9.3.1.3 Absolute 2-Center on an Unweighted Tree Network (Daskin 1995)

To solve the absolute 2-center on an unweighted tree, we can modify the algorithm used to find the absolute 1-center on an unweighted tree. Steps of this algorithm are as follows:

1. Use the algorithm for the absolute 1-center and find the absolute 1-center.
2. If the absolute 1-center is on a node, delete one of the arcs incident on the center which is on the path from v_s to v_t, then delete the arc between v_s and v_t. Now, we have two disconnected subtrees.
3. Use the absolute 1-center algorithm to find the absolute 1-center of each subtree. This would be a solution to the absolute 2-center problem.

To illustrate the algorithm, consider again the tree shown in Fig. 9.3. As the Fig. 9.6 indicates, the absolute 1-center lies on the link *BD*. Removing this link results in the two trees shown in Fig. 9.7. After applying the absolute 1-center algorithm to each subtree, we obtain locations of x_1 and x_2 as shown. The objective function value is 10.5 (maximum between two objective function values).

9.3.1.4 Absolute 1-Center on a Weighted Tree Network (Daskin 1995)

In this section, we are seeking an absolute center on a weighted tree or a tree in which the weights associated with each of the nodes are not equal. Consider the simple network in Fig. 9.8. In this case, we want to minimize the maximum demand-weighted distance between a demand node and its nearest facility. In this simple case, to locate the facility, a point at X units from node A is selected such that or $X = 4$. Now the demand-weighted distance between each node and the facility is 24. This is also shown in Fig. 9.9. It is obvious that the solution involves locating closer to the larger demand node.

For a simple tree with only two nodes, computing the absolute 1-center is easy, but when there is a more complicated tree, it becomes more difficult.

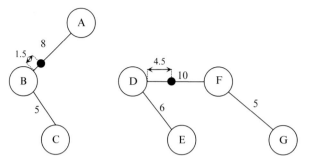

Fig. 9.7 Absolute 2-center on a tree network

Fig. 9.8 Simple network for the weighted problem on tree

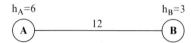

Fig. 9.9 Maximum demand-weighted distance = 24

However we can generalize the approach as follows. Consider two nodes i and j. In the case that the center is located on the path between them, we must solve the following equations for the location X:

$$h_i d(i, x) = h_j d(j, x), \quad (9.12)$$

$$d(i, X) + d(X, j) = d(i, j). \quad (9.13)$$

From the (9.12)–(9.13) we obtain (9.14): (After solving for $d(i, X)$, we have (9.15) or (9.16))

$$h_i d(i, X) = h_j [d(j, X) - d(i, X)], \quad (9.14)$$

$$d(i, X) = \frac{h_j d(i, j)}{h_i + h_j}, \quad (9.15)$$

$$d(X, j) = \frac{h_i d(i, j)}{h_i + h_j}. \quad (9.16)$$

So, if we were to locate a facility at this point, both nodes i and j would be

$$\frac{h_i h_j d(i, j)}{h_i + h_j}, \quad (9.17)$$

demand-weighted distance units from that center. This center is located $d(i, X)$ units from node i and on the path between node i and node j. we can compute this value for every pair of nodes in the tree and select the pair that has the largest value to obtain the optimal solution. The approach is as follows:

- Compute β_{ij} for every pair of nodes i and j:

$$\beta_{ij} = \frac{h_i h_j d(i, j)}{(h_i + h_j)}. \qquad (9.18)$$

- Find: $\beta_{st} = \max_{ij}(\beta_{ij})$. Corresponding nodes are s and t.
- Locate at a point $[h_t/(h_s + h_t)]d(s, t)$ from node s on the unique path from s to t.

Since n is the number of nodes in the tree, this approach involves computing $O(n^2)$ terms β_{ij}. The approach can be simplified by computing only a portion of the bound matrix $B = (\beta_{ij})$. The algorithm is as follows:

1. Compute one row of the β_{ij} elements in the matrix.
2. Find the maximum element in that row (if the maximum element is in a column that was already computed, stop)
3. Compute the elements β_{ij} in the column in which the maximum β_{ij} element occured in step 2.
4. Find the maximum element in the column that was just computed (if the maximum element is in a row that was already computed, stop).
5. Compute the elements β_{ij} in the row in which the maximum β_{ij} occurred in step 4. Go to step 2.

For more explanation of this method consider the network of Fig. 9.10.

In the first step, elements in the row corresponding to node A are computed. The partial matrix in Table 9.1 shows the results.

As shown in Table 9.1, the element in the column corresponding to node G is the largest one, so in the 4*th* step, we will compute elements in corresponding column. The results are shown in Table 9.2.

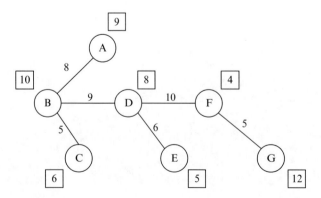

Fig. 9.10 A weighted tree

9 Center Problem

Table 9.1 A partially computed matrix of β_{ij} terms

β_{ij}	A	B	C	D	E	F	G
A	0	37.89	46.8	72	73.92	74.76	164.57

Table 9.2 A partially computed matrix of β_{ij} terms

β_{ij}	A	B	C	D	E	F	G
A	0	37.89	46.8	72	73.92	74.76	164.57
B							130.90
C							116
D							72
E							74.11
F							15
G							0

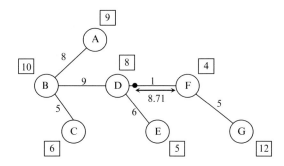

Fig. 9.11 Location of the weighted absolute 1-center for the weighted tree of Fig. 9.10

The largest element corresponds to the row associated with node A, so we stop. The optimal location is at the point 13.71 units away from node G on the path from node G to node A or 8.71 units from node F to node D on the link from node F to node D shown by Fig. 9.11.

$$\frac{h_A}{h_G + h_A} d(A, G) = 13.71. \quad (9.19)$$

Note that we only had to compute 11 of the β_{ij} elements instead of 21 elements. (The actual number of elements that must be computed is $n(n-1)/2$ or 21 in this case).

9.3.1.5 Absolute P-Center on a Weighted Tree Network (Francis et al. 1992)

In this section, the p-center problem on a tree will be solved by solving a sequence of covering problems.

We are given a set $Y = \{y_1, \ldots, y_p\}$ of center locations, and each center in some edge. For each demand node v_i, $i = 1, \ldots, n$, and any Y, we have the closest center assumption as follows:

$$D(Y, v_i) = \min\{d(y_1, v_i), \ldots, d(y_p, v_i)\}. \quad (9.20)$$

It means that each demand node v_i receives service from a closest center (facility). Now the objective function of interest would be as follows:

$$G(Y) = \max\{h_1 D(Y, v_1), \ldots, h_n D(Y, v_n)\}. \tag{9.21}$$

We seek an absolute p-center Y^* which minimizes $G(Y)$. Note that if $p \geq n$, the problem has a trivial solution (one center at each vertex).

To solve this problem, we shall use the fact that there is some 1-center problem whose minimal value is equal to the minimal value of $G(Y)$. Thus, the search for the minimal objective function value can be limited to the positive entries in the bound matrix $B = (\beta_{ij})$.

Minimal Objective Function Value Property
The minimal objective function value for the p-center problem, say z_p, is some entry in the bound matrix $B=(\beta_{ij})$.

Suppose that we have a p-center problem with n nodes and $Y = \{y_1, \ldots, y_p\}$ in an absolute p-center. We can write the p-center problem as follows:

$$\text{Min } G(Y). \tag{9.22}$$

Subject to

$$G(Y) = \max\{h_1 D(Y, v_1), \ldots, h_n D(Y, v_n)\}, \tag{9.23}$$
$$|Y| = p. \tag{9.24}$$

Equivalently we can

$$\text{Min } z. \tag{9.25}$$

Subject to

$$D(Y, v_i) \leq \frac{z}{h_i} \quad i = 1, \ldots, n, \tag{9.26}$$
$$|Y| = p. \tag{9.27}$$

Consider z_p as the minimal objective function value, so z_p is the smallest value of z such that there exist a p-center Y for which Y and z satisfy (9.26)–(9.27). Consider R to be the set of entries in the B matrix. According to minimal objective function value property, we can say that z_p will be one of the numbers in the set R. So we conclude that z_p is the smallest number z in R for which there exist a Y that Y and z satisfy (9.26)–(9.27). We let $C(z)$ denote the following covering problem:

$$C(z) : \text{Min } |Y|. \tag{9.28}$$

9 Center Problem

Subject to

$$D(Y, v_i) \le \frac{z}{h_i} \quad i = 1, 2, \ldots, n, \qquad (9.29)$$

$C(z)$ is the equivalent covering problem and in this problem, z would be the parameter of the covering problem. So each time we change z, we will have a different covering problem.

If z_p is the minimal objective function value for p-center problem and $q(z)$ is the minimal objective function of the covering problem, we conclude that z_p is the minimal element r in R for which $q(r) \le p$.

As you see, the p-center problem can be solved by solving a sequence of covering problems.

We use discrete values in R as possible values of z_p and there is as many as $n(n-1)/2$ elements in B. So a good procedure is needed for searching among these elements to find z_p. A search procedure that is often used is called *bisection search*. The algorithm is as follows (Francis et al. 1992):

1. Construct the set R consisting of all distinct positive values β_{ij}.
2. Repeat step 3 until R consists of a single element.
3. Find a median entry in R, say r. Solve the covering problem $C(r)$ and compute $q(r)$. If $q(r) \le p$, delete all elements greater than r form R, otherwise, delete all elements not greater than r (including r).
4. Let z_p be the single element in R. Solve $C(z_p)$ and obtain its optimal solution Y^*. If $|Y^*| = p$, take Y^* as an optimal p-center and stop. If $|Y^*| = p_1 < p$, choose any convenient p-p_1 centers append to Y^* to obtain an optimal p-center and stop.

Using bisection search is a good idea, because it reduces the number of elements in R by half at each iteration. That is, even if R initially consists of 1,000,000 elements, bisection search would have to solve at most 21 covering problems!

9.3.2 Center Problems on a General Graph

In this section, center problems on a general graphs are discussed. A general graph is a network $N = (V, A)$ which has at least one cycle. A path in a network is called a cycle if the initial and final vertices in the path are identical (Francis et al. 1992).

9.3.2.1 Vertex 1-Center on a General Graph (Francis et al. 1992)

To find a vertex center, we need to compute the Matrix $D = (d_{ij})$. The entry in row i and column j in this matrix is $d(v_i, v_j)$ that implicates the shortest path between the node i and the node j in the graph (One can use *Floyd*'s algorithm to compute these distances).

Fig. 9.12 Example of a general graph

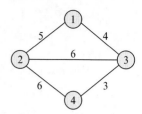

Table 9.3 Example of a vertex 1-center on a general graph

D'		Weight of node v_j				$g(v_i)$
		2	3	4	2	
v_i		0	15	16	14	16
		10	0	24	12	24
		8	18	0	6	18
		14	18	12	0	18

In the next step, in order to obtain the new matrix D', every entry in each column must be multiplied by h_j. For each row of the new matrix, the maximum entry $g(v_i)$ is determined and placed in the right margin. Any row with the smallest value in the right margin identifies a vertex center.

Consider the general graph of Fig. 9.12 with weights of 2, 3, 4, and 2 for vertices 1–4, respectively. Computation results are shown in Table 9.3. With $g(v_1) = 16$, we can see that v_1 is a vertex 1-center on this general graph.

9.3.2.2 Vertex P-Center Problem on a General Graph (with Integer Distances) (Daskin 1995)

A solution approach to solve the unweighted vertex p-center on a general graph is outlined in this section. We assume that all link distances are integer values. (Since all rational values can be converted to integer values by multiplying them by a sufficiently large number, this is not a restrictive assumption). In this approach, we search over the range of coverage distances to find the smallest one that allows all nodes to be covered by a vertex center.

The search procedure is called *binary search*. In this procedure, we define initial lower and upper bounds for the objective function value of the p-center problem. Using the average of the lower and upper bounds, we solve the set covering problem. If the number of facilities needed to cover all nodes is less than or equal to p, we will find out that the objective function of the p-center problem cannot be larger than this coverage distance. So we replace the upper bound to the current coverage distance. If the number of facilities needed to cover all nodes is greater than p, then similarly we will find out that the objective function value of the p-center problem must be larger than the current value, because we have to cover all nodes with a smaller number of centers and hence a larger coverage distance. In this case we would replace the lower bound with the current coverage distance plus 1.

9 Center Problem

Let $q(r)$ denote the optimal value of the set covering problem when the coverage distance is r. also let R^L and R^H as lower and upper bounds on the p-center objective function value. The initial values of lower and upper bounds are defined as follows:

$$R^L = 0, \tag{9.30}$$

$$R^H = (n-1)\max_{ij}(d_{ij}), \tag{9.31}$$

where n is the number of nodes in the graph and d_{ij} is the length of link (i, j). The binary search algorithm would be as follows:

1. Set R^L and R^H. Using equations in (9.30)–(9.31). Note that by setting these values in this manner, we make sure that every possible value for the coverage distance is considered.
2. Set r as shown in (9.32). Where $\lfloor x \rfloor$ denotes the largest integer less than or equal to x.

$$r = \left\lfloor \frac{R^H + R^L}{2} \right\rfloor. \tag{9.32}$$

3. Solve a set covering problem with a coverage distance of r and let the solution be $q(r)$.
4. If $q(r) \leq p$, reset R^H to r; else reset R^L to $r+1$.
5. If $R^H \neq R^L$, go to step 2; otherwise, stop, r is the optimal value for the objective function of p-center problem and optimal locations for the p-center problem, are the locations corresponding to the set covering solution for this coverage distance.

To illustrate this algorithm, consider the graph of Fig. 9.13. All distances are integer in this graph. Let $p = 2$. The maximum link distance is 6 and there are five nodes. Therefore, we initially set $R^H = 24$ and $R^L = 0$. Table 9.4 summarizes the iterations of the algorithm for this problem. The optimal value for the objective function is $r = 4$. From the covering problem, when coverage distance is 4, optimal locations of two centers are nodes B and C or nodes D and C.

The discussed algorithm can be extended to solve the weighted vertex p-center problem. All steps are similar in this case except that the initial upper bound R^H, must be replaced by

$$R^H = (n-1)[\max_{ij}(d_{ij})][\max_{ij}(h_i)]. \tag{9.33}$$

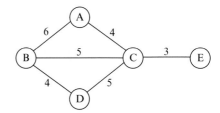

Fig. 9.13 Example of a general network with integer distances

Table 9.4 Summary of Iterations of the vertex 2-center algorithm

Iteration	R^L	R^H	r	$q(r)$
1	0	24	12	1
2	0	12	6	1
3	0	6	3	4
4	4	6	5	1
5	4	5	4	2
6	4	4	Stop!	

Note that in solving the set covering problem, demand node i is covered by candidate site j only if $h_i d_{ij} \leq r$.

9.3.2.3 Absolute P-Center on a General Graph (Francis et al. 1992)

In this section we will introduce the concept of distance function. Consider the simple graph of Fig. 9.13. If we are to locate a center in a point X on the link between node B and node C and x units from node B, the distance between this point and node A would be:

$$d(X, A) = \min\{d(B, X) + d(B, A), d(X, C) + d(C, A)\}. \tag{9.34}$$

Let $d(B, A) = d_{BA}$ is the shortest path between node B and Node A, and $d(C, A) = d_{CA}$. Since we have $d(B, X) = x$ and $d(X, C) = l_{BC} - x$, we can write the (9.33) again:

$$d(X, A) = \min\{x + d_{BA}, (l_{BC} - x) + d_{CA}\}. \tag{9.35}$$

If we substitute the values, we will have:

$$d(X, A) = \min\{x + 6, -x + 9\}. \tag{9.36}$$

Figure 9.14 illustrates $d(X, A)$, the minimum distance between node A and point X. so the shortest path between node A and point X is a piecewise function, that depends on the distance of point X from node B, say x.

Now if we consider all other nodes with point X, we will have the graph of Fig. 9.15.

If we let $g(X)$ denote the maximum of weighted distances involving X, then we have

$$g(X) = \max\{h_A d(X, A), \ldots, h_E d(X, E)\}. \tag{9.37}$$

With all weights equal to one, the thick piecewise line in Fig. 9.15, illustrates $g(X)$. If the absolute center of the graph is to be located on the link BC, the optimal value of objective function would be the minimum of $g(X)$. In this case, the minimum is on node C.

Fig. 9.14 Graph of $d(X, A)$, for the network of Fig. 9.13

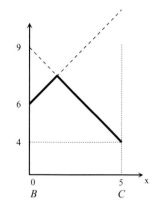

Fig. 9.15 Graphs of distances on the link BC

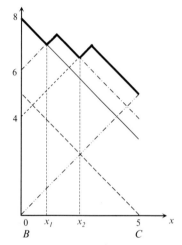

$$g(X) = \begin{cases} h_E d(X, E) & 0 \le x \le 1 \\ h_A d(X, A) & 1 \le x \le 2.5 \\ h_D d(X, D) & 2.5 \le x \le 5 \end{cases} \qquad (9.38)$$

We call x_1 and x_2 the intersection points. Intersection point is defined by exactly two distinct weighted distance functions being equal. At this point, one of the two functions increases locally as x moves away from the point in one direction, while the other increases as x moves away from the point in the other direction. For example, consider the intersection point x_1 in the graph of Fig. 9.15. At this point, we have $h_D d(X, D) = h_A d(X, A)$, while $h_A d(X, A)$ increases as x decreases locally from 2.5, $h_D d(X, D)$ increases as x increases locally from 2.5.

As it is indicated, it is also possible to have local minima at the endpoints of the arc. For example, point C is not defined by an intersection point, but it is the minimum of $g(X)$.

Now after this introduction, we conclude that to find the absolute center in a network, we have to find all intersection points on every arc and choose the one with minimum distance to all other nodes and also evaluate $g(v_i)$ at every vertex and finally choose the best point among all intersection points and vertices.

Consider the p-center problem, in which $X = \{x_1, \ldots, x_p\}$ is a collection of centers. We let $D(X, v_i)$ be the distance between vertex v_i and a closest center in X, so the objective would be to find an absolute p-center X^* that minimizes:

$$G(X) = \max\{h_1 D(X, v_1), \ldots, h_n D(X, v_n)\}. \tag{9.39}$$

The VIP property for the p-center problem is the following:

Vertex and Intersection Point (VIP) Property
There exists at least one absolute p-center for which each center is at a vertex or an intersection point. Thus it is sufficient to consider only vertex and intersection point locations in order to find an absolute p-center.
This property reduces the p-center problem with infinite number of points to be considered to a problem with a finite number of points to be considered.

Although now we have a finite set of potential center locations, it would be possibly very large. To improve our enumeration approach, we will avoid enumeration of intersection points on some arcs. If we have a current best *trial* solution, X', with function value $g(X')$. If we know a number b_{pq} so that $g(X) \geq b_{pq}$ for all X in arc $[v_p, v_q]$, and also $b_{pq} > g(X')$, no location on the $[v_p, v_q]$ can be an absolute center.

Arc Exclusion-Bounding Property
$b_{ipq} = \min\{h_i d(v_p, v_i), h_i d(v_q, v_i)\}$
$b_{pq} = \max\{b_{ipq}. i = 1, \ldots, n\}$
If $b_{pq} > g(X')$, no point in arc $[v_p, v_q]$ is an absolute 1-center.

9.3.2.4 Formulating the P-Center Problem (Francis et al. 1992)

Now that we have limited the solution of absolute p-center to a finite set of potential center locations using VIP and Arc exclusion-bounding properties, we can formulate the p-center problem. In this case, there is binary decision for every potential location to include it in the p-center or not. Define $Q = \{q_1, q_2, \ldots, q_m\}$ to be the set of all potential center location. First n members of Q correspond to vertices of the graph.

We associate each intersection point q_k with a bound value b_k, that is simply the weighted distance from on of the two vertices used to define the intersection point. For example, consider the intersection point x_1 in Sect. 3.2.3. x_1 is defined by vertices A and E, so the bound value for x_1 is 7.

9 Center Problem

Decision variables:

- $x_j = 1$ if a center is located at q_j and 0 otherwise

Now the p-center problem can be formulated as follows:

$$\text{Min } z_p. \tag{9.40}$$

Subject to

$$z_p \geq \min\{h_i d_{ij} \mid j \in \theta(X)\} i = 1, \ldots, n, \tag{9.41}$$

$$\sum_j x_j \leq p, \tag{9.42}$$

$$x_j \in \{0, 1\} j = 1, \ldots, m. \tag{9.43}$$

The set $\theta(X)$ in (9.41) is the set of potential center locations that are used in the solution. This is a mathematical statement of the p-center problem, but there is no direct solution procedure for it. But the indirect approach is used to solve this problem and consists of solving a sequence of related covering problems. In Sect. 3.2.5, we will discuss the relationship between p-center problem and covering problem.

9.3.2.5 Relationship Between P-Center Problem and Covering Problem (Francis et al. 1992)

We used covering problem to solve center problems earlier in this chapter. Now in this section, we will discuss the relationship between them in general.

Suppose that (z^*, X^*) is the optimal solution to p-center problem. Covering problem is as follows:

Decision variables:

- $a_{ij} = 1$ if $h_i d_{ij} \leq z$ and 0 otherwise

$$CP(z) : \text{Minimize } p = \sum_j x_j \tag{9.44}$$

Subject to

$$\sum_j a_{ij} x_j \geq 1 \; i = 1, \ldots, n, \tag{9.45}$$

$$x_j \in \{0, 1\} j = 1, \ldots, m. \tag{9.46}$$

Now suppose that z^1 and z^* are specific values for parameter z, and the optimal solution to CP(z^1) is (p^1, X^1). The relationship between two problems is as follows, offered without proof:

1. If (z^*, X^*) is a solution to p-center problem, then (p, X^*) solves CP(z^*)

2. If (z^*, X^*) is a solution to p-center problem and (p^1, X^1) solves $\text{CP}(z^1)$, then:
   (a) If $p^1 > p$, then $z^1 < z^*$.
   (b) If $p^1 \leq p$, then $z^1 \geq z^*$.

To explain these claims, part 1 states that if we knew the z^*, we could use $\text{CP}(z^*)$ to determine X^*. Part 2 states that if we can guess a value z^1 for z^*, and solve $\text{CP}(z^1)$, in case (a), we obtain a lower bound on z^* and in case (b), we obtain a feasible solution or an upper bound on z^*. Earlier in this chapter we had a similar discussion on this, for vertex p-center on a general graph with integer distances.

9.4 Approximate Solution Approaches

Kariv and Hakimi (1979) showed that the p-center problem on a general graph is NP-hard. In this section, some of the approximate solution approaches suggested for solving p-center problem are discussed.

Many heuristic and metaheuristic solution approaches were designed for the p-center problem in recent years; here we will mention some of them.

- Pallottino et al. (2002) represented a local search heuristic for the capacitated vertex p-center.
- Bespamyatnikh et al. (2002) represented a polynomial time algorithm for p-center problem on circular arc graphs.
- Burkard and Dollani (2003) represented a number of algorithms with low computational complextity for p-center problem with *pos/neg* weights on trees and general graphs.
- Caruso et al. (2003) represented four algorithms that solve p-center problems. Two exact algorithms and two heuristics. All these methods are based on solving a sequence of set covering problems. Two heuristics can solve problems up to 900 nodes in a few seconds.
- Hochbaum and Pathria (1997) represented approximation algorithms for two closely related problems p-SetSupplier and p-SetCenter.
- Khuller et al. (2000) represented polynomial time approximation algorithm to solve the *fault tolerant p-center problem* in which every vertex must have at least α centers close to it.
- Khuller and Sussmann (2000) represented an approximation algorithm for the capacitated p-center problem.
- Panigrahy and Vishwanathan (1998) represented an approximation algorithm for the asymmetric p-center. The authors repeatedly employed a greedy set covering algorithm.
- Pelegrin and Canovas (1998) presented new versions of seed point algorithms. In these algorithms, the first step is to generate p points for the p-center problem and then generating a partition of the demand points. They proposed a new assignment rule based on partitions.

- Andersson et al. (1998) represented an approximation algorithm based on demand point aggregation method.
- Dyer and Frieze (1985) presented a greedy algorithm in which the first center is chosen at random. This variant of greedy is called *Greedy Plus* (GrP).
- Drezner (1984) represented two heuristic algorithms for the p-center problem. These heuristics resemble algorithms for other location-allocation problems.
- Hochbaum and Shmoys (1985) represented a 2-approximation heuristic for the p-center problem.
- Hassin et al. (2003) introduced a local search strategy in which solutions are compared lexicographically rather than by their worst coordinate. They applied this approach to p-center problem.
- Mladenovic et al. (2003) suggested metaheuristic approaches for the first time as a means for solving p-center problems. They represented a basic Variable Neighborhood search and two Tabu search metaheuristics and a multi-start local search for the p-center problem.
- Bozkaya and Tansel (1998) proposed a spanning tree approach for the absolute p-center problem on cyclic networks (general graphs). The approach was motivated by the fact that the problem is NP-hard on general networks but solvable in polynomial time on trees.
- Pacheco and Casado (2005) proposed a metaheuristic procedure based on the scatter search approach for solving p-center problem. The procedure incorporates procedures based on different strategies such as local search, GRASP and path relinking. The aim was solving problems with real data.
- Cheng et al. (2007) modeled the network of p-center problem as an interval graph whose edges all have unit lengths and provide a polynomial time algorithm to solve the problem under the assumption that the endpoints of the intervals are sorted.

9.5 Case Study

In this section we introduce a real-world case study related to p-center problems.

9.5.1 A Health Resource Case (Pacheco and Casado 2005)

In Pacheco and Casado (2005) a real health resource allocation problem was surveyed in Burgos, a rural area in the north of Spain. As mentioned in their paper, the authorities have limited budget, hence less than ten facilities considered to be located. With dispersed population in this area, it was essential to design a method to provide good solutions with a low number of facilities.

Real data in this case refer to the estimation of diabetes cases in that area. Four hundred and fifty two locations with at least one known case of diabetes were taken into account within the area and 152 of these locations were considered suitable for the project.

They dealt with two problems, first one was minimizing the maximum distance between users and facilities (*p-center*) and the second one was minimizing the population further away from its closest available facility than a previously fixed time (*maximum covering*).

References

Andersson G, Francis RL, Normak T, Rayco MB (1998) Aggregation method experimentation for large-scale network location problems. Location Sci 6:25–39

Bespamyatnikh S, Bhattacharya B, Keil M, Kirkpathrick D, Segal M (2002) Efficient algorithms for centers and medians in interval and circular-arc graphs. Networks 39(3):144–152

Bozkaya B, Tansel B (1998) A spanning tree approach to the absolute p-center problem. Location Sci 6:83–107

Burkard RE, Dollani H (2003) Center problems with pos/neg weights on trees. Eur J Oper Res 145:483–495

Caruso C, Colorni A, Aloi L (2003) Dominant an algorithm for the p-center problem. Eur J Oper Res 149:53–64

Cheng TCE, Kang L, Ng CT (2007) An improved algorithm for the p-center problem on interval graphs with unit lengths. Comput Oper Res 34:2215–2222

Daskin MS (1995) Network and discrete location: Models, algorithms, and applications. Wiley, New York

Dyer ME, Frieze AM (1985) A simple heuristic for the p-center problem. Oper Res Lett 3:285–288

Drezner Z (1984) The p-center problem: heuristics and optimal algorithms. J Oper Res Soc 35: 741–748

Francis RL, McGinnis LF Jr, White JA (1992), Facility layout and location: An analytical approach. Prentice-Hall, Englewood Cliffs, NJ

Hakimi SL (1964) Optimum location of switching centers and the absolute centers and medians of a graph. Oper Res 12:450–459

Hakimi SL (1965) Optimum location of switching centers in a communications network and some related graph theoretic problems. Oper Res 13:462–475

Handler GY (1973) Minimax location of a facility in an undirected tree graph. Transport Sci 7: 287–293

Hassin R, Levin A, Morad D (2003) Lexicographic local search and the p-center problem. Eur J Oper Res 151:265–279

Hochbaum DS, Pathria A (1997) Generalized p-center problems: Complexity results and approximation algorithms. Eur J Oper Res 100(3):594–607

Hochbaum DS, Pathria A (1998) Locating centers in a dynamically changing network, and related problems. Location Sci 6:243–256

Hochbaum DS, Shmoys DB (1985) A best possible heuristic for the k-center problem. Math Oper Res 10(2):180–184

Kariv O, Hakami SL (1979) An algorithmic approach to network location problems. Part I: the p-center problem. SIAM J Appl Math 37:513–538

Khuller S, Sussmann YJ (2000) The capacitated K-center problem. SIAM J Discrete Math 13:403–418

Khuller S, Pless R, Sussmann Y (2000) Fault tolerant K-center problems. Theor Comput Sci 242:237–245

Klein CM, Kincaid RK (1994) The discrete anti-p-center problem. Transport Sci 28:77–79

Mladenovic N, Labbe'M, Hansen P (2003) Solving the p-center problem with tabu search and variable neighborhood search. Networks 42:48–64

Ozsoy FA, Pinar MC (2006) An exact algorithm for the capacitated vertex p-center problem. Comput Oper Res 33:1420–1436

Pacheco JA, Casado S (2005) Solving two location models with few facilities by using a hybrid heuristic: a real health resources case. Comput Oper Res 32(12):3075–3091

Pallottino S, Scappara MP, Scutellà MG (2002) Large scale local search heuristics for the capacitated vertex p-center problem. Networks 43(4):241–255

Panigrahy R, Vishwanathan S (1998) An O(log* n) Approximation algorithm for the asymmetric p-center problem. J Algorithms 27:259–268

Pelegrin B, Canovas A (1998) A new assignment rule to improve seed points algorithms for the continuous k-center problem. Eur J Oper Res 104:366–374

Pérez-Brito D, Moreno-Perez JA, Rodriguez-Martin I (1998) The 2-facility centdian network problem. Location Sci 6:369–381

Tamir A (1987) On the solution value of the continuous p-center location problem on a graph. Math Oper Res 12(2):340–349

Tamir A (2001) The k-centrum multi-facility location problem. Discrete Appl Math 109:293–307

Tansel BC, Francis RL, Lowe TJ (1983) Location on networks: A survey. Part I: The p-center and p-median problems. Manage Sci 29(4):482–497

Chapter 10
Hierarchical Location Problem

Sara Bastani and Narges Kazemzadeh

In the basic models presented in previous chapters, it is assumed that there was only one type of facility being located. As the systems that provide services/products usually consist of two or more levels of facilities, we discuss hierarchical facility systems in this chapter.

Many facility systems are hierarchical in nature. These facilities are usually hierarchical in terms of the types of services they provide. For example, the health care delivery system consists of local clinics, hospitals and medical centers (Fig. 10.1). In this system a local clinic provides basic health care and diagnostic services. A hospital provides out-patient surgery in addition to those provided by a local clinic; and a medical center provides out-patient surgery and a full range of in-patient services. As another example of a hierarchical system, consider a solid waste disposal system. The solid waste is collected from the source of solid waste and shipped to transfer stations or landfill stations by trucks. Other examples of a hierarchical system are: education system, postal system, banking system and production–distribution system (Narula 1986; Daskin 1995).

In the examples above, facilities cannot be located independently at each level. Thus, there is a need to consider them as a hierarchical system.

In this chapter, location-routing problem, which is confused with the hierarchical location problem, is not discussed. In the location-routing problem, the locations of the primary facilities and the demand points are fixed and given; the objective is to locate intermediate facilities and design tours originating at the primary facilities to serve the secondary facilities and tours emanating from secondary facilities to serve the demand points. The location-routing problem is presented in Chap. 18.

This chapter is organized as follows. In Sect. 10.1, we give a definition about hierarchical location problem, its applications and classifications. In Sects. 10.2–10.5 mathematical models for the problem are given. We present solution methods in Sect. 10.3. We conclude the chapter with some case studies in Sect. 10.4.

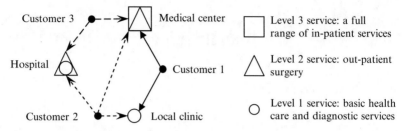

Fig. 10.1 An example of a health care delivery system

10.1 Applications and Classifications

Many applications of hierarchical location problem are:

- Health care systems are one of the most studied real-life applications of the hierarchical facility location problem. Such systems can consist of local clinics, hospitals and medical centers. Some works in this area are Calvo and Marks (1973), Dökmeci (1977), Okabe et al. (1997), Rahman and Smith (1999), Marianov and Taborga (2001), Galvão et al. (2002, 2006) and Smith et al. (2009). Researches for considering location problems in health systems, including hierarchical problems is reviewed by Rahman and Smith (2000).
- Solid waste disposal system consists of transfer stations and landfill stations. A work for this application is Barros et al. (1998).
- Production–distribution system consists of factories, warehouses and retail outlets. Some works in this area are Scott (1971), Ro and Tcha (1984), Tcha and Lee (1984), Van Roy (1989) and Eben-Chaime et al. (2002).
- Education system consists of kindergartens, guidance schools and high schools. Moore and ReVelle (1982) and Teixeira and Antunes (2008) represented some models in this area. Teixeira and Antunes (2008) considered two levels for school system: public and private schools.
- Emergency medical service (EMS) systems consist of basic life support and advance life support. Some works in this area are Charnes and Storbeck (1980), Mandell (1998) and Şahin et al. (2007).

Some other applications have been presented for hierarchical facility locations. For example Banerji and Fisher (1974) presented an application of successively inclusive hierarchical systems for area planning. Chan et al. (2008) is another application presented for hierarchical models. They applied a hierarchical maximal-coverage location–allocation for the case of search and rescue.

A hierarchical system of facilities consists of m levels in which level 1 is the lowest level of service or facility and level m is the highest level. Level 0 presents demand nodes.

Narula (1986) considers two types of facility hierarchies and three types of service in relation to a hierarchical system. Daskin (1995) refers to this as two ways in which services are offered and three types in terms of the regions to which services are provided.

- In a *successively inclusive facility hierarchy*, a facility at level k ($k = 1, \ldots, m$) provides services 1 through k.
  - A successively inclusive facility hierarchy is said to have a *locally inclusive service hierarchy* if a level k facility ($k = 1, \ldots, m$) at location j offers services of level $1, \ldots, k$ only to demands at location j and only level k services to demands at location $i \neq j$.
  - A successively inclusive facility hierarchy is said to have a *successively inclusive service hierarchy*, Daskin (1995) refers to this as *globally inclusive service hierarchy*, when a level k facility ($k = 1, \ldots, m$) at location j provides level $1, \ldots, k$ services to all demand nodes.
- In a *successively exclusive facility hierarchy*, a facility level k ($k = 1, \ldots, m$) provides only services of level k.
  - A successively exclusive facility hierarchy is said to have a *successively exclusive service hierarchy* if a level k facility at location j provides type k services to all demand nodes.

Narula (1984) considers two types of *flow discipline*. The flow is *integrated* when it can be from any lower-level facility to any higher-level facility. The flow is *discriminating* if it is from any lower-level facility k to the next higher-level facility $k+1$.

Şahin and Süral (2007) classify the hierarchical location problem with respect to *flow pattern, service variety, spatial configuration, objective, horizontal interactions* and *capacity limits on facilities*.

- Flow pattern refers to demand flow through levels of a hierarchical system. In a *single-flow* pattern, demand begins at level 0, passes through all levels, and finally ends at the highest level; or vice versa. In a *multi-flow* pattern, demand begins and ends at any level k ($k = 1, \ldots, m$). Flow pattern is similar to the flow discipline described in Narula (1984). We can consider flow pattern in a *referral* or *non-referral* system. In a referral system, lower-level facility refers a proportion of customers to the higher-level facility.
- Service variety specifies the service availability at the levels of hierarchy. *Nested* and *non-nested* features, respectively resembles Narula's successively inclusive and exclusive systems.
- Spatial configuration refers to the coherency of a hierarchical system. A *coherent* hierarchical system is one in which all customers of the same low level facility are also customers of the same high level facility.
- For locating facilities in hierarchical location problem models, three types of objectives are considered: *median, fixed charge*, and *covering* objectives.

Teixeira and Antunes (2008) consider three types of *spatial pattern* according to which demands are assigned to facilities: *closest assignment, single assignment* and *path assignment*. In closest assignment, a demand node is assigned to the closest facility located. In single assignment, a demand node is assigned only to one facility located. In path assignment, when a given facility is located at location j, all demands near the path travelled by the customers to reach the facility are also assigned to it. In following Sects. 10.2–10.5, we introduce categories of hierarchical location models presented and developed as mathematical models.

10.2 Flow-Based Hierarchical Location Problem

Aardal et al. (1999) considers flow-based formulation with fixed-charge objective in which allocations is represented by a variable that is more common to network flow models and establishes flow from one level of the hierarchy to another. Şahin and Süral (2007) present this model with median objective.

10.2.1 Flow-Based Formulation for Single-Flow Systems (Şahin and Süral 2007)

Şahin and Süral (2007) consider a two-level single-flow system, in which flow begins from demand node, passes a level 1 facility and ends at a level 2 facility.

10.2.1.1 Model Assumptions

Model assumptions of this model are as follows:

- The objective function is *MiniSum*.
- The solution space is *discrete* and *finite*.
- The formulation represents a two-level, single-flow, non-nested, *non-coherent*, *capacitated* system.
- The number of facilities at each level is known (*exogenous* model).

10.2.1.2 Model Inputs

Model inputs of this model are as follows:

$c_{jj'}$: unit cost of flow between facilities level 2 at candidate location j' and level 1 at candidate location j
c_{ij}: unit cost of flow between level 1 facility at candidate location j and demand node at i
d_i: the amount of demand at node i
$M_{j'}$: the capacity of level 2 facility at candidate location j'
M_j: the capacity of level 1 facility at candidate location j
p': the number of level 2 facilities to be located
p: the number of level 1 facilities to be located

10.2.1.3 Model Outputs (Decision Variables)

Model outputs of this model are as follows:

$x_{j'} = 1$ if level 2 facility located at j', zero otherwise
$y_j = 1$ if level 1 facility located at j, zero otherwise
$v_{jj'}$: amount of flow between level 2 facility at location j' and level 1 facility at location j
u_{ij}: amount of flow between level 1 facility at location j and demand at location i

10.2.1.4 Objective Function and its Constraints

The objective function of this model and its related constraints are as follows:

$$\text{Min} \sum_i \sum_j u_{ij} c_{ij} + \sum_j \sum_{j'} v_{jj'} c_{jj'}. \tag{10.1}$$

Subject to

$$\sum_j u_{ij} = d_i \ \forall \ i, \tag{10.2}$$

$$\sum_{j'} v_{jj'} = \sum_i u_{ij} \ \forall \ j, \tag{10.3}$$

$$\sum_i u_{ij} \leq M_j y_j \ \forall \ j, \tag{10.4}$$

$$\sum_{j'} v_{jj'} \leq M_i x_i \ \forall \ j', \tag{10.5}$$

$$\sum_j y_j = p, \tag{10.6}$$

$$\sum_{j'} x_{j'} = p', \tag{10.7}$$

$$u_{ij} \geq 0 \ \forall \ i, j, \tag{10.8}$$

$$v_{jj'} \geq 0 \ \forall \ j, j', \tag{10.9}$$

$$y_j = 0, 1 \ \forall \ j, \tag{10.10}$$

$$x_{j'} = 0, 1 \ \forall \ j'. \tag{10.11}$$

Equation (10.1) minimizes the total demand-weighted distance from demand nodes to level 1 facilities and from level 1 facilities to level 2 facilities. Equations (10.2) ensure that the total demand of a node is completely satisfied by level 1 facilities. Equations (10.3) ensure that the demand referred to a level 2 facility by a level 1 facility is equivalent to the total demand of that level 1 facility.

Equations (10.4)–(10.5) are for facility capacities. Equations (10.6)–(10.7) locate the required numbers of level 1 and 2 facilities, respectively. Equations (10.8)–(10.9) are non-negativity; (10.10)–(10.11) are integrality constraints.

10.2.2 Flow-Based Formulation for Multi-Flow Systems (Şahin and Süral 2007)

Şahin and Süral (2007) consider a two-level multi-flow, nested system, in which demand at location i is provided either directly or via a level 1 facility for its level 2 demands and can be served by a level 2 facility for its both level 1 and 2 demands. Since facilities are capacitated, a portion of level 1 demand is provided by a level 1 facility and the remaining portion by a level 2 facility. The same model can be seen in Narula and Ogbu (1985).

10.2.2.1 Model Assumptions

The assumptions of this model are similar to previous model except that there is the following difference:

- The formulation represents a two-level, multi-flow, nested, non-coherent, capacitated system.

10.2.2.2 Model Inputs

Model inputs are similar to previous model in addition to the following parameter:

$c_{ij'}$: unit cost of flow between level 2 facility at candidate location j' and demand node at i

10.2.2.3 Model Outputs (Decision Variables)

Model outputs are similar to previous model in addition to the following decision variable:

$w_{ij'}$: amount of flow between level 2 facility at location j' and demand at location i

10.2.2.4 Objective Function and its Constraints

The objective function is similar to previous model in addition to the following term:

$$\sum_i \sum_{j'} w_{ij'} c_{ij'}. \tag{10.12}$$

The differences between the constraints of this model and previous model are as follows:
- Equations (10.2) and (10.5) are omitted.
- The following constraints are added to the formulation:

$$\sum_j u_{ij} + \sum_{j'} w_{ij'} = d_i \ \forall \ i, \tag{10.13}$$

$$\sum_{j'} v_{jj'} + \sum_i w_{ij'} \leq M_i x_i \ \forall \ j', \tag{10.14}$$

$$w_{ij'} \geq 0 \ \forall \ i, j'. \tag{10.15}$$

Equation (10.12) in the objective function minimizes the total demand-weighted distance from demand nodes to level 2 facilities. Equations (10.13) replace (10.2) for which the first-level demand can be assigned to either level facility. Equations (10.14) replace (10.5) for which a level 2 facility capacity can be utilized either by the second-level demand at a node or the referred demand from level 1. Equations (10.15) are non-negativity.

10.3 Median-Based Hierarchical Location Problem (Daskin 1995)

Mirchandani (1987) presents a generalized median-based hierarchical location model which allows various allocation schemes. Daskin (1995) represents median-based formulations in which demand at location i is assigned to a set of facilities one from each level.

10.3.1 Median-Based Formulation for Globally Inclusive Service Hierarchies

A model for a successively inclusive facility hierarchy operating under a globally inclusive service hierarchy is formulated by Daskin (1995).

10.3.1.1 Model Assumptions

Model assumptions of this model are as follows:
- The objective function is *MiniSum*.
- The solution space is *discrete* and *finite*.
- The formulation represents a successively inclusive facility hierarchy operating under a globally inclusive service hierarchy.
- The number of facilities at each level is known (*exogenous* model).

10.3.1.2 Model Inputs

Model inputs of this model are as follows:

h_{ik}: the amount of demand for type k services at node i
d_{ij}: the distance between node i and candidate location j
p_k: the number of type k facilities to be located

10.3.1.3 Model Outputs (Decision Variables)

Model outputs of this model are as follows:

$X_{jk} = 1$ if a facility of type k is located at candidate location j, zero otherwise
$Y_{ijk} = 1$ if demand at node i for type k services is assigned to a facility at candidate location j, zero otherwise

10.3.1.4 Objective Function and its Constraints

The objective function of this model and its related constraints are as follows:

$$\text{Min} \sum_i \sum_j \sum_k h_{ik} d_{ij} Y_{ijk}. \tag{10.16}$$

Subject to

$$\sum_j Y_{ijk} = 1 \ \forall \ i, k, \tag{10.17}$$

$$\sum_j X_{jk} = p_k \ \forall \ k, \tag{10.18}$$

$$Y_{ijk} \leq \sum_{h=k}^{m} X_{jh} \ \forall \ i, j, k, \tag{10.19}$$

$$X_{jk} = 0, 1 \ \forall \ j, k, \tag{10.20}$$

$$Y_{ijk} = 0, 1 \ \forall \ i, j, k. \tag{10.21}$$

Equations (10.16) minimizes the demand-weighted total distance. Equations (10.17) stipulates that all demand levels at all locations must be assigned to some facility. Equation (10.18) limits the total number of level k facilities located to p_k. Equation (10.19) ensure that demands at node i for level k services are assigned to the facility at location j when there is a level k or higher level facility located at location j. They are the linkage constrains. Equations (10.20)–(10.21) are the integrality constraints.

10.3.2 Median-Based Formulation for Locally Inclusive Service Hierarchies

A model for a successively inclusive facility hierarchy operating under a locally inclusive service hierarchy is formulated by Daskin (1995).

10.3.2.1 Model Assumptions

The assumptions of this model are similar to previous model except that there is the following difference:

- The formulation represents a *successively inclusive facility hierarchy* operating under a *locally inclusive service hierarchy*.

10.3.2.2 Model Inputs

Model inputs are similar to previous model.

10.3.2.3 Model Outputs (Decision Variables)

Model outputs are similar to previous model.

10.3.2.4 Objective Function and its Constraints

The objective function is similar to previous model. The differences between the constraints of this model and previous model are as follows:

- Equations (10.19) are omitted
- The following constraints are added to the formulation:

$$Y_{ijk} \leq X_{jk} \ \forall \ j,k; \ \forall \ i \neq j, \tag{10.22}$$

$$Y_{jjk} \leq \sum_{h=k}^{m} X_{jh} \ \forall \ j,k. \tag{10.23}$$

Equations (10.22) ensure that demands at node i for level k service are assigned to the facility at location j when there is a level k facility located at location j. Equations (10.23) state that demands for level k service are assigned to the level k or higher level facility when the demand node and candidate facility location are the same.

10.3.3 Median-Based Formulation for Successively Exclusive Service Hierarchies

A model for a successively exclusive facility hierarchy operating under a successively exclusive service hierarchy is formulated by Daskin (1995).

10.3.3.1 Model Assumptions

The assumptions of this model are similar to globally inclusive service hierarchy model except that there is the following difference:

- The formulation represents a *successively exclusive facility hierarchy* operating under a *successively exclusive service hierarchy*.

10.3.3.2 Model Inputs

Model inputs are similar to globally inclusive service hierarchy model.

10.3.3.3 Model Outputs (Decision Variables)

Model outputs are similar to globally inclusive service hierarchy model.

10.3.3.4 Objective Function and Its Constraints

The objective function is similar to previous model. The differences between the constraints of this model and previous model are as follows:

- Equations (10.19) are omitted
- The following constraints are added to the formulation:

$$Y_{ijk} \leq X_{jk} \ \forall \ i, j, k. \tag{10.24}$$

Equations (10.24) ensure that demands at node i for level k service are provided by the level k facility at location j.

10.4 Coverage-Based Hierarchical Location Problem (Daskin 1995)

There are basically three different approaches to formulate covering problems. The set covering location problem seeks to minimize the number of open facilities (or the cost of opening facilities) while ensuring that all demand points are within the coverage area of some open facility. The p-center problem locates a given number (p) of facilities while minimizing the maximum distance between demands and facilities. The most studied covering problem in hierarchical location literature is the maximum covering problem that seeks to maximize the amount of demand covered.

A hierarchical location problem with a coverage objective is formulated by Daskin (1995). This formulation considers maximal covering with two approaches for defining covered demands.

10.4.1 Hierarchical Maximal Covering Location Problem

This model for hierarchical maximal covering location problem is presented by Daskin (1995).

10.4.1.1 Model Assumption

- The objective is to *maximize* the total number of demands that are covered while the number of facilities at each level is known.
- The formulation represents a *nested* system.

10.4.1.2 Model Inputs

Model inputs are similar to median-based hierarchical model in addition to the following parameter:

$a_{ij}^{kq} = 1$ if a level q facility located at candidate location j can provide service k to demands at node i, zero otherwise.

10.4.1.3 Model Outputs (Decision Variables)

Model outputs of this model are as follows:

$X_{jq} = 1$ if we locate a level q facility at candidate location j, zero otherwise.
$Z_{ik} = 1$ if demands for service k at node i are covered, zero otherwise.

10.4.1.4 Objective Function and its Constraints

The objective function of this model and its related constraints are as follows:

$$\text{Max} \sum_i \sum_k h_{ik} Z_{ik}. \tag{10.25}$$

Subject to

$$\sum_j X_{jq} = P_q \ \forall q, \qquad (10.26)$$

$$Z_{ik} \leq \sum_j \sum_q a_{ij}^{kq} X_{jq} \ \forall i,k, \qquad (10.27)$$

$$0 \leq Z_{ik} \leq 1 \ \forall i,k, \qquad (10.28)$$

$$X_{jq} = 0, 1 \ \forall j,q. \qquad (10.29)$$

Equation (10.25) maximizes the total number of demands of all levels that are covered. Equations (10.26) stipulate that exactly P_q level q facilities are to be located. Equations (10.27) stipulate that demand for service k at node i cannot be counted as being covered unless we locate at least one facility at one or more of the candidate locations which are able to provide service k to demand node i. Equations (10.28)–(10.29) are the nonnegative and standard integrity constraints, respectively. Note that the coverage variables (Z_{ik}) explicitly do not need to accept only integer values.

10.4.2 Hierarchical Maximal Covering Location Problem with Covering all Kinds of Demands

In some situations, demands at each demand node can only be counted as being covered if all of the services that are demanded at the node i are covered. Moore and ReVelle (1982) introduced a maximal covering model with this assumption. Daskin (1995) also represented the model as follows.

10.4.2.1 Model Assumption

The model assumptions are similar to previous model, except that in this model, demands at each demand node can only be counted as being covered if all kind of the services that are demanded at the node i are covered.

10.4.2.2 Model Inputs

Model inputs are similar to median-based hierarchical model in addition to the following parameters:

h_i: The demand at node i. This is probably a function of the service specific demands (h_{ik}) at node i such as: $\Sigma_k \ h_{ik}$ or $\Sigma_k \ \alpha_k \ h_{ik}$ or $\max_k \{h_{ik}\}$ where $_k$ is a weight associated with demands for service level k.
$\delta_{ik} = 1$ if $h_{ik} > 0$, zero otherwise

10.4.2.3 Model Outputs (Decision Variables)

Model outputs of this model are as follows:

$W_i = 1$ if demands at node i are covered, zero otherwise

10.4.2.4 Objective Function and its Constraints

The objective function of this model and its related constraints are as follows:

$$\text{Max} \sum_i h_i W_i. \tag{10.30}$$

Subject to

$$\sum X_{jq} = P_q \; \forall q, \tag{10.31}$$

$$Z_{ik} \leq \sum_j \sum_q a_{ij}^{kq} X_{jq} \; \forall i, k, \tag{10.32}$$

$$W_i \leq Z_{ik} + (1 - \delta_{ik}) \; \forall i, k, \tag{10.33}$$

$$0 \leq Z_{ik} \leq 1 \; \forall i, k, \tag{10.34}$$

$$X_{jq} = 0, 1 \; \forall j, k, \tag{10.35}$$

$$0 \leq W_i \leq 1 \; \forall i. \tag{10.36}$$

Equation (10.30) maximizes the number of covered demands.

Equations (10.31)–(10.32) are identical to (10.26)–(10.27) respectively. Equations (10.33) stipulates that demands at node i cannot be covered unless all services that are required at demand node i are covered. If there exists demand for service level k at node i ($\delta_{ik}=1$), then (10.33) stipulates that $W_i \leq Z_{ik}$, meaning that node i cannot be covered unless demands for service level k at node i are covered. However, if there is no demand for level k services at node i, then node i can be covered even if $Z_{ik} = 0$. Finally, (10.34)–(10.36) are the nonnegative and integrity constraints on the problem's decision variables.

10.4.2.5 Extensions and Comments on the Model

A complication associated with hierarchical covering location problem is that the critical distance for lower-level services should be significantly less than that for the higher-level services. However, in nested systems, the critical distance definition changes since one can cover demand for lower-level services with a higher-level facility as long as the multi-flow setting exists. To consider critical distance, it can be assumed that demand i is covered if:

- Lower-level facility is within a distance d_l of node i and higher-level facility is within a distance d_h of node i or
- Higher-level facility is within a distance d of node i, where $d_l < d < d_h$.

This definition is presented by Moore and ReVelle (1982) and then used by Mandell (1998), Espejo et al. (2003) and Jayaraman et al. (2003).

Mandell (1998) presented a probabilistic version of this model. Capacity of facilities constraints were added to hierarchical maximal covering location problem by Jayaraman et al. (2003). Marianov and Serra (2001) proposed a hierarchical covering model within a queuing approach that also guarantees a service level. This approach is also mentioned in Boffey et al. (2007). Serra et al. (1992) and Marianov and Taborga (2001) considered this model in condition of competition with existing facilities.

10.5 Median-Based Hierarchical Relocation Problem (Teixeira and Antunes 2008)

Teixeira and Antunes (2008) presented a model for relocating hierarchical facilities. The model considers openings and closures.

10.5.1 Median-Based Hierarchical Relocation Problem with Closest Assignment

The model assumes that customers attend the closest facility offering a particular level of service (Teixeira and Antunes 2008).

10.5.1.1 Model Assumptions

- The objective function is *MiniSum*.
- The solution space is *discrete* and *finite*.
- The formulation represents a *nested* and *capacitated* system.
- The type of spatial pattern is *single* and *closest assignment*.
- The number of facilities at each level is known (*exogenous* model).

10.5.1.2 Model Inputs

Model inputs are similar to globally inclusive service hierarchy model in addition to these new parameters:

J_k^0: the set of locations with existing type k facilities
B_{ik}: the maximum capacities of level k facility at candidate location j

b_{jk}: the minimum capacities of level k facility at candidate location j
q_k: the number of type k facilities to be closed
D_k: the maximum user-to-facility distance for demand level k

10.5.1.3 Model Outputs (Decision Variables)

Model inputs are similar to globally inclusive service hierarchy model in addition to one new variable:

Z_{jkt}: the capacity occupied with demand level k of a level t facility located at candidate location j

10.5.1.4 Objective Function and its Constraints

The objective function of this model and its related constraints are as follows:

$$\text{Min} \sum_i \sum_j \sum_k h_{ik} d_{ij} Y_{ijk}. \tag{10.37}$$

Subject to

$$\sum_j Y_{ijk} = 1 \ \forall \ i,k, \tag{10.38}$$

$$Y_{ijk} \leq \sum_{h=k}^{m} X_{jh} \ \forall \ i,j,k, \tag{10.39}$$

$$\sum_{h=k}^{m} Z_{jkt} \leq \sum_i u_{ik} Y_{ijk} \ \forall \ j,k, \tag{10.40}$$

$$\sum_{h=k}^{m} Z_{jkt} \geq b_{jk} X_{jk} \ \forall \ j,k, \tag{10.41}$$

$$\sum_{h=k}^{m} Z_{jkt} \geq B_{jk} X_{jk} \ \forall \ j,k, \tag{10.42}$$

$$\sum_{d_{ih} \leq d_{ij}} Y_{ihk} \geq X_{jk} \ \forall \ i,j,k | t \geq k, \tag{10.43}$$

$$\sum_j X_{jk} \leq p_k \ \ \forall \ k, \tag{10.44}$$

$$\sum_j X_{jk} \geq |J_k^0| - q_k \ \forall \ k, \tag{10.45}$$

$$Y_{ijk} = 0 \ \forall \ i, j, k | d_{ij} \geq D_k, \qquad (10.46)$$

$$X_{jk} = 0, 1 \ \forall \ j, k, \qquad (10.47)$$

$$Y_{ijk} = 0, 1 \ \forall \ i, j, k, \qquad (10.48)$$

$$Y_{jkt} \geq 0 \ \forall \ j, k, t. \qquad (10.49)$$

Equations (10.38) ensure that all demands of all levels from all nodes are satisfied. Equations (10.39) impose that a given level of demand can only be satisfied by a facility of equal or higher level. Equations (10.40) define capacity variables Z_{jkt} by stating that the demand of each level assigned to a node has to be served by some facility of equal or higher level located there. Equations (10.41)–(10.42) impose maximum and minimum limits on capacity, according to facility type. Closest assignment Equations (10.43) are written separately per demand level and state that each demand level must be assigned to the closest facility of equal or higher level. Equations (10.44)–(10.45) limit the number of new facilities to be opened and existing facilities to be closed. Equations (10.46) limit the maximum travel distance between demand nodes and facilities. Finally, Equations (10.47)–(10.49) define decision variables and enforce single assignment.

10.5.2 Median-Based Hierarchical Relocation Problem with Path Assignment

The model assumes that when a given facility is located at location j, all demands near the path travelled by the customers to reach the facility are also assigned to it (Teixeira and Antunes 2008).

10.5.2.1 Model Assumptions

The assumptions of this model are similar to previous model except that there is the following difference:

- The type of spatial pattern is *single* and *path assignment*.

10.5.2.2 Model Inputs

Model inputs are similar to previous model in addition to one new parameter:

$|P_{ij}|$: the cardinality of the subset of demand nodes that are near the shortest path from v to j

10.5.2.3 Model Outputs (Decision Variables)

Model outputs are similar to previous model.

10.5.2.4 Objective Function and its Constraints

The objective function of this model and its related constraints are as follows:
- Equations (10.43) are omitted
- The following constraints are added to the formulation:

$$\sum_{h} Y_{hjk} \geq |P_{ij}| \cdot Y_{ijk} \ \forall \ i, j, k \ . \tag{10.50}$$

In (10.50) the assignments of different levels are independent, while in (10.43) the location of higher-level facilities influences lower-level assignments.

10.6 Solving Algorithms for Hierarchical Location Problem

Many algorithms are represented to solve different types of hierarchical facility location problems. Similar to single-level location problems, Lagrangian relaxations, specialized branch and bound procedures and conventional heuristic methods are developed for hierarchical location problems. Also a group of studies developing combinatorial approximation algorithms have appeared in recent years. We review the related literatures of solving algorithms for hierarchical facility location problems.

- Scott (1971) presented a heuristic algorithm for the hierarchical location–allocation problem. The algorithm involves a steady movement from a high value of the objective function, to progressively lower values, and this is accomplished through a series of iterative stages each of which seeks out a locally optimal solution.
- Dökmeci (1977) used a heuristic method. In this method at first an ideal theoretic solution is obtained from the heuristic procedure. Then by repeating the foregoing heuristic and adjustment procedures for each level, the environmentally adjusted optimal locations of the facilities are obtained.
- Moore and ReVelle (1982) used relaxed linear programming, supplemented by branch and bound where necessary, to solve the integer programming problem which is extension of the 2-level hierarchical maximal covering location problem.
- Considering the hierarchical maximum covering location problem presented by Moore and ReVelle (1982), Espejo et al. (2003) defined a combined Lagrangian–surrogate (L–S) relaxation which reduces to a 0–1 knapsack

problem. A Lagrangian and a surrogate relaxation of the problem, which are particular cases of (L–S) relaxation, are also discussed. Then they developed a subgradient-based heuristic using the proposed relaxations to solve this problem.

- Tcha and Lee (1984) represented a branch and bound algorithm for the multi-level uncapacitated facility location problem. In this method, the dual based scheme of "dual ascent procedure" is applied. Also the convergence rate to an optimal solution for this branch and bound algorithm has been further accelerated by employing two other devices, node simplification procedure and primal descent procedure.
- For the two-level uncapacitated facility location problem with some side constraints. Ro and Tcha (1984) proposed a branch and bound solution procedure, employing a set of new devices for lower bounds and simplifications which are obtained by exploiting the submodularity of the objective function and the special structure of the side-constraints.
- Narula and Ogbu (1985) developed the Lagrangian relaxation of the uncapacitated 2-hierarchical location–allocation problem and proposed a subgradient optimization procedure to solve it.
- Hodgson (1986) solved the nested hierarchical location–allocation problem with allocations based on facility size by employing a heuristic method which allows all levels to be located simultaneously. He reformulated the model based upon the Reilly law of retail gravitation, because of the difficulties encountered with the traditional inverse square Reilly law, using a negative exponential allocation rule which has been a popular way of overcoming the inability to model trips over short distances.
- Van Roy (1989) used standard features and techniques for solving linear programming (LP) and mixed integer programming (MIP) problems with an improved formulation based on pre- and post-processing of the problem and dynamic cut generation procedures for speed up the solution of MIP problems.
- Okabe et al. (1997) used the optimization procedure with two steps for a system of successively inclusive hierarchical facilities. The first step optimizes a system of exclusive hierarchical facilities by an analytical method. Using this optimal solution, the second step optimizes a system of successively inclusive hierarchical facilities by a computational search method.
- Barros et al. (1998) represented a heuristic method based on linear relaxation.
- Aardal (1998) presented some classes of inequalities to strengthen the linear relaxation for obtaining a good lower bound on the optimal solution in branch and bound.
- Aardal et al. (1999) developed a randomized algorithm for the hierarchical facility location problem. The algorithm is a randomized rounding procedure that use an optimal solution of a linear programming relaxation and its dual to make a random choice of facilities to be opened.
- Goncharov and Kochetov (2000) presented a probabilistic Tabu search algorithm for multi stage uncapacitated facility location problem.
- Marianov and Taborga (2001) proposed a heuristic algorithm to solve their model.

- A simple dual ascent method for the hierarchical facility location problem is presented by Bumb and Kern (2001). The algorithm is deterministic and based on the primal-dual technique.
- Bumb (2001) presented a 0.47-approximation algorithm for the maximization version of the two level uncapacitated facility location problem. For the analysis of this algorithm the assumption that there are only two levels of facilities is essential. The generalization of the algorithm to the case when the facilities are located on k levels, with $k > 2$, makes the analysis of the algorithm much more difficult.
- For the nested hierarchical queuing covering location problem, Marianov and Serra (2001) offered a bi-level heuristic with two phases. A construction phase using a greedy adding procedure with random substitution (GRASP) and an improvement phase by using a vertex-substitution heuristic and a tabu search procedure.
- Eben-Chaime et al. (2002) proposed a heuristic solution schemes and lower bounds on objective values for capacitated location–allocation problem on a line.
- Galvão et al. (2002) represented Lagrangian-based decomposition of the hierarchical location problem and proposed three heuristic methods to solve this model: a 3 p-median heuristic which consists of successively locating each level services and then applying a vertex substitution algorithm, a Lagrangian heuristic which uses a subgradient optimization algorithm, and a modified Lagrangian heuristic.
- Galvão et al. (2006) used a Lagrangian heuristic for capacitated version of their previous model presented in Galvão et al. (2002).
- A Lagrangian relaxation methodology coupled with a heuristic was employed by Jayaraman et al. (2003) for hierarchical maximal covering location problem.
- Ageev et al. (2004) presented improved combinatorial approximation algorithms for the k-level facility location problem. In this research they applied path reduction and greedy for an approximation algorithm. Also they represented a recursive path reduction Algorithm for approximate this problem.
- A quasi-greedy algorithm for approximating the classical uncapacitated two-level facility location problem is presented by Zhang (2006).
- A hybrid multistart heuristic for the uncapacitated facility location problem was presented by Resende and Werneck (2006). Their method has two phases. The first is a multistart routine with intensification using a process called path-relinking. The second phase is post-optimization.
- Ignacio et al. (2008) presented a two-level hierarchical model for the location of concentrators and routers in computers networks. They used Lagrangian relaxation to provide lower bounds for the problem. A tabu search meta-heuristic is then developed to provide approximate solutions. A feasible solution of good quality is obtained by the TS algorithm.
- Chan et al. (2008) presented a nonlinear model for generalized search-and-rescue problem. This problem is modeled using a multiobjective linear integer program (MOLIP), which is an approximation of a highly nonlinear integer program. As a solution algorithm, the MOLIP is converted to a two-stage network-flow

formulation that reduces the number of explicitly enumerated integer variables. Non-inferior solutions of the MOLIP are evaluated by a value function, which identifies solutions that are similar to the more accurate nonlinear model.

10.7 Case Study

In this section we will introduce some real-world case studies related to hierarchical location problems.

10.7.1 A Hierarchical Model for the Location of Maternity Facilities in the Municipality of Rio de Janeiro (Galvão et al. 2002 and 2006)

Galvão et al. (2002) represented a 3-level hierarchical model that addresses the location of levels of facilities associated with maternal and perinatal care in Rio de Janeiro including basic units, maternity homes and neonatal clinics.

Since the overall aim is to develop a location model that aids health care authorities to reduce the perinatal mortality rate in the municipality, good access to facilities is needed. Therefore the model seeks to optimize the surrogate objective of total distance travelled by mothers-to-be. By the description of the different types of facility, they developed a successively inclusive model. Some other assumptions are considered for this model.

The model is solved for real 1995 data of the municipality of Rio de Janeiro. Also results are given for available problems, for networks ranging from 10 to 400 vertices.

Galvão et al. (2006) completed their model by adding some form of capacity constraints, which are needed especially in the higher, resource intensive level of the hierarchy. This model is solved exactly for a small problem and approximately for the 152-vertex Rio de Janeiro data.

10.7.2 Locational Analysis for Regionalization of Turkish Red Crescent Blood Services (Şahin et al. 2007)

Şahin et al. (2007) represented the location problem of the blood services of Turkish Red Crescent (TRC) at a regional level to increase the countrywide service level of the blood services, which is an integral part of the national health care system. They developed location–allocation models to solve the problems of regionalization based on a hierarchical structure.

The problem was considered as a 2-level hierarchical system in which the regional blood centers (RBCs) are the upper-level facilities whereas the blood centers, blood stations, and mobile units are the lower-level facilities.

The entire problem was decomposed into three stages. In Stage 1 they formulated a 2-level hierarchical pq-median problem in which the locations of the regional centers, the allocation of blood centers to the regional centers together with their service-referral levels, and the allocation of demand points to the blood centers were determined. A hierarchical set covering problem was formulated in Stage 2 to increase the service level. This second sub-problem finds the minimum number of blood stations such that every demand point is covered by at least one facility within a given maximal service distance or time. To help increase the service level even further, an integer programming model was formulated as the third sub-problem in Stage 3 to determine the fleet size for the mobile units in each region.

10.7.3 School Network Planning in Coimbra, Portugal (Teixeira and Antunes 2008)

Teixeira and Antunes (2008) presented a study on the redeployment of Coimbra's primary school network in Portugal. Three objectives were pursued by the education authorities. Three scenarios for the redeployment of the school network were considered. First, they solved median-based hierarchical relocation problem with closest assignment constraints. For this model, no feasible solutions could be found for any one of the three scenarios. The solutions were obtained for the three scenarios using median-based hierarchical relocation problem with path assignment constraints.

References

Aardal K (1998) Reformulation of capacitated facility location problems: how redundant information can help. Ann Oper Res 82:289–308
Aardal K, Chudak FA, Shmoys DB (1999) A 3-approximation algorithm for the k-level uncapacitated facility location problem. Inf Process Lett 72:161–167
Ageev A, Ye YY, Zhang JW (2004) Improved combinatorial approximation algorithms for the k-level facility location problem. SIAM J Discrete Math 18(1):207–217
Banerji S, Fisher HB (1974) Hierarchical location analysis for integrated area planning rural in India. Papers Sci Assoc 33:177–194
Barros AI, Dekker R, Scholten V (1998) A two-level network for recycling sand: a case study. Eur J Oper Res 110(3):199–214
Boffey B, Galvão RD, Espejo L (2007) A review of congestion models in the location of facilities with immobile servers. Eur J Oper Res 178:643–662
Bumb A (2001) An approximation algorithm for the maximization version of the two level uncapacitated facility location problem. Oper Res Lett 29:155–161

Bumb AF, Kern W (2001) A simple dual ascent algorithm for the multilevel facility location problem. Lecture notes in computer science 2129. Springer, Berlin, pp 55–62

Calvo AB, Marks DH (1973) Location of health care facilities: an analytical approach. Socio-Econ Plan Sci 7:407–422

Chan Y, Mahan JM, Chrissis JW, Drake DA, Wang D (2008) Hierarchical maximal coverage location allocation: Case of generalized search-and-rescue. Comput Oper Res 35:1886–1904

Charnes A, Storbeck J (1980) A goal programming model for the siting of multilevel EMS systems. Socio-Econ Plan Sci 14:155–161

Daskin MS (1995) Network and discrete location: Models, algorithms, and applications. Wiley, New York

Dökmeci VF (1977) A quantitative model to plan regional health facility systems. Manage Sci 24(4):411–419

Eben-Chaime M, Mehrez A, Markovich G (2002) Capacitated location–allocation problems on a line. Comput Oper Res 29:459–470

Espejo LGA, Galvão RD, Boffey B (2003) Dual-based heuristics for a hierarchical covering location problem. Comput Oper Res 30:165–180

Galvão RD, Espejo LGA, Boffey B (2002) A hierarchical model for the location of perinatal facilities in the municipality of Rio de Janeiro. Eur J Oper Res 138:495–517

Galvão RD, Espejo LGA, Boffey B (2006) Load balancing and capacity constraints in a hierarchical location model. Eur J Oper Res 172:631–646

Goncharov E, Kochetov Y (2000) Probabilistic tabu search algorithm for the multi-stage uncapacitated facility location problem. Operations research proceedings. Springer, Berlin, pp 65–70

Hodgson MJ (1986) A hierarchical location–allocation model with allocations based on facility size. Ann Oper Res 6:273–289

Ignacio AAV, Filho VJMF, Galvão RD (2008) Lower and upper bounds for a two-level hierarchical location problem in computer networks. Comput Oper Res 35:1982–1998

Jayaraman V, Gupta R, Pirkul H (2003) Selecting hierarchical facilities in a service-operations environment. Eur J Oper Res 147:613–628

Mandell MB (1998) Covering models for two-tiered emergency medical services systems. Location Sci 6:355–368

Marianov V, Serra D (2001) Hierarchical location allocation models for congested system. Eur J Oper Res 135:195–208

Marianov V, Taborga P (2001) Optimal location of public health centers which provide free and paid services. J Oper Res Soc 52(4):391–400

Mirchandani PB (1987) Technical note: generalized hierarchical facility locations. Transport Sci 21(2):123–125

Moore GC, ReVelle C (1982) The hierarchical service location problem. Manage Sci 28(7):775–780

Narula SC (1984) Hierarchical location–allocation problems: A classification scheme. Eur J Oper Res 5:93–99

Narula SC (1986) Minisum hierarchical location–allocation problems on a network: A survey. Ann Oper Res 6:257–272

Narula SC, Ogbu UI (1985) Lagrangian relaxation and decomposition in an uncapacitated 2-hierarchical location–allocation problem. Comput Oper Res 12(2):169–180

Okabe A, Okunuki K, Suzuki T (1997) A computational method for optimizing the hierarchy and spatial configuration of successively inclusive facilities on a continuous plane. Location Sci 5(4):255–268

Rahman SU, Smith DK (1999) Deployment of rural health facilities in a developing country. J Oper Res Soc 50(9):892–902

Rahman SU, Smith DK (2000) Use of location–allocation models in health service development planning in developing nations. Eur J Oper Res 123(3):437–452

Resende MGC, Werneck RF (2006) A hybrid multistart heuristic for the uncapacitated facility location problem. Eur J Oper Res 174:54–68

Ro H, Tcha DW (1984) A branch and bound algorithm for the two-level uncapacitated facility location problem with some side constraints. Eur J Oper Res 18:349–358

Şahin G, Süral H (2007) A review of hierarchical facility location models. Comput Oper Res 34:2310–2331

Şahin G, Süral H, Meral S (2007) Locational analysis for regionalization of Turkish Red Crescent blood services. Comput Oper Res 34:692–704

Scott AJ (1971) Operational analysis of nodal hierarchies in network systems. Oper Res Quart 22:25–36

Serra D, Marianov V, ReVelle C (1992) The maximum-capture hierarchical location problem. Eur J Oper Res 62:363–371

Smith HK, Harper PR, Potts CN, Thyle A (2009) Planning sustainable community health schemes in rural areas of developing countries. Eur J Oper Res 193: 768–777

Tcha DW, Lee B (1984) A branch-and-bound algorithm for the multi-level uncapacitated facility location problem. Eur J Oper Res 18:35–43

Teixeira JC, Antunes AP (2008) A hierarchical location model for public facility planning. Eur J Oper Res 185:92–104

Van Roy TJ (1989) Multi-level production and distribution planning with transportation fleet optimization. Manage Sci 35(12):1443–53

Zhang J (2006) Approximating the two-level facility location problem via a quasi-greedy approach. Math Program 108(1):159–176

Chapter 11
Hub Location Problem

Masoud Hekmatfar and Mirsaman Pishvaee

One of the novel topics in location problems is the hub location problem. There are plenty of applications for the hub location problem; therefore, this section is dedicated to introducing this problem to readers. The preface is composed of three parts: apprehensions, definitions, and classifications of the hub location problem.

In this chapter we discuss services such as, movement of people, commodities and information which occurs between an origin-destination pair of nodes (see A–B in Fig. 11.1 as an origin-destination pair). Each origin-destination pair needs a service different from other pairs. Thus, the commodities carried from i to j are not interchangeable with the commodities carried from j to i.

If we have N nodes and if each node can be either an origin or a destination, we'll have $N(N-1)$ origin-destination pairs of nodes in a network which form a fully connected network (a network in which all nodes are connected together). Notice that $i-j$ pair is different from $j-i$ pair. A sample network with six nodes is presented in Fig. 11.1 (Daskin 1995).

Assuming that we have different traffic services in this network and that each vehicle can service *five* origin-destination pairs every day, with 18 vehicles, we will be able to service *ten* nodes every day.

If we set one of the nodes as a hub[1] node and connect it to all of the other nodes, which are introduced as spoke, we will have $2(N-1)$ connections to service all origin-destination node pairs. This network is presented in Fig. 11.2 (Daskin 1995). In this network, if there are different traffic services and if each vehicle can service five origin-destination pairs every day, with 18 vehicles, we will be able to service 46 nodes every day.

Thus, with fixed traffic resources, we can service more cities with a hub network than with a completely connected network[2].

---

[1] Hub means the ball in the center of a wheel and Campbell (1994) defined it as "the facilities that are servicing many origin-destination pairs as transformation and tradeoff nodes, and are used in traffic systems and telecommunications."

[2] This argument ignores vehicles' capacity. It should be clear that the volume of goods or the number of people transported on each link in the hub-and-spoke network will be considerably greater than the number transported on each link of the fully connected network. This also ignores differences in the distances between nodes as it assumes that the number of origin-destination pair trips a vehicle can service is independent from the distances between the nodes.

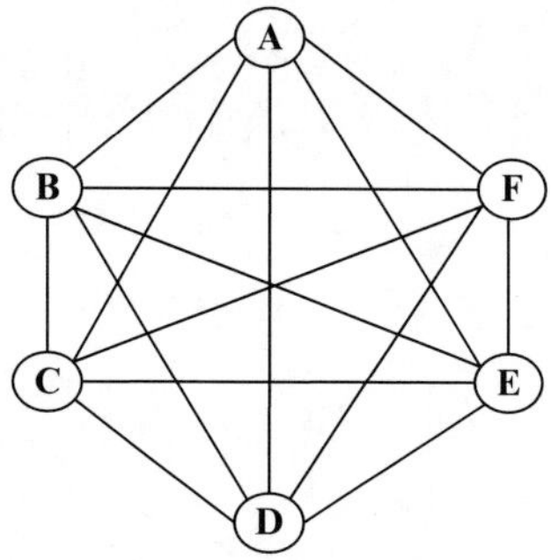

Fig. 11.1 A fully connected network with 6 nodes and 30 origin-destination pairs (Daskin 1995)

Fig. 11.2 A hub and spoke network with 6 nodes and *30* origin-destination pairs (Daskin 1995)

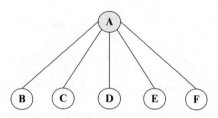

The main disadvantage of such system (regarding all nodes except the hub node) is that more than one trip is required to travel between each origin-destination pair since we have to pass the hub node to be able to travel from one non-hub node to another.

In multi hub networks, we assume that the hub nodes are completely connected to one another and that each non-hub node is connected to exactly (at least) one hub node such as Fig. 11.3 (Daskin 1995). In Fig. 11.3, there are 15 cities and *three* hubs. The number of passengers or commodities carried from one hub to another is greater than the number of passengers or commodities moved from each non-hub node to that hub; for example if the traffic between each origin-destination pair is *ten* units, there will be 140 traffic units between each non-hub city and the hub it is connected to, but there will be 250 traffic units between two hubs.

It is not reasonable to establish direct paths between every pair of nodes; for example assume that we establish direct paths between each pair of nodes in a connective network such as, a route network or a computer network (Camargo et al. 2008). Thus, hub nodes are used to resolve this problem. One of the advantages of using hubs is that we gain economic profits by establishing more qualitative paths between the hubs (Camargo et al. 2008). In road networks, when there are a large number of relationships between two nodes, it is economic to establish a highway with several lines between those two nodes, and obtain faster movement of vehicles, and less waste in fuel, and, thus, savings in time and cost.

In computer networks, fiber-optic cables are only used to connect hubs and it is not economic to use them to join any two nodes.

Fig. 11.3 Example of a three-hub network (Daskin 1995)

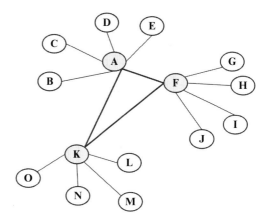

This chapter is organized as follows. In Sect. 11.1, some applications of hub location problem and its classifications are given, and Sect. 11.2 presents some models developed for the problem. Some relevant algorithms to solve hub models are given in Sect. 11.3. Finally, Sect. 11.4 represents some real world case studies with a short summary.

11.1 Applications and Classifications

Many applications of hub problem are given in the following:

- Airlines and air ports: Some works in this area are Toh et al. (1985), Shaw (1993), Aykin (1995), Jaillet et al. (1996), Bania et al. (1998), Sasaki et al. (1999), Martin and Roman (2003) and Adler and Hashai (2005). In Adler and Hashai (2005), airlines and transportations based on open sky policy are surveyed in the Middle East. It is interesting that based on their research, the four cities selected as optimized hub airports are, in order of utility, Cairo, Tehran, Istanbul, and Riyadh. Dubai which now works as an important center for airport transportation, is not an optimal hub airport. This means that, politic and economic problems have dominated over optimized location.
- Transportation and handling problems: Some works in this area are Don et al. (1995), Lumsdenk et al. (1999), Aversa et al. (2005), Baird et al. (2006), Cunha and Silva (2007), Yaman et al. (2007) and Eiselt (2007). In Eiselt (2007), finding the optimized land dump locations, with respect to garbage transportation stations, is discussed.
- Post delivery services and fast delivery packing companies: Kuby et al. (1993), Krishnamoorthy et al. (1994), Ernst and Krishnamoorthy (1996) and Ebery et al. (2000) represent models in this area.

- Telecommunication systems and massage delivery networks: Some works in this area are Lee et al. (1996) and Klincewicz (1998).
- Emergency services: Hakimi (1964) and Berman et al. (2007) represented models in emergency services. Berman et al. (2007) discussed the location of a hub for rescue helicopters.
- Chain stores in supply chain (like Wall-Mart): A work in this area is Campbell et al. (2002).
- Productive companies in basis transportation correctly: Every assembly plant probably wants to find an optimized solution for its material storage and handling such that each production facility can receive its required materials effectively.

Some practical examples of hub problems are as follows:

- A classical example is Hungarian railway system with Budapest as its hub.
- Two huge American airlines based in Atlanta and Chicago, use hub networks.
- Dubai airport is a hub for many flights in the Middle East.

The hub location problem has a short history. The first paper on hub location problem was published by Toh et al. (1985). This paper was on the application of hub location problem in airlines and airports. Although Hakimi (1964) first published a paper on hub location, since next paper on this topic was not published until two decades later, it is assumed that the hub location problem has been first discussed in 1980s.

O'Kelly (1987) developed hub location models. He had an important role in developing the first modeling of hub problems (O'Kelly 1987, 1992). Later, Campbell (1994) played a major role in completing hub modeling. His papers are among the most important papers on types of hub modeling (Campbell 1994, 1996). Also, some authors played important roles in improving this topic (Aykin 1994, 1995; Klincewicz 1991, 1992).

Many papers have been published on hub location problem so far (since 1980s). Daskin (1995) has written a book on "Network and Discrete location" and only a brief section of this book is dedicated to hub location. Figure 11.4 shows that the number of papers has increased in recent years. The number of published papers on hubs shows a significant increase in 1996, which is presumably the time when the modeling of hub problems has reached maturity. The emphasis of papers was on modeling in the early years, on optimizing and completing the models in the following years, and, finally, on solution methods in recent years. Thus, hub location problem is a rather new topic and a good area for research and development activities.

A classification of different types of hub problems and their properties is represented as follows:

- Area solution: *discrete, continual*
- Objective function: *MiniMax, MiniSum*
- Determination of the number of hubs: *exogenous, endogenous*
- Number of hubs: one hub, more than one hub
- Hub capacity: *unlimited (uncapacitated), limited*

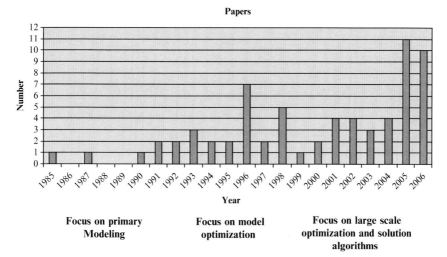

Fig. 11.4 Revolution of Hub location problem papers[3]

- Cost of hub location: no cost, *fixed cost*, *variable cost*
- Node connections to hub: to one hub, to more than one hub
- The cost of connection to a hub: no cost, *fixed cost*, *variable cost*

Researchers have worked on a variety of hub modeling problems. However, no research has been conducted on many types of hub modeling problems resulted from multiplying the above items. On the other hand, some of the new models do not have any applications in the real world and, therefore, are not really worth modeling.

Since most of the applications of hub problems in real world are discrete, the models developed so far are mostly discrete models.

11.2 Models

In this section we introduce hub models represented and developed as mathematical models.

11.2.1 Single Hub Location Problem (O'Kelly 1987)

O'Kelly (1987) was the first to introduce the single hub model which has only one hub node.

---

[3] This information is based on Springer-Verlag and Elsevier (Science Direct) websites.

11.2.1.1 Model Assumptions

Model assumptions of this model are as follows:

- The objective function is *MiniSum*.
- The solution space is *discrete* and *finite*.
- There is only one hub node.
- All of the nodes are connected to the hub node and each non-hub node is connected to every other non-hub node via the hub node.
- The number of hub nodes is known (*exogenous* model).
- The installation cost of the hub node is not considered.
- The capacity of the hub node is *unlimited* (*uncapacitated* model).
- All decision variables of the model are binary (0–1) variables.

11.2.1.2 Model Inputs

Model inputs of this model are as follows:

h_{ij}: demand or flow between origin i and destination j
C_{ij}: unit cost of local (non-hub to hub) movement between nodes i and j

11.2.1.3 Model Outputs (Decision Variables)

Model outputs of this model are as follows:

X_j = a hub is located at node j
Y_{ij} = node i is connected to a hub located at node j

11.2.1.4 Objective Function and its Constraints

The objective function of this model and its related constraints are as follows:

$$\text{Min} \sum_i \sum_j \sum_k h_{ik} \left(C_{ij} + C_{jk} \right) y_{ij} y_{kj}. \tag{11.1}$$

Subject to

$$\sum_j X_j = 1, \tag{11.2}$$

$$Y_{ij} - X_j \leq 0 \; \forall_{i,j}, \tag{11.3}$$

$$X_j = 0, 1 \; \forall_j, \tag{11.4}$$

$$Y_{ij} = 0, 1 \; \forall_{i,j}. \tag{11.5}$$

Equation (11.1) minimizes the total cost associated with the transport through the hub. Equation (11.2) ensures that we locate only one hub. Equation (11.3) ensures that demand node i cannot be connected to a hub at j unless we locate the hub at j. Equations (11.4) and (11.5) are standard integrity constraints.

11.2.1.5 Linearizing the Objective Function

The objective function is quadratic since it involves the product of decision variables. However since there is only one hub, if node i is assigned to a hub at node j, then all nodes $k(k \neq i)$ must be assigned to the hub at node j. Thus we can rewrite (11.1) as follows:

$$\sum_i \sum_j \sum_k h_{ik} (C_{ij} + C_{jk}) y_{ij} y_{kj} = \sum_i \sum_j C_{ij} y_{ij} \left(\sum_k h_{ik} \right) + \sum_j \sum_i C_{ji} y_{ij} \left(\sum_k h_{ki} \right) = \sum_i \sum_j C_{ij} y_{ij} (O_i + D_i), \quad (11.6)$$

where O_i: the total outflow of node i; D_i: the total inflow of node i.

Having transformed (11.1)–(11.6), we can find the optimal 1-hub location with minimum objective function value by total enumeration in $O(N^2)$ time.

11.2.2 P-Hub Location Problem (O'Kelly 1987)

This model is referred to as single allocation P-hub location problem, since each non-hub node is assigned to one hub node (O'Kelly 1987).

11.2.2.1 Model Assumptions

Model assumptions are as follows:

- The objective function is *MiniSum*.
- The solution space is *discrete* and *finite*.
- All of the hub nodes are connected to one another and each non-hub node is connected to (exactly, at least) a hub.
- The number of hub nodes is known (*exogenous*).
- To travel between two non-hub nodes, one or two hubs have to be passed, i.e. two non hub nodes are never connected directly.
- The installation cost of the hub nodes is not considered.
- The capacities of the hub nodes are *unlimited* (*uncapacitated* model).
- All decision variables of the model are binary variables (0–1).

11.2.2.2 Model Inputs

We have all the inputs in previous model in addition to the following inputs:

α = discount factor for line-haul movement between hubs ($0 \leq \alpha < 1$).

As transportation cost between two hubs is less than transportation cost between a hub node and a non-hub node, we multiply α by C_{ij} in calculating the movement cost between two hubs.

P = the number of hubs to locate.

11.2.2.3 Model Outputs (Decision Variables)

The outputs of this model are similar to the previous model.

11.2.2.4 Objective Function and its Constraints

The objective function of this model and its related constraints are as follows:

$$\text{Min} \sum_i \sum_k C_{ik} Y_{ik} \left(\sum_j h_{ij} \right) + \sum_k \sum_i C_{ki} Y_{ik} \left(\sum_J h_{ji} \right)$$

$$+ \alpha \sum_i \sum_j \sum_k \sum_m h_{ij} C_{km} y_{ik} y_{jm}. \quad (11.7)$$

Subject to

$$\sum_j y_{ij} = 1 \ \forall i, \quad (11.8)$$

$$\sum_j x_j = P, \quad (11.9)$$

$$y_{ij} - x_j \leq 0 \ \forall i, j, \quad (11.10)$$

$$x_j = 0, 1 \ \forall j, \quad (11.11)$$

$$y_{ij} = 0, 1 \ \forall i, j. \quad (11.12)$$

Equation (11.7) minimizes the total cost associated with the P hubs locations and the assignment of nodes to the hubs. The first term is the cost of connecting all trips originating at node i to the hub k to which node i is attached. The second term is the cost of connecting all trips destined for node i to hub k, to which node i is attached (sum on all i, k). The third term is a hub-to-hub connection cost (sum of two hubs). Equation (11.8) ensures that each node i is assigned to exactly one hub. Equation (11.9) ensures that the number of hub nodes is P. Equation (11.10) states that demand node i cannot be connected to a hub at j unless we locate the hub at j. Equations (11.11) and (11.12) are standard integrity constraints.

11.2.3 Multiple Allocation P-Hub Location Model (P-Hub Median Location Model) (Campbell 1991)

The objective function of the previous model was nonlinear; so Campbell (1991) represented the following model with a linear objective function. He formulated this model like P-median problem and called it P-hub median location model. We discuss P-hub median problems in which each non-hub node can be connected to more than one hub, and therefore, are called multiple allocation P-hub location problem. Notice that this property is not fixed, so we also discuss models with one allocation between each hub node and non-hub node (discussed in Sect. 11.2.5).

11.2.3.1 Model Assumptions

Model assumptions are similar to the ones of P-hub problem model except that the Z_{ij}^{km} variables is relaxed ($Z_{ij}^{km} \geq 0$) and each non-hub node can be connected to more than one hub node.

11.2.3.2 Model Inputs

Model inputs are similar to P-hub problem model except that the C_{ij} variables are defined as follows:

C_{ij}^{km} = unit cost of travel between origin i and destination j when going via hubs at nodes k and m

$$\left(C_{ij}^{km} = C_{ik} + \alpha C_{km} + C_{mj}\right). \tag{11.13}$$

11.2.3.3 Model Outputs (Decision Variables)

The model outputs of this model are as follows:

X_j = a hub is located at node j
Z_{ij}^{km} = flow from origin i to destination j uses hubs at candidates sites k and m.

11.2.3.4 Objective Function and its Constraints

The objective function of this model and its related constraints are as follows:

$$\text{Min} \sum_i \sum_j \sum_k \sum_m C_{ij}^{km} h_{ij} Z_{ij}^{km}. \tag{11.14}$$

Subject to

$$\sum_k x_k = P, \tag{11.15}$$

$$\sum_k \sum_m Z_{ij}^{km} = 1 \; \forall i, j, \tag{11.16}$$

$$Z_{ij}^{km} \leq x_m \; \forall i, j, k, m, \tag{11.17}$$

$$Z_{ij}^{km} \leq x_k \; \forall i, j, k, m, \tag{11.18}$$

$$Z_{ij}^{km} \geq 0 \; \forall i, j, k, m, \tag{11.19}$$

$$x_k = 0, 1 \; \forall k. \tag{11.20}$$

Equation (11.14) minimizes the demand-weighted total travel cost. Equation (11.15) stipulates that exactly P hubs should be located. Equations (11.16) ensure that each origin-destination pair (i, j) must be assigned to exactly one hub pair. Equations (11.17) and (11.18) stipulate that flow from origin i to destination j cannot be assigned to a hub at location k or m unless a hub is located at these candidate nodes (when we travel from one node to another node via one hub node, m and k are coincided with each other). Equations (11.19) are standard integrality constraints. Equations (11.20) are relaxed decision variable constraints.

One of the key difficulties associated with this hub location model should also be evident from this formulation. The number of assignment variables (Z_{ij}^{km}) can be extremely large. In fact, if every origin or destination node is a candidate hub, there will be $O(N^4)$ of such variables. For a relatively small problem with 32 origins and destinations, we would have over one million such decision variables. In short, the size of these problems grows very quickly with the number of nodes in the problem unless some a priori means of eliminating candidate hub locations is used. The use of quadratic formulation (11.7) reduces the number of decision variables dramatically but does not make solving the problem any easier.

11.2.4 P-Hub Median Location Problem with Fixed Costs (O' Kelly 1992)

P-hub median location model with respect to fixed cost of hub locations is represented by O' Kelly (1992).

11.2.4.1 Model Assumptions

The model assumptions are similar to the ones of P-hub problem model except that there are two differences:

- The number of hub nodes is not known beforehand (*endogenous*).
- A *fixed cost* of hub location is incorporated into the model.

11.2.4.2 Model Inputs

Model inputs are similar to the inputs of P-hub problem model in addition to two new variables:

$B = $ a weight on the capital or fixed costs to allow exploration of the tradeoff between capital costs and transport (or operating) costs
$f_k = $ the fixed cost of hub location in candidate node k

11.2.4.3 Model Outputs (Decision Variables)

The outputs are similar to P-hub problem model.

11.2.4.4 Objective Function and its Constraints

The differences between the objective function of this model and P-hub problem model are as follows:

- Equations (11.9) are eliminated
- The following term is added to the objective function:

$$B \sum_k f_x x_k. \tag{11.21}$$

11.2.5 Single Spoke Assignment P-Hub Median Location Problem (Single Allocation P-Hub Location Problem) (Daskin 1995)

Equation (11.14)–(11.20), P-hub median location model, allow each of the spoke nodes to be assigned to multiple hubs. Thus, for example, the assignment shown in Fig. 11.5 (Daskin 1995) is entirely possible as a result of solving this model. In this figure two origin-destination flows are shown: origin i to destination j_1 and origin i to destination j_2. Origin i is assigned to two different hubs: k_1, k_2.

Fig. 11.5 Schematic representation of multiple spoke assignment (Daskin 1995)

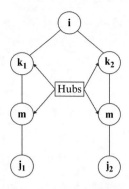

Fig. 11.6 Schematic representation of single spoke assignment (Daskin 1995)

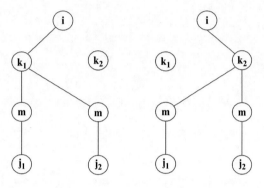

In many cases, it is desirable (for operational reasons) to have each of the spoke nodes assigned to a single hub. This might result in one of the assignments shown in Fig. 11.6 (Daskin 1995).

The single spoke assignment P-hub median location model is formulated as Daskin (1995)'s model.

11.2.5.1 Model Assumptions

The assumptions of this model are similar to median P-hub model except that there are the two following differences:

- Each non-hub node is assigned to only one hub.
- All of the variables are binary variables (0–1).

11.2.5.2 Model Inputs

Model inputs are similar to median P-hub model.

11.2.5.3 Model Outputs (Decision Variables)

Model outputs are similar to median P-hub model in addition to the following decision variables:

Y_{ik} = non-hub node i is assigned to a hub node k

11.2.5.4 Objective Function and its Constraints

The objective function of this model and its related constraints are as follows:

$$\text{Min} \sum_i \sum_j \sum_k \sum_m C_{ij}^{km} h_{ij} Z_{ij}^{km}. \tag{11.22}$$

Subject to

$$\sum_k X_k = P, \tag{11.23}$$

$$\sum_k \sum_m Z_{ij}^{km} = 1 \; \forall \, i, j, \tag{11.24}$$

$$Y_{ik} \leq X_k \; \forall \, i, k, \tag{11.25}$$

$$\sum_k Y_{ik} = 1 \; \forall i, \tag{11.26}$$

$$Y_{ik} + Y_{jm} - 2Z_{ij}^{km} \geq 0 \; \forall i, j, k, m, \tag{11.27}$$

$$X_k = 0, 1 \; \forall k, \tag{11.28}$$

$$Y_{ik} = 0, 1 \; \forall i, k, \tag{11.29}$$

$$Z_{ij}^{km} = 0, 1 \; \forall i, j, k, m. \tag{11.30}$$

Equation (11.22)–(11.24) are identical to those of (11.14)–(11.16). Equations (11.25) ensure that spoke i cannot be assigned to a hub at location k unless we locate a hub at location k. Equations (11.26) are key constraints that stipulate that each spoke node i is assigned to exactly one hub. Equations (11.27) state that the flow from origin i to destination j cannot be routed through hubs at nodes k and m, unless spoke node i is assigned to a hub at k and spoke node m is assigned to a hub at j. Equations (11.28)–(11.30) are standard integrity constraints.

11.2.6 The Extension Model of Fixed Cost for Connecting a Spoke to a Hub (Campbell 1994)

Instead of forcing each spoke node to be assigned to a single hub, we may want to stipulate a fixed cost to any spoke/hub connection. Alternatively, we could incorporate a fixed cost for connecting a spoke to a hub. Campbell (1994) shows how these extensions can be formulated.

11.2.6.1 Model Assumptions

The assumptions of this model are similar to median P-hub model except that there is a fixed cost for connecting a spoke to a hub.

11.2.6.2 Model Inputs

Model inputs are similar to median P-hub model in addition to the following parameter:

g_{ik}: the fixed cost of connecting spoke node i to a hub at candidate location k.

11.2.6.3 Model Outputs (Decision Variables)

Model outputs are similar to single allocation median P-hub model.

11.2.6.4 Objective Function and its Constraints

The objective function is similar to median P-hub model in addition to the following term:

$$\sum_i \sum_k g_{ik} Y_{ik}. \tag{11.31}$$

11.2.7 Minimum Value Flow on any Spoke/Hub Connection Problem (Campbell 1994)

Instead of forcing each spoke node to be assigned to a single hub, we may want to stipulate that the flow along any spoke/hub connection exceed some minimum value. Campbell (1994) represented this model, which is similar to single allocation P-hub location problem.

11.2.7.1 Model Assumptions

The assumptions of this model are similar to median P-hub model except that there is a minimum flow for each spoke/hub connection.

11.2.7.2 Model Inputs

Model inputs are similar to median P-hub model in addition to the following parameter:

l_{ik}: the minimum flow between spoke i and hub k.

11.2.7.3 Model Outputs (Decision Variables)

Model outputs are similar to single allocation median P-hub model.

11.2.7.4 Objective Function and its Constraints

The objective function is similar to median P-hub model except that the following constraints are added to median P-hub model's constraints:

$$Y_{ik} + Y_{jm} - 2Z_{ij}^{km} \geq 0 \ \forall i,j,k,m, \tag{11.32}$$

$$\sum_m \sum_j h_{ij} Z_{ij}^{km} + \sum_P \sum_s h_{pi} Z_{Pi}^{sk} \geq L_{ik} Y_{ik} \ \forall i,k. \tag{11.33}$$

Equations (11.32) were explained before. The first term of constraints (11.33) are the flow from spoke node i to hub k and then from there to any hub/destination pair. The second term is the flow from any origin/hub pair to hub k and then from there to destination i. The sum of these two flows is the total flow between two nodes i, k.

11.2.8 Capacity Limitation of Hub Location Problem (Campbell 1994)

Capacity limitation of hub node means that the total flows, incoming or outgoing, must be less than or equal to a fixed value and is called capacitated hub location problem. This model is represented by Campbell (1994).

11.2.8.1 Model Assumptions

The assumptions of this model are similar to median P-hub model except that the capacities of the hub nodes are limited.

11.2.8.2 Model Inputs

Model inputs are similar to median P-hub model in addition to the following parameter:

θ_k = the capacity of a hub at candidate node k.

11.2.8.3 Model Outputs (Decision Variables)

Model outputs are similar to median P-hub model.

11.2.8.4 Objective Function and its Constraints

The objective function is similar to median P-hub model except that the following constraints are added to median P-hub model's constraints:

$$\sum_m \sum_i \sum_j h_{ij} Z_{ij}^{km} + \sum_s \sum_i \sum_j h_{ij} Z_{ij}^{sk} \leq \theta_k X_k \ \forall k. \tag{11.34}$$

The left side of the above inequality shows the total incoming and outgoing flows of node k.

11.2.9 P-Hub Center Location Problem (Campbell 1994)

The center location problem is an important problem for its applications such as emergency facility location or the worst situation scenario. The P-hub center location problem is similar to P-center location problem. If an origin-destination pair in a hub location problem is introduced as a demand node in P-center problem, the meaning of a hub center problem is a set of hubs that minimizes the maximum cost of each origin/destination pair. This problem is used for decomposable goods or sensitive goods in a hub system. This model is represented by Campbell (1994).

11.2.9.1 Model Assumptions

The assumptions of this model are similar to median P-hub model except that X_k variables are relaxed and the objective function is *MiniMax*.

11.2.9.2 Model Inputs

Model inputs are similar to median P-hub model.

11.2.9.3 Model Outputs (Decision Variables)

Model outputs are similar to median P-hub model.

11.2.9.4 Objective Function and its Constraints

The objective function of this model and its related constraints are as follows:

$$\text{Min Max} \left\{ C_{ij}^{km} h_{ij} Z_{ij}^{km} \right\}. \tag{11.35}$$

Subject to

$$\sum_k X_k = P, \quad (11.36)$$

$$\sum_k \sum_m Z_{ij}^{km} = 1 \ \forall \ i, j, \quad (11.37)$$

$$Z_{ij}^{km} \leq X_k \ \forall i, j, k, m, \quad (11.38)$$

$$Z_{ij}^{km} \leq X \ \forall i, j, k, m, \quad (11.39)$$

$$0 \leq X_k \leq 1 \ \forall k, \quad (11.40)$$

$$0 \leq Z_{ij}^{km} \leq 1 \ \forall i, j, k, m. \quad (11.41)$$

Equation (11.35) minimizes the maximum cost of transportation between each origin/destination pair. Equations (11.36)–(11.41) are similar to Median P-hub location problem.

Campbell et al. (2007) represented a new optimization of P-hub center problems (P-HC) and analyzed the complexity of the model and then represented algorithms to solve them.

11.2.10 Hub Covering Location Problem (Campbell 1994)

This model can be used to solve P-hub center model. If an origin-destination pair in a hub location problem is introduced as a demand node in hub covering location problem, the meaning of a hub covering problem is:

The origin/destination pair (i, j) is covered by (m, k) pair of hub nodes, if the cost of i node to j node via m, k hubs is less than or equal to a certain fixed value (number).

$$C_{ij}^{km} \leq \gamma_{ij}. \quad (11.42)$$

Campbell (1994) represented this model and we share this model to two models: hub set covering location model and hub maximal Covering location model.

11.2.10.1 Hub Set Covering Location Problem

Hub set covering location model is a special case of hub covering location model. We introduce this model as follows:

Model assumptions. The assumptions of this model are similar to median P-hub model except that the number of hubs is not known (*endogenous*) before solving and a *fixed cost* of hub location is incorporated in the model.

Model inputs. The model inputs of this model are as follows:

$F_k = $ the fixed hub location cost in candidate node k

C_{ij}^{km} = transportation cost from origin i to destination j via hubs at candidate nodes k and m

γ_{ij} = maximum cost for going from origin i to destination j (distance covering)

V_{ij}^{km} = node hubs m, k cover the origin-destination i, j

Model outputs (decision variables): Model outputs are similar to median P-hub model.

Objective function and its constraints. The objective function of this model and its related constraints are as follows:

$$\text{Min} \sum_{k} F_K X_K. \qquad (11.43)$$

Subject to

$$Z_{ij}^{km} \leq X_k \; \forall i,j,k,m, \qquad (11.44)$$

$$Z_{ij}^{km} \leq X_m \; \forall i,j,k,m, \qquad (11.45)$$

$$\sum_{k}\sum_{m} V_{ij}^{km} Z_{ij}^{km} \geq 1 \; \forall i,j, \qquad (11.46)$$

$$0 \leq X_k \leq 1 \; \forall k, \qquad (11.47)$$

$$0 \leq Z_{ij}^{km} \leq 1 \; \forall i,j,k,m. \qquad (11.48)$$

Equation (11.43) minimizes the total hub location costs. Equations (11.46) ensure that all of origin-destination pairs are covered at least once. The other equations are similar to those of the previous models.

11.2.10.2 Hub Maximal Covering Location Problem

Hub maximal covering location model is a special case of hub covering location model. We introduce it as follows:

Model assumptions. The assumptions of this model are similar to median P-hub model except that the number of hubs is known (*exogenous*) before solving the model and that the fixed cost of hub location is not considered in the model.

Model inputs. The model inputs are as follows:

h_{ij} = the demand flow from origin i to destination j

Model outputs (decision variables). Model outputs are similar to median P-hub model.

Objective function and its constraints. The objective function of this model and its related constraints are as follows:

$$\text{Max} \sum_{i}\sum_{j}\sum_{m} h_{ij} Z_{ij}^{km} V_{ij}^{km}. \qquad (11.49)$$

11 Hub Location Problem

Subject to

$$\sum_k X_k = P, \qquad (11.50)$$

$$\sum_k \sum_m Z_{ij}^{km} = 1 \ \forall \ i,\ j, \qquad (11.51)$$

$$Z_{ij}^{km} \leq X_k \ \forall i, j, k, m, \qquad (11.52)$$

$$Z_{ij}^{km} \leq X_m \ \forall i, j, k, m, \qquad (11.53)$$

$$0 \leq X_k \leq 1 \ \forall k, \qquad (11.54)$$

$$0 \leq Z_{ij}^{km} \leq 1 \ \forall i, j, k, m. \qquad (11.55)$$

Equation (11.49) maximizes the covered demand value. The other equations of this model are similar to P-hub median model introduced before.

11.3 Solution Techniques

Many algorithms are represented to solve difference types of hub location problems. We review the related literatures and introduce some of the proposed associated algorithms.

11.3.1 Various Kinds of Algorithms

To solve small hub problems, integer programming optimization methods are used. However, for larger problems, heuristic methods or Meta heuristic methods are utilized.

In the past, few solving methods were proposed for hub location problems in which the number of hubs is a decision variable and the fixed cost of establishing a hub is considered. Nevertheless, with the growth of meta heuristic methods, number of methods to solve such problems has been increased.

- To solve the two-hub case, a procedure is given by Ostresh (1975) to solve the two-center location–allocation problem (location–allocation problem with no interaction between the sources where each destination is assigned to the closest source).
- O'Kelly (1987) formulated the P-hub median problem (P-HLMP) as a quadratic integer programming problem. He showed that the problem is NP-hard, and proposed two enumeration-based heuristics to solve it.
- Exchange clustering methods are presented by Klincewicz (1991).
- Greedy search methods, Tabu search and Grab are given by Klincewicz (1992).

- Tabu search methods are given by Skorin-Kapov and Skorin-Kapov (1994).
- Genetic algorithm methods are given by Abdinnour-Helm and Venkataramanan (1998).
- A mixed method, Tabu search and genetic algorithm by Abdinnour-Helm (1998);
- A mixed method, Simulated Annealing and Tabu search given by Chen (2007);
- Genetic algorithm method given by Topcouglu et al. (2005);
- Solving uncapacitated single allocation hub location problem with installed fixed cost simulated annealing is represented by Aykin (1995).
- Greedy Interchange, Alflo, Maxflo given by Campbell (1996);
- Shortest Path method given by Sohn (1998);
- Greedy Algorithm for one stop state (traveling form an origin to a destination through only one hub node) given by Sasaki et al. (1999), are discussed in this section. Two networks are studied with 32 nodes and 2 or 5 hubs, and 50 nodes and 2 or 4 hubs, respectively. Comparisons between the greedy and branch and bound algorithms have shown that the greedy algorithm needs less machine time.
- Ebery et al. (2000) represented a heuristic algorithm with shortest path method to solve capacitated multiple allocation hub location problem (CHLP-M), and then used the gained upper bound in branch and bound procedure in basic linear programming.
- Ernst and Krishnamoorthy (1999) represented methods to solve capacitated single allocation hub location problem (CHLP-S).
- Aykin (1994) represented procedures based on Lagrangian relaxation to solve capacitated hub location problems (CHLP).
- Camargo et al. (2008) represented a bender decomposition method to solve uncapacitated multiple allocation hub location problem (UHLP-M).
- Canovas et al. (2007) represented a dual ascent method, and a heuristic method, to solve uncapacitated multiple allocation hub location problem (UHLP-M).
- Rodriguez et al. (2007) represented a solution method based on simulated annealing to solve capacitated hub location problem (CHLP). In this method each hub is assumed to be an $M/M/1$ queuing system and has solved for a network with 52 nodes.
- Martine Labbe et al. (2005) represented a solution method based on branch and cut algorithm to solve uncapacitated single allocation hub location problem (UHLP-S). In this method, the network connecting the hub nodes is called backbone Network and the connected network of the terminal nodes is called access network.
- Marianov et al. (2003) represented Tabu search algorithm in airlines location in which each hub node is assumed to be an $M/D/C$ queue. In this method, only a part of feasible solution is surveyed and the best neighborhood is selected as a new hub node with respect to continuous iterations on neighborhood nodes of former hub, even the target function gains a worse solution. This method works best for networks of up to 50 nodes with 4 or 5 hubs. However, the efficiency of method decreases as the number of nodes increases and reaching a feasible solution is guaranteed.

11 Hub Location Problem

- Wagner (2007) represented a clustering method using Tabu search and genetic algorithm. This method was used to solve traveling salesman problem (TSP).
- Pamuk et al. (2001) represented a single relocating heuristic by Tabu search to solve P-hub center problems (P-HLCP). Two single-allocation schemes were used in the evaluation phase of the algorithm. A greedy local search was employed to improve the resulting allocations.
- Cunha and Silva (2007) represented an efficient hybrid genetic algorithm (GA) approach for the hub and spoke location problem for the less-than-truckload (LTL) services in Brazil. This problem can be seen as a modified version of the uncapacitated hub location problem with single allocation (UHLP-S), in which the discount factor on the hub to hub links is not constant but may vary according to the total amount of cargo between hub terminals.
- Thomadsen and Larsen (2007) represented branch-and-price algorithm or IP column generation (the combination of column generation and branch-and-bound algorithm) to solve a two-layered network (a hierarchical network) consisting of clusters of nodes, each defining an access network and a backbone network. The two layers in the network are: the backbone network and the access networks. The backbone network connects disjoint clusters of nodes, each including an access network. The node connecting an access network to the backbone network is called a hub.
- Costa et al. (2008) represented a bi-criteria integer linear programming to solve the capacitated single allocation hub location problems (CHLP-S).
- Bollapragada et al. (2005) represented a new network-planning model and an effective greedy solution heuristic to solve a model that is most closely related to the capacitated hub maximum-covering location problem with multi allocations (CHMCLP-M).
- The quality of the heuristic algorithm is evaluated by comparing its coverage with the optimal (for small problems) or with an upper bound obtained by solving a linear-programming relaxation.
- Rodriguez-Martin et al. (2008) represented a mixed integer linear programming formulation and described two branch-and-cut algorithms based on decomposition techniques to solve a capacitated multi allocation hub location problem (CHLP-M)
- Yaman (2008) represented a heuristic algorithm based on Lagrangian relaxation and local search to solve P-hub location median single allocation problems (P-HLMP-S).
- Wagner (2008) represented LP-relaxation to solve uncapacitated multi allocation P-hub location median problems (P-HLMP-M).
- Kratica et al. (2007) represented two genetic algorithms for solving the uncapacitated single allocation P-hub location median problem (P-HLMP-S).

A wide array of solution methods are represented in Table 11.1. It's shown that methods lose their efficiency, need much time to be solved when the number of nodes is increased over 50.

Table 11.1 Solution methods for hub location problem

Reference	Problem	Solving method	Efficient number of nodes (number of hubs)
O'Kelly (1986)	1-HLP-S	Nearest distance	
Ostresh (1975)	2-HLP	Location–allocation (shortest route)	
O'Kelly (1987)	P-HLMP	Nearest distance-quadratic integer	
Klincewicz (1991)	P-HLMP	Clustering	
Klincewicz (1992)	P-HLMP	Tabu search and greedy random algorithm	
Skorin-Kapov and Skorin-Kapov (1994)	P-HLMP-S	Tabu search	
Skorin-Kapov et al. (1996)	P-HLMP-S & P-HLMP-M	Linear programming	
Campbell (1991)	P-HLMP-M	Integer programming	
Campbell (1994)	P-HLMP-M	Integer programming	
O' Kelly (1992)	UHLP-S	Heuristic algorithm	
Abdinnour-Helm and Venkataramanan (1998)	UHLP-S	Genetic algorithm	
Abdinnour-Helm (1998)	UHLP-S	Genetic algorithm and tabu search (GATS)	
Chen (2007)	UHLP-S	Tabu search and simulated annealing	200
Topcouglu et al. (2005)	UHLP-S	Genetic algorithm	200 (5)
Aykin (1995)	UHLP-S	Simulated annealing (greedy interchange) B & B	
Campbell (1996)	P-HLMP-M	Greedy- interchange	
Sohn and Park (1998)	P-HLMP-M	Nearest distance	25 (3–4)
Sasaki et al. (1999)	P-HLMP-M	B&B algorithm and greedy algorithm	50 (2–4)
Ebery et al. (2000)	CHLP-M	Nearest distance – B & B	200
Ebery (2001)	P-HLMP-S	Mixed integer linear programming	50 (2–3)
Aykin (1994)	P-HLMP-S	B & B (lagrangian relaxation)	
Camargo et al. (2008)	UHLP-M	Benders decomposition	200
Canovas et al. (2007)	UHLP-M	Means of a dual ascent technique- B & B	120
Rodriguez et al. (2007)	CHLP-M	Simulated annealing	52
Labbe et al. (2005)	UHLP-S	Branch & cut (B & C)	
Sung and Jin (2001)	P-HLMP-M	Clustering (dual-based approach)	
Wagner (2007)	UHLP-M	Clustering (genetic algorithm & Tabu search)	
Marin (2005)	CHLP-M	Integer linear programming	40
Marianov and Serra (2003)	UHLP-M	Tabu search	50 (4–5)
Klincewicz (1996)	UHLP-M	Dual ascent and dual adjustment techniques within a B & B scheme	

(continued)

Table 11.1 (continued)

Reference	Problem	Solving method	Efficient number of nodes (number of hubs)
Mayer and Wagner (2002)	UHLP-M	Dual ascent approach	
Yaman et al. (2007)	CHLP-S	Tabu search (with greedy algorithm) – B & C	49
Cunha and Silva (2007)	UHLP-S	Genetic algorithm	25
Pamuk and Sepil (2001)	UHLP-M	Tabu search (with greedy local algorithm)	25 (5)
Thomadsen and Larsen (2007)	UHLP-M	Branch and price (combination of column generation and B & B)	25
Costa et al. (2008)	CHLP-S	Bi-criteria integer linear programming	40
Bollapragada et al. (2005)	CHMCLP-M (maximum covering)	Greedy algorithm	
Rodriguez-Martin and Salazar-Gonzalez (2008)	CHLP-M	Mixed integer linear programming with B & C based on decomposition method	25 (10)
Yaman (2008)	P-HLMP-S	Lagrangian relaxation and local search	81 (25)
Pirkul and Schilling (1998)	P-HLP-S	Lagrangian relaxation	25
Wagner (2008)	P-HLMP-M	LP relaxation	50 (5)
Kratica et al. (2007)	P-HLMP-S	Genetic algorithm	200 (20)

11.3.2 Some Relevant Algorithms

O'Kelly (1987) represented two heuristic methods to solve uncapacitated single allocation hub location problem.

In the first heuristic method each demand node is allocated to the nearest hub node. It is known that when $\alpha = 0$, the third part of the nonlinear (11.7) will be zero and the problem is reduced to a P-Median Problem. This method works well when $\alpha < 0.5$.

In the second heuristic method all ways to allocate non-hub nodes to the nearest or second nearest hub nodes are analyzed. If we have N nodes to select P hubs, we will have $N!/P!.N!$ ways. For each one of the $N!/P!.N!$ ways, all of the 2^{N-P} ways to allocate non-hub nodes to the nearest and second nearest hub nodes are studied. By increasing the number of nodes solution time is increased.

The second heuristic method results in better solution compared to the first heuristic method. Also, the second heuristic gives a tighter upper bound on the objective function than the first one.

11.3.2.1 Greedy Heuristic Algorithm

Greedy algorithm was first presented by Sasaki et al. (1999) to solve the 1-stop uncapacitated multiple allocation hub location problem. One stop means that to travel between each origin-destination pair, we have to pass only one hub node. The application of this method is for small networks such as Japan inner airlines network.

11.3.2.2 Genetic Algorithm

Topcuoglu et al. (2005) represented this algorithm to solve uncapacitated single allocation hub location problem with fixed cost of location.

A genetic algorithm (GA) is a search algorithm for finding the near-optimal solutions in large spaces, which is inspired from population genetics. The general idea was introduced by Holland (1975). Genetic algorithms have been applied to a large set of problems in various fields in the literature.

Two example sources for detailed information on GA are the books written by Goldberg (1989) and Mitchell (1998).

11.3.2.3 Benders Decomposition Method

Camargo et al. (2008) represented this method based on an old algorithm in 1962 which proposed a partitioning method for solving mixed linear and nonlinear integer programming problems. Camargo et al. (2008) defined a relaxation algorithm for solving a problem through partitioning it into two simpler problems: an integer problem, known as MP, and a linear problem, known as SP.

The MP is a relaxed version of the original problem with a set of integer variables and its associated constraints, while SP is the original problem with the values of the integer variables temporarily fixed by the MP.

The algorithm solves each one of the two simpler problems iteratively, one at a time. At each iteration, a new constraint, known as Benders cut, is added to the MP. This new constraint is originated by the dual problem of the SP. The algorithm goes on until the objective function value of the optimal solution to the MP is equal to that of the SP, when it stops obtaining the optimal solution of the original mixed integer problem.

11.4 Case Study

In this section we will introduce some real-world case studies related to hub location problems.

11.4.1 The Policy of Open Skies in the Middle East (Adler and Hashai 2005)

In Adler and Hashai (2005), airlines and transportations based on open sky policy were surveyed in the Middle East.

Conclusions drawn from this investigation may enable both researchers and policy makers to develop a greater understanding of the social welfare impacts of deregulation in the regional air-transport industry and the economic benefits to individual air carriers, countries and passengers alike, once peace restraints in the region. This analysis had led to the conclusion that the increase in both leisure and business air traffic due to the reduction in violence in the Middle East may lead to an increase of 51% in inter-country passenger flow under the assumption of deregulation of the regional air-transport industry.

It is interesting that based on their research the four cities selected as optimized hub airports are, in order of utility, Cairo, Tehran, Istanbul, and Riyadh. Dubai which now works as an important center for airport transportation, is not an optimal hub airport. This means that, politic and economic problems have dominated over optimized location.

11.4.2 A Hub Port in the East Coast of South America (Aversa et al. 2005)

Aversa et al. (2005) formulated a mixed planning model for selecting a hub port, from eleven ports servicing to transportation demands, in the east coast of South America.

It was recommended that minimisation of transport costs, is often given unwarranted significance, usually by "awkward" river ports, such as Antwerp and Hamburg, while the importance of port costs, in these ports, is at the same time purposely downplayed.

In this research many ports were researched such as, ports in Brazil, Argentina and Uruguay. Their model consists of 3,883 variables and 4,225 constraints. After solving the model, port Santos, Brazil was chosen as the hub port.

11.4.3 A Hub Model in Brunswick, Canada (Eiselt 2007)

Eiselt (2007) represented an application of location models to the siting of landfills. The landfill and transfer station location problem was formulated similar to a hub location problem. The problem included a parameter that measures the discount factor of the transportation between transfer stations and landfills in comparison to the unit transportation cost between customers and transfer stations.

The Province of New Brunswick was used to compare optimized facility locations with facility locations that had been chosen by the planners. In order to make such comparison, the major towns and villages were chosen on the basis of the statistical data available from the latest census. The result of the calculations was that, the optimized solutions were between 10 and 40% less costly as compared to the observed solutions. Still, the optimized locations of the landfills were quite close to those found in the optimization runs. The only exception was a case in which the planners deviated from their plan due to public opposition. Their first choice of location also appeared in some of the optimized runs. Some additional optimization was also performed on a smaller subset of the 93 points which were the basis of the optimization reported above.

11.4.4 A Hub/Spoke Network in Brazil (Cunha and Silva 2007)

Cunha and Silva (2007) represented the problem of configuring hub-and-spoke networks for trucking companies that operate less-than-truckload services in Brazil. The problem consists of determining the number of consolidation terminals (also known as hubs), their locations and the assignment of the spokes to the hubs, aiming to minimize the total cost, which is composed of fixed and variable costs.

References

Abdinnour-Helm S (1998) A hybrid heuristic for the uncapacitated hub location problem. Eur J Oper Res 106:489–99

Abdinnour-Helm S, Venkataramanan MA (1998) Solution approaches to hub location problems. Ann Oper Res 78:31–50

Adler N, Hashai N (2005) Effect of open skies in the Middle East region. Transport Res 39:878–894

Aversa R, Botter RC, Haralambides HE, Yoshizaki HTY (2005)A mixed integer programming model on the location of a hub port in the East Coast of South America. Maritime Econ Logist 7:1–18

Aykin T (1994) Lagrangian relaxation based approaches to capacitated hub-and-spoke network design problem. Eur J Oper Res 79:501–523

Aykin T (1995) Networking policies for hub-and-spoke systems with application to the air transportation system. Transport Sci 29(3):201–221

Baird AJ (2006) Optimizing the Container transshipment hub location in northern Europe. J Transport Geograph 14(3):195–214

Bania N, Bauer P, Zlatoper TU (1998) Air passenger service: A taxonomy of route network, hub location, and competition. Logist Transport Rev 34:53–74

Berman O, Drezner Z, Wesolowsky G (2007) The transfer point location problem. Eur J Oper Res 179(3):978–989

Bollapragada R, Camm J, Rao US, Wu J (2005) A two-phase greedy algorithm to locate and allocate hubs for fixed-wireless broad bound access. Oper Res Lett 33:134–142

Camargo RS, Miranda Jr G, Luna HP (2008) Benders decomposition for the uncapacitated multiple allocation hub location problem. Comput Oper Res 35(4):1047–1064

Campbell JF (1991) Hub location problems and the p-hub median problem. Center for Business and Industrial Studies, University of Missouri, St. Louis, MO

Campbell JF (1994) Integer programming formulations of discrete hub location problems. Eur J Oper Res 72:387–405

Campbell JF (1996) Hub location and P-hub median problem. Oper Res 44(6):923–935

Campbell JF, Ernst A, Krishnamoorthy M (2002) Hub location problems. In: Drezner Z, Hammacher H (eds) Facility location: applications and theory. Berlin, Springer

Campbell AM, Lowe TJ, Zhang L (2007) The P-hub center allocation problem. Eur J Oper Res 176(2):819–835

Canovas L, Garcia S, Marin A (2007) Solving the uncapacitated multiple allocation hub location problem by means of a dual-ascent technique. Eur J Oper Res 179:990–1007

Chen JF (2007) A hybrid heuristic for the uncapacitated single allocation hub location problem. Omega 35(2):211–220

Costa MG, Captivo ME, Climaco J (2008) Capacitated single allocation hub location problem-A bi-criteria approach. Comput Oper Res 35(11):3671–3695

Cunha CB, Silva MR (2007) A genetic algorithm for the problem of configuring a hub-and-spoke network for a LTL trucking company in Brazil. Eur J Oper Res 179:747–758

Daskin MS (1995) Network and discrete location: Models, algorithms, and applications. Wiley, New York

Don T, Harit S, English JR, Whicker G (1995) Hub and spoke networks in truckload trucking: configuration testing and operational concerns. Logist Transport 31:209–237

Ebery J (2001) Solving large single allocation p-hub problems with two or three hubs: Eur J Oper Res 128:447–458

Ebery J, Krishnamoorty M, Ernst A, Boland N (2000) The capacitated multiple allocation hub location problem: formulation and algorithms. Eur J Oper Res 120:614–631

Eiselt HA (2007) Locating landfills – optimization vs. reality. Eur J Oper Res 179(3): 1040–1049

Ernst A, Krishnamoorthy M (1996) Efficient algorithms for the uncapaciterted single allocation P-hub median problem. Location Sci 4:139–154

Ernst A, Krishnamoorthy M (1999) Solution algorithms for the capacitated Single allocation hub location problem. Ann Oper Res 86:141–159

Goldberg DE (1989) Genetic algorithms in search, optimization and machine learning. Addison-Wesley, Reading, MA

Hakimi SL (1964) Optimum location of switching centers and the absolute centers and medians of a graph. Oper Res 12:450–459

Holland JH (1975) Adaptation in natural and artificial systems. University of Michigan Press, Michigan

Jaillet P, Song G, Yu G (1996) Airline network design and hub location problems. Location Sci 4(3):195–212

Klincewicz JG (1991) Heuristics for the P-hub location problem. Eur J Oper Res 53:25–37

Klincewicz JG (1992) Avoiding local optima in the P-hub location problem using tabu search and grasp. Ann Oper Res 40:283–302

Klincewicz JG (1996) A dual algorithm for the uncapacitated hub location problem. Location Sci 4(3):173–184

Klincewicz JG (1998) Hub location in backbone tributary network design: A review. Location Sci 6:307–335

Kratica J, Stanimirovic Z, Tosic D, Filipovic V (2007) Two genetic algorithms for solving the uncapacitated single allocation p-hub median problem. Eur J Oper Res 182:15–28

Krishnamoorthy M, Mills G, Sier D (1994) Strategic configuration of the mail processing network: location–allocation modeling-stage 1, CSIRO, Technical Report DMS-C94/9 Division of Mathematics and statistics CSIRO, Australia

Kuby MJ, Gray RG (1993) Hub network design problem with stoppers and feeders: Case of federal express. Transport Res 27:1–12

Labbe M, Yaman H, Gourdin E (2005) A branch and cut algorithm for hub location problems with single assignment 102:371–405

Lee Y, Lim B, Park J (1996) A hub location problem in designing digital data service networks: Lagrangian relaxation approach. Location Sci 4:183–194

Lumsdenk, Dallari F, Ruggeri R (1999) Improving the efficiency of the hub and spoke system for the SKF European distribution network. Int J Phys Distrib Logist Manage 29:50–64

Marianov V, Serra D (2003) Location models for airline hubs behaving as M/D/c queues. Comput Oper Res 30:983–1003

Marin A (2005) Formulating and solving splittable capacitated multiple allocation hub location problems. Comput Oper Res 32:3093–3109

Martin JC, Roman C (2003) Hub location in the South-Atlantic airline market: A spatial competition game. Transport Res A: Policy Pract 37(10):865–888

Mayer G, Wagner B (2002) Hub Locator: an exact solution method for the multiple allocation hub location problem. Comput Oper Res 29:715–39

Mitchell M (1998) An introduction to genetic algorithms. MIT Press, Cambridge, MA

O'Kelly ME (1986) The location of interacting hub facilities, Transport Sci 20:92–106

O'Kelly ME (1987) A quadratic integer program for the location of interacting hub facilities. Eur J Oper Res 32:393–404

O' Kelly ME (1992) Hub facility location with fixed costs. Papers in Regional Science 71:292–306

Ostresh LMJr (1975) An efficient algorithm for solving the two center location – allocation problem. J Region Sci 15:209–216

Pamuk FS, Sepil C (2001) A solution to the hub center problem via a single-relocation algorithm with Tabu search. IIE Trans 33:399–411

Pirkul H, Schilling DA (1998) An efficient procedure for designing single allocation hub and spoke systems. Manage Sci 44(12):235–242

Rodriguez V, Alvarez MJ, Barcos L (2007) Hub location under capacity constraints. Transport Res Part E: Logist Transport Rev 43:495–505

Rodriguez-Martin I, Salazar-Gonzalez JJ (2008) Solving a capacitated hub location problem. Eur J Oper Res 184(2):468–479

Sasaki M, Suzuki A, Drezner Z (1999) On the selection of hub airports for an airline hub-and-spoke system. Comput Oper Res 26:1411–1422

Shaw SL (1993) Hub structures of major US passenger airline. J Transport Geograph 1(1):47–58

Skorin-Kapov D, Skorin-Kapov J (1994) On Tabu search for the location of interacting hub facilities, Eur J Oper Res 73:502–509

Skorin-Kapov D, Skorin-Kapov J, O'Kelly M (1996) Tight linear programming relaxations of uncapacitated p-hub median problems. Proc Natl Decis Sci Conf, Boston 94:582–593

Sohn J, Park S (1998) Efficient solution procedure and reduced size formulation for P-hub location problem. Eur J Oper Res 108:118–126

Sung CS, Jin HW (2001) Dual-based approach for a hub network design problem under non-restrictive policy. Eur J Oper Res 132:88–105

Thomadsen T, Larsen J (2007) A hub location problem with fully interconnected backbone and access networks. Comput Oper Res 34:2520–2531

Toh RS, Higgins RC (1985) The impact of hub and spoke network centralization and route monopoly on domestic airline profitability. Transport J 24:16–27

Topcuoglu H, Corut F, Ermis M, Yilmaz G (2005) Solving the uncapacitated hub location using genetic algorithms. Comput Oper Res 32:467–984

Wagner B (2007) An exact solution procedure for a cluster hub location problem, Eur J Oper Res 178:391–401

Wagner B (2008) A note on location of hubs in a competitive environment. Eur J Oper Res 184(1):57–62

Yaman H (2008) Star P-hub median problem with modular arc capacities. Comput Oper Res 35(9):3009–3019

Yaman H, Kara BY, Tansel BC (2007) The latest arrival hub location problem for cargo delivery systems with stopovers. Transport Res B 41:906–919

Chapter 12
Competitive Location Problem

Mohammad Javad Karimifar, Mohammad Khalighi Sikarudi,
Esmaeel Moradi, and Morteza Bidkhori

A large part of location theory in operational research has been built around the (mostly implicit) modeling assumption of a spatial monopoly: the facility to be located offers a unique product or service and is the single player in the part of the market that is considered. Most situations in practice do not fit such models and the need arises to incorporate competition with other players. This has long been understood by economists who have studied competition, including its spatial aspects, for some 70 years.

A location model is said to be about competitive facilities when it explicitly incorporates the fact that other facilities are already (or will be) present in the market and that the new facilities will have to compete with them for its (their) market share. The apparent simplicity of this statement hides several implicit and explicit notions which have to be made more precise before a clear and well-defined model arises.

This chapter is organized as follows. In Sect. 12.1, we consider literatures, definitions and classifications of competitive location problem. Section 12.2 presents some models with continuous and discrete space developed for the problem, and also some relevant algorithms to solve these models are given in this section. Finally, Sect. 12.3 represents some real world case studies with a short summary.

12.1 Applications and Classifications

Hotelling's work (Hotelling 1929) on two terms competing in a linear market (with consumers distributed uniformly along the line) set the foundations of what is today the burgeoning field of competitive location.

During the late thirties and early forties, several papers using the same spatial representation as Hotelling but modifying some of the economic assumptions appeared in the economic literature (Hoover 1936; Lerner and Singer 1937; Smithies 1941).

There followed several decades of stagnation in the contribution of new insights in the field of competitive location in linear markets have been past.

Since the late seventies however, a myriad of different models have appeared in the literature of spatial economics and industrial organization (Gabszewicz and Thisse 1991).

Parallel to the development of this body of literature, a new field on location modeling was growing in the late sixties and seventies at a fast rate, namely facility location analysis. This field of research, coming basically from the fields of operations research, regional science and geography, dealt with the problem of locating new facilities in a spatial market in order to optimize one or several geographical and/or economic criteria. These criteria included overall distance minimization and transport and manufacturing cost minimization. The literature in facility location analysis is extensive: good sources of references can be found in Chhajed et al. (1993). Although most of these models used more realistic spatial representations than the line, such as networks and planes, most of them dealt exclusively with non-competitive situations, and little attention was paid to the characterization of market equilibrium.

From the late seventies, considerations on the interaction between competing facilities in discrete space have been developed following several different approaches. An extensive bibliographic survey with over 100 citations on competitive location can be found in Eiselt et al. (1993).

One of the first questions that is addressed by several authors is whether or not a set of locations in the vertices of a network exist that will ensure a Nash equilibrium, that is, a position where neither firms have incentives to move. Wendell and McKelvey (1981) considered the location of two competitive firms with one server each and tried to and a situation where a firm would capture at least 50% of the market regardless of the location of its competitor. Results showed that there was not a general strategy for the firm that would ensure this capture if locations were restricted to vertices of the network. Hakimi (1986) also analyzed extensively the problem of competitive location on vertices and proved that, under certain mathematical conditions such as concave transportation costs functions, that there exists a set of optimal locations on the vertices of the network.

A similar problem was studied by Lederer and Thisse (1990). Their problem not only looked at the specification of a site but also at the setting of a delivered price. They formulated the problem as a two stage game, where in the first stage both firms choose locations and in the second stage them simultaneously set delivery price schedules, and the result is that there is sub-game perfect Nash equilibrium. As Hakimi (1992) did, they also proved that if firm's transport costs are strictly concave, then the set of locally choices of the firm is reduced to the vertices of the network. As a consequence, the location problem can be reduced to a 2-median problem if social costs are minimized. A similar result was obtained by Hakimi et al. (1992).

The problem of two firms competing in a spatial market has also been studied in the case where the market is represented by a tree. Eiselt et al. (1993) proved that in such a case there is not a sub-game perfect Nash equilibrium if both prices and locations are to be determined. Eiselt et al. (1993) extended the problem to the location of three facilities in a tree. They found that the existence of equilibrium depended on the distribution of the demand in the geographical space in question. In both models, firms were allowed to locate on the edges of the network.

The game-theoretical models presented so far restrict themselves to the location of firms with one facility each that compete against each other.

Tobin and Friesz (1986) examined the case of a profit-maximizing firm that entered a market with several plants. They considered price and production effects on the market, since the increase in the overall production level from the opening of new plants in a spatial market stimulates reactions in the competitors. These reactions might a fact not only production levels, but also prices and locations.

Tobin and Friesz developed two models: (1) spatial price equilibrium model which determines equilibrium in prices and production levels for a given number of firms and (2) a Cournot–Nash oligopolistic model in which a few profit maximizing firms compete in spatially separated markets. They used both models to analyze the case of an entering firm that is going to open several new plants in spatially separated markets, and knows that its policy will have impact on market prices. Since profits depend on location and price-levels and these depend on the reaction of the competitors, it is not possible to use a standard plant location model. To tackle the problem, they used sensitivity analysis on variation inequalities to relate changes in production to changes in price to obtain optimal locations. The model was solved using a heuristic procedure where in the first step a spatial competitive equilibrium model was obtained and, in the second step, a sensitivity analysis of profit to production changes was performed to select locations and production levels likely to maximize total profits.

This model was generalized by Friesz et al. (1989) to allow the entering firm to determine not only production levels and the sites of its plants, Due to the mathematical complexity of these models, Miller et al. (1992) developed several heuristic methods to tackle the problem using the approach of variation inequalities.

Price-location modeling has been studied in a non-competitive model by Hanjoul et al. (1990). They develop three incapacitated plant location models where different alternative spatial price policies are considered.

Another body of literature on competitive location deals with the sitting of retail convenience stores. This type of store is characterized by (1) a limited and very similar product offering across outlets, (2) similar store image across firms, and (3) similar prices. Therefore, location is a major determinant of success.

Ghosh and Craig (1984) considered the location of several retail facilities by two servers. The problem is to locate retail facilities in a competitive market knowing that a competing firm will also enter this market. They used a MiniMax approach, where the entering firm maximizes its profit given the best location of the competitor. The firm's objective is to maximize the net present value of its investment over a long-term planning horizon. The model did not allow location at the same site for both firms and therefore did not examine the issue of ties. Ghosh and Craig used a heuristic algorithm to obtain solutions. The algorithm is as follows: for each possible set of locations of firm, the best sitting strategy is found for firm B. The final result is the set of locations where Firm A's objective maximum given the best reactive location strategy of its competitor. A Teitz and Bart hill climbing heuristic was used to determine the sites for both firms. The model is adapted to examine other strategies such as preemption, i.e., the identification of locations that are robust against competitive action. In a similar model, Dobson and Karmarkar (1987) introduced the notion of stability in the location of retail outlets by two profit maximizing firms in a competitive market.

Most competitive decision location models in discrete space assume that consumers patronize the closest shop. Karkazis (1989) considered two criteria that customers may use to decide which shop to patronize: a level criterion based on the preferences of a customer on the size of the facility and a distance criterion based on closeness to the store. He developed a model that would determine the location and number of servers to enter the market when there are other firms already operating in the market by maximizing the profit subject to a budget constraint.

Another model that examines competition among retail stores in a spatial market was developed by ReVelle (1986). The maximum capture problem (MAXCAP) has formed the foundation of a series of models. These models The MAXCAP model, based on the classical maximal location covering problem of Church and ReVelle (1974), consists of the location of servers by an entering firm so as to maximize its market share capture in a market in which competitor servers are already in position. Eiselt and Laporte (1989a, b) modified the MAXCAP formulation to include attraction parameters based on gravity models and Voronoi diagrams. ReVelle and Serra (1991) extended the formulation to allow relocation of existing servers as well as the location of new servers.

The MAXCAP model has also been adapted to consider facilities that are hierarchical in nature and where there is competition at each level of the hierarchy (Serra et al. 1992).

Regarding Medianoid of Network, as what Hakami says that only about the equal situation of MAXCAP, as discussed by ReVelle, is different.

Those individuals who have in the recent years also very much studied in this connection, have been Drezner, Eiselt, Laporte, Choedhury, Koval, Wesolowsky, Benati, Berman, Freisz, Tobin and Miller.

From the year 1997 onwards, the number of articles increased very much and the peak period in these years, was the year 2000.

The recent years' have focused towards the expansion of applications and assumptions and to cite an example, in an article written by Aboolian et al. (2006) three objects have been followed. The first one being, is the number of facilities that must be located and the second one is the location of such facilities and the last one which quietly differs from the other articles, is the facility terms, from the point of size, type and volume of services given, etc.

12.1.1 Game Theories (Winston and Wayne 1995)

Game theories or competitive strategies, are mathematical theories, in which competitive opportunities have been noticed. This viewpoint is advantageous, when two or more individuals or organizations with specific objects, who have tried to take decisions and the decision of anyone of them, effect others' decisions. (This theory does not show the playing of implementation of the game but in fact, shows the description of methods and principles of selection of the games).

This theory has been mentioned by Mr. Phone Newman and whose theory, taking into consideration the base of MiniMax, each competitor, acts in such a manner in order to reduce his maximum losses into minimum.

Regarding this theory, many examples can be given, such as playing of two players in a chess game, competition between members of parliament and competition of trading companies for safeguarding their shares in the market. The peculiarities of competitive games are:

- The number of participants or competitors is limited.
- The participant has a limited list of those activities that can be implemented and it's possible that such a list may not be the same for all.
- Each participant is aware of the possible selections made by others but does not know which one would be selected by them.
- A game can only be considered as over, when each participant would have implemented any one of his selected games. (on assumption that all the games would be played at the same time).
- Any actions taken by anyone of the individual participants, has an advantage for him and which could be either positive or negative.
- The advantage that each participant would have does not depend only upon his own actions but also depends on the actions of others.

In this theory, it's necessary that explanation for some of the parameters are studied, some of which are as under:

- *Game.* Actions taken between two or more participants and which has either profit or loss for him.
- *Player.* Each participant or competitor is called a player in the game.
- *Strategy.* Rules have been set earlier already, based on which, the player while playing, takes decision about his own actions from the list of his own (actions).
- *Pure strategy.* Rule for taking decision for permanent selection, is a special action.
- *Impure strategy.* Is a decision that is taken from the pure strategies, with fixed probabilities.
- *Zero total game.* Game of N player, in which the total advantages are zero.
- *Optimal strategy.* Is a strategy in which the value of Minimax is equal to MaxiMin.

As already shown in the last explanation, in this theory, we can arrive at an optimal result, when the value of MiniMax (that is, maximum loss is turned into minimum) equal to value of MaxiMin (that is, minimum advantage is turned into maximum).

Accordingly, in view of the initial explanations and definitions regarding game theories, we shall continue in subsequent sections, by continuing with facility locations.

Some of studies of game theory deals with situations where there are only two decision makers (or players), but there are the situations with n (where $n > 2$) players. For more details about game theory see Winston and Wayne (1995).

12.1.2 Static Competition

The simplest competitive models arise when competition is assumed to be already present in the market. The whereabouts and characteristics of this competition are known in advance and assumed to be fixed. Such models correspond to a short term view: they are based on the assumption that the time and/or effort/cost needed for the competition to react is sufficiently long to harvest the main benefits of the new facility. These models also form the basis on which more complex models may be built. These kind of static situations are discussed in more detail in the remainder of this part.

12.1.3 Competition with Foresight

The situation becomes quite different when a virgin market is entered in the knowledge that other competing actors will enter it soon afterwards.

It will, then, be necessary to make decisions with foresight about this competition, which itself will enter a market where competition is already present. The ensuing Stackelberg type models, where each evaluation of the main objective involves the solution of the competitor's nontrivial optimization model, quickly become extremely complex. We enter here the realm of sequential models, which were recently extensively surveyed in (Eiselt and Laporte 1996a, b).

12.1.4 Dynamic Models and Competitive Equilibrium

Existing competition will most probably alter its strategy when it loses part of or even all of its market shares to a newcomer, implying that the competitive environment changes. This leads to dynamic models which aim at describing the action/reaction cycles of the competing actors.

One of the traditional questions in this respect is the possible (in) existence of equilibrium situations, dear to economists, to which such a system might evolve. It is in fact this point of view that forms the root of competitive location theory thanks to the seminal paper of Hotelling (1929). This large area of research has been most often surveyed, see e.g. (Eiselt and Laporte 1989a, b, 1996a, b) and will not be discussed here.

12.1.5 Point vs. Regional Demand

Where does demand originate? Is it discrete, i.e., concentrated in a finite set of points or rather continuously dispersed over a region? In both cases a precise description is needed of its spatial distribution.

In case of point demand its volume, be it expressed in terms of quantity, frequency and/or currency (then sometimes called "buying power" at each demand point should be given. For regional demand this is described by a continuous spatial distribution, often assumed to be uniform.

It may be argued that in principle individual customers form a discrete set, so should be described by a point distribution. However, there are usually too many individuals involved and their location in space is not fixed in time, hence a continuous distribution might also be necessary and/or adequate. Observe, however, that regional demand typically has meaning only in a continuous or network environment (see below).

Next, it must be determined whether demand is elastic or inelastic with respect to quality. In other words, does the volume of demand, depend on the (conditions of) supply or may it be considered as fixed.

This will largely be determined by the product type. It is customary to consider demand for essential goods, such as bread, to be inelastic (within time-periods during which populations may be considered as constant), as opposed to inessential goods, e.g., luxury, for which demand may be highly supply/price sensitive.

Demand may also vary independently of the supply, due to the inevitable uncertainties in the market's description, or due to inherent randomness, e.g., weather effects. Such situations then are patronizing by stochastic demand. For models of this type we refer to (Drezner and Drezner 1996; Peeters 1997).

12.1.6 Patronizing Behavior

In order to be able to determine the market share of a facility it is necessary to describe in a precise manner which part of the demand will be captured by each of the competing facilities. This involves the way customers behave when making the choice which of several facilities to patronize.

It is generally considered that each customer feels some attraction towards each of the competing facilities. It is the way these attraction forces determine the actual patronizing choice which leads to two quite different types of customer behavior models.

This choice is deterministic when the full demand of each customer is served by the facility to which it is mostly attracted. This conceptually simple patronizing rule is the most common one in the literature. Basically it assumes that as long as the supply side remains unchanged customers will always patronize one and the same facility.

The deterministic rule stated above does not clarify what happens in the case of ties, in other words when a customer feels equally and maximally attracted towards several facilities, including a new one. Several tie resolution rules may be considered: either the demand is (equally?) split over all tied facilities, or it goes fully towards the new facility, or may stick to the competing facilities.

A deterministic choice rule does not allow for the "changing mood" of customers. The choice is probabilistic when each customer splits its volume of demand over the different facilities, with probabilities determined some way by the attraction felt towards each facility. At present this seems to be the only alternative proposed to the deterministic "all or nothing" rule.

12.1.7 Attraction Function

The attraction function describes how a customer's attraction (also often called utility, particularly in economics) towards a facility is obtained. In location theory it is always assumed that some notion of distance between customer and facility plays a crucial role in this attraction.

Typically, attraction will decrease with distance and the attraction function describes in what precise way. In case all competing facilities, existing and new, are uniform, i.e., apart from their site they are further indistinguishable in the sense that they offer exactly comparable, and thus substitutable, products and services at the same prices, the distance will be the sole determinant in the attraction.

It may be observed that in this case it is usually considered that only deterministic behavior applies. In many cases, however, facilities are multiform, i.e., they do differ in other aspects than the mere site where they are located, and customers will take these differences into account in the way they feel attracted to them. These differences should then be incorporated into the attraction function as additional parameters on top of the distance. There are basically two standard ways in which this may be done.

In Economics it is often considered that the product's observed price primarily determines the customer's choice. A notion of attraction in such a setting is therefore fully price based. In the traditional mill pricing system the price actually paid for the product is given at the facility, but the customer should travel to the facility and its travel cost, determined by the distance of travel, should be included in the full observed price. Typically this leads to additive attraction functions.

Apart from distance, one may consider the price as just one of several ingredients in the overall attraction process, in which other features like floor area, number of cashing counters, product mix, publicity, etc. also play an important role. All these properties (excluding distance) may be summarized into a single measure for which the unattractive word "attractiveness" has been used, and which we prefer to simply call the quality. In this context one usually finds proposalsfor multiplicative attraction functions. Note that this type of attraction function has recently been criticized since it might imply that a choice of facility may change during the trip towards the facility.

12.1.8 Decision Space

In competitive location models one finds back the three traditional spatial settings of location theory: discrete space, a network, and continuous space. Observe that a complete description of space should also include the distance measure used.

In discrete space there is only a (relatively small) finite list of candidate sites and the market is always assumed to consist of point demand. Distances may then in principle be obtained in a very precise way including all possible special features necessary for an adequate description of reality.

Indeed the full set of demand (candidate) facility site pairs is fully known and finite. The central difficulty in practice resides in the amount of data to be collected. In network environment both demand and facilities may lie anywhere along the edges of the network. The nodes of the network are just the points where edges meet. Since travel is assumed to be restricted to the network, distance is typically calculated as shortest path distance. Location of new facilities might be further restricted to only part of the network, as defined by a set of edge segments.

It should be observed that the term network location is often used in a more restrictive sense, where only nodes of the network are candidate sites. In our terminology such problems are considered as discrete problems, and the network setting is only used in order to obtain a standard way to calculate distances by shortest paths.

On the other hand, theoretical developments in network setting most often lead to the identification (and efficient construction) of finite sets of points which are guaranteed to contain at least one or all optimal sites for the location problem at hand. Such localization theorems then allow reducing the original network location problem to a discrete one by restricting the search for optimal sites to this "finite dominating set", thereby generating the situation described in previous paragraph. Similar discrimination results often appear in continuous setting too.

Continuous space refers to a location space determined by a coordinate system in which in principle any real coordinate values are admissible.

One-dimensional space is equivalent to the simplest possible network: a linear segment (or line), a very popular setting for competitive equilibrium studies in virtue of its simplicity. Other settings are of course the geographical space fucoids as a two-dimensional plane or possibly a sphere. Applications in e.g., product positioning may involve even higher dimensional settings.

In continuous space it is necessary to specify the type of distance which is used. Classically this will often be the patronizing distance, but many other distance measures may be considered, like LP ($1 \leq p \leq +\infty$) of which the rectangular (or Manhattan) distance ($p = 1$) and Euclidean distance ($p = 2$) are special instances, or block norms, obtained by shortest paths using only a finite set of travel directions and velocities and even their asymmetric cousins block gauges which usually lead to easily manageable linearity properties.

12.2 Models

In this part we introduce four models which have different kinds of solution space; the first of them is in continuous space and other three subsequent models solve in discrete space.

12.2.1 Gravity Problem

Before starting of the models we can illustrate the continuous space before and after of competition. In Fig. 12.1 there are just one player and it has all the market but in Fig. 12.2 there are two players and the market is shared between them.

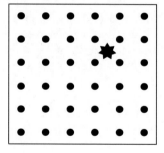

Fig. 12.1 A continuous space with one player (no competition)

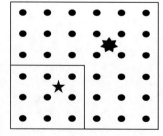

Fig. 12.2 A continuous space with two player and sharing the market (with competition)

12 Competitive Location Problem

12.2.1.1 Model Assumptions

Model assumptions of this model are as follows:

- Existing competition is known and fixed.
- Customers' patronize the most attracting facility with their full demand, i.e., "the winner gets it all" principle.
- The probability that a customer patronizes a facility is proportional to its attractiveness and inversely proportional to a power of the distance to it.
- When p new facilities are opened in an area, the total market share T attracted by these facilities and by those already part of the franchise.
- This model finds the best location for new facilities whose individual measures of attractiveness are known.

12.2.1.2 Model Inputs (Indexes and Sets)

Model inputs of this model are as follows:

i: be the sub index of demand point
j: be the sub index of existing facilities
m: be the set of new facilities

12.2.1.3 Model Outputs (Decision Variables)

Model outputs of this model are as follows:

(x_m, y_m): the location of new facility m, for $m = 1, \ldots, p$

12.2.1.4 Parameters

Parameters of this model are as follows:

n: the number of demand points (each demand point represents a small area around it)
(a_i, b_i): the location of demand point $i = 1, \ldots, n$
B_i: the available buying power at demand point i for $i = 1, \ldots, n$
K: the number of existing competing facilities
C: the number of existing facilities which are part of one's own chain
P: the number of new facility to be locating in the area
$(x_m - y_m) = \sqrt{(x_m - a_i)^2 + (y_m - b_i)^2}$: the distance between demand point i and new facility m. $i = 1, \ldots, n; m = 1, \ldots, p$
E_j: the measure of attractiveness of existing facility j for $j = 1, \ldots, k$
A_m: the measure of attractiveness of existing facility m for $m = 1, \ldots, p$
λ: the power to which the distance is raised

12.2.1.5 Objective Function and its Constraints

The objective function of this model as follows:

$$T = \sum_{i=1}^{n} B_i \frac{\sum_{m=1}^{p} \frac{A_m}{d_i^\lambda (x_m, y_m)} + \sum_{j=1}^{c} \frac{E_j}{d_{ij}^\lambda}}{\sum_{m=1}^{p} \frac{A_m}{d_i^\lambda (x_m, y_m)} + \sum_{j=1}^{k} \frac{E_j}{d_{ij}^\lambda}}. \tag{12.1}$$

The objective is to find the best location in the plane that maximizes the total market share captured T using (12.1).

A sequence of algebraic manipulations (Drezner 1995) leads to a somewhat simpler minimization problem, one of minimizing the total buying power not attracted by the chain.

$$F = \sum_{i=1}^{n} B_i \frac{\sum_{j=c+1}^{k} \frac{E_j}{d_{ij}^\lambda}}{\sum_{m=1}^{p} \frac{A_m}{d_i^\lambda (x_m, y_m)} + \sum_{j=1}^{k} \frac{E_j}{d_{ij}^\lambda}}. \tag{12.2}$$

The total sums for existing facilities are constants. Let

$$G_i = B_i \sum_{j=c+1}^{k} \frac{E_j}{d_{ij}^\lambda}, \quad H_i = \sum_{j=1}^{k} \frac{E_j}{d_{ij}^\lambda}. \tag{12.3}$$

These definitions lead to:

$$\text{Min} : \left\{ F = \sum_{i=1}^{n} \frac{G_i}{H_i + \sum_{m=1}^{p} \frac{A_m}{d_i^\lambda (x_m, y_m)}} \right\}. \tag{12.4}$$

12.2.1.6 Solution Gravity Problem

- *Algorithm 1*

Randomly generate p sites for the p new facilities.

Perform Weisfeld iteration for each of the facilities while holding the other rooted in their places (Drezner 1995).

After all p facilities were relocated one by one in step 2, calculate the changes in their locations. If the location changes are less than a perspective ε, terminate the algorithm.

The following are two practical approaches to solving (12.4) (Drezner 1995):

- *The AMPL approach*

Instead of pursuing a specialized algorithm for the solution of these problems, standard non-linear programming codes available for the solution of non-linear programming problems like (Drezner 1995) can be used. The student version of AMPL (Drezner 1995) was used to solve this problem. Since these standard programs assume that the objective function is convex, one still needs to resolve the problem repeatedly with various starting points and select the best solution for implementation. Also, the no convexity of the objective function may cause difficulties in the solution procedure itself. The AMPL modeling program is quite easy to write, is very short and compact, and is easy to follow. The full program is given in (Drezner 1995).

- *The excel approach*

Spreadsheet software now incorporates optimization capabilities. The "solver" option in Excel can be used to solve. In Excel 4.0, this option is found under "formula". A spread sheet is built to calculate the objective function, and the solver provides the optimal solution with the calculated market share at the point. Since the problem is not convex, the procedure has to be repeated using many randomly generated starting location and the best solution is selected for implementation.

12.2.2 The Maximum Capture Problem Model (MAXCAP) (Serra and ReVelle 1995)

12.2.2.1 Model Assumptions

Model assumptions of this model are as follows:
- Existing competition is known and fixed.
- Customers' patronize the most attracting facility with their full demand, i.e., "the winner gets it all" principle.
- This model leads to combinatorial optimization models similar to covering, as exhaustively reviewed in.

12.2.2.2 Model Inputs (Indexes and Sets)

Model inputs of this model are as follows:
- i, I: be the sub index and set of demand points
- p_i: set of sites s which i would patronize if a new facility would be opened there
- T_i: set of sites for i tied with the currently patronized competitor's facility

12.2.2.3 Model Outputs (Decision Variables)

Model outputs of this model are as follows:

y_i: the fully captured for i
z_i: the tied with a competitor for i

12.2.2.4 Parameters

Parameters of this model are as follows:

w_i: the demand of customer for $i \in I$
x_s: the facility be opened at s

12.2.2.5 Objective Function and its Constraints

The objective function of this model and its related constraints are as follows:

$$\text{Max} \sum_{i \in I} w_i y_i + \sum_{i \in I} \frac{w_i}{2} z_i. \tag{12.5}$$

Subject to

$$Y_i \leq \sum_{s \in p_i} x_s \ (i \in I), \tag{12.6}$$

$$Z_i \leq \sum_{s \in T_i} x_s \ (i \in I), \tag{12.7}$$

$$Y_i + Z_i \leq 1 \ (i \in I), \tag{12.8}$$

$$\sum_{s \in S} x_s \leq P, \tag{12.9}$$

$$Y_i, Z_i \in \{0, 1\} \ x_s \in \{0, 1\}. \tag{12.10}$$

12.2.2.6 Solution Maximum Capture Problem

Discrete models without split demand lead to the maximal covering type location model introduced in (Church and ReVelle 1974). This is a simplified version of the maximal capture problem given above, in which all tie sets t_i are empty, and therefore without the auxiliary tie variables z_i. Typically, these models will have many optimal solutions, a feature which is troublesome for standard exact search branch and bound methods, but makes heuristic approaches particularly appealing. A recent proposal (Benati and Laporte 1995) for solving large-scale models of this type consists of a Tabu search method.

Since in network and continuous setting ties appear whenever a site is chosen which is exactly at break-even distance from the demand point, the deterministic allocation rule inevitably leads to discontinuity of the capture function at such points, and previous rule of even split enhances this. Without split one at least retains semi-continuity. Two extreme situations without split demand may now be considered.

First there is conservatism, stating that in case of tie with a new facility; customers will go on patronizing the existing facility they patronized before. This is the rule followed in (Hakimi 1990) introducing the NP-hard (r, x_p) medianoid problem: find r sites on a network maximizing the total weight of demand vertices lying closer (in terms of shortest paths) to one of them than to any of the competitors x_p.

Second, the opposite assumption of novelty orientation, i.e., in case of tie the new facility gets all demand (Hanjoul and Thill 1987), gives rise to closed captured markets, a feature of particular importance in the next section. With this tie-resolution rule there corresponds to each demand point a (closed) subset of the location space of all sites for the new facility(ies) that would capture that demand. In other words, we have a collection of subsets, each related to a given demand volume. For a particular site the total captured demand is then obtained by summation of the volumes of all sets it lies in. Maximizing the captured demand now means finding (a point in) a no void intersection of such sets corresponding to the highest total volume. In the Euclidean plane these sets are circular balls and it is easy to show that optimal solutions will always exist among all intersection points of two of the boundary circles, an easily enumerated finite set of candidates. Dresdner (Drezner 1981) shows how to do this efficiently for a single facility, while (Mehrez and Stulman 1982) suggest a dynamic programming approach for the multi facility version.

These types of model have also been advocated in marketing studies for brand positioning and even in political science, see (Schmalensee and Thisse 1988). In the first case, product characteristics are taken as coordinates in a feature space, consumer groups having a common ideal brand-description represent demand, and attraction towards a brand is expressed by way of the (Euclidean) distance between the points representing the ideal and the real brand. This leads to ball intersection problems in higher dimensions, which turn out to be NP-hard when dimension is part of the input, but polynomial in fixed dimension. Several solution approaches have been developed recently, all relying on geometric construction and evaluation of a finite dominating set.

12.2.3 The Maximum Capture Problem with Price Model (PMAXCAP) (Serra and ReVelle 1998)

We will introduce the max capture model with price which is a kind of location and design problem that contains the price of the product in its output.

12.2.3.1 Model Assumptions

Model assumptions of this model are as follows:
- Existing competition is known and fixed.
- Customers' patronize the most attracting facility with their full demand, i.e., "the winner gets it all" principle.

- The space is discrete and is defined by a connected graph. On each vertex of the graph there is a demand whit a distinct size, the set of local markets that are located on the vertices of the graph.
- The consumer's decision on patronizing a store is based on transportation costs and price. Consumers always go the outlet with the lowest total price, regardless of its ownership.
- There is an existing firm (from now on, Firm B) operating with q outlets. A new firm (Firm A) wishes to enter and establish p servers. (The product sold in this industry is homogeneous).
- Suppose the demand is elastic then the demand of local market i is a function of the market's characteristics and the price customer faces and is denoted as $D_i(\Pi_i)$. Thus it could be said that $D_i(p + td_{ib})$ is the demand for the local market i, shopping at its closest outlet. Therefore, the demand function for each local market i for Firm A is defined as follows: if b_i^A is the closest Firm A's server to i and b_i^B the closest Firm B's server, then:

$$D_i^A(\pi^A, \pi^B) = \begin{cases} D_i(\pi^A) & if \ p^A + td_{ib_i^A} < p^B + td_{ib_i^B} \\ 0 & if \ p^A + td_{ib_i^A} \geq p^B + td_{ib_i^B} \end{cases}. \quad (12.11)$$

- Equation (12.11) is, Firm A will capture the demand of local market i if the total price Π_i^A (mill price plus transport costs) faced by consumers is lower than the total price Π_i^B that defined the in the same way for B. Assume that production entails for each outlet a fixed set-up cost f_j, and a constant marginal cost v, per unit. Thus the total cost for each outlet is given by $f_j + v_s$. s is the number of products in this facility. S is the number of products in this facility. If j^A is the set of actual outlet locations ($J^A \subset J$), then profits for firm A can be written as follows:

$$\prod\nolimits^A = (p^A - v) \sum D_i^A(\pi^A, \pi^B) - \sum_{j \in J^A} f_j. \quad (12.12)$$

- Equation (12.12) for firm A is determining j^A and p^A to maximize profits. This profit also depends on other model parameters such as the location and prices of the competitor firm and the demand function of consumers among others.

12.2.3.2 Model Inputs (Indexes and Sets)

Model inputs of this model are as follows:

i,I: be the sub index and the set of local markets that are located on the vertices of the graph

j, J: be the sub index and set of potential locations for Firm A's outlets.

J_B: be the set of actual locations of the outlets of Firm B.

12.2.3.3 Model Outputs (Decision Variable)

Model outputs of this model are as follows:

P^A: as the mill price to its customers irrespective of this location. (Continuous decision Variable)
$y_i^A = 1$, if firm A captures demand node i; 0, if not
$x_i^A = 1$, if firm A locates a server at node j; 0, if not

12.2.3.4 Parameters

Parameters of this model are as follows:

b_i^A: be the closest firm A's server to i
b_i^B: be the closest firm B's server to j
p^B: be the mill price to its customers irrespective of this location
d_{ij}: be the network (shortest) distance between local markets i and an outlet in j.
n^A = number of firm an outlet servers

12.2.3.5 Objective Function and its Constraints

If the demand function (12) of the local markets is totally inelastic with respect to prices, it can be written as $D_i = a_i$, where ai is the total demands that market i will purchase.

The objective function of this model and its related constraints are as follows:

$$\text{Max} \prod = (P^A - v)(\sum_{i \in I} a_i y_i) - \sum_{j \in J} f_j x_j. \tag{12.13}$$

Subject to

$$y_i^A \le \sum_{j \in N_I(b_i^B)} X_j^A \quad \forall i \in I, \tag{12.14}$$

$$\sum_{j=1}^{n} x_j^A = n^A, \tag{12.15}$$

$$y_i^A, x_j^A = (0, 1) \quad \forall i \in I, \forall j \in J. \tag{12.16}$$

Where additional notation is:

$$N_i(b_i^B) = \left\{ \forall j \in J, p^A + td_{ij} < p^B + td_{ib_i^B} \right\}. \tag{12.17}$$

PMAXCAP is the problem which maximizes profit capture as opposed to population captured.

Equations (12.14) depends on the set N_i (b_i^B), which is known as capture aria of the demand i. Each one of the demand nodes i has an associated set N_i (b_i^B) which contains all the potential nodes at which Firm A can locate a server and capture the demand of local market i. Therefore, if one of the variables x_i^A belonging to the corresponding constraint is equal to 1 (a facility is located within the capture area of node i), then capture variable y_i^A is allowed to be 1, which indicates that node i has been captured by Firm A. Finally, (12.15) sets the number of servers that Firm A is going to locate. The objective function defines the total profits that Firm A can achieve. For each local market If $y_i^A = 1$, then $(p^A - v)a_i$ is added to the revenues. Fixed costs are multiplied by x_j, so if an outlet established; its associated fixed cost is subtracted from the objective.

If we want to consider the number of A's established servers as inborn, then its enough to eliminate (12.15).

The basic difference between the MAXCAP problem and the PMAXCAP problem formulation are in three points: on the sets N_i in restriction, in the objective function, and in the equality case. Indeed the above formula does not pay any incidence to equality model. Of course it did not make any mistake because both value and place are variable and the possibility of the equality is very low.

The N_i (b_i^B) set contains all candidate nodes where if the server is established there the demand of node i will be captured. While in the MAXCAP problem, these sets were known preferment for each node, in the PMAXCAP model while in the MAXCAP problem these sets were known preferment for each node, in the PMAXCAP model these are variable because the price is variable therefore (12.14) cannot be written extensively. In this formulation that was given for PMAXCAP, the objective function is nonlinear.

12.2.3.6 Solution Maximum Capture Problem with Prices

If the demands function is elastic, then the PMAXCAP problem has to be reformulated using a P-median like approach which is called PMAXMED (Serra and ReVelle 1998) for solving the PMAXMED model in both cases that said before, a barred searching based method was given because using the branch and bound methods is difficult (Serra and ReVelle 1998).

12.2.4 Flow Capturing Location Allocation Problem Model (FCLAP)

12.2.4.1 Model Assumptions

Model assumptions of this model are as follows:
- Nowadays, many customers do their shopping in their daily travels between home and work or vice versa, instead of set a special travel for buying a good. Thus, in

such an area, the demand in the network is like a flow instead of a node. the goal is to establish the servers in the places as they can capture the maximum demand.
- In the articles (Berman et al. 1992; Fouska 1988) the writers had studied this subject. Which Hodgson called "flow capturing location allocation problem" (FCLAP) (Hodgson 1990). It is concluded in all papers that the optimal set of locations must be on the nodes.
- In most of the studies cited thus far, customers can visit only service facilities located at points on paths of the network. That is, no deviation from the pre-planned path is allowed. But new articles have overruled this assumption (Berman et al. 1995). Thus customer can pervert his from his predetermined way. The extra distance traveled in this case is called the "deviation distance".
- $D(p, j)$ the deviation distance from path p to node j, $d(i, j)$ being the shortest distance from node i to node j in the network; and s, e represent the starting and ending nodes for path p.

$$D(p, x) = d(s, x) + d(x, e) - d(s, e). \tag{12.18}$$

12.2.4.2 Model Inputs (Indexes and Sets)

Model inputs of this model are as follows:

K: set for existing competing facilities.
M: number of facilities to be located
$G(N, A)$: N, set of nodes with cardinality n; A, the set of arcs
$\underline{P}$: set of nonzero flow paths through network nodes and arcs
p: a path in $\underline{P}$
i: be the sub index that are not located on the vertices of the graph.
j: be the sub index that are available
t: be the sub index that are new

12.2.4.3 Model Outputs (Decision Variable)

Model outputs of this model are as follows:

$X_{pti} = 1$, if customers on path p visit facility t located on node i; 0, if not
$Y_{ti} = 1$, if facility t is located on node i; 0, if not.

12.2.4.4 Parameters

Parameters of this model are as follows:

f_p: number of customers in path P
M: number of facilities to be located
(x_m, y_m): location of new facility m, for $m = 1, 2, \ldots, M$

d_{ij}: distance between demand point i and existing facility j, $i = 1,\ldots,n$; $j = 1,\ldots,k$

$d_{ij}(x_m, y_m)$: euclidean distance between demand point i and new facility $i = 1,\ldots,n$; $m = 1,\ldots,M$

E_j: measure of attractiveness of existing facility j; $j = 1,\ldots,k$

A_m: measure of attractiveness of new facility m, $m = 1,\ldots,M$

λ: power to which distance is raised

T: total market share attracted by facilities of one chain

N_p: set of nodes capable of capturing flow on path P

12.2.4.5 Objective Function and its Constraints

The objective function of this model and its related constraints are as follows:

$$\text{Max} \sum_{P \in \underline{P}} f_p \frac{\sum_{t=1}^{M} \sum_{i \in N-K} \frac{A_i}{DD^\lambda(p,i)} x_{pti}}{\sum_{t=1}^{M} \sum_{i \in N-K} \frac{A_i}{DD^\lambda(p,i)} x_{pti} + \sum_{j \in K} \frac{E_j}{DD^\lambda(p,i)}}. \quad (12.19)$$

Subject to

$$\sum_{t=1}^{M} x_{pti} \leq 1 \; \forall p \in P, \forall i \in N - K, \quad (12.20)$$

$$\sum_{i \in N-K} x_{pti} = 1 \; \forall p \in P, t = 1,\ldots,M, \quad (12.21)$$

$$y_{ti} - x_{pti} \geq 0 \; \forall i \in N - K, t = 1,\ldots,M, \quad (12.22)$$

$$\sum_{t=1}^{M} \sum_{i \in N-K} y_{ti} = M, \quad (12.23)$$

$$x_{pti}, y_{ti} \in \{0, 1\}, \quad (12.24)$$

$$\forall p \in \underline{P}, \forall i \in N - K, t = 1,\ldots,M. \quad (12.25)$$

Equation (12.19) represents the objective to be maximized: flow captured by these new facilities.

Equations (12.20) requires that for each node, at most one facility can be located there. Equations (12.21) indicates that each new facility can be located on only one node. Equations (12.22) guarantees that the flow on path p can be captured only if the corresponding facility is located. Equation (12.23) assures that M facilities are to be located.

The binary requirements for all decision variables are expressed in (12.24).

12.2.4.6 Solution Flow Capturing Location Allocation Problem

Upon model is nonlinear which might make problems in the calculation phase. Wu and Lin (2003) had changed this model to liner, based on the method presented by Wu (1997), but the result will not always redound to simplicity. Also those man had presented an inventive method for solving the model base on a greedily procedure which is too similar to what Berman et al. (Berman et al. 1995; Berman and Krass 1998) had developed for FCLAP problem.

12.3 Case Study

In this section we will introduce some real-world case studies related to Competitive location problems.

12.3.1 A Case in Toronto (Aboolian et al. 2006)

A company would like to enter the metropolitan Toronto market by locating one or several supermarket-type retail facilities there. There are two choices for facility designs: a regular facility, with approximately 15,000 square feet of retail space, and a large facility with approximately 45,000 square feet of retail space. These values were chosen based on data from the Food Marketing Institute which lists 15,000 square feet as the size of a typical supermarket and 40,000–50,000 square feet as the size of a superstore. The budget that the company has allocated for the Toronto expansion is sufficient to locate one large facility or up to three regular facilities anywhere in the city.

In this case, the following competitive situation is assumed: a competitor providing similar service has already entered the Toronto market, using the same facility design alternatives. For the competitor, the same two choices regarding the number and sizes of the facilities are considered: one large or three small. For each combination of values of problem parameters described below, optimal locations for the competitor's facilities is selected. The company now has to decide on the location and sizes of its own facilities given the existing locations of competitive facilities.

The network that is used corresponded to the geography of metropolitan Toronto. The lease costs for retail real estate vary significantly throughout the city, the cost data per square foot is used from the April 2004 Commercial Reality Watch report produced by the Toronto Real Estate Board. Since each node of network represents an area that can contain multiple facilities, own and competitive facilities are allowed to be co-located within the same nodes.

The problem described above is analyzed under three values for demand elasticity parameter, which represent respectively very high elasticity, moderate elasticity, and low elasticity; three values for the size sensitivity parameter, which represent, respectively, very high sensitivity, moderate sensitivity, and low sensitivity; and two values for the distance sensitivity, which represent respectively, high and moderate values. Aboolian et al. (2006) wanted to see the extent to which the optimal location and sizing decisions depend on the problem parameters and on the sizes and locations of pre-existing competitive facilities.

The following conclusions can be made based on the results of the case study in Toronto:

- It is always optimal to locate three regular facilities when either the size sensitivity is small, or size sensitivity is moderate and distance sensitivity is high.
- When distance and size sensitivities are both moderate, three regular facilities are also preferred, except when demand is very elastic, in which case one large facility performs better.
- When size sensitivity is high, one large facility is generally optimal, except when distance sensitivity is high and demand is not very elastic.
- The optimal sizes of own facilities appear to depend only on problem parameters the sizes/number of competitive facilities do not seem to affect own design decisions. However the locations of own facilities are certainly influenced by both, the number and locations of competitive facilities, as well as by the problem parameters.
- When demand is very elastic, co-locations are very common i.e., one or more of own facilities are located in the same FSAs as the competitive facilities, we can loosely interpret these as shopping mall solutions. On the other hand, when demand elasticity is low, co-location never happens owns facilities tend to be located away from the competitive ones.

12.3.2 A Case in Yuanlin Taiwan (Wu and Lin 2003)

The decision objective for service providers is to find the optimal locations for such service facilities to Maximize the number of customers "captured". This sort of problem is usually called a "flow capturing location allocation problem" (FCLAP), that in the earlier seasons of this book is discussed. In this article a mathematical model and heuristic solving method is developed based on the greedy solving method, and this solving method in the instance study of real networks in Yuanlin, Changhua which was accomplished in Taiwan is surveyed.

Yuanlin is a township in Changhua County, Central Taiwan with an approximate area of 33 : 72 km^2 and a 1998 population of 126,395.

A newly established retail chain is planning to enter the local convenience-store market and locate a number of new stores in Yuanlin. For this analysis, The Household Registration Office of Yuanlin provided data such as geographical zoning, and the population of each zone from a 1998 update.

In this analysis, there is a network with 39 nodes and 1482 paths and several assumptions made in this analysis are described as follows: These criteria consist of product mix (c1), price (c2), interior layout and design (c3), personnel (c4), overall cleanliness (c5), floor space (c6), traffic congestion in the surrounding area (c7), and frequency of promotional sales (c8). Information regarding the location and attractiveness score is gathered for each existing store.

The greedy heuristic and the enumeration method developed are used for solving this authentic network. The results enumeration approaches are nodes 19, 27, 3 and the results greedy approach summarized are nodes 8, 27, 19. The deviation from the optimal of the greedy heuristic is 5.73%, with 7.141 s taken, which is more than 340 times faster than the 2,484.658 s required by the enumeration method are.

References

Aboolian R, Berman O, Krass D (2006) Competitive facility location and design problem. Eur J Oper Res 182:40–62
Benati S, Laporte G (1995) Tabu search algorithms for (r|Xp) medianoid and (r|p) centroid problems. Location Sci 2:193–204
Berman O, Krass D (1998) Flow intercepting spatial interaction model: A new approach to optimal location of competitive facilities. Location Sci 6:41–65
Berman O, Larson RC, Fouska N (1992) Optimal location of discretionary service facilities. Transport Sci 26:201–221
Berman O, Bertsimas D, Larson RC (1995) Locating discretionary service facilities II: maximizing market, minimizing inconvenience. Oper Res 43:623–632
Chhajed D, Francis RL, Lowe TJ (1993) Contributions of operations research to location analysis. Location Sci 1(4):263–287
Church R, ReVelle C (1974) The maximal covering location problem. Papers of the Regional Science Association 32:101–118
Dobson G, Karmarkar US (1987) Competitive location on a network. Oper Res 35(4):565–574
Drezner Z (1981) On a modified one-center problem. Manage Sci 27:848–851
Drezner T (1995) Competitive location problem in the plane, In: Drezner Z (ed) Facility location: A survey of application and methods. Springer, Berlin
Drezner T, Drezner Z (1996) Competitive facilities: Market share and location with random utility. J Region Sci 36:1–15
Eiselt HA, Laporte G (1989a) Competitive spatial models. Eur J Oper Res 39:231–242
Eiselt HA, Laporte G (1989b) The maximum capture problem on a weighted network. J Region Sci 29:433–439
Eiselt HA, Laporte G (1996a) Equilibrium results in competitive location models. Middle East Forum 1:63–92
Eiselt HA, Laporte G (1996b) Sequential location problems. Eur J Oper Res 96:217–223
Eiselt HA, Laporte G, Thisse JF (1993) Competitive location models: A framework and bibliography. Transport Sci 27(1):44–54
Fouska N (1988) Optimal location of discretionary service facilities, MS Thesis, Operation Research Center. MIT, Cambridge, MA, USA
Friesz T, Tobin L, Miller T (1989) Existence theory for spatially competitive network facility location models. Ann Oper Res 18:267–276
Gabszewicz J, Thisse JF (1991) Location. In: Auman R, Hart S (eds) Handbook of game theory with economic applications. North-Holland, Amsterdam
Ghosh A, Craig CS (1984) A location-allocation model for facility planning in a competitive environment. Geograph Anals 20:39–51
Hakimi SL (1986) p-median theorems for competitive location. Ann Oper Res 5:79–88
Hakimi SL (1990) Locations with spatial interactions: Competitive locations and games. In: Francis RL, Mirchandani PB (eds) Discrete location theory. Wiley, New York, pp 439–447

Hakimi SL, Labbe M, Schmeichel E (1992) The Voronoi partition of a network and its implications in location theory. ORSA J Comput 4:412–417

Hanjoul P, Thill JC (1987) Elements of planar analysis in spatial competition. Region Sci Urban Econ 17:423–439

Hanjoul P, Hansen P, Peeters D, Thisse JF (1990) Uncapacitated plant location under alternative spatial policies. Manage Sci 36(1):41–57

Hodgson J (1990) A flow-capturing location-allocation model. Geograph Anal 22:270–279

Hoover E (1936) Spatial price discrimination. Rev Econ Stud 4:182–191

Hotelling H (1929) Stability in competition. Econ J 39:41–57

Karkazis J (1989) Facilities location in a competitive environment: A promethee based multiple criteria analysis. Eur J Oper Res 42:294–304

Lederer P, Thisse JF (1990) Competitive location on networks under delivery pricing. Oper Res Lett 9:147–153

Lerner A, Singer HV (1937) Some notes on duopoly and spatial competition. J Political Econ 39:145–186

Mehrez A, Stulman A (1982) The maximal covering location problem with facility placement on the entire plane. J Region Sci 22:361–365

Miller T, Friesz TL, Tobin RL (1992) Heuristic algorithms for delivered price spatially competitive network facility location problems. Ann Oper Res 34:177–202

Peeters PH (1997) Static competitive location models on networks. Master's thesis, Vrije Universiteit Brussel, Brussels, Belgium, pp 65

ReVelle C (1986) The maximum capture or sphere of in influence problem: Hotelling revisited on a network. J Region Sci 26(2):343–357

ReVelle C, Serra D (1991) The maximum capture problem including relocation. Inf Oper Res 29(2):130–138

Schmalensee R, Thisse JF (1988) Perceptual maps and the optimal location of new products: An integrative essay. Int J Res Market 5:225–24

Serra D, ReVelle C (1995) Competitive location in discrete space. In: Drezner Z (ed) Facility location: a survey of applications and methods. Springer, Berlin, pp 367–386

Serra D, ReVelle C (1998) Competitive location and pricing on networks. J Econ Lit Classif C61, R32, L81, R12

Serra D, Marianov V, ReVelle C (1992) The hierarchical maximum capture problem. Eur J Oper Res 62(3):58–69

Smithies A (1941) Optimum location in spatial competition. J Political Econ 49:423–439

Tobin R, Friesz TL (1986) Spatial competition facility location models: Definition, formulation and solution approach. Ann Oper Res 6:47–74

Wendell R, McKelvey RD (1981) New perspectives in competitive location theory. Eur J Oper Res 6:174–182

Winston, Wayne L (1995) Introduction to mathematical programming, 2nd ed. Duxbury Press, North Scituate, MA

Wu TH (1997) A note on a global approach for general 0–1 fractional programming. Eur J Oper Res 101:220–223

Wu TH, Lin JN (2003) Solving the competitive discretionary service facility location problem. Eur J Oper Res 144:366–37

Chapter 13
Warehouse Location Problem

Zeinab Bagherpoor, Shaghayegh Parhizi, Mahtab Hoseininia,
Nooshin Heidari, and Reza Ghasemi Yaghin

Finding the optimal location for industrial facilities has always been of a crucial importance and priority from geographers' and economists' view point. Although economics play the main role in presenting location theories by resorting to its theories, geographers, with their focus on locative and spatial changes leading to natural phenomenon, have also had a share in complimenting these location theories and finding optimal points to locate industrial activities location. From this point of view, materials, market and other manufacturing factors have not been concentrated in one point, and their spatial separation necessitates traveling distances which, in turn, brings about costs. That is why optimal industrial location is also a part of geographical studies.

By location theories, we mean "a series of principals with resorting to which, the optimal location of industrial activities is determined (point conjoining on the most benefit)". The history of location theories goes back to nineteenth century in Germany. The first industrial location theory was presented by Shuffle in 1878 A.D. He was successful in applying the gravity model in the way industries are located:

$$M_{ij} = P_i P_j - D_{ij}^{-2}, \qquad (13.1)$$

where P&D represent population and distances, respectively. In this way, industries are located adjacent to huge cities as a response to demand and market factors.

The most dominating principle in finding the optimal location is based on the basis of the least cost. Lanhart is another scientist in this field who represented his theory in 1882. According to his reasoning, the position of industries depends on the significant factor of transportation. In other words, the ideal point for locating industry is a point where the total transportation cost, including material, final products and fuel, are at minimum.

At the mercy of myriad business, logistics and government initiatives, including just in time production, quick response, research on quality, enhanced customer satisfaction, operators' safety, and environmental protection, warehouse operations have been and are continuously revolutionized (Tompkins et al. 1996). Warehouses can play each of the following roles in a distribution network:

- They can be used as a balance and storage point because of the difference between the time scheduling and manufacturing demand. For this reason, the

warehouses are usually located at the manufacturing point. Complete pallets flow in and out. Warehouses whose role is limited to this can have monthly and seasonal demands until progressing to the next step in distribution.
- They can be utilized for storing and commixing outputs coming from different manufacturing points in one company or more companies, before being send to the customers. This part usually responses to the weekly or monthly orders.
- They can be dispersed to reach the shortest transportation distances to be able to quickly respond to the customer's demand. Items are often chosen individually and similar items can be sent daily.

If possible, two or more of these roles must be consolidated in the same warehouses. Today's changes have necessitated this consolidation to make inputs accessible and to decrease transportation costs. Small items with great value and unpredictable demands, in particular, are often distributed from a single source through a global network (Tompkins et al. 1996).

13.1 Classifications

A classification of different types of warehouse location problems is represented as follows:

- Area solution: discrete, continual
- Warehouse installation cost: Fixed installation cost, Without fixed installation cost
- Determination of the number of warehouses: exogenous, endogenous
- Determination of the number of products: Single product, Multiple product
- Determination of number of periods: singe period and multi period.
- Warehouse capacity: unlimited capacity, Limited capacity
- Constraint on relationship between warehouses and customer: In some models, customer's demand could be served by any number of warehouses but in others there are constraints on relationship between customers and warehouses and each warehouse can serve only a limited number of customers.

The purpose of these problems is to minimize the total cost of locating warehouses in candidate points and allocating customers to the warehouses in each period. These problems also make clear assumptions about costs. The curve in Fig. 13.1 indicates the required cost to build facilities as a function of output quantity and the curve in Fig. 13.2 indicates the incurred transportation costs as a function of shipment size (in fact, transportation costs increase with the size of shipment). It may be difficult to estimate the cost items. We may also encounter questions such as "How long does a period last?", "How many periods should be considered?", and "How much are the administering costs of the warehouse?". Such questions can be examined in the special problem.

13 Warehouse Location Problem

Fig. 13.1 Warehouse cost model

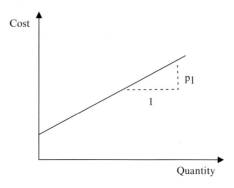

Fig. 13.2 Transportation cost model

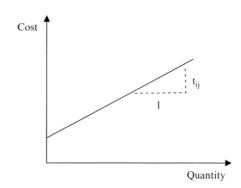

13.2 Models

In this section, we introduce warehouse location models represented and developed as mathematical models.

13.2.1 Warehouse Location Problem without Fixed Installation Costs (William et al. 1958)

In this section, fixed costs of warehouse installation are not considered in the warehouse location problem and, therefore, there are changes in the problem variables which convert it to a transportation problem (William et al. 1958).

13.2.1.1 Model Assumptions

Model assumptions are as follows:

- The location problem is viewed as a discrete problem.
- The capacities of facilities are assumed to be equal and infinite.

- Transportation costs are an increasing function of shipment sizes.
- The number of warehouses should not be more than the number of candidate points.
- Each customer's demand should be estimated and customers should be allocated to the warehouses.

13.2.1.2 Model Inputs

i: factory ($i = 1, 2, \ldots, m$)
j: warehouse ($j = 1, 2, \ldots, n$)
k: retailer ($k = 1, 2, \ldots, q$)
C_{ijk}: cost of the shipment (from factory i to retailer k through warehouse j) including the relevant inventory cost
Q_i: quantity shipped from factory i
R_j: capacity of warehouse j
S_k: quantity required at destination k

13.2.1.3 Model Outputs (Decision Variables)

X_{ijk}: quantity shipped from factory i via warehouse j to retailer k
A_{ijk}: amount of inventory remained in warehouse j from the flow X_{ijk}

13.2.1.4 Objective Function and its Constraints

The problem is to minimize the total delivery costs, i.e., to minimize the following:

$$\text{Min } Z = \sum_{i,j,k} C_{ijk}\left(X_{ijk}\right), \tag{13.2}$$

Subject to

$$\sum_{jk} X_{ijk} = Q_i \; i = 1, 2, \ldots, m, \tag{13.3}$$

$$\sum_{i,k} A_{ijk}\left(X_{ijk}\right) \leq R_j \; j = 1, 2, \ldots, n, \tag{13.4}$$

$$\sum_{i,j} X_{ijk} = S_k \; k = 1, 2, \ldots, q. \tag{13.5}$$

Equation (13.3): all goods must be shipped out of the factory
Equation (13.4): no warehouse capacity can be exceeded
Equation (13.5): all customers' demands must be met

The resemblance to the standard transportation problem is obvious and there are only three differences:

(a) The possible nonlinearity of (13.2)
(b) The presence of the warehouse-capacity (13.4)
(c) The need for a three subscript notation for the variables X_{ijk} (three dimensional X variables) resulting from the necessity of routing each flow through a warehouse.

Of course, a nonlinear objective function is not necessarily ruled out for the transportation problem, and can be ignored. The warehouse capacity limitations in the problem, can be also be ignored because a firm never ends up renting more than a small fraction of the public warehouse space available at any location.

Elimination of difference (c), i.e., the three-subscript notation, becomes a trivial matter because of the following rule: An optimal (least cost) solution will involve shipment of all goods that go from factory i^* to destination k^* via that (those) warehouse (s) j^* for which $C_{i^*j^*k^*} = \text{Min } jC'_{i^*jk^*}$

In the other ways, it will always pay to make any shipment via the warehouse that offers the lowest delivery cost. The solution of the program is now simple.

For each factory-destination combination, $i^* - k^*$, select a value j^* for which (13.5) is satisfied. This can be done by simple inspection of the C_{ijk} data. We can now revise our notation by letting $X_{i^*j^*k^*} = X'_{i^*k^*}$, $C_{i^*j^*k^*} = C'_{i^*k^*}$ (since in an optimal solution all other $X_{i^*jk^*}$'s will be equal zero). Substituting this notation in (13.2), (13.4), and (13.5) will obviously leave us with a standard transportation problem whose optimum solution can be found by the standard methods.

13.2.2 Warehouse Location Problem with Fixed Cost of Establishment (Akinc and Khumawala 1977)

All assumptions in this problem are similar to the previous case; the only difference is the fixed cost of location.

13.2.2.1 Model Inputs

k: customer ($k = 1, 2, \ldots, q$)
j: candidate points ($j = 1, 2, \ldots, n$)
f_j: cost of locating a warehouse in point j
r_k: customer's demand
v_{kj}: the cost of shipment to customer k from point j for each unit

$$c_{kj} = v_{kj} + r_k,$$

where usually $q > n$.

13.2.2.2 Model Outputs (Decision Variables)

x_{kj}: a fraction of r_k which is transported from j to customer k
y_i: Will be equal one if the candidate point j is selected, otherwise it will be equal to zero.

13.2.2.3 Objective Function and its Constraints

The warehouse location model is formulated as a mix integer programming problem, as follows:

$$\text{Min } Z = \sum_{j=1}^{n} f_j y_j + \sum_{j=1}^{n}\sum_{k=1}^{q} c_{kj} x_{kj}, \tag{13.6}$$

Subject to

$$\sum_{j=1}^{n} x_{kj} = 1; \quad k = 1, \ldots, q, \tag{13.7}$$

$$-x_{kj} + y_j \geq 0, \tag{13.8}$$

$$0 \leq x_{kj} \leq 1, \tag{13.9}$$

$$y_j \in \{0, 1\}. \tag{13.10}$$

Notice that $r_k{}^* x_{kj}$ is the amount transported from point j to customer k (x_{kj} is a fraction of r_k which is transported from point j to customer k).

Equation (13.7) insure that a customer's demand is satisfied and that the maximum quantity of x_{kj} is equal to 1. Equation (13.8) insure that a warehouse in point j serves customer k if a warehouse has been located in that point.

This formulation shows that WLP is, in fact, a special type of n-Median in which the number of facilities is ignored.

13.2.2.4 The Other Way of Formulation

In this section, another WLP formulation is presented which is discussed in the last section. Here, by adding up of (13.8) over k, the mentioned WLP is converted to the following problem:

$$\text{Min } z' = \sum_{j=1}^{n} f_j y_j + \sum_{j=1}^{n}\sum_{k=1}^{q} c_{kj} x_{kj} \quad (\text{WLP}'), \tag{13.11}$$

Subject to

$$\sum_{j=1}^{n} x_{kj} = 1, \quad k = 1, \ldots, q, \tag{13.12}$$

$$\sum_{k=1}^{q} x_{kj} - qy_j \leq 0, \quad j = 1, \ldots, n, \tag{13.13}$$

$$0 \leq x_{kj} \leq 1, \quad k = 1, \ldots, q; j = 1, \ldots, n, \tag{13.14}$$

$$y_j \in \{0, 1\}. \tag{13.15}$$

Both problems have the same optimal solution. However, they have different relaxations. In fact, WLP' can be solved through scanning, since the following equation holds:

$$\sum_{k=1}^{q} x_{kj}{}^* = qy^*{}_j. \tag{13.16}$$

Reducing $y_j{}^*$ results in the objective function value to reduce as well. Therefore, the constraints of $y_j{}^*$ can be solved and replaced in the objective function:

$$\text{Min} \sum_{j=1}^{n} \sum_{k=1}^{q} (\frac{f_j}{q} + c_{kj}) x_{kj}, \tag{13.17}$$

Subject to

$$\sum_{j=1}^{n} x_{kj} = 1, \quad k = 1, \ldots, q, \tag{13.18}$$

$$0 \leq x_{kj} \leq 1, \quad k = 1, .., q; \ j = 1, .., n. \tag{13.19}$$

By this WLP compact method, the warehouse with the least $f_j/q + c_{kj}$ is chosen. The relaxation of WLP' presents a weak low bound for the WLP and it is not clear how it can be used to solve WLP.

Therefore, mathematical models with less number of constraints are not necessarily better. For warehouse location models, the extended model of $-x_{kj} + y_j \geq 0$ is preferred to the following compact model:

$$\sum_{k=1}^{q} x_{kj} - qy_j \leq 0. \tag{13.20}$$

Even if it increases the size of the model (WLP is called strong LP, and WLP' is called weak LP) (Akinc and Khumawala 1977).

13.2.3 Capacitated Warehouse Location Problem with Constraints in Customers Being Serviced (Nagy 2004)

In the pervious models, a customer's demand could be served by any number of warehouses, but in this model there is a constraint on the warehouses, and, therefore, each warehouse can serve only a limited number of customers and each customer must be supplied by exactly one open warehouse. The objective is to determine which warehouses to open, and the allocation of the customers to the opened warehouses, such that the sum of the maintenance and supply costs is minimized (Nagy 2004).

13.2.3.1 Model Inputs

k: is the number of customer
j: is the number of warehouses
c_{kj}: is a table containing the cost associated to the supply
c_f: is the fixed cost
$Capacity_j$: the max number of stores that it can supply

13.2.3.2 Model Outputs (Decision Variables)

O_j: is a vector of Booleans indicating what warehouses have been opened.
S_{kj}: is a matrix of Booleans indicating if customer k is supplied by warehouse j

13.2.3.3 Objective Function and its Constraints

$$\text{Min} \sum_{k,j} S_{kj} c_{kj} + c_f \sum_j O_j, \quad (13.21)$$

Subject to

$$\sum_j S_{kj} = 1, \quad \forall k, \quad (13.22)$$

$$\sum_k S_{kj} \leq Capacity_j, \quad \forall j, \quad (13.23)$$

$$\sum_k S_{kj} \leq O_j, \quad \forall k, j. \quad (13.24)$$

Equation (13.22) insure that a customer must be supplied by exactly one warehouse. Equation (13.23) insure that each warehouse has a fixed capacity. Equation (13.24) insure that a customer can be supplied only by an open warehouse (Nagy 2004).

13.2.4 Single Stage Capacitated Warehouse Location Model (Sharma and Berry 2007)

In this section, new formulations and relaxations of the single stage capacitated warehouse location problem (SSCWLP) are described.

13.2.4.1 Model Inputs

i: plant
j: warehouse
k: market
D_k: demand for the commodity at market k
d_k: $D_k / \sum D_k$ demand at market k as a fraction of total market demand
S_i: supply available at plant i
s_i: $S_i / \sum D_k$ supply available at plant i as a fraction of the total market demand
f_j: fixed cost of locating a warehouse at j
C_{ijk}: cost of transporting a quantity of goods from i to j to market k
CAP_j: capacity of warehouse j
cap_j: $CAP_j / \sum D_k$ capacity of the warehouse at location j as a fraction of the total market demand

13.2.4.2 Model Outputs (Decision Variables)

X_{ijk}: quantity of commodity transported from plant i to warehouse j to market k
x_{ijk}: $X_{ijk} / \sum D_k$ quantity transported as a fraction of total market demand
y_j: will be equal 1 if warehouse is located at location j, 0 otherwise

13.2.4.3 Objective Function and its Constraints

$$\text{Min } Z = \sum_i \sum_j \sum_k c_{ijk} {}^* x_{ijk} + \sum_j f_j {}^* y_j, \qquad (13.25)$$

Subject to

$$\sum_i \sum_j \sum_k x_{ijk} = 1, \qquad (13.26)$$

$$\sum_j \sum_k x_{ijk} \leq s_i, \quad \forall i, \qquad (13.27)$$

$$\sum_i \sum_j x_{ijk} \geq d_k, \quad \forall k, \qquad (13.28)$$

$$\sum_i \sum_k x_{ijk} \leq cap_j, \quad \forall j, \qquad (13.29)$$

$$x_{ijk} \geq 0, \quad \forall i, j, k. \qquad (13.30)$$

Equation (13.26) ensures that the flow through the entire network is equal to the total demand of all markets. Equation (13.27) ensure that the outflow from a supply point is less than its supply. Equation (13.28) ensure that the inflow at a market point meets the demand of that point. Equation (13.29) are non-negativity constraints (Sharma and Berry 2007).

Now, we list the constraints that link real variables and the 0–1 integer (location) variables as follows:

$$\sum_i \sum_k x_{ijk} \leq cap_j \, y_j, \quad \forall j, \tag{13.31}$$

$$\sum_i \sum_k x_{ijk} \leq y_j, \quad \forall j, \tag{13.32}$$

$$\sum_i x_{ijk} \leq d_k \, y_j, \quad \forall j, \tag{13.33}$$

$$\sum_k x_{ijk} \leq s_i \, y_j, \quad \forall i, j, \tag{13.34}$$

$$\sum_i \sum_k x_{ijk} + M \left(1 - y_j\right) \geq 0, \quad \forall j,$$

$$\sum_i \sum_k x_{ijk} + M \, y_j \geq 0, \quad \forall j, \tag{13.35}$$

$$\sum_i \sum_k x_{ijk} - M \, y_j \leq 0, \quad \forall j,$$

$$\sum_i x_{ijk} - M \left(1 - y_j\right) \leq d_k, \quad \forall j, k,$$

$$\sum_i x_{ijk} + M \, y_j \geq 0, \quad \forall j, k, \tag{13.36}$$

$$\sum_i x_{ijk} - M \, y_j \geq 0, \quad \forall j, k,$$

$$\sum_k x_{ijk} - M \left(1 - y_j\right) \leq s_i, \quad \forall j, i,$$

$$\sum_k x_{ijk} + M \, y_j \geq 0, \quad \forall j, i, \tag{13.37}$$

$$\sum_k x_{ijk} - M \, y_j \leq 0, \quad \forall j, i,$$

$$y_j = [0, 1], \quad \forall j, \tag{13.38}$$

$$y_j \geq 0, \quad \forall j. \tag{13.39}$$

It should be noted that the (13.32) are the "weak relaxation" constraints and (13.33) form the "strong relaxation" constraints. Since (13.34) are similar to (13.33), they are also referred to as "strong relaxation" constraints. Equation (13.31) are as "capacity" constraints. Thus, given one kind of linking constraints (that link 0–1 integer variables and real variables), we get six formulations for SSCWLP (Sharma and Berry 2007).

1. GG_Weak
   min (13.25)
   s.t. (13.26)–(13.30), (13.32) and (13.39).

2. GG_Strong_1
   min (13.25)
   s.t. (13.26)–(13.30), (13.33) and (13.38).
3. GG_Strong_2
   min (13.25)
   s.t. (13.26)–(13.30), (13.35) and (13.36).
4. GG_BigM_1
   min (13.25)
   s.t. (13.27)–(13.31), (13.35)–(13.36) and (13.38).
5. GG_BigM_2
   min (13.25)
   s.t. (13.26)–(13.30), (13.36)–(13.37), and (13.38).
6. GG_BigM_3
   min (13.25)
   s.t. (13.26)–(13.30), (13.37), (13.33) and (13.38).
   Considering two types of linking constraints (capacity constraints along with weak, strong (two types) and BigM (three types)) in one formulation, we get six other formulations for SSCWLP.
7. GG_Capacity_Weak
   min (13.25)
   s.t. (13.26)–(13.28), (13.30), (13.31), (13.32) and (13.38).
8. GG_Capacity_Strong_1
   min (13.25)
   s.t. (13.26)–(13.28), (13.30), (13.31), (13.33) and (13.38).
9. GG_Capacity_Strong_2
   min (13.25)
   s.t. (13.26)–(13.28), (13.30), (13.31), (13.34) and (13.38).
10. GG_Capacity_BigM_1
    min (13.25)
    s.t. (13.26)–(13.28), (13.30), (13.31), (13.35) and (13.38).
11. GG_Capacity_BigM_2
    min (13.25)
    s.t. (13.26)–(13.28), (13.30), (13.31), (13.36) and (13.38).
12. GG_Capacity_BigM_3
    min (13.25)
    s.t. (13.26)–(13.28), (13.30), (13.31), (13.37) and (13.38).

13.2.5 Redesigning a Warehouse Network (Melachrinoudis and Min 2007)

To take advantage of the economies of scale, a growing number of firms have begun to explore the possibility of integrating supply chain activities. The advent of such a possibility would necessitate the redesign of a warehouse network. The consolidation or redesign of warehouses can help a firm save transportation, inventory, and warehousing costs due to economies of scale (Melachrinoudis and Min 2007).

In this section, a mixed-integer programming model is developed to solve the warehouse redesign problem.

13.2.5.1 Problem Definition

Typically, a warehouse redesign problem involves the consolidation of regional warehouses into a fewer number of master stocking points and the subsequent phase-out of redundant or underutilized warehouses without deteriorating customer service (see Table 13.1) (Melachrinoudis and Min 2007).

Table 13.1 Differences in strategic network planning among warehouse redesign alternatives

	Retention of existing warehouses	Closure of existing warehouses	Establishment of new warehouses
Key checkpoints	• Which existing Warehouses are still viable for sustaining customer services? • How to maintain the best balance between customer service and logistics costs?	• How to determine the level of redundancy among existing warehouses? • Which existing warehouses are considered redundant with nearby warehouses? • When to phase-out redundant warehouses without disruptions?	• How to identify potential sites for new warehouse locations? • What is the level of strategic risks involved in new start-up investment? • Are there any changes in locations of customer bases?
Key factors	• Customer service • Maintenance cost	• Closure cost • Relocation/moving cost • Warehouse utilization rate • Severance pay for laid-off warehouse employees	• Setup cost • Start-up risk • Labor availability • Regional tax incentives • Local regulation
Main advantages	• Presence of near customer locations • Stability	• Cost saving potential • Flexibility	• Proximity to major customer bases • Capacity expansion
Major shortcomings	• Inflexibility • Depreciation • Obsolescence	• Downsizing • Service disruptions • Low employee morale	• Overlap risk • High cost of investment • Learning curve

13.2.5.2 Model Assumptions

1. The warehouses are owned by the company (private).
2. When a warehouse is consolidated into another warehouse, its whole capacity is relocated.
3. The restructuring plan covers a planning horizon within which no substantial changes are likely in the customer demands and in the transportation infrastructure.
4. Although the company distributes its products in various quantities, customer orders are aggregated into a single product.

13.2.5.3 Model Inputs

i: index for manufacturing plants i,
k: index for customers; $k \in K$,
j: index for existing warehouses and new candidate sites for relocation and consolidation; $j \in A$,
sets: $A = E \cup N$; $(j, l) \in (E \times A)$
E: set of existing warehouses
N: set of new candidate sites for relocation and consolidation.
V_{ij}: Unit production cost (including storage cost) at manufacturing plant i plus unit transshipment cost between manufacturing plant i and warehouse j
S_{jk}: Unit warehousing cost at warehouse j and unit transportation cost between warehouse j and customer k
r_{lj}: Cost of moving and relocating unit capacity l to consolidated site $j^{(l \neq j)}$
c_j: Throughput capacity of existing warehouse j
q_i: Production capacity of manufacturing plant i
d_k: Demand of customer k
f_{cj}: Cost per unit capacity of warehouse j
f_{mj}: Fixed cost of maintaining warehouse j, excluding capacity cost
f_{sj}: Cost savings resulting from the closure of existing warehouse j
t_{jk}: Truck delivery time (in hours) from warehouse j to customer k
τ: Maximum of customer access time (in hours) from serving warehouses

$$C(j) = \{k | t_{jk} \leq \tau\}, \qquad (13.40)$$
$$D(k) = \{j | t_{jk} \leq \tau\}. \qquad (13.41)$$

13.2.5.4 Model Outputs (Decision Variables)

X_{jk}: Volume of products shipped from warehouse j to customer k
Y_{ij}: Volume of products supplied by plant i to warehouse j

z_{jl} will be equal to 1 if capacity of warehouse j, is relocated to site l, or if existing warehouse j remains open and otherwise it will be equal to 0

w_j will be equal to 1 if a new warehouse established at site j and otherwise it will be equal to 0

13.2.5.5 Objective Function and its Constraints

$$\text{Min} \sum_{i \in I} \sum_{j \in A} v_{ij} y_{ij} + \sum_{j \in A} \sum_{k \in C(j)} s_{jk} x_{jk} + \sum_{l \in E} \sum_{j \in A} r_{lj} z_{lj} + \sum_{j \in A} f_j^c \sum_{l \in E} c_l z_{lj}$$
$$+ \sum_{j \in E} f_j^m z_{jj} + \sum_{j \in N} f_j^m w_j - \sum_{l \in E} \left[f_l^s \left(1 - \sum_{j \in A} z_{lj} \right) + f_l^m \sum_{\{j \in E, j \neq l\}} z_{lj} \right],$$
(13.42)

Subject to

$$\sum_{j \in A} y_{ij} \leq q_i \quad \forall i \in I, \tag{13.43}$$

$$\sum_{i \in I} y_{ij} = \sum_{k \in C(j)} x_{jk} \quad \forall j \in A, \tag{13.44}$$

$$\sum_{k \in C(j)} x_{jk} \leq \sum_{l \in E} c_l x_{lj} \quad \forall j \in A, \tag{13.45}$$

$$\sum_{j \in D(k)} x_{jk} = d_k \quad \forall k \in K, \tag{13.46}$$

$$\sum_{l \in E} z_{lj} \leq |E| z_{jj} \quad \forall j \in E, \tag{13.47}$$

$$\sum_{l \in E} z_{lj} \leq |E| w_j \quad \forall j \in N, \tag{13.48}$$

$$\sum_{j \in A} z_{lj} \leq 1 \quad \forall l \in E, \tag{13.49}$$

$$x_{jk} \geq 0 \quad \forall j \in A, \ k \in K, \tag{13.50}$$

$$y_{ij} \geq 0 \quad \forall i \in I, \ j \in A, \tag{13.51}$$

$$z_{lj}, w_j \in \{0, 1\} \quad \forall l \in E, \ j \in A. \tag{13.52}$$

Equation (13.42) minimizes total supply chain costs comprised of production, transportation, warehousing, and relocation costs, while maximizing the cost savings resulting from the closure or consolidation of redundant warehouses. Equation (13.43) assure that the total volume of products shipped to warehouses do not exceed the capacity of the manufacturing plant supplying those products. Equation (13.44) insure that the total volume of products supplied by the manufacturing plant to each warehouse matches the total volume of products shipped from that warehouse to its customers. In other words, inbound shipping volume for each warehouse must be equal to its outbound shipping volume. Equation (13.45) insure that the total volume of products shipped to customers can not exceed the throughput capacity (after consolidation) of the warehouse serving them. Equation (13.46) ensure that the customer demand is satisfied. Equation (13.47) state that the current resources (i.e., capacity) of an existing warehouse can not be consolidated into another existing warehouse, unless such a consolidated warehouse remains open. Equation (13.48) state that the capacity of an existing warehouse cannot be relocated to a new site, unless a warehouse is established at the new site. Equation (13.49) consider various options for an existing warehouse j. These options include: keeping the warehouse open ($z_{jj} = 1$), consolidating its capacity into another existing warehouse $j \in E$, $j \neq l(z_{lj} = 1)$, relocating its capacity to a new site $i \in N(z_{lj} = 1)$, or closing the existing warehouse l $(z_{lj} = 0 \; \forall i \in A)$. Equations (13.50)–(13.51) assure the non negativity of decision variables x_{jk}, y_{ij}. Equation (13.52) state that z_{il} and w_j are zero-one variables (Melachrinoudis and Min 2007).

13.3 Solution Methods

To solve small WLPs, integer programming optimization methods are used. However, for larger problems, heuristic methods or Meta heuristic methods are utilized.

13.3.1 Exact Solution Methods

The UWLP has attracted considerable attention in mathematical programming. Khumawala (1972) developed a branch and bound algorithm for uncapacitated warehouse location problems. Akinc and Khumawala (1977) developed a branch and bound algorithm for capacitated warehouse location problems. Also based on dual and primal–dual approaches branch and bound algorithms were developed (Erlenkotter 1978; Korkel 1989). Dual-based and primal–dual algorithms are very effective for the UWLP on the OR Library benchmarks. However, they experience significant difficulties and exhibit exponential behavior on the M* instances (Kratica et al. 2001). These instances stimulate real situations, have a large number of suboptimal solutions, and exhibit a strong tension between transportation and fixed costs, which makes it difficult to eliminate many warehouses early in the search (Michel and Hentenryck 2004).

Lagrangian relaxation is a well known technique for calculating lower bounds in branch and bound algorithms. In order to solve CWLP, Geoffrion and Graves (1974), Geoffrion and Nauss (1977), and Christofides and Beasley (1983) have used a Lagrangian relaxation of the demand constraints.

Baker (1986) proposed another Lagrangian relaxation for the demand constraints to obtain lower band. In order to converge to optimal set of multiplier, he proposed a heuristic algorithm. The computational result shows that the algorithm based on partial dual approach has performed well and generally produced results which are as good as, or better than those of the previously accepted based on a Lagrangian relaxation of demand constraints.

Beasley (1988) presented a lower bound for the capacitated warehouse location problem based upon Lagrangian relaxation of a mixed-integer formulation of the problem. Feasible solution exclusion constraints are used together with problem reduction tests derived from both the original problem and the Lagrangian relaxation. By incorporating the lower bound and the reduction tests into a tree search procedure solving problems involving up to 500 potential warehouse locations and 1,000 customers is possible.

Subgradient optimization is a popular method of finding a good set of multipliers for use in Lagrangian relaxation. Baker and Sheasby (1999) developed a model for obtaining faster convergence. The method was developed within a study of the generalised assignment problem (GAP) and its application to vehicle routing. The method was applied to benchmark capacitated warehouse location problems (CWLPs).

Lee (1993) presented an algorithm for solving multi products capacitated warehouse location problem based on cross-decomposition, to reduce the computational difficulty by incorporating Benders decomposition and Lagrangian relaxation. The algorithm solves problems of practical sizes in acceptable times.

Sweeny and Tatham (1976) presented a mixed integer programming formulation for the single period warehouse location model with a dynamic programming procedure for finding the optimal sequence of configurations over multiple periods.

Kelly and Marucheck (1984) proposed an algorithm for dynamic WLP. First, the model is simplified and then a partial optimal solution is obtained through iterative examinations by both upper and lower bounds on savings realized if a site is opened in a given time period. A complete optimal solution is obtained by solving the reduced model with Benders' decomposition procedure. The optimal solution is then tested to determine which time periods contain tentative decisions that may be affected by post-horizon data. The relationship between the lower (or upper) bounds utilized in the model simplification time period is analyzed.

Dupont (2008) presented a branch and bound algorithm for a facility location problem with concave site dependent costs.

Sharma et al. (2007) presented new formulations and relaxations for single stage capacitated warehouse location problem. In this paper different formulations and relaxations were compared with each other.

13.3.2 Heuristic and Metaheuristic Methods

Because of the nature of many warehouse location problems, the exact methods can not be used to solve them, so heuristic & Meta heuristic methods can be used.

Genetic algorithms have been shown to be very successful on the UWLP. In a series of papers spanning over several, Kratica et al. (2001) have shown that genetic algorithms find optimal solutions on the OR Library and the M* instances (whenever the optimal solutions are known) with high frequencies and very good efficiency. Their final algorithm uses clever implementation techniques such as caching and bit vectors to avoid recomputing the objective function which is quite costly on large-scale problems. Also, the speed-up of the genetic algorithm over mathematical programming approaches increases exponentially with problem size on the M^* instances.

Various heuristic search algorithms have also been proposed but have been less successful. Alves and Almedia (1992) presented simulated annealing algorithms which produce high-quality solutions but are quite expensive in computation times (Michel and Hentenryck 2004).

Al-Sultan and Al-Fawzan (1999) presented a tabu-search algorithm. The algorithm generates $5n$ neighbors at each iteration and moves to the best neighbor which is not tabu and improves the current value of the objective function. Each of these iterations takes significant computing time, which limits the applicability of the algorithm. Michel and Hentenryck (2004) presented another tabu search algorithm. The algorithm uses a linear neighborhood and essentially takes $O(m \log n)$ time per iteration. It finds optimal solutions on the OR Library and the M^* instances (whenever the optimal solution is known) with high frequencies. It also outperforms the state of the-art genetic algorithm of Kratica et al. (2001), both in efficiency and robustness.

Kuehn and Hamburger (1963) and Whitaker (1985) presented Greedy- Bump and Shift (Interchange) heuristics algorithms. In the Greedy process, warehouses are located at the most economical positions, one at a time, until no additional warehouses can be added without increasing the total cost. In the Bump process, those warehouses that became uneconomical as a result of the placement of subsequent warehouses are eliminated. In the Shift process, a warehouse is shifted to another potential location in the same territory if the relocation causes a reduction of the total cost.

Heras and Larrosa (2006) analyzed the effect of heuristic orders at three levels of increasing overhead: (a) compute the order prior to search and keep it fixed during the whole solving process (this is called a static order), (b) compute the order at every search node using current sub problem information (this is called a dynamic order) and iii) compute a sequence of different orders at every search node and sequentially enforce the local consistency for each one (this is called dynamic reordering).They performed experiments in three different problems: Max-SAT, Max-CSP and warehouse location problems. They did not find an alternative better than the rest for all the instances.

Lee (1996) proposed an optimal solution algorithm based on the cross decomposition method for multi type capacitated distribution center location problem. The cross decomposition method can be applied to solve this problem because both the primal and dual sub problems are relatively easy to solve and both sub problems quickly converge. Tight lower and upper bounds can be obtained in just a few iterations of the proposed algorithm. This algorithm can be used as a heuristic which produces not just a feasible solution but also a confidence interval to measure the quality of the solution. The algorithm was implemented in FORTRAN.

13.4 Case Study

In this section, we describe some applications of the warehouse location problem in real world.

13.4.1 Redesigning a Warehouse Network (Melachrinoudis and Min 2007)

The model which was described in the last section is a case study of a firm which plans to redesign its warehouse network and reduce its total logistics costs. Beta has its main manufacturing plant in Terre Haute, Indiana, and currently operates 21 warehouses to serve a total of 281 customers scattered around the United States and Canada. The warehouse consolidation problem (WCP) facing Beta differs from the classical warehouse location problem in that the former is primarily concerned with determining which existing warehouses to keep open, which new warehouses to establish, and which warehouses to phase-out among the existing locations, whereas the latter is primarily concerned with selecting the optimal site among the alternatives of new locations. In this problem, 25 warehouse locations, including 4 candidate sites were existed. The target problem was solved and analyzed by LINGO optimization software.

Out of the 281 customers, only four have non-unique warehouse assignments and each one of those four customers receives partial demand allocations from exactly two warehouses.

13.4.2 Warehouse Location Problems for Air Freight Forwarders (Wan et al. 1998)

The move of Hong Kong International Airport from the city centre to a suburban area in July 1998 provided sufficient capacity to meet the increasing demand of passenger and air-cargo flows in Hong Kong in the foreseeable future. However, the move has had adverse side effects such as causing the readjustment of many existing systems and creating many imminent strategic problems. One of such problems is the warehouse location of freight forwarders: They have to decide whether they should locate their warehouses in the new airport, in current locations, or in new locations somewhere in the city.

In this case, air freight forwarders had then been facing the decision on whether they should (1) move their warehouses to the new airport, (2) stay in the current locations, (3) move the warehouses to new locations in the city, (4) keep the current warehouses and add an additional one in Chek Lap Kok (CLK), and (5) move the current warehouses to new locations in city and add one in CLK.

With the special structure of a toll bridge for the (CLK) airport, this problem is in exactly the same form as the one-median location problem on a tree network by using a decomposition approach. The problem can be solved by the Chinese algorithm or its modified version, the majority algorithm.

References

Akinc U, Khumawala BM (1977) An efficient branch and bound algorithm for the capacitated warehouse location problem. Manage Sci 23(6):585–594

Alves ML, Almedia MT (1992) Simulated annealing algorithm for simple plant location problems. Revista Investigacao Operationanl 12

Al-Sultan KS, Al-Fawzan MA (1999) A tabu search approach to the uncapacitated facility location problem Ann Oper Res 86:91–103

Baker BM (1986) A partial dual algorithm for the capacitated warehouse location problem. Eur J Oper Res 23:48–56

Baker BM, Sheasby J (1999) Accelerating the convergence of subgradient optimization. Eur J Oper Res 117:136–144

Beasley JE (1988) An algorithm for solving large capacitated warehouse location problems. Eur J Oper Res 33:314–323

Christofides N, Beasley JE (1983) Extensions to a Lagrangian relaxation approach for the capacitated warehouse location problem. Eur J Oper Res 12:19–28

Dupont L (2008) Branch and bound algorithm for a facility location problem with concave site dependent costs. International Journal of Production Economics 112(1):245–254

Erlenkotter D (1978) A dual-based procedure for uncapacitated facility location. Eur J Oper Res 26(6):992–1009

Geoffrion AM, Graves GV (1974) Multicommodity distribution system design by benders decomposition. Manage Sci 20(5):882–844

Geoffrion AM, Nauss R (1977) Parametric and postoptimality analysis in integer linear programming. Manage Sci 23(5):453–466

Heras F, Larrosa J (2006) Intelligent variable orderings and re-orderingsin DAC-based solvers for WCSP. J Heuristics 12:287–306

Kelly DL, Maruchek AS (1984) Planning horizon results for the dynamic warehouse location problem. J Oper Manage 4(3):279–294

Khumawala BM (1972) An efficient branch and bound algorithm for the warehouse location problem. Manage Sci 18(12):585–594

Korkel M (1989) On the exact solution of large-scale simple plant location problems. Eur J Oper Res 39:157–173

Kratica J, Tosic D, Filipovic V, Ljubic I (2001) Solving the simple plant location problem by genetic algorithm. Oper Res 35:127–142

Kuehn A, Hamburger MJ (1963) A heuristic program for locating warehouses. Manage Sci 9:643–666

Lee CY (1993) The multi product warehouse location problem: Applying a decomposition algorithm. Int J Phys Distrib Logist Manage 23(6):3–13

Lee CY (1996) An algorithm for a two-staged distribution system with various types of distribution centers. INFOR 34(2):105–117

Melachrinoudis E, Min H (2007) Redesigning a warehouse network. Eur J Oper Res 176:210–229

Michel L, Hentenryck PV (2004) A simple tabu search for warehouse location. Eur J Oper Res 157:576–591

Nagy T (2004), Warehouse location problem. Available online at http://www.freehackers.org

Nuass RM (1978) An improved algorithm for the capacitated facility location problem. J Oper Res Soc 29(12):1195–1201

Sharma RRK, Berry V (2007) Developing new formulations and relaxations of single stage capacitated warehouse location problem (SSCWLP): Empirical investigation for assessing; relative strengths and computational effort. Eur J Oper Res 177:803–812

Sweeny DJ, Tatham RL (1976) An improved long-run model for multiple warehouse location. Manage Sci 7:748–758

Tompkins JA, White JA, Bozer YA, Frazelle EH, Tanchoco JMA, Trevino J (1996) Facility planning, 2nd ed. Wiley, New York

Wan YW, Raymond K, Cheung, Liu J, Judy H, Tong (1998) Warehouse location problems for air freight forwarders: A challenge created by the airport relocation. J Air Transport Manage 4:201–207

Whitaker RA (1985) Some add-drop and drop-add interchange heuristics for non-linear warehouse location. J Oper Res Soc 36:61–70

William J, Baumol, Wolfe P (1958) A warehouse-location problem. Oper Res 6:252–263

Chapter 14
Obnoxious Facility Location

Sara Hosseini and Ameneh Moharerhaye Esfahani

In general, facilities are divided in two groups, the first one are desirable to the nearby inhabitants which try to have them as close as possible such as hospitals, fire stations, shopping stores and educational centers. The second group turns out to be undesirable for the surrounding population, which avoids them and tries to stay away from them such as garbage dump sites, chemical plants, nuclear reactors, military installations, prisons and polluting plants. In this sense, Daskin (1995) discussed that Erkut and Neuman in 1989 distinguished between *Noxious* (hazardous to health) and *Obnoxious* (nuisance to lifestyle) facilities, although both can be simply regarded as Undesirable. Moreover, in the last decade, a new nomenclature has been developed to define these oppositions: *NIMBY* (not in my back yard), *NIMNBY* (not in my neighbor's back yard), and *NIABY* (not in anyone's back yard).

We survey two types here:

- *Dispersion problems*: in which there are only facilities to be located in such a way as to affect each other the least possible. Usually, Cases such as sales representative of some organizations are addressed in this type. The mother organization intends to minimize the comparison among its sales representative and cover more areas via maximizing distance between them. Note that in some cases, investors interestedly try to minimize the distance between their sales representative, for instance you can imagine two restaurants with same ownership, although they are placed in one area for making more customers, not only they don't lose their customers, but also make more profits.

- *Undesirable facilities problems*: Because of sanitation, security or people's welfare, some facilities are not desirable and we try to far them away from demand centers. Despite these undesirable facilities being necessary, in general, to the community, for instance garbage dump sites, the location of such facilities might cause a certain disagreement in the population. High opening cost of these facilities beside high total transport cost of undesirable materials make decision makers to solve a bi-objective problem (to minimize transport cost and to maximize distance from demand centers). Furthermore, to maintain security and because of transportation of hazardous materials generated at these centers, transport routing should be pointed out. About 5% of GNP of more developing countries is consumed to campaign with growth of air pollution, noises, accidents

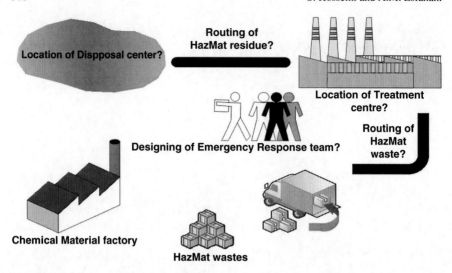

Fig. 14.1 The example of Obnoxious problem

and traffic problems. Nevertheless, the advantages of a convenient transportation system are much more than these costs, so, existence of such system appears essential. An example of obnoxious problem is shown in Fig. 14.1.

14.1 Applications and Classifications

14.1.1 Applications

Some Applications of these problems can be as follows:

- Locating chemical plants
- Locating nuclear reactor plants
- Locating pollution plants
- Locating garbage dump sites
- Routing and location – routing of these applications are considered in recent years.

14.1.2 Revolution of Undesirable Facility Problem

Obnoxious facilities location problem was first introduced at 1975 by Goldman and Dearing (cited in (Rakas et al. 2004) and first solution was presented at 1978 by Church and Garfinkel in $O(mn\log n)$ time. McGinnis and White (1978) first introduced a bicriteria problem, using the minisum–minimax criteria. Drezner and Wesolowsky (1983) first introduced the rectilinear maximin problem for locating an obnoxious facility. Ting devised a linear time algorithm for the 1-maxisum problem on tree networks at 1984. Mehrez et al. (1986) suggested an improvement of previous algorithm, based on bounds, which reduced the size of model. Batta and Chiu (1988) present a hazardous material transportation model on a network in which sum of distances of container within a threshold limit from demand centers, is minimized. Ratick and White (1988) develop a multiobjective model, minimizing costs and people's repulsion simultaneously. In this case Wayman and Kuby (1994) present a model with three objectives: Minimization of risk and cost and maximization of equity. Gopalan et al. (1990) model the equity of the HazMat transport risk and present a heuristic solution. At 1995, Melachrinoudis and Smith extended an algorithm with "m" edges and "n" nodes as obnoxious facilities, assuming Euclidean spatial distances. But that was not the end of researches and different types of these problems with various assumptions were reviewed at those years. Marianov and ReVelle (1998) model a linear vehicle routing problem, minimizing cost and risk simultaneously. Erkut and Verter (1998) model transport risk completely and review various methods. Rogers (1998) propose a model to minimize the global repulsion of the inhabitants of the region. Results show that insecurity of region is the most important reason for negative reaction of people. Giannikos (1998) use the goal-programming technique for obnoxious facility location-routing problem. In 1999, Melachrinoudis developed a bicriteria location model for locating a new semi-obnoxious[1] facility in an existing layout which is solved by an adaptation of the *Fourier–Motzkin* elimination method. Zagrafos and samara presented a methodological framework for developing a *decision support system* (DSS) for hazardous materials emergency response operations (Erkut and Alp 2007). Cases such as Routing emergency response teams and evacuation of region from people and cars were considered in this paper. Fernandez et al. (2000) address a continuous location within a given geographical region of an undesirable facility considering environmental aspects. Akgün et al. (2000) review cases which decision maker seeks for various transport routes. Zhang et al. (2000) devise a routing hazardous materials algorithm, using GIS^2 technique and a Gaussian Plume model for their dispersion model. One of its applications is to transport urban hazardous wastes. Katz et al. (2002) propose a maximin model for multi-facility location. Here the distance between each facility and demand centers should be considered beside distances among facilities.

Cappanera et al. (2004) addressed the problem of simultaneously locating obnoxious facilities and routing obnoxious materials between a set of built-up areas and the facilities. Rakas et al. (2004) propose a multiobjective model with fuzzy data for the location of undesirable facilities. Castillo (2004) reviewed the issues related to hazmat transportation risks and discussed the modeling tool available for

---

[1] These facilities service to demand points; nevertheless, they are undesirable for them.
[2] Geographic information system

routing problem of hazardous materials. Also, a route optimization model is developed as a decision support tool. Rodriguez et al. (2006) considered Euclidean travel distances for obnoxious facilities location problem. Colebrook et al. (2005) have developed a new bound and a new $O(mn)$ algorithm to solve the network maxian problem. Erkut and Ingolfsson (2005) formulated the *tree* design problem as an integer programming problem aiming at trade off between cost and risk. Díaz-Báñez et al. (2005) computed shortest paths for transportation of hazardous material in continuous spaces. They proposed an approximate algorithm based on the bisection method and reduced the optimization problem to a decision problem, where one needs to compute the shortest path such that the minimum distance to the demand points is not smaller than a certain amount r. Pisinger (2006) present an exact algorithm for finding a number of fast upper bounds for P-dispersion problems in which these bounds can be derived in $O(n)$ time. Bell (2006) considered mixed rout strategies for the risk-averse shipment of hazardous materials. He believes, for repeated shipments on the arc with unknown incident probabilities, the safest strategy is to use a mix of routes.

Berman et al. (2007) extended an optimum model for designing emergency response networks for hazardous materials transportation that would be applicable for large-scale problems.

Alumur and Kara (2007) develop a comprehensive multi objective model for the hazardous waste location-routing problem that covers various problems of this field. For exact solving in a case study, GIS technique and CPLEX software were used. Akgün et al. (2007) consider effects of weather systems on HazMat transportation. They introduced weather system effects as circle areas with different probabilities on accident rate, speed, delays and others. They use time dependent shortest path problem in form of an exact model and four heuristic models. They concluded in such weather systems accident rates can be double. Carotenuto et al. (2007) model a hazmat shipment routing and scheduling problem. They develop a tabu search algorithm to assign a minimum and equitable risk route to each hazmat shipment and schedule these shipments on the assigned routes.

14.1.3 Classification of Undesirable Facility Problems

- Area solution: *Discrete, Continual*
- Number of Objective function: *Multiobjective, Single objective*
- Category: *Location, Routing, Location-Routing*
- Determine the number of nodes: *Exogenous, Endogenous*
- Facility capacity: *Unlimited, Limited*
- Technology assignment: non-assignment, assignment
- Number of type of hazardous waste: one type, more than one type

14.2 Models

14.2.1 Dispersion Problem (Daskin 1995)

In this problem, suppose that there are some candidate centers for installation facilities. The purpose is to find P points for locating in order that maximize the minimum distance between located facilities. In other word, the decision maker knows the number of locatable facilities and candidate centers then, he tries to select set of points that maximize the minimum distance between them.

14.2.1.1 Model Assumptions

- The problem is investigated on the discrete network and nodes are representative of candidate points.
- This network is general or it's possible to have loops.
- The facilities often are general. In other word, investor (government) focuses on keeping away facilities from population centers. In these cases, environmental costs and some other ones are more important than installation costs.
- The numbers of facilities are predetermined.
- All of facilities are obnoxious and should be kept away from population centers.
- All of facilities are similar and all of services are equal too.
- The installation cost is not considered.
- The facilities replacement is not considered.
- All of parameters are deterministic.
- The problem is formulated in static form. It means that, the problem's inputs are not dependent to time.

14.2.1.2 Model Inputs

d_{ij}: it is distance between i and j
M: it is large elected digit and it is often larger than the maximum distance between candidate points
P: the number of facility to locate
D: the minimum distance between facilities

14.2.1.3 Model Outputs (Decision variables)

X_j: 1 if facility is installed in node j; 0 otherwise

14.2.1.4 Objective Function and its Constraints

$$\text{Max } D \tag{14.1}$$

Subject to

$$\sum_j X_j = P \tag{14.2}$$

$$D \leq d_{ij} + (M - d_{ij}).(1 - X_i) + (M - d_{ij}).(1 - X_j) \quad \forall j; \forall i \prec j. \tag{14.3}$$

$$X_j \in \{0, 1\} \quad \forall j \tag{14.4}$$

Equation (14.1) maximizes the minimum distance between facilities. Equation (14.2) represents that number of located facilities, should be P.

Equation (14.2) determines the minimum distance along distance between each pair of facilities and finally the third constraint shows that X_j is 0, 1 variable.

To achieve better perception of (14.2), consider the following explanations:

- If $X_i = X_j = 1$ (install facility in node i, j), so $D \leq d_{ij}$ and it means that the minimum distance between each pair of facilities can't be more than from distance between facilities, certainly it is obvious.
- If $Xi = 0$, $X_j = 1$ or $X_i = 1$, $X_j = 0$ means that, only one facility is located in node i, j.
- So, (14.2) will be $D \leq M$. It's clear because M is more than all of couple distances.
- Now, consider the case that $X_i = 0, X_j = 0$. In this case, (14.2) will be $M \geq Max_{i,j} \{d_{ij}\}$ and, it's reasonable too.

Researchers didn't focus much on relationship between dispersion models and other models. As one example in this case, we can refer to Kuby (1987). He has illustrated the relationship between P-Dispersion and $(P-1)$ Center.

14.2.2 Undesirable Facility Location Problem (Daskin 1995)

Locating some facilities such as fire stations and shopping centers, are considered in recent decades. For example in locating a shopping center, we know that it should be near and available to population centers. But it's so important that, we consider in locating factors such as decreasing noise, heavy traffic in that center, related crimes and people's tranquility of mind. These factors make problem more complex. The investigated model in this section is P-Median transformed model and for the reason that facilities are undesirable, the objective function is maximization. In Median problems because of desirability of facilities such as hospitals and fire stations, the

14 Obnoxious Facility Location

objective function is minimization. But in Maxisum models, the subject is locating facilities such as incinerators that, decision maker attend to far it from demand centers. Of course, it is obvious that we can't eliminate transportation cost.

14.2.2.1 Model Inputs

P: the number of facilities should be located

14.2.2.2 Model Outputs (Decision Variables)

h_i: demand of node i
Distance between demand nodes i and candidate place j d_{ij}:
X_j: 1 if facility is located at node j; 0 otherwise
Y_{ij}: 1 if demand of node i was provided by located facility at node j; 0 otherwise

14.2.2.3 Objective Function and its Constraints

$$\text{Max} \sum_i \sum_j h_i d_{ij} y_{ij}, \tag{14.5}$$

$$\sum_j Y_{ij_{ij}} = 1 \quad \forall i, \tag{14.6}$$

$$\sum_j X_{j_{ij}} = P, \tag{14.7}$$

$$Y_{ij} \leq X_j \quad \forall i, j, \tag{14.8}$$

$$X_j = 0, 1 \quad \forall j, \tag{14.9}$$

$$Y_{ij} = 0, 1 \quad \forall i, j. \tag{14.10}$$

Equation (14.5) minimizes the weighted sum of demands and distances.
The (14.6) represent that demands of all nodes should responded by just one facility. The (14.7) considers the number of all facilities equal P. Equation (14.8) ensures that if any facility is located at node j, demand of this node should responded by itself. Equations (14.9) and (14.10) are integer limitations.
Example 14.1 was illustrated that the above model in reality doesn't express nature of mentioned problem.

14.2.2.4 Example 14.1

A,B,C,D are demand centers, digits in boxes are demand amount of each place and on the line numbers represent distance between places that are connected with line

Fig. 14.2 Example 14.1

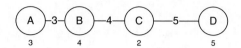

Table 14.1 Nearest facility to each center

Demand of node i	m = 1	M = 2	m = 3	m = 4
A	A	B	C	D
B	B	A	C	D
C	C	B	D	A
D	D	C	B	A

together (Fig. 14.2). After solving the problem with above way, the followed yield was resulted:

$$X_A = X_D = 1$$
$$X_B = X_C = 0$$
$$Y_{AD} = Y_{BD} = Y_{CA} = Y_{DA} = 1.$$

Objective function value is 146 that seem so appropriate. In this example, demand of center A was responded by center D. Of course, it is not reasonable that demand of center A was responded by center D when there is a facility at node A. but the above model results center A was responded by center D. This solution obviously has bad effect on C, D nodes.

Therefore, the model should have some corrections or reformations to meet reality. After adding some constraints into the previous model, the *corrected model* will be as followed:

$$-X_{[m]_i} + \sum_{k=1}^{m} Y_{i[k]_i} \geq 0 \quad \forall i; m = 1, 2, \ldots, N - 1. \quad (14.11)$$

$[m]i$ represents the *mth* candidate place from demand node i (see Table 14.1). To illustrate complete formulation of model, additional constraint was explained below:

$$X_B \leq Y_{BB}, \quad (14.12)$$
$$X_A \leq Y_{BB} + Y_{BA}, \quad (14.13)$$
$$X_C \leq Y_{BB} + Y_{BA} + Y_{BC}, \quad (14.14)$$
$$X_D \leq Y_{BB} + Y_{BA} + Y_{BC} + Y_{BD}. \quad (14.15)$$

Equation (14.12) ensures that, if a facility is located at node B, demand of node B was provided by node B.

Equation (14.13) says if a facility is located at node A, demand of node B can be provided by node A or B. Of course, if a facility is located at node B, demand of

Table 14.2 Compared Maxisum and median models

P	Model MaxiSum		Model median	
	Center	Objective function value	Center	Objective function value
1	A	86	B	62
2	A,B	53	B,D	17
3	A,B,C	25	A,B,D	8
4	A,B,C,D	0	A,B,C,D	0

node B was provided by node B and (14.13) will be satisfied. Other constraints are justified with this way.

The complete formulation of Example 14.1 and final results were brought. Incidentally, comparison between Median and Maxisum models was brought in Table 14.2.

$$Max \quad 9Y_{AB} + 21Y_{AC} + 36Y_{AD} + 12Y_{BA} + 16Y_{BC} + 36Y_{BD} + 14Y_{CA}$$
$$+ 8Y_{CB} + 10Y_{CD} + 60Y_{DA} + 45Y_{DB} + 25Y_{DC}.$$

Subject to

$$X_A + X_B + X_C + X_D = P$$
$$Y_{AA} + Y_{AB} + Y_{AC} + Y_{AD} = 1 \quad Y_{CA} + Y_{CB} + Y_{CC} + Y_{CD} = 1$$
$$Y_{BA} + Y_{BB} + Y_{BC} + Y_{BD} = 1 \quad Y_{DA} + Y_{DB} + Y_{DC} + Y_{DD} = 1$$

$$\begin{bmatrix} Y_{AA} \leq X_A & Y_{BA} \leq X_A & Y_{CA} \leq X_A & Y_{DA} \leq X_A \\ Y_{AB} \leq X_B & Y_{BB} \leq X_B & Y_{CB} \leq X_B & Y_{DB} \leq X_B \\ Y_{AC} \leq X_C & Y_{BC} \leq X_C & Y_{CC} \leq X_C & Y_{DC} \leq X_C \\ Y_{AD} \leq X_D & Y_{BD} \leq X_D & Y_{CD} \leq X_D & Y_{DD} \leq X_D \end{bmatrix}$$

$$\begin{bmatrix} -X_A + Y_{AA} \geq 0 \\ -X_B + Y_{AA} + Y_{AB} \geq 0 \\ -X_C + Y_{AA} + Y_{AB} + Y_{AC} \geq 0 \end{bmatrix} ; \begin{bmatrix} -X_B + Y_{BB} \geq 0 \\ -X_A + Y_{BB} + Y_{BA} \geq 0 \\ -X_C + Y_{BB} + Y_{BA} + Y_{BC} \geq 0 \end{bmatrix} ;$$

$$\begin{bmatrix} -X_C + Y_{CC} \geq 0 \\ -X_B + Y_{CC} + Y_{CB} \geq 0 \\ -X_D + Y_{CC} + Y_{CB} + Y_{CD} \geq 0 \end{bmatrix} ; \begin{bmatrix} -X_D + Y_{DD} \geq 0 \\ -X_C + Y_{DD} + Y_{DC} \geq 0 \\ -X_B + Y_{DD} + Y_{DC} + Y_{DB} \geq 0 \end{bmatrix}$$

$$X_A, X_B, X_C, X_D = 0, 1$$
$$\text{All } Y_{ij} \geq 0$$

14.2.3 Hazardous Materials Routing Problem

Hazardous materials that are briefly called *HazMats*, consist of explosives, flammable substances, oxidizing substances, poisonous substances, radioactive materials, infected materials, corrosives and hazardous wastes (Erkut and Verter 1995). Basically these materials are used in many facilities and processes in the industry such as petroleum refineries, chemical plants and nuclear reactors or hospital's wastes. Due to the nature of hazmats, many risks related to production, storage and transportation of these materials could arise. In the case of transporting hazmats, the selection of routes considering economic and risk issues is a very important problem and needs to an integrated transport and risk management. Therefore, the term "optimal routes" means the route that best fulfils the objectives by the stakeholders associated with transporting and distributing of HazMats within the study area.

It's not possible to completely avoid risks, nevertheless risk management activities such as mitigation and prevention would be useful. These activities are reviewed as two groups: proactives and reactives. Some cases such as driver training, restriction of driving hours and container specifications are considered in proactives and some cases such as firefighting, emergency response and evacuation of region from inhabitants and cars are of reactives.

To understand its importance, we mention some examples of transporting HazMats:

- Every year, approximately, 4 billions shipments of these materials are transported, in other word, 20% of traveling trucks (one in every five) in USA carry HazMats.
- The difference between the transportation of HazMats and any other ones is, in this case any accident may cause serious damages for people, animals and plants.
- In 1976, as the explosion of a small chemical plant in small city of Seveso and released Dioxin, 190 persons damaged seriously and thousands of birds were killed.
- Afghanistan, 1982, the explosion of a truck, carrying gasoline, in a tunnel killed 2,700 persons.
- India, 1984, the Methil-Iso-Cianate leakage in Bhopal area, killed 400 persons.

Annually, about 2.5 million tons of garbage are generated in Tehran that management cost of these huge volumes is 600 billion rials. It is evident that applying a quick and efficient transportation system is one of the most important ways for reduction of such costs. From other hand, management of hospital-garbage is one of the most important problems that exist in our country.

Basically, routing of HazMats is done by governments, also because of high sensitivity of society toward these accidents, fixed costs of opening facilities are not be considered in most of these models, in contrast, risk and equity assessment methods are always be considered. Routing of HazMat is as important as locating them, because these two issues are relevant to each other strictly. In recent decades, researchers had more studies in this matter.

One of the recent research studies was published by Akgün et al. (2007) investigated HazMat routing problem with weather systems considerations. Weather system effects on accident probability, speed, time duration, risk and cost related to HazMat transportations. For example it can lead to change routs, reduce speed, delaying shipment, increase parking times and other issues. Due to the dynamic nature of weather system and hence the time varying nature of the weights on links in the transportation network, *time-dependent shortest paths problems (TDSPP)* should be considered. TDSPP was first introduced by Cook and Halsey with using finite departure times from every node to the destination. TDSPP approach was developed continuously after that. For example, Ziliakopoulos and Mahmassani introduced an algorithm that calculates the TDSP's from all nodes to the destination for every time step over a given time horizon. Cia et al., Erkut and Alp and Nozik researches were focused on TDSPP. Akgün et al. (2007) focused on the effect of weather systems on hazmat routing. They characterized the time dependent attributes of a link due to movement of the weather system. They aimed to find a least risk path for hazmat transportation under variable weather system. They applied one exact model for routing, Time-dependent shortest Path problem, and four heuristic model such as k-shortest path heuristic (*KPATH*), dissimilar path heuristic (*DISSIM*), Iterative weather system heuristic (*IWS*) and finally Myopic shortest path heuristic (*MYOPIC*). They compared exact model with heuristics and heuristics with each others too. They consider a circle area for weather system that can move by time and weights that in some methods were constant and in some others were inconstant.

14.2.3.1 Risk Evaluation for Hazardous Waste Transportation

Risk management activities could result in an accurate assessment of the risks and therefore it would be possible to create strategies for reduction of risk level to its lowest level. We have expanded models with different conditions in subject of risk evaluation. Erkut and Verter (1998) suggested much evaluation risk models. The simplest model in this category yields the product of the accident consequences, the probability of a hazardous waste accident, activity volume.

$$\text{Risk} = \text{accident consequences probability of a hazardous waste} \times \text{accident activity volume}.$$

Generally, the accident consequences are measured by population exposure and the accident probability depends on material type and rout nature. In practice, the rout is divided to equal segments (k/m or mile) then; the consequences probability is calculated for all segments by population exposure in accident place.

In this equation assumed that, if an accident happens at center A, people are influenced in circle with radius of R. The assumed radius is considered 0–7 km and the consequences accident is measured through the Worst-case. It means that without considering geographical, climate and topography conditions, all exposure people in assumed circle will perish. Other developed way for calculating the consequences accident, presented by Raj and Glikman who discussed about effects of wind and air instability in the consequences accident in 1991 (see Fig. 14.3). It made the model so complex, but so similar to reality.

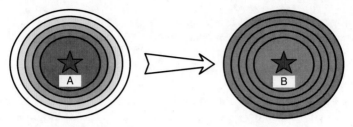

Fig. 14.3 Accident worst-case

The accident probability of hazardous materials usually ranges from 0.1 to 0.8 in each million mile. Of course it depends on the nature of rout, culture problems, transportation time (day, night) and security cases. Undoubtedly, to estimate realistic probability we need accurate information. After recognizing accident probability and consequences for each segment (with assumption probability is equal in all segments of rout and, stopping the travel if any accident happened) the formulation of rout risk will be:

$$PR = PC + (1-P)\,PC + (1-P)^2\,PC + \ldots + (1-P)^{n-1}\,PC. \qquad (14.16)$$

P is accident probability and C is accident consequences. According to past paragraph, the accident probability is nearly 1 million in each mile, therefore we can eliminate terms with P_n for $n > 1$ and simplify the above formulation:

$$PR = \sum_{J=1}^{n-1} (P_j C_j). \qquad (14.17)$$

Erkut and Verter (1998) confirmed that effect of the assumption "negligibility the product of more than two probabilities" is insignificant especially for long routs.

ReVelle et al. (1991) believed that in transportation of hazardous material, population was exposed in dangerous consequences. So, in the cases such as atomic waste transportation, the influenced population should be minimized.

Saccomanno and Chan (1985) pretended that in the reason of the accident consequences are so violent, the problem should be modeled through minimizing the accident probability. It means that, even one accident is not forgivable. Consequently, the accident probability should be nearly zero.

Some researchers claimed that people count an accident with low probability and high consequences more unreasonable than an accident with high probability and low consequences. So, in risk evaluation it is bettor to apply PC_q model for $q > 1$ because this model increases the value of accident consequence and results solution with less consequences. There was a difficulty even after Abkowitz's model and this was an assumption that the rout was exposed by accident, was usable after accident happened. But it is clear, after accruing accident the rout should be

Table 14.3 Different types of risk evaluation models (Erkut and Ingolfsson 2005)

Model	Formulation
Traditional risk	$\text{TR}(P) = \sum_{i \in p} P_i C_i$
Population exposure	$\text{PE}(P) = \sum_{i \in p} T_i$
Incident probability	$\text{IP}(P) = \sum_{i \in p} P_i$
Perceived risk	$\text{PR}(P) = \sum_{i \in p} P_i C_i$
Conditional risk	$\text{CR}(P) = \frac{\sum_{i \in P} P_i C_i}{\sum_{i \in P} P_i}$
Mean-variance	$\text{MV}(P) = \sum_{i \in P} (P_i C_i + k P_i C_i^2)$
Disutility	$\text{DU}(P) = \sum_{i \in P} P_i (\exp(k C_i) - 1)$
Minimax	$\text{CR}(P) = \max_{i \in P} C_i$

obstructed temporarily or permanent and occasionally the optimum rout should be designed again. The rout obstruction cost and also redesigning new rout are such subjects that lead to brilliancy for importance of correct routing for hazardous material transportation.

Sivakumar et al. (1993, 1995) expanded the conditional risk model that, the consequences minimized in first accident. The final discussion in modeling of hazardous material transportation risk is looping proposition. It was discussed in Erkut and Verter (1998).

Table 14.3 reviewed modeling method for hazardous material transportation risk.

14.2.3.2 Risk Equality

Certainly in spite of all discussed conditions, we can not find a rout or place without any risk or any effect on the environment. Consequently, the decision maker should divide the risk among segments and reach to minimum variance. This subject is named "*risk equality*" in hazardous waste literature and can formulate in different ways. The general type of it was followed here:

$$\text{Risk Equity} = \sum_{y} a\, y(N - y) P(y); a < 0. \tag{14.18}$$

In (14.18), N represents population of a center, y determines the number of accident casualties and constant $\underline{a}$ is less than *zero*. It is simply provable that, minimum equality will be obtained, when the number of accident casualties is half of population. With moving away from each side, the equality increases and in ultimate it reaches to zero value and it is best state. For example in an accident when doesn't take place any casualties or maybe when all population of center perishes, the maximum equality is obtained. The fuzzy risk equality modeling seems remarkable direction for future researches.

14.2.3.3 Designing Optimum Routes for Material Transportation

Nowadays with improvement in technology, the hazardous transportation problem is as significant for governments as they establish inflexible regulations for it. These regulations include prohibiting hazardous material transportation in centers, different times, and beneficiaries' commitment for at most transportation safety. Simultaneously the governments design optimum routs and monitor material transportation.

- We can classify the problems in designing optimum transportation routs that increases problem. It seems that the best possible solution may be the transportation at farther distances from the demand centers; however, its extra costs are imposed to consumers. In the other word, the transport organizations try to reduce the transport costs, however, the governments emphasize to the reduction of transport risks.
- On the other hand, the governments tend to design routs with lowest risk, but they can't force transport organizations to drive in these routs, furthermore, designing a unique path for HazMat transport is not applicable.
- Even if that would be possible to design optimum routs for each OD (origin-destination) pair, there's not any assurance for optimization of set of these routs.
- Solving a real problem requires so many nodes and edges which is not simply obtainable with present solution techniques.

Erkut and Alp (2007) proposed using an optimum tree network for simplifying of solution. In the better word; it's not permitted to pass through any replaced path. Their considered network is similar to the *"optimum communication spanning tree network" (OCST)*, where the objective is to minimize the weighted sum of the length of the paths between each pair of nodes on a tree.

Let N be the set of nodes on a city road network and E be the set of undirected edges (i, j) that connect these nodes. Let $i < j$ for the edges in set E. let C be the set of pairs of nodes (u, v) such that $u < v$, where there exists a positive shipment between nodes u (origin) and v (destination). Moreover, let take:

14.2.3.4 Model Inputs

N: number of nodes in N
A: $\{(i, j), (j, i) : (i, j) \in E\}$
S_{uv}: number of shipments between nodes u and v where $(u, v) \in C$
r_{ij}: risk per shipment on arc $(i, j) \in A$
l_{ij}: length of arc $(i, j) \in A$

14.2.3.5 Model Outputs (Decision variables)

$$X_j = \begin{cases} 1 & \text{if a facility is located at } j, \\ 0 & \text{otherwise.} \end{cases}$$

$$Z_{ij}^{uv} = \begin{cases} 1 & \text{if region i uses facility } j, \\ 0 & \text{otherwise} \end{cases}.$$

14.2.3.6 Objective Function and its Constraints

Bi − Level :
$$\underset{X_{ij} \in \{0,1\}}{\text{Min}} \sum_{(i,j) \in A} \sum_{(u,v) \in C} s_{uv} r_{ij} Z_{ij}^{uv}, \qquad (14.19)$$

$$\sum_{(i,k) \in A} z_{ik}^{uv} - \sum_{(k,i) \in A} Z_{ki}^{uv} = \begin{cases} +1 & i = u \\ -1 & i = v \\ 0 & o.w. \end{cases} \forall i \in N, (u,v) \in C, \quad (14.20)$$

$$Z_{ij}^{uv} \leq X_{ij} \quad \forall (i,j) \in A; (u,v) \in C, \qquad (14.21)$$
$$Z_{ij}^{uv} \in \{0,1\}. \qquad (14.22)$$

Here, we negligee from constraints discussion. The problem can be converted to a single level optimization problem by writing out the *KKT*[3] optimally conditions using additional variables and a large number R.

14.2.3.7 Objective Function and its Constraints

$$\underset{X_{ij} \in \{0,1\}}{\text{Min}} \sum_{(i,j) \in A} \sum_{(u,v) \in C} s_{uv} r_{ij} Z_{ij}^{uv}, \qquad (14.23)$$

$$\sum_{(i,k) \in A} z_{ik}^{uv} - \sum_{(k,i) \in A} Z_{ki}^{uv} = \begin{cases} +1 & i = u \\ -1 & i = v \\ 0 & o.w. \end{cases} \forall i \in N, (u,v) \in C, \quad (14.24)$$

$$Z_{ij}^{uv} \leq X_{ij} \quad \forall (i,j) \in A; (u,v) \in C, \qquad (14.25)$$
$$v_{ij}^{uv} \leq R(1 - Z_{ij}^{uv}) \quad \forall (i,j) \in A; (u,v) \in C, \qquad (14.26)$$
$$\lambda_{ij}^{uv} \leq R(1 - (X_{ij} - Z_{ij}^{uv})) \quad \forall (i,j) \in A; (u,v) \in C, \qquad (14.27)$$
$$v_{ij}^{uv} \geq 0 \quad \lambda_{ij}^{uv} \geq 0 \quad w_i^{uv} \ free \quad Z_{ij}^{uv} \in \{0,1\} \quad X_{ij} \in \{0,1\}. \qquad (14.28)$$

---
[3] Karush-Kuhn-Tucker optimality conditions

Solving this mixed integer programming problem with n nodes, k OD pairs, and m arcs contains $nk + 4mk$ constraints, $m(k + 1)$ binary variables, and $2k(m + n)$ non-negative continuous variables. For example, with 100 nodes, 30 OD pairs, and 200 arcs, the mathematical problem has 27,000 constraints, 6,200 binary variables, and 18,000 continuous variables. However the problem size may make it difficult to solve realistic versions of the problem. We now provide the formulation for OCST. This formulation is later extended to *minimum risk hazmat tree (MRHT)*.

14.2.3.8 Objective Function and its Constraints

$$\text{OCST:} \quad \text{Min} \sum_{(i,j) \in A} \sum_{(u,v) \in C} s_{uv} r_{ij} Z_{ij}^{uv}. \tag{14.29}$$

Subject to

$$\sum_{(i,j) \in A} Z_{ij}^{uv} - \sum_{(j,i) \in A} Z_{ji}^{uv} = \begin{cases} 1 & \forall i \in N, (u,v) \in C, i = u. \\ 0 & \forall i \in N, (u,v) \in C, i \neq u, v. \end{cases} \tag{14.30}$$

$$Z_{ij}^{uv} + Z_{ji}^{uv} \leq X_{ij} \quad \forall (i,j) \in E, (u,v) \in C, \tag{14.31}$$

$$\sum_{(i,j) \in E} X_{ij} = n - 1, \tag{14.32}$$

$$Z_{ij}^{uv} \in \{0,1\} \quad \forall i \in N, (u,v) \in C. \tag{14.33}$$

$$X_{ij} \in \{0,1\} \quad \forall (i,j) \in E. \tag{14.34}$$

Equation (14.30) provides the flow conservation constraints for each shipment. Equation (14.31) guarantees that if there is a shipment on an arc, and then it must be part of the hazmat tree. Equation (14.32) guarantees the construction of a tree network. Equations (14.33) and (14.34) declare the decision variables as binary.

The nodes are classified in two sets: *mandatory* and *non-mandatory* nodes. Origins and destinations are mandatory nodes, and the rest are non-mandatory. Let S and $T : S \cup T = N, S \cap T = \phi$ be the set of mandatory and non-mandatory nodes, respectively.

14.2.3.9 Objective Function and its Constraints

$$\text{MRHT : Min} \sum_{(i,j) \in A} \sum_{(u,v) \in C} s_{uv} r_{ij} Z_{ij}^{uv}. \tag{14.35}$$

Table 14.4 A comparison of the problem size of the bi-level model and MHRT as a function

	Constraints	Binary var.	Continuous var.
Bi-level	$nk + 4mk$	$m(k+1)$	$2k(m+n)$
MRHT	$nk + mk/2 + s$	$m(k+1)$	0

Subject to

$$\sum_{(i,j)\in A} z_{ij}^{uv} - \sum_{(j,i)\in A} z_{ji}^{uv} = \begin{cases} 1 & \forall i \in N, (u,v) \in C, i = u. \\ 0 & \forall i \in N, (u,v) \in C, i \neq u,v. \end{cases} \quad (14.36)$$

$$Z_{ij}^{uv} + Z_{ji}^{uv} \leq X_{ij} + X_{ji} \quad \forall (i,j) \in E, (u,v) \in C, \quad (14.37)$$

$$\sum_{j \in N} X_{ij} = 0 \quad for\ i = 1, \quad (14.38)$$

$$\sum_{j \in N} X_{ij} = 1 \quad for\ i \neq 1\ and\ i \in S, \quad (14.39)$$

$$\sum_{j \in N} X_{ij} \leq 1 \quad for\ i \in T, \quad (14.40)$$

$$Z_{ij}^{uv} \in \{0,1\} \quad \forall (i,j) \in A, (u,v) \in C, \quad (14.41)$$

$$X_{ij} \in \{0,1\} \quad \forall (i,j) \in A. \quad (14.42)$$

For a design problem with n nodes (of which s are mandatory), m arcs and k OD pairs, Table 14.4 compares the problem sizes for the bi-level model and MRHT as a function of problem parameters.

For example with 100 nodes (of which 20 arc mandatory), 30 OD pairs, and 200 arcs, MRHT will have 6,200 variables and 6,020 constraints.

14.2.4 Obnoxious Facilities Location-Routing Problem

Obnoxious facilities location problem is usually considered along with routing of undesirable materials. Most of these obnoxious facilities, such as garbage dump citing and chemical plants are producer or consumer of Undesirable materials, so we should consider routing problem with location of these facilities simultaneously.

Cappanera et al. (2004) defined a discrete combined location-routing model, at 2004s, which we refer to as *obnoxious facilities location and routing model (OFLR)*. OFLR is a NP-Hard problem, for which a *Lagrangean heuristic* approach is presented. The Lagrangean relaxation proposed allows decomposing of OFLR into a location sub problem and a routing sub problem. An effective branch and bound algorithm is then presented, which aims at reducing the gap between the above mentioned lower and upper bounds. This is accomplished by using a bundle method to solve at each node the Lagrangean dual. Before 1970s scientists have mainly focused their attention on classical location problem i.e. service facilities location such as hospitals, supermarkets, post-offices and warehouses in which minimizing the distance between facilities and demand centers is one of objective functions. Gradually, some problems such as reactor dump citing and chemical plants locating with maximizing objectives were surveyed. However costs of material transportation to these facilities grow up by increasing distances. On the other hand, recently increasing attention of environmental-friend groups and repulsion of people forces governments to consider routing problems beside location of undesirable facilities and that imposes high costs to governments. In the last ten years for instance, the Italian electric society has attended to locate at least four electric power supplier networks and failed in all the cases due to the public opposition. Here, the *obnoxious facility location and routing (OFLR) problem* is formulated as a capacitated minimum cost network flow model.

14.2.4.1 Model Assumptions

- The model is single commodity, i.e. a single obnoxious material is considered.
- The affected sites are represented as point in the plane.
- In this network there are some nodes that they don't use hazardous material and they don't produce hazardous material too, but they influenced by hazardous material transportation consequences.
- For each site, location and routing exposure thresholds are given.

14.2.4.2 Model Inputs

The model is considered as $G = (V, A)$ graph, A is set of arcs and the set of vertices V is the union of the following three sets:

$R = \{1 \ldots m\}$: the set of affected sites
$N = \{1 \ldots n\}$: the set of candidate location to establish the new facilities
$T = \{1 \ldots t\}$: the set of transshipment nodes

Let us define:

δ_i ($\delta_i <= 0$): the demand of vertex i. Each node $i \in R$ can be a hazardous material source.
α_{ijk}: the exposure caused by a unitary flow along the arc (i, j) to affected site K
τ_k: the threshold of affected site K relative to the exposure induced by the establishment of obnoxious materials
a_{ij}: the exposure caused by the opening of a facility in location j to affected site i
t_i: the threshold of affected site I relative to the exposure induced by the establishment of obnoxious facilities
U_j: the capacity of located facility in site j
C_j: the opening cost of facility located in site jth
γ_{ij}: the transporting cost of a unitary flow along the arc (i, j)

14.2.4.3 Model Outputs (Decision Variables)

Y_j: 1 if a new facility is established at node j; 0 otherwise
X_{ij}: the amount of transported flow along the arc (i, j)

An artificial node P was added to set V, each site $j \in N$ is connected to this node via artificial arc (j, p) of zero cost. The demand of this node is $-\sum_{i \in \Re} \delta_i$ and represents demand of each influenced site $i \in R$ is completely disposed of.
V' and A' are the extended set of nodes and arcs respectively,

$$i.e.\ V' = V \bigcup \{P\},\ A' = A \bigcup \{(j, p) : j \in N\}. \tag{14.43}$$

Subject to

$$OFLR : \text{MINIMIZE} \sum_{j \in N} C_j Y_j + \sum_{(i,j) \in A} \gamma_{ij} X_{ij}, \tag{14.44}$$

$$\sum_{j:(j,i) \in A'} X_{ji} - \sum_{j:(i,j) \in A'} X_{ij} = \delta_i \quad \forall i \in V', \tag{14.45}$$

$$\sum_{(i,j) \in A} \alpha_{ij}^k X_{ij} \leq \tau_k \quad \forall k \in R, \tag{14.46}$$

$$\sum_{j \in N} a_{ij} Y_j \leq t_i \quad \forall i \in R, \tag{14.47}$$

$$X_{ij} \geq 0 \quad \forall (i, j) \in A, \tag{14.48}$$

$$Y_j \in \{0, 1\} \quad \forall j \in N. \tag{14.49}$$

The OFLR model is like above model. The objective and constraints are explained below:

Equation (14.44) minimizes sum of establishment and transportation costs.

Equation (14.45) represents that demand of each site is disposed of entirely.

Equation (14.46) considers that the sum of yield affected of hazardous material transportation among network arcs, must not exceed the threshold τ_k.

Equation (14.47) represents that the sum of yield affected of establishing facilities for each site, must not be over the fixed threshold.

Equation (14.48) ensures that if any facility is not located at node j, this node just can be applied as transshipment node, i.e. we can't vacate undesirable flow at node j and if a facility is located at this node, vacated amount shouldn't be more than capacity. Finally the (14.49) is the common constraint of location problems.

- The above model is compared with the models by zagrafos and samara (cited in (Erkut and Alp 2007)) and by List and Mirchandani (cited in (Erkut and Alp 2007)). A *goal programming model* was presented by zagrafos and samara which simultaneously minimizes Routing risk, Location risk and routing cost. The main differences between OFLR and the model by Zografos and Samara are following:

- In goal programming model each affected site suffers from the nearest open facility only, whilst in OFLR, each affected site is exposed to a set of open obnoxious facilities, according to the value of the a_{ij}' s.
- In goal programming model the total risk given by location and routing activities is minimized, i.e. risks are summed up over all of the affected sites differently from OFLR where, for each affected site, given exposure thresholds must not be exceeded
- In goal programming model the number of facilities to open is fixed while in OFLR is variable
- In goal programming model there are capacity constraints on the arcs of network versus uncapacitated arcs in OFLR.
- A *multi-objective model* is proposed by List and Mirchandani (cited in (Erkut and Alp 2007)) which risk, cost and risk equality are considered jointly. In this problem a set of non-overlapping zones are considered as the region of concern. For each zone, the risk from routing of obnoxious material along nearby arcs and the establishment of nearby facilities is taken into account and the total risk is minimized, which is given by the sum of the zonal risks. Equality is regarded by minimizing the maximal zonal risk. The main issues that characterize the model proposed by List and Mirchandani (cited in (Erkut and Alp 2007)) are the following:
- In the multi-objective model against OFLR, different types of obnoxious wastes and materials are considered
- Impact from both routing and location are assumed to be additive while in OFLR they are considered separately
- The multi-objective model is uncapacitated.

Alumur and Kara (2007) presented a comprehensive multi-objective model for the hazardous waste location-routing problem.

Hazardous waste management includes the collection, transportation, treatment and disposal of hazardous wastes. The aim of proposed model is to answer the following cases: 1 – locating treatment center and assigning proportional technologies, 2 – locating disposal centers, 3 – routing different types of hazardous wastes to compatible treatment technologies and 4 – routing waste residues to disposal centers.

The exclusive limitation of the model that was not incorporated into previous models is the treatment technology compatibility limitation with type of hazardous waste should be treated.

The other specialties of model are: 1 – considering different types of hazardous waste, 2 – grouping them for transportation and treatment and 3 – possibility to recycle them in treatment and disposal centers.

14.2.4.4 Mathematical Model

The Schematic of Mathematical model is shown in Fig. 14.4.

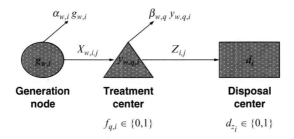

Fig. 14.4 Schematic modeling

14.2.4.5 Model Inputs

$N = (V, A)$ transportation network
$G = \{1 \ldots g\}$ generation nodes
$T = \{1 \ldots t\}$ potential treatment nodes
$D = \{1 \ldots d\}$ potential disposal nodes
$T_r = \{1 \ldots tr\}$ transshipment nodes
$W = \{1 \ldots w\}$ hazardous waste types
$Q = \{1 \ldots q\}$ treatment technologies
$c_{i,j}$: cost of transporting one unit of hazardous waste on link (i,j)
$cz_{i,j}$: cost of transporting one unit of waste residue on link (i,j)
$fc_{q,i}$: fixed annual cost of opening a treatment technology $q \in Q$ at treatment node $i \in T$
fd_i: fixed annual cost of opening a disposal facility at disposal node $i \in D$
POP_{wij}: number of people in the bandwidth for hazardous waste type $w \in W$ along link $(i, j) \in A$
$g_{w,i}$: amount of hazardous waste type $w \in W$ generated at generation node $i \in G$
$\alpha_{w,i}$: recycle percent of hazardous waste type $w \in W$ generated at generation node $i \in G$
$\beta_{w,q}$: recycle percent of hazardous waste type $w \in W$ treated with technology $q \in Q$
$r_{w,q}$: percent mass reduction of hazardous waste type $w \in W$ treated with technology $q \in Q$
$t_{q,i}$: capacity of treatment technology $q \in Q$ at treatment node $i \in T$
$t^m_{q,i}$: minimum amount of hazardous waste for treatment technology $q \in Q$ at treatment node $i \in T$
dc_i: disposal capacity of disposal site $i \in D$
$com_{w,q}$: 1 if waste type $w \in W$ is compatible with technology $q \in Q$; 0 otherwise

14.2.4.6 Model Outputs (Decision Variables)

$x_{w,i,j}$: amount of hazardous waste type w transported through link (i,j)
$z_{i,j}$: amount of waste residue transported through link (i,j)

$y_{w,q,i}$: amount of hazardous waste type w to be treated at treatment node i with technology q

d_i: amount of waste residue to be disposed of at disposal node i

$f_{q,i}$: 1 if treatment technology q is established at treatment node i; 0 otherwise

dz_i: 1 if disposal site is located at disposal node i; 0 otherwise

14.2.4.7 Objective Function and its Constraints

$$\text{Min} \sum_{(i,j)\in A} \sum_w c_{i,j} x_{w,i,j} + \sum_{(i,j)} cz_{i,j} z_{i,j} + \sum_i \sum_q fc_{q,i} f_{q,i}$$
$$+ \sum_i fd_i dz_i, \qquad (14.50)$$

$$\text{Min} \sum_{(i,j)} \sum_w POP_{w,i,j} x_{w,i,j}, \qquad (14.51)$$

Subject to

$$(1 - \alpha_{w,i}) g_{w,i} = \sum_{j:(i,j)\in A} x_{w,i,j} - \sum_{j:(j,i)\in A} x_{w,i,j}$$
$$+ \sum_q y_{w,q,i}, \ w \in W, i \in V, \qquad (14.52)$$

$$\sum_q \sum_w y_{w,q,i}(1 - r_{w,q})(1 - \beta_{w,q}) - d_i = \sum_{j:(i,j)\in A} z_{i,j} - \sum_{j:(j,i)\in A} z_{j,i}, \ i \in V, \qquad (14.53)$$

$$\sum_w y_{w,q,i} \leq t_{q,i} f_{q,i}, \quad q \in Q, i \in T, \qquad (14.54)$$

$$d_i \leq dc_i dz_i, \quad i \in D, \qquad (14.55)$$

$$\sum_w y_{w,q,i} \geq t_{q,i}^m f_{q,i}, \quad q \in Q, i \in T, \qquad (14.56)$$

$$y_{w,q,i} \leq t_{q,i} com_{w,q}, \quad w \in W, q \in Q, i \in T, \qquad (14.57)$$

$$\sum_q \sum_w y_{w,q,i} = 0, \quad i \in (V - T), \qquad (14.58)$$

$$d_i = 0, \ i \in (V - T), \qquad (14.59)$$

$$x_{w,i,j}, z_{w,i,j} \geq 0, \ w \in w, (i,j) \in A, \qquad (14.60)$$

$$y_{w,q,i} \geq 0, \quad w \in W, q \in Q, i \in T, \qquad (14.61)$$

$$d_i \geq 0, \quad i \in D, \qquad (14.62)$$

$$f_{q,i} \in \{0, 1\}, \quad q \in Q, i \in T, \qquad (14.63)$$

$$dz_i \in \{0, 1\}, \quad i \in D. \qquad (14.64)$$

Equation (14.50) is the cost objective minimizes the total cost of transporting hazardous wastes and residues and the fixed annual cost of opening a treatment technology and a disposal facility.

Equation (14.51) is the risk objective that minimizes the transportation risk.

Equation (14.52) is the flow balance constraint for hazardous waste and ensures that all generated non-recycled hazardous waste is transported and treated at a treatment facility.

Equation (14.53) is the flow balance constraint for waste residues.

Equations (14.54) and (14.55) are the capacity constraints for treatment and disposal centers.

Equation (14.56) is the minimum amount of requirement constraint for opening a treatment center.

Equation (14.57) is the compatibility constraint, which ensures that a hazardous waste type is treated only with a compatible treatment technology.

Equations (14.58) and (14.59) ensure that treatment and disposal centers should be located in candidate centers.

The model's advantages are:

- It has capability to apply in large scale problems. In spite of the prior models were responsible only to a network with 10–15 nodes and 3–4 candidate centers, this model can cover a network with 90 nodes and 15–20 candidate places in reasonable time.
- Considering the residue waste issue.
- Proposing several method for treatment (with compatibility constraint)
- The above model was solved with *CPLEX* software. We can focus on heuristic techniques for future direction.
- This model can be applied in real problems. For example, a age scale implementation of the model in the *Central Anatolian region of Turkey* is presented in Sect. 14.4.1.

14.2.5 Multiobjective Obnoxious Facilities Location Problem (Rakas et al. 2004)

In the real world, usually we should consider multiple objectives to ensure the adaptation of model with real conditions.

In this way Rakas et al. (2004) proposed a multiobjective model as followed:

14.2.5.1 Model Inputs

$i = 1, 2, \ldots,$: representatives of demand points
$j = 1, 2, \ldots, N$: representatives of supply points
P_i: population of region i
Cp: the amount of produced waste by everyone

$d_i = C_p * P_i$: the amount of produced waste by each region
C_j^{Min}: minimum capacity of each candidate point
C_j: the maximum capacity of every point
L_{ij}: the length between two points i and j
$C_{ij} = C_w * L_{ij}$: the transport cost for wastes between i and j
$f_j(k)$: the cost of opening facility in j with size k
V_i: the error cost of experiment in the region i
O_i: repulsion reason in region i
S_j: capacity of each candidate point

14.2.5.2 Model Outputs

$$X_j = \begin{cases} 1 & \text{if a facility is located at } j, \\ 0 & \text{otherwise} \end{cases}$$

$$Y_{ij} = \begin{cases} 1 & \text{if region i uses facility } j, \\ 0 & \text{otherwise} \end{cases}$$

14.2.5.3 Objective Function and its Constraints

C: the total cost
TC: the transport cost
IIC: primary investment cost

$$C = TC + IIC,$$

$$TC = d_i * C_{ij} * Y_{ij},$$

$$IIC = f_j(S_j) * X_j,$$

$$\text{Min } Z_1 = \sum_{i=1}^{M} \left(\sum_{j=1}^{N} (d_i * C_{ij} * Y_{ij}) \right) + \sum_{j=1}^{N} (f_j(S_j) * X_j), \quad (14.65)$$

$$\text{Min } Z_2 = \sum_{i=1}^{M} \sum_{j=1}^{N} (O_i * Y_{ij}). \quad (14.66)$$

Subject to

$$\sum_{j=1}^{N} Y_{ij} = 1 \quad \forall i, \quad (14.67)$$

$$Y_{ij} \leq X_j \quad \forall i, \forall j, \quad (14.68)$$

$$\sum_{i=1}^{M}(d_i{}^*Y_{ij}) \leq S_j \quad \forall j, \tag{14.69}$$

$$C_j^{Min} \leq S_j \leq C_j^{Max} \quad \forall j. \tag{14.70}$$

Equation (14.65) minimizes sum of opening and transportation cost and (14.66) minimizes the people opposition. Equation (14.67) declares each region is covered by only one facility. Equation (14.68) shows that region i can use facility j only if one facility is located in j. Equation (14.69) is capacity constraint of each candidate point and (14.70) proposes the capacity of every point between two limits.

For solving this continuous model, two models are solved separately and $Z_1{}^{Opt}$, $Z_2{}^{Opt}$ are obtained. Then using weighting method, two objective functions are integrated and following model is solved:

$$\text{Min } Z_3 = \text{Weight 1}^* \frac{Z_1}{Z_1^{Opt}} + \text{Weight 2}^* \frac{Z_2}{Z_2^{Opt}}. \tag{14.71}$$

Because of uncertainty in data estimation, required data are solved as fuzzy data that are described in (Rakas et al. 2004) in detail.

14.3 Solutions and Techniques

In this section we review some researches in obnoxious facility location field focusing on solutions and techniques.

- Melachrinoudis (1999) developed a bicriteria location model for locating a new semi-obnoxious facility in an existing layout which is solved by an adaptation of the Fourier–Motzkin elimination method
- Zhang et al. (2000) devise a routing hazardous materials algorithm, using GIS technique and a Gaussian Plume model for their dispersion model
- Akgün et al. (2000) to find dissimilar paths for transporting HazMat, solved the capacitated flow problem:
    - Iterative penalty method(IPM)
    - Minimax method
    - Gateway shortest path (GSP) method

  By increasing the size of problem, calculations volume rises up strongly. They used GIS method as a facilator to test different network roads. Finally they proposed a P-Dispersion problem and solved it with constructing a candidate set m of K-shortest paths.
- Kara et al. (2003) present two path- selection algorithms for hazmat transport problems with selection of a minimum risk path. One of the proposed procedures is a modified version of shortest path algorithm and the other is an adaptation of a link-labeling algorithm developed for urban transportation.

- Cappanera et al. (2004) proposed a Lagrangean heuristic approach allows to decompose obnoxious facility location routing (OFLR) into a location subproblem and routing subproblem. Then, an effective branch and bound algorithm was offered for reduction of the gap between lower and upper bounds.
- Colebrook et al. (2005) presented a new bound for the undesirable 1-median problem (Maxian) on networks. they proposed an undesirable center and median models and implemented Multicriteria-anti-cent-dian problem (MACDP). They created a heuristic algorithm for MACDP.
- Díaz-Báñez et al. (2005) for solving the obnoxious short path problem in continuous spaces presented an approximate algorithm based on the bisection method. They transformed optimization problem into decision problem and could provide efficient algorithm. They proposed:
  - A general method of voroni diagram with daguare geometry
  - Shortest path avoiding obstacles
- Erkut et al. (2005) formulated the tree design problem as an integer programming problem aiming at trade off between cost and risk. They developed a simple heuristic to expand the solution of the tree design problem by adding node segments.
- Erkut and Alp (2007) formulate the tree design problem for hazardous materials routes in and through a major population center as an integer programming model with an objective of minimizing the total transport risk. They propose the use of a new model for finding a minimum risk hazmat tree called Optimum Communication Steiner Tree. Then a construction heuristic that adds paths incrementally and permits local authorities to balance between risk and cost was developed.
- Zhang et al. (2005) proposed a new model that is a variant of the vehicle routing problem with time windows (VRPTW) by adding load upper bounds on the road segments. The objective is to find a schedule to guarantee the safety of all vehicles. They propose a sophisticated Tabu search heuristic with novel neighborhood operators such as dynamic penalty mechanism to obtain good solutions.
- Zhang et al. (2005) used a heuristic algorithm based on greedy to solve a multiobjective approach (analysing cost minimization, potential risk minimization and risk equity maximization) to assist decision makers in analysing combined location/routing decisions involving hazmats.
- Dadkar et al. (2008) Identified geographically diverse routes for the transportation of hazardous materials by applying k-shortest path algorithm with stochastic objective and varying over time. They also implemented Mixed Integer Programming.
- Erkut and Gzara (2008) develop and test a heuristic for a bilevel network design problem for hazmat transportation that finds stable solutions. This heuristic exploits the network flow structure at both levels to overwhelm the difficulty and instability of the bilevel integer programming model.
- Pisinger (2006) present an exact algorithm for finding a number of fast upper bounds for P-dispersion problems in which these bounds can be derived in $O(n)$ time.

- Bell (2006) considered mixed rout strategies for the Risk-Averse shipment of hazardous materials. A minimax problem was formulated to determine the safest set of routs and safest share of traffic between these routs. A simple heuristic based on a shortest path algorithm and the method of successive averages is proposed. Connections to game theory can be seen in the nature of the solution.
- Yapicioglu et al. (2007) offer a new model for the semi obnoxious facility location problem composed of a weighted minisum function for transportation cost and a distance- based piecewise function for the obnoxious effects of the facility. They devise a single objective particle swarm optimizer (PSO) and a bi-objective PSO to solve this problem.
- Carotenuto et al. (2007) For finding minimum and equitable risk routes for HazMat shipment present a mathematical model and solved with Lagrangian relaxation and two heuristic algorithms based on the Yen's k-shortest path:

  – Greedy algorithm (GD)
  – Randomized Greedy algorithm (RGD)

- Carotenuto et al. (2007) implemented a Tabu Search algorithm for scheduling and routing of HazMat transportation. They focus on scheduling to decrease traffic volume of HazMat transportation as well as on a network road.

14.4 Case Study

14.4.1 Obnoxious Facility Location and Routing in Anatolian Region of Turkey (Alumur and Kara 2007)

In Central Anatolian region of Turkey, there are 184 administrative districts. The population of districts ranges from 3,700 to 77,000 people. It assumed that the districts with a population more than 25,000 produce hazardous waste.

The data on the amount of hazardous waste produced by each districts in Turkey are not available presently. So, assumed that the amount of hazardous waste generated by each district is proportional to the population times the industrial activity level of the district. The GIS system is applied in collecting geographical information. In this region three types of hazardous waste are generated and two treatment methods are determined. The first type waste can be incinerated, the second type is suitable for chemical treatment, and the third type can be treated by both incineration and chemical process. The proposed model assumed that treatment and disposal centers can be located at the same nodes. The candidate point's selection is so important because of cost considerations. So that, the model was considered in two conditions: A: 15 candidate places, B: 20 candidate places. After solving the problem with *CPLEX* resulted that final answers are not mainly different. Therefore, in the reason of economic considerations the 15 candidate place state was selected.

14.4.2 Designing Emergency Response Network for Hazardous Materials Transportation (Berman et al. 2007)

In addition to government's policies for decreasing HazMats accidents, detrimental effects of these accidents are such that we should consider various alternatives for locating, routing and improving of emergency teams performance to reduce these consequences. Critical factor is quick arrival of emergency teams at the accident site. Arrival time, itself, is related to selected paths and location of teams, therefore such designs are essential to consider.

In this way, Berman et al. (2007), proposed a *maximal arc-covering model* for optimal design of such networks. Their model improves solution capability relative to previous models by adding some binary variables. Moreover, they developed a *greedy heuristic* to solve their model efficiently.The advantages of new formulation are:

- Reducing the number of variables,
- Reducing time of solution,
- Compatibility with existing software and large scale problems,
- Proposed model is explicit and easy to understand,
- The new model constitutes a basis for an efficient heuristic.

Proposed model was efficiently applied for emergency response infrastructure for gasoline incidents on the highway networks of *Quebec and Ontario in Canada*. They derived the model parameters from a GIS-based representation of the two provinces. This application shows the possibility of a significant improvement in response capability via relocation of the existing stations. Also, a noticeable decrease in the threshold time of coverage for gasoline incidents is considered.

14.4.3 Locating Waste Pipelines to Minimize their Impact on Marine Environment (Ceceres et al. 2007)

Ceceres et al. (2007), suggested a methodology for locating waste pipelines to minimize their impact on marine environment. A waste pipeline, as an undesirable facility, is to be located in a coastal region. The coastal fringe is the territory where marine, air and terrestrial environments interrelate. Here very diverse and fragile ecosystems coexist, although subjected in many cases to increasing degradation due to industrial and urban developments disrespectful to the environment.

Pasidonia oceanica (Linnaeus) Delile is a plant with leaves, flowers and fruit, similar to those plants which live in forests and gardens, but which lives in the sea between the surface and a depth of 50 m.

It is endemic to the Mediterranean Sea and, by providing the principal source of oxygenation of the Mediterranean Sea; it is its most important ecosystem. Due to its ecological role, this sea-grass is a protected species in Spain and in France. Here

Fig. 14.5 The area Voronoi diagram

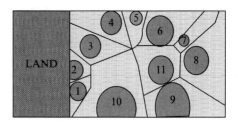

a methodology is described to obtain an efficient set of points where the extreme of a marine pipeline should be located. Two criteria are taken into account, the Euclidean distance from a given set of protected areas and a utility function related to the pipeline length, both to be maximized.

The region under study has been assumed to be a rectangle which includes zones of biological interest, geometrically modeled as rectangles and circles. They used *Voronoi diagram* shown in Fig. 14.5.

The length of the pipe has been associated to a utility function described by a generalized gamma function. Since intensity of pollution has been assumed to be inversely proportional to the Euclidean distance, the location problem was formulated as a bi-criterion problem in which both the minimum distance to protected zones and the utility function had to be maximized.

An efficient set of solutions has been identified along edges of the zone Voronoi diagram by means of an approach based upon the *NISE*[4] method.

References

Akgün V, Erkut E, Batta R (2000) On finding dissimilar paths. Eur J Oper Res 121:232–246
Akgün V, Parekh A, Batta R, Rump C (2007) Routing of a hazmat tuck in the presence of weather systems. Comput Oper Res 34:1351–1373
Alumur S, Kara B (2007) A new model for the hazardous waste location-routing problem. Comput Oper Res 34:1406–1423
Batta R, Chiu SS (1988) Optimal obnoxious path on a network: Transportation of hazardous materials. Oper Res 36(1):84–92
Bell MGH (2006) Mixed strategies for the risk-averse shipment of hazardous materials. Spat Econ 6:253–265
Berman O, Verter V, Kara B (2007) Designing emergency response networks for hazardous materials transportation. Comput Oper Res 34:1374–1388
Cappanera P, Gallo G, Maffioli F (2004) Discrete facility location and routing of obnoxious activities. Discrete Appl Math 133:3–28
Carotenuto P, Giordani S, Ricciardelli S, Rismondo S (2007) A tabu search approach for scheduling hazmat shipments. Comput Oper Res 34:1328–1350
Castillo JE (2004) Route optimization for hazardous materials transport. International Institute for geo-Information science and earth observation, Enschede, The Netherlands

---

[4] Non-Inferior set estimation

Ceceres T, A.Mesa J, Ortega F (2007) Locating waste pipelines to minimize their impact on marine environment. Eur J Oper Res 179(3):1143–1159

Colebrook M, Guti J, Sicilia J (2005) A new bound and an O (mn) algorithm for the undesirable 1-median problem (Maxian) on networks. Comput Oper Res 32:309–325

Dadkar Y, Jones D, Nozick L (2008) Identifying geographically diverse routes for the transportation of hazardous materials. Transportation Research Part E: Logistics and Transportation Review 44(3):333–349

Daskin MS (1995) Network and discrete location: models, algorithms and applications. Wiley, New York

Díaz-Báñez JM, Gómez F, Toussaint GT (2005) Computing shortest paths for transportation of hazardous materials in continuous spaces. J Food Eng 70:293–298

Drezner Z, Wesolowsky GO (1983) Location of an obnoxious facility with rectangular distances. J Reg Sci 23:241–248

Erkut E, Verter V (1995) Hazardous Materials Logistics. Springer Series in Oper Res, Chapter 20

Erkut E, Verter V (1998) Modeling of transport risk for hazardous material. Oper Res 46(5):625–642

Erkut E, Alp O (2007) Designing a network for hazardous materials shipments. Comput Oper Res 34(5):1389–1405

Erkut E, Gzara F (2008) Solving the hazmat transport network design problem. Comput Oper Res 35(7):2234–2247

Erkut E, Ingolfsson A (2005) Transport risk models for hazardous materials: revisited. Oper Res Lett 33:81–89

Fernandez J, Fernandez P, Pelegrin B (2000) A continuous location model for siting a non-noxious undesirable facility within a geographical region. Eur J Oper Res 121:259–274

Giannikos I (1998) A multi-objective programming model for locating treatment sites and routing hazardous wastes. Eur J Oper Res 104:333–342

Gopalan R, Kolluri KS, Batta R, Karwan MH (1990) Modeling equity of risk in the transportation of hazardous materials. Oper Res 38(6):961–973

Kara BY, Erkut E, Verter V (2003) Accurate calculation of hazardous materials transport risks. Oper Res Lett 31:285–292

Katz MJ, Kedem K, Segal M (2002) Improved algorithms for placing undesirable facilities. Comput Oper Res 29:1859–1872

Kuby MJ (1987) Programming models for facility dispersion: the p-dispersion and maxisum dispersion problems. Geographical Analysis 19:315–329

Marianov V, ReVelle C (1998) Linear, no-approximated models for optimal routing in hazardous environments. J Operl Res Society 48:157–164

McGinnis LF, White JA (1978) A single facility rectilinear location problem with multiple criteria. Transport Sci 12:217–231

Mehrez A, Sinuany-Stern Z, Stulman A (1986) An enhancement of the Drezner–Wesolowsky algorithm for single facility location with maximin of rectilinear distance. J Oper Res Soc 37:971–977

Melachrinoudi E (1999) Bicriteria location of a semi-obnoxious facility. Comput Oper Res 37:581–593

Pisinger D (2006) Upper bounds and exact algorithms for p-dispersion problems. Comput Oper Res 33:1380–1398

Rakas J, Teodorovic D, Kim T (2004) Multi-objective modeling for determining location of undesirable facilities. Transport Re D9:125–138

Ratick S, White A (1988) A risk sharing model for locating noxious facilities. Environment Plan 165–179

ReVelle C, Cohon J, Shobrys D (1991) Simultaneous siting and routing in the disposal of hazardous wastes. Transportation Science 25(2):138–145

Rogers GO (1998) Sitting potentially hazardous facilities: What factors impact perceived and acceptable risk? Landsc Urban Plan 39:265–281

Rodriguez JJ, Garcia GC, Muñoz Pérez J Mérida Casermeiroa E (2006) A general model for the undesirable single facility location problem. Oper Res Lett 34(4):427–436

Saccomanno FF, Chan A (1985) Economic evaluation of routing strategies for hazardous road shipments. Transp. Res. Record 1020:12–18

Sivakumar R, Batta R, Karwan MH (1993) A network- based model for transporting extremely hazardous materials. Oper Res Lett 13(2):85–93

Sivakumar R, Batta R, Karwan MH (1995) A multiple route conditional risk model for transporting hazardous materials. INFOR 33:20–33

Wayman MM, Kuby M (1994) Proactive optimization: General framework and a case study using a toxic waste location model with technology choice. International symposium on locational decisions, ISOLDE VI, Lesvos and Chios, Greece

Yapicioglu H, Smith AE, Dozier G (2007) Solving the semi- obnoxious facility location problem using bi-objective particle swarm. Eur J Oper Res 177:733–749

Zhang J, Hodgson J, Erkut E (2000) Using GIS to assess the risk of hazardous materials transport in networks. Eur J Oper Res 121:316–329

Zhang L, Guo S, Zhu Y, Lim A (2005) A tabu search algorithm for the safe transportation of hazardous materials. Proceedings of the ACM symposium on Applied computing, SESSION: Evolutionary computation and optimization (ECO), pp 940–946

Zografos KG, Androutsopoulos KN (2004) A heuristic algorithm for solving hazardous materials distribution problems. Eur J Oper Res 152:507–519

Zografos KG, Vasilakis GM, Giannouli IM (2000) Methodological framework for developing decision support system (DSS) for hazardous materials emergency response operations. J Hazardous Mater 71:503–521

Chapter 15
Dynamic Facility Location Problem

Reza Zanjirani Farahani, Maryam Abedian, and Sara Sharahi

Facility location is a strategic management decision. This decision is usually made, however, with respect to the current parameters (like weights) which represent population, infrastructure, service requirements and others (Drezner 1995; Francis and Lowe 1992; Mirchandani and Francis 1990). Much of the research published on location theory is drawn from the models such as single/multi facility location, covering, P-median, P-center problems, and their applications and extensions. Solving many of these problems can be extremely difficult. Thus, it is not surprising that so much work has focused on statistic and deterministic problem formulations. While such formulations are reasonable research topics, they do not capture many of the characteristics of real-world location problems.

The strategic nature of facility location problems requires that any reasonable model consider some aspects of future uncertainty. Since the investment required by location or relocation facilities is usually large, facilities are expected to remain operable for an extended time period (Owen and Daskin 1998). Thus, the problem of facility location truly involves an extended planning horizon. Decision makers must not only select robust locations which will effectively serve changing demand over time, but must also consider the timing of facility expansions and relocations in the long term (Daskin et al. 1992).

It is generally true of facilities that they are expected to serve over a long period of time. During this time, many of the "constants" of the problem, such as demands and distribution costs, are likely to change. It is also generally true that relocation cannot be accomplished without cost (Wesolowsky 1973). Thus, decision makers must select sites that will not simply perform well according to the current system state, but that will continue to be profitable for the facility's lifetime (Owen and Daskin 1998). Considering the fact that changes in static problem parameters can be forecasted, optimization requires the balance between the benefits of planned location changes and their costs (Wesolowsky 1973).

There are two different types of dynamic facility location Problems: Location and Location–Relocation. These two types are different in the following ways:

- In a time-dependent location problem, the decision maker selects a site which is profitable for a defined time horizon.
- In location–relocation problem, the decision maker selects a primary location, relocation or development times and the facility's location after relocation.

In the remainder of this chapter, first, some classifications of time-dependant facility location problems will be presented. Then, some of the related mathematical models will be reviewed. Next, some lemmas and solution techniques will briefly be presented. And finally, some real-world case studies will be introduced.

15.1 Classifications

Facility location problems can be divided into static and dynamic problems, These can also be further classified on the basis of different criteria. This section provides a brief description of different classifications of dynamic facility problem.

- *Cause of change*. The first and the most important way for the classification of dynamic facility location problem is based on the cause of change and uncertainty. According to this criterion, dynamic facility location problems are divided into two categories (Owen and Daskin 1998):
  - Uncertainty related to planning for future conditions, and
  - Uncertainty due to the limited knowledge of model input parameters.

  Note that in the first category, although there are changes in the conditions, they are deterministic and time-dependent. In other words, the pattern of changes is distinctive and deterministic. In the second category, although the pattern of changes may be distinctive, it is not deterministic and time dependent, rather, it is stochastic (Rosental et al. 1978).

- Denoting the weight of facility parameter by "W_i", deterministic and stochastic changes can be classified as follows:
  - Deterministic changes can be further classified based on whether or not:

1. "W_i" changes in each period of time horizon but it is fixed and distinctive in every period.
2. The weight parameter, "W_i", is a function of time, say $w_i(t)$.

Stochastic changes can be classified into three types where:

1. "W_i" has a probabilistic distribution with fixed parameters.
2. "W_i" has a probabilistic distribution with variable parameters where the parameters are functions of time.
3. There is no information about the alteration of the parameters and the weight of the facility.

- Dependency variable: *Time-dependent weights*, *Distance-dependent weights*. This chapter is mainly dedicated to time-dependent weights. However, some works such as the one by Huang et al. (1990) consider the weights as a function of distance between the new facility and the existing facilities; this application can be found in marketing area.

- The number of relocations: *Single relocation, Multiple relocation*. In the first category, there is only one relocation (Emamizadeh and Z.-Farahani 1997a, b) whereas in the second category the location of the new facility is allowed to change several times during the time horizon, i.e. n changes are allowed during the time span.
- Classification by the number of relocating facilities (Owen and Daskin 1998; Chand 1988): *Single facility, Multiple facility*. In the first category, only one facility can be relocated whereas in the second, more than one facility can be considered for relocating (Scott 1971).
- Classification by the Relocation Time: *Discrete, Continuous*. In the first category, relocation can take place only at pre-determined points (Wesolowsky 1973) of time whereas in the second category, relocation can take virtually any time in the defined time horizon (Drezner and Wesolowsky 1991).
- Time horizon: *Finite, Infinite*. Daskin et al. (1992) acknowledge that the difficulty in solving dynamic facility location problems arises from the uncertainty surrounding future conditions. Even establishing an appropriate time horizon length is a non-trivial problem which is ignored in most formulations. They argue that the best way to mange uncertainty is postponing decision making as much as possible, collecting information and improving forecasts as time advances. Since the first period decisions are the ones to be implemented immediately, the authors claim that the goal of dynamic location planning should not be to determine locations and/or relocations for the entire horizon, but to find an optimal or near-optimal first period solution for the problem over an infinite horizon.

15.2 Mathematical Formulations

15.2.1 Static Model (Wesolowsky 1973)

Perhaps the best known of static location models is the generalized Weber problem. The problem requires the location of a facility among m destinations. Costs are assumed to be proportional to distances. Location is achieved by solving:

$$\text{Min} \sum_{i=1}^{m} w_i . d_i(x, y) \tag{15.1}$$

where:

$d_i(x, y)$: is the distance between the facility to be located at (x, y) and destination i located at (a_i, b_i).
w_i: is a constant transforming distances into costs.

To simplify notation in the succeeding section, model (15.1) is set in common notation.

$$\text{Min} \sum_{i=1}^{m} f_i(x, y). \tag{15.2}$$

The static model given in (15.2) is now extended to a model with a planning horizon of r time periods. This means that the demands, costs and destination locations are forecasted for r time periods in advance, and the optimal planned location of the facility in each period must be found. Consider the following problem:

$$\text{Min} \sum_{k=1}^{r} \sum_{i=1}^{m_k} f_{ki}(x_k, y_k) + \sum_{k=2}^{r} C_k . z_k, \tag{15.3}$$
$$z_k = 0 \quad if \quad d_{k,k-1} = 0.$$

where:

m_k: is the number of destinations in period k.
$f_{ki}(x_k, y_k)$: is the present value of the cost of shipping from the facility at (x_k, y_k) in period k to destination i.
C_k: is the cost of moving at the beginning of period k.
$d_{k-1,k}$: the distance the facility is moved at the beginning of period k.

The above model makes the following assumptions:

- Each term $f_{kd}(x_k, y_k)$ is adjusted to represent its present value at time 0. It can also be adjusted by a factor reflecting confidence in the forecast.
- Each "moving" cost C_k is independent from the distance the facility is to be moved and is also independent from the number of periods it will remain at the new location (Wesolowsky 1973).

15.2.2 Dynamic P-Median Model (Owen and Daskin 1998)

We will examine the P-median problem under the scenario planning approach.

15.2.2.1 Model Inputs

k: index of possible scenarios
h_{ik}: demand at node i under scenario k
d_{ijk}: distance from node i to facility site j under scenario k
$\hat{v}_k$: optimal P-median solution value for scenario k
q_k: scenario probability for scenario k.

15.2.2.2 Decision Variables

$Y_{ijk} = 1$ if demand node i is assigned to facility j under scenario k, otherwise is 0
$X_j = 1$ if facility site j locates at potential, otherwise is 0

15 Dynamic Facility Location Problem

The regret associated with scenario k is, thus, given by:

$$R_k = v_k - \hat{v}_k,$$

where v_k the value of the demand is weighted total distance (i.e., the P-median objective value) under the compromise locations

$$v_k = \sum_i \sum_j h_{ik}.d_{ijk}.Y_{ijk}.$$

15.2.2.3 Objective Function and its Constraints

The expected regret problem can thus be formulated as follows:

$$\text{Minimise} \sum_k q_k R_k, \tag{15.4}$$

$$\sum_j X_j = p, \tag{15.5}$$

$$\sum_j Y_{ijk} = 1 \quad \forall i,k, \tag{15.6}$$

$$Y_{ijk} - X_j \leq 0 \quad \forall i,j,k, \tag{15.7}$$

$$R_k - \sum_i \sum_j (h_{ik} d_{ijk} Y_{ijk} - \hat{V}_k) = 0 \quad \forall k, \tag{15.8}$$

$$X_j = \{0,1\} \quad \forall j, \tag{15.9}$$

$$Y_{ijk} = \{0,1\} \quad \forall i,j,k. \tag{15.10}$$

The objective function minimizes the expected regret, with regret defined in (15.8). The remaining constraints are the scenario planning equivalents to the standard P-median constraints.

Note that the locations are common to all scenarios and must be determined before knowing which scenario is realized. The demand assignments, however, are scenario-specific. In essence, they are the result of optimizing the assignments conditional to the chosen sites after we know which scenario is realized. This formulation requires the decision maker to input probability values q_k for each scenario, values which must be typically estimated. To avoid making such estimates, we can instead minimize the maximum regret across all scenarios. This objective is more conservative, and is formulated with the same constraints as above, but with the following objective function:

$$\text{Min Max}_k R_k. \tag{15.11}$$

15.2.3 Multiperiod Model (Wesolowsky and Truscott 1975)

A dynamic or multiperiod location–allocation formulation is the problem of locating G facilities among M possible sites to serve N demand points.

The goal is to devise a plan of optimal locations and relocations in response to predicted changes in the demand volume originating at demand points over a planning horizon of K periods.

15.2.3.1 Model Inputs

A_{jik}: the present value of the cost of assigning node i to node j in period k.
c'_{jk}: the present value of the cost of removing a facility from site j in period k.
c''_{jk}: the present value of the cost of establishing a facility at site j in period k.
m_k: the maximum number of facility location changes allowed in period k.

15.2.3.2 Decision Variables

$$x_{jik} = \begin{cases} 1 & \text{if node } i \text{ is assigned to node } j \text{ in period } k \\ 0 & \text{Otherwise} \end{cases}.$$

$$y'_{jk} = \begin{cases} 1 & \text{if a facility is removed from site } j \text{ in period } k \\ 0 & \text{Otherwise} \end{cases}.$$

$$y''_{jk} = \begin{cases} 1 & \text{if a facility is established at site } j \text{ in period } k \\ 0 & \text{Otherwise} \end{cases}.$$

15.2.3.3 Objective Function and its Constraints

The model is:

$$\text{Min} \sum_{k=1}^{K}\sum_{i=1}^{N}\sum_{j=1}^{M} A_{jik} x_{jik} + \sum_{k=2}^{K}\sum_{j=1}^{M} (c'_{jk} y'_{jk} + c''_{jk} y''_{jk}), \quad (15.12)$$

Subject to

$$\sum_{j=1}^{M} x_{jik} = 1 \quad \forall i, k, \quad (15.13)$$

$$\sum_{i=1}^{N} x_{jik} \leq N x_{jjk} \quad \forall j, k, \quad (15.14)$$

$$\sum_{j=1}^{M} x_{jik} = G \quad \forall k, \tag{15.15}$$

$$\sum_{j=1}^{M} y'_{jk} \leq m_k \quad \forall k \geq 2, \tag{15.16}$$

$$x_{jjk} - x_{jj\,k-1} + y'_{jk} - y''_{jk} = 0 \quad \forall j, k \geq 2, \tag{15.17}$$

$$x_{jik} \geq 0 \,\forall i \neq j \; y'_{jk}, y''_{jk} \geq 0, \; \forall j, k \; x_{jjk} \in \{0,1\}, \forall j, k. \tag{15.18}$$

The objective function is to minimize the costs of distribution from the facilities to the demand centers. Based on (15.13), each node i is assigned to exactly one node j. In (15.14) node i can be assigned to node j only if node j is self assigned. Equation (15.15) guarantee that G self-assignments are made among the M nodes. Equation (15.16) limit the number of sites vacated in each of periods 2 through K. Since constant number of facilities, G, is required in all periods by (117), placing an upper bound on the number of facility removals in a period is equivalent to limiting the number of facility location changes in the period. Equation (15.18) in conjunction with the second term of (15.12) ensure that the appropriate relocation costs are charged. The required minimization of costs forces the following binary values of y'_{jk} and y''_{jk} for each possible combination of values for x_{jjk} and $x_{jj,k-1}$ in (15.17).

15.2.4 Probabilistic Model (Rosental et al. 1978)

The specific model concerns making dynamic relocation decisions for a new facility (server) that must interact with existing facilities (customers) whose relocations are stochastic processes. The two distinguishing features of the problems considered here are (1) probabilistic location of existing facilities; and (2) dynamic relocation of new and existing facilities. These two features are treated together.

Costs are location-dependent and are incurred in two ways: (1) when the server makes choice relocations; and (2) when the server interacts with customers.

We allow both new facility and existing facility to change locations, but the distinction between a new facility and an existing facility is that the location of a new facility is under a decision maker's control. The model is relocation policy that minimizes the expected discounted sum of costs.

X_t: server location at time t, decision variable,
A_t: customer location at time t, stochastic,
$N: \{1,...,n\}$: known set of possible locations for both,
F: known server relocation cost matrix, $n \times n$,
G: known service cost matrix, $n \times n$,
P: known Markov transition matrix for customer location, $n \times n$,
B: known discount factor.

A discrete-time process evolves as follows:

- The decision-maker observes (X_{t-1}, A_{t-1}) and chooses X_t,
- The relocation cost $f(x_{t-1}, x_t)$ is incurred,
- The chance probabilistic A_t, is realized and
- The service cost $g(X_t, A_t)$ is incurred.

Then the process repeats. The problem is to find a policy for choosing server locations, so as to minimize the expected present worth of all costs, i.e.,

$$\text{Minimize } E\left[\sum_{t=1}^{a}\{F(X_{t-1}, X_t) + G(X_t, A_t)\}B^{t-1}\right]. \tag{15.19}$$

15.3 Solution Techniques

Some of the common methods used in dynamic Facility location are as follows:

- Exact Techniques as in:
  - *Mixed integer programming.* Some works in this area are Wesolowsky and Truscott (1975), Hormozi and Khumawala (1997) and Z.-Farahani et al. (2009).
  - *Complete enumeration.* Wesolowsky (1973) represented a method based on complete enumeration.
  - *Nonduplicating enumeration.* This method was used by Wesolowsky (1973).
  - *Dynamic programming (DP).* Some examples in this area are Hormozi and Khumawala (1997), Chand (1988), Canel et al. (2001) and Romauch and Hartl (2005).
  - *B&B.* This method was used by Canel et al. (2001) and Wesolowsky and Truscott (1975).
  - *Graphs and networks.* An example of this method is Andretta and Mason (1994).
  - *Primal-dual.* Dias et al. (2004, 2007) used this method to solve their problems.

- *Heuristic technique.* This method was used by Romauch and Hartl (2005).

- Meta heuristic techniques as in:
  - *Simulated annealing (SA).* Antunes and Peeters (2000) used SA to solve their problem.
  - *Lagrangean relaxation (LR).* This method was used by Snyder et al. (2007).
  - *Tabu search (TS).* Rajagopalan et al. (2008) used TS for their problem.

15.3.1 Fundamental Lemmas

In this section, we will first propound some lemmas regarding the location and relocation of new facilities.

Lemma 15.1. *When there are no relocations and the facility is located only at the start time, such that the total location costs are minimized, we use the following weights, and by solving a simple single facility location problem, we can find the best location. The resulting point is optimal location* (Drezner and Wesolowsky 1991).

$w_i(t)$: weight associated with demand point i.
m: Number of current facilities.

$$w_i = \int_0^T w_i(t)\,\mathrm{d}t. \tag{15.20}$$

Lemma 15.2. *When there are no relocation costs* (Drezner and Wesolowsky 1991)

$$F^*_{k+1} \leq F^*_k, \tag{15.21}$$

where F^*_k is the cost of optimal k time break solution. Based on this Lemma, the cost of optimal $k+1$ time break solution can only be lower than the cost of optimal k time breaks solution. Thus, we should use all opportunities for relocating the facility to the best locations. The best way to manage uncertainty is postponing decision making as much as possible, collecting information and improving forecasts as time advances. Since the first period decisions are the ones to be implemented immediately, the goal of dynamic location planning should not be to determine locations and/or relocations for the entire horizon, but to find an optimal or near-optimal first period solution for the problem over an infinite horizon (Z.-Farahani et al. 2009).

Lemma 15.3. *The objective cost function is additive.*

Consider Fig. 15.1 b_{j1}, b_j and b_{j+1} are some points in the time horizon. It is obvious that the location of the new facility can be determined independently during $[(b_{j1}, b_j)$ and $(b_j, b_{j+1})]$, given that the relocation takes place at b_j.

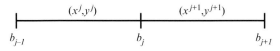

Fig. 15.1 New facility locations and relocation time

The objective function is:

$$F = \int_{b_{j-1}}^{b_j} \sum_{i=1}^{m} d(X^{j-1,j}, p_i) w_i(t) dt + \int_{b_j}^{b_{j+1}} \sum_{i=1}^{m} d(X^{j,j+1}, p_i) w_i(t) dt$$

$$= g_1(x^{j-1}, y^{j-1}) + g_2(x^j, y^j), \qquad (15.22)$$

where X_{jk} is the optimal facility location during the $[b_j, b_k]$. This shows the additivity of the objective function. Therefore, given b_j, the optimal location of the new facility before and after the relocation time can be determined independently (Z.-Farahani et al. 2009).

Therefore, if there are predetermined time breaks, we can find the best location at that time by solving a simple single facility location problem.

Lemma 15.4. *For optimal facility location during the $[b_j, b_{j+1}]$ use Lemma 1:*

$$\overset{j}{\underset{i}{w}} = \int_{b_j}^{b_{j+1}} w_i(t).dt. \qquad (15.23)$$

Lemma 15.5. *The cost of every relocation is at least equal to cost of no relocation.*

If $F^*1(B)$ is the cost of optimum location with one relocation at time $B, 0 < B < T$, and $F^*(0)$ is the cost of optimum location with no relocation, then:

$$F_1^*(B) \le F^*(0). \qquad (15.24)$$

Based on lemma 5 $F_1(B) \le F^*(B = 0)$ and what we have: $F_1(B) \le F^*(B = T)$.

15.3.2 Single Relocation at Discrete Time

If we consider Fig. 15.2 without t_1 and t_n, there will be $ñ2$ candidates for relocation. We must select one point for relocation, such that the total location and relocation costs is minimized.

Suppose that t_j is selected, according to Fig. 15.3 we must locate facility at this time and calculate cost function.

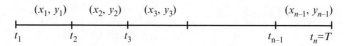

Fig. 15.2 Relocation at discrete time

15 Dynamic Facility Location Problem

Fig. 15.3 Relocation at t_j

According to Lemma 4, we solve the optimal location problem for intervals $[t_1, t_j], [t_j, t_n]$ and $(x^{1j}, y^{1j}), (x^{jn}, y^{jn})$ are reached. Location and relocation costs are:

$$F_j = \int_0^{t_j} \sum_{i=1}^m w_i(t).d(x^{1j}, p_j) dt + \int_{t_j}^T \sum_{i=1}^m w_i(t).d(x^{jn}, p_j) dt. \quad (15.25)$$

If this procedure is repeated for $t_j (j = 2, \ldots, \tilde{n}1)$, there will be $\tilde{n}2$ cost functions as $F_j (j = 2, \ldots, (\tilde{n}1))$.

The minimum F_j is the optimal location and relocation cost, t_j is the optimal relocation time, (x^{1j}, y^{1j}) is the optimal location of facility during $[0, t_j]$ and (x^{jn}, y^{jn}) is the optimal location of facility during $[t_j, T]$.

15.3.3 Multiple Relocations at Discrete Times Without Relocation Costs (Z.-Farahani et al. 2009)

This dynamic problem requires the location of a specified number of facilities among a predetermined set of potential sites and the allocation of demand centers to these facilities.

A more interesting problem arises when the location of the new facility is allowed to change several times during the time horizon i.e. n changes are allowed during the time span $[0, T]$. The variables to be determined are the time breaks $B = (b_1, \ldots, b_n)$ at which the changes take place and the associated optimal solution. Defining $b_0 = 0$ and $b_{n+1} = T$ then, we will have n time breaks. Of course, T can be infinite.

Given the specific weight functions in time, it could be more economical to relocate the new facility some time in the future, so that the total location and relocation costs is minimized. It is assumed that the relocation can take place only at pre-determined points in time. The total location cost, therefore, is the sum of the location costs before and after the relocation. The total cost depends on the optimal relocation time and the facility's optimal locations before and after the relocation.

Refering to Fig. 15.4; C_{jk} is the cost of locating the facility during period $[b_j, b_k)$. In the simplest case (without relocation cost and with finite time horizon $[0, T]$), the goal is to find the shortest path from b_0 to b_{n+1}.

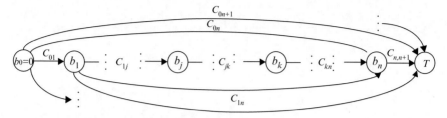

Fig. 15.4 New facility locations and relocations time

Lemma 3 helps us to find the best relocation times and new locations. However, using Lemma 3 in different situations related to time horizon and relocation cost, may be different. The time horizon can be either finite or infinite and relocation costs can exist or not; in the existence of relocation cost, various alternatives can occur. These situations will be investigated in following sections. Therefore when there are no relocation costs, we apply Lemma 2.

15.3.4 Multiple Relocations at Discrete Times with Relocation Costs

When more than one break is permissible, we have a multiple relocation problem. Drezner and Wesolowsky (1991) investigate multiple time break and linear change of weights over time. They consider location on multiple time breaks and devise two algorithm for minimax location problem. They solve the problem optimally for any number of time breaks and any distance metric.

First, it can be shown that for a vector $Z = (z_2, z_3, \ldots, z_r)$ problem (3) can be decomposed into static location problems, where:

$$z_j = \begin{cases} 1 & \text{Relocation at the beginning of period } j \\ 0 & \text{Otherwise} \end{cases}.$$

If n' be the number of 1's in the vector Z, the number of different locations for the facility over the planning period, will be $n = \acute{n} + 1$.

If S_j is the number of periods in the jth sequence that begins with either the first period or with a period p where $z_p = 1$, and ends either with the last period or before a period i where $z_l = 1$. the number of periods in sequence j will be $\tilde{i}\,p + 1$. The location of the facility during sequence j can be found by solving the static problem by a method appropriate to the model (Wesolowsky 1973):

$$\text{Min} \sum_{k=p}^{l-1} \sum_{i=1}^{m_k} f_{ki}(x_k, y_k). \tag{15.26}$$

15 Dynamic Facility Location Problem

Hence, for any vector Z, the solution of n static problems will specify the successive optimal locations. The optimal solution to the original problem (3) can now be found by evaluating the cost of the location patterns for every possible Z vector (Wesolowsky 1973).

15.3.5 Complete Enumeration

The optimal solution to the problem (15.3) can now be found by evaluating the cost of the location patterns for every possible Z vector. There are 2^{r-1} such vectors and each vector requires the solution of $(\tilde{r}1)/2 + 1$ static problems on the average. Hence, the total number of static problems that must be solved is $2^{\tilde{r}1}[1 + (\tilde{r}1)/2]$.

$$\sum_{i=0}^{r-1}(i+1)\binom{r-1}{i} = \sum_{i=0}^{r-1} i \cdot \binom{r-1}{i} + \sum_{i=0}^{r-1}\binom{r-1}{i}$$

$$= (r-1).2^{r-2} + 2^{r-1} = 2^{r-1}.\left[\tfrac{r-1}{2} + 1\right]$$

(15.27)

This total enumeration may be feasible for a small r but it is not necessary, since there exists a much more efficient way of obtaining a solution (Wesolowsky 1973).

15.3.6 Non-Duplicating Enumeration

Reflection on the above described enumeration procedure yields the following observation. Once a move is specified by the Z vector, subsequent succeeding locations are independent of the previous one. This leads to the conclusion that many of the static problems solved in the process of the total enumeration of the Z vectors are identical – a better method of enumeration, one that avoids the recalculation of static problems.

In this method, one begins the evaluation at the rth period. If there is a move at the beginning of the rth period, $C_j(1)$, the sum of the cost of the static problem and the moving cost C_r, can be calculated. Similarly, in the rt1th period, $C_s(1,1)$ can be found by adding the sum of the costs of the static problem in the rt1th period and the change cost C_{rt1} to $C_s(1)$.

Also $C_s(1,0)$ can be found by adding the cost of the static problem in the last two periods to the change cost C_{r-1}.

One can thus evaluate the cost of the 2^{r-1} vectors Z without duplicating the calculation of any static problems. It turns out that this enumeration method calls for the solution of $2^{\tilde{r}1}$ static problems (Wesolowsky 1973).

15.3.7 Incomplete DP

Noted that there is no need to evaluate all of the branches. At each stage, as one proceeds from the last period to the first, only those branches where c, is not greater than the stage minimum need be kept. The saving in the number of static problems that needs to be evaluated is considerable. If one chooses only one of the branches in the case where a tie exists at any stage, the total number of static problems to be evaluated is $r(r+1)/2$ (Wesolowsky 1973).

$$1 + 2 + 3 + r = r(r+1)/2. \tag{15.28}$$

15.3.8 An Especial BIP

There are some points for relocation and we must select some of them, so that the total cost is minimized. For example, we calculate the cost of the policy that there are two relocations at time 3 and 4.

$$f_{13} = \sum_{i=1}^{m} w_i(t).d(x^{13}, p_i) \quad t \in [t_1, t_3]$$
$$f_{34} = \sum_{i=1}^{m} w_i(t).d(x^{34}, p_i) \quad t \in [t_3, t_4]. \tag{15.29}$$
$$f_{46} = \sum_{i=1}^{m} w_i(t).d(x^{46}, p_i) \quad t \in [t_4, t_6]$$

The total cost of this policy is:

$$F = \int_{t_1}^{t_3} f_{13} dt + \int_{t_3}^{t_4} f_{34} dt + \int_{t_4}^{t_6} f_{46} dt. \tag{15.30}$$

This policy can be shown with binary variable: $Z_{13} = Z_{34} = Z_{46} = 1$. We propose a binary integer programming (BIP) model composed of six steps (Z.-Farahani et al. 2009).

Step 1 There are $ñ2$ time candidates for relocation. Adding $t_1 = 0$ and $tn = T$ as relocation points yields the total of n points. The interval $[0,T]$ is divided into $ñ1$ subintervals. There are m demand points. Calculate:

$$w_i^j = \int_{t_j}^{t_{j+1}} w_i(t) dt \quad j = 1, ..., n-1 \quad i = 1, ..., m \tag{15.31}$$

15 Dynamic Facility Location Problem

Step 2 Define w_i^{jk}:

$$w_i^{jk} = \int_{t_j}^{t_k} w_i(t)dt \quad k = j+1, ..., n \quad j = 1, 2, ..., n-1 \quad i = 1, 2, ..., m \quad j < k. \tag{15.32}$$

For every demand point i, Calculate the value of w_i^{jk} for all values of j and k. This generates the integrated weight associated with the ith demand point for the location of the facility during the time interval $[t_j, t_k)$.

Step 3 For each interval $[b_j, b_k)$, find the optimal location of the facility (x_{jk}, y_{jk}). By the value of w_i^{jk} and the coordinates of the existing facilities (a_i, b_i), the optimal solution for facility location is used.

Step 4 If the new facility has the same location during the time interval $[t_j, t_k)$, calculate C_{jk}, the location cost, using the following relationship:

$$C_{jk} = \sum_{i=1}^{m} w_i^{jk} \cdot d(X.P_i), \tag{15.33}$$

where $d(X^{jk}, p_i)$ is the distance between the optimal location of the new facility and demand point i for $[t_j, t_k)$ and X_{jk} is calculated in step 3.

Step 5 Using the cost coefficients in step 4, the following model is used to find the optimal relocation times:

m: number of existing facilities

w_i^j: the weight associated with demand point i in period j

$w_i(t)$: the weight associated with demand point i at time t

w_i^{jk}: the integrated weight associated with the ith demand point during the time interval of $[t_j, t_k)$.

(x^{jk}, y^{jk}): the optimal location of the new facility during the time interval of $[t_j, t_k)$.

S_j: is the relocation cost at time j.

$d(X^{jk}, p_i)$: the distance between the new facility and ith demand point during the time interval of $[t_j, t_k)$.

Z_{jk}: binary variable equal to 1 if the current relocation takes place at t_j and the next one at t_k, and is 0 otherwise.

$$\text{Min } F = \sum_{j=1}^{n-1} \sum_{k=j+1}^{n} C_{jk} \cdot Z_{jk} + \sum_{j=2}^{n-1} \sum_{k=j+1}^{n} S_j Z_{jk}, \tag{15.34}$$

$$\sum_{k=2}^{n} Z_{1k} = 1, \tag{15.35}$$

$$\sum_{j=1}^{k-1} Z_{jk} = \sum_{l=k+1}^{n} Z_{kl} \quad \forall k = 2, \ldots, n-1, \tag{15.36}$$

$$\sum_{j=1}^{n-1} Z_{jn} = 1 \quad \forall j, k, \tag{15.37}$$

$$Z_{jk} = 0, 1 \quad \forall j, k. \tag{15.38}$$

This is a binary integer programming (BIP) model with n constraints and $n(n+1)/2$ variables.

Equation (15.35) ensures that the relocation decision starts at time $t_1 = 0$.

Equation (15.36) enforce the consideration of the next relocation time exactly after the last relocation time.

Equation (15.37) guarantee that the decision making will continue to the end of planning horizon, T. The BIP model can be solved using optimization software such as LINGO and CPLEX.

The solution to this BIP model yields the times for relocation. The facility location for each time interval is found in step 3. The total cost of this policy is F.

Step 6 After solving the model, the following solution is obtained:
$Z_{1b} = Z_{bc} = \ldots = Z_{st} = Z_{tn} = 1$ and all the other variable are equal to 0. So $t_1, t_b, \ldots, t_c, t_s, t_t$ are relocation times and $(x^{tn}, y^{tn}), (x^{st}, y^{st}), \ldots, (x^{bc}, y^{bc})$, (x^{1b}, y^{1b}) are the locations of the new facilities after relocation. The total cost of this policy is F.

In this model there are no constraints on the number of relocations. The maximum number of possible relocations is:

$$N = \sum_{j=1}^{n-1} \sum_{k=j+1}^{n} Z_{jk}. \tag{15.39}$$

If we wish to limit this number to L, the following constraint is added to model.

$$\sum_{j=1}^{n-1} \sum_{k=j+1}^{n} Z_{jk} \leq L. \tag{15.40}$$

15.3.8.1 Location Dependent Relocation Cost

Another situation closer to real world applications is the case in which relocation cost depends on the location of the facility; i.e. the facility relocation cost at the time t_j is $S_j(X = x, y)$ instead of S_j, where $X = (x, y)$ is the location of facility. For instance, one major part of the cost for locating facility is the price of land. Price of land for locating a facility will differ from one location to another.

In this model, we solve the problem similar to the procedure described in the pervious section. The only difference is that the cost of the best location during $[t_j, t_k)$ will be the minimum of the function:

$$C_{jk} = S_j(X) + \sum_{i=1}^{m} w_i^{jk} \times d(X^{jk}, p_i). \qquad (15.41)$$

This means that the second term of the objective function is not independent of the first term.

If $S_j(X = x, y)$ is differentiable, the minimum of C_{jk} could be calculated directly. When squared Euclidean distances are used, C_{jk} is differentiable and there is no need to use Hyper approximation procedure (HAP) for the calculation of the optimal C_{jk} (Z.-Farahani et al. 2009).

15.3.8.2 Relocation Cost Depend on the Location of Facility Before and After Relocation

Sometimes, relocation cost at the time t_j depends on the location of facility before and after t_j. In practical cases, there are situations in which the cost of relocating to a closer location is lower than relocating to a farther location. For example, in mobile facilities, the relocation cost will be a function of distance between the location of facility before and after relocation time. In this case the objective function is:

$$C_{jk} = u(t_j) \times d(X^{hj}, X^{jk}) + \sum_{i=1}^{m} w_i^{jk} \times d(X^{jk}, p_i). \qquad (15.42)$$

where th is the last relocation point before t_j, $d(X^{hj}, X^{jk})$ is the distance between the location of facility before t_j (X^{hj}) and after t_j (X^{hk}). In addition, $u(t_j)$ is the unit distance cost for relocating a facility from its location to another new location, at the time t_j. In this case, Lemma 3 is not satisfied and the objective function is not additive.

For a finite time horizon, we propose to perform complete enumeration and find all of feasible paths from t_0 to t_{n+1}. When n is large we must resort to heuristic algorithms. For each feasible solution, we should calculate the objective function and select the minimum. The number of these feasible paths can be calculated with respect to the number of relocations (0, 1, 2) as follows:

$$1 + \binom{n}{1} + \binom{n}{2} + \ldots + \binom{n}{n} = 2^n. \qquad (15.43)$$

For solving the objective function of each feasible path, note that if both $d(X^{jk}, p_i)$ and $d(X^{hj}, X^{jk})$ are rectilinear distance, we can solve an equivalent LP substituting the absolute function with new variables and constraints. If both $d(X^{jk}, p_i)$ and $d(X^{hj}, X^{jk})$ are squared Euclidean distance, the objective function is differentiable and the problem can easily be solved. If the type of distances related to $d(X^{jk}, p_i)$ and $d(X^{hj}, X^{jk})$ is different or both are Euclidean, we can use the HAP (Francis and Lowe 1992).

15.3.9 Relocation at Continues Times

As it was noted, relocation can take place only at pre-determined points in time or, at any point in the time horizon. In this section, first, we will propound a lemma and then we will study the facility location–relocation problem with linear time dependent weights.

Roll Theorem (Leithold 1976). If $f(x)$ is continuous in $[0,T]$ and differentiable in $(0,T)$ and if $f(a) = f(b)$, then there is a c such that $a < c < b$ and $f(c) = 0$.

Suppose that there are no candidate times for relocation, and relocation can take place at any point in the time horizon $[0,T]$. Therefore, time break (B) enters the cost objective function. The cost objective function will be:

$$F(B, x_1, y_1, x_2, y_2) = \int_0^B \sum_{i=1}^m w_i(t).d(X_1, p_i).dt + \int_B^T \sum_{i=1}^m w_i(t).d(X_2, p_i).dt, \quad (15.44)$$

where $0 < B < T$.

Given a distinct time break (B), other variables are calculated, and for every B there is only one point (x_1, y_1) and (x_2, y_2). In other words, (x_1, y_1) and (x_2, y_2) functions of B).

$$x_1 = f_1(B)\ y_1 = f_2(B)\ x_2 = f_3(B)\ y_2 = f_4(B). \quad (15.45)$$

According to (15.44) and (15.45), the cost function is:

$$F(B, x_1, y_1, x_2, y_2) = F(B, f_1(B), f_2(B), f_3(B), f_4(B)). \quad (15.46)$$

Relation (15.46) shows that the cost function is function of time break and we can use F as $F(B)$ according to (15.44):

$$F(B = 0) = F(B = T). \quad (15.47)$$

The approximate rectilinear distance is (Francis and Lowe 1992):

$$|x - a_i| + |y - b_i| = \sqrt{(x - a_i)^2 + \varepsilon} + \sqrt{(y - b_i)^2 + \varepsilon}. \quad (15.48)$$

Using this approximation, the cost function of (15.47) is continuous in $[0, T]$ and derivable in $(0, T)$.

According to Roll Theorem, there is at least one B, such that $0 < B < T$ and is an extreme point for cost function.

It is important to note that the weights, $w_i(t)$, cannot be negative in the $[0, T]$. For the linear weights the following holds:

$$u_i \geq 0, \quad v_i \geq -\frac{u_i}{T}. \quad (15.49)$$

15 Dynamic Facility Location Problem

For single relocation, linear weight function is put in the cost function (15.44):

$$\int_0^B \sum_{i=1}^m w_i(t).d(X_1, p_i).dt + \int_B^T \sum_{i=1}^m w_i(t).d(X_2, p_i).dt =$$

$$\int_0^B \sum_{i=1}^m d(X_1, p_i).(u_i + v_i.t).dt + \int_B^T \sum_{i=1}^m d(X_2, p_i).(u_i + v_i.t).dt. \quad (15.50)$$

Integration and sigma are replaced:

$$\sum_{i=1}^m \int_{.}^B d(X_1, p_i).(u_i + v_i.t).dt + \sum_{i=1}^m \int_B^T d(X_2, p_i).(u_i + v_i.t).dt =$$

$$\sum_{i=1}^m d(X_1, p_i).(u_i.t + \frac{1}{2}v_i.t^2)\Big|_0^B + \sum_{i=1}^m d(X_2, p_i).(u_i.t + \frac{1}{2}v_i.t^2)\Big|_B^T =$$

$$\sum_{i=1}^m d(X_1, p_i).(u_i.B + \frac{1}{2}v_i.B^2) + \sum_{i=1}^m d(X_2, p_i).(u_i.(T-B)$$

$$+ \frac{1}{2}v_i.(T^2 - B^2)). \quad (15.51)$$

For approximate rectilinear function, (15.51) will be differentiable and concave and, therefore, we will have:

$$\frac{\partial F}{\partial B} = \frac{\partial}{\partial B}\left\langle \sum_{i=1}^m d(X_1, p_i).(u_i.B + \frac{1}{2}v_i.B^2) \right\rangle$$

$$+ \frac{\partial}{\partial B}\left\langle \sum_{i=1}^m d(X_2, p_i).(u_i.(T-B) + \frac{1}{2}v_i.(T^2 - B^2)) \right\rangle. \quad (15.52)$$

Integration and sigma are replaced:

$$\frac{\partial F}{\partial B} = \sum_{i=1}^m \frac{\partial}{\partial B}\left\langle d(X_1, p_i).(u_i.B + \frac{1}{2}v_i.B^2) \right\rangle + \sum_{i=1}^m \frac{\partial}{\partial B}\left\langle d(X_2, p_i).(u_i.(T-B) \right.$$

$$\left. + \frac{1}{2}v_i.(T^2 - B^2)) \right\rangle = \sum_{i=1}^m d(X_1, p_i).(u_i + v_i.B)$$

$$+ \sum_{i=1}^m d(X_2, p_i).(-u_i - v_i.B) \quad (15.53)$$

$$= \sum_{i=1}^m d(X_1, p_i).(u_i + v_i.B) - \sum_{i=1}^m d(X_2, p_i).(u_i + v_i.B).$$

In the optimal point (15.53) must be equal to zero:

$$\sum_{i=1}^{m} \langle d(X_1, p_i).(u_i + v_i.B) - d(X_2, p_i).(u_i + v_i.B)\rangle$$

$$= 0 \Rightarrow \sum_{i=1}^{m} \langle (u_i + v_i.B)(d(X_1, p_i) - d(X_2, p_i))\rangle$$

$$= 0 \Rightarrow \sum_{i=1}^{m} u_i.(d(X_1, p_i) - d(X_2, p_i))$$

$$- \sum_{i=1}^{m} v_i B.(d(X_1, p_i) - d(X_2, p_i)) = 0. \tag{15.54}$$

Therefore, B will be equal to:

$$B = -\frac{\sum_{i=1}^{m} u_i.(d(X_1, p_i) - d(X_2, p_i))}{\sum_{i=1}^{m} v_i B.(d(X_1, p_i) - d(X_2, p_i))}. \tag{15.55}$$

Note that to make sure that B is at minimum, the second derivation must be positive.

$$\frac{\partial^2 F}{\partial B^2} > 0 \qquad \frac{\partial^2 F}{\partial B^2} = \frac{\partial}{\partial B}\left(\frac{\partial F}{\partial B}\right) =$$

$$\frac{\partial}{\partial B}\left(\sum_{i=1}^{m} d(X_1, p_i).(u_i + v_i.B) - \sum_{i=1}^{m} d(X_2, p_i).(u_i + v_i.B)\right) \Rightarrow$$

$$\frac{\partial^2 F}{\partial B^2} = \sum_{i=1}^{m} v_i.(d(X_1, p_i) - d(X_2, p_i)) > 0. \tag{15.56}$$

According to lemmas 3 and 4, if the relocation times are determined then:

$$w_i^{(1)} = \int_0^B (u_i + v_i t).dt = u_i t + \frac{1}{2}v_i t^2 \Big|_0^B = u_i B + \frac{1}{2}v_i B^2$$

$$w_i^{(2)} = \int_B^T (u_i + v_i t).dt = u_i t + \frac{1}{2}v_i t^2 \Big|_B^T = u_i(T-B) + \frac{1}{2}v_i(T^2 - B^2). \tag{15.57}$$

Therefore, using $w_i^{(1)}$ we can solve facility location problem and obtain the location of the facility before relocation, (x_1, y_1), then using $w^{(2)}{}_i$, the location of facility after relocation (x_1, y_1) is reached.

15 Dynamic Facility Location Problem

Obviously, doing these calculations with hand, particularly for large problems, is very difficult. However, nowadays, with the technological advances, doing this calculation with computer is not so difficult and time consuming. Thus, in this subsection, we present an algorithm that obtains optimal point in this problem.

15.3.10 Iterative Algorithm for Obtaining Optimal Solution

In this algorithm, first an optional B in interval $[0, T]$ is selected, and $w_i^{(1)}$ and $w_i^{(2)}$ are calculated using (15.57). Then, (x_1, y_1) and (x_2, y_2) are calculated through solving the two obtained location problems based on $w_i^{(1)}$ and $w_i^{(2)}$. Next, by substituting these four variables in (15.55), a new B value is obtained. All the mentioned steps are repeated using this new B. It can be shown by Roll theorem that these iterations converge to a B point.

Not that (15.56) must be satisfied in order to have the F function minimized for the given B value, otherwise, we cannot claim that the obtained B minimizes F. Even if (15.56) is satisfied, there is no proof that the obtained point is global minimum. To solve this problem, repeat the algorithm with different Bs as a starting point. Therefore, if a local minimum exists, we can obtain global minimum.

As it was explained before, the steps of the global minimum algorithm for the obtained break time and optimal location are as fallows:

Step 1 Generate a reasonable number for search steps. The smaller this value, the more accurate and the slower the algorithm, and vice versa. Set $count = 0, k = 1$, $F^* = \infty$. Enter coordinates of the existing facilities, linear functions parameters (u_i, v_i), and permissible errors.

Step 2 Set $count = count + step$ if $count \geq T$ then go to step 10 else go to next step.

Step 3 Set $B^{k1} = count$.

Step 4 As described before and by considering B^{k1}, calculate values of (x_1^{k-1}, y_1^{k-1}) and (x_2^{k-1}, y_2^{k-1}).

Step 5 calculate the result of (15.55) as follows:

$$B^k = -\frac{\sum_{i=1}^{m} u_i \cdot (d(X_1^{k-1}, p_i) - d(X_2^{k-1}, p_i))}{\sum_{i=1}^{m} v_i B \cdot (d(X_1^{k-1}, p_i) - d(X_2^{k-1}, p_i))}. \quad (15.58)$$

Step 6 If $\left|B^k - B^{k-1}\right| > \delta$ then set $k = k + 1$ and go to step 4 else go to the next step.

Step 7 calculate the result of (15.56) as follows:

$$\sum_{i=1}^{m} v_i \cdot (d(X_1^{k-1}, p_i) - d(X_2^{k-1}, p_i)). \quad (15.59)$$

If this value is negative then set $k = 1$ and go to step 2 else go to the next step.

Step 8 calculate the cost using the following equation:

$$\begin{aligned}F = &\sum_{i=1}^{m}(d(X_1^{k-1}, p_i) - d(X_2^{k-1}, p_i)).(u_i.B^k + \tfrac{1}{2}v_i.B^{k2})\\ &+ \sum_{i=1}^{m} d(X_2^{k-1}, p_i).(u_i.T + \tfrac{1}{2}v_i.T^2)).\end{aligned} \quad (15.60)$$

Step 9 If $F < F^*$ then set $F^* = F, B^* = B^k, (x_1^*, y_1^*) = (x_1^{k-1}, y_1^{k-1})$, $(x_2^*, y_2^*) = (x_2^{k-1}, y_2^{k-1})$, $k = 1$ and go to step 2 else without changes go to step 2

Step 10 $B^*, (x_1^*, y_1^*), (x_2^*, y_2^*)$ and F^* are optimal solutions.

Note that there is also another approach for solving single relocation and multi relocation time-independent problems that interested readers are referred to Owen and Daskin (1998) for detailed information.

15.3.11 Static Stochastic Techniques

The dynamic models described in the previous sections attempt to locate facilities assuming that input parameters are known values or vary deterministically over time.

In stochastic location problems, any number of system parameters might be taken as uncertain. Stochastic location problems can be broken down into probabilistic approach and the scenario planning approach (Owen and Daskin (1998)).

15.3.11.1 Probabilistic Approach

Sometimes, we examine models which capture the stochastic aspects of facility location through explicit consideration of the probability distributions associated with modeled random quantities.

These distributions can be incorporated into standard mathematical programs, or in a queuing framework (Owen and Daskin 1998).

15.3.11.2 Scenario Planning Approach

Scenario planning is a method in which decision makers capture uncertainty by specifying a number of possible future states. The objective is to find solutions which perform well under all scenarios. In some applications, scenario planning replaces forecasting as a way to evaluate trends and potential changes in the business environment. Firms can thus develop strategic responses to a range of environmental changes, more adequately preparing themselves for the uncertain future. Under such circumstances, scenarios are qualitative descriptions of plausible future states, derived from the present state with consideration of potential major industry events. In other applications, scenario planning is used as a tool for formulating and solving specific operational problems (Owen and Daskin 1998).

The goal of scenario planning is to specify a set of scenarios, which represent the possible realizations of unknown problem parameters and to consider the range of scenarios in determining a compromise (robust) location solution (Owen and Daskin 1998). There are at least three approaches to incorporating scenario planning into location modeling:

- Optimizing the expected performance over all scenarios,
- Optimizing the worst-case performance, and
- Minimizing the expected or worst-case regret across all scenarios. (Owen and Daskin 1998).

Scenario planning approach, though invaluable in dealing with conditions where there is uncertainty about input parameter information, has two disadvantages:

- Defining scenario and assigning probabilities to them is difficult
- Because of the high calculation efforts required, the number of evaluated scenarios are kept low and therefore, the future condition is restricted (might not be realistic enough) (Snyder 2006).

The regret associated with a scenario is calculated by comparing the performance of the optimal locations for the scenario (had planners known for certain that the scenario would be realized) with the performance of the compromise locations when the scenario is realized. (Owen and Daskin 1998)

In other words, by extent of loss, also referred to as "opportunity loss" it is meant what the decision maker pays for performing under the conditions of not knowing about the occurrence of a scenario as compared with his/her performance in the compromise locations when the scenario has already realized (Snyder 2006).

Thus, using a regret-based objective allows us to evaluate robust solution alternatives with respect to the optimal solution obtained under data certainty.

One should use this measure in objectives which:

- Require assessment of scenario realization probabilities, and
- Assume that all scenarios are of equal probability.

15.4 Case Study

In this section, we will introduce some case studies related to Dynamic Facility location problems.

15.4.1 A Dynamic Model for School Network Planning (Antunes and Peeters 2000)

This case study describes a dynamic multi-period optimization model that has been used in Portugal to formulate planning proposals for the evolution of several school networks. The solution to this problem gives information about where and when new schools should be built, what their sizes should be, which schools should be kept open and which ones should be closed. Additionally, for the schools which remain open, it identifies which schools should maintain the same size and which should be resized, becoming larger or smaller.

This model considers the following features:

- Over the planning horizon, each site will not change its state more than once;
- Both setup and operation costs have a component dependent on capacity and a component dependent on attendance; and
- Facility size is limited to pre-defined standards, expressed in terms of an architectural module, for instance, a given number of classrooms.

The objective function of this model minimizes the total discounted (socio-economic) costs of a set of facilities. Facility costs are divided into three parts: fixed costs; capacity-variable costs proportional to the number of modules; and attendance-variable costs proportional to the number of users, a significant part of which will normally consist of transport costs.

The approaches that had been used to solve this model are as following:

- Branch and bound (B&B), but this method is unsuccessful to solve a few $10 \times 10 \times 3$ (centers × sites × periods) problems.
- Dual-based and LR exact methods. However, this kind of method would hardly be successful in the current case.
- The "myopic" and "panoramic" approaches (heuristics). These methods in the presence of severe capacity inadequacy and important demand decreases _ the situation encountered in many Portuguese regions when the expansion of elementary education was decided _ didn't have successful function.
- SA: For 50 problems in 17, SA was unable to find the optimum B&B solution. Moreover, in all these 17 problems, it came quite close to it, as the difference was always smaller than 1%. In the remaining 33 problems, SA behaved at least as efficiently as B&B.

15.4.2 A Multiperiod Set Covering for Dynamic Redeployment of Ambulances (Rajagopalan et al. 2008)

The dynamic available coverage location model was formulated to determine the minimum number of ambulances and their locations for each time cluster in which significant changes in demand pattern take place while meeting coverage requirements with a predetermined reliability.

A straightforward search algorithm was developed to determine the minimum number of servers to provide the coverage and availability requirements. The algorithm starts with an estimated fleet size for the first time interval, which is called a reactive Tabu search (RTS) algorithm. A look-ahead procedure (LAP) within the RTS was used to compute server specific busy probabilities and the resulting coverage. Results showed that the RTS with LAP takes them very close to number of servers required to satisfy the coverage constraint generally 2–3 times faster than the algorithm without LAP.

15.4.3 *A Multi-period Model for Combat Logistics (Gue 2003)*

In the past, logistics support for amphibious warfare has depended on a large, land-based infrastructure, with trucks accomplishing most of the distribution. New war fighting concepts for the US Marine Corps emphasize small, highly-mobile forces supported instead from the sea. The goal of logistics planners is to support these forces with as little inventory on land as possible. But the best distribution system depends on a number of operational levers.

For better conception, this study has considered a sea base containing combat and support units. Each combat unit is required to reach a particular set of objectives on land; support units are positioned to provide supplies as needed. Combat units consume food, water, ammunition, and fuel during each time period. Quantities may vary depending on the intensity of conflict or other concerns. Supply units are free to deploy, move, and to build up and deplete inventories as necessary to meet demand. A fleet of vehicles is available to transport combat units to objectives or intermediate points, to move entire supply units, or to transport supplies between units. Naturally, vehicle types are constrained to transport only between feasible origin–destination pairs. The problem is to determine the locations of supply units for each time period and the shipments of each commodity between units, such that there is as little land-based inventory as possible.

In this case a multi-period, facility location and multi-commodity flow model is formulated as a mixed integer program. The battle space is modeled as a network of two types of nodes, combat and supply nodes. In model, it is assumed that the combat nodes are given in a battle plan and that supply units may not occupy them. And also that intelligence could provide a set of candidate locations for supply units. The objective is to minimize the total inventory of land-based support units, in keeping with the primary purpose of sea-based logistics. Decisions in the model are, for each time period, the locations of support units, inventories held by the units, and the amounts shipped between units.

Two limitations of this model are:

- Transportation capacity is modeled in units of lb mile, the model could propose a solution that is impossible to implement in practice.
- A solution could also require more transporters than are available.

References

Andretta G, Mason FM (1994) A not on a perfect forward procedure for a single facility dynamic location/relocation problem. Oper Res Lett 15:81–83

Antunes A, Peeters D (2000) A dynamic optimization model for school network planning. Socio Econ Plan Sci 34(2):101–120

Canel C, Khumawala B, Law J, Loh A (2001) An algorithm for the capacitated, multi-commodity multi-period facility location problem. Comput Oper Res 28:411–427

Chand S (1988) Decision/forecast horizon results for a single facility dynamic location/relocation problem. Oper Res Lett 7(5):247–251

Daskin MS, Hopp WJ, Medina B (1992) Forecast horizon and dynamic facility location planning. Ann Oper Res 40:125–151

Dias J, Captivo E, Climaco J (2004) Dynamic multi-level capacitated and uncapacitated location problems: an approach using primal-dual heuristics. Inesc-Coimbra Research Report 26

Dias J, Captivo E, Climaco J (2007) Efficient primal-dual heuristic for a dynamic location problem. J Comput Oper Res 34:1800–1823

Drezner Z (1995) Facility location: a survey of applications and methods. Springer, New York

Drezner Z, Wesolowsky GP (1991) Facility location when demand is time dependent. Naval Res Logist 38:763–777

Emamizadeh B, Z-Farahani R (1997a) Facility location and relocation in global manufacturing strategy. Paper presented at the FAIM conference, Middlesbrough, England

Emamizadeh B, Z-Farahani R (1997b) Facility location and relocation with time-dependent weight. Paper presented at the DSI Conference, Sidney, Australia

Francis RL, McGinnis LF, White JA (1992) Facility layout and location: an analytical approach, 2nd edn. Prentice Hall, Englewood Cliffs, NJ

Gue k (2003) A dynamic distribution model for combat logistics. Comput Oper Res 30:367–381

Hormozi AM, Khumawala BM (1997) An improved algorithm for solving a multi-period facility location problem. IIE Trans 28:105–114

Huang WV, Batta R, Babu AJG (1990) Relocation-promotion problem with Euclidean distance. Eur J Oper Res 46:61–72

Leithold L (1976) The calculus with analytic geometry, 3rd edn. Harper & Row, New York

Mirchandani PB, Francis RL (1990) Discrete location theory. Wiley, New York

Owen S, Daskin M (1998) Strategic facility location: a review. Eur J Oper Res 111:423–447

Rajagopalan H, Saydamb C, Xiaoc J (2008) A multiperiod set covering location model for dynamic redeployment of ambulances. Comput Oper Res 35:814–826

Romauch M, Hartl RFH (2005) Dynamic facility location with stochastic demands. Lecture notes in computer science (Stochastic algorithms: foundations and applications), vol 3777

Rosental R, White J, Young D (1978) Stochastic dynamic location analysis. Manage Sci 124(6):645–653

Scott AJ (1971) Dynamic location–allocation systems: some basic planning strategies. Environ Plan 3:73–82

Snyder LV (2006) Facility location under uncertainty: a review. IIE Trans 38(7):547

Snyder LV, Daskin MS, Teo CP (2007) The stochastic location model with risk pooling. Eur J Oper Res 179:1221–1238

Wesolowsky GO (1973) Dynamic facility location. Manage Sci 19(11):1241–1248

Wesolowsky GO, Truscott WG (1975) The multiperiod location–allocation problem with relocation of facilities. Manage Sci 22(1):57–65

Z.-Farahani R, Drezner Z, Asgari N (2009) Single facility location and relocation problem with time-dependent weights and discrete planning horizon. Ann Oper Res 167(1):353–368

Chapter 16
Multi-Criteria Location Problem

Masoud Hekmatfar and Maryam SteadieSeifi

Decision-making is the process of selecting a possible subset of decisions from all the available alternatives (feasible space). We introduced many decision-making models including one objective function, so far. Almost there are many criteria for judging the optimality of decision. In this situation, we will be faced with the multi-criteria decision-making (MCDM). There are many methods to solve the MCDM problems, but all of them are common in some factors that are as follows (Hwang and Masud 1979; Hwang and Yoon 1981):

- Multiple objectives/attributes
- Conflict among criteria
- Incomparable units
- Design or selection: solutions to these problems consist of two classes, one of them designs the best alternative and the second one selects the best solution among the specified finite alternatives

The MCDM is classified into two categories:

- The multi-objective decision-making (MODM), and
- The multi-attribute decision-making (MADM)

First, briefly, we define some prevalent important terms used in this area (Hwang and Masud 1979; Hwang and Yoon 1981):

- Criteria: Criteria are standards of judgment or rules to test acceptability
- Goal: Goals are a priori levels of aspiration that are determined by decision makers (DMs) with explicit term
- Objective: Objectives are the directions that increase the inspiration of DMs (Maybe it seems that the two recent terms have a common meaning, while objectives give the desired direction, goals give a desired level to achieve.)
- Optimal solution: Optimal solution is one which results in maximum value of each of the objective functions. Because of the conflicting objectives, this solution will not usually exist
- Efficient solution (Nondominated solution): $\tilde{x}$ is an efficient solution if there exists no other feasible solution that will yield an improvement in one objective without causing a reduction in at least one other objective

- Preferred solution: A preferred solution is selected by DM from efficient solutions
- Satisfing solution: A Satisfing solution Satisfies a minimum acceptable level for all attributes of the problem

The MCDM comprises some general techniques that can be used in many types of application including facilities location.

The remainder of this chapter will first present some classifications, objective functions and mathematical models of MCLPs. Next, solution techniques will be briefly reviewed. Finally, in Sect. 16.3 some real-world case studies will be introduced.

16.1 Applications and Classifications

Multi-criteria analysis of location problems has received considerable attention within the scope of *continuous and network models* in recent years. There are several problems that are accepted as classical ones:

- The point-objective problem (Wendell and Hurter 1973; Hansen et al. 1980; Pelegrin and Fernandez 1988; Carrizosa et al. 1993)
- The continuous multi-criteria min–sum facility location problem (FLP) (Hamacher et al. 1996; Puerto and Fernandez 1999)
- The network multi-criteria median location problem (Hamacher and Nickel 1998; Wendell et al. 1977)

So far, multi-criteria analysis of *discrete location models* has attracted less attention. Several authors have dealt with problems and applications of multi-criteria decision analysis in this field. For instance,

- Ross and Soland (1980) worked on multi-activity multi-facility problems and proposed an interactive solution method to compute non-dominated solutions to compare and choose from
- Lee et al. (1981) studied an application of integer goal programming for facility location with multiple competing objectives
- Solanki (1991) applies an approximation scheme to generate a set of non-dominated solutions to a bi-objective location problem
- Ogryczak (1999) looks for symmetrically efficient location patterns in a multi-criteria discrete location problem

In general, none of the above papers focuses on the complete determination of the whole set of non-dominated solutions. The only exception is the paper by Ross and Soland (1980) that gives a theoretical characterization but does not exploit its algorithmic possibilities.

16.2 Models

Although location problems have a long history, we can assume that the modern location has been started from Weber research on one vehicle location problem with the objective function based on minimizing the total rectilinear distances. This trend was continued up to 1960s, minimizing the total distances (min–sum).

In 1960s, Hakimi (1964) represented a new kind of problems, minimizing the maximal distance (min–max). In this decade, many operation researchers worked on location problems (Eiselt and Laporte 1995).

In the mid 1970s, it seems that the topic of obnoxious location problem was represented by some researchers such as Goldman and also Church and Granfinkel for the first time (Eiselt and Laporte 1995). Maybe we can assume that after coming up of this topic in multi-objective problems, the MCDM techniques were started to be used to solve the MCDM problems.

Since the aim of this section is FLPs from objective functions point of view, in the following sections we try to represent the main classification of objective functions, conflicting of contradictory objectives and at last some case study of location problems.

We concentrate to display these problems and their classifications based on their objective functions.

16.2.1 Private and Public Facilities

Problems that are naturally multi-objectives are generally discussed in public facilities, semi-noxious facilities and desirable facilities. Cohon (1978) represented MCLPs in a separate section. He divided FLPs into two main classes:

- Facility location in private sections
- Facility location in public sector

In the first group, problems have almost only one objective and the main purpose is almost minimizing the cost of construction, production and transportation, or the purpose is maximizing the profit earned from constructing the facility. This kind of problems is located in class of classic location problems.

In the second group, problems that are efficient in governments' final decision-making (directly or indirectly), are divided into three classes:

- Facilities with ordinary services
- Facilities with emergency services
- Facilities with undesirable effect

In ordinary services like libraries, hygienic clinics etc., the purpose usually consists of the maximizing of service to more people.

In emergency services like fire stations the purpose is usually consisted of maximizing the minimal covering.

In undesirable facilities, there is an undesirable facility like a place for repulsing refuses, wastes, etc., and the purpose is consisted of minimizing the effect of this area on the residents near it.

It seems that the Cohon's (1978) classification has some problems and it can be possible to represent better classification. We represent some of them in later parts.

In public sectors, the main problem is the lack of proper criteria and their different natures. For example in a fire station location problem, there are two conflicting objectives, one of them is consisted of minimizing the cost of facility and the other one is consisted of preserving the human life. so how the human life can be evaluated?

In Cohon (1978), two location problems are represented, emergency services location problem (construction of a fire station in Baltimore) and power generation location problem in a power station. Readers can refer to Cohon (1978) for more details.

16.2.2 Balancing Objective Functions

A group of objective functions are discussed in public facility and services and the purpose is consisted of maximizing the equity and balanced services among users. These problems are introduced as fairness functions, balancing functions and equity functions.

Displaying the value of equity is varied in different problems, but it can be possible to generate a new class of objective functions based on a development from min–sum functions and a statistic view.

In prevalent min–sum functions, it is easy to show that minimizing the total distances of demand points from facility is statistically equal to minimizing the average of distances _ with assuming one facility and locating in one dimension. (see Eq. 16.1).

$$\min : \sum_{i=1}^{n}(x_i - L) = n \times \frac{\sum_{i=1}^{n}(x_i - L)}{n} \rightarrow n \times \mu_d \qquad (16.1)$$

where L is the situation of facility.

We can assume some other functions like the total squared distance of demands from facility or cubical distance of demands.

From statistics point of view, the total distances (first torque) are related to average distances, total squared distances (second torque) are related to variance of distances, and cubical distances (third torque) are related to scale of symmetry for point distribution around facility location place. In other words, by minimizing the second torque we can obtain a set of solutions in which the distance oscillation of demand points from the facility location are minimized.

With minimizing the total cubical distances, the set of solutions will finally have less asymmetry. It means that there is not anyone who lives very close or very far from the facility.

Balancing objective functions can reach a better solution in dealing with public FLPs and if we see these three functions simultaneously, it will be necessary to use techniques of multi-objective programming (Eiselt and Laporte 1995).

16.2.3 Pull, Push and Pull–Push Objectives

The various types of facilities from customer point of view were represented by Eiselt and Laporte (1995) as follows:

- Desirable
- Undesirable
- Partly desirable
- Partly undesirable
- Indifferent

According to an acceptable classification which was represented by Krarup et al. (2002), Curtin and Church (2003), and Eiselt and Laporte (1995), objective functions are divided into two main classes: Pull and Push. The combination of these two classes is introduced as pull–push term and is a major topic in multi-objective real problems.

Another kind of classifications is related to service distribution and establishment of equity which is represented as balancing objective by Eiselt and Laporte (1995).

Pull Objectives The classic location problems, desirable facilities and generally older location problems have pull objective functions. For example, it is tried to minimize the distance between production plants and consuming markets which yielded minimizing the cost of transportation, maximizing the availability of customers and increasing part of the market.

The classic pull-objective functions are generally divided into four classes: P-median (min–sum), P-center (min–max), UFLP[1] (min–sum) and QAP (min–sum).

Push Objectives Most of the undesirable location problems such as obnoxious and noxious and also dispersion models have push objective functions. It means that in these problems the purpose is consisted of decreasing the noxious effect of facility on demand points. Since in most cases the noxious effect has an inverse relation with the distance, the purpose of these problems is consisted of maximizing the distance between facility and demand points. A complete survey of these problems has been represented by Curtin and Church (2003).

Erkut and Neuman (1990) made a comparison of dispersion models and divided them into four main classes: P-dispersion (max–min–min), P-defense (max–sum–

---

[1] Uncapacitated Facility Location Problem

min), Anti-hub (max–min–sum) and Maxi-sum dispersion/P-maxian (max–sum–sum). It can be seen that they employed a three-syllable naming convention for objective functions with maximizing aim to distinguish between different types of dispersion. Using this convention, the first syllabus for each model was "Max" denoting that all models attempt to maximize the amount of dispersion among selected facility sites. Both the second and third syllables were either "sum" or "min". In the second syllable, a "sum" operator indicates a concern for overall system performance while a "min" operator indicates a concern for worst-case performance (here least distance). The third syllable is again either "sum" or "min", and it refers to which facility interactions comprise the minimum distance to be considered by the formulation. When the "min" operator is employed, the objective function is only forced by the minimum distance between *any two* facilities in a given solution. The "sum" operator indicates that the distances from each facility to all other facilities will force the objective function.

Push–Pull Objectives As it was indicated in the previous sections, in most of the real problems, simultaneously there are some conflicted objectives. It means that objective functions are combined with desirable and undesirable effects. It is noticed that these problems deal with interference of government like municipal, ecological organization, etc. as an example of these conflicted objectives, assume that the purpose is consisted of both increasing the distance between production plants and residential places and also increasing the cost of transportation, decreasing the attraction of professions, etc.

There is a clear example about these types of problems. In establishing a superstore or a sport club, the purpose of investors is decreasing the distance between their buildings and residential places to attract more customers, but residents prefer to live not too far and not too close to these facilities. Such problems are introduced with terms like "close but not too close" and "never in my back yard". These classes of problems had not been surveyed until 1970s.

A complete review about discrete location problems with push–pull objectives is represented by Krarup et al. (2002).

As it has been mentioned in previous sections, there is a classification of classical location problems with pull-objectives and desirable facilities: P-median, UFLP, QAP with min–sum objective function and P-center with min–max objective function. In QAP demand points and facilities are the same things and the demand is equal to material flow or information between facilities.

Also there is a classification of classical location problems with push-objectives: The first group is consisted of undesirable facilities which have noxious effect on health like chemical wastes and obnoxious effect on environment like the noise of sports clubs. The second group is consisted of dispersion models (Erkut and Neuman 1990) which there are classically undesirable effects between their facilities.

Krarup et al. (2002) represented that there is a famous problem, apparently first formulated in the early 1600s by Fermat, together with kind of a companion problem termed complementary problem (ComP). For a given triangle, Fermat asks for a fourth point such that the sum of its Euclidean distances, each weighted by $+1$, to the three given points is minimized. ComP differs from Fermat in that the weight associated with one of these points is -1 instead of $+1$.

It can be possible to divide push–pull problems into two major groups:

- Problems that only inter-facility interactions are considered, some being desirable, and some undesirable, this group is called a semi-dispersion model. There are some cases in this group such as: QAP with undesirable effect, quadratic knapsack problem that a number of facilities may be established at some predefined locations and then undesirable effect will be occurred, P-defense-sum problem and P-dispersion (Krarup et al. 2002)
- Problems that involve a set of demand points which pull the facilities towards them, whereas the undesirable part will be concerned with another set of subjects which push the facilities away. These problems are modeled as bi-objective with the attractions and the repulsions as two quite opposing objectives, each of which might still be multi-objective (Krarup et al. 2002)

The strategies that are used to solve these bi-objective problems are summarized as follows:

- Treat the bi-objective problem as really bi-objective and derive (approximations to) the Pareto-set
- Fix a bound on the obnoxious effects as a (set of) constraint(s) and optimize the desirable objective. This leads to standard pull objectives with additional restrictions
- Fix a bound for the desirable objective part and optimize the undesirable objective. This leads to standard push objectives with an additional constraint
- Combine the push and pull objectives into a single objective

16.2.4 Mathematical Models

In this section, some multi-objective problems with their mathematic models which Krarup et al. (2002) called them general push–pull will be represented. First, there are some remarks, which are represented as follows:

- The type of modeling has a major effect on final solution. It means that the style of exhibition in an undesirable effect (as you can see in following sections) will be affected on type of the objective function (the problem will be single objective or multiple objective)
- The type of objective functions is usually very different between desirable effect and undesirable effect. For example in a network problem, assume that the purpose is consisted of establishing a plant which pollutes the air. In one part of objective function with desirable effect, we can use shortest route method on the network to represent objective function with minimizing the transportation costs. In another part of objective function with undesirable effect (e.g. air pollution), we should use Euclidean distance to represent objective function, therefore the

problem will be NP-hard and we can not use the network properties to find the optimal solution
- Objectives with distance measuring unit are ascending functions in desirable effect and are descending functions in the undesirable effect with a negative (too negative) slope in minimal covering. Since one of the purposes of multi-objective functions is consisted of conflicting between objectives, it is necessary to use techniques of multiple objective functions to solve location problems (e.g. push–pull objectives)

16.2.4.1 Push–Pull Models

These models consider FLPs in which a set of individuals are specified, which are negatively (potentially) affected by the facilities. All the models considered are NP-hard to solve and thus the solution techniques must rely on some kind of enumerative methods. Heuristic approaches may also be applied for the solution of large-size instances (Krarup et al. 2002).

UFLPs with Additive Noxious Effects: The UFLP has some assumptions as follows:

- Finite set I of demand points (users)
- Finite set J of candidate points for demands (users)
- Each demand point (user) uses a certain facility
- Facilities are uncapacitated
- The number of facilities are exogenous
- Costs include variable cost of customer services and fixed cost f_j, the cost of establishing the facility in jth point

In this problem, the set k is consisted of a set of points such as candidate points and demand points. a_{kj} express the noxious effect of facility j on point k.

The initial model is formulated as follows:

$$\min Z : \left(\sum_{i \in I} \sum_{j \in J} c_{ij} y_{ij} + \sum f_j x_j \right) + \left(\sum_{k \in K} \sum_{j \in J} a_{kj} x_j \right) \quad (16.2)$$

Subject to

$$\sum_{j \in I} y_{ij} = 1, \quad i \in I \quad (16.3)$$

$$y_{ij} \leq x_j, \quad i \in I, \quad j \in J, \quad (16.4)$$

$$x_j \in \{0, 1\}, y_{ij} \in \{0, 1\}, \quad i \in I \quad j \in J. \quad (16.5)$$

If we change the model like $\tilde{f}_j = f_j + \sum_{k \in K} a_{kj}$, then the model will be converted to a UFLP standard model facility with single objective. We can see the importance of modeling in such problems.

UFLPs with Minimal Covering as Noxious Effects: In several situations, however, it is not reasonable to assume that the obnoxious effects are additive. For example, the facilities poison the subsoil water, every affected subject in some predefined radius will have to connect to the public water supply instead of using its own pump.

If pollution occurs in a certain radius, after that the other facilities do not have a noxious effect in that area. In other words, pollution occurs by establishing one facility and increasing in the number of facilities has not any effect on that.

Therefore, the cost of undesirable effect is constant and does not depend on the number of facilities located close to the subject. Since this is an obnoxious effect of minimal covering type, we obtain a different model which may be formulated as follows:

$$\min Z \left(\sum_{i \in J} \sum_{j \in J} c_{ij} y_{ij} + \sum_{j \in J} f_j x_j \right) + \sum_{k \in K} a_k z_k \qquad (16.6)$$

Subject to

$$\sum_{j \in I} y_{ij} = 1, \quad i \in I \qquad (16.7)$$

$$y_{ij} \leq x_{ij} \quad i \in I, \quad j \in J, \qquad (16.8)$$

$$x_j \leq z_k, \quad j \in C_k, \quad k \in K, \qquad (16.9)$$

$$x_j \in \{0,1\}, \quad y_{ij}, z_k \in \{0,1\}, \quad i \in I, \quad j \in J, \quad k \in K. \qquad (16.10)$$

where the variable z_k here is used to indicate whether subject k is affected by any facility or not.

If a facility is established around C_k from point k, it will be resulted in $z_k = 1$ and $a_k \geq 0$.

This problem will be solved by a bi-objective problem with minsum–minsum objective function. The represented method to solve this problem is approximation of Pareto-set and finally comparing and selecting by the DM (Krarup et al. 2002).

Another more stringent push objective is the worst-case like maxmin type, where one wants to minimize the maximal effect any subject feels from any of the facilities. When this objective is considered next to the minsum pull objective of the UFLP, another bi-objective model arises.

As before, we use a_{kj} to express the noxious effect of a facility at site j on subject k. Introducing $\tilde{a}_j = \max_{k \in K} a_{kj}$ and an auxiliary variable z for the second objective, we arrive at the linear, bi-objective MIP formulation:

$$\min \left(\sum \sum c_{ij} y_{ij} + \sum f_j x_j \right) \qquad (16.11)$$

$$\min z \tag{16.12}$$

Subject to

$$\sum y_{ij} = 1, \quad i \in I \tag{16.13}$$
$$y_{ij} \leq x_j, \quad i \in I, \quad j \in J, \tag{16.14}$$
$$x_j \in \{0,1\}, \quad y_{ij}, z_k \in \{0,1\}, \quad i \in I, \quad j \in J, \quad k \in K. \tag{16.15}$$

Since undesirable facility problems have multi-objective functions in real world, there are many case studies in the new topic of location science. Therefore, we will introduce some literature review of multi-objectives briefly.

Rakas et al. (2004) represented a multi-objective model for undesirable facilities based on fuzzy programming.

Erkut and Neuman (1989) displayed the necessity of using multi-objectives in undesirable FLPs. They added that the weakness of single objective problems has been emphasized in location science like repulsion place of urban wastes.

ReVelle (2000) has emphasized the importance of equity functions in undesirable FLPs. When wastes are generated by residents of an area, it is not fair to consider just negative effects of wastes on this area; therefore we should use the multi-objective models.

Ratick and White (1988) developed a three-objective for undesirable FLPs.

Erkut and Tansel (1992) expanded the Ratick and White (1988) models and solved the problem under condition of facilities with variable capacity by enumerating the possible solutions for possible capacities. This method is useful only for small size problems.

Wayman and Kuby (1994) represented a three-objective model for undesirable FLPs. They assumed the following objectives:

Minimizing the fixed cost and transportation cost, minimizing the risk and minimizing the inequity.

Rahman and Kuby (1995) developed a multi-objective model for locating a facility to transport wastes. They represented a bi-objective model with minimizing the installation cost and minimizing the public opposition as their objectives. The public opposition is a descending function from distance to residential places.

Giannikos (1998) represented a goal programming model for locating and carrying the dangerous wastes by transportation networks. In this model, it is not only assumed to minimize the operation costs and the total available risks, but also it is assumed to consider the distribution of risk and the desirability among populated centers.

Berman et al. (2000) developed a multi-objective location routing problem (LRP) on the network.

Berman and Drezner (2000) represented a bi-objective to find the best point on the network to establish a dangerous waste repulsion center.

It was a brief review of undesirable FLPs and it needs more research to find further subjects in this area.

16.2.4.2 The MCLP on the Network

Hamacher et al. (1996, 1998, 2002) surveyed MCLP on the network in different situations such as models with desirable effect and semi-noxious effect. Their models are usually consisted of single objective function but multiple weighted vectors (the first group of MCLPs). The results of their researches are consisted of representing a set of solution algorithms with polynomials under states of set-pareto and lexicography solution. Most of the proofs are based on a trick series and graph theory.

A review of solved problems in this area, their solution codes, complexity of these problems can be found in their papers. Readers can refer to Hamacher et al. (1996, 1998, 2002) to find more related subjects. In the followings, MCLP on the network based on properties and final solution can be seen in brief:

- On the network, graph without any direction, distance node to node, function min–sum, lexicography solution (final solution on the node)
- On the network, graph without any direction, distance node to allocation point, function min–sum, lexicography solution (final solution on the node)
- Graph with direction, distance node to node and node to allocation point, function min–sum, lexicography solution (final solution on the node)
- Graph without any direction and with direction, distance node to node, pareto solution (final solution on the node)
- Graph without any direction, distance node to allocation point, pareto solution (final solution on the node and vectors)
- Graph with direction, distance node to allocation point, pareto solution (final solution on the node) and
- Graph without any direction and with direction, function min–sum with respect to desirable and undesirable effects (final solution on the node)
- There are some complicated algorithms with anti-center objective function that are represented by Hamacher et al. (1996, 1998, 2002), too

16.3 Solution Techniques

16.3.1 The MCDM Techniques

Naturally, these techniques include both the MADM and the MODM techniques.

16.3.1.1 The MADM Techniques

The distinguishing feature of the MADM problems is that there are usually a limited number of predetermined alternatives. These alternatives satisfy each objective in a specified level and the DM selects the best solution (or solutions) among all alternatives according to the priority of each objective and the interaction between them. There are many techniques, which are used to tackle the MADM problems. The most popular ones are as follows: dominant, maximin, maximax, conjunctive method, disjunctive method, lexicographic method, elimination by aspects, permutation method, linear assignment method, simple additive weighting (SAW), hierarchical additive weighting, ELECTRE, TOPSIS, hierarchical trade-offs, LINMAP, interactive SAW method and MDS with ideal point (Hwang and Yoon 1981).

16.3.1.2 The MODM Techniques

In the MODM problems the purpose is to design the best alternative by considering the various interactions within the design constraints which best satisfy the DM by way of attaining some acceptable levels of a set of some objectives. The MODM problems have various components, but the common characteristics of them are as follows:

- A set of quantifiable and quality objectives
- A set of well defined constraints
- A process of obtaining some tradeoff information

There are many techniques, which are used to tackle the MODM problems. The most popular ones are as follows: global criterion method, utility function, metric L-P methods, bounded objective method, lexicographic method, goal programming, goal attainment method, method of Geoffrion, interactive GP, surrogate worth trade-off, method of satisfactory goals, method of Zionts-Wallenius, STEM and related method, SEMOPS and SIGMOP method, method of displaced ideal, GPSTEM method, method of Steuer, parametric method, C-constraint method and adaptive search method (Hwang and Lin 1987; Hwang and Masud 1979; Szidarovszky et al. 1986; Ulungu and Teghem 1994; Zionts 1979).

However, in solving the MODM problems, without respect to the used technique, investigating the following general steps is needed:

- *Conflicting Objectives*: It is in the nature of the MODM problems to have conflicting objectives
- *Efficient Solution*: An ideal solution to a MODM problem is one that results in the optimum value of each of the objective functions simultaneously. An efficient solution (Ulungu and Teghem 1994) (also known as non-inferior solution or non-dominated solution) is one in which no one objective function can be improved without a simultaneous detriment to the other objectives
- *A preferred Solution*: A preferred solution (also known as the best solution) is an efficient solution, which is chosen by the DM as the final decision. We have used some of simple MODM methods and some sensibility analysis to choose a preferred solution

16.3.2 Metaheuristics for the MODM

Various approaches have been utilized to solve multi objective optimization problems. In general, these approaches can be divided into three categories. The approaches in first category, which is named classical, such as weighted sum approach attempt to convert the multi objective problem into a single objective problem and optimize new single objective problem (Hajela and Lin 1992; Murata and Ishibuchi 1995). Optimizing this single objective problem yields a single solution; but the DMs need diverse options in the real condition. In addition, some classical approaches require knowing the optimal solution of each objective; acquiring this information about problem is expensive and time consuming. Their dependency to chosen weights, special in the case of non deterministic situation, is another fault of these approaches. Therefore, determination of these weights is really difficult. The second category of approaches includes those act based on Pareto optimal. In this case, a set of solutions are acquired when the problem is solved. These approaches, often, utilize evolutionary algorithms to solve multi objective problem which are more complicated than those that can be solved by deterministic optimization approaches like linear programming. So, these approaches, due to utilizing evolutionary algorithms, require little information about the problem in addition to yield a set of solutions. Some of these approaches are MOGA[2] (Fonseca and Fleming 1993), NSGA[3] (Srinivas and Deb 1994) and NSGA II[4] (Deb et al. 2002). Nevertheless, there are some approaches which neither convert the multi objective into single objective nor act based on Pareto optimal. These approaches are settled in the third category. Some of these approaches are: Vector Evaluated Genetic Algorithm (Schaffer 1985), Lexicographic Ordering, Weight Min–Max Method and Distance Method.

16.3.3 Multi-Objective Combinatorial Optimization

Nowadays, *multi-objective combinatorial optimization* (MOCO) (see Ehrgott and Gandibleux 2000; Ulungu and Teghem 1994) provides an adequate framework to tackle various types of discrete multi-criteria problems. Within this emergent research area several methods are known to handle different problems such as dynamic programming enumeration (Villarreal and Karwan (1981), for a methodological description; Klamroth and Wiecek (2000), for a recent application to knapsack problems) and implicit enumeration (Zionts and Wallenius 1980; Zionts 1979; Klein and Hannan 1982; Rasmussen 1986; Ramesh et al. 1986). Another approach based on labeling algorithms can be seen in Captivo et al. (2000). It is worth noting that most of MOCO problems are NP-hard and intractable (Ehrgott and

---

[2] Multi Objective Genetic Algorithm
[3] Non-dominate Sorting Genetic Algorithm
[4] Fast Non-dominate Sorting Genetic Algorithm

Gandibleux 2000, for further details). Even in most of the cases where the single-objective problem is polynomially solvable, the multi-objective version becomes NP-hard. This is the case of spanning tree problems and min-cost flow problems, among others. In the case of uncapacitated plant location problem, the single-objective version is already NP-hard (Krarup and Pruzan 1983). This ensures that the multi-objective formulation is not solvable in polynomial time. In this context, when time and efficiency become real issues, different alternatives can be used to approximate the Pareto optimal set. One of them is the use of general-purpose MOCO heuristics (Gandibleux et al. 2000). Another possibility is designing "ad hoc" methods based on one of the following strategies:

- Computing the supported non-dominated solutions
- Performing a partial enumeration of the solutions space

Obviously, the second strategy does not guarantee the non-dominated character of all the generated solutions since we only consider the solutions obtained during the partial search. Nevertheless the reduction in computation time can be remarkable.

16.4 Case Study

In this section we will introduce some real-world case studies related to MCLP.

16.4.1 LRP (Lin and kwok 2006)

In this paper an integrated logistic system are surveyed, where decisions on location of depot, vehicle routing and assignment of routes to vehicles are considered simultaneously. Total cost and workload balance are common criteria influencing decision-making. Literature on LRPs addressed the location and vehicle routing decisions with a common assumption of assigning one route to one vehicle. However, the cost of acquiring vehicles (and crew) is often more significant than the routing cost. This notion of assigning several routes to a vehicle during the routing procedure is explored in their integrated model. Meta heuristics of tabu search and simulated annealing are applied on real data and simulated data, to compare their performances under two versions: simultaneous or sequential routes assignment to vehicles. Results show that the simultaneous versions have advantage over the sequential versions in problems where routes are capacity-constrained.

Logistics operations often involve sending out staff from their offices or depots to customers in various areas to perform on-site tasks. There are several decisions to be considered as follows:

- Selecting the depot locations
- Scheduling routes from selected depots to customers
- Assigning routes to vehicles/crew

These decisions are often inter-dependent and each change has influenced other decisions.

The total cost is an obvious and primary concern of management. This includes the fixed cost of selected depots, traveling cost of the routes and cost of vehicles and crew.

This paper examined the integrated model on the total cost and workload balance criteria that are important to both management and operational staff.

LRP consists of two sub problems:

- FLP
- Vehicle Routing Problem

Both of them are shown to be NP-hard.

In the MCDM problems, after establishing the location of depots and delivery routes for vehicles, demands of customers will be satisfied and management will reach its purposes.

Readers can refer to Lin and Kwok (2006) to find further subjects about structure of used algorithms.

16.4.2 Facility Layout (Chiang et al. 2006)

Most of researches have been managed on the facility layout problem, much of it based on the QAP formulation. The QAP objective is to minimize the transportation cost which expressed as the product of the quantity of workflow and the distance traveled.

In addition of the common purpose to minimize the transportation costs, the focus of this research is also consisted of minimizing the intersections between transportation routes. This problem is used in production lines of plants and traffic problems, because of the increasing number of intersections, it will derive more queues and more delays in transportation.

To illustrate the effect of conducting a layout analysis that fails to account for workflow interference, they consider an eight-department example with the workflow matrix. The solution to this problem using traditional layout analyses (QAP is solved using Euclidean distances) is provided. This layout arrangement minimizes the total distance traveled.

Chiang et al. (2006) modeled workflow interference in facility layout design as a quadratic assignment problem, and developed a branch-and-bound procedure and a tabu search heuristic to solve the problem.

In this paper, to solve the problem, first the problem is separated into two certain problems which their objective functions are consisted of minimizing the product of traveled distance and the number of transportations and minimizing the number of intersections among routes respectively.

The first problem can be expressed as a QAP and the second problem will be converted to QAP after adding some constraints to the original model.

16.4.3 Fire Station Locations

Location of fire stations is an important factor in its fire protection capability. Yang et al. (2007) aim to determine the optimal location of fire station facilities. The proposed method is the combination of a fuzzy multi-objective programming and a genetic algorithm. The fuzzy multiple objectives are converted to a single unified min–max goal, which makes it easy to apply a genetic algorithm for the problem solving. Compared with the existing methods of fire station location this approach has three distinguishing features:

- Considering fuzzy nature of a DM in the location optimization model
- Fully considering the demands for the facilities from the areas with various fire risk categories
- Being more understandable and practical to DM

The case study was based on the data collected from the Derbyshire fire and rescue service and tried to illustrate the application of the method for the optimization of fire station locations.

Determination of where to locate fire stations and how many fire stations to have in a given area is the most important decision faced by any Chief Fire Officer. The optimum solution is deduced to minimize the sum of losses from fire and the cost of providing the service. The fire station location problems have multi-objective functions which are NP-hard.

Multiple objectives often conflict with each other and require multi-objective approaches. Tzeng and Chen (1999) considered three objectives in the optimal location of airport fire stations:

- Minimizing the total setup cost of fire stations and total loss cost of an incident
- Minimizing the longest distance from the fire stations to any incident point
- Minimizing the longest distance from any fire station to the high-risk area

Badri et al. (1998) considered 11 objectives in a general MODM for locating fire stations.

- Minimize fixed cost
- Minimize total annual operating cost
- Maximize service of those areas that have most probability based on number of forecasted accidents
- Minimize average distance travelled from station to accident sites
- Minimize maximum distance travelled from station to accident sites
- Minimize average time travelled from station to accident sites
- Minimize maximum time travelled from station to accident sites
- Attain the number of fire stations required
- Minimize service overlaps of fire stations
- Attain the favored condition of areas
- Minimize locating where water availability could be a problem

The main concept of multi-objective problems based on fuzzy approach is consisted of finding the highest level of availability among conflicting constraints. Two common goals usually used in many emergency-location (ambulance, fire station etc.) related studies:

- To minimize the fixed cost and the total loss cost of incidents
- To minimize the distance from the fire station to any incident site

Tzeng and Chen (1999) represented an approach for the first objective, to obtain the optimal number of fire stations, and they use a fuzzy multi-objective model for the second objective to address the recommendation made by the Home Office on the time limits for attendance at incident sites.

16.4.4 The 2-Facility Centdian Network Problem (Perez-Brito et al. 1998)

The P-facility centdian network problem consists of finding the P points that minimize a convex combination of the P-center and P-median objective functions. The vertices and local centers constitute a dominating set for the 1-facility centdian.

In this paper, the problem of selecting several points of a network is considered in order to minimize a function that is distance dependent with respect to given points of the network. The median and the center problems are two well-known problems with numerous possible applications.

In many real world problems, the objective to be optimized in a model is a combination of (possibly conflicting) goals. For example, when locating a fire station, there may be two objectives as follows:

- To minimize the distance between stations and farthest potential customer
- To minimize the distance between stations and majority of customers

The first function is a center problem and the second one is a median problem. It is reasonable, because to locate the fire station centers, the purpose consisted of both minimizing the distance between center and the farthest potential incident point (center problem) and minimizing the distance between center and the most densely populated point (median problem).

Halpern (1978) represented this multi-objective approach for locating a facility on a network (who coined the term centdian for this problem). Hakimi (1964) demonstrated that the set of vertices (nodes) is a finite dominating set for the P-median problem. Moreno (1985) proved that the set of vertices and local centers (points, in the internal of the edges, which have equal distance and balanced with respect to two vertices) is a finite dominating set for the P-center problem. Halpern (1978) proved that the set of vertices and local centers of the network is a finite dominating set for the single facility centdian problem. Hooker et al. (1991) considered a theoretical result that extended the finite dominating sets of the single facility problems to the corresponding P-facility problems, and applied it to the

P-facility centdian problem. It is not reasonable; therefore a counterexample has been given by Perez-Brito et al. (1998). In this paper finally an optimal solution consisting of vertices and local centers is presented as a set of final solution for solving the 2-centdian on the network. It also presented a solution procedure for a network that improves the complexity of the exhaustive search in the dominating set. It also provided a very efficient algorithm that solves the 2-centdian on a tree network with complexity $O(n^2)$.

16.4.5 Military Logistics (Z-Farahani and Asgari 2007)

The case of this research relates to the MCDM (including the MADM and the MODM) and set covering problem. In this paper, it is represented to locate some warehouses as distribution centers in a real-world military logistics system. This study looks for finding the least number of distribution centers and locating them in the best possible locations. The objectives of the problem are as follows:

- Maximizing the utility of the selected locations. Utility of a potential point depends on 23 attributes
- Minimizing the number of supportive centers

The first objective deduced the minimum cost of locating the facilities and the latter expresses the quality of the distribution centers locations, which is evaluated by studying the value of appropriate attributes affecting the quality of a location. Quality of a warehouse location depends on a number of attributes; so the value of each location is determined by using the MADM methods (hereby, TOPSIS). Then, regarding the obtained values and the minimum number of distribution centers, the two objective functions are formed. Constraints imposed on these two objectives cover all centers, which must be supported by the distribution centers. Using the MODM techniques (hereby, utility function), the locations of distribution centers are determined. In the final phase, a simple set partitioning model is represented to assign each supported center to only one of the located distribution centers.

16.4.6 A Paper Recycling System (Pati et al. 2008)

Since reducing and reutilizing waste being defined as one of the requirements for substantial development, the reverse logistic concept of a supply chain has been used to optimize the recycling system of the paper industry of India.

There are five levels of facilities in this reverse distribution network: customer, dealer, godown owner, supplier and the manufacturer. Also, there are two varieties of wastepaper. Based on the requirements of the problem, the goals/objectives are:

1. Minimizing the reverse logistics cost (minimizing the positive deviation from the planned budget)

2. Minimizing the quantity on non-relevant wastepaper in the reverse distribution network (minimizing the positive deviation from the maximum limit of non-relevant wastepaper target)
3. Maximizing the wastepaper collection at source (minimizing the negative deviation from the minimum desired waste collection)

A mixed integer goal programming (MIGP) model has been proposed for this FLP in which these objectives are lexicographically minimized and the Pareto inefficient or dominated solutions are produced, based on six priority structures CWN,CNW, NCW, NWC, WCN and WNC where C, N and W represent each of above objectives respectively.

Afterwards, the Pareto optimality of the solution is detected by constructing a new achievement function from non-weighted deviational variables and is compared with the initial optimal solution. The new achievement objective is to maximize the sum of deviational variables which are not present in the achievement function of the MIGP model.

In conclusion, for each priority, the network sub-entities to be closed or opened are determined along with the associated route and quantity of flow for different varieties of papers in this multi-item, multi-echelon and multi-facility network.

References

Badri MA, Mortagy AK, Alsayed CA (1998) A multi-objective model for locating fire stations. Eur J Oper Res 110(2):243–260

Berman O, Drezner Z (2000) A note on the location of an obnoxious facility on a network. Eur J Oper Res 120:215–217

Berman O, Drezner Z, Wesolowsky G (2000) Routing and location on a network with hazardous threats. J Oper Res Soc 51:1093–1099

Captivo ME, Climaco J, Figueira J, Martins E. Santos JL (2000) Solving multiple criteria knapsack problems using labeling algorithms. Paper presented at IO2000, Setubal

Carrizosa E, Conde E, Fernandez FR, Puerto J (1993) Efficiency in Euclidean constrained location problems. Oper Res Lett 14(5):291–295

Chiang WC, Kouvelis P, Urban TL (2006) Single- and multi-objective facility layout with workflow interference considerations. Eur J Oper Res 174:1414–1426

Cohon JL (1978) Multiobjective programming and planning. In: Mathematics in science and engineering. vol 140 Academic, NY

Curtin KM, Church RL (2003) A family of location models for multiple-type discrete dispersion. Geogr Anal 38:248–270

Deb K, Pratap A, Agarwal S, Meyarivan T (2002) A fast and elitist multi objective genetic algorithm. NSGA-II", IEEE Trans Evol Comput 6(2):182–197

Ehrgott M, Gandibleux X (2000) An annotated bibliography of multicriteria combinatorial optimization OR-Spectr 22(4) 425–460

Eiselt HA, Laporte G (1995) Objectives in location problems, in facility location. In: Drezner Z (ed) A survey of application and methods Springer, NY, pp 151–180

Erkut E, Neuman S (1989) Analytical models for locating undesirable facilities. Eur J Oper Res 40:275–291

Erkut E, Neuman S (1990) Comparison of four models for dispersing facilities. INFOR 29(2):68–86

Erkut E, Neuman S (1992) A multi-objective model for locating undesirable facilities. Ann Oper Res 40:209–227
Fonseca CM, Fleming PJ (1993) Multi objective genetic algorithms. In: IEE colloquium on genetic algorithms for control systems engineering vol 130, London, May
Gandibleux X, Jaszkiewicz A, Freville A, Slowinski R (2000) Multiobjective metaheuristics J Heurist 6(3):291–431
Giannikos I (1998) A multi-objective programming model for locating treatment sites and routing hazardous wastes. Eur J Oper Res 104:333–342
Hajela P, Lin CY (1992) Genetic search strategies in multi criterion optimal design. Struct Optim 4(2):99–107
Hakimi SL (1964) Optimum locations of switching center and the absolute center and medians of a graph. Oper Res 12:450–459
Halpern J (1978) Finding minimal center median convex combination (centdian) of a graph. Manage Sci 24(5):535–544
Hamacher HW, Nickel S (1996) Multicriteria planar location problems. Eur J Oper Res 94:66–86
Hamacher HW, Labbe M, Nickel S (1998) Multicriteria network location problems with sum objective. Networks 33:79–92
Hamacher HW, Labbe M, Nickel S (2002) Multicriteria semi-obnoxious network location problems (MSNLP) with sum and center objectives. Ann Oper Res 110:33–53
Hansen P, Perreur J, Thisse JF (1980) Location theory, dominance and convexity: some further results. Oper Res 28:1241–1250
Hooker JN, Garfinkel RS, Chen CK (1991) Finite dominating sets for network location problems. Oper Res 39(1):100–118
Hwang CL, Lin ML (1987) Group decision-making under multiple criteria. Springer, New York
Hwang CL, Masud ASM (1979) Multiple objective decision-making. Springer, New York
Hwang CL, Yoon K (1981) Multiple attribute decision-making. Springer, New York
Klamroth K, Wiecek M (2000) Dynamic programming approach to the multiple criteria knapsack problem. Naval Res Logist 47:57–76
Klein D, Hannan E (1982) An algorithm for the multiple objective integer linear programming problem. Eur J Oper Res 9:378–385
Krarup J, Pruzan PM (1983) The simple plant location problem: survey and synthesis. Eur J Oper Res 12:36–81
Krarup J, Pisingera D, Plastriab F (2002) Discrete location problems with push–pull objectives. Discrete Appl Math 123:363–378
Lee SM, Green GI, Kim C (1981) A multiple criteria model for the location-allocation problem. Comput Oper Res 8:1–8
Lin CKY, Kwok RCW (2006) Multi-objective meta heuristics for a location-routing problem with multiple use of vehicles on real data and simulated data. Eur J Oper Res 175:1833–1849
Moreno JA (1985) A correction to the definition of local center. Eur J Oper Res 20:382–385
Murata T, Ishibuchi H (1995) MOGA: multi-objective genetic algorithms. In: Proceedings of the IEEE international conference on evolutionary computation, Perth, WA, IEEE, Australia, 29 November–1 December
Ogryczak W (1999) On the distribution approach to location problems. Comput Ind Eng 37:595–612
Pati RK, Vrat P, Kumar P (2008) A goal programming model for paper recycling system. Omega 36:405–417
Pelegrin B, Fernandez FR (1988) Determination of efficient points in multiple objective location problems. Naval Res Logist Quart 35:697–705
Perez-Brito D, Moreno-Perez JA, Rodriguez-Martin I (1998) The 2-facility centdian network problem. Location Sci 6:369–381
Puerto J, Fernandez FR (1999) Multicriteria mini-sum facility location problems. J Multicriteria Decision Anal 8:268–280
Rahman M, Kuby M (1995) A multi-objective model for locating solid-waste transfer facilities using an empirical opposition function. INFOR 33:34–49

Rakas J, Teodorovic D, Kim T (2004) Multi-objective modeling for determining location of undesirable facilities. Transp Res Pt 9:125–138

Ramesh R, Zionts S, Karwan M (1986) A class of practical interactive branch and bounds algorithms for multicriteria integer programming. Eur J Oper Res 26:161–172

Rasmussen LM (1986) Zero-one programming with multiple criteria. Eur J Oper Res 26:83–95

Ratick, White A (1988) A risk-sharing model for locating noxious facilities. Environ Plan 15:165–179

ReVelle C (2000) Research challenges in environmental management. Eur J Oper Res 121:218–231

Ross GT, Soland RM (1980) A multicriteria approach to location of public facilities. Eur J Oper Res 4:307–321

Schaffer JD (1985) Multiple objective optimization with vector evaluated genetic algorithms. In: Proceedings of the international conference on genetic algorithm and their applications

Solanki R (1991) Generating the noninferior set in mixed biobjective linear programs: an application to a location problem. Comput Oper Res 18:1–15

Srinivas N, Deb K (1994) Multi objective optimization using non dominated sorting in genetic algorithms. J Evol Comput 2(3):221–48

Szidarovszky F, Gershon ME, Duchstein L (1986) Techniques for multi-objective decision-making in systems management. Elsevier, Amsterdam

Tzeng GH, Chen YW (1999) The optimal location of airport fire stations: a fuzzy multi-objective programming and revised genetic algorithm approach. Transport Plan Technol 23:37–55

Ulungu EL, Teghem J (1994) Multi-objective combinatorial optimization problems: a survey. J Multi-criteria Decisions Anal 3:83–104

Villarreal B, Karwan MH (1981) Multicriteria integer programming: a (hybrid) dynamic programming recursive approach. Math Program 21:204–233

Wayman MM, Kuby M (1994) Proactive optimization: general framework and a case study using a toxic waste location model with technology choice. Paper presented at the international symposium on locational decisions, ISOLDE VI, Lesvos and Chios, Greece

Wendell RE, Hurter AP (1973) Location theory, dominance and convexity. Oper Res 21:314–320

Wendell RE, Hurter AP Jr, Lowe TJ (1977) Efficient points in location problems. AIIE Trans 9(3):238–246

Yang L, Jones BF, Yang SH (2007) A fuzzy multi-objective programming for optimization of fire station locations through genetic algorithms. Eur J Oper Res 181:903–915

Z.-Farahani R, Asgari N (2007) Combination of MCDM and covering techniques in a hierarchical model for facility location: a case study. Eur J Oper Res 176:1839–1858

Zionts S (1979) A survey of multiple criteria integer programming methods. Ann Discrete Math 5:389–398

Zionts S, Wallenius J (1980) Identifying efficient vectors: some theory and computational results. Oper Res 23:785–793

Chapter 17
Location-Routing Problem

Anahita Hassanzadeh, Leyla Mohseninezhad, Ali Tirdad,
Faraz Dadgostari, and Hossein Zolfagharinia

The aim of this chapter is to survey the state of the art in location-routing. The location-routing problem (LRP) is a research area within location analysis, with the distinguishing property of paying special attention to underlying issues of vehicle routing.

Since the Vehicle-Routing Problem (VRP), which is a complex problem itself, is known as a basic component of LRPs, the main concepts of VRP are introduced in the first section. In the second section, the definition, applications and classifications of LRP are discussed. The next section is dedicated to the LRP models and introduces some basic mathematical models of this field. Solution techniques are presented in the fourth section. Finally, three case studies regarding applications of LRP in real world are briefly reviewed.

17.1 An Introduction to VRP

Since LRPs are extensions of classical VRPs, here we provide a brief introduction to VRP including its definition, major applications and classification.

17.1.1 Definition of VRP

The VRP is one of the most studied among the combinatorial optimization problems, due both to its practical relevance and to its considerable difficulty. The VRP is concerned with the determination of the optimal routes used by a fleet of vehicles, based on one or more depots, to serve a set of customers.

Typical applications of this problem are, for instance, solid waste collection, street cleaning, school bus routing, dial-a-ride systems, transportation of handicapped persons, routing of salespeople, and of maintenance units.

The distribution of goods, in a given time period, concern the service of a set of customers by a set of vehicles, which are located in one or more depots, are operated by a set of crews (drivers), and perform their movements by using an appropriate road network. In particular, the solution of a VRP calls for the determination of a set of routes, each performed by a single vehicle that starts and ends at its own depot, such that all the requirements of the customers are fulfilled, all the operational constraints are satisfied, and the global transportation cost is minimized. Here, we describe the typical characteristics of the routing and scheduling problems by considering their main components (road networks, customers, depots, vehicles, and drivers), the different operational constraints that can be imposed on the construction of routes, and the possible objectives to be achieved in the optimization process.

The road networks, used for the transportation of goods, is generally described through a graph, whose arcs represent the road sections and whose vertices correspond to the road junctions and to the depot and customer locations. The arcs (and consequently the corresponding graphs) can be directed or undirected, depending on whether they can be traversed in only one direction (for instance, because of the presence of one-way streets, typical of urban or motorway networks) or in both directions, respectively. Each arc is associated with a cost, which generally represents its length, and a travel time, which is possibly dependent on the vehicle type or on the period during which the arc is traversed.

Typical characteristics of customers are:

- Vertex of the road graph in which the customer is located
- Amount of goods (demand), possibly of different types, which must be delivered or collected at the customer
- Periods of the day (time windows) during which the customer can be served (for instance, because of specific periods during which the customer is open or the location can be reached, due to traffic limitations)
- Time required to deliver or collect the goods at the customer location (unloading or loading times, respectively), possibly dependent on the vehicle type
- Subset of the available vehicles that can be used to serve the customer (for instance, because of possible access limitations or loading and unloading requirements)

Sometimes, it is not possible to fully satisfy the demand of each customer. In these cases, the amounts to be delivered or collected can be reduced, or a subset of customers can be left unserved. To deal with these situations, different priorities associated with the partial or total lack of service, can be assigned to the customers.

The routes performed to serve customers start and end at one or more depots, and are located at the vertices of the road graph. Each depot is characterized by the number and types of vehicles associated with it and by the global amount of goods it can deal with. In some real-world applications, the customers are a priori partitioned among the depots, and the vehicles have to return to their home depot at the end of each route. In these cases, the overall VRP can be decomposed into several independent problems, each associated with a different depot.

Transportation of goods is performed by using a fleet of vehicles whose composition and size can be fixed or can be defined according to the requirements of the customers. Typical characteristics of the vehicles are:

- Home depot of the vehicle, and the possibility to end service at a depot other than the home one
- Capacity of the vehicle, expressed as the maximum weight, or volume, or number of pallets, the vehicle can load
- Possible subdivision of the vehicle into compartments; each characterized by its capacity and by the types of goods that can be carried
- Devices available for the loading and unloading operations;
- Subset of arcs of the road graph which can be traversed by the vehicle
- Costs associated with utilization of the vehicle (per distance unit, per time unit, per route, etc.)

Drivers operating the vehicles must satisfy several constraints laid down by union contracts and company regulations (for instance, working periods during the day, number and duration of breaks during service, maximum duration of driving periods, overtime). In the following, the constraints imposed on drivers are imbedded in those associated with the corresponding vehicles.

The routes must satisfy several operational constraints, which depend on the nature of the transported goods, on the quality of the service level, and on the characteristics of the customers and the vehicles. Some typical constraints are the following: along each route, the current load of the associated vehicle can not exceed the vehicle capacity; the customers served in a route can require only the delivery or the collection of goods; or both possibilities can exist; and customers can be served only within their time windows and the working periods of the drivers associated with the vehicles visiting them. Precedence constraints can be imposed on the order in which the customers served in a route are visited. One type of precedence constraint requires that a given customer be served in the same route serving a given set of other customers and that the customer must be visited before (or after) the customers belonging to the associated subset. This is the case, for instance, of the so-called pickup and delivery problems, wherein the routes can perform both the collection and the delivery of routes, and the goods collected from the pickup customers must be carried to the corresponding delivery customers by the same vehicle.

Another type of the precedence constraints impose that if customers by different types are served in the same route, the order in which customers are visited is fixed. This situation arises, for instance, for the so-called VRP with back hauls, wherein again, the routes can perform both the collection and the delivery of goods, but constraints associated with the loading and unloading operations, and the difficulty in rearranging the load of the vehicle along the route, mean that all deliveries must be performed before the collections (Toth and Vigo 2002).

17.1.2 The Traveling Salesman Problem

There exist a few exact methods formed to solve LRPs, and most of them are represented in recent years. These algorithms are usually on the based on the linear integer models in the VRPs, which include the locating dimension, too. Hence, it is useful to have an overview of an exact method that is considered in the field of VRPs.

The first integer linear programming formulation for the Traveling Salesman Problem (TSP) belongs to Dantzig and Fulkerson (1954).
Define:

$N = \{1, 2, ..., n\}$ a set of nodes (points customers or cities)

$C = (c_{ij}), (i, j \in I \cup J)$: a distance matrix (undefined if $i, j \in I$)

x_{ij}: a 0–1 variable equal to 1 if and only if edge (i, j) is chosen in the optimal solution. x_{ij} only need to be defined if $i \prec j$. Here and elsewhere, x_{ij} must be interpreted as x_{ij} whenever $i \succ j$.

The problem is then to

$$\text{Minimize} \sum_{i,j \in J} c_{ij} x_{ij} \tag{17.1}$$

Subject to

$$\sum_{i \prec k} x_{ik} + \sum_{k \prec j} x_{kj} = 2 \quad (k \in N) \tag{17.2}$$

$$\sum_{i,j \in S} x_{ij} \leq \frac{1}{2} \Delta(S) - 1 \quad (S \subset N; 2 \leq |S| \leq n - 2) \tag{17.3}$$

$$x_{ij} = 0, 1 \quad (i \in I) \tag{17.4}$$

In this formulation, (17.2) are degree constrains: they specify the degree of each node. Equation (17.3) are subtour elimination constrains: they prevent the formation of subtours over proper subsets of N. Equation (17.4) are integrality constrains (Laporte et al. 1988).

17.1.3 A Classification of Capacitated VRP

Here we concentrate on the basic version of the VRP, the Capacitated VRP (CVRP). In the CVRP, all the customers correspond to deliveries and the demand are deterministic, known in advance, and may not be split. The vehicles are identical and based on a single central depot, and only the capacity restrictions for the vehicles are imposed. The objective is to minimize the total cost to serve all the customers (Toth and Vigo 2002).

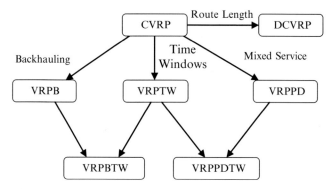

Fig. 17.1 The basic problems of the VRP class and their interconnections (Toth and Vigo 2002)

Figure 17.1 shows a classification corresponding to the basic problems of the VRPs and their interconnections. In this figure, CVRP stands for Capacitated VRP, DCVRP for Capacitated and Distance Constrained VRP, VRPB for VRP with Backhauls, VRPTW for VRP with Time Windows, VRPPD for VRP with Pickup and Delivery, VRPBTW for VRP with Backhauls and Time Windows, VRPPDTW for VRP with Pickup and Delivery and Time Windows.

17.2 LRP

The basic concepts of LRPs were introduced by Boventer (1961), Maranzana (1965), Webb (1968), Lawrence and Pengilly (1969), Higgins (1972) and Christofides and Eilon (1969). These primary studies did not consider the complexity of LRP as a combined problem. Introduction and extensions of LRP as a combined problem commenced at the late 1970s and early 1980s. These studies include articles of Or and Pierskalla (1979), Jacobsen and Madsen (1978) and Laporte and Norbert (1981). Such popularity of LRP studies almost parallels the advent of an integrated logistics concept and the growth of international trade which necessitated distribution efficiency (Min et al. 1998).

According to the articles which have been published from 1972 to 1996, the potential future research areas are:

- Stochastic LRPs
- Time windows LRPs
- Dynamic LRPs
- LRPs with multiple objectives

We may distinguish between two types of dynamic problems, in one, the depots are located sequentially. In the other, the depots are located at the beginning of the planning horizon and vehicle routes vary with the variations in customer demand.

The former case is more applicable if demand is increasing and the latter if demand is fluctuating (Nagy and Salhi 2007).

In order to understand the relation between LRP and the classical location problems, it seems necessary to define its place among location problem. Therefore, we firstly concentrate on the types of trips in which the main difference between the LRP and the classical location-allocation problem (see Chap. 5) lies. Usually, it is assumed that users or customers are directly connected to facilities. These types of trips between customers and facilities are called out-and-back, direct, or return trips.

But there exist many cases in which the trip commences from a facility and covers many customers. In addition to identifying the number and location of the facilities, the followings must be determined:

- The allocation of customers to the facilities
- The allocation of customers to the routes
- The order of visiting the customers in a route

These two kinds of trips are presented in Fig. 17.2 (Daskin 1995).

From the customer servicing point of view, location problems can be divided to two categories:

- The customers are being serviced in their own locations
- The customers take trips to facilities to get serviced

The common examples of the second category are schools and hospitals.

In general, two cases occur in the first category. The server must return to the facility after serving the customer, like fire engines (direct trips) or the server can visit many customers in a tour, like repairers and postmen (tour trips). Figure 17.3 demonstrates this division.

Therefore, if there exist direct trips, the problem is a location-allocation problem (see Chap. 5), and if there exist tour trips, the problem is a LRP. Hence, a LRP contains both location and tours (Min et al. 1998; Lin and Kwok 2006).

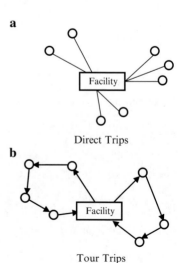

Fig. 17.2 Two types of trips between customers and facilities (Daskin 1995) (**a**) direct trips (**b**) tour trips

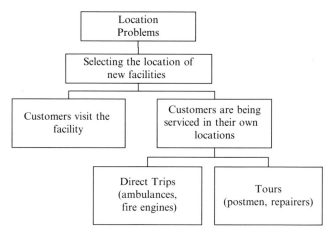

Fig. 17.3 Different types of servicing the customers

LRPs are clearly related to both classical location problem and VRP. In fact, both of the latter problems can be viewed as special cases of the LRP. If we require all customers to be directly linked to a depot, the LRP becomes a standard location problem. If, on the other hand, we fix the depot locations, the LRP reduces to a VRP (Nagy and Salhi 2007).

After defining the place of the problem, the LRP can be defined as follows: A feasible set of potential facility sites and locations and expected demands of each customer which are given. Each customer is to be assigned to a facility which will supply its demand. The shipments of customer demand are carried out by vehicles which are dispatched from the facilities, and operate on routes that include multiple customers. The location of distribution facilities and the distribution of products from these facilities to customers are two key components of a distribution system.

In various different settings, these two components are interdependent; therefore it is necessary to consider the facility location and the distribution decisions simultaneously (Tuzun and Burke 1999).

Figure 17.4 is a simple representation of LRP sub problems and their interdepenence.

17.2.1 Applications of LRP

Although most of the applications of location-routing focus on distribution of consumer goods or parcels, there are also some applications in health, military and communications. Some of these applications are in:

- Food and drink distribution
- Waste collection

Fig. 17.4 The relationship between LRP components (Min et al. 1998)

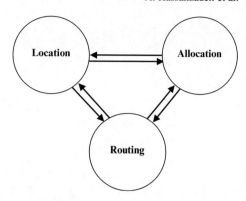

Table 17.1 A summary of LRP applications

Author	Application area	Country/region
Watson et al. (1973)	Food and drink distribution	United Kingdom
Bednar and Strohmeier (1979)	Consumer goods distribution	Australia
Or and Pierskalla (1979)	Blood bank location	United States
Jacobsen and Madsen (1980)	Newspaper distribution	Denmark
Nambiar et al. (1989)	Rubber plant location	Malaysia
Perl and Daskin (1985)	Goods distribution	United States
Labbe and Laporte (1986)	Postbox location	Belgium
Nambiar et al. (1989)	Rubber plant location	Malaysia
Semet and Taillard (1993)	Grocery distribution	Switzerland
Kulcar (1996)	Waste collection	Belgium
Murty and Djang (1999)	Military equipment location	United States
Bruns et al. (2000)	Parcel delivery	Switzerland
Chan et al. (2001)	Medical evacuation	United States
Lin et al. (2002)	Bill delivery	Hong Kong
Lee et al. (2003)	Optical network design	Korea
Wasner and Zäpfel (2004)	Parcel delivery	Australia
Billionnet et al. (2005)	Telecom network design	France
Gunnarsson et al. (2006)	Shipping industry	Europe

- Blood bank location
- Newspaper distribution

Table 17.1 summarizes the main characteristics of papers describing practical applications (Nagy and Salhi 2007).

17.2.2 Classifications of LRP

Various classification schemes are available in the literature to categorize LRPs (Min et al. 1998).

A classification of LRP with regard to its problem perspective is presented in Table 17.2.

Table 17.2 Classification of LRP with regard to its problem perspective (Min et al. 1998)

I.		Hierarchical level
		A. Single stage
		B. Two stages
II.		Nature of demand
		A. Deterministic
		B. Stochastic
III.		Number of facilities
		A. Single facility
		B. Multiple facilities
IV.		Size of vehicle fleets
		A. Single vehicle
		B. Multiple vehicles
V.		Vehicle capacity
		A. Uncapacitated
		B. Capacitated
VI.		Facility capacity
		A. Uncapacitated
		B. Capacitated
VII.		Facility layer
		A. Primary
		B. Secondary
VIII.		Planning horizon
		A. Single period
		B. Multiple periods
IX.		Time restriction
		A. Unspecified time with no deadline
		B. Soft time windows with loose deadlines
		C. Hard time windows with strict deadlines
X.		Objective function
		A. Single objective
		B. Multiple objectives
XI.		Types of model data
		A. Hypothetical
		B. Real world

These classification schemes do not require a specific description. The only vague ones may be:

- Hierarchical level, which can be in one or two stages. One stage means one type of facility and two stages mean two types. (For example one manufacturing plant and one distribution center)
- Facility layer, which will be described in Sect. 17.2.2.1
- Objective function, which is usually a single objective of cost reduction, but several other objectives may be considered (Averbakh and Berman 1995a, b; Jamil et al. 1994)

17.2.2.1 Classification of LRP Regarding Layer Diagram

If we consider users or customers on the one hand, and facilities to be located on the other hand, we can theoretically arrive at the definition of four different types of problems depending on whether users or facilities are assumed to belong to discrete or continues sets (Laporte 1988). We also temporarily assume that users and facilities belong to disjoint sets.

Several distribution centers can be represented by a layer diagram such as the one depicted by Fig. 17.5. In this example, there are three layers which have been identified as primary facilities, secondary facilities, and users. Frequently, the primary facilities will represent factories, secondary facilities will correspond to depots or warehouses, and users will be customers. Primary facilities and users are usually situated at known and fixed locations. On the other hand, the location of secondary facilities will frequently not be determined a priori: the number or locations of these facilities, together with the associated distribution routes constitute decision variables.

Several problems can be defined according to the distribution mode M_t used by vehicles based on a facility located at layer t. Usually, these vehicles will make trips to layer $t + 1$. We consider two distribution modes:

$M_t = R$: all trips from layer t must be return trips. (i.e. trips to and from a single user or facility);

$M_t = T$: trips from layer t may be tours. (i.e. round-trips through several users or facilities)

The distribution modes used for the whole system will be represented by the expression $\lambda/M_1/M_2/\ldots/M_{\lambda-1}$, where λ is the number of layers. Thus, in a three-layer system, we will have the four following possibilities:

$3/R/R$: mostly, Occurs when shipments of a generally bulky material (e.g. lumber, cement) have to be made in full loads between successive layers, as is depicted in Fig. 17.5.

$3/R/T$: Here, large shipments arriving at the secondary facilities are broken up and dispatched in smaller loads to customers, as is depicted in Fig. 17.6. This situation is encountered in food industry, for example.

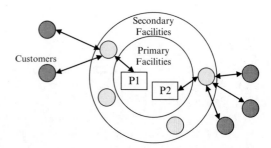

Fig. 17.5 $3/R/R$ layer diagram (Laporte 1988)

Fig. 17.6 $3/R/T$ layer diagram (Laporte 1988)

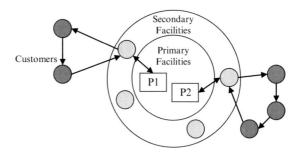

Fig. 17.7 $3/T/R$ layer diagram (Laporte 1988)

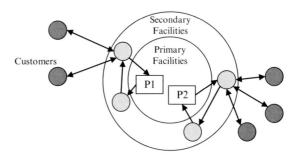

Fig. 17.8 $3/T/T$ layer diagram (Laporte 1988)

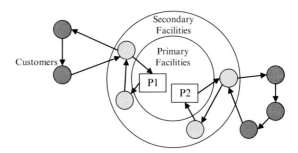

$3/T/R$: As in Fig. 17.7, in this situation, trips are often made from the users who bring goods to the secondary facilities. These goods are then collected in round-trips and brought to primary facilities.

$3/T/T$: This case is frequently encountered in the newspaper industry. Here, the primary facilities are printing plants; newspapers are dispatched daily to secondary facilities (transfer points) and then again to retail outlets. This situation is presented in Fig. 17.8.

In LRPs,

- Location decisions must be made for at least one layer (otherwise, the problem reduces to a pure routing problem)
- Tours ($M_t = T$) must be allowed to at least once (otherwise the problem becomes a pure location problem)

Therefore, problems of the form $\lambda/R/R/\ldots/R$ will not be covered in this study.

Table 17.3 LRP applications (Laporte 1988)

Type	Application	Layers (with number of sites)				References
		1	2	3	4	
2/T	Optimal location of blood banks	Blood banks[a] (3)	Hospitals (17)			Or and Pierskalla (1979)
2/T	Aircraft operating locations	Military airports[a] (5)	Military bases (84)			McLain et al. (1984)
3/R/T	Distribution of consumer goods	Factories	Depots[a]	Customers		Watson-Gandy and Dohrn (1973)
3/T/R	Rubber collection	Rubber processing factories[a] (8)	Collection stations (50)	Small holders (3750)		Nambiar et al. (1989)
3/T/T	Newspaper delivery	Printing plants (21)	Transfer points (37)	Retailers (4500)		Jacobsen and Madsen (1980)
4/R/R/T	Distribution of consumer goods	Factories	Warehouses[a]	Depots[a]	Customers	Mercer et al. (1978)

[a]indicates locational decision

Case studies describing various LRP implementations have been reported by a number of authors. These cover several fields of government and economic activities. Some of the most interesting cases are summarized in Table 17.3.

17.3 Models

17.3.1 Classifications

Min et al. (1998) represent the Laporte's classification of exact methods as follows:
- Direct tree search
- Dynamic programming
- Integer programming
- Nonlinear programming

Since the majority of solution approaches consist of integer programming, here we concentrate on them and examine them further.

Using the classification of Magnanti (1981), Laporte (1988) puts the integer programming algorithms into the following four categories:
- Set partitioning algorithms
- Commodity flow algorithms
- Vehicle flow algorithms

Here in this chapter, the described integer models are related to the third class; therefore, a brief description of it is provided here.

Vehicle flow models deal with the optimal circulation of vehicles and users in the system and do not include costs and constraints directly related to the actual flow of goods. The TSP and the p-median problem fall into this category.

It is often convenient to classify these models according to the number of indices of the flow vehicles. Common cases are:

- Two-index vehicle flow formulations
- Three-index vehicle flow formulations

There are certain advantages and disadvantages in using two-index or three-index variables in VRP or LRP formulations. Two-index formulations are concise and involve a relatively small number of variables (particularly in the symmetrical case). However, they can not take into account different vehicle costs and characteristics and can therefore only be applied under the assumption that the vehicle fleet is homogenous. Successful implementations of such formulations are reported by Laporte et al. (1985), for example. Three-index formulations are more versatile but, at the same time, more costly. Classical examples of such formulations are the vehicle flow models proposed by Golden et al. (1977) However, Laporte (1988) states that three-index formulations have never led to the successful implementation of an exact algorithm for the VRP.

17.3.2 Mathematical Models

The exact methods generally act on the basis of mathematical programming. They often include relaxations and redefining constrains as follows:

- Subtour elimination: all tours must include only one distribution center
- Chain barring: the distribution centers should not be connected through the routes
- Integrality: the variables should be integers (or binary)

Exact methods provide significant insights into problems, but due to the complexity of location-routing they can only tackle relatively small instances. General location-routing instances with up to 40 potential depot locations or 80 customers have been solved to optimality (Laporte et al. 1988; Laporte and Norbert 1981).

17.3.2.1 The Classical 3/R/T LRP Model

The classical $3/R/T$ model presented by Laporte 1988) consists of simultaneously

- Selecting facility sites at the second layer
- Determining the composition of the vehicle fleet based at each facility
- Constructing optimal delivery routes from the supply sources to the facilities located at the second layer and from these facilities to users

The solution must be such that

- The total system cost is minimized
- All user requirements are satisfied without exceeding vehicle capacities
- The number of vehicles used does not exceed a given bound
- Route length are within a given maximum distance
- Route durations do not go beyond a present time
- Vehicle routes pass through only one facility
- Facility throughput capacities are respected

In order to formally express these constrains and objective, the following notation is introduced. Define sets as following.

L: the set of all supply sources (first layer)
I: the set of all potential facility sites (second layer)
J: the set of all users (third layer)
K: the set of all vehicle routes

Parameters are defined as below:

$\bar{m} = |K|$: the maximum allowed number of vehicle routes
$C = (c_{ij}), (i, j \in I \cup J)$: a distance matrix (undefined if $i, j \in I$)
$T = (t_{ijk}), (i, j \in I \cup J; k \in K)$: a three-dimensional travel time array for all routes and for all pairs of facilities and users
g_i: the fixed cost of establishing facility $i \in I$
v_i: the variable cost per throughput unit at facility $i \in I$
V_i: the maximum throughput at facility $i \in I$
s_{li}: the unit transportation cost from $l \in L$ to $i \in I$
d_j: the requirement of user $j \in J$
T_{kj}: the time required by the vehicle used on route k to unload at user $j \in J$
D_k: the capacity of the vehicle used on route k
E_k: the maximum allowable length (in distance units) of route k
T_k: the maximum allowed duration of route k
p_k: the cost per distance unit of delivery vehicle on route k
q_{ij}: a fixed cost incurred for delivering from facility $i \in I$ to user $j \in J$

Variables are as following:

X_{ijk}: is equal to 1 if i immediately precedes j on route k, otherwise is 0
Y_j: is equal to 1 if a facility is located at site I, otherwise is 0
Z_{ij}: is equal to 1 if user j is served from facility i, otherwise is 0
w_{li}: quantity of goods shipped from supply source $l \in L$ to facility $i \in I$.

Then the problem formulation is as follows:

$$\text{Min} \sum_{i \in I} g_i y_i + \sum_{l \in L} \sum_{i \in I} s_{li} w_{li} + \sum_{i \in I} \sum_{j \in J} (v_i d_j + q_{ij}) z_{ij}$$
$$+ \sum_{k \in K} \sum_{i \in (I \cup J)} \sum_{j \in (I \cup J)} p_k c_{ij} x_{ijk} \qquad (17.5)$$

Subject to

$$\sum_{k \in K} \sum_{i \in (I \cup J)} x_{ijk} = 1 \quad (j \in J) \tag{17.6}$$

$$\sum_{j \in J} \sum_{i \in (I \cup J)} d_j x_{ijk} \leq D_k (k \in K) \tag{17.7}$$

$$\sum_{i \in (I \cup J)} \sum_{j \in (I \cup J)} c_{ij} x_{ijk} \leq E_k \quad (k \in K) \tag{17.8}$$

$$\sum_{j \in J} \sum_{i \in (I \cup J)} \tau_{kj} x_{ijk} + \sum_{i \in (I \cup J)} \sum_{j \in (I \cup J)} t_{ijk} x_{ijk} \leq T_k \quad (k \in K) \tag{17.9}$$

$$\sum_{k \in K} \sum_{i \in S} \sum_{j \in (I \cup J) - S} x_{ijk} \geq 1 \quad (2 \leq |S| \leq |I \cup J|; S \subseteq |I \cup J|; S \cap J \neq O) \tag{17.10}$$

$$\sum_{i \in I} \sum_{j \in J} x_{ijk} \leq 1 \quad (k \in K) \tag{17.11}$$

$$\sum_{j \in (I \cup J)} x_{jik} - \sum_{j \in (I \cup J)} x_{ijk} = 0 \quad (k \in K, i \in I \cup J) \tag{17.12}$$

$$\sum_{l \in L} w_{li} - \sum_{j \in J} d_j z_{ij} = 0 \quad (i \in I) \tag{17.13}$$

$$\sum_{l \in L} w_{li} \leq V_i y_i \quad (i \in I) \tag{17.14}$$

$$-z_{ij} + \sum_{u \in I \cup J} (x_{iuk} + x_{ujk}) \leq 1 \quad (i \in I; j \in J, k \in K) \tag{17.15}$$

$$x_{ijk} = 0, 1 \quad (i \in I; j \in J, k \in K) \tag{17.16}$$

$$y_i = 0, 1 \quad (i \in I) \tag{17.17}$$

$$z_{ij} = 0, 1 \quad (i \in I; j \in J) \tag{17.18}$$

$$w_{li} \geq 0 \quad (l \in L; i \in I) \tag{17.19}$$

In this formulation, the objective function is the sum of facility fixed costs, first level delivery costs, variable warehousing costs and delivery costs, respectively. Equations (17.6) ensure that every user belongs to one and only one route. Equations (17.7)–(17.9) guarantee that vehicle capacities, maximum route length and maximum route durations, respectively, are respected. Equation (17.10) are connectivity constrains: they ensure that every user is on a route connected to the set of facilities. Equation (17.11) are flow conservation equations: any point of $(I \cup J)$ must be entered and left by the same vehicle. Equation (17.12) stipulated that a vehicle can depart only from a facility. This prevents cases where a vehicle leaves the same facility for two different users and also passes through more than one facility. Equation (17.13) ensure that the flow entering a facility is equal to the flow exiting that facility. Equation (17.14) limit the flow through a facility to the capacity of that facility. Equation (17.15) specify that z_{ij} must be equal to 1 if facility i and user j belong to the same route k. Finally, (17.16)–(17.19) impose bounds and integrality conditions on the variables.

17.3.2.2 The TSP with Single Depot

We described the TSP model in part 1, as a basic model in VRP. Here, we extend this model in order to solve the LRP.

In this very simple form of LRP, we consider a set N of users and a subset $I \subseteq N$ of potential sites for a single facility, in order to minimize the total routing cost for a fleet of exactly m vehicles based at that facility (Laporte 1988).

The first step is to define a binary variable y_i equal to 1 if and only if the facility is located at node i. The remaining notation is as in TSP. The problem is then to

$$\text{Min} \sum_{i,j \in J} c_{ij} x_{ij} \tag{17.20}$$

Subject to

$$\sum_{i \in I} y_i = 1 \quad (i \in I) \tag{17.21}$$

$$\sum_{i \prec k} x_{ik} + \sum_{k \prec j} x_{kj} = 2 + 2(m-1) y_i \quad (k \in I) \tag{17.22}$$

$$\sum_{i \prec k} x_{ik} + \sum_{k \prec j} x_{kj} = 2 \quad (k \in N - I) \tag{17.23}$$

$$\sum_{i,j \in S} x_{ij} \leq \tfrac{1}{2} \Delta(S) - 1 \quad (S \subset N; 2 \leq |S| \leq n - 2) \tag{17.24}$$

$$y_i = 0, 1 \quad (i \in I) \tag{17.25}$$

Most constrains of this model are self-explanatory. Equation (17.24) are derived as follows: any feasible solution must correspond to a connected graph, therefore the following constrains must hold:

$$\sum_{i \in S, j \in \bar{S}} X_{ij} \geq 2 \quad (S \subset N; 2 \leq |S| \leq n - 2) \tag{17.26}$$

$$or$$

$$i \in \bar{S}, j \in S$$

In Laporte and Norbert (1981), this model is solved by means of a constraint relaxation method inspired by the branch and bound algorithm for the TSP. The model is solved through initially relaxing the subtour elimination constrains and the integrality conditions on the variables (but by retaining their upper bound). Integrality is gradually regained by branch and bound; at an integer solution, a check for violated subtour elimination constrains is made, the constraint corresponding to the subtour involving the least number of nodes is introduced and the problem is reoptimized.

17.3.2.3 The TSP with Multi Depot

All the assumptions and objectives of this category are just like the single-depot problem, the only difference is locating at most p facilities, instead of one. In addition, the triangle ineguality is assumed to be satisfied in I, i.e.

$$c_{ki} + c_{ij} \geq c_{kj} \quad (i \in I) \tag{17.27}$$

Under this condition, it can be shown that there will be only one vehicle for each opened facility in the optimal solution. (i.e. the m-TSP solution is then dominated by a TSP tour). As in previous model, we define g_i as the fixed cost of opening a facility at site $i \in I$. Then the problem can be formulated as following, with $m = 1$: number of vehicles per new facility, and p: maximum number of facilities.

$$\text{Min} \sum_{i,j \in N} c_{ij} x_{ij} + \sum_{i \in I} g_i y_i \tag{17.28}$$

Subject to

$$\sum_{i \in I} y_i \leq p (i \in I) \tag{17.29}$$

$$\sum_{i \prec k} x_{ik} + \sum_{k \prec j} x_{kj} = 2 \quad (k \in N) \tag{17.30}$$

$$\sum_{i,j \in S} x_{ij} \leq \tfrac{1}{2}\Delta(S) - 1 \quad (S \subset N; 2 \leq |S| \leq n-2) \tag{17.31}$$

$$y_i = 0, 1 \quad (i \in I) \tag{17.32}$$

Equation (17.29) has been changed as compared with the previous model, ensuring that the number of new facilities should not exceed a maximum of p ones. Equation (17.22) used in the single-depot model is not applicable here because with respect to the triangle inequality m will be equal to 1, and (17.23)–(17.24) are here appeared in form of (17.30).

Problems were solved by adapting a former Reverse Algorithm for the TSP that checks for violated subtour elimination constrains even at fractional solutions by Laporte and Norbert (1981). The solution procedure may be summerized in three steps:

- Step 1. Solve the multi-depot TSP by relaxing (17.31) and the integrality conditions on the variables
- Step 2. Identify violated subtour elimination constrains (even if the solution at hand is not necessarily integer) and introduce one such constrain for each illegal component remains
- Step 3. Reach integrality by gradually introducing Gomory cuts. Stop if a feasible solution has been reached. Otherwise, proceed to step 2

17.4 Solution Techniques

Some solution methods for LRPs were mentioned during the previous chapters. Since the exact models are frequently so complicated with numerous constrains and variables, they are often solved by applying approximate methods. So the mathematical models are applicable for special cases. Some examples of the exact methods and the solution techniques of them are presented in Table 17.4. Table 17.4 shows some examples of these methods.

17.4.1 Heuristic Methods

Karp (1972) showed that location is NP Hard and also vehicle routing decisions is NP-hard, thus the LRPs also belongs to the class of NP-hard problems. Due to its complexity, exact solution approaches to the LRP have been very limited and so it is more common to use the heuristic methods.

This algorithms often divide the problem into its components and then solve it. The components are: facility location; allocation of users to facilities; and vehicle routing. These three sub-problems are closely interrelated and cannot be optimized seperately without running the risk of arriving at a suboptimal solution. Laporte (1988) classifies these algorithms in two categories:

- Location–Allocation–Routing Algorithms: facilities are located, users are then allocated to the facilities and routes are finally defined. Watson-Gandy and Dohrn (1973) execute these three steps sequentially while other authors combine the location and allocation steps (see, for example, Bedner and Strohmeier (1979) Or and Pierskalla (1979))

Table 17.4 Solution methods for LRP exact models (Nagy and Salhi 2007)

Problem type	Solution method	Paper	Facilities	Customers
General deterministic LRP	Cutting planes	Laporte et al. (1983)	40	40
	Branch-and-bound	Laporte et al. (1988)	3	80
Round-trip location	Numerical optimisation	Drezner (1982)	1	10,000
Eulerian location	Branch-and-cut	Ghiani and Laporte (1999)	50	200
Minmax TS location	Graph theoretical	Averbakh and Berman (2002)	1	Not given
Plant cycle location	Branch-and-cut	Labbé et al. (2004)	30	120

- Allocation–Routing–Location: the allocation and routing steps are often simultaneous: sets of routes are first constructed, assuming all facilities "open"; locations are then selected by dropping various facilities from the system and updating the location and routing decisions. The SAV-DROP heuristic of Jacobsen and Madsen (1980) and the algorithm of Srikar and Srivastava (1984) constitute examples of these algorithms

Although this classification is applicable for many heuristic algorithms, not all the heuristic algorithms can be categorized into them. For example, the algorithm proposed by Nambiar et al. (1989). did not contain the allocation phase.

Also Nagy and Salhi (2007), have divided the heuristic methods as below:

1. Clustering-based method
2. Iterative method
3. Hierarchical method

17.4.2 Metaheuristic Methods

One recent development in the solution of combinatorial problems is the introduction of metaheuristics such as tabu search, genetic algorithms, simulated annealing, and neural networks (Tuzun and Burke 1999).

All of these metaheuristics aim to search the solution space more electively than conventional approaches using deferent strategies. They show great promise in solution of difficult combinatorial problems such as the LRP. Among these, TS explores the solution space by moving from a solution to its best neighbor, even if this results in a deterioration of the objective function value. This strategy allows the search to move out of the local optima and explore other regions of the solution space (see Glover 1995; Glover et al. 1993, for overviews of TS).

17.5 Case Study

17.5.1 Bill Delivery Services (Lin et al. 2002)

In this research, a local case of integrated facility location and distribution planning problem is described. Distribution of bills to customers is a major issue to a telecommunication service company in Hong Kong that serves a large customer base of business and residential customers. The customer region is divided to 31 housing states and four potential depots. This problem is constrained by operating constraints such as:

- Daily working hours
- Capacity of a vehicle
- The capacity of a potential depot

There is no time window constraint as customers need not be present during the delivery. If multiple routes could be assigned to a vehicle without exceeding the staff working hours, further cost reduction could be achieved.

Considering the above interdependent decisions, the basic questions to address are: given a set of demand nodes (target housing estates) and a set of potential facilities (delivery depot sites), where should the facilities be established? How should routes be formed from a facility and what is the routing sequence to the demand nodes such that all demand nodes are served? What is the smaller number of vehicles (vehicle fleet size) to be used for a given set of established routes? The primary objective of the above location, routing and loading problems is to minimize the sum of facility costs, staff costs, vehicle rental and operating costs.

For solving the problem, based on five different subproblems, the solutions and CPU time of five algorithms TA, SA, (TA, SA), (SA, TA), and branch and bound are calculated and finally the (TA, SA) algorithm is applied to the actual problem. The solution demonstrates that with two depots and 11 routes, the whole customers can be serviced while the costs are minimized.

17.5.2 Contaminated Waste Disposal (Caballero et al. 2007)

This work presents a model to find the best location for up to two incineration plants shared between several preestablished locations in Andalusia (Spain) that will be used to dispose solid animal waste and simultaneously find the best routes to transport the waste from each slaughterhouse to the plants opened. Thus, we are dealing with a location (deciding which plants should be opened) routing (designing the routes to transport the waste from the slaughterhouses) problem.

When evaluating potential locations for the new plants, different factors should be considered; therefore, a multi-objective problem does exist. Five different objectives are formulated while taking into account two major aspects:

- Economic objectives (start-up, maintenance, and transport costs)
- Social objectives (social rejection by towns on the truck routes, maximum risk as an equity criterion, and the negative implications for towns close to the plant)

In the application, we face a problem with six possible locations (where at most we can choose two of them), 93 clients to serve, five objectives to optimize, and constraints on truck capacity and on the duration of the route.

To solve this problem, the researchers have adapted a metaheuristic for multi-objective combinatorial optimization problems based on tabu search, the multi-objective metaheuristic using an adaptative memory procedure method. This adaptation consists of some specific neighborhood definitions inspired by the movements used for a similar problem in the literature, a single-objective LRP with capacitated vehicles. The solution presents a set of efficient solutions considering the five objectives to the decision maker.

17.5.3 Logistics System (Lin and Kwok 2006)

This paper addresses an integrated logistic system where decisions on location of depot, vehicle routing and assignment of routes to vehicles are considered simultaneously. Total cost and workload balance are common criteria influencing decision-making. Metaheuristics of tabu search and simulated annealing on real data and simulated data are applied, to compare their performances under two versions: simultaneous or sequential routes assignment to vehicles. A new statistical procedure is proposed to compare two algorithms on the strength of their multi-objective solutions.

This research has the following contributions:

- A multi-objective LRP integrated with the routes assignment decisions is considered, and real instances from a local delivery service are used
- Certain methods to estimate unavailable data are proposed: the use of GIS to estimate the travel times and a regression method to estimate the on-site service (delivery) time
- A new statistical procedure based on the hypothesis testing of difference between two population proportions (Z-test) is proposed, in order to compare the relative non-dominance of multi-objective solutions between tabu search and simulated annealing
- The effect of allowing multiple use of vehicles in the routes formation stage with the sequential approach of routing before assignment is examined

References

Averbakh I, Berman O (1995a) Probabilistic sales-delivery man and sales-delivery facility location problems on a tree. Transport Sci 29:184–197

Averbakh I, Berman O (1995b) Routing and location-routing p-delivery men problems on a path. Transport Sci 28:162–166

Averbakh I, Berman O (2002) Minmax p-traveling salesmen location problems on a tree. Ann Oper Res 110:55–62

Bender V, Strohmeier E (1979) Largerstandorto imierung und Fuhrparkeinsatzplanung in der konsumguter-industrie. Zen Sconrift Fur Oper Res 23:89–104

Billionnet A, Elloumi S, Grouz-Djerbi L (2005) Designing radio-mobile access networks based on synchronous digital hierarchy rings. Comput Oper Res 32:379–394

Boventer V (1961) The relationship between transportation costs and location rent in transportation problems. J Regional Sci 3:27–40

Bruns A, Klose A, Stähly P (2000) Restructuring of Swiss parcel delivery services. OR Spektrum 22:285–302

Caballero R, Gonzalez M, Guerrero FM, Molina J, Paralera C (2007) Solving a multiobjective location routing problem with a metaheuristic based on tabu search. Application to a real case in Andalusia. Eur J Oper Res 177(3):1751–1763

Chan Y, Carter WB, Burnes MD (2001) A multiple-depot, multiple-vehicle, location-routing problem with stochastically processed demands. Comput Oper Res 28:803–826

Christofides N, Eilon S (1969) An algorithm for the vehicle dispatching problem. Oper Res Quart 20:309–318

Dantzig GB, Fulkerson DR (1954) Minimizing the number of tankers to meet a fixed schedule. Nav Res Logist Q 1:217–222

Daskin MS (1995) Network and discrete location: Models, algorithms, and applications. Wiley, New York

Drezner Z (1982) Fast algorithms for the round trip location problem. IIE Trans 14:243–248

Ghiani G, Laporte G (1999) Eulerian location problems. Networks 34:291–302

Glover F (1995) Tabu search fundamentals and uses. Technical paper, University of Colorado, Boulder, CO

Glover F, Taillard E, De Werra D (1993) A user's guide to tabu search. Ann Oper Res 41:3–28

Golden BL, Magnanti TL, Nguyen HQ (1997) Implementing vehicle routing algorithms. Networks 7:113–148

Gunnarsson H, Rönnqvist M, Carlsson D (2006) A combined terminal location and ship routing problem. J Oper Res Soc 57:928–938

Higgins JC (1972) On the merits of simple models in distribution planning. Int J Phys Distrib 2:144–148

Jacobsen SK, Madsen OBG (1978) On the location of transfer points in a two-level newspaper delivery system – a case study. Presented at the international symposium on locational decisions, 24–28

Jacobsen SK, Madsen OBG (1980) A comparative study of heuristics for a two-level routing-location problem. Eur J Oper Res 5:378–387

Jamil M, Batta R, Malon DM (1994) The traveling repairperson home base location problem. Transp Sci 28:150–161

Karp R (1972) Reducibility among combinatorial problems. Plenum, New York, pp 85–104

Kulcar T (1996) Optimizing solid waste collection in Brussels. Eur J Oper Res 90:26–44

Labbé M, Rodríguez-Martín I, Salazar-Gonzalez JJ (2004) A branch-and-cut algorithm for the plant-cycle location problem. J Oper Res Soc 55:513–520

Laporte G (1988) Location-routing problems. In: Methods and studies. North-Holland, Amsterdam, pp 163–198

Laporte G, Norbert Y (1981) An exact algorithm for minimizing routing and operating costs in depot location. Eur J Oper Res 6:224–226

Laporte G, Nobert Y, Pelletier P (1983) Hamiltonian location problems. Eur J Oper Res 12:82–89

Laporte G, Nobert Y, Desrochers M (1985) Optimal routing under capacity and distance restrictions. Oper Res 33:1050–1073

Laporte G, Nobert Y, Taillefer S (1988) Solving a family of multi-depot vehicle routing and location-routing problems. Transp Sci 22:161–172

Lawrence RM, Pengilly PJ (1969) The number and location of depots required for handling products for distribution to retail stores in South-East England. Oper Res Quart 20:23–32

Lee Y, Kim S-I, Lee S, Kang K (2003) A location-routing problem in designing optical internet access with WDM systems. Photon Netw Commun 6:151–160

Lin CKY, Chow CK, Chen A (2002) A location-routing-loading problem for bill delivery services. Comput Ind Eng 43:5–25

Lin CKY, Kwok RCW (2006) Multi-objective metaheuristics for a location-routing problem with multiple use of vehicles on real data and simulated data. Eur J Oper Res 175:1833–1849

Magnanti TL (1981) Combinatorial optimization and vehicle fleet planning: perspectives and prospect. Networks 11:179–214

Maranzana FE (1965) On the location of supply points to minimize transport costs. Oper Res Quart 15:261–270

McLain DR, Durchholz ML, Wilborn WB (1984) U.S.A.F. EDSA routing and operating location selection study. Report XPSR84-3, Operations Research Division, Directorate of Studies and Analysis

Mercer A, Canley MF, Rand GK (1978) Operational distribution research. Taylor and Francis, London

Min H, Jayaraman V, Srivastava R (1998) Combined location-routing problems: a synthesis and future research directions. Eur J Oper Res 108:1–15

Murty KG, Djang PA (1999) The U.S. army national guard's mobile training simulators location and routing problem. Oper Res 47:175–182

Nagy G, Salhi S (2007) Location-routing: issues, models and methods. Oper Res 177:649–672

Nambiar JM, Gelders LF, Van Wassenhove LN (1989) Plant location and vehicle routing in the Malaysian rubber smallholder sector: a case study. Eur J Oper Res 38:14–26

Or I, Pierskalla WP (1979) A transportation, location-allocation model for regional blood banking. AIIE Trans 11:86–95

Perl J, Daskin MS (1985) A warehouse location-routing problem. Transp Res 5:381–396

Semet F, Taillard E (1993) Solving real-life vehicle routing problems efficiently using tabu search. Ann Oper Res 41:469–488

Srikar B, Srivastava R (1984) Solution methodology for location routing problem. In: ORSA/TIMS conference

Toth P, Vigo D (2002) An overview of vehicle routing problems. In: Toth P, Vigo D (eds) The vehicle routing problem. pp 1–26, Society for Industrial and Applied Mathematics, Philadelphia

Tuzun D, Burke LI (1999) A two-phase tabu search approach to the location routing problem. Eur J Oper Res 116:87–99

Wasner M, Zäpfel G (2004) An integrated multi-depot hub location vehicle routing model for network planning of parcel service. Int J Prod Econ 90:403–419

Watson-Gandy CDT, Dohrn PJ (1973) Depot location with van salesmen – a practical approach. Omega 11:321–329

Webb MHJ (1968) Cost functions in the location of depots for multiple-delivery journeys. Oper Res Quar 19:11–320

Chapter 18
Storage System Layout

Javad Behnamian and Babak Eghtedari

A warehouse consists of a number of parallel aisles. The items are stored on both sides of the aisles. Order pickers are assumed to be able to traverse the aisles in both directions and to change direction within the aisles. Their major roles include: buffering the material flow along the supply chain to accommodate variability caused by factors such as product seasonality and/or batching in production and transportation; consolidation of products from various suppliers for combined delivery to customers; and value-added-processing such as kitting, pricing, labeling, and product customization.

Usually the items in a warehouse exhibit varying characteristics with respect to dimensions, weight, demand, and other properties. It is natural to apply certain storage and retrieval strategies depending upon the product families or individual products within families. Products need to be put into storage locations before they can be picked to fulfill customer orders. A storage policy is considered optimal if it minimizes the average time required to store and retrieve a unit load while satisfying the various constraints placed upon the system. A storage assignment policy is a set of rules which determines where the unit loads of different products will be located in a warehouse. With regard to storing unit loads, two major classes of storage policies can be distinguished (Koster et al. 2007; Goetschalckx and Ratliff 1990; Van den Berg et al. 1999) in other word, The storage location assignment problem (SLAP) is to assign incoming products to storage locations in storage departments/zones in order to reduce material handling cost and improve space utilization. Different warehouse departments might use different SLAP policies depending on the department-specific SKU profiles and storage technology (Gu 2005).

A basic rule in assigning products to storage locations is storing "better" products in the "better" locations in the order picking system. A "the most desirable locations" is a location, which provides faster and more ergonomic access to the product stored.

The definition of "the most desirable locations" depends on the system as well as the travel pattern. For example, if traversal routing policy is used for traveling in a conventional multi-parallel-aisle system, the desirability of locations are measured in terms of aisles where the most desirable locations are in the aisle that is closest to the I/O point (This leads to the so-called organ pipe storage location assignment) (Gu et al. 2007).

A measure of "goodness" of an item could have been the frequency with which it is requested. If an item is requested frequently, it is logical to keep that item in an easily accessible location. But if the item is too heavy, it may be too much time consuming to replenish that item to that favored location. Another measure of "goodness" for an item is occupying smaller space. On the other hand if an item is requested very infrequently, it is not necessary at all to assign it to a favored position, just because it occupies little space. If that practice were followed, the "best" locations could be filled with lots of small products that are not really requested much.

Another basic rule in assigning products to storage locations is taking the dimensions into consideration. Cube matching of the items with the storage locations is essential to eliminate space inefficiencies. Shelf dimensions should be spacious enough to allow easy picking, but tight enough to avoid unused space. Here is a bad usage of shelf space vs. good usage.

An effective storage location assignment policy may reduce the mean travel times for storage/retrieval and order-picking. Also, by distributing the activities evenly over the warehouse subsystems, congestion may be reduced and activities may be balanced better among subsystems, thus increasing the throughput capacity (Van den Berg et al. 1999).

18.1 Assumptions and Classifications

The storage system considered here contains multiple products with stores and retrieves performed in a single-command mode[1] (i.e., there is only one store or one retrieve on each round trip). Most of the concepts extend in a straight forward manner to the dual-command mode (i.e., a store and a retrieve on each round trip). Although there is the potential for more efficient storage using a dual-command mode, the single-command mode continues to be widely used. This is primarily because of the additional coordination required to unload one truck and simultaneously load another.

We assume that all products in the system are stored and moved in unit loads. We also assume that each unit load requires the same space and that the expected cost of storing or retrieving a unit load from a storage location is independent of which unit is stored in that location. This assumption allows computation of the expected travel cost for each location before any storage assignment has been made (Goetschalckx and Ratliff 1990).

---

[1] In a single-command cycle either a storage or a retrieval is performed between two consecutive visits of the input and output station. In a dual-command cycle the S/R machine consecutively performs storage, travels empty to a retrieval location and performs retrieval. The empty travel between the storage and retrieval location is referred to as interleaving travel (Van den Berg et al. 1999).

The physical location where arriving items will be stored Subject to performance criteria and constraints such as:

1. Storage capacity and efficiency
2. Picker capacity and efficiency based on the picker cycle time
3. Response time
4. The compatibility between products and storage locations and the compatibility between products
5. Item retrieval policy such as FIFO (first-in, first-out), LIFO (last-in, first-out), BFIFO (batch first-in, first-out). When using the BFIFO policy, items that arrived in the same replenishment batch are considered to be equivalent.

In typical warehouse operations, the physical storage infrastructure and its characteristics are known when planning the storage location assignment. The availability of storage locations is always known in automated warehouses and often known in mechanized warehouses (Gu 2005).

Trade-offs inevitably occur between *throughput* and *storage space* in designing storage systems. The term *throughput* is used as a measure of the number of storages and retrievals performed per time period. It can be expressed directly as a rate (e.g., 320 storages per 8-h day). Alternatively it can be given inversely in terms of the time required to perform storage (e.g., 1.5 min per storage). Space is a measure of the static nature of storage. Throughput however is a measure of the activity or the dynamic nature of storage; it represents the flow occurring in storage.

The *size* of the storage system depends on a number of parameters and variables. For example, the size of the storage system is influenced by storage, throughput, and cost parameters. The decision variables that influence the size of storage include the storage methods and the storage layout.

The *material characteristics* and *inventory profile* establish the storage and throughput parameters. Included in the former are the characteristics that influence the way material is stored, handled, and controlled. The material characteristics of interest include size, weight, shape, value, shelf life, stack ability, toxicity, flammability, explosiveness; and environmental requirements, among others. The inventory profile includes both the amount of each product stored over time and the input/output functions that generate the activity requirements for storing and retrieving material.

The input/output functions will depend on; the mission of the storage system. As an example, consider a distribution center for finished goods produced at various company-owned manufacturing plants. If a push system is used, the production plants push inventory to the distribution center and the input function will be determined by the production schedules at the plants. The output or demand function might be represented by a forecasting equation developed for the marketing department. The cumulative differences in the input and output functions will determine the storage requirements in the distribution center over time.

Among the *cost parameters* that influence the size of the storage system are the costs of providing storage vs. the costs of not providing storage. The former includes the costs of providing storage internally vs. leasing space or contracting with a public warehouse to provide the storage space. The costs of providing storage space include the costs associated with space, personnel, and equipment resources.

The cost of not providing storage reflects the impact of a space shortage and includes the cost of lost business, goodwill costs, and the cost to the total business due to inadequate space.

The *storage method* used includes the specification of the unit load and/or container to be stored, handled, and controlled, as well as the storage/retrieval device, storage equipment, and other material handling equipment. A number of alternative methods exist for storing and retrieving material, including manually storing items on shelving, storing unit loads in pallet rack with lift trucks, storing unit loads in pallet rack with automated storage/retrieval machines, and manually storing small parts in carousel conveyors. Material can be moved to/from storage manually or mechanically via conveyors and industrial trucks, or automatically via automatic guided vehicles and automated monorails, among others.

The storage system layout includes the height, length, and width of storage, the location of the individual items in storage, and the location and configuration of any required support functions. Both the storage capacity and the throughput capacity of the storage system will be influenced by the layout used.

In this chapter we consider the layout of the storage system. However, to accomplish our objective, it will be necessary to determine the size of the storage requirement. Storage size depends on the number of storage locations required; in turn, the number of storage locations depends on the storage location policy used.

The storage location assignment problem (SLAP) is formally defined as follows:

- Information on the storage area, including its physical configuration and storage layout.
- Information on the storage locations, including their availability, physical dimensions, and location.
- Information on the set of items to be stored, including their physical dimensions, demand, quantity, arrival and departure times.

The storage assignment problem can be divided into three classes depending on the amount of information known about the arrival and departure of the products stored in the warehouse:

1. Product information,
2. Item information
3. No information.

Different operational policies exist for each of these classes, and their implementation and performance have been discussed extensively in the literature. Most of the research has focused on unit-load warehouses. Of course, these SLAP policies can be applied to non unit-load warehouses as well, but it is usually much more difficult to provide analytical results because of the complexity of computing the associated material handling times and cost involved in a non unit-load warehouse (for example when batching and routing are used) (Gu 2005).

18.2 Storage Location Assignment Problem Based on Product Information

Most of the times, only product information is known about the items to be stored, and items are instances of products. Products may be classified into product classes. The assignment problem now assigns an individual item to a product class based on its product characteristics, and assigns a product class to storage locations. The location of an item in its class is most often done using some simple rule, such as nearest location, or randomly. If the number of classes is equal to the number of products, then this policy is called dedicated storage. If the number of classes is equal to one, this policy is denoted as random storage. In real-life warehousing operations, a small number of classes ranging from 3 to 5 are used. This policy is called class-based storage (Gu 2005).

18.2.1 Dedicated Storage Location Policy

In this method each product is stored at a fixed location, which is called dedicated storage (Koster et al. 2007). The dedicated storage location policy is shown Fig. 18.1.

Dedicated storage is used when an SKU is assigned to a specific storage location or a set of locations. The term fixed slot is used to describe the dedicated storage. Two methods of dedicated storage are commonly used:

- Store items in parts number sequence
- Dedicate a location for an SKU based on its activity and inventory level.

The latter method is preferred when there are significant differences in either the activity level or the inventory level for SKUs. Dedicated storage has low space utilization, but the warehouse is easier to manage since it has a permanent assignment of products to locations.

The class-based storage policy and the dedicated storage policy attempt to reduce the mean travel times for storage/retrieval by storing products with high demand at

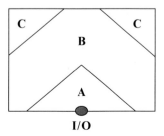

Fig. 18.1 Dedicated storage location policy

locations that are easily accessible (Van den Berg et al. 1999). This method requires more storage space than class-based storage since sufficient storage locations have to be reserved for the maximum inventory of each product, and therefore increases warehouse space cost and material handling cost. On the other hand, dedicated storage has the advantage that the controlling of the warehouse is very simple, since items of a product will always be stored in the same locations and sufficient space is always available for all of the items in replenishment batches. The simplicity advantage is decreasing in importance because the introduction of information technologies such as WMS, bar coding, and radio frequency tags provides a real-time accurate inventory map of the warehouse. The advantages of robustness and simplicity of dedicated storage must be traded off against the increased required storage space and material handling cost (Gu 2005).

A disadvantage of dedicated storage is that a location is reserved even for products that are out of stock. Moreover, for every product sufficient space has to be reserved such that the maximum inventory level can be stored. Thus, the space utilization is lowest among all storage policies. An advantage is that order pickers become familiar with product locations. In retail warehouses, often the product-to-location assignment matches the layout of the stores. This can save work in the stores, because the products are logically grouped. Finally, dedicated storage can be helpful if products have different weights. Heavy products have to be on the bottom of the pallet and light products on top. By storing products in order of weight and routing the order pickers accordingly, a good stacking sequence is obtained without additional effort. Dedicated storage can be applied in pick areas, with a bulk area for replenishment that may have, for example, random storage. In this way, the advantages of dedicated storage still hold, but the disadvantages are only minor because dedicated storage is applied only to a small area (Koster et al. 2007).

Kallina and Lynn (1976) discussed the implementation of the COI rule in practice. The COI rule is easy to implement and has the intuitive appeal of locating compact, fast-moving items in readily accessible locations. Furthermore, the COI rule is proved to be optimal for dedicated storage when the following assumptions are satisfied:

1. The objective is to minimize the long-term average order picking cost.
2. The travel cost depends only on locations. Examples that do not satisfy this assumption include the case when the travel cost is item dependent or when there are multiple I/O points, and products have different probability of moving from/to the I/O points, i.e., it does not satisfy the factoring assumption as defined in Mallette and Francis (1972).
3. When dual or multi-command order picking is used, there is no dependence between the picked items in the same picking tour.
4. Certain routing policies are assumed for multi-command order picking, e.g., Jarvis and McDowell (1991) assume using the traversal routing policy for the conventional multi-aisle order picking system.
5. There are no compatibility constraints that limit the storage location assignment, e.g., certain items must and/or cannot be put together (Gu 2005).

18.2.1.1 Space Requirements

With dedicated storage, products are assigned to specific locations. Also, one and only one product is assigned to a storage location. Hence *the number of storage locations assigned to a product must be capable of satisfying the maximum storage requirement for the product*. With multiproduct storage, the storage space required equals the sum of the maximum storage requirements for each of the products (Francis et al. 1992).

18.2.1.2 Sizing on the Basis of Service Levels

One approach that can be used to size storage under dedicated storage conditions is a *service-level* approach. Specifically, when demand for storage is a random variable, storage capacity can be determined on the basis of the probability of a shortage of space. With dedicated storage, Q_j storage sots are assigned t product i for $i = 1, \ldots, n$. Therefore, the probability of there bring a sufficient number of storage positions for product i is simply the probability of storage demand being less than or equal to Q_j. Thus the probability is given by the cumulative distribution function $F_j(Q_j)$.

If the storage demands for the various products are statistically independent, the probability of there being one or more shortages 0 storage space is given by

$$Pr \text{ (1 or more shortages)} = 1 - Pr \text{ (no shortages)}. \tag{18.1}$$

Since the terms on the right-hand side of (18.2) are the cumulative probabilities, (18.2) can be expressed as

$$Pr \text{ (no shortages)} = \prod_{j=1}^{n} p_r, \tag{18.2}$$

$$Pr \text{ (no shortages)} = \prod_{j=1}^{n} F_j(Q_j). \tag{18.3}$$

Therefore, on substituting (18.3) in (18.1), we obtain

$$Pr \text{ (1 or more shortages)} = 1 - \prod_{j=1}^{n} F_j(Q_j). \tag{18.4}$$

18.2.1.3 Sizing on the Basis of Costs

The previous analysis of space requirements for dedicated storage was based entirely on, service-level considerations. Under deterministic conditions, the size of the storage system was determined to be equal to the sum of the maximum requirements for each product. When random conditions exist, two approaches were considered in order to minimize the amount of space required to ensure that the probability of a shortage is no greater than a prespecified quantity and, given the storage capacity, allocate the space among the products so that the probability of no shortage is maximized.

Alternatively, storage size can be determined using cost models. Such models might reflect the costs of owning and operating space vs. contracting space or incurring a space shortage. To motivate the consideration of cost of models in sizing storage, consider a situation in which the cost to provide Q_j storage slots for product j is equal to the sum of a fixed cost of building Q_j slots, a variable cost of storing product j each time period, and a variable cost that occurs when the requirement for space exceeds Q_j. One formulation of such a situation, under deterministic conditions, follows:

$$\text{Min } TC(Q_1 \ldots Q_n) = \sum_{j=1}^{n} C_0 Q_j + \\ + \sum_{t=1}^{T} C_{1,t} [\min(d_{t,j}, Q_j)] + C_{2,t} [\max(d_{t,j}, Q_j, 0)]\}]. \tag{18.5}$$

Q_j = owned storage capacity for product j
T = length of the planning horizon in time periods,
$d_{t,j}$ = storage space required for product j during period t
$TC(Q_1 \ldots Q_n)$ = total cost over the planning horizon as a function of the set of storage capacities.
C_0 = discounted present worth cost per unit storage capacity owned during the planning horizon of T time periods.
$C_{1,t}$ = discounted present worth cost per unit stored in, owned space during time period t.
$C_{2,t}$ = discounted present worth cost per unit stored in leased space or per unit of space shortage during time period t.

where

$$\min(d_{t,j}, Q_j) = d_{t,j} \text{ if } d_{t,j} < Q_j,$$
$$\min(d_{t,j}, Q_j) = Q_j \text{ if } d_{t,j} \geq Q_j,$$
$$\max(d_{t,j} - Q_j, 0) = 0 \text{ if } d_{t,j} - Q_j < 0,$$
$$\max(d_{t,j} - Q_j, 0) = d_{t,j} - Q_j \text{ if } d_{t,j} - Q_j \geq 0.$$

In (18.5) the discounted present worth cost of building the space for product j is $C_0 Q_j$. The operating cost each time period is based on the amount of *product j in* storage, either the storage requirement ($d_{t,j}$) or the storage capacity (Q_j), whichever i the smallest. If the storage requirement is greater than the storage capacity, a space shortage occurs. Under such conditions, we assume that the excess requirement $(d_{t,j} - Q_j)$ is met via leased storage at an incremental cost of $C_{2,t}$ per, unit stored in leased space during period t.

Due to the separable nature of (18.5), the optimum storage capacity can be determined independently for each product. The total cost function given by (18.5) can be shown to be piecewise linear and convex. Consequently, a simple solution procedure can be used to determine the optimum capacity. Before stating the procedure, let $C' = C_0/C_2 - C_1$ the optimum capacity can be obtained as follows:

1. Sequence the demands for space in decreasing order.
2. Sum the demand frequencies over the sequence.
3. When the partial sum is first equal to or greater than C, stop; the optimum capacity equals that demand level.

18.2.1.4 Assigning Products to Storage/Retrieval Locations

With dedicated storage, products are assigned to storage/retrieval locations in an attempt to minimize the time required to perform the storage and retrieval operations. Of course, for dedicated storage to be feasible, you must have a sufficient number of storage slots to dedicate slots to products. In such a situation, the assignment problem becomes a matter of assigning products to slots according to an appropriate criterion. In our case the criterion will be to minimize some function 0 the distance traveled to store and retrieve the assigned products. To formulate the dedicated storage assignment problem, let

s = number of storage slots or locations
n = number of products to be stored
m = number of input/output (I/O) points
S_j = storage requirement for product j, expressed in number of storage slots;
T_j = throughput requirement or activity level for product j, expressed by the number of storage/retrievals performed per unit time i
$P_{i,j}$ = percent of the storage/retrieval trips for product j that are from/to input/out put (I/O) point $t_{i,k}$ = time required to travel between I/O point i and storage/retrieval location k
$X_{j,k}$ = 1, if product j is assigned to storage/retrieval location k = 0, otherwise
$I(x)$ = expected time required to satisfy the throughput requirement for the system the formulation of the dedicated storage assignment problem is

$$\text{Min} \sum_{i=1}^{m} \sum_{j=1}^{n} \sum_{k=1}^{s} \frac{T_j}{S_j}(p_{i,j}\ t_{i,k}\ x_{j,k}). \tag{18.6}$$

Subject to

$$\sum_{j=1}^{n} x_{j,k} = 1 \qquad k = 1, \ldots, s, \tag{18.7}$$

$$\sum_{j=1}^{s} x_{j,k} = S_j \qquad j = 1, \ldots, n, \qquad (18.8)$$

$$x_{j,k} = 0, 1 \qquad \forall j, k. \qquad (18.9)$$

Equation (18.6) gives, the expected time required to perform the required storages and retrievals during a time period. In particular, if product j is assigned to storage/retrieval location k ($X_{j,k} = 1$), then it takes $t_{i,k}$ time units to travel from input point i to storage location k and it takes $t_{i,k}$ time units to travel from retrieval location k to output point i. Since the total number of storage/retrieval locations for product j equals S_j, the probability of the storage/retrieval trip being from/to storage/retrieval location k is $1/S_j$ for those locations assigned to product j the total number of storage/retrieval trips performed per time period for. product j equals $1j$; however, only $p_{i,j}$ percent of the total trips for product j are performed from/to I/O point i, Hence the expected time required to travel between storage/retrieval location k and I/O point i for product j is given by the product of T_j/S_j and $P_{i,j}.t_{i,k}.x_{j,k}$ Summing over all I/O points, products, and storage locations yields $I(x)$. Equation (18.7) ensures that only one product is assigned to storage/retrieval location k, (18.8) ensures that the number of storage/retrieval locations assigned to product j equals S_j.

Again, our formulation of the storage/retrieval location assignment problem assumes that each of the S_j loads of product j is equally likely to be retrieved and that each of the S_j storage locations assigned to product j is equally likely to be selected for storage. If a first-in, first-out retrieval policy is used and storage is always performed at the location that has been empty the longest period of time, our assumptions will be valid.

On examining (18.6), notice that it can be written equivalently as

$$F(x) = \sum_{j=1}^{n} \frac{T_j}{S_j} \sum_{k=1}^{s} x_{j,k} \sum_{i=1}^{m} (p_{i,j}, t_{i,k}). \qquad (18.10)$$

The term in parentheses represents the average amount of time required for product j to travel between storage/retrieval location k and the m I/O points. Letting

$$\bar{t}_{j,k} = \sum_{i=1}^{m} p_{i,j} t_{i,k}. \qquad (18.11)$$

The objective function can be written as

$$F(x) = \sum_{j=1}^{n} \sum_{k=1}^{s} c_{j,k} x_{j,k}, \qquad (18.12)$$

where $C_{j,k} = (T_j/S_j)\,\bar{t}_{j,k}$. Thus the dedicated storage assignment problem can be formulated as a transportation problem (Francis et al.1992).

18.2.2 Cube-Per-Order Index (COI)

Cube-per-order index (COI) rule is one of the earliest dedicated storage algorithms (Lai et al. 2002, Zapfel et al. 2006). The cube per order index (COI) is perhaps the most common storage dispatching rule. It is defined as the ratio of the number of storage addresses allocated to an item, to the number of transactions per period. It is applied by routing incoming items with the lowest COI values to the most accessible storage addresses of a facility (Malmborg et al. 2000).

The algorithm consists of locating the items with the lowest COI closest to the dock, and assigning items to locations progressively farther away from the dock by increasing COI. Harmatuck showed that COI yields an optimal solution when the system is: of a single-command (one clamp truck trip fulfils one task, stock or retrieve); has a single I/O, with no compatibility constraints; and the traveling of different items are independent. Malmborg and Krishnakumar (2000) have shown that under the Euclidean distance, COI produces the shortest traveling cycle time for a multiple-command system (Lai et al. 2002).

18.2.3 Class-Based Storage Location Policy

The class-based storage location policy distributes the products, based on their demand rates, among a number of classes and reserves a region within the storage area for each class. Accordingly, an incoming load is stored at an arbitrary open location within its class (Van den Berg et al. 1999). The concept of class-based storage combines some of the methods mentioned so far. In class based storage if the number of classes is equal to the number of products, then this policy is called dedicated storage (Gu et al. 2007). The class-based storage location policy is shown Fig. 18.2.

In inventory control, a classical way for dividing items into classes based on popularity is Pareto's method. The idea is to group products into classes in such a way that the fastest moving class contains only about 15% of the products stored but contributes to about 85% of the turnover each class is then assigned to a dedicated area of the warehouse. Storage within an area is random. Classes are determined by some measure of demand frequency of the products, such as COI or pick volume.

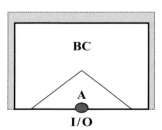

Fig. 18.2 Class-based storage location policy

Fast moving items are generally called A-items. The next fastest moving category of products is called B-items, and so on. Often the number of classes is restricted to three, although in some cases more classes can give additional gains with respect to travel times (Koster et al. 2007).

This storage policy in the literature seems to be a compromise between the dedicated and the randomized storage policies. It divides products into classes based on their turnover ratio. The class with the highest ratio is located closest to the I/O. The implementation of class based storage (i.e., the number of classes, the assignment of products to classes, and the storage locations for each class) has significant impact on the required storage space and the material handling cost in a warehouse (Gu et al. 2007).The implementation of class-based storage (i.e., the number of classes, the assignment of products to classes, and the storage locations for each class) has significant impact on the required storage pace and the material handling cost in a warehouse. Research on this problem has been largely focused on AS/RS, especially single-command AS/RS.

18.2.3.1 Criteria for Assigning a Product (Class) to Storage Locations

Different criteria can be used to assign a product (class) to storage locations. The three most frequently used criteria are (Gu 2005):

1. Popularity (defined as the number of storage/retrieval operations per unit time period). For the popularity policy, product classes are ranked by decreasing popularity and the classes with the highest popularity are assigned the most desirable locations.
2. Maximum inventory (defined as the maximum warehouse space allocated to a product class). For the maximum inventory policy, product classes are ranked by increasing maximum inventory and the classes with the lowest maximum inventory are assigned the most desirable locations.
3. Cube-per-order index (COI, which is defined as the ratio of the retrieval operations per unit time/ maximum allocated storage space to the number of storage). The COI policy takes into consideration both a SKU's popularity and its storage space requirement. Product classes are ranked by increasing COI value and the classes with the high COI are stored in the most desirable locations.

The implementation of the above policies depends on the types of warehouse systems and, therefore there may be have different variations in that, for example:

1. If storage space is measured in units (e.g., shelves and bays), each unit can be treated as an individual product by appropriately apportioning demand. This is most commonly used in unit load warehouses and sometimes in less-than-unit-load warehouses. Since each unit load occupies the same amount of storage space, the popularity policy based on the apportioned popularity is essentially the same as the COI policy. However, it is different from the popularity policy without apportioning. For example, suppose that product A has three unit loads and a popularity of three picks per day, and product B has one unit load and a popularity of two picks a day. The popularity policy without apportioning will

rank product A ahead of product B. On the other hand, if product A is treated as three products (denoted as A1, A2, and A3), each of them will have an apportioned popularity of 1 pick per day. So the popularity policy based on the apportioned popularity will now rank product B ahead of product A1, A2, and A3, which can be easily verified to be equivalent to the COI policy.
2. The definition of "the most desirable locations" depends on the system as well as the travel pattern. For example, if traversal routing policy is used for traveling in a conventional multi-parallel-aisle system, the desirability of locations are measured in terms of aisles where the most desirable locations are in the aisle that is closest to the I/O point. This leads to the so-called organ pipe storage location assignment.
3. The above three policies are simple and flexible enough to be implemented in different warehouse systems. Among them, the COI policy has been the most comprehensively studied one. The COI policy was first described without a proof of its optimality.

18.2.3.2 Assigning a Product (Class) to Storage Locations Based on Popularity

Model parameters:

Q_k = Number of storage locations requested at any single operational period for the storage of SKU i
S = Quantity of storage at any single operational period for the storage of SKU i
R = Quantity of retrieval at any single operational period for the storage of SKU i

Storage policy: calculate S/R ratio

- If $S/R < 1$: locate nearer to receiving
- If $S/R > 1$: locate nearer to shipping
- If $S/R = 1$: does not matter

18.2.4 Class-Based Dedicated Storage Location Policy (COI)

As a compromise between dedicated storage and randomized storage, *class-based, dedicated storage* is frequently used. With class-based dedicated storage, products are divided into three, four, or five classes based on their throughput (T)-to-storage (S) ratios. The relatively few fast movers are categorized as class 1 products, next are class 2 products, and then class 3 products, and so on. Dedicated storage is used for the classes and randomized storage is used within a class.

It should be noted that the entire discussion of dedicated storage given in Sect. 18.2.1 applies to class-based dedicated storage, if, instead of dealing with; products, one deals with classes of products. For this reason, our class-based dedicated storage treatment focuses on the formation of classes of products.

18.2.4.1 Model for Class-Based Storage Location

Van den Berg (1999) presents a polynomial time dynamic programming algorithm that partitions products and locations into classes such that the mean single command cycle time is minimized. The algorithm works under any demand curve, any travel time metric, any warehouse layout and any positions of the input station and output station. We use the following notation:

Q_i = independent random variables representing the number of unit-loads present of product i at an arbitrary epoch,
P_k = set of products in class $k = 1, 2, \ldots, K$. Due to the demand and supply processes the inventory level fluctuates. We estimate the storage space requirement such that the storage space in every class suffices for at least a fraction $0 < \alpha < 1$ of the time. In other words, the probability of a stock overflow is less than 1α-. Let Q^k be a random variable representing the inventory level of class k at an arbitrary epoch, i.e.

$$Q^k = \sum_{i \in P_k} Q_i. \tag{18.13}$$

Now, we want to find the smallest size Sku for the class-region of class k such that

$$P(Q^k \leq S^k) \geq \alpha. \tag{18.14}$$

Let $t_j{}^{in}$ denote the travel time between the input station and location j and let $t_j{}^{out}$ denote the travel time between the output station and location j.

Every stored unit-load is retrieved some time later, so that over a long time period half of the single command cycles are storages and half are retrievals.

Accordingly, the mean single command cycle time to location $j \in L$ equals:

$$\frac{1}{2}(2t_j^{in} + 2t_j^{out}) = (t_j^{in} + t_j^{out}). \tag{18.15}$$

The single command cycle time, $E(SC)$, is defined as

$$E(SC) = \sum_{k=1}^{k} \frac{\sum_{i \in P_k} E(D_i)}{\sum_{i \in P} E(D_i)} \cdot \sum \frac{(t_j^{in} + t_j^{out})}{|L_k|}, \tag{18.16}$$

where L_k denotes the set of storage locations of class k. The First factor represents the probability that a request concerns class k. The second factor represents the mean travel time to a location in class k.

In order to minimize the expected single command cycle time, we assign the products i that constitute the largest demand per reserved space and the locations j with the smallest $(t_j{}^{in} + t_j{}^{out})$ to the First class and we assign the products i that constitute the next largest demand per reserved space and the locations j with the next smallest $(t_j{}^{in} + t_j{}^{out})$ to the second class, and so on. Accordingly, the locations are ranked according to non-decreasing $(t_j{}^{in} + t_j{}^{out})$ and the products are ranked according to nonincreasing demand per reserved space. We define $g_k(p, l)$ as the contribution of classes $1, 2, \ldots, k$ to (18.16) when products $1, 2, \ldots, p$ and storage locations $1, 2, \ldots, l$ are distributed among these classes such that $g_k(p, l)$ is minimal. Then $g_k(p, l)$ satisfies

$$g_k(p, l) = \min{}_{1 \le i \le p, 1 \le j \le l} \left\{ h_{i+1, p}^{j+1, l} + g_{k-1}(i, j) \right\}, \qquad (18.17)$$

where $h_{i+1, p}^{j+1, l}$ denotes the contribution to (18.16) if the products $i + 1, \ldots, p$ and the locations $j + 1, \ldots, l$ form one class k. Recalling that the number of locations required in each class is determined by (18.15) the values $g_k(p, l)$ are found by iteratively solving the dynamic programming (18.17) Each $g_k(p, l)$ corresponds to an optimal solution of the sub problem with k classes and the First p products and the First l storage locations when ranked as indicated before. We may use the algorithm to determine the optimal class-partition for $1, 2, \ldots, k$ classes. Subsequently, the number of classes among $1, 2, \ldots, k$ may be selected that constitutes an acceptable mean travel time and space requirement (Van den Berg et al. 1999).

Research on this problem has been largely focused on AS/RS, especially single command AS/RS. Hausman et al. (1976) show that for single-command AS/RS with the Chebyshev metric, the ideal shape of storage regions is L-shaped. For such systems, the problem reduces to determining the number and boundaries of the classes. Explicit analytical solutions for the class boundaries can be derived for the case with 2 or 3 classes, as shown by Hausman et al. (1976), Kouvelis and Papanicolaou (1995), and Eynan and Rosenblatt (1994). For the general n-class case, Rosenblatt and Eynan (1989) and Eynan and Rosenblatt (1994) suggest a one-dimensional search procedure to find the optimal boundaries. The implementation of class-based storage in multi-command AS/RS is discussed in Guenov and Raeside (1992).

18.2.5 Full Turn-over Based Storage

For the turnover policy, products are ranked by the ratio of their demand rate divided by their maximum inventory. Products with the highest turnover are stored in the most desirable locations. The turnover policy is the most comprehensively studied one in the literature.

This policy distributes products over the storage area according to their turnover. The products with the highest sales rates are located at the easiest accessible locations, usually near the depot. Slow moving products are located somewhere towards the back of the warehouse. An early storage policy of this type is the cube-per-order index (COI) rule, A practical implementation of full turnover policies would be easiest if combined with dedicated storage (Koster et al. 2007). It is applicable when space requirements for individual items are identical and, like the COI, has the objective of maximizing throughput capacity (Malmborg et al. 2000). Gu (2005) showed that the turnover based policy for dedicated storage was first described by Heskett in 1963 and 1964 as the cube-per-order index (COI) rule without a proof of its optimality.

Gu (2005) discussed that some researchers compared randomized storage, dedicated storage, and class-based storage in single-command and dual-command AS/RSs using both analytical models and simulations. The results show that the turnover-based policy for class-based storage with relatively few classes could achieve good performance in terms of both material-handling cost and storage capacity.

The turnover or COI policy has been shown to be optimal for the case with restrictive assumptions such as single command, dedicated storage, and product-independent travel costs. However, simulation typically has been used to show that the turnover policy nearly always performs the best in more general cases (Gu 2005).

The main disadvantage is that demand rates vary constantly and the product assortment changes frequently. Each change would require a new ordering of products in the warehouse resulting in a large amount of reshuffling of stock. A solution might be to carry out the restocking once per period. The loss of flexibility and consequently the loss of efficiency might be substantial when using full-turnover storage. Based on simulation experimental results, Petersen et al. (2004) show that with regards to the travel distance in a manual order-picking system, full turnover storage outperforms class-based storage (Koster et al. 2007). Meanwhile, a class based storage policy allocates zones to specific product groups, often based upon their turnover rate (Gu et al. 2007).

18.2.5.1 Solution Algorithm for Full Turn-over Based Storage

1. Rank all the available storage locations in increasing distance from the I/O point, d_j.
2. Rank all SKU's in decreasing "turns", TH_i/N_i
3. Move down the two lists, assigning to the next most highly ranked SKU i, the next N_i locations.

Model inputs

d_j = Storage locations distance from the I/O point
N_i = Number of storage locations
TH_i = Number of units handled per unit of time

Note

- In case that the material transfer is performed through a forklift truck (or a similar type of material handling equipment), a proper distance metric is the, so-called, rectilinear or Manhattan metric (or L_1 norm):

$$d_j = |x_j - x_{I/O}| + |y_j - y_{I/O}|. \qquad (18.18)$$

- For an AS/RS type of storage mode, where the S/R unit can move simultaneously in both axes, with uniform speed, the most appropriate distance metric is the, so-called Tchebychev metric (or L_∞ norm):

$$d_j = \max\{|x_j - x_{I/O}|, |y_j - y_{I/O}|\}. \tag{18.19}$$

Decision variables: $X_{ij} = 1$ if location j is allocated to SKU i; 0 otherwise.

18.2.5.2 Problem Representation

The schematic of problem presentation for full turn-over based storage is shown in Fig. 18.3.

Formulation

$$\text{Min} \sum_i \sum_j \left[\left(\frac{TH_i}{N_i}\right) \cdot d_j\right] x_{ij}. \tag{18.20}$$

Subject to

$$\sum_j x_{ij} = N_i \quad \forall i, \tag{18.21}$$

$$\sum_i x_{ij} = 1 \quad \forall j, \tag{18.22}$$

$$x_{ij} \in \{0, 1\}, x_{ij} \geq 0 \quad \forall i, j. \tag{18.23}$$

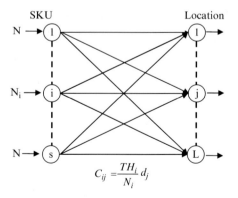

Fig. 18.3 Problem presentation for full turn-over based storage

Remarks

- The previous problem representation corresponds to a balanced transportation problem: Implicitly it has been assumed that: $L = \sum_i N_i$
- For the problem to be feasible, in general, it must hold that: $L \geq \sum_i N_i$

18.3 Storage Location Assignment Problem Based on Item Information (SLAP/II)

In the SLAP/II problem, it is assumed that complete information is known about the arrival and departure time of the individual items. It is very unlikely that information on individual items will be available in typical warehousing operations, but it may be available in the case of short term planning of container ports or airport gates (Gu 2005).

1. Assignment problem and vector assignment problem
2. Shared storage policies for balanced input and output (Goetschalckx and Ratliff 1990)
3. Duration-of-stay storage policy
4. Shared storage policies for unbalanced input and output (Goetschalckx and Ratliff 1990)

    - Static shared storage policies
    - Adaptive shared storage policies

18.3.1 Assignment Problem and Vector Assignment Problem

The resulting problem is a specially structured assignment problem (AP), where items are assigned to storage locations. The special structure derives from the property that two items can occupy the same storage location, provided that they do not occupy it at the same time. This problem has been called the vector assignment problem (VAP), since the occupation is no longer expressed as a single binary status variable but as a vector over the different time periods (Goetschalckx 1998). The optimal solution of this problem for typical warehousing operations is computationally impractical because of the very large problem instances. The problem is of interest to academic research in warehouse operations because it provides a cost lower bound or performance upper bound. An example of a heuristic SLAP/II policy is the duration-of-stay (DOS) policy of Goetschalckx and Ratliff (1990).

18.3.2 Shared Storage Policies

Shared storage policies allow for more flexible use of space than that allowed by dedicated storage policies. This provides the potential both to reduce the maximum-effective storage area and to better utilize the more desirable storage locations. Both of these factors reduce average travel time.

The biggest disadvantage of shared storage is the increased data and computational requirements to keep track of where each retrieved load is located and to determine where each received load should be stored. Using dedicated storage systems. A location will always be used to store the same product and the picker can "learn" where each product is stored (Goetschalckx and Ratliff 1990).

Dedicated storage policies require the warehouse to be large enough to store the maximum inventories of all products simultaneously. If shared storage is allowed and if products are not replenished simultaneously, then total storage requirements vary over time depending on how the material input and output are distributed over time. The required rack size is equal to the maximum number of locations during the planning horizon used by the storage policy. The ideal situation occurs when the input and output flows are balanced. That is, arrival of each unit of new stock occurs just at the time when an old unit is removed from the system. For this ideal case, the warehouse need only be large enough to hold the sum of the average product inventories.

Turnover rate is a product characteristic since all unit loads of the same product have the same turnover rate. The time in storage or "duration-of-stay" for different units of the same product is a unit characteristic since it may differ among different unit loads of the same product. To illustrate this difference, assume that a replenishment batch of units of a product has just arrived and there is no inventory of the product already in storage. The first unit retrieved will stay the length of one demand interarrival time. The last unit retrieved will stay, on the average, the length of the demand interarrival time multiplied by the batch size of the product. It is shown in Sect. 3.2.1 that a duration-of-stay-based policy is optimal under an assumption of perfectly balanced inputs and outputs.

18.3.2.1 Optimal Shared Storage Policy for a Perfectly Balanced System

A system is balanced if for every period t, the number of arriving units is equal to the number of departing units. In a balanced system there is never an empty location at the end of any period and there is always an open location available for an arriving unit. In this case the warehouse is of minimal size and is equal to the sun1 of average inventories of all products.

A system is perfectly, balanced if for any period t, the number of departing units that have duration of stay of p is equal to the number of arriving units that have a DOS of p for all p. The number of units arriving in period t with a DOS of y will be denoted by $n_p(t)$. The system is then perfectly balanced if for all p and t the following relationship holds: $n_p(t) = n_p(t + p)$.

For a balanced system the aggregate input flow is equal to the aggregate output flow. For a perfectly balanced system the input flow is equal to the output flow for each class of units that have the same DOS. Hence perfectly balanced implies balanced, but not the reverse.

For a perfectly balanced system, let z_p be the total number of units arriving during any p consecutive time periods that have a DOS equal top. Then z_p equals to the number's of slots in the warehouse required for storing units which have DOS equal to p, since the units arriving at time period $p+1$ will exactly replace the units arrived at time period one. Note, from the definition of the perfectly balanced system, that z_p is constant over time. For a perfectly balanced system the expression for z_p is

$$Z_p = \sum_{i=1}^{p} n_p(i). \tag{18.24}$$

The following theorem provides a procedure for determining an optimal shared storage policy for a perfectly balanced system

Theorem 18.1. *A shared storage policy which minimizes both travel time and required storage space for a perfectly balanced system is to allocate for each $p = 1, 2, \ldots$ the z_p, unallocated storage locations having the smallest travel time to unit loads with DOS equal to p.*

18.3.3 Duration-of-Stay Storage Policy

In an attempt to reduce the storage space requirement for dedicated storage, some warehouse managers use a variation of dedicated storage in which the assignment of products to spaces is managed carefully. In particular, over time, different products use the same storage slot, albeit only one product occupies the slot when it is occupied. The location policy used is here referred to as *shared storage*.

To motivate our consideration of shared storage, consider the arrival of 100 pallet loads of a particular fast mover product to be stored in pallet rack. Pallet loads will be retrieved and shipped at a rate of five pallet loads per day over a 20-day period. With randomized storage, 100 empty storage slots are randomly selected for the product; no recognition is given to the fact that the product is a fast mover.

With dedicated storage, on the other hand, at least 100 empty slots must be available among the premium locations assigned to the fast-mover product. If randomized storage is used, each time a pallet load is removed from storage, the slot is available for use by the next product requiring storage. However, with dedicated storage, each removal of a pallet from storage creates an empty slot that will not possibly be filled until, at the earliest, the arrival of the next shipment of the same product. Shared storage recognizes that while the product might be considered to be a fast mover, each pallet load stays in storage different lengths of time. Depending on the amount of the product in inventory at the time the shipment arrives, it is possible that five pallet loads will be in storage for only 1 day, whereas five other pallet loads within the same shipment will be in storage for 20 days. From the perspective of the storage positions in the warehouse, five pallet loads appear to be super fast movers; the remaining pallet loads are viewed as being less fast, perhaps even medium or slow movers. *Shared storage recognizes and takes advantage of the inherent differences in lengths of time that individual pallet loads remain in storage* (Francis et al. 1992).

An example of a heuristic SLAP/II policy is the duration-of-stay policy of Goetschalckx and Ratliff (1990). In DOS-based storage policies, the expected DOS of the ith unit of a SKU with replenishment lot size Q is i/λ for $i = 1, 2 \ldots Q$, where λ is the demand rate of that SKU.

$$DOS = i/\lambda. \qquad (18.25)$$

Then the items of all the different products having the shortest DOS are assigned to the closest locations. Hence, the items of a single replenishment batch of a single product are not stored together in the warehouse. Under some unrealistic assumptions on the scheduling and size of product replenishments, it can be shown that the DOS storage policy is optimal for both materials handling effort and required storage capacity. In practice, DOS-based policies are difficult to implement since it requires the tracking and management of each stored unit in the warehouse. Also the performance of DOS-based policies depends greatly on factors such as the skewness of demands, balance of input and output flows, inventory control policies, and the detailed implementations. Kulturel et al. (1999) compared class-based storage and DOS-based storage using simulation and showed that the former consistently outperforms the latter in practical settings.

Goetschalckx and Ratliff (1990) and Thonemann and Brandeau (1998) theoretically showed that DOS-based storage policies are the most promising policy in terms of minimizing traveling costs. In practice, DOS-based policies are difficult to implement since they require the tracking and management of each stored unit in the warehouse. Also, the performance of DOS-based policies depends greatly on factors such as the skewness of demands, balance of input and output flows, inventory control policies, and the detailed implementations (Gu 2005).

18.3.3.1 Space Requirements

The storage space requirements for shared storage range from that required for randomized storage to that required for dedicated storage, depending on the amount of information available regarding the inventory levels over time for each product. As noted above, the distinction between shared storage and randomized storage is that the former involves total specificity regarding the storage locations for products, whereas with the latter, the locations depend solely on the mergence of empty slots within the warehouse. Shared storage and dedicated storage differ due to the distinction made by the former regarding *the time that each load of a product spends*, formally the shared storage policy. Relatively little experience has been gained in applying the policy to large-scale problems optimally; furthermore, as will be seen, it is not immediately obvious how one might go about making optimum location decisions for large-scale applications. We present the policy because (a) multiple products sharing storage space is quite common in some industries, and (b) its features are sufficiently attractive to warrant our further attention. Since the material might be of less interest to those interested in tried and true storage policies, this section may be omitted without jeopardizing an understanding of the remaining material in the chapter (Francis et al.1992).

In storage; dedicated storage assigns the total replenishment lot of a product to a number of storage positions based on *the average time spent in storage for the replenishment lot*.

A situation that naturally suggests the use of shared storage is a production line that is used to produce multiple products. Since products are produced sequentially rather than simultaneously, inventory replenishments are distributed over time. A beverage bottling line is an example of the type of situation we have in mind; other examples include production lines for paint, bleach, and industrial chemicals.

In each case cited, the same production equipment is used to produce different package sizes of the same product, as well as different products. A new setup or changeover is required between the production of different sizes or products Hence it is not possible for the inventory levels of the various sizes and products produced on the same production line to be increasing at the same time. While one product is being produced, the inventory levels of the other products are decreasing. Not all products can be at their maximum inventory levels simultaneously. Hence the use i of dedicated storage would result in some empty storage slots, existing at all times.

18.3.4 Shared Storage Policies for Unbalanced Input and Output

A perfectly balanced system is a much idealized situation which is unlikely to occur in real storage systems. However, the analysis of the perfectly balanced systems provides:

1. A bound on how much improvement can be expected from the use of shared storage policies, and
2. Insights which allow development of attractive heuristics for more realistic situations.

Shared storage policies for systems which are not perfectly balanced need to be distinguished in terms of when information is available to make the storage decisions. We will define static storage policies as those where all the information affecting the storage and retrieval decision is available at the beginning of the planning period. In this case, all assignments of items to locations can be made prior to the beginning of the planning horizon. We define adaptive policies as those using information which becomes available during the planning period to influence the storage and retrieval decisions. Based on the knowledge gained from the perfectly balanced case, we develop heuristics for both static and adaptive policies and then compare them (Goetschalckx and Ratliff 1990).

18.3.5 Static Shared Storage Policies

First consider a static system where we know the arrival and departure time of each item during the planning horizon. From the results we conclude that for all shared storage systems that satisfy the travel independence condition, any storage policy that relies only on the ranking of the travel times to the locations (and not on their actual value) is optimal if and only if it simultaneously maximizes the number of items stored in the first, first two, ..., first N locations. This is a very restrictive condition and thus finding optimal policies based only on the ranking of the storage locations will most likely be restricted to special cases. Goetschalckx (1992) shows that solving the optimal storage policy will require a prohibitive computational effort in a warehousing setting. However, if we know the exact arrival and departure time of each unit during the planning horizon (i.e., the system is static), then an efficient heuristic (GREEDY) can be formulated.

GREEDY is based on the fact that we can efficiently maximize the number of units stored in the first location. Given the assignment of units to the first location, we can maximize the number of units stored in the second location. In general, given the assignment of units to the first locations we can maximize the number of units stored in location $n + 1$. To accomplish this we first order all the units, which will be stored during the planning horizon, by nondecreasing departure time. If there are any ties, then they are broken by ordering the units by nondecreasing arrival time. This tie-breaker fills up early locations as much as possible, thereby increasing flexibility for later decisions. The storage locations are ordered by nondecreasing travel time. We then assign the units in order to the open location with the smallest travel time.

The computational effort required by GREEDY is small, since it requires only a sort of the locations and a sort of the items. The effort is of the order of $O(K \log (K)) + O(N \log (N))$ where K is the number of units stored during the planning horizon and N is the number of slots in the warehouse (Goetschalckx and Ratliff 1990).

18.3.6 Adaptive Shared Storage Policies

Most real life storage systems are adaptive systems, because complete and perfect information is not available at the beginning of the planning horizon. Most of the time, the only information available is with regard to average material flow and, in some cases, what is arriving during the next period. The policy developed in this section involves establishment of classes within the warehouse based on average arrivals and departures of items with different durations of stay. This can be viewed as a variation of the Hausman et al. (1976) class based storage concept, but with the classes based on unit duration of stay rather than product turnover rate.

Let $n_p(t)$ be the number of units with DOS equal to p which arrives in period t. Let $\bar{n}_p$ be the average number of items arriving in a period with DOS equal to p. For a perfectly balanced system $\bar{n}_p$ is equal to z_p/p. Hence, for those items with DOS equal to p, we define a zone of size $p\bar{n}_p$ which is exactly the right size each period.

For systems which are not perfectly balanced, some periods have $n_p(t)$ different from the number of open locations in the zone of size $p\bar{n}_p$. Hence, a zone of size pi & is too large for some periods and too small for other periods. One approach to handling this variation is to establish the zones in exactly the same fashion as for the perfectly balanced case. That is, let $z_p = p\bar{n}_p$ be the zone size for items with DOS equal to p. Then for $p = 1, 2\ldots$ reserve the z, remaining locations with the smallest travel time for items with DOS equal to y.

There are two difficulties with this approach which must be overcome. The first is that z, may not be an integer number of slots since $p\bar{n}_p$ is not necessarily integer. This can be handled by rounding z, to the nearest integer. When z, is small the relative impact of this rounding is greater than when z, is larger. For example if $z_1 = 1.5$ the zone size could double, based on which way z_1 value is rounded. An alternative is to aggregate items into a class until the z, for the aggregate class can be rounded without large relative Impact. It is shown that for that case the increase in average distance traveled which results from combining two adjacent DOS classes is $\bar{n}_p^2 C/2$ where c is the slot width. This result indicates that the impact of combining classes is strongly affected by the number of items arriving in a class, but not by the DOS itself. Hence, we would be more inclined to combine DOS classes with small $\bar{n}_p$.

The second difficulty occurs when an item arrives with DOS equal to p and the zone allocated for items with DOS equal to p is full. It seems logical to assign the item either to the nearest zone higher than p with an open location or the nearest zone lower than p with an open location. To better understand the impact of putting an item in a zone different from its own, consider the following situation. Suppose that one slot in a zone corresponding to DOS equal to p is always used for items with DOS equal to q and one slot in a zone corresponding to DOS equal to q is always used for items with DOS equal to p. Further, assume that both slots remain full. Let t_p and t_q, be the average travel time to zones p and q respectively.

If the slots had been used for the correct items, then the expected travel time would have been $t_p/p + t_p/q$. By interchanging the slot usage, the expected travel time becomes $t_p/p + t_p/q$ which is an increase of

$$(q-p)(t_q - t_p)/pq. \qquad (18.26)$$

From this we see that the impact of interchange becomes less a p and q get larger (i.e., the penalty for placing an item in the wrong zone decreases with increasing duration of stay).

For the computation experiments discussed in the next section, the zones for the dynamic shared storage policy were determined by the following ADAPTIVE algorithm with cumulative rounding. The average time between two demands for an item of product i is denoted by dit_i.

18.3.6.1 Adaptive Algorithm

1. For each duration of stay p do
$$n_p = 0. \tag{18.27}$$

For each item $k = 1 \ldots q_i$ in replenishment batch of produce i do
$$P = k.di_n. \tag{18.28}$$
$$n_p = n_p + 1/(q_i.dit_i). \tag{18.29}$$

2. for each duration of stay p do
$$z_p = n_p.p. \tag{18.30}$$

Cumulative remainder $= 0$, *prev bound* $= 0$, *zone* $= 0$.

3. for each duration of stay p do
   Cumulative remainder = *cumulative remainder* $+z_p$
   If cumulative remainder > 1 *then,*
   Zone = *zone* $+ 1$,
   Zone size (zone) = *round to integer (cumulative remainder),*
   Lower dos (zone) = *prev bound* $+1$,
   Upper dos (zone) $= p$,
   Cumulative remainder = *cumulative remainder* $-$ *zone size (zone),*
   Prev bound $= p$.

In step 1 of the algorithm the average number of items arriving for each duration of stay is computed, based on the fact that during $q_i dit_i$, time periods one item belonging to product i with duration of stay p will arrive in the system. In step 2 the required zone size z_p is computed for each duration of stay and the bookkeeping variables for step three are initialized. In step 3 of the algorithm, for each dos the required zone size is added to the cumulative remainder, until the cumulative remainder is larger than one location.

Then, the new zone is set equal to the cumulative remainder size rounded to the nearest integer and the DOS bounds for this new zone are set. The size of this new zone is then subtracted from the cumulative remainder. This is consistent with the properties that zones with large z_n's and corresponding large z_n's should not be combined and zones with small z_n's can be combined without incoming a large penalty. It also solves the problem on how to round the fractional zone sizes to integer numbers.

Once the zones are determined, ADAPTIVE executes in the same way as the optimal policy. At the time of its arrival, the DOS of every unit is estimated and that unit is stored in its corresponding zone. If that zone is full, the unit is stored in the open location with the smallest value for expression (Goetschalckx and Ratliff 1990).

18.4 Storage Location Assignment Problem Based on No Information (SAP/NI)

If no information is available on the characteristics of the arriving items, only very simple storage policies can be constructed. In this case the most frequently used policies are

1. Closest-open-location (COL),
2. Farthest-open-location (FOL),
3. Random (RAN)
4. Longest-open-location (LOL).

The first two policies pick an open location based on its distance to the receiving dock; the last policy picks the location that has been vacant for the longest time. It is not known if there is any significant performance difference between them.

18.4.1 Randomized Storage Location Policy

Randomized storage, also referred to as *floating slot storage*, allows the storage location for a particular product to change or float over time. In practice, randomized storage is defined as follows (Fig. 18.4).

When a load arrives for storage it is placed in the closest open feasible location; retrievals occur on a first-in, first-out basis. If there s more than one input point, the storage location selected is the one closest to the input point through which the unit load enters the storage facility. In modeling randomized storage, it is commonly assumed that each empty storage slot is equally likely to be chosen for storage when a storage operation is performed; similarly, it is assumed that each unit of a particular product is equally likely to be retrieved when multiple storage locations exist for a product and a retrieval operation is performed. When the warehouse is relatively full, there are no significant differences in the travel distances obtained via the "equal likelihood" assumptions and those resulting from the closest open slot practice. However, for a "sparse warehouse" there can be significant differences in the travel distances obtained.

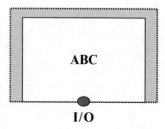

Fig. 18.4 Randomized storage location policy

The random storage policy will only work in a computer-controlled environment (Malmborg et al. 2000). If the order pickers can themselves choose the location for storage we would probably get a system known as closest open location storage. The first empty location that is encountered by the employee will be used to store the products. This, typically, leads to a warehouse where racks are full around the depot and gradually more empty towards the back (if there is excess capacity). Hausman et al. (1976) argue that closest open location storage and random storage have a similar performance if products are moved by full pallets only (Koster et al. 2007). Closest open location refers to the placement of stored items in the closest available address to minimize expected cycle times in randomized storage systems (Malmborg et al. 2000).

18.4.1.1 Space Requirements

With randomized storage, products can be stored in any available storage slot Hence, the storage space requirements will equal the maximum of the aggregate storage. requirements for the products.

We have considered two approaches in sizing a storage facility determining the minimum size that satisfies; service-level objective (expressed as a probability of a space shortage), and determining the size on the basis of trade-offs in the costs of providing space vs. having insufficient space. In this section, both approaches are considered in sizing a storage facility for randomized storage.

Due to the dynamic conditions that typically exist in the replenishment of products it is very difficult to *exactly* predict the storage requirement for randomized storage. For this reason, storage capacity levels are sometimes established by treating inventory levels of the products as random variables (Francis et al. 1992).

18.4.1.2 Sizing Randomized Storage Based on "Service Level" Requirements

Q = max number of storage locations requested at any single operational period (a random variable)

$$P_k = Pr\,(Q = k),\ k = 0, 1, 2 \ldots \text{ (Probability mass function for } Q), \quad (18.31)$$

$$F(k) = Pr\,(Q_k) = \sum_{j=0\ldots k} p_j \text{ (Cumulative distribution function for } Q). \quad (18.32)$$

Problem formulation. Find the smallest number of locations N, which will satisfy a requested service level s for storage availability, i.e.,

$$\min N. \quad (18.33)$$

Subject to

$$F(N) \geq s, \qquad (18.34)$$
$$N \geq 0. \qquad (18.35)$$

Solution

$$N = \min \{k : \sum_{j=0,\ldots,k} p_j \geq s\}. \qquad (18.36)$$

18.5 Comparing Storage Policies

- The class-based storage location policy and the dedicated storage location policy attempt to reduce the mean travel times for storage/retrieval by storing products with high demand at locations that are easily accessible (Van den Berg et al. 1999).
- Dedicated storage requires more space than randomized storage. If an out-of-stock condition exists for a given SKU, the empty slot continues to remain "active" with dedicated storage; whereas, it would not be the case with randomized storage. If multiple slots are assigned for a given SKU, as the inventory level decreases, the number of empty slots will increase (Koster et al. 2007).
- Comparing dedicated storage with random storage, the former has the advantage of locating fast moving and compact SKUs close to the I/O points, and therefore is beneficial for efficient material handling. However, it also requires more storage space since sufficient storage locations must be reserved for the maximum inventory of each product. In class-based storage, additional decisions are to determine the number of classes and to assign products to classes (Gu et al. 2007).
- *Dedicated storage* policies require that a particular storage location be reserved for units of a single product during the entire planning horizon. *Shared storage* policies allow the successive storage of units of different products in the same location (Goetschalckx and Ratliff 1990).

18.6 Family Grouping

All storage assignment policies discussed so far have not entailed possible relations between products. For example, customers may tend to order a certain product together with another product. In this case, it may be interesting to locate these two products close to each other. An example of this is called family-grouping, where similar products are located in the same region of the storage area. Clearly, grouping of products can be combined with some of the previously mentioned storage policies. For example, it is possible to use class-based storage and simultaneously group related items. However, the decision in which class to locate the products has to depend on a combination of the properties of all products in the group. Roll and Rosenblatt (1983) compare the space requirements for the random and grouped storage for a port warehouse and show that the grouped storage assignment increases space requirements compared to random storage assignment. Rosenblatt and Roll (1984) set up a model for warehousing costs, taking the effect of space requirements into account. To apply family grouping, the statistical correlation between items (e.g. frequency at which they appear together in an order, should be known or at least be predictable. In the literature, two types of family grouping are mentioned. The first method is called the complementary-based method, which contains two major phases. In the first phase, it clusters the items into groups based on a measure of strength of joint demand ("complementary").

In the second phase, it locates the items within one cluster as close to each other as possible (Wascher 2004). Rosenwein (1994) shows that the clustering problem can be formulated as a p-median problem. For finding the position of clusters, Liu (1999) suggests that the item type with the largest demand should be assigned to the location closest to the depot (volume-based strategy), while Lee (1992) proposes to take into account also the space requirement (COI-based strategy). The second type of family-grouping method is called the contact based method. This method is similar to the complementary method, except it uses contact frequencies to cluster items into groups. For a given (optimal) routing solution, a contact frequency between item type i and item type j is defined as the number of times that an order picker picks either item type I directly after item type j, or item type j directly after item type i. However, the routing decision is dependent on the location of the item types, which demonstrates the strong interrelationship between item location and routing. Due to the fact that finding a joint optimal solution for both problems is not a realistic approach, at least not for problem instances of the size encountered in practice, contact-based solution methods alternate between the two problem types (Koster et al. 2007). The contact-based method is considered, for example, in Van Oudheusden et al. (1988).

18.7 Continuous Warehouse Layout

In this section we assume that the set of storage locations can be represented adequately as "continuous" planar region, a set of positive area, rather than a set of discrete locations. The reasons for studying continuous warehouse layout are threefold. First, results from continuous formulations can provide insights concerning the underlying discrete problem. Second, many storage problems involve such a large number of storage locations that a continuous representation is quite appropriate. Third, the continuous problem may be easier to solve than the corresponding discrete problem.

18.7.1 Storage Region Configuration

Perhaps after some reflection it should be; apparent that the shape of the continuous storage region for a product can be defined by a contour line. In this chapter apply these concepts in defining the boundaries of storage regions within a warehouse. In this chapter we let the existing facilities be the source (input) and destination output) points for travel to/from storage; the percentage of travel between storage and the I/O points represent the weights between existing and new facilities By definition, a contour line encloses all points having an expected distance raveled less than or equal to the value of the contour line; we call the set of such points a level set or contour set. In this chapter we will be interested in constructing level sets of a given area in defining the storage regions to be used in a warehouse.

A storage region defined by a level set of area A will have an expected distance less than or equal to the expected distance for any other set of equal area. Based on the use of contour lines to define storage regions, the problem of determining storage configurations for continuous warehouse layouts reduces to a geometry problem.

18.8 Dynamic Storage Location Assignment Problems (Gu 2005)

The version of the SLAP problem studied in the literature is most often static, i.e., it assumes that the incoming and outgoing material flow patterns are stationary over the planning horizon. In reality, the material flow changes dynamically due to factors such as seasonality and the life cycles of products. Therefore, the storage location assignment should be adjusted to reflect changing material flow requirements. One possibility is to relocate those items whose expected retrieval rate has increased (decreased) closer to (farther from) the I/O point. Such relocations are only beneficial when the expected saving in order picking outweighs the corresponding relocation cost. Therefore, decisions must be made carefully concerning which set of items to be relocated, where to relocate them, and how to schedule the relocations. Another type of relocation might take place as a result of the uncertainty in incoming shipments. For example, Roll and Rosenblatt (1987) describes the situation when the storage area is divided into separate zones and any incoming shipment must be stored within a single zone. It might happen that none of the zones has sufficient space to accommodate an incoming shipment. In such cases, it is advisable to free some space in a certain zone to accommodate the incoming shipment by shifting some stored products in that zone to other zones (Gu 2005).

18.9 Case Study

This section lists some real industrial case studies, which not only provide applications of the various design and operation methods in practical contexts, but more

Table 18.1 A summary of the literature on SLAP case studies

Citation	Problems studied	Type of warehouse
Zeng et al. (2002)	Storage location assignment; warehouse dimensioning; storage and order picking policy	A distribution center
Van Oudheusden et al. (1988)	Storage location assignment; batching; routing	A man-on-board AS/RS in an integrated steel mill
Kallina and Lynn (1976)	Storage location assignment using the COI rule	A distribution center

importantly also identify possible future research challenges from the industrial point of view. Table 18.1 lists these case studies with the problems and the types of warehouse they investigated. The detailed results and discussions are too cumbersome to be presented here. Interested readers should refer to the original papers (Gu 2005).

References

Eynan A, Rosenblatt MJ (1994) Establishing zones in single-command class-based rectangular AS/RS. IIE Trans 26(1):38–46
Francis RL, McGinnis LF, White JA (1992) Facility layout and location: An analytical approach. Englewood Cliffs, NJ: Prentice-Hall
Goetschalckx M (1992) An interactive layout heuristic based on hexagonal adjacency graphs. Eur J Oper Res 63:304–321
Goetschalckx M (1998) A review of unit load storage policies in warehouse operations. Proceedings of EURO XVI Conference, Brussels, July 12–15
Goetschalckx M, Ratliff HD (1990) Shared storage policies based on the duration stay of unit loads. Manage Sci 36(9):1120–1132
Gu JX (2005) The forward reserve warehouse sizing and dimensioning problem. Working Paper, Virtual Factory Laboratory Georgia Institute of Technology
Gu JX, Goetschalckx M, McGinnis LF (2007) Research on warehouse operation: A comprehensive review. Eur J Oper Res 177(1):1–21
Guenov M, Raeside R (1992) Zone shapes in class based storage and multicommand order picking when storage/retrieval machines are used. Eur J Oper Res 58:37–47
Hausman WH, Schwarz LB, Graves SC (1976) Optimal storage assignment in automatic warehousing systems. Manage Sci 22(6):629–638
Jarvis JM, McDowell ED (1991) Optimal product layout in an order picking warehouse. IIE Trans 23(1):93–102
Kallina C, Lynn J (1976) Application of the cube-per-order index rule for stock location in a distribution warehouse. Interfaces 7(1):37–46
Koster Rd, Le-Duc T, Roodbergen KJ (2007) Design and control of warehouse picking order: A literature review. Eur J Oper 182(2):481–501
Kouvelis P, Papanicolaou V (1995) Expected travel time and optimal boundary formulas for a two-class-based automated storage/retrieval system. Int J Prod Res 33(10):2889–2905
Kulturel S, Ozdemirel NE, Sepil C, Bozkurt Z (1999) Experimental investigation of shared storage assignment policies in automated storage/retrieval systems. IIE Trans 31(8):739–49

Lai KK, Xue J, Zhang G (2002) Layout design for a paper reel warehouse: A two-stage heuristic approach. Int J Prod Econ 75:231–243
Lee MK (1992) A storage assignment policy in a man-on-board automated storage/retrieval system. Int J Prod Res 30(10):2281–2292
Liu CM (1999) Clustering techniques for stock location and order-picking in a distribution center. Comp Oper Res 26:989–1002
Mallette AJ, Francis, RL (1972) A generalized assignment approach to optimal facility layout. AIIE Trans 4(2):144–147
Malmborg CJ, Al-Tassan K (2000) An integrated performance model for order picking systems with randomized storage. Appl Math Model 24(2):95–111
Petersen CG, Aase G (2004) A comparison of picking, storage, and routing policies in manual order picking. Int J Prod Econ 92:11–19
Roll Y, Rosenblatt MJ (1983) Random versus grouped storage policies and their effect on warehouse capacity. Mater Flow 1:199–205
Roll Y, Rosenblatt MJ (1987) Shifting in warehouses. Mater Flow 4:147–157
Rosenblatt MJ, Eynan A (1989) Deriving the optimal boundaries for class-based automatic storage/retrieval systems. Manage Sci 35(12):1519–1524
Rosenblatt MJ, Roll Y (1984) Warehouse design with storage policy considerations. Int J Prod Res 22(5):809–821
Rosenwein MB (1994) An application of cluster analysis to the problem of locating items within a warehouse. IIE Trans 26(1):101–103
Thonemann UW, Brandeau ML (1998) Optimal storage assignment policies for automated storage and retrieval systems with stochastic demands. Manage Sci 44(1):142–148
Van Oudheusden DL, Tzen YJ, Ko HT (1988) Improving storage and order picking in a person-on-board AS/R system: a case study. Eng Costs Prod Econ 13:273–283
Van den Berg JP, Zijm WHM (1999) Models for warehouse management: Classification and examples. Int J Prod Econ 59:519–528
Wascher G (2004) Order picking: A survey of planning problems and methods. In: Supply Chain Management and Reverse Logistics, pp 323–347
Zapfel G, Wasner M (2006) Warehouse sequencing in the steel supply chain as a generalized job shop model. Int J Prod Econ 104:482–501
Zeng AZ, Mahan M, Fluet N (2002) Designing an efficient warehouse layout to facilitate the order-filling process: an industrial distributor's experience. Prod Invent Manage J 43(3):83–88

Chapter 19
Location-Inventory Problem

Mohamadreza Kaviani

Traditionally, logistics analysts have divided decision levels into strategic, tactical and operational (Miranda and Garrido 2006). There are also three important decisions within a supply chain: facilities location decisions; inventory management decisions; and distribution decisions (Shen and Qi 2007). For example, in a distribution network, we could mention location of Distribution centers (DCs) as a strategic decision, distribution decisions as a tactical decision and inventory service level as a tactical or operational decision. Often, for modeling purposes, these levels are considered separately. And this may conduce to make non-optimal decisions, since in reality there is interaction between the different levels (Miranda and Garrido 2006). For example, most well-studied location models do not consider inventory costs, and shipment costs are estimated by direct shipping. Although one may argue that tactical inventory replenishment decisions and shipment schemes are not at the strategic level, and we should not consider them in the strategic planning phase, however, failure to take the related inventory and shipment costs into consideration when deciding the locations of facilities can lead to sub-optimality, since strategic location decisions have a big impact on inventory and shipment costs (Shen and Qi 2007). On the other hand firms would like to consider cost and service levels simultaneously. It is good to have many DCs, since this reduces the cost of transporting product to customers (/retailers) and will provide better service. Also, it is good to have few DCs, since this reduces the cost of holding inventory via pooling effects, and reduces the fixed costs associated with operating DCs via economies of scale (Erlebacher and Meller 2000).

Nozick and Turnquist (1998) discussed that in 1997, Thomas provided the data that show total logistics costs (inventory plus transportation) in the U.S. declined from about 13% of Gross Domestic Product (GDP) in 1985, to about 10.5% in 1993, largely as a result of increasing emphasis on controlling inventories throughout the supply chain. "However, since 1993, logistics costs (as a percentage of GDP) have been essentially constant. The "easy" cost reductions have been made, and further improvements will require more effective tools" (Nozick and Turnquist 1998).

Nozick and Turnquist (2001) also discussed that in 1997, Thomas provided inventory and freight transportation costs for the US economy in 1985, and through the 1990s. "Freight transportation costs have been nearly constant (at about 6%

of Gross National Product) over the entire period of the data. Inventory costs fell significantly between 1985 and 1992, as companies implemented just-in-time systems and the economy grew steadily. However, since 1992 there has been almost no change in inventory costs, and total physical distribution costs seem to have reached a plateau" (Nozick and Turnquist 2001).

On the basis of the above, managing inventory has become a major challenge for firms as they simultaneously try to reduce costs and improve customer service in today's increasingly competitive business environment (Daskin et al. 2002). The goal of cost reduction is to provide motivation for centralization of inventories. On the other hand, the goal of customer responsiveness is to provide motivation for having goods as near to the final consumer as possible. Thus, there is a basic conflict between these objectives, and locating DCs is a critical decision in finding an effective balance between them (Nozick and Turnquist 2001). Many companies face the strategic decision of deciding on the number of DCs, their location, and which customers they serve. One objective for a company facing this decision is to maintain acceptable service while minimizing the fixed costs of operating the DCs, inventory holding costs at the DCs, and transportation costs between plants and DCs, and DCs and customers (Erlebacher and Meller 2000). Inventory theory literature tends to focus on finding optimal inventory replenishment strategies at the DCs and the retailer outlets. This work usually assumes that the number and locations of the DCs are given. On the other hand, location theory tends to focus on developing models for determining the number of DCs and their locations, as well as the DC-retailer assignments. This work usually includes fixed facility setup costs and transportation costs, but the operational inventory and shortage costs are typically ignored (Daskin et al. 2002).

The location-inventory problem is presented bellow. A set of suppliers and customers are spatially dispersed in a geographical region. Typically, the customers face stochastic demand for an array of products offered by the suppliers (Miranda and Garrido 2008). We consider a three-tiered system consisting of one or more suppliers, DCs and customers shown in Fig. 19.1. We assume that the locations of the suppliers and the customers are known and that the suppliers have infinite capacity at least from the perspective of the system being modeled. The problem is to determine the optimal number of DCs, their locations, the customers assigned to each DC, and the optimal ordering policy at the DCs (Daskin et al. 2002).

For example, consider a blood bank that supplied roughly 30 hospitals in the greater Chicago area. Our focus was on the production and distribution of platelets, the most expensive and most perishable of all blood products. If a unit of platelets is not used within 5 days of the time it is produced from whole blood, it must be destroyed. The demand for platelets is highly variable as they are needed in only a limited number of medical contexts. The hospitals supplied by the blood bank collectively owned the blood bank and set prices. As a result they could return a unit of platelets up to the time it outdated and not be charged for it. Thus, there was little incentive to manage inventories in an efficient manner. Many of the larger hospitals ordered almost twice the number of platelet units that they used each year resulting in the need to destroy thousands of units of this expensive blood product.

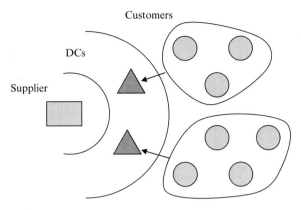

Fig. 19.1 A three-tiered system

Other hospitals ordered almost all of their needed platelets on an emergency basis. The blood bank often had to ship the units to these hospitals using a taxi or express courier at significant expense to the system. Clearly an improved system was needed (Daskin et al. 2002). Or General Motors is instituting a "customer express delivery" system in an attempt to provide better availability of a wide range of vehicles to customers, while reducing the amount of inventory held on dealer lots. With the customer express delivery program, new vehicles would be held at DCs and be made available to the dealers on order, using a 24-h delivery standard (Nozick and Turnquist 2001).

This chapter is organized as follows. In Sect. 19.1, literature and classification of location-inventory problem are given, and Sect. 19.2 presents some models developed for the problem. Some relevant approaches to solve Location Inventory models are given in Sect. 19.3. Finally, Sect. 19.4 represents a short summary of a real world case study.

19.1 Applications and Classifications

The literature presents different approaches to model and solve the problem. The inventory literature tends to ignore the strategic location decision and its associated costs, whereas the location literature tends to ignore the operational inventory and shortage costs, as well as the demand uncertainty and the effects that reorder policies have on these and shipping costs (Shen et al. 2003).

In the literature, many papers have been seen that study the integration and coordination of any two of the three important decisions: location routing models, inventory-routing models, and location-inventory models as below:

- Nozick and Turnquist (1998) demonstrate a way of approximating the costs of safety stock for a set of products as a linear function of the number of DCs. This allows the costs of safety stock to be included directly in a fixed-charge form of the facility location model

- Erlebacher and Meller (2000) formulate a highly nonlinear integer location-inventory model. They attack the problem by using a continuous approximation as well as a number of constructions and bounding heuristics
- Daskin et al. (2002) and Shen et al. (2003) studied the joint location-inventory model in which location, shipment and nonlinear safety stock inventory costs are included in the same model. They developed an integrated approach to determine the number of DCs to establish, the location of the DCs, and the magnitude of inventory to maintain at each center
- Shen et al. (2003) derived a cross-level model to analyze decisions about inventory control and facility location, specially suited to urban settings, where the storage space is scarce and the vehicles' capacity is usually restricted. Both conditions, on the one hand make the problem difficult to solve optimally, on the other hand make it more realistic and useful in practice. Shen et al. (2003) reformulate the problem as a Set Covering Problem, which is then solved through a hybrid heuristic mixing columns generation and branch and bound methods. While Daskin et al. (2002) apply Lagrangian relaxation to solve this problem
- Miranda and Garrido (2006) present a simultaneous nonlinear-mixed integer model of inventory control and facility location decisions, which considers two novel capacity constraints. The first constraint states a maximum lot size for the incoming orders to each warehouse, and the second constraint is a stochastic bound to inventory capacity. This model is NP-hard and presents nonlinear terms in the objective function and a nonlinear constraint
- Snyder et al. (2007) present a stochastic version of the location model with risk pooling that optimizes location, inventory, and allocation decisions under random parameters. The goal of their model is to find solutions that minimize the total cost (including location, transportation, and inventory costs) of the system across all scenarios. The location model explicitly handles the economies of scale and risk-pooling effects that result from consolidating inventory sites. They present a Lagrangian-relaxation–based exact algorithm for the model. The Lagrangian sub problem is a non-linear integer program, but it can be solved by a low-order polynomial algorithm
- Shen and Qi (2007) formulated a nonlinear integer programming model to minimize the total cost that includes location costs and inventory costs at the DCs, and distribution costs in the supply chain, for which they propose a Lagrangian relaxation based solution algorithm. By exploring the structure of the problem, they find a low-order polynomial algorithm for the nonlinear integer programming problem that must be solved in solving the Lagrangian relaxation sub-problems
- Miranda and Garrido (2008) developed an efficient heuristic to solve a joint location–distribution–inventory model for a three layered supply chain. The solution approach is based on Lagrangian relaxation, improved with validity constraints derived from the finite set of all possible combinations of mean demand and variance. The optimal solution's lower bound is found through the optimal solution of the dual problem

19 Location-Inventory Problem

A classification of different types of location inventory problems and their properties is represented as follows:

- Area solution: *Discrete, Continual*
- Objective function: *MiniMax, MiniSum*
- Variables: *integer, mixed integer*
- Determine the number of DCs: *Exogenous, Endogenous*
- DC capacity: *Unlimited, Limited*
- Cost of DC location: *No cost, fixed cost, Variable cost*
- Solution methods: *Exact, Heuristic, Meta heuristic*

19.2 Models

In this section, we introduce location-inventory models represented and developed as mathematical models.

19.2.1 Model of Shen et al. (2003)

The first model that is present here is easy to understand. Shen et al. (2003) assume that location costs are incurred when DCs are established. Line-haul transportation costs are incurred for shipments from the single supplier to the DCs. Local transportation costs are incurred in moving the goods from the DC to the retailers. Inventory costs are incurred at each DC and consist of the carrying cost for the average inventory used over a period of time, as well as safety stock inventory that is carried to protect against stock outs that might result from the uncertain retailer demand. Inventory costs are also incurred at each retailer.

19.2.1.1 Model Inputs

Model inputs of this model are as follows:

μ_i : Mean (yearly) demand at retailer i, for each $i \in I$
σ_i^2 : Variance of (daily) demand at retailer i, for each $i \in I$
f_i : fixed (annual) cost of locating a regional DC (RDC) at retailer j, for each $j \in I$
$v_j(x)$: cost to ship x units from the main supplier (the plant) to a RDC located at retailer j, for each $j \in I$
d_{ij} : cost per unit to ship from retailer j to retailer i, for each $i \in I$ and $j \in I$
α : Desired percentage of retailer's orders satisfied
β : Weight factor associated with the transportation cost

θ : Weight factor associated with the inventory cost
z_α : Standard normal deviate such that $P(z \leq z_\alpha) = \alpha$
h : Inventory holding cost per unit of product per year
$w_j(x)$: Total annual cost of working inventory held at DC j if the expected daily demand at j is x for each $j \in I$
F_j : fixed cost of placing an order at DC j, for each $j \in I$
L : lead time in days

19.2.1.2 Model Outputs (Decision Variables)

Model outputs of this model are as follows:

$X_j = 1$, if retailer j is selected as a DC location, and 0 otherwise for each $j \in I$
$Y_{ij} = 1$, if retailer i is served by a DC based at retailer j, and 0 otherwise for each $i \in I$ and each $j \in I$

19.2.1.3 Objective Function and its Constraints

The objective function of this model and its related constraints are as follows:

$$\text{Min} \sum_j \left\{ f_j X_j + \beta \sum_i \mu_i d_{ij} Y_{ij} + w_j \left(\sum_i \mu_i Y_{ij} \right) + \theta h z_\alpha \sqrt{\sum_i \sigma_i^2 Y_{ij}} \right\} \quad (19.1)$$

Subject to

$$\sum_j Y_{ij} = 1 \quad \forall i \quad (19.2)$$

$$Y_{ij} \leq X_j \quad \forall i, j \quad (19.3)$$

$$Y_{ij} \in \{0, 1\} \quad \forall i, j \quad (19.4)$$

$$X_j \in \{0, 1\} \quad \forall j \quad (19.5)$$

Equation (19.1) minimizes the weighted sum of the following four costs: the fixed cost of locating facilities, the shipping cost from the DCs to the non-DC retailers, the expected working inventory cost, and the safety stock costs. Equation (19.2) ensures that each retailer is assigned to exactly one DC. Equation (19.3) states that retailers can only be assigned to candidate sites that are selected as DCs. Equations (19.4) and (19.5) are standard integrity constraints.

19.2.2 Model of Nozick and Turnquist (1998)

Assume that there are n retail outlets assigned to the DC, each with a Poisson demand process whose mean rate is λ_i where $1 \leq i \leq n$. Each time an item is demanded at a retail outlet, a replacement is ordered immediately from the DC. Therefore, the demand at the DC is Poisson with a mean rate:

$$\Lambda = \sum_i \lambda_i \tag{19.6}$$

Assume that the DC has a total of s items either in inventory or on order, and it orders from the plant each time an item is sent to a retail outlet. We will define μ and σ^2 to be the mean and variance of the delivery time of a product from the plant to the DC once an order is placed. Then the performance measures for the single DC and assigned retail outlets are the same as those for an M/G/s queue with an arrival rate of Λ, a mean and variance for the service time distribution of μ and σ^2, respectively, and s servers.

The stock out rate is the percentage of demand that can not be satisfied from on-hand inventory. In the queuing system representation, this is analogous to the probability that when a customer enters the system, a server is not available (i.e. wait time, denoted by W, is greater than zero). The probability of waiting (stock out), $P(W \succ 0)$ in an M/G/s queue can be approximated quite accurately by $P(W \succ 0)$ in an M/M/s queue.

They use two equations to approximate $r = P(W \succ 0)$ for two conditions to find the minimum inventory necessary for a given stock out rate.

If there is a constant total expected demand across all retail outlets, the total safety stock required is related to the number of DCs used. Consider a product with an expected demand of 800 units per year. Furthermore, assume that this expected demand is divided equally among N DCs. Based on these assumptions; they provided a histogram for this case that shows the safety stock necessary for various numbers of DCs, given a stock out rate of 5%, and the predicted safety stock based on a linear regression model:

$$\text{Safety stock} = a + bN = 22 + 1.8N$$

where $N =$ number of DCs.

19.2.2.1 Model Inputs

Model inputs of this model are as follows:

f_j : fixed cost of locating a facility at candidate site j
h_i : demand at location i
d_{ij} : distance from demand location i to candidate site j
α : cost per unit distance per unit demand

19.2.2.2 Model Outputs (Decision Variables)

Model outputs of this model are as follows:

$X_j = 1$ if a facility is to be located at candidate site j, and 0 otherwise
Y_{ij} = fraction of demand at location i which is served by a facility at j

19.2.2.3 Objective Function and its Constraints

The objective function of this model and its related constraints are as follows:

$$\text{Min} \sum_j f_j X_j + \alpha \sum_i \sum_j h_i d_{ij} Y_{ij} \tag{19.7}$$

Subject to

$$\sum_j Y_{ij} = 1 \quad \forall i \tag{19.8}$$

$$Y_{ij} \leq X_j \quad \forall i, j \tag{19.9}$$

$$X_j = 0, 1 \quad \forall j \tag{19.10}$$

$$Y_{ij} \geq 0 \quad \forall i, j \tag{19.11}$$

Equation (19.7) minimizes the sum of the following two costs: the fixed cost of locating facilities and the shipping cost from the DCs to the demand locations assigned to the DC. Equation (19.8) ensures that each retailer is assigned to exactly one DC. Equation (19.9) states that retailers can only be assigned to candidate sites that are selected as DCs. Equations (19.10) and (19.11) are standard integrity constraints.

19.2.3 Model of Erlebacher and Meller (2000)

19.2.3.1 Model Assumptions

Model assumptions of this model are as follows:

- The problem is represented by a unit-square grid structure with C columns and R rows
- Uniform customer demand across any grid
- Distances are measured rectilinearly between plants and DC locations, and DC locations and continuously-represented customer locations
- Each DC operates under a continuous-review inventory system
- The location and capacity of each plant is known and fixed

19.2.3.2 Model Inputs

Model inputs of this model are as follows:

i: Index for DCs; $i = 1, \ldots, N$
j: Index for customer grids; $j = 1, \ldots, M$
p: Index for plants; $p = 1, \ldots, P$
(c_j, r_j): Location of customer grid j (right-hand side of grid, $x = c_j$; bottom of grid, $y = r_j$)
d_j: Average demand for customer j; D = total average demand = $\sum_{j=1}^{M} d_j$
(a_p, b_p): Location of plant p
v_p: Volume capacity at plant p
F: Annual cost of operating a DC
s: Unit DC-to-customer transportation (shipping) cost
l: Unit plant-to-DC transportation (logistic) cost
A, h, z, σ: Order cost, holding cost, safety-stock parameter, and standard deviation of total demand during lead-time, respectively

19.2.3.3 Model Outputs (Decision Variables)

Model outputs of this model are as follows:

$Z_i = 1$ if DC_i opened, and 0 otherwise
N = number of DCs to open = $\sum i Z_i$
(x_i, y_i) = location of DC_i
$w_{ij} = 1$ if DC_i serves customer grid j, and 0 otherwise
t_{ip} = average distance from DC_i to customer grid j
u_{pi} = demand shipped from plant p to DC_i
q_{pi} = distance from plant p to DC_i

19.2.3.4 Objective Function and Its Constraints

The objective function of this model and its related constraints are as follows:

$$\text{Min } F \sum_{i=1}^{r} Z_i + \sum_{i=1}^{r} Z_i \left(\sqrt{2Ah} + \frac{z\sigma}{\sqrt{D}} h \right) \sqrt{\sum_{j=1}^{M} d_j w_{ij}} + l \sum_{p=1}^{p} \sum_{i=1}^{r} Z_i u_{pi} q_{pi}$$

$$+ s \sum_{i=1}^{r} \sum_{j=1}^{M} Z_i \left(t_{ij}^x + t_{ij}^y \right) d_j w_{ij} \qquad (19.12)$$

where:

$$q_{pi} = |x_i - a_p| + |y_i - b_p| \qquad (19.13)$$

$$t_{ij}^x = \begin{cases} \frac{1}{2}[x_i - (c_j - 1)]^2 + \frac{1}{2}(c_j - x_i)^2; & if \quad c_j - 1 \leq x_i \leq c_j \\ \frac{1}{2}|x_i - (c_j - 1)| + \frac{1}{2}|c_j - x_i|; & otherwise \end{cases} \quad (19.14)$$

$$t_{ij}^y = \begin{cases} \frac{1}{2}[y_i - (r_j - 1)]^2 + \frac{1}{2}(r_j - y_i)^2; & if \quad r_j - 1 \leq y_i \leq r_j \\ \frac{1}{2}|y_i - (r_j - 1)| + \frac{1}{2}|r_j - y_i|; & otherwise \end{cases} \quad (19.15)$$

Subject to

$$\sum_{i=1}^{M} w_{ij} = 1 \quad \forall j \quad (19.16)$$

$$\sum_{j=1}^{M} w_{ij} \leq Z_i \quad \forall i \quad (19.17)$$

$$\sum_{p=1}^{P} u_{pi} = \sum_{j=1}^{M} d_j w_{ij} \quad \forall i \quad (19.18)$$

$$\sum_{j=1}^{r} u_{pi} \leq v_p \quad \forall p \quad (19.19)$$

$$Z_i \in \{0, 1\} \quad \forall i \quad (19.20)$$

$$w_{ij} \in \{0, 1\} \quad \forall i, j \quad (19.21)$$

$$u_{pi} \geq 0 \quad \forall p, i \quad (19.22)$$

Equation (19.12) minimizes the sum of the following four costs: the fixed cost of locating facilities, total DC inventory costs, and total transportation costs from plants to DCs, and from DCs to customers. Equations (19.13)–(19.15) compute the rectilinear distances from the plants to the DCs, and the DC locations to the continuously-represented customer locations. Equation (19.16) ensures that each retailer is assigned to exactly one DC. Equation (19.17) states that retailers can only be assigned to candidate sites that are selected as DCs. Equation (19.18) ensures that each DC is fully supplied. Equation (19.19) checks each plant's capacity. Equations (19.20)–(19.22) are standard integrity constraints.

19.2.4 Model of Daskin et al. (2002)

The formulation that they obtain is a mixed integer non-linear programming problem which can be viewed as an extension of the traditional uncapacitated fixed charge facility location problem. In addition to the standard facility location and local distribution costs, the model includes cost components representing working and safety stock inventories at the DCs as well as transport costs from the supplier(s) to the DCs. These inventory and supplier-to-DC transport costs introduce significant nonlinearities into the model.

19.2.4.1 Model Assumptions

- The formulation allows for multiple production plants but assumes that the uncapacitated DCs receive the product from the (uncapacitated) plant with the smallest total shipping cost to the DC
- Plant to DC lead time is the same for all plant/DC combinations
- DC using a (Q, r) inventory model
  - Axsater (1996) notes that it is common to approximate the (Q, r) model using two steps with the order quantity determined by an EOQ model in which the mean demand is used to represent the stochastic demand process and the reorder point is determined in a second step
- We know which customers are to be assigned to a specific DC

With these assumptions, the model is mathematically equivalent to assuming that there is only a single plant.

19.2.4.2 Model Inputs

Model inputs of this model are as follows:

I: set of retailers indexed by i
J: set of candidate DC sites indexed by j
f_j: fixed cost of locating a DC at candidate site j, for each $i \in I$ and $j \in J$
d_{ij}: cost per unit to ship between retailer i and candidate DC site j, for each $i \in I$ and $j \in J$
χ: Days per year (used to convert daily demand and variance values to annual values)
μ_i: Daily mean demand at each retailer
σ_i^2: Daily variance demand at each retailer
S: Set of customers assigned to the DC
L: Lead time in days for deliveries from the supplier to the DC
Z_α: Is a standard Normal deviate ($P(Z \leq Z_\alpha) = a$)
D: Expected annual demand ($D = \chi \Sigma_i \mu_i$)
h: holding cost per item per year
F: fixed cost of placing an order from the DC to the supplier
n: (unknown) number of orders per year
$v(x)$: cost of shipping an order of size x from the supplier

β and θ are weights that we assign to transportation and inventory costs respectively so that we can later test the effects of varying the importance of these costs relative to the fixed facility costs

g: Fixed cost of a shipment from the plant to the DC
a: Volume dependent cost of a shipment from the plant to the DC

19.2.4.3 Model Outputs (Decision Variables)

Model outputs of this model are as follows:

$X_j = 1$ if a facility is to be located at candidate site j, and 0 otherwise
$Y_{ij} = 1$ if demands at retailer i are assigned to a DC at candidate site j, and 0 otherwise

The annual cost of ordering inventory from the supplier at the DC is:

$$Fn + \beta v \left(\frac{D}{n}\right) n + \theta \frac{hD}{2n} \tag{19.23}$$

Taking the derivative of this expression with respect to n, the number of orders per year, and setting the derivative to zero, we obtain:

$$F + \beta v \left(\frac{D}{n}\right) - \beta n v' \left(\frac{D}{n}\right) \frac{D}{n^2} - \theta \frac{hD}{2n^2} = 0 \tag{19.24}$$

$$n = \sqrt{\theta h D / (2(F + \beta g))} \tag{19.25}$$

Substituting this into the cost function we obtain an annual working inventory cost of

$$\sqrt{2\theta h D (F + \beta g)} + \beta a D \tag{19.26}$$

19.2.4.4 Objective Function and its Constraints

The objective function of this model and its related constraints are as follows:

$$\begin{aligned}\text{Min} \sum_{j \in J} f_j X_j &+ \left(\beta \sum_{j \in J} \sum_{i \in I} \chi d_{ij} \mu_i Y_{ij}\right) \\ &+ \left(\sum_{j \in J} \sqrt{2\theta h (F_j + \beta g_j) \sum_{i \in I} \chi \mu_i Y_{ij}} + \sum_{j \in J} a_j \sum_{i \in I} \chi \mu_i Y_{ij}\right) \\ &+ \theta h Z_\alpha \sum_{j \in J} \sqrt{\sum_{i \in I} L \sigma_i^2 Y_{ij}} \end{aligned} \tag{19.27}$$

Subject to

$$\sum_{j \in J} Y_{ij} = 1 \quad \forall i \tag{19.28}$$

$$Y_{ij} \leq X_j \quad \forall i, j \tag{19.29}$$

$$X_j \in \{0, 1\} \quad \forall j \tag{19.30}$$

$$Y_{ij} \in \{0, 1\} \quad \forall i, j \tag{19.31}$$

Equation (19.27) minimizes the sum of the following four costs: the fixed cost of locating facilities, local delivery cost, total working inventory cost, and the safety stock inventory cost. Equation (19.28) ensures that each retailer is assigned to exactly one DC. Equation (19.29) states that retailers can only be assigned to candidate sites that are selected as DCs. Equations (19.30) and (19.31) are standard integrity constraints.

19.2.5 Model of Shen and Qi (2007)

They propose a supply chain design model, which considers the impacts of the strategic facility location decisions on the tactical inventory and shipment decisions in a three-tiered supply chain. They assume that each customer has uncertain demand that follows a certain probability distribution. They assume that the customers are uniformly scattered in a connected area. Several DCs will be opened and each DC is served directly by the supplier and distributes products to customers. Each customer will order at the beginning of the period, the DC combines the orders from different customers and order from the supplier. The number and locations of DCs are not given a priori. They assume that at every DC, there is a delivery truck with fixed capacity. A key problem is that the demand that is seen by each DC is a function of the demands at the customers assigned to that DC, which is a function of the assignment of customers to the DC. They assume the transportation costs and the inventory costs exhibit economies of scale under which the average unit cost decreases as the total volume of activity increases. This realistic assumption will result in several nonlinear terms in the formulation.

19.2.5.1 Model Assumptions

- The customers are uniformly scattered in a connected region, S
- The area of S is A
- The customer demands are independent and follow Normal distributions

19.2.5.2 Model Inputs

Model inputs of this model are as follows:

I : Set of customers
J : Set of candidate DC locations
μ_i : Mean (yearly) demand at customer i, for each $i \in I$
σ_i^2 : Variance of (daily) demand at retailer i, for each $i \in I$
f_j : Fixed (annual) cost of locating a DC at j, for each $j \in J$
α : Desired percentage of customer's orders satisfied (fill rate)
β : Weight factor associated with the shipment cost
θ : Weight factor associated with the inventory cost
Z_α : Standard normal deviate such that $P(Z \leq Z_\alpha) = \alpha$
h : Inventory holding cost per unit of product per year
F_j : Fixed administrative and handling cost of placing an order at DC j, for each $j \in J$
L : DC order lead time in days
g_j : Fixed shipment cost per shipment from the plant to DC j
$\bar{a}_j$: Cost per unit of a shipment from the plant to candidate site j
χ : Denote the number of visits in a year
m : Total number of customers served by a specific DC j
$\bar{q}$: Vehicle capacity
d_{ij} : Distance between customer i and DC j
T_j^* : Length of the optimal traveling salesman tour that visits DC j and the customers it serves

19.2.5.3 Model Outputs (Decision Variables)

Model outputs of this model are as follows:

X_j : 1, if j is selected as a DC location, and 0, otherwise
Y_{ij} : 1, if customer i is serviced by a DC based at j, and 0, otherwise

The annual cost of ordering inventory from the supplier at the DC is provided exactly similar to Daskin et al. (2002) as:

$$\sqrt{2\theta h D_j (F_j + \beta g_j)} + \beta \bar{a}_j D \qquad (19.32)$$

And for approximate Routing cost they assume each DC sends a truck to visit its customers at a fixed frequency, say every day or every week and estimate the routing distance from DC j to the customers it serves by the following formulation (see Chap. 17: LRP):

$$V_j \approx \left[2 \left(\sum_i \mu_i d_{ij} Y_{ij} \right) \bigg/ \bar{q} + \chi \left(1 - 1/\bar{q} \right) \Phi \sum_i Y_{ij} \sqrt{\frac{A}{N}} \right] = \sum_i \hat{b}_{ij} Y_{ij} \qquad (19.33)$$

19.2.5.4 Objective Function and its Constraints

The objective function of this model and its related constraints are as follows:

$$\text{Min} \sum \left\{ f_j X_j + \beta \bar{a}_j \sum_i \mu_i Y_{ij} + RC_j \left(\sum_i \hat{b}_{ij} Y_{ij} \right) \right.$$
$$\left. + K_j \sqrt{\sum_i \mu_i Y_{ij}} + q \sqrt{\sum_i \sigma_i^2 Y_{ij}} \right\} \quad (19.34)$$

Subject to

$$\sum_j Y_{ij} = 1 \quad \forall i \quad (19.35)$$

$$Y_{ij} \leq X_j \quad \forall i, j \quad (19.36)$$

$$Y_{ij} \in \{0, 1\} \quad \forall i, j \quad (19.37)$$

$$X_j \in \{0, 1\} \quad \forall j \quad (19.38)$$

where:

$$K_j = \sqrt{2\theta(F_j + \beta g_j)h}$$
$$q = \theta h Z_\alpha \sqrt{L}$$

Equation (19.34) minimizes the sum of the following five costs: the fixed cost of locating facilities, the annual shipment cost from the supplier to the DCs, The annual shipment cost from the DCs to the customers, working inventory cost, the safety stock inventory cost. Equation (19.35) ensures that each retailer is assigned to exactly one DC. Equation (19.36) states that retailers can only be assigned to candidate sites that are selected as DCs. Equations (19.37) and (19.38) are standard integrity constraints.

The constraints of the model are identical to those of the uncapacitated facility location (UFL) problem, thus the problem we are studying is more difficult than the standard UFL problem, which is already a notorious NP-hard problem.

19.2.6 Model of Miranda and Garrido (2008)

The problem is that of locating a set of facilities with constrained storage and ordering capacities, to serve a set of known and fixed spatially distributed clients with stochastic demands, which must be satisfied to a given level of service.

19.2.6.1 Model Inputs

Model inputs of this model are as follows:

M : Number of clients to be served
N : Number of potential DCs
i : Index for DC i
j : Index for customer j
d_j : Mean daily demand for each customer j
v_j : Variance of the daily demand for each customer j
$Q_{\max}$: Order size capacity
I_{cap} : DC inventory capacity
FC_i : Daily fixed installation and operating costs for DC i
TC_{ij} : Total daily transportation cost from DC i to client j
UOC_i : Unit cost per order to be transported from a plant to DC i
OC_i : Fixed ordering costs for DC i
HC_i : Daily holding cost per unit of product at DC i
$1 - \alpha$: Level of service linked to the safety stock level at each DC
$1 - \beta$: Level of service linked to the inventory capacity constraint at each DC
Z_θ : Value of the cumulative standard normal distribution up to a probability of θ
LT_i : Deterministic lead time when ordering from DC i

19.2.6.2 Model Outputs (Decision Variables)

Model outputs of this model are as follows:

$X_i = 1$ if a DC is installed at site i, and 0 otherwise
$Y_{ij} = 1$ if DC i serves client j, and 0 otherwise
$D_i = $ Mean daily demand to be assigned to DC i
$V_i = $ Variance of the daily demand assigned to DC i
$Q_i = $ Order size at warehouse i

19.2.6.3 Objective Function and its Constraints

The objective function of this model and its related constraints are as follows:

$$\text{Min} \sum_i FC_i X_i + \sum_i \sum_j (UOC_i d_j + TC_{ij}) Y_{ij} + \sum_i \left(OC_i \frac{D_i}{Q_i} + HC_i \frac{Q_i}{2} \right)$$

$$+ \sum_i HC_i Z_{1-\alpha} \sqrt{LT_i V_i} \qquad (19.39)$$

Subject to

$$\sum_i Y_{ij} = 1 \quad \forall j \qquad (19.40)$$

$$Y_{ij} \leq X_j \quad \forall i,j \qquad (19.41)$$

$$D_i = \sum_j Y_{ij} d_j \quad \forall i \qquad (19.42)$$

$$V_i = \sum_j Y_{ij} v_j \quad \forall i \qquad (19.43)$$

$$0 \leq Q_i \leq Q_{\max} \quad \forall i \qquad (19.44)$$

$$Q_i + (Z_{1-\alpha} + Z_{1-\beta})\sqrt{LT_i V_i} \leq I_{cap} X_i \quad \forall i \qquad (19.45)$$

$$X_j \in \{0,1\} \quad \forall j \qquad (19.46)$$

$$Y_{ij} \in \{0,1\} \quad \forall i,j \qquad (19.47)$$

Equation (19.39) represents the total daily system costs and minimizes the sum of the following four costs: the fixed and operating cost of locating facilities, daily transport cost between each DC and its assigned customers, plus the transportation and ordering costs between the plant and DCs, total ordering and working inventory cost, and the safety stock inventory cost. Equation (19.40) ensures that each retailer is assigned to exactly one DC. Equation (19.41) states that retailers can only be assigned to candidate sites that are selected as DCs. Equations (19.42) and (19.43) link the mean and the variance of each DC demand, to the mean and the variance of the demand of each customer assigned to it. Equation (19.44) sets the accepted range for the lot size. Equation (19.45) is the stochastic inventory capacity restriction. Equations (19.46) and (19.47) are standard integrity constraints.

19.3 Solution Approaches

Among algorithms that are represented to solve different types of location-inventory problems, we introduce some of the proposed associated approaches:

19.3.1 Solution Approach of Erlebacher and Meller (2000)

Since the problem they are solving is NP-hard, finding an optimal solution could require enumerating overall values of N and all customer-to-DC allocations. This enumeration could be time consuming for realistic-sized problems. To that end, they first develop an analytical model based on some simplifying assumptions to determine a good starting point for a search on N. Then present bounds of N to limit the search. And finally, they consider heuristics for allocating customers to DCs.

19.3.1.1 Solution Approach

- Determining the optimal number of DCs
  - Stylized model for the optimal number of DCs
  - Examples with stylized model
  - Considering plant locations in the stylized model
- Using bounds to determine a range on the optimum number of DCs
- Location-allocation heuristics
  - Location problems
  - The allocation heuristics
  - Considering plant locations in the heuristic

19.3.2 Solution Approach of Daskin et al. (2002)

To solve this problem, they use Lagrangian relaxation embedded in branch and bound.

19.3.2.1 Solution Approach

- Using a Lagrangian relaxation:

- Finding a lower bound for number of DCs
- Finding an upper bound for number of DCs
  - Retailer reassignments (try to improve the bounds)
  - DC exchange algorithm improvements (try to improve the bounds)
- For each DC in the current solution, find the best substitute DC that is not in the current solution and retailers are assigned in a *greedy manner* to the DC
  - Variable fixing technique
  - Branch and bound

19.3.3 Solution Approach of Shen and Qi (2007)

Shen and Qi (2007) propose a Lagrangian relaxation based solution algorithm embedded in branch and bound to solve the problem, similar to Daskin et al. (2002). By exploring the structure of the problem, they find a low-order polynomial algorithm for the nonlinear integer programming problem that must be solved in solving the Lagrangian relaxation sub-problems.

19.3.3.1 Solution Approach

- Finding a lower bound
- Finding an upper bound
- Variable fixing

19.3.4 Solution Approach of Miranda and Garrido (2006)

Their model is NP-hard and presents nonlinear terms in the objective function and a nonlinear constraint. A heuristic solution approach is introduced, based on Lagrangian relaxation and the sub gradient method.

19.3.5 Solution Approach of Miranda and Garrido (2008)

Their mathematical model is highly complex due to the incorporation of non-linear terms into the constraints and objective function, making the standard FLP methods difficult to apply. For this reason, a new solution method is developed based on Lagrangian relaxation in conjunction with a complex heuristic (which, due to its complexity is used only in a fraction of the iterations). The heuristic is based on a greedy procedure and local improvement methods of the k-opt type. Finally, they propose a set of inequalities that help to tighten the dual bounds as a part of the relaxation process. These inequalities arise from the feasible boundaries that emerge from all the possible combinations of means and variances of different clusters of demand points.

19.3.5.1 Solution Approach

- Relaxation and decomposition
- Characterization of the feasible space
- An exact procedure
- Lagrangian heuristic

19.4 Case Study

In this section, we will introduce a real-world case study related to location-inventory problem:

19.4.1 Distribution System for Finished Automobiles in US (Nozick and Turnquist 1998)

Consider a distribution system for finished automobiles. The current distribution system for finished automobiles relies on large networks of independent dealers to provide the inventory of vehicles from which customers choose. Dealers order new vehicles from the manufacturer in the models and colors. These orders typically require 6–12 weeks to fill and make up the dealer stock. But most customers are unwilling to wait about 6–12 weeks for a vehicle, so most vehicles are sold out of the finished vehicle inventory held on dealer lots. The system of relying on dealers to maintain separate pools of inventory is costly because dealers are forced to maintain a large inventory of cars. As an illustration of the magnitude of inventory costs in the auto industry, consider that in a typical year about 15 million new cars and light trucks are sold in the U.S., and the average value of those vehicles, is about $18,500. If the average dealer holds 60 days' inventory, total on-hand inventory is approximately 2.5 million vehicles, representing an investment of over $46 billion. If inventory carrying costs are about 22% of inventory value, then dealer stock generates annual inventory holding costs on the order of $10 billion.

One alternative method of managing this inventory is through a series of RDCs which would hold most of the inventory and dealers served by a given RDC and would have access to its entire inventory.

The questions of how many RDCs are necessary, and where should they be located, are critical to the success of the venture.

This example will focus on identifying how many RDCs are necessary and where they should be located in order to minimize transportation, fixed facility, and inventory costs for new vehicles. In this case study the manufacturer serves demands across the continental U.S., organized into 698 demand areas. For the purposes of this analysis, the demand within each of the demand areas is assumed to occur at the centroid of the demand area.

The fixed-charge model yields a recommendation of 23 RDCs, also determines the assignment of demand areas to RDCs, and gives an indication (using line thickness) of the volume of demand allocated to each RDC.

They also illustrate the sensitivity of this solution to changes in the per-RDC fixed-charge coefficient. It is important to notice that within a range of $\pm 10\%$, the number of RDC's recommended does not change.

References

Axsater S (1996) Using the deterministic EOQ formula in stochastic inventory control. Manage Sci 42:830–834

Daskin MS, Coullard CR, Shen ZM (2002) An inventory-location model: formulation, solution algorithm and computational results. Ann Oper Res 110:83–106

Erlebacher SJ, Meller RD (2000) The interaction of location and inventory in designing distribution systems. IIE Trans 32:155–166

Miranda PA, Garrido RA (2006) A simultaneous inventory control and facility location model with stochastic capacity constraints. Netw Spat Econ 6:39–53

Miranda PA, Garrido RA (2008) Valid inequalities for Lagrangian relaxation in an inventory location problem with stochastic capacity. Transport Res E 44:47–65

Nozick LK, Turnquist MA (1998) Integrating inventory impacts into a fixed-charge model for locating distribution centers. Transport Res E-Log 34(3):173–186

Nozick LK, Turnquist MA (2001) Inventory, transportation, service quality and the location of distribution centers of distribution centers. Eur J Oper Res 129:362–371

Shen ZM, Qi L (2007) Incorporating inventory and routing costs in strategic location models. Eur J Oper Res 179:372–389

Shen ZM, Coullard C, Daskin MS (2003) A joint location-inventory model. Transport Sci 37(1):40–55

Snyder LV, Daskin MS, Teo CP (2007) The stochastic location model with risk pooling. Eur J Oper Res 179:1221–1238

Chapter 20
Facility Location in Supply Chain

Meysam Alizadeh

A supply chain (SC) is the network of facilities and activities that performs the function of product development, procurement of material from vendors, the movement of materials between facilities, the manufacturing of products, the distribution of finished goods to customers, and after-market support for sustainment (Mabert and Venkataramanan 1998). The supply chain not only includes the manufacturer and suppliers, but also transporters, warehouses, retailers, and customer themselves. Within each organization, the supply chain include, but not limited to, new product development, marketing, operations, distribution, finance, and customer service (Chopra 2003).

A supply chain is dynamic and involves the constant flow of information, product, and funds between different stages. A typical supply chain may involve a variety of stages. These supply chain stages include:

- Customers
- Retailers
- Wholesalers/distributors
- Manufacturers
- Component/raw material suppliers

SC systems can be studied and analyzed from several viewpoints. Yet there are three major perspectives of SC systems: (a) "material flow", (b) "information flow", and (c) "buyer-seller relations" (Fazel Zarandi et al. 2002). The objective of every supply chain is to maximize the overall value generated. Supply chain management involves the management of flows between and among stages in a supply chain to maximize totally supply chain profitability (Chopra 2003).

20.1 Design Phases in Supply Chain

Successful supply chain management requires many decisions relating to the flow of information, product, and funds. These decisions fall into three categories or phases, depending on the frequency of each decision and the time frame over which a decision phase has an impact:

1. Supply chain strategy or design;
2. Supply chain planning or tactical level; and
3. Supply chain operations.

In the supply chain design phase, strategic decisions, such as facility location and technology selection decisions play major roles. While the supply chain configuration is determined, the focus shifts to decisions at the tactical and operational levels, such as inventory control and distribution decisions. The five major supply chain drivers include:

- Production: what, how, and when to produce;
- Inventory: how much to make and how much to store;
- Location: where best to do what activities;
- Transportation: how and when to move product;
- Information: the basis for making these decisions.

Facility location may be the most critical and most difficult of the decisions needed to realize an efficiency supply chain. Transportation, inventory, and information sharing decisions can be readily re-optimized in response to changes in the underlying conditions of the supply chain; but facility location decisions are often fixed and difficult to change even in the intermediate term.

Therefore, the facility location decision is a strategic decision in supply chain management and play a crucial role in the logistics activities involved in SCM.

20.2 Network Design in Supply Chain

20.2.1 The Role of Network Design in the Supply Chain

Supply chain network design decisions include the location of manufacturing, storage, or transportation-related facilities and the allocation of capacity and roles to each facility. Supply chain network design decisions are classified as follows:

1. Facility role: what role should each facility play? What processes are performed at each facility?
2. Facility location: where should facilities be located?
3. Capacity allocation: how much capacity should be allocated to each facility?
4. Market and supply allocation: what market should each facility serve?

Which supply sources should feed each facility?

All network design decisions affect each other and must be made taking this fact into consideration.

Facility location decisions have a long-term impact on a supply chain's performance because it is very expensive to shut down a facility or move it to a different location. A good location decisions can help a supply chain to be responsive while keeping its costs low.

20.2.2 Factors Influencing Network Design Decisions

There are seven factors that influence network design decisions in supply chains:

- Strategic factors,
- Technological factors,
- Macroeconomic factors,
- Political factors,
- Infrastructure factors,
- Competitive factors, and
- Operational factors.

In the next section we discuss models for making facility location and capacity allocation decisions during Phase II and IV.

20.3 Classical Models

Managers use network design models in two different situations. First, these models are used to decide on locations where facilities will be established and the capacity to be assigned to each facility. Second, these models are used to assign current demand to the available facilities and identify lanes along which product will be transported. The following information must be available before the design decision can be made:

- Location of supply sources and markets,
- Location of potential facility sites,
- Demand forecast by market,
- Facility, labor, and material costs by site,
- Transportation costs between each pair of sites,
- Inventory costs by site as well as a function of quantity,
- Sale price of product in different regions,
- Taxes and tariffs as product is moved between locations,
- Desired response time and other service factors.

Given this information, either gravity or network optimization models may be used to design the network.

In this section, we review several traditional facility location models, beginning with the classical fixed charge location model. We then show how the model can be extended to incorporate additional facets of the supply chain design problem.

20.3.1 Fixed Charge Facility Location Problem (Daskin et al. 2005)

This problem is a classical location problem and forms the basis of many location models that have been used in supply chain design. The problem can be stated simply as follows. We are given a set of customer locations with known demands and a set of candidate facility locations. If we select to locate a facility at a candidate site, we incur a known fixed location cost. There is a known unit shipment cost between each candidate site and each customer location. The problem is to find the locations of the facilities and the shipment pattern between the facilities and the customers to minimize the combined facility location and shipment costs subject to a requirement that all customer demands be met (Daskin et al. 2005).

Specifically, we introduce the following notation:

20.3.1.1 Model Inputs

I: Set of customer locations, indexed by i
J: Set of candidate facility locations, indexed by j
h_i: demand at customer location $i \in I$
f_i: fixed cost of locating a facility at candidate site $j \in J$
c_{ij}: unit cost of shipment between candidate facility site $j \in J$ and customer location $i \in I$

20.3.1.2 Model Outputs (Decision Variables)

$$X_j = \begin{cases} 1, & \text{if we locate at candidate site } j \in J \\ 0 & \text{if not} \end{cases},$$

Y_{ij}: Fraction of the demand at customer location $i \in I$ that is served by a facility at site $j \in J$.

20.3.1.3 Objective Function and its Constraints

The problem is then formulated as the following integer program (Balinski 1965):

$$\text{Min } \Sigma_{j \in J} f_j X_j + \Sigma_{j \in J} \Sigma_{i \in I} h_i c_{ij} Y_{ij}. \tag{20.1}$$

Subject to

$$\sum_{j \in J} Y_{ij} = 1 \quad i \in I. \tag{20.2}$$
$$Y_{ij} - X_j \leq 0 \quad i \in I; j \in J, \tag{20.3}$$
$$X_j \in \{0, 1\} \quad j \in J, \tag{20.4}$$
$$Y_{ij} \geq 0 \quad i \in I; j \in J. \tag{20.5}$$

The objective function (20.1) minimizes the total cost (fixed facility location + shipment) of setting up and operating the network. Equation (20.2) stipulates that each demand node is fully assigned. Equation (20.3) states that a demand node cannot be assigned to a facility unless we open that facility. Equation (20.4) enforces that each candidate site is either open or closed and (20.5) are a simple non-negativity equations.

20.3.2 Uncapacitated Facility Location Model with Single Sourcing

The formulation given in previous section assumes that facilities have unlimited capacity; the problem is sometimes referred to as the uncapacitated fixed charge location problem. It is well known that at least one solution to this problem involves assigning all of the demand at each customer location $i \in I$ fully to the nearest open facility site $j \in J$ (Daskin et al. 2005). in other words, $Y_{ij} \in \{0, 1\}$. Many firms insist on or strongly prefer such single sourcing solutions as they make the management of the supply chain considerably simpler.

20.3.3 Capacitated Facility Location Model

One natural extension of the problem is to consider capacitated facilities. If we let b_j be the maximum demand that can be assigned to a facility at candidate site $j \in J$ (20.1)–(20.5) can be extended to incorporate facility capacities by including the following additional equation (Daskin et al. 2005):

$$\sum_{i \in I} h_i Y_{ij} - b_j X_j \leq 0 \quad j \in J. \tag{20.6}$$

Equation (20.6) limits the total assigned demand at facility $j \in J$ to a maximum of b_j. From the perspective of the integer programming problem, this constraints obviates the need for (20.3) since any solution that satisfies (20.5) and (20.6) will also satisfy (20.3).

For fixed values of the facility location variables, X_j, the optimal values of the assignment variables can be found by solving a traditional transportation problem.

The embedded transportation problem is most easily recognized if we replace $h_i Y_{ij}$ by Z_{ij}, the quantity shipped from distribution center j to customer i. The transportation problem for fixed facility locations is then (Daskin et al. 2005):

$$\text{Min } \sum_{i \in I} \sum_{j \in J} c_{ij} Z_{ij}. \tag{20.7}$$

Subject to

$$\sum_{j \in J} Z_{ij} = h_i \quad i \in I, \tag{20.8}$$

$$\sum_{i \in I} Z_{ij} \leq b_j X_j \quad j \in J, \tag{20.9}$$

$$Z_{ij} \geq 0 \quad i \in I; j \in J, \tag{20.10}$$

where we denote the fixed (known) values of location variables by $\hat{X}$.

The solution to the transportation problem (20.7)–(20.10) may involve fractional assignments of customers to facilities. This means that the addition of (20.6) will not automatically satisfy the single sourcing condition. To restore the single sourcing condition, we can replace the fractional definition of the assignment variables by a binary one:

$$Y_{ij} = \begin{cases} 1, & \text{if demands at customer site } i \text{ are served by facility at candidate site } j \\ 0, & \text{if not} \end{cases}$$

The problem becomes considerably more difficult to solve since there are now far more integer variables.

Daskin and Jones (1993) observed that, in many practical contexts, the number of customers is significantly greater than the number of distribution centers that will be sited. As such, each customer represents a small fraction of the total capacity of the distribution center to which it is assigned. Also, if the single sourcing requirement is relaxed, the number of multiply sourced customers is less than or equal to the number of distribution centers minus one. Thus, relatively few customers will be multiply-sourced in most contexts. They further noted that warehouse capacities, when measured in terms of annual throughput as is commonly done, are rarely known with great precision, as they depend on many factors, including the number of inventory turns as the warehouse. They therefore proposed a procedure for addressing the single sourcing problem that involves (20.1) ignoring the single sourcing constraint and solving the transportation problem, (20.2) using duality to find alternate optima to the transportation problem that require fewer customers to be multiply sourced, and (20.3) allowing small violations of the capacity constraints to identify solutions that satisfy the single sourcing requirement.

20.3.4 Locating Plants and Distribution Centers with Multiple Commodity

In a classic paper, Geoffrion and Graves (1974) extend the traditional fixed charge facility location problem to include shipments from plants to distribution centers and multiple commodities. They introduce the following additional notation:

20.3.4.1 Model Inputs

K: Set of plant locations, indexed by k
L: Set of commodities, indexed by l
D_{li}: demand for commodity $l \in L$ at customer $i \in I$
S_{lk}: supply of commodity $l \in L$ at plant $k \in K$
$\underline{V}_j$, V_j: minimum and maximum annual throughput allowed at distribution center $j \in J$
v_j: variable unit cost of throughput at candidate site $j \in J$
c_{lkji}: unit cost of producing and shipping commodity $l \in L$ between plant $k \in K$, candidate facility site $j \in J$ and customer location $i \in I$

20.3.4.2 Model Outputs (Decision Variables)

$$Y_{ij} = \begin{cases} 1, & \text{if demands at customer site } i \text{ are served by facility at candidate site } j \\ 0, & \text{if not} \end{cases}$$

Z_{lkji} = quantity of commodity $l \in L$ shipped between plant $k \in K$, candidate facility site $j \in J$ and customer location $i \in I$

20.3.4.3 Objective Function and its Constraints

The problem is then formulated as the following (Geoffrion and Graves 1974):

$$\text{Min } \Sigma_{j \in J} f_j X_j + \Sigma_{j \in J} v_j (\Sigma_{i \in I} \Sigma_{l \in L} D_{li} Y_{ij}) + \Sigma_{l \in L} \Sigma_{k \in K} \Sigma_{j \in J} \Sigma_{i \in I} c_{lkji} Z_{lkji}. \tag{20.11}$$

Subject to

$$\Sigma_{j \in J} \Sigma_{i \in I} Z_{lkji} \leq S_{lk} \quad k \in K; l \in L, \tag{20.12}$$

$$\sum_{k \in K} Z_{lkji} = D_{li} Y_{ij} \quad l \in L; j \in J; i \in J, \tag{20.13}$$

$$\sum_{j \in J} Y_{ij} = 1 \quad i \in I, \tag{20.14}$$

$$V_j X_j \leq \sum D_{li} Y_{ij} \leq V_j X_j \quad j \in J, \tag{20.15}$$

$$X_j \in \{0,1\} \; j \in J, \tag{20.16}$$

$$Y_{ij} \in \{0,1\} \; i \in I; j \in J, \tag{20.17}$$

$$Z_{lkji} \geq 0 \quad i \in I; j \in J; k \in K; 1 \in L. \tag{20.18}$$

The objective function (20.11) minimizes the total fixed and variable costs of the supply chain network. Equation (20.12) states that the total amount of commodity $l \in L$ shipped from plant $k \in K$ cannot exceed the capacity of the plant to produce that commodity. Equation (20.13) says that the amount of commodity $l \in L$ shipped to customer $i \in I$ via distribution center (DC) $j \in J$ must equal to amount of that commodity produce at all plants that is destined for that customer and shipped via that DC. Equation (20.14) is the now-familiar single-sourcing constraint. Equation (20.15) imposes lower and upper on the throughput processed at each distribution center that is used.

20.4 Integrated Decision Making Models

As Shen (2007) discussed in his paper, in the literature, we have seen many papers that study the integration and coordination of any two of the three important supply chain decisions. He review these papers based on the following three categories: (1) location/routing (LR) models; (2) inventory/routing (IR) models; and (3) location/inventory (LI) models.

20.4.1 Integrated Location-Routing Models (LR)

An important limitation of the fixed charge location model, and even a multi-echelon, multi-commodity extension of Geoffrion and Graves, is the assumption that full truckload quantities are shipped from a distribution center to a customer (Daskin et al. 2005). In many contexts, shipments are made in less-than-truckload (LTL) quantities from a facility to customers along a multiple-stop route. In the case of full truckload quantities, the cost of delivery is independent of the other deliveries made, whereas in the case of LTL quantities, the cost of delivery depends on the other customers on the route and the sequence in which customers are visited. During the past three decades, a sizeable body of literature has developed on integrated location/routing models.

Integrated location/routing problems combine three components of supply chain design: facility location, customer allocation to facilities and vehicle routing. Laporte (1998) reviews early work on location routing problems; he summarizes the different types of formulations, solution algorithms and computational results of work published prior to 1988. More recently, Min et al. (1998) develop a hierarchical taxonomy and classification scheme that they is used to review the existing location routing literature. They categorize papers in terms of problem characteristics and solution methodology. One means of classification is the number of layers of facilities. Typically, three-layer problems include flows from plants to distribution centers to customers, while two-layer problems focus on flows from distribution centers to customers.

Like three-layer formulation of Perl, two-layer location routing formulations (e.g., Laporte et al. 1998) usually are based on integer linear programming formulations for the vehicle routing problem (VRP). Flow formulations of the VRP are often classified according to the number of indices of the flow variable. The size and structure of these formulations make them difficult to solve using standard integer programming or network optimization techniques. Motivated by the successful implementation of exact algorithms for set-partitioning-based routing models, Berger (1997) formulates a two-layer location/routing problem, she formulates the routes in terms of paths, where a delivery vehicle may not be required to return to the distribution center after the final delivery is made. In the latter case, the time to return from the last customer to the distribution center is much less important than the time from the facility to the last customer. Thee is a recent study from Chan et al. (2001), in which they apply the three-dimensional space-filling curve. More recent literature review can be found in Nagy and Salhi (2007).

20.4.2 Integrated Inventory-Routing Models (IR)

There are four characteristics associated with IR models: demands; fleet size, i.e., the number of available vehicles, which is limited or unlimited; length of the planning horizon; and number of demand points visited on a vehicle trip.

Kleywegt et al. (2002) provide an excellent survey and classification of IR models using the above four categories plus a fifth category on the research contribution of the models. More recent literature review can be found in Kleywegt et al. (2002) and Adelman (2003).

20.4.3 Integrated Location-Inventory Models (LI)

The fixed charge location problem ignores the inventory impacts of facility location decisions; it deals only with the tradeoff between facility costs, which increase with the number of facilities, and the average travel cost, which decreases approximately as the square root of the number of facilities located (call it N). Baumol and Wolfe (1958) recognized the contribution of inventory to distribution costs. Eppen (1979) argued that safety stock costs also increase as the square root of N.

While the contribution of inventory to distribution costs has been recognized, many papers study the location, inventory, and distribution coordination issues, but most of these papers either ignore the inventory costs, or approximate the nonlinear costs with linear functions. Recently there are a few papers that consider nonlinear cost terms in their models. Erlebacher and Meller (2000) formulate a non-linear integer location/inventory model. Shen et al. (2003), Daskin et al. (2001) propose the joint location/inventory in which location, shipment and nonlinear safety stock inventory costs are included in the same model. They develop an integrated approach to determine the number of DCs to establish, the location of the DCs, and the magnitude of inventory to maintain at each center.

All of the models that will be reviewed in the remainder of this chapter are built on the basic model described in the next section.

20.5 Basic Model Formulation

Shen (2007) considers the design of a three-tiered supply chain system consisting of one or more suppliers, DCs, and retailers. Each retailer has uncertain demand. The problem is to determine how many DCs to locate, where to locate them, which retailers to assign to each DC, how often to reorder at the DC and what level of safety stock to maintain, so as to minimize total cost, while ensuring a specified level of service.

20.5.1 Model Inputs

I: set of retailers
J: set of candidate DC location
μ_i: mean (daily) demand at retailer i, for each $i \in I$
σ_i^2: variance of (daily) demand at retailer i, for each $i \in I$
f_j: fixed (annual) cost of locating a DC at j, for each $j \in J$
d_{ij}: cost of shipping a unit from DC_j to retailer i, for each $i \in I$ and $j \in J$
α: desired percentage of retailer orders satisfied (fill rate)
β: weight factor associated with the shipment cost
θ: weight factor associated with the inventory cost
h: inventory holding cost per unit of product per year
F_j: fixed administrative and handling cost of placing an order at DC_j, for each $j \in J$
L: DC order lead time in days
g_i: fixed shipment cost per shipment from the supplier to DC_j
$\bar{a}_j$: cost per unit of a shipment from the supplier to DC_j
χ: a constant used to convert daily demand into annual demand

20.5.2 Model Outputs (Decision Variables)

$X_j = 1$, if retailer j is selected as a DC location, and 0 otherwise, for each $j \in J$

$Y_{ij} = 1$, if retailer i is served by a DC based at location j, and 0 otherwise, for each $i \in I$ and $j \in J$

20.5.3 Objective Function and its Constraints

$$\text{Min } \Sigma_{j \in J}\{f_j X_j [\Sigma_{i \in a}(\beta \mu_i d_{ij} + \beta a_j \mu_j)\chi Y_{ij}]\} + \sqrt{2\theta h(F_j + \beta g_j)}\sqrt{\Sigma \mu_i \chi Y_{ij} + \theta h z_\alpha}\sqrt{\Sigma L \sigma_i^2 Y_{ij}}. \quad (20.19)$$

Subject to

$$\Sigma_{j \in J} Y_{ij} = 1 \ \forall i \in I, \quad (20.20)$$

$$Y_{ij} - X_i \leq 0 \ \forall i, \quad (20.21)$$

$$Y_{ij} \in \{0, 1\} \ \forall i \in I, j \in J, \quad (20.22)$$

$$X_j \in \{0, 1\} \ j \in J. \quad (20.23)$$

The first two terms of the objective function are structurally identical to those of the uncapacitated facility location (UFL) model, which include the fixed cost of locating facilities, and the delivery costs from the DCs to the retailers as well as the marginal cost of shipping a unit from a supplier to a DC. The last two terms are related to inventory costs. Equation (20.20) requires that each retailer is assigned to exactly one DC. Equation (20.21) states that retailers can only be assigned to candidate site that are selected as DCs. Equations (20.22) and (20.22) are standard integrality constraints.

Daskin et al. (2001) and Shen et al. (2003) have discovered some interesting properties of this model.

20.6 Model with Routing Cost Estimation

In this section, we consider a more realistic modeling of the shipment costs from DCs to retailers. We consider a three-tiered supply chain system consisting of one or more suppliers, DCs, and retailers. We assume that each retailer has uncertain demand that follows a certain probability distribution. The locations of the suppliers are known, but the exact locations of the retailers are not known. We assume the retailers are uniformly scattered in a connected area. We assume that the transportation cost exhibits economies of scale under which the average unit cost decrease as the travel distance increases.

All of the models we reviewed so far assume that the locations of the retailers are given. However, during the supply chain design phase, usually not much information is given about retailer locations. Thus, they should not be fixed in the supply chain design stage. Continuous approximation models, which use continuous functions to represent distributions of retailer location and demand, have been developed to provide insights into complicated mathematical programming models. It is also widely recognized that continuous models should supplement mathematical programming models, not replace them (Geoffrion 1976; Hall 1986). In this section, we plan to use continuous models to approximate the routing cost in our integrated supply chain model.

We study an integrated stochastic supply chain design model in which we relax two major assumptions in the models from Sect. 20.4.3. Instead of assuming that the decision maker knows exactly where the retailers are located, we assume that the retailers are scattered in a connected region according to a certain distribution. Furthermore, we model the shipment from a DC to its retailers using a vehicle routing model instead of the linear direct shipping model. We also assume that there is a dedicated truck in each DC that delivers to the retailers every period using a certain route. It is reasonable to assume that, under some conditions (e.g., the driver does not have to work overtime), the transportation cost related to this route is concave in the distance travelled.

Let $\bar{\iota}$ be the vehicle capacity, d_{ij} be the distance between retailer i and DC_j. The integrated supply chain model can then be formulated as:

$$\sqrt[q]{\sum \sigma_i^2 Y_{ij}}. \tag{20.24}$$

Subject to (20.20)–(20.23)
where $\hat{g}_{ij} = 2\mu_i d_{ij}/\bar{\iota} + \chi(1 - 1/\bar{\iota})\Phi \sqrt{A/N} \geq 0$.

20.7 Model with Capacitated DCs

Ozsen et al. (2003) introduce a capacitated version of the model in Sect. 20.4.3. They assume that the DCs have capacity restrictions. The capacity constraints are defined based on how the inventory is managed. Thus, the relationship between the capacity of a DC and the inventory levels are embedded in the model.

Assume that the inventory is managed by a (r, Q) model with a type-I service level constraint at each DC. Define the following notation for each $j \in J$:

C_j: the capacity of DC_j
r_j: the reorder point at DC_j
Q_j: the reorder quantity at DC_j

It is easy to see that the inventory at DC_j reaches its maximum when there is no demand during the lead time. Thus, the maximal accumulation at DC_j equals $Q_j + r_j$, and r_j = safety stock+ E[demand during lead time]. Let D_j be the expected annual demand of retailers served by DC_j We can write the capacity constraint for DC_j as:

$$Q_j + r_j \leq C_j.$$

Adding this constraint to (20.20)–(20.23) in Sect. 20.4.3, we obtain a new model with nonlinear terms in both the objective function and the constraints.

20.8 Model with Multiple Levels of Capacity (Amiri 2006)

This section addresses the distribution network design problem in a supply chain system that involves locating production plants and distribution warehouses, and determining the best strategy for distributing the product from the plants to the warehouses and from the warehouses to the customers. The goal is to select the optimum numbers, locations and capacities of plants and warehouses to open so that all customer demand is satisfied at minimum total costs of the distribution network. Unlike most of past models, this model allows for multiple levels of capacities available to the warehouses and plants. Amiri (2006) develop a mixed integer programming model and define the following notations:

20.8.1 Model Inputs

N: index set of customers zones,
M: index set of potential warehouse sites,
L: index set of potential plant sites,
R: index set of capacity levels available to the potential warehouses,
H: index set of capacity levels available to the potential plants,
C_{ij}: cost of supplying one unit of demand to customer zone i from warehouse at site j,
$\overline{C}_{jk}$ cost of supplying one unit of demand to warehouse at site j from plant at site k,
F_j^r: fixed cost per unit of time for opening and operating warehouse with capacity level r at site j,
G_k^h: fixed cost per unit of time for opening and operating plant with capacity level h at site k,
a_i: demand per unit of time of customer zone I,
b_j^r: capacity with level r for the potential warehouse at site j,
e_k^h: capacity with level h for the potential plant at site k.

20.8.2 Model Outputs (Decision Variables)

U_{ij}: fraction (regarding a_i) of demand of customer zone i delivered from warehouse at site j,
Y_{jk}^r: fraction (regarding b_j^r) of shipment from plant at site k to warehouse at site j with capacity level r,
$X_j^r = \begin{cases} 1, & \text{if a warehouse with capacity level } r \text{ is located at site } j \\ 0, & \text{otherwise} \end{cases}$
$V_k^h = \begin{cases} 1, & \text{if a plant with capacity level } h \text{ is located at site } k \\ 0, & \text{otherwise} \end{cases}$

20.8.3 Objective Function and its Constraints

In terms of the above notation, Amiri (2006) formulated the problem as follows:

$$\text{Min } \Sigma_{i \in N} \Sigma_{j \in M} C_{ij} a_i X_{ij} + \Sigma_{r \in R} \Sigma_{j \in M} \Sigma_{k \in L} \overline{C_{jk}} b_j^r Y_{jk}^r$$
$$+ \sum_{j \in M} \sum_{r \in R} F_j^r U_j^r + \sum_{k \in L} \sum_{h \in H} G_k^h V_k^h. \qquad (20.25)$$

Subject to

$$\Sigma_{j \in M} X_{ij} = 1 \quad \forall i \in N, \qquad (20.26)$$
$$\sum_{i \in N} a_i X_{ij} \le \sum_{r \in R} b_j^r U_j^r \quad \forall j \in M, \qquad (20.27)$$
$$\sum_{r \in R} U_j^r \le 1 \quad \forall j \in M, \qquad (20.28)$$
$$\sum_{i \in N} a_i X_{ij} \le \sum_{k \in L} \sum_{r \in R} b_j^r Y_{jk}^r \quad \forall j \in M, \qquad (20.29)$$
$$\sum_{j \in M} \sum_{r \in R} b_j^r Y_{jk}^r \le \sum_{h \in H} e_k^h V_k^h \quad \forall k \in L, \qquad (20.30)$$
$$\sum_{h \in H} v_k^h \le 1 \quad \forall k \in L, \qquad (20.31)$$
$$X_{ij} \ge 0 \quad \forall i \in N \text{ and } j \in M, \qquad (20.32)$$
$$u_j^r \in (0, 1) \quad \forall j \in M \text{ and } r \in R, \qquad (20.33)$$
$$Y_{jk}^r \ge 0 \quad \forall k \in L, j \in M \text{ and } r \in R, \qquad (20.34)$$
$$V_k^h \in (0, 1) \quad \forall k \in L \text{ and } h \in H. \qquad (20.35)$$

20.9 Model with Service Considerations

When designing supply chains, firms are often faced with the competing objectives of improving customer service and reducing cost. We extend the basic model in Sect. 20.4.3 to include a customer service element and develop practical methods for quick and meaningful evaluation of cost/service tradeoffs. Service is measured by the fraction of all demands that are located within an exogenously specified distance of the assigned DC.

Ross and Soland (1980), in one of the earliest papers on multi-objective location problems, argue that practical problems involving the location of public facilities should be modeled as multi-objective problems. Cost and service are the typical objectives, although there exist several distinct objectives in each of those two categories: fixed investment cost, fixed operating cost, variable operating cost, total operating cost, and total discounted cost are all reasonable cost objectives to consider; and both demand served and response time (or distance traveled) are appropriate objectives for service measurement. They treat such multi-objective problems in the framework of a model for selecting a subset of M sites where public facilities are established to serve client groups located at N distinct points. For a review of other multi-objective location models, we refer the reader to Shen (2005).

Model (20.20)–(20.23) in Sect. 20.4.3 captures important facility location, transportation and inventory costs. Some retailers may be served very well, in the sense that they are located very close to the DCs to which they are assigned, while other retailers may be served very poorly by this criterion. The maximal covering location problem (Church and ReVelle 1974) maximizes the number of customers that can be covered by a fixed number of facilities. Customer i is covered if node i is assigned to a facility that is within dc of node i, where dc is the coverage distance. Instead of maximizing covered demand volume, for fixed total demand, we can minimize the uncovered demand volume. In a manner similar to Daskin (1995), we can then formulate a model that simultaneously minimizes the fixed costs of the facilities and a weighted sum of the uncovered demand volume as follows:

$$\text{Min} \sum_{j \in J} f_j X_j + \sum_{j \in J} \sum_{i \in I} \hat{d}_{ij} Y_{ij}. \quad (20.36)$$

Subject to (20.20)–(20.23)

Where W is the weight on the uncovered demand volume and $U_{ij} = \chi \mu_i$, if $d_{ij} > d_c$, and 0, if not.

This model is structurally identical to basic model. The only difference is that we penalize all assignments of demand nodes to DCs that are more than dc away from the DC. By varying the weight W on uncovered demand volume, we can trace out an approximation to the set of non-inferior solutions to the tradeoff between location-inventory costs and customer responsiveness. Altiparmak et al. (2006) presented mixed-integer non-linear programming model for multi-objective optimization of SCN. They considered three objectives: (1) minimization of total cost comprised of fixed costs of plants and distribution centers (DCs), inbound and outbound distribution costs, (2) maximization of customer services that can be rendered to customers in terms of acceptable delivery time (coverage), and (3) maximization of capacity utilization balance for DCs (i.e., equity on utilization ratios). To deal with multi-objective and enable the decision maker to evaluate a greater number of alternative solutions, two different weight approaches were implemented in the proposed GA.

20.10 Profit Maximizing Model with Demand Choice Flexibility

Minimizing total cost has been the primitive objective in most of the supply chain network design models. These models typically require that every customer's demand has to be satisfied. However, for a profit-maximizing business, it may not always be optimal to satisfy all potential demands, especially if the additional cost is higher than the additional revenue associated with servicing these customers. Furthermore, if the company is facing competition, sometimes it might be more profitable to lose some potential customers to competitors since the cost of maintaining these customers can be prohibitively high. Most supply chain related costs, such as location, transportation, and inventory related costs of an item depend on total demand volume, and no clear method exists for determining a customer's profitability a priori, based solely on the characteristics of this customer. Shen addresses this problem by proposing a profit-maximizing supply chain design model in which a company can choose whether to satisfy a customer's demand.

The literature on integrating cost-minimizing supply chain network design models with profit-maximizing microeconomic theory is limited. Hansen et al. (1987) and Hansen et al. (1995) provide surveys on profit-maximizing location models.

Zhang (2001) considers a profit-maximizing location model, where a firm needs to decide where to locate a single DC to serve the customers and to set the price for its product, so as to maximize its total profit. He shows that under certain assumptions on the complexity counts, a special case of this problem can be solved in polynomial time. However, he does not consider any cost related terms in his model, not even the DC location costs.

Another location model is proposed by Meyerson (2001), where he considers a profit earning facility location problem for a given set of demand points, and the decision maker needs to open some facilities such that every demand may be satisfied from a local facility and the total profit is maximized. Instead of incurring a cost, opening a facility can gain a certain profit which is a function of the amount of demand the facility satisfies. Since this profit-earning problem is NP-hard, Meyerson develops an approximation algorithm that is based on linear program rounding.

Demand choice flexibility in inventory models is proposed by Geunes et al. (2004). Their models address economic ordering decisions when a producer can choose whether to satisfy multiple markets. They assume the per unit revenue from serving a specific customaries exogenously given, not a decision variable. Furthermore, their models are pure inventory models; supply chain design related decisions, such as location decisions, are absent from the models.

Shen (2006) considers not only location decisions and customer-DC assignment decisions, but also production and inventory related decisions within a supply chain network. It is assumed that after production, the product is shipped to several DCs, and then from DCs to each customer the company has decided to serve. Contrary to Meyerson's model, assumes opening a facility incurs a certain cost, however, by serving the customers assigned to this facility, a certain amount of profit will be gained, which is also a function of the total demand served by the facility.

The profit-maximizing supply chain network design problem can be described as following: Given a production site o, a set I of customers and a set J of candidate DC locations, the decision maker wants to determine (a) the number and locations of the DCs, (b) the assignments of customers to DCs, (c) the inventory replenishment strategy at each DC, and (d) the sale price of the product at each region, so that the total profit is maximized. The profit is equal to the revenue minus the total cost, which includes the DC location cost, inventory holding cost at DCs, and delivery cost to DCs.

To model this problem, we define the following additional notation:

$f_j(x)$ (annual) cost of locating and operating a DC at j, for each $j \in J$. it is a concave function of the annual demand x flowing through DC_j
K: fixed cost of delivering product from the production site to a DC
d_{oj}: distance from the production site o to DC_j, $j \in J$
d_{ij}: distance from the DC_j to customer i, for $i \in I$, $j \in J$
$c(d_{oj})$ delivery cost per unit from the production site o to DC_j it has the following structure:

$$C(d_{oj}) = \begin{cases} c_1, & if\ 0 < d_{oj} < d_1 \\ c_2, & d_1 < d_{oj} < d_2 \\ \ldots, & \\ c_t, & d_{t-1} < d_{oj} < d_t \end{cases}.$$

It is typically assumed that $c_1 < c_2 < \ldots < c_t$

p_j: sale price per unit at the region served by DC_j
u_i: customer i's reserve price $g(d_{ij})$ delivery cost per unit charged to customer if delivery is made from DC_j. it has the following structure:

$$g(d_{ij}) = \begin{cases} v_1, & if\ 0 < d_{ij} < d_1 \\ v_2, & d_1 < d_{ij} < d_2 \\ \ldots, & \\ v_t, & d_{t-1} < d_{ij} < d_t \end{cases}.$$

it is typically assumed that $v_1 \leq v_2 \leq \ldots \leq v_t$

Shen (2006) assumes the company will lose a customer if the price a customer has to pay is higher than the customer's reserve price, i.e., if $u_i < p_j + g(d_{ij})$. He defines

$$R_i(p_i + d_{ij}) = \begin{cases} p_j + g(d_{ij}) - c(d_{oj}), & p_j + g(d_{ij}) \leq u_i \\ 0, & p_j + g(d_{ij}) > u_i \end{cases}.$$

Shen (2006) formulates the decision problem as a set-covering model, and present a branch-and-price algorithm to solve this model. To solve the resulting pricing problem, it suffices to find, for every $DC_j \in J$, a maximum-reduced-cost set $R_j^* \subset I$, that uses j as the designated DC. Thus, the pricing problem reduces to finding R_j^* for each $j \in J$. To find R_j^*, the following integer programming problem must be solved:

$$\text{Min} \sum_{i \in S} a_i Y_{ij} - \sqrt{2kh \sum_{i \in S} \mu_i Y_i} - h Z_\alpha \sqrt{\sum_{i \in S} \sigma_i^2 Y_i} - f_j \left(\sum_{i \in S} \mu_i Y_i \right). \tag{20.37}$$

Subject to

$$Y_i \in \{0, 1\}, \quad \forall i \in S, S \subseteq \Omega. \tag{20.38}$$

20.11 Model with Multiple Commodities

Nowadays, retailers carry thousands of different products and the amount of data involved in a supply chain design model can be overwhelming. It is not necessary, and may not be possible, to account for all distinct products in the strategic supply chain design phase. Aggregated information at the product category level should be used instead (Simchi-Levi et al. 2000).

Shen (2007) states that Warszawski and Peer (1973) and Warszawski (1973) are among the first to study the multi-commodity location problem. These models consider fixed location costs and linear transportation costs, and assume that each warehouse can be assigned at most one commodity.

Geoffrion and Graves (1974) consider the capacitated version of the multi-commodity location problem in which they impose capacity constraints on the suppliers and the DCs. They also assume that each customer must be served with all the products it requires from a single DC or directly from a supplier.

Shen (2005) multi-commodity supply chain design model can be stated as follows: We are given a set of alternative facility locations, a set of retailers, a set of different products, and a certain activity whose cost can be modeled using a concave function. The objective is to design a supply chain system that can serve outside demand at minimum cost.

Shen (2007) use the following additional notation:

L: set of commodities;
I_l: set of retailers that have demand for commodity $l \in L$
μ_{il}: mean annual demand from retailer i for commodity l.

Decision variables

$X_j = 1$, if j is selected as facility location, and 0 otherwise, for each $j \in J$
$Y_{ijl} = 1$, if the demand for commodity l of retailer i is served by j, and 0 otherwise, for each $i \in I$, $j \in J$, $l \in L$

With this notation, Shen (2005) formulates the problem as follows:

$$\text{Min} \sum_{j \in J} \left\{ f_j X_j + \sum_{l \in L} \left[\sum_{i \in I} (d_{ijl} \mu_{il}) Y_{ijl} + G_{jl} \left(\sum_{i \in I} \mu_{il} Y_{ijl} \right) \right] \right\}. \tag{20.39}$$

Subject to

$$\sum_{j \in J} Y_{ijl} = 1, \quad \forall i \in I, l \in L, \tag{20.40}$$

$$Y_{ijl} - X_j \le 0 \quad \forall i \in I, j \in J, l \in L, \tag{20.41}$$

$$Y_{ijl} \in \{0, 1\}. \forall i \in I, j \in J, l \in L, \tag{20.42}$$

$$X_j \in \{0, 1\}. \forall j \in J. \tag{20.43}$$

20.12 Model with Unreliable Supply

A supply chain network is a complex system in which there are many uncertainties, such as demands from the customers and delivery reliability. Because most supply chain design decisions (e.g., facility location) are irreversible, it is critical to take these uncertainties into account.

As Shen (2007) discussed, Qi and Shen consider the multi-period problem that in each period, multiple retailers order a specific product from a supplier, and the supplier ships the product to some intermediate facilities selected from a set of candidate locations. However, the amount of final product delivered on time to a retailer may not be exactly the amount this retailer requests from the supplier, because of the quality issues resulting from different production/assembly capabilities in different facilities, mistakes made during the assembly/packaging operations, the weather or other factors that may impact the on-time delivery from facilities to retailers. Thus, the decision maker needs to take this unreliability issue into consideration when designing the supply chain.

As Snyder and Daskin (2007) surveyed, a more formal review of this body of literature is presented by Snyder et al. (2006). Owen and Daskin (1998), Daskin et al. (2005), and Snyder (2006) all provide reviews of stochastic location models (generally considering uncertainty in demand, rather than disruptions to facilities). See Birge and Louveaux (1997) or Higle (2005) for an introduction to general stochastic programming techniques. Snyder and Daskin (2005) introduce several models, based on classical facility location problems, in which facilities may fail with a given probability. They minimize a weighted sum of two objectives, one of which is a classical objective (ignoring disruptions) and the other is the expected cost after accounting for disruptions. Customers are assigned to several facilities, one of which is the "primary" facility that serves it under normal circumstances, one of which serves it if the primary facility fails, and so on.

As Snyder and Daskin (2007) surveyed in their paper, Church and Scaparra (2005) and Scaparra and Church (2005, 2006) consider the fortification, rather than design, of facilities – that is, the network is assumed to exist and the firm has resources to prevent disruptions at some of them, thus partially fortifying the network. Their model finds the best facilities to fortify assuming that an interdictor will attempt to cause worst-case losses for the firm by disrupting a fixed number of the un-fortified facilities. Similarly, Daskin et al. (2005) allow the firm to choose whether each facility opened is reliable or unreliable; reliable facilities come at a higher cost.

20.12.1 Model Inputs

Based on basic model that discussed in Sect. 20.4.3, Qi and Shen define the following additional notation for this problem:

c: purchasing price from the supplier per unit of product
χ: number of periods per year
R_j: the reliability coefficient associated with facility j, $j \in J$, which is a random variable between 0 and 1. Let $\theta_j = E(R_j)$ and $\tau_j^2 = \text{Var}(Rj)$
p_i: retail price at retailer i per unit of product, $i \in I$
π_i: penalty cost of lost good will at retailer i per unit of product, $i \in I$
v_i: salvage value at retailer i per unit of product, $i \in I$

20.12.2 Model Outputs (Decision Variables)

$$X_j = \begin{cases} 1, & \text{facility } j \in J \text{ is open} \\ 0, & \text{otherwise} \end{cases},$$

Q_{ij}: order quantity at facility $j \in J$ from retailer $i \in I$ in each period.

20.12.3 Objective Function and its Constraints

Qi and Shen assume that the per-unit purchase and transportation costs are based on the quantity ordered, not the quantity actually received by the retailers. Based on this assumption, they formulate the following integrated model:

$$\text{Min} - \sum_{j \in J} \left\{ f_j X_j + c\chi \sum_{i \in I} Q_{ij} + a_j \chi \sum_{i \in I} Q_{ij} + K_J \sqrt{\sum_{i \in I} Q_{ij}} \right\}$$
$$+ \chi \sum_{i \in I} T_i(Q) = \phi(Q) - \sum_{j \in J} f_j X_j. \tag{20.44}$$

Subject to

$$1 - e^{-\beta Q_{ij}} \leq X_j \quad i \in I, j \in J, \tag{20.45}$$
$$Q_{ij} \geq 0 \quad i \in I, j \in J, \tag{20.46}$$
$$X_j \in \{0, 1\} \quad j \in J. \tag{20.47}$$

The objective function maximizes the expected annual profit of the entire system including all facilities and retailers. The first term represents the facility location cost for opening facilities and the second term is the annual purchasing cost from the supplier. The third and fourth term represent the working inventory cost and the safety stock cost associated with each facility. The last term is profit earned at retailers. Equation (20.45) requires that retailers can only order from open facilities. An exponential function is used to formulate this restriction because of the quick convergence property of the exponential function. The positive constant β is used to expedite the convergence.

20.13 Model with Facility Failures (Snyder 2003)

Once a set of facilities has been built, one or more of them may from time to time become unavailable, for example, due to inclement weather, labor actions, natural disasters, or changes in ownership. These facility "failures" may result in excessive transportation costs as customers previously served by these facilities must now be served by more distant ones. In this section, we discuss models for choosing facility locations to minimize fixed and transportation costs while also hedging against failures within the system. The goal is to choose facility locations that are both inexpensive and reliable.

The models discussed in this section are based on the fixed charge location problem; they address the tradeoff between operating cost (fixed location costs and day-to-day transportation cost, the classical fixed charge problem objective) and failure cost (the transportation cost that results after a facility has failed). The first model considers the maximum failure cost that can occur when a single facility fails, while the second model considers the expected failure cost given a fixed probability of failure.

In addition to the notation defined earlier, let

$$Y_{ijk} = \begin{cases} 1, & \text{if facility } j \in J \text{ serves as the primary facility and facility} \\ & k \in J \text{ serves as the secondary facility for customer } i \in I \\ 0, & \text{if not} \end{cases}$$

And let V be a desired upper bound on the failure cost that may result if a facility fails.

20.13.1 Objective Function and its Constraints

Snyder (2003) formulates the maximum-failure-cost reliability problem as follows:

$$\text{Min} \sum_{j \in J} f_j X_j + \sum_{i \in I} \sum_{j \in J} \sum_{k \in J} h_i c_{ij} Y_{ijk}. \quad (20.48)$$

Subject to

$$\sum_{j \in J} \sum_{k \in J} Y_{ijk} = 1 \quad \forall i \in I, \quad (20.49)$$

$$\sum_{k \in J} Y_{ijk} \leq X_j \quad \forall i \in I, \forall j \in J, \quad (20.50)$$

$$Y_{ijk} \leq X_k \quad \forall i \in I, \forall j \in J, \forall k \in J, \quad (20.51)$$

$$\sum_{i \in I} \sum_{j \in J} \sum_{k \in J} h_i c_{ij} Y_{ijk} + \sum_{i \in I} \sum_{k \in J} h_i c_{ij} Y_{ijk} \leq V \quad \forall j \in J, \quad (20.52)$$

$$Y_{ijj} = 0 \quad \forall i \in I, \forall j \in J, \quad (20.53)$$

$$X_j \in \{0, 1\} \quad \forall j \in J, \quad (20.54)$$

$$Y_{ijk} \geq \{0, 1\} \quad \forall i \in I, \forall j \in J, \forall k \in J. \quad (20.55)$$

The objective function sums the fixed cost and transportation cost to customers from their primary facilities. Equation (20.49) requires each customer to be assigned to one primary and one backup facility. Equation (20.50) and (20.51) prevent a customer from being assigned to a primary or a backup facility, respectively, that has not been opened. Equation (20.52) is the reliability constraint and requires the failure cost for facility j to be no greater than V. The first summation computes the cost of serving each customer from its primary facility if its primary facility is not j, while the second summation computes the cost of serving customers assigned to j as their primary facility from their backup facilities. Equation (20.53) requires a customer's primary facility to be different from its backup facility, and (20.54) and (20.55) are standard integrality and non-negativity constraints. This model can be solved for small instances using an off-the-shelf IP solver, but larger instances must be solved heuristically.

The expected-failure-cost reliability model (Snyder and Daskin 2003) assumes that multiple facilities may fail simultaneously, each with a given probability q of failing. In this case, a single backup facility is insufficient, since a customer's primary and backup facilities may both fail. Therefore, we define:

$$Y_{ijr} = \begin{cases} 1, & \text{if facility } j \in J \text{ serves as the level} - r \text{ facility for customer } i \in I \\ 0, & \text{if not} \end{cases}.$$

A "level-r" assignment is one for which there are r closer facilities that are open. If $r = 0$, this is a primary assignment; otherwise it is a backup assignment. The objective is to minimize a weighted sum of the operating cost (the fixed charge location problem objective) and the expected failure cost, given by

$$\sum_{i \in I} \sum_{j \in J} \sum_{r=0}^{|J|-1} h_i c_{ij} q^r (1-q) Y_{ijr}.$$

Each customer i is served by its level-r facility (call it j) if the r closer facilities have failed (this occurs with probability qr) and if j itself has not failed (this occurs with probability $1 - q$). The full model is omitted here.

20.14 Planning Under Uncertainty (Snyder et al. 2007)

Long-term strategic decisions like those involving facility locations are always made in an uncertain environment. However, classical facility location models like the fixed charge location problem treat data as though they were known and deterministic, even though ignoring data uncertainty can result in highly sub-optimal solutions. Unfortunately, as Vidal and Goetschalckx (2000) discussed in their paper, critical parameters such as customer demands, prices, and resource capacities are quite uncertain. Moreover, the arrival of regional economic alliances, for instance the Asian Pacific Economic Alliance and the European Union, have prompted many corporations to move more and more towards global supply chains, and therefore to become exposed to risk factors such as exchange rates, reliability of transportation channels, and transfer prices.

Daskin et al. (2003) said that most approaches to decision making under uncertainty fall into one of two categories: stochastic programming or robust optimization. In stochastic programming, the uncertain parameters are described by discrete scenarios, each with a given probability of occurrence; the objective is to minimize the expected cost. In robust optimization, parameters may be described either by discrete scenarios or by continuous ranges; no probability information is known, however, and the objective is typically to minimize the worst-case cost or regret.

According Daskin et al. (2003), Sheppard (1974) was one of the first authors to propose a stochastic approach to facility location. He suggests selecting facility locations to minimize the expected cost, though he does not discuss the issue at length. Weaver and Church (1983) and Mirchandani et al. (1985) present a multi-scenario version of the P-median problem. Their model can be translated into the context of the fixed charge location problem as follows. Let S be a set of scenarios. Each scenario $s \in S$ has probability of occurring and specifies a realization of random demands and travel costs. Location decisions must be made now, before it is known which scenario will occur. However, customers may be assigned to facilities after the scenario is known. Other stochastic facility location models include those of Louveaux (1986), Franga and Luna (1982), Berman and LeBlanc (1984), Carson and Batta (1990), and Jornsten and Bjorndal (1994).

The earlier models assume the decision maker knows the demand parameters. That is, the mean μ_i and the standard deviation σ_i of retailer i's demand are known parameters. Snyder et al. (2007) present a stochastic version of the model in Sect. 20.4.3 that explicitly handles parameter uncertainty by allowing parameters to be described by discrete scenarios, each with a specified probability of occurrence. The goal is to choose DC locations, assign retailers to DCs, and set inventory levels at DCs to minimize the total system wide cost. To model this problem, Snyder et al. (2007) define the following additional notation:

20.14.1 Model Inputs

- S: set of scenarios, indexed by s,
- μ_{is}: mean daily demand at retailer i in scenario s, for $i \in I$, $s \in S$,
- d_{ijs}: per-unit cost to ship from DC_j to retailer i in scenario s, for $i \in I$, $j \in J$,
- q_s: probability that scenario s occurs, for $s \in S$.

20.14.2 Model Outputs (Decision Variables)

- $x_j = 1$, if j is selected as a facility location, and 0 otherwise, for each $j \in J$,
- $y_{ijs} = 1$, if retailer $i \in I$ is served by DC_j $j \in J$ in scenario $s \in S$, and 0 otherwise.

20.14.3 Objective Function and its Constraints

$$\sum_{s \in S} \sum_{j \in J} \left\{ f_j X_j + \left(\sum_{i \in I} \beta \chi \mu_{is}(d_{ijs} + a_j) Y_{ijs} \right) \right. \\ \left. + K_j \sqrt{\sum_{i \in I} \mu_{is} Y_{ijs}} + q \sqrt{\sum_{i \in I} L_j \sigma_i^2 Y_{ijs}} \right\}. \quad (20.56)$$

Subject to

$$\sum_{j \in J} Y_{ijs} = 1, \quad \forall i \in I, s \in S, \quad (20.57)$$
$$Y_{ijs} - X_j \leq 0 \quad \forall i \in I, j \in J, s \in S, \quad (20.58)$$
$$Y_{ijs} \in \{0, 1\} \quad \forall i \in I, j \in J, s \in S, \quad (20.59)$$
$$X_i \in \{0, 1\} \, \forall j \in J, \quad (20.60)$$

where $q = \theta h z_\alpha$.

20.15 Solution Techniques

A number of solution approaches have been proposed for the supply chain design models. We review the related literatures.

- To solve the uncapacitated fixed charge location model, Maranzana (1964) proposed a neighborhood search improvement algorithm for the closely related p-median problem that exploits the ease in finding optimal solutions to 1-median problem: it partitions the customers by facility and then finds the optimal location within each partition. If any facility changes, the algorithm repartitions the customers and continues until no improvement in the solution can be found.
- Teitz and Bart (1968) proposed an exchange or "swap" algorithm for the P-median problem that can also be extended to the fixed charge facility location problem.
- Hensen and Mladenovic (1997) proposed a variable neighborhood search algorithm for the P-median problem that can also be used for the fixed charge location problem.
- Heuristics that be applied to the P-median problem will not perform well for fixed charge facility location problem if the starting number of facilities is suboptimal. Thus, we should apply more sophisticated heuristics to the problem. Al-Sultan and Al-Fawzan (1999) applied tabu search to the uncapacitated fixed charge location problem.
- Daskin (1995) review the use of Lagrangian relaxation algorithms in solving the uncapacitated fixed location problem.
- When embedded in branch and bound, Lagrangian relaxation can be used to solve the fixed charge location problem optimally (Geoffrion 1974).
- Daskin et al. apply Benders decomposition to locating plants and distribution centers simultaneously with multiple commodities after noting that, if the location and assignment variables are fixed, the remaining problem breaks down into $|L|$ transportation problems, one for each commodity.
- Shen et al. (2003) outline a column generation approach to solve the basic model that presented in Sect. 20.4.3. Daskin et al. (2001) proposes a Lagrangian relaxation approach for the same problem.
- To solve the model with routing cost estimation, Shen and Qi (2004) develop a Lagrangian relaxation based solution algorithm. By exploiting the structure of the problem, they find an $O(|I|^2 \log(|I|))$ time algorithm for the similar problem that must be solved in the Lagrangian relaxation subproblems.
- Ozsen et al. (2003) apply a Lagrangian relaxation solution algorithm to solve the capacitated DCs problems that presented in Sect. 20.4.4. The Lagrangian subproblem is also a non-linear integer program, and they propose an efficient algorithm for the continuous relaxation of this problem.
- Amiri (2006) studied the designing a distribution network in a supply chain system with allow for multiple levels of capacities available to the warehouses and plants. He develop a mix integer programming model and present a Lagrangian based solution procedure for the problem.

- Two solution approaches was presented by Shen and Daskin (2005) for the model with service consideration, one based on the weighting method and the other based on genetic algorithms. The genetic algorithm performs very well compared to the weighting method, and it is the only feasible approach for large-sized problem instances, since the weighting method requires excessive computational time in such cases.
- A branch-and-price algorithm, a variant of branch-and-bound in which the nodes are processed by solving linear-programming relaxation via column-generation, was presented by Shen (2006) to solve the profit maximizing model with demand choice flexibility.
- Shen (2005) proposes Lagrangian relaxation embedded in a branch and bound algorithm to solve the model with multiple commodities.
- Yeh (2005) present a hybrid heuristic algorithm for the multistage supply chain network problem (MSCN). The proposed algorithm employs a simple greedy method and a hybrid local search method combining the XP, RP and IP to solve the MSCN. From the computation experiments, both the speed in finding the solution and the quality of the obtained solutions were good enough to solve the larger MSCN problem.
- Yeh (2006) has also proposed a memetic algorithm (MA) which is a combination of GA, greedy heuristic, and local search methods for the same problem. The author has extensively investigated the performance of the MA on the randomly generated problems.
- Romeijn et al. (2007) proposed a framework for the two-echelon supply chain design problem that incorporates location decisions as well as location-specific transportation cost and two-echelon inventory costs. Their approach is to formulate the problem as a set-covering model. They propose to solve this problem using column generation to deal with the fact that the number of variables (columns) in this formulation is exponentially large.
- Altiparmak et al. (2006) propose a new solution procedure based on genetic algorithms to find the set of Pareto-optimal solutions for multi-objective SCN design problem. To deal with multi-objective and enable the decision maker for evaluating a greater number of alternative solutions, two different weight approaches are implemented in the proposed solution procedure.
- Altiparmak et al. (2007) presents a solution procedure based on steady-state genetic algorithms (ssGA) with a new encoding structure for the design of a single-source, multi-product, multi-stage SCN. The effectiveness of the ssGA has been investigated by comparing its results with those obtained by CPLEX, Lagrangian heuristic, hybrid GA and simulated annealing on a set of SCN design problems with different sizes.
- Hinojosa et al. (2008) formulating the problem that deal with a facility location problem where they build new facilities or close down already existing facilities at two different distribution levels over a given time horizon. In addition, they allow carrying over stock in warehouses between consecutive periods. They propose a Lagrangian approach which relaxes the constraints connecting the distribution levels. A procedure is developed to solve the resulting, independent

subproblems and, based on this solution, to construct a feasible solution for the original problem.
- Jayaraman and Pirkul (2001) have developed a heuristic approach based on Lagrangean relaxation for the single-source, multi-product, multi-stage SCN design problem. Another heuristic approach based on Lagrangean relaxation and simulated annealing has been developed by Syam (2002) for a multi-source, multi-product, multi-location framework.
- Jang et al. (2002) have presented a combined model of network design and production/distribution planning for a SCN. While they have used a Lagrangian heuristic for the design of SCN, a genetic algorithm (GA) has been proposed for integrated production and distribution planning problem.
- Syarif et al. (2002) have developed a spanning tree-based GA approach for the multi-source, single-product, multi-stage SCN design problem based on Prüfer numbers.
- Jayaraman and Ross (2003) have also proposed a heuristic approach based on simulated annealing for the designing of distribution network and management in supply chain environment.
- Shen (2007) states that Qi and Shen propose an algorithm based on the bisection search and the outer approximate algorithm. They show that their algorithm is more efficient that the outer approximation algorithm when being applied to the model with unreliable supply.
- To solve the model with parameter uncertainty, Snyder et al. (2007) present a Lagrangian-relaxation based solution algorithm. They show the Lagrangian subproblem is non-linear integer program, but it can be solved by a low-order polynomial algorithm. They present qualitative and quantitative computational results on problems with up to 150 nodes and nine scenarios, and describe both algorithm performance and solution behavior as key parameters change.

Solution methods discussed above are outlined in Table 20.1. This table shows that the use of heuristics and meta-heuristics based solution algorithms increase in recently papers.

20.16 Case Study

In this section we will introduce two real-world case studies related to supply chain design problems.

20.16.1 An Industrial Case in Supply Chain Design and Multilevel Planning in US (Sousa et al. 2008)

Souse et al. (2007) address a case study, inspired by a real agrochemicals supply chain, with two main objectives, structured in two stages. In the first stage they

Table 20.1 Solution methods for supply chain design problem

References	Problem	Solution method
Maranzana (1964)	Uncapacitated fixed charge location model	Neighborhood search improvement algorithm
Teitz and Bart (1968)	Fixed charge facility location problem	Exchange or "swap" algorithm
Hensen and Mladenovic (1997)	Fixed charge facility location problem	Variable neighborhood search algorithm
Al-Sultan and Al-Fawzan (1999)	Uncapacitated fixed charge location problem	Tabu search
Galvo (1993) and Daskin (1995)	Uncapacitated fixed charge location problem	Lagrangian relaxation algorithms
Geoffrion (1974)	Fixed charge location	Lagrangian relaxation algorithms
Shen et al. (2003)	Basic model	Column generation approach
Shen and Qi (2004)	Model with routing cost estimation	Lagrangian relaxation based solution algorithm
Ozsen et al. (2003)	Capacitated Dcs problems	Lagrangian relaxation solution algorithm
Amiri (2006)	Designing a distribution network in a supply chain system with allow for multiple levels of capacities	Lagrangian based solution procedure
Shen and Daskin (2005)	Model with service consideration	Weighting method
Shen and Daskin (2005)	Model with service consideration	Genetic algorithms
Shen (2006)	Profit maximizing model with demand choice flexibility	Branch-and-price algorithm
Shen (2005)	Model with multiple commodities	Lagrangian relaxation embedded in a branch and bound algorithm
Yeh (2005)	Multistage supply chain network problem (MSCN)	Hybrid heuristic algorithm
Yeh (2006)	Multistage supply chain network problem (MSCN)	Memetic algorithm (MA)
Romeijn et al. (2007)	Two-Echelon supply chain design problem	Column generation
Altiparmak et al. (2006)	Multi-objective SCN design problem	New solution procedure based on genetic algorithms
Altiparmak et al. (2007)	Design of a single-source, multi-product, multi-stage SCN	Solution procedure based on steady-state genetic algorithms (Ssga)
Hinojosa et al. (2008)	Dynamic supply chain design with inventory	Lagrangian approach which relaxes the constraints connecting the distribution levels
Jayaraman and Pirkul (2001)	Single-source, multi-product, multi-stage SCN design problem	Heuristic approach based on Lagrangean relaxation
Jang et al. (2002)	Design of SCN	Lagrangian heuristic

(continued)

Table 20.1 (continued)

References	Problem	Solution method
Syarif et al. (2002)	Multi-source, single-product, multi-stage SCN design problem	Spanning tree-based GA approach
Jayaraman and Ross (2003)	Designing of distribution network and management in supply chain environment	Heuristic approach based on simulated annealing
Shen (2007)	Model with unreliable supply	Algorithm based on the bisection search and the outer approximate algorithm
Snyder et al. (2007)	Model with parameter uncertainty	Lagrangian-relaxation based solution algorithm

redesign the global supply chain network and optimize the production and distribution plan considering a time horizon of 1 year, providing a decision support tool for long term investments and strategies. The output decisions from the first stage, mainly the supply chain configuration and allocation decisions, are the input parameters for the second stage where a short term operational model is used to test the accuracy of the derived design and plan. The outputs of this stage are detailed production and distribution plans and an assessment of the customer service level.

20.16.2 Multi-Objective Optimization of Supply Chain Networks in Turkey (Altiparmak et al. 2006)

The problem considered in this paper has been from a company which is one of the producers of plastic products in Turkey. The company is planning to produce plastic profile which is used in buildings, pipelines and consumer materials. The company wishes to design of SCN for the product, i.e., select the suppliers, determine the subsets of plants and DCs to be opened and design the distribution network strategy that will satisfy all capacities and demand requirement for the product imposed by customers. The problem is a single-product, multi-stage SCN design problem. Considering company managers' objectives, they formulated the SCN design problem as a multi-objective mixed-integer non-linear programming model.

References

Adelman D (2003) A price-directed approach to stochastic inventory/routing. Working Paper, University of Chicago

Al-Sultan KS, Al-Fawzan MA (1999) A tabu search approach to the uncapacitated facility location problem. Ann Oper Res 86:91–103

Altiparmak F, Gen M, Lin L, Paskoy T (2006) A genetic algorithm approach for multi-objective optimization of supply chain networks. Comput Ind Eng 51:197–216

Altiparmak F Gen M, Lin L, Karaoglan I (2007) A steady-state genetic algorithm for multi-product supply chain network design. Comput Ind Eng, in press, Corrected Proof, Available online 2 June 2007

Amiri A (2006) Designing a distribution network in a supply chain system: Formulation and efficient solution procedure. Eur J Oper Res 171:567–576

Balinski ML (1965) Integer programming: Methods, uses, computation. Manage Sci 12:253–313

Baumol WJ, Wolfe P (1958) A warehouse-location problem. Oper Res 6:252–263

Berger RT (1997) Location-routing models for distribution system design. Ph.D. Dissertation, Department of Industrial Engineering and Management Sciences, Northwestern University, Evanston, IL

Birge JR, Louveaux F (1997) Introduction to stochastic programming. Springer-Verlag, New York

Carson, YM, Batta Y (1990) Locating an ambulance on the Amherst Campus of the State University of New York at Buffalo. Interfaces 20(5):43–49

Chan Y, Carter WB, Burnes MD (2001) A Multiple-depot, multiple-vehicle, location-routing problem with stochastically processed demands. Comput Oper Res 28:803–826

Chopra S (2003) Supply chain management: Strategy, planning, and operation. Prentice-Hall, India

Church RL, ReVelle CS (1974) The maximal covering location problem. Papers Region Sci Assoc 32:101–118

Daskin MS (1995) Network and discrete location: Models, algorithms, and applications. Wiley, New York

Daskin MS, Jones PC (1993) A new approach to solving applied location/allocation problems. Microcomput Civil Eng 8:409–421

Daskin M, Coullard C, Shen ZJ (2001) An inventory-location model: Formulation, solution algorithm and computational results. Ann Oper Res 110:83–106

Daskin MS, Snyder LV, Berter RT (2003) Facility location in supply chain design, forthcoming in logistics systems. In: Langevin A, Riopel D (eds) Design and optimization. Kluwer, Dordecht

Daskin MS, Snyder LV, Berger RT (2005) Facility location in supply chain design. In: Langevin A, Riopel D (eds) Logistics systems: Design and operation. Springer, New York, pp 39–66

Eppen G (1979) Effects of centralization on expected costs in a multi-location newsboy problem. Manage Sci 25(5):498–501

Erlebacher SJ, Meller RD (2000) The interaction of location and inventory in designing distribution systems. HE Trans 32:155–166

Fazel Zarandi MH, Turksen IB, Saghiri S (2002) Supply chain: crisp and fuzzy aspects. Int J Appl Math Comput Sci 12(3)423–435

Franga PM, Luna HPL (1982) Solving stochastic transportation-location problems by generalized Benders decomposition. Transport Sci 16:113–126

Geoffrio AM (1974) Lagrangian relaxation for integer programming. Math Program Study 2: 82–114

Geoffrion AM (1976) The purpose of mathematical programming is insight, not numbers. Interfaces 7:81–92

Geoffrion AM, Graves GW (1974) Multicommodity distribution system design by Benders decomposition. Manage Sci 20(5):822–844

Geunes J, Shen ZJ, Romeijn HE (2004) Economic ordering decisions with market choice flexibility. Naval Res Logist 51:117–136

Hall RW (1986) Discrete models/continuous models. Omega, Int J Mgmt Sci 14:213–220

Hansen P, Labbe M, Peeters D, Thisse JF (1987) Facility location analysis. Fundam Pure Appl Econ 22:1–70

Hansen P, Peeters D, Thisse JF (1995) The profit-maximizing weber problem. Location Sci 3: 67–85

Higle JL (2005) Stochastic programming: Optimization when uncertainty matters. In: Greenberg HJ (ed) TutORials in operations research. INFORMS, Baltimore, pp 30–53

Hinojosaa Y, Kalcsicsb J, Nickelc S, Puertod J, Veltene S (2008) Dynamic supply chain design with inventory. Comput Oper Res 35:373–391

Jang YJ, Jang SY, Chang BM, Park (2002) A combined model of network design and production/distribution planning for a supply network. Comput Ind Eng 43:263–281

Jayaraman V, Pirkul H (2001) Planning and coordination of production and distribution facilities for multiple commodities. Eur J Oper Res 133:394–408

Jayaraman V, Ross A (2003) A simulated annealing methodology to distribution network design and management. Eur J Oper Res 144:629–645

Jornsten K, Bjorndal M (1994) Dynamic location under uncertainty. Stud Region Urban Plan 3:163–184

Kleywegt A, Nori VS, Savelsbergh MWP (2002) Dynamic programming approximations for a stochastic inventory routing problem. Working Paper, Georgia Inst. of Technology

Laporte G (1998) Location-routing problems. In: Golden BL, Assad AA (eds) Vehicle routing: methods and studies. North-Holland, Amsterdam, Holland, pp 163–197

Louveaux FV (1986) Discrete stochastic location models. Ann Oper Res 6:23–34

Mabert VA, Venkataramanan MA (1998) Special research focus on supply chain linkages: Challenges for design and management in the 21st century. Dec Sci 29(3):537–552

Maranzana FE (1964) On the location of supply points to minimize transport costs. Oper Res Quart 15:261–270

Meyerson A (2001) Profit-earning facility location. STOC 2001, Hersonissos, Crete, Greece

Min H, Jayaraman V, Srivastava R (1998) Combined location-routing problems: a synthesis and future research directions. Eur J Oper Res 108:1–15

Mirchandani PB, Oudjit A, Wong RT (1985) Multidimensional extensions and a nested dual approach for the m-median problem. Eur J Oper Res 21:121–137

Nagy G, Salhi S (2007) Location-routing: Issues, models and methods. Eur J Oper Res 177: 649–672

Owen SH, Daskin MS (1998) Strategic facility location: A review. Eur J Oper Res 111:423–447

Ozsen L, Daskin MS, Coullard CR (2003) Capacitated facility location model with risk pooling. Networks, Submitted

Romeijn HE, Shu J, Teo CP (2007) Designing two-echelon supply networks. Eur J Oper Res 178:449–462

Ross GT, Soland RM (1980) A multicriteria approach to location of public facilities. Eur J Oper Res 4:307–321

Shen ZJ (2005) Multi-commodity supply chain design problem. IIE Trans 37:753–762

Shen ZJ (2006) A profit-maximizing supply chain network design model with demand choice flexibility. Oper Res Lett 34:673–682

Shen ZJ (2007) Integrated supply chain design models: A survey and future research directions. J Ind Manage Optimiz 3(1):1–27

Shen ZJ, Daskin M (2005) Trade-offs between customer service and cost in integrated supply chain design. M& SOM 7:188–207

Shen ZJ, Qi L (2004) Incorporating inventory and routing costs in strategic location models. To appear in Eur J Oper Res

Shen ZJ, Coullard C, Daskin M (2003) A joint location-inventory model. Transport Sci 37:40–55

Sheppard ES (1974) A conceptual framework for dynamic location-allocation analysis. Environ Plan 6:547–564

Simchi-Levi D, Kaminsky P, Simchi-Levi E (2000) Designing and managing the supply chain. Irwin McGraw-Hill, New York

Snyder LV (2003) Supply chain robustness and reliability: Models and algorithms. PhD Dissertation, Department of Industrial Engineering and Management Sciences, Northwestern University, Ewantson, IL 60208

Snyder LV (2006) Facility location under uncertainty: A review. IIE Trans 38:537–554

Snyder LV, Daskin MS (2005) Reliability models for facility location: The expected failure cost case. Transport Sci 39:400–416

Snyder LV, Daskin MS (2007) Models for reliable supply chain network design. Critical Infrastructure, Murray AT, Grubesic TH. Springer, Berlin, pp 257–289

Snyder LV, Scaparra MP, Daskin ML, Church RC (2006) Planning for disruptions in supply chain networks. In: Greenberg HJ (ed) Tutorials in operations research. INFORMS, Baltimore, forthcoming

Snyder LV, Daskin MS, Teo CP (2007) The stochastic location model with risk pooling. Eur J Oper Res 179(3):1221–1238

Sousa R, Shah N, Papageorgiou LG (2008) Supply chain design and multilevel planning: An industrial case. Comput Chem Eng 32(11):2643–2663

Syam SS (2002) A model and methodologies for the location problem with logistical components. Comput Oper Res 29:1173–1193

Syarif A, Yun Y, Gen M (2002) Study on multi-stage logistics chain network: A spanning tree-based genetic algorithm approach. Comput Ind Eng 43:299–314

Teitz MB, Bart P (1968) Heuristic methods for estimating the generalized vertex median of a weighted graph. Oper Res 16:955–961

Vidal CJ. Goetschalckx M (2000) Modeling the effect of uncertainties on global logistics systems. J Bus Logist 21(1):95–120

Warszawski A (1973) Multi-dimensional location problems. Oper Res Quart 24:165–179

Warszawski A, Peer S (1973) Optimizing the location of facilities on a building site. Oper Res Quart 24:35–44

Weaver, JR, Church RL (1983) Computational procedures for location problems on stochastic networks. Transport Sci 17:168–180

Yeh WC (2005) A hybrid heuristic algorithm for the multistage supply chain network problem. Int J Adv Manuf Technol 26:675–685

Yeh WC (2006) An efficient memetic algorithm for multi-stage supply chain network problem. Int J Adv Manufact Technol 29(7–8):803–813

Zhang S (2001) On a profit maximizing location model. Ann Oper Res 103:251–260

Chapter 21
Classification of Location Models and Location Softwares

Sajedeh Tafazzoli and Marzieh Mozafari

According to the importance and advantages of classification, the first section of this chapter is dedicated to some presented classifications of location models, which help in having more disciplined understanding of location models. In the second section, some location softwares will be introduced briefly.

21.1 Classification of Location Models

Nowadays, with the increasing development of science in all branches, need for a systematic arrangement or proposing a classification scheme for easy access to scientific researches seems necessary. Location science is a branch of optimization science, which formally introduce by Alfred Weber in 1909. It has been growing so rapidly for years that now without a systematic classification of models, continuing the procedure of researches would be so difficult. Therefore, several efforts in classifying location models have been made that, some of them will be mentioned in this section.

21.1.1 Taxonomy vs. Classification Scheme

Classification scheme and taxonomy are two terms often used interchangeably. Though there may be subtle differences in different examples. These two terms are considered as follows:

Taxonomy is a classification of similar objects or concepts into a group, based on their separating characteristics. For example in location models based on "topological structure" criteria, location problems can be classified into three categories, planar (continuous), discrete and network. Taxonomy could be presented by proposing few criteria and classifying the concepts based on them.

Classification scheme is a more general term, an arrangement or division of objects into groups based on characteristics common between the objects. The aim of a classification scheme which makes it different from taxonomy is to encompass the whole subject. But in taxonomy, it is not necessary to cover the whole subject. Regarding, the comprehensiveness of a classification scheme, it is used for encoding data which could have many benefits. Some of the advantages of using a classification scheme are mentioned below:

- Lets a user to find an object in a large collection quickly
- Makes detecting duplicate objects easier
- Present a meaning for an object, which may not be conveyed by its name or definition
- Makes concise problem statement, as opposed to verbal ambiguous descriptions
- Makes data encoding and information retrieval in bibliographical information system and software libraries simple
- Facilitate referencing in literature
- Provides a scheme of defined models and help in detecting models which could be worked on by researchers
- Assists in assigning a predefined model to a real problem

21.1.2 Taxonomy

21.1.2.1 Taxonomy of Francis and White (1974)

One of the first taxonomies presented for layout and location problems, is the classification of Francis and White. In this classification six major elements considered: (1) New facility characteristics, (2) existing facility location, (3) new and existing facility interaction, (4) solution space characteristics (5) distance measure, and (6) objective (Fig. 21.1).

21.1.2.2 Taxonomy of Tansel et al. (1983)

Tansel et al. (1983) present a tree structure as a conceptual framework for their survey of network location models. In this taxonomy, models are classified into point-location or path-location models, which are shown in Fig. 21.2.

21.1.2.3 Taxonomy of Brandeau and Chiu (1989)

Brandeau and Chiu (1989) present a taxonomy of location models based on three criteria, objective, decision variable(s) and system parameters in a table format (Table 21.1). This taxonomy was made according to more than 50 different problem types.

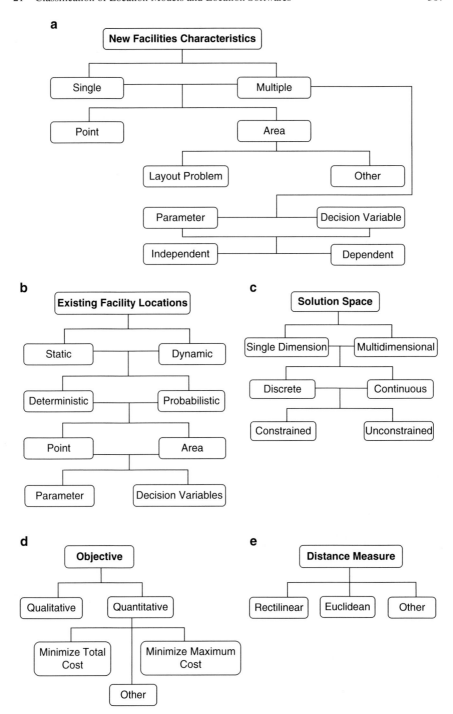

Fig. 21.1 Classification of location models (**a**) new facilities characteristicsm (**b**) existing facility locations (**c**) solution space (**d**) objective (**e**) distance measure, (**f**) new/existing facility interaction (Francis and White 1974)

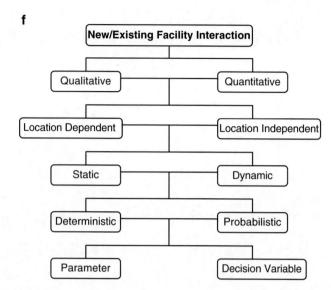

Fig. 21.1 (continued)

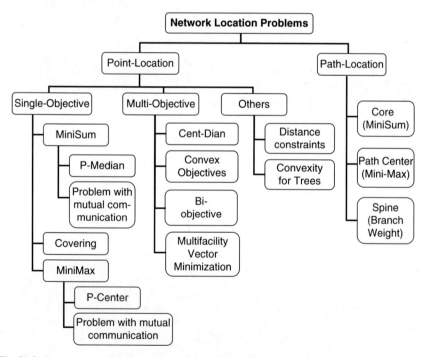

Fig. 21.2 Tree structure for network location problems (Tansel et al. 1983)

Table 21.1 Taxonomy developed by Brandeau and Chiu (1989)

I. Objective	Optimizing:
	Minimize average travel time/average cost
	Maximize net income
	Minimize average response time
	Minimize maximum travel time/cost
	Maximize minimum travel time/cost
	Maximize average travel time/cost
	Minimize server cost subject to a minimum service constraint
	Optimize a distance-dependent utility function
	Other
	Non-optimizing
	Type of location dependence of objective function:
	Server-demand point distances
	Weighted vs. unweighted
	Some vs. all demand points
	Routed vs. closest
	Inter-server distances
	Absolute server location[a]
	Server-distribution facility distances
	Distribution facility-demand point distances
	Other
II. Decision variables	Server/facility location
	Service area/dispatch priorities
	Number of servers and/or service facilities
	Server volume/capacity
	Type of goods produced by each server (in a multi-commodity situation)
	Routing/flows of server or goods to demand points
	Queue capacity
	Other
III. System parameters	Topological structure:
	Link vs. tree vs. network vs. plane vs. n-dimensional space[a]
	Directed vs. undirected
	Travel metric:
	Network-constrained vs. rectilinear vs. Euclidean vs. block norm vs. round norm vs. L, vs. other
	Travel time/cost:
	Deterministic vs. probabilistic
	Constrained vs. unconstrained
	Volume-dependent vs. nonvolume-dependent
	Demand:
	Continuous vs. discrete
	Deterministic vs. probabilistic
	Cost-Independent vs. cost-dependent
	Time-invariant vs. time-varying
	Number of servers
	Number of service facilities
	Number of commodities
	Server location:
	Constrained vs. unconstrained
	Finite vs. infinite number of potential locations

(continued)

Table 21.1 (continued)

	Fixed vs. dependent on system status
	Zero vs. nonzero relocation cost
	Deterministic vs. probabilistic location
	Zero vs. nonzero fixed cost
	Server capacity:
	Capacitated vs. uncapacitated
	Reliable vs. unreliable
	Service area and dispatch priorities:
	Cooperating vs. noncooperating servers
	Closest distance vs. nonclosest-distance service Area
	Service discipline:
	FCFS vs. priority classes vs. spatially-oriented rule vs. other
	Queue capacity

[a] For certain product design and product positioning problems.

Table 21.2 Taxonomy proposed by (Daskin 1995)

Criteria	Classification		
Topological structure	Planar	Discrete	Network
Network type	Tree problems	General graph	
Distance measure	Manhattan	Euclidean	Lp
Number of facilities to locate	Single facility	Multi-facility	
Time dependency	Static	Dynamic	
Certainty	Deterministic	Probabilistic	
Product diversity	Single product	Multi product	
Public/private sector	Public	Private	
Number of objectives	Single objective	Multi objective	
Demand elasticity	Elastic	Inelastic	
Capacity of facilities	Capacitated	Uncapacitated	
Demand allocation type	Nearest facility	General allocation demand	
Hierarchical structure	Single-level	Hierarchical	
Desirability of facility	Desirable	Undesirable	

21.1.2.4 Taxonomy of Daskin (1995)

Daskin (1995) proposed a classification based on 14 criteria: (1) Topological structure, (2) network type, (3) distance measure, (4) number of facilities to locate, (5) time dependency, (6) certainty, (7) commodity (product) diversity, (8) public/private sector, (9) number of objectives, (10) demand elasticity, (11) capacity of facilities, (12) demand allocation type, (13) hierarchical structure, and (14) desirability of facility. This classification is summarized in Table 21.2.

21.1.2.5 Taxonomy of Nagy and Salhi (2007)

Nagy and Salhi (2007) used eight aspects of problem structure to classify location-routing problems, (a) Hierarchical structure, (b) Type of input data (deterministic/stochastic), (c) Planning period (single/multi-period), (d) Solution method (exact/heuristic), (e) Objective function, (f) Solution space, (g) Number of depots (single/multiple), (h) Number and types of vehicles (homogeneous/ heterogeneous), and (i) Route structure.

21.1.2.6 Taxonomy of ReVelle et al. (2008)

ReVelle et al. (2008) provided a brief taxonomy of broad field of facility location modeling in a bibliography in two branches of discrete location science (1) median and plant location models and (2) center and covering models. In this taxonomy, location models are classified into four categories:

1. *Analytic models* are based on large simplifying assumptions (fixed cost of locating a facility dependent of where it will locate, demand uniformly distributed, etc). Despite valuable insight which this class of models provides, they cannot be used for real decision-making purposes
2. *Continuous models* assume that facilities can be located anywhere in service area, while demands are often taken as being at discrete locations
3. *Network models* assume that topological structure of the location model is a network composed of lines and nodes. Much of the literature in this area is concerned with finding special structures that can be exploited to derive low-order polynomial time algorithms
4. *Discrete models* assume that the set of demands and candidate location for facilities are discrete. These problems often formulate in integer or mix-integer programming that most of them are NP-hard on general network

In addition of these classifications, location models can also be distinguished based on other attributes (Klose and Drexl 2004; Jia et al. 2007).

21.1.3 Classification Schemes

In several branches of optimization, classification schemes have been proposed and used by authors successfully (schemes in scheduling (Graham et al. 1979) and queuing theory (Kendall 1951)). Classification schemes are also proposed in location science that few of them will be mentioned here.

21.1.3.1 Classification Scheme of Handler and Mirchandani (1979)

The first classification scheme was proposed by Handler and Mirchandani (1979). They suggested a 4-position scheme which is applicable to network location models with objective functions of the center type.

Pos1/Pos2/Pos3/Pos4
Position 1: information about the new facilities
Position 2: information about existing facilities
Position 3: number of new facilities
Position 4: network type

21.1.3.2 Classification Scheme of Eiselt et al. (1993)

Eiselt et al. (1993) suggested a 5-position scheme for classifying competitive location models (those based on a game-theory approach).

Pos1/Pos2/Pos3/Pos4/Pos5

Position 1: information about the decision space (linear segment, line, circle, bounded subset of m-dimensional real space, m-dimensional real space, network, tree)

Position 2: number of players (specified number, any arbitrary fixed number, markets with free entry)

Position 3: a description of the pricing policy (mill pricing, uniform delivered pricing, perfect spatial discriminatory pricing)

Position 4: rules of the game under consideration (Cournot-Nash equilibrium, subgame perfect Nash equilibrium, Stackelberg equilibrium)

Position 5: behavior of the customers (minimization of distance, minimization of a deterministic or random utility)

21.1.3.3 Classification Scheme of Carrizosa et al. (1995)

Carrizosa et al. (1995) presented a 6-position scheme for classifying planar models where both demand rates and service times are given by a probability distribution.

21.1.3.4 Classification Scheme of Hamacher and Nickel (1998)

Hamacher and Nickel (1998) proposed a 5-position classification scheme for location models that covers not only classes of specific location models, as in the references above, but also covers all of them in a single scheme. Furthermore, this scheme can describe models which are not of the classical type and problems which have not been solved yet. The classification scheme has been in use since 1992 and has been proven to be helpful in research, software development, classroom teaching, and for overview articles. The software library, Library of location algorithms (LoLA) has been developed (Hamacher et al. 1996) based on this classification scheme. The classification scheme consists of the following five positions:

Pos1/Pos2/Pos3/Pos4/Pos5,

where position 1 contains information about the number and type of new facilities. Position 2 indicates type of the location model with respect to the decision space.

Position 3 describes the particulars of the specific location model, such as information about the feasible solutions, capacity restrictions, etc. In position 4, relation between new and existing facilities is defined by a distance function or by assigned costs. In position 5 a description of the objective function is given.

A list of symbols is available for each position that covers a large variety of location models. In Table 21.3, some examples of these symbols, according to the three main areas of location theory (i.e. continuous location, network location and discrete location) is given.

If there are not any special assumptions in a position, this is indicated by •. For example, a • in position 5 means that any objective function are looked or the • in position 3 means that standard assumptions for the model described in the remaining four positions hold. It is assumed by default that weights are non-negative and the objective function is to be minimized. If these assumptions do not hold this has to be stated respectively in positions 3 and 5.

In the following, some examples from the literature are given that indicate the ability of the 5-position classification scheme to describe various kinds of location models. Of course the 5-position classification scheme cannot represent the complete contents of a paper, but it can reflect the major particulars of the models investigated.

- Brandeau (1992): $1/P/queue/l_P/\sum_{prob}$
- Erkut and Tansel (1992): $1/T/w_m : f(.)/d(V,G)/\Sigma$
- Eiselt and Laporte (1993): $3/T/./d(V,G)/\Sigma_{comp}$
- Mirchandani et al (1996): $\#/D/F = line, cap/./\Sigma_{cov}$
- Burkard et al. (2000): $P/G/w_m ><0/d(V,G)/\Sigma$
- Klamroth (2004): $1/P/B_C/l_{2,B_C}/f\ convex$
- Gomes et al. (2007): $N/P/alloc/l_2/\Sigma$
- Colebrook and Sicilia (2007): $1/G/./d(V,G)/Q - CD_{par}$

21.2 Facility Location Softwares

In previous chapters, many models and algorithms have been discussed for solving different facility location problems. Of course, in large real world problems, it is impossible to implement these algorithms manually. In this point computer programs or special software come into play.

Some of the major facility location software is introduced in this section. Although they cannot cover all of the facility location models, they are still under development.

Table 21.3 Some examples of the classification scheme symbols (Hamacher and Nickel 1998)

	Location model	Symbol	Description
Position 1	Continuous	(empty string)	n points are to be located
		L	n lines are to be located
		P	n paths are to be located
		A	n general areas are to be located
	Network	(empty string)	n points are to be located
		P	n paths are to be located
		T	n trees are to be located
		G	n subgroups are to be located
	Discrete	$n \in \{1, \ldots, n\}$	Number of new facilities
		#	Number of new facilities is not known in advance
Position 2	Continuous	R^d	D-dimensional space
		P	Euclidean plane i.e., $P = R^2$
		H	General Hilbert space
	Network	G	General undirected graph
		G_d	General directed graph
		T	A tree
	Discrete	D	Discrete
Position 3	Continuous	F	Feasible region
		R	Forbidden region
		B	Barrier
		$w_m = 1$	Unweighted problem
		$alloc$	Allocation of existing facilities to new facilities
	Network		The same possibilities as in the continuous case
	Discrete	cap	Capacity restrictions
		bdg	Budget restrictions
		$queue$	Service of new facilities is modeled using queuing theory
Position 4	Continuous	l_P	Distance is defined by an l_p-norm
		γ	General gauge
		γ_{pol}	Polyhedral gauge
		$\|.\|$	General norm
	Network	$d(V, V)$	New and existing facilities must be nodes of the graph
		$d(V, G)$	Existing facilities are at nodes and few facilities can be any points on the graph.
		$d(V, T)$	Analogous to d(V, G), where G is a tree
	Discrete		Any restrictions and particulars of given cost Cij can be specified
Position 5	Continuous	Σ	The classical Weber or sum objective function
		max	The maximum objective function
		CD	Cent-Dian objective function
		$\int$	Continuous demand satisfying the distribution specified in position 3

(continued)

Table 21.3 (continued)

Location model	Symbol	Description
	Σ_{prob}	Sum objective with some probabilistic influences, like, for example, different scenarios or weights which are random variables
	$Q - \Sigma_{par}$	Q-criteria Weber model, where we are looking for Pareto locations
Network		Any of the objective functions listed for the continuous case which are meaningful in the network environment
Discrete	Σ_{comp}	Competitive location model
	QAP	Quadratic assignment objective function
	$\Sigma_{cov} + \Sigma_{uncov}$	Covering objective function
	Σ_{hub}	Hub location objective function

21.2.1 LoLA

LoLA is a collection of efficient algorithms for solving planar, network and discrete facility location problems (Hamacher et al. 1996). LoLA uses the classification scheme of Hamacher and Nickel (1998) for accessing to the implemented algorithms. A part of the algorithms is known from the literature whereas others are the results of current research. LoLA can solve a number of different location models including Median, Center, Q-median and Q-center that Q is the number of facilities in a multi-facility problem or the number of objective functions in a multi-objective problem. The algorithms available in LoLA can be found in Hamacher et al. (1996).

LoLA has been designed to address several different user groups. It fulfills the needs of students and teachers as well as researchers and practitioners.

LoLA provides a graphical user interface that allows its simple application in industrial projects as well as for demonstrations in high school and university teaching. In addition, a Text-based user interface is available to call algorithms of LoLA from other applications. To solve individual facility location problems, a programming interface allows the direct incorporation of specific algorithms of the program library into the implementation of extended routines (Callable Library).

21.2.1.1 LoLA and Interface with Geographical Information System

Geographical information systems (GIS) are designed for visualizing real world data of countries, states, cities, etc. with map data and additional information that allow decision makers to find solutions to problems such as locating facilities, routing, etc. The software library LoLA has the ability to be linked with GIS to easily get real world data and solve real world problems. An example of a GIS is ArcView

GIS using script language called Avenue. This language has been implemented to combine ArcView GIS with LoLA (Bender et al. 2002).

Via LoLA ArcView® Link it is possible to read data out of the ArcView GIS database and convert them into a LoLA input file, then call LoLA Libraries to solve the model and finally monitor the results and get the solution back to ArcView GIS.

21.2.1.2 LoLA Example

Here a simple example (from software package) is used to illustrate the ideas involved and the basic data required in LoLA.

Consider uncapacitated facility location (UFL) problem, by choosing the characteristics of 5-position classification scheme from software menus, LoLA exhibit the classification by symbols, $\#/D/ \bullet / \bullet / \Sigma$ (Pos1: Number of facilities to locate determine by model, Pos2: Discrete solution space, Pos3: No special conditions in model, Pos4: Metric define by cost matrix as input, Pos5: Sum (median) objective function).

Input format of this discrete location model contains information about:

- Demand point (x, y, b, n) where x and y are coordinates, b is the customer demand and n is the facility name, for example: 54.00 15.00 5,000 [Palermo]
- Cost matrix ($n \times n$ matrix defines travel or transport cost or time from facility i to j).

This model is solved for a UFL problem to identify the cities in Italy from which to service demand of customer sites in a total of 39 cities (supply point must be placed on demand points).

The optimal result consists of:

- The number and location of supply points (opt1 is Lucca and opt2 is Viterbo, Fig. 21.3)
- objective function value
- and allocation of demand points to each supply point (Fig. 21.3)

21.2.2 SITATION

SITATION (Daskin 2002) is a facility location software that accompanies Daskin's text (Network and discrete location: models, algorithms, and applications). The SITATION software now solves a number of different discrete and network facility location problems including:

- P-median
- P-center
- Set covering
- Maximal covering

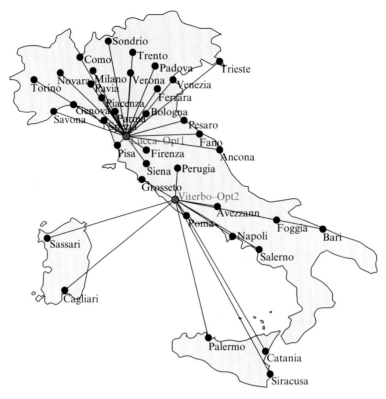

Fig. 21.3 LoLA result

- Partial set covering
- Partial P-center
- Uncapacitated fixed charge
- 1-Source capacitated fix charge problems
- SCD integrated inventory location model
- Inventory location
- Profit maximization

SITATION allows the user to choose from a variety of heuristics and optimization-based approaches for each of the different models. Some examples of SITATION available algorithms according to different classes of problems are given in Table 21.4.

In addition, SITATION has the ability to solve multi objective facility location models such as the covering-median tradeoff problem by using the weighting method.

Menu-OKF, Net Spec and Modify Distances are additional softwares which accompany SITATION and make it more efficient. The program Menu-OKF solves network problems using the Out-of-kilter flow algorithm. The program Modify

Table 21.4 Some examples of SITATION available algorithms

Problem to solve	Available algorithms
P-median	Myopic
	Variable neighborhood
	Genetic algorithm
	Exchange
	Lagrangian relaxation
P-center	Lagrangian relaxation
Set covering	Lagrangian relaxation
Maximum covering	Greedy adding
	Greedy adding and substitution
	Lagrangian relaxation
Partial set covering	Lagrangian relaxation
Partial P-center	Lagrangian relaxation
Uncapacitated fixed charge	Add
	Drop
	Exchange
	Variable neighborhood
	Lagrangian relaxation
Integrated Inv/Loc model (SCD)	Lagrangian relaxation

Distances modifies distance files used by SITATION. The program Net Spec allows user to specify the inputs for network problems to be solved in SITATION.

Other SITATION capabilities are as follows:

- Entirely menu-driven and relatively easy to understand
- Allows the user to add or delete facilities from a solution and also exchange facilities locations manually, thereby allowing the user to gain confidence in the solutions determined by the program or to test his or her own solutions
- Includes branch and bound capabilities that allow the user to obtain very tight (usually provably optimal) solutions
- Includes good reporting and mapping capabilities for illustrating the solutions
- Able to solve problems up to 300 nodes scale (latest version, 5.7.0.26)

21.2.2.1 SITATION Example

Here, one test problem in the software package is used as an example. A P-median problem where the demand nodes are defined by the data contained in the 150-city data set found in SITATION. The inter-nodal distances are computed by software, using great circle distances. The coverage distance and cost per mile are defined 300 and 1 respectively (Daskin 2002).

The model could be run under different number of facilities (different scenarios). Fig. 21.4 illustrates map result of running model for locating 15 facilities with Lagrangian relaxation.

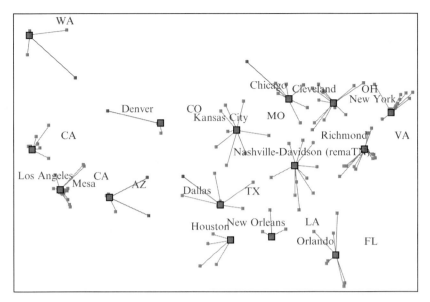

Fig. 21.4 SITATION result

21.2.3 S-Distance

S-distance is a standalone Spatial Decision Support System, mainly focused on location-allocation analysis (Sirigos and Photis 2005).

S-distance is able to solve quite large classical discrete and network location-allocation problems, including:

- P-median
- P-center
- Maximal covering
- Multi-objective

Current version of the software (version 0.7) offers a number of heuristic and optimization-based algorithms such as:

- Greedy and randomized algorithms
- Local search heuristics
- Meta-heuristics
- Lagrange relaxation

While still being in an early stage, S-distance software is functional and has been tested on many classical Operation Research instances, as well as on several real-world problems.

Other S-distance capabilities are as follows:

- Able to read data from various file formats, such as OR-library files and databases with network/point topology in dbf format

- Provides all Pairs Shortest Paths calculation using Dijkstra's (2-ary heap) or Floyd's algorithms, for network problems
- Incorporate an interactive solution process within a simplified GIS framework
- Allows the user straight-forward creation and evaluation of different solutions both numerically and graphically

21.2.4 Other Facility Location Softwares

There is some other facility location software specialized on solving a specific problem and limited more in their functionalities than the three software introduced above. Some examples are given in the following:

- *RLP* is a program package for solving restricted 1-facility location problems in a user friendly environment (Nickel and Hamacher 1992)
- *Optimal locating air polluting facilities* is a general modeling system to evaluate and optimize the location of an air polluting facility (Fliege 2001)
- *Jure Mihelic's K-center algorithms* is a program for solving k-Center location problems (Mihelic 2004)
- **Minimum enclosing circle applet** is a program package for solving the Minimal Enclosing Circle problem (Eliosoff and Unger 1998). It is useful for planning the location of a shared facility
- *Excel template for facility location* includes model for center-of-gravity method for locating distribution centers
- *GAMBINI* is a small GIS-utility which calculates draws and exports multiplicative weighted Voronoi diagrams (Tiefelsdorf and Boots 1997). A point location data structure can be built on top of the Voronoi diagram in order to find the object that is nearest to a given point
- *Mathematical programming softwares* such as CPLEX, LINGO, LINDO and GAMS which are useful when having mathematical models for facility location problems

References

Bender T, Hennes H, Kalcsics J, Melo MT, Nickel S (2002) Location software and interface with GIS and supply chain management. In: Drezner Z, Hammacher H (eds) Facility location: applications and theory. Berlin, Springer

Brandeau ML (1992) Characterization of the stochastic median queue trajectory in a plane with generalized distances. Oper Res 40(2):331–341

Brandeau ML, Chiu SS (1989) An overview of representative problems in location research. Manage Scie 35:645–674

Burkard RE, Cela E, Dollani H (2000) 2-Medians in trees with pos/neg weights. Discrete Appl Math 105:51–71

Carrizosa EJ, Conde E, Munoz M, Puerto J (1995) The generalized weber problem with expected distances. RAIRO 29:35–57

Colebrook M, Sicilia J (2007) A polynomial algorithm for the multicriteria cent-dian location problem. Eur J Oper Res 179:1008–1024

Daskin MS (1995) Network and discrete location: models, algorithms, and applications. Wiley Interscience, NY

Daskin MS (2002) SITATION-facility location software. Department of Industrial Engineering and Management Sciences, Northwestern University, Evanston, IL. http://users.iems.northwestern.edu/~msdaskin/

Eiselt HA, Laporte G (1993) The existence of equilibria in the 3-facility Hotelling model in a tree. Transport Sci 27(1):39–43

Eiselt HA, Laporte G, Thisse JF (1993) Competitive location models: a framework and bibliography. Transport Sci 27:44–54

Eliosoff J, Unger R (1998). MEC – minimum enclosing circle applet. http://www.cs.mcgill.ca/~cs507/projects/1998/jacob/welcome.html

Erkut E, Tansel BC (1992) On parametric medians of trees. Transport Sci 26(2):149–156

Fliege J (2001) OLAF – a general modeling system to evaluate and optimize the location of an air polluting facility. OR Spektrum 23:117–136

Francis RL, White JA (1974) Facility layout and location: an analytical approach. Prentice-Hall, Englewood Cliffs

Gomes H, Ribeiro AB, Lobo V (2007) Location model for CCA-treated wood waste remediation units using GIS and clustering methods. Environ Model Softw 22:1788–1795

Graham RE, Lawler EL, Lenstra JK, Rinnoy Kan AHG (1979) Optimization and approximation in deterministic sequencing and scheduling: a survey. Ann Discrete Math 4:287–326

Hamacher HW, Nickel S (1998) Classification of location models. Location Sci. 6:229–242

Hamacher HW, Klamroth K, Nickel S, Schoebel A (1996) Library of location algorithms. University of Kaiserslautern. http://www.mathematik.uni-kl.de/lola/

Handler GY, Mirchandani PB (1979) Location on networks theory and algorithms. MIT Press, Cambridge

Jia H, Ordonez F, Dessouky M (2007) A modeling framework for facility location of medical services for large-scale emergencies. IIE Trans 39:41–55

Kendall D (1951) Some problems in the theory of queues. J R Stat Soc 13:151–153

Klamroth K (2004) Algebraic properties of location problems with one circular barrier. Eur J Oper Res 154:20–35

Klose A, Drexl A (2004) Facility location models for distribution system design. Eur J Oper Res 162:4–29

Mihelic J (2004) Jure Mihelic k-center algorithms. Department of Computer and Information Science, University of Ljubljana

Mirchandani P, Kohli R, Tamir A (1996) Capacitated location problems on a line. Transport Sci 30(1):75–80

Nagy G, Salhi S (2007) Location-routing: issues, models and methods. Eur J Oper Res 177:649–672

Nickel S, Hamacher HW (1992) RLP: a program package for solving restricted 1-facility location problems in a user friendly environment. Eur J Oper Res 62:116–117

ReVelle CS, Eiselt HA, Daskin MS (2008) A bibliography for some fundamental problem categories in discrete location science. Eur J Oper Res 184:817–848

Sirigos S, Photis YN (2005) S-distance software. Department of Planning and Regional Development (DPRD), University of Thessaly, Greece

Tansel BC, Francis RL, Lowe TJ (1983) Location on networks: a survey. Part I: the p-center and p-median problems. Manage Sci 29:482–497

Tiefelsdorf M, Boots B (1997) GAMBINI multiplicative weighted voronoi diagrams. http://www.wlu.ca/wwwgeog/special/download/gambini.htm

Chapter 22
Demand Point Aggregation Analysis for Location Models

Ali NaimiSadigh and Hamed Fallah

When selecting locations for facilities, such as hospitals, fire stations schools, warehouses and retail outlets, one has to take into account the demand for the service provided by the facility. In many instances, such facilities serve a large number of individuals, and it may not be realistic to model each individual as a separate demand point (DP). To reduce the problem size to a manageable one, an analyst is usually forced to aggregate the demand (population) data by representing a collection of individuals as one DP. While this is a practical solution, it perturbs the original problem and may introduce errors to subsequent analysis (Erkut and Bozkaya 1999).

Many location problems can be formulated as minimizing some location objective function subject to upper bounds on other location constraint functions. When such functions are sub additive and no decreasing in the distances, worst-case DP aggregation error bounds are known. It is shown how to solve a relaxation and a restriction of the aggregated problem in such a way as to obtain lower and upper bounds on the optimal value of the original problem (Francis et al. 2002).

Location problems often involve finding locations of new facilities that provide services of some kind to existing facilities, also called DPs. When such problems take place in urban contexts, each private residence can be a DP. Thus there can be too many DPs to be modeled individually, and aggregation of the DPs becomes necessary; indeed, sometimes only aggregated data is available. This aggregation creates a more tractable model, but also introduces model error.

It is naturally of interest to examine how much error is introduced, and the effect of the level of aggregation upon the error. Essentially the modeler is faced with a tradeoff: less model accuracy for more model tractability, or vice versa.

Hillsman and Rhoda (1978) were perhaps the first to study errors associated with DP aggregation for the K-median problem. Their classification of aggregation errors was further studied by Current and Schilling (1987), Erkut and Bozkaya (1999) and Zhao and Batta (1999). Plastria (2001), in an effort to reduce aggregation error, further refined the Hillsman–Rhoda error classification, and made a strong case for using the centroid of each aggregation group as the representative point for the group in the reduced K-median problem. Current and Schilling (1987) considered errors due to aggregation for the (discrete) covering problem.

Methods for reducing DP aggregation error have been proposed by Current and Schilling (1987), Bowerman et al. (1999), and Hodgson and Neuman (1993).

General background discussions on DP aggregation and resulting errors can be found in Zhao and Batta (1999, 2000) and Plastria (2001).

Zhao and Batta (2000) point out that there is another kind of aggregation error; it is perhaps less obvious but often occurs. Due to budgetary constraints, only a subset of the set of all possible feasible solutions may be considered. For example, potential location sites of interest may be enumerated in a list. Sites might be added to the list with more resources to consider sites of interest, additional. This approach is usually viewed as solving a restriction of the actual problem, but it can also be viewed as a "solution space" aggregation, since a large collection of potential sites is, in effect, aggregated into a smaller collection. Zhao and Batta (1999, 2000) also give a general background discussion of DP aggregation, as do Francis et al. (2002).

22.1 Applications

22.1.1 P-Median Problem

A network location model is defined with respect to a connected graph and a set of weighted DPs on the graph; generally, p new facilities are to be established to service these DPs. The problem of optimally locating the p new facilities so that the sum of the weighted network distances between the DPs and their respective closest new facilities is smallest is called the p-median problem (Andersson et al. 1998).

The p-median model is arguably the most popular model in the facility location literature dealing with multiple facilities. Given n DPs in some space (such as Euclidean plane or road network), the goal of the model is to locate p service facilities, and allocate the n DPs to these service facilities such as to minimize the total distance to be traveled for service. It is possible to solve medium-sized instances ($n = 200$) of this problem optimally. Furthermore, efficient heuristics are available to solve larger instances of the problem ($n = 1,000$) to near optimality.

Unfortunately, for most realistic instances of the facility location problem, the number of DPs is much larger. For example, if we wish to locate facilities (such as retail outlets, post offices, or bank machines) in a city, then each resident is a potential DP. Given that the population of many large cities exceeds one million, the need for some aggregation becomes apparent (Erkut and Bozkaya 1999).

22.1.2 P-Center Problem

A model frequently proposed for locating emergency service facilities is the p-center model. Its solution recommends locations for such facilities to minimize the maximum time (or distance) in order to respond to an emergency at some DP. In an urban context, there could be millions of possible emergency DPs. Thus, it is common to aggregate DPs.

Location models are generally *NP-hard*. Furthermore, real-world location problems are often large in scale, and are not solvable to optimality within reasonable time and effort. Thus, in practice, approximate representations of problems are created by means of DP aggregation (Rayco et al. 1999).

22.1.3 Covering Problem

Covering models measure effectiveness through assessment of whether demand can receive service from located facilities (Church and ReVelle 1974). The key concept in these models is the acceptable proximity or coverage. Usually a maximum value, known as the service standard, is preset with respect to either distance or travel time, though the latter can be converted to a distance measure. Demand is said to be suitably served if it can be reached by any facility within this maximum coverage standard. For example, fire department response time should be less than 6 min to an accident or structure fire after a call for service has been received (Tong and Murray 2006).

22.2 Aggregation Errors

22.2.1 Spatial Aggregation Demand

Spatial aggregation of demand units is a common technique used in the solution of LA models. As mentioned previously, many location problems, including the p-median problem, are NP-hard. Spatial aggregation of the demand units results in a reduction of the size of these problems to make them computationally more tractable.

The aggregation process reduces the number of distinct demand units so that the m unaggregated demand units indexed by U are aggregated to $q < m$ aggregated demand units indexed by the set $A = \{1, \ldots, q\}$ with the demand of each unaggregated demand unit assigned to its respective aggregated demand unit. More precisely, if the set U_j identifies the unaggregated demand units that are associated with aggregated demand unit $j \in A$ then the total demand of this aggregated demand unit is given by:

$$\omega = \sum_{i \in U_j} w_i \quad j \in A \qquad (22.1)$$

$$f_U(X) = \sum_{i \in U} w_i D(X, u_i) \qquad (22.2)$$

In this way, the function f given in (22.2) can be approximated by:

$$f_A(X) = \sum_{j \in A} \omega_j D(X, a_j) \tag{22.3}$$

Where a_j is the jth aggregated demand unit and $D(X, a_j)$ is a measure of the distance between a_j and the element of X that serves the corresponding demand. Different approximations results by varying the way in which a_j and D(X, a_j), $j \epsilon A$, are defined. In any case, solving the p-median problem defined by (22.3) is computationally more attractive than solving the one defined by (22.2) simply because $q < m$. In what follows, we will use the terms basic spatial unit (BSU) and aggregated spatial unit (ASU) to distinguish between unaggregated and aggregated demand units, respectively. This process of demand aggregation can induce errors in the evaluation of the cost of a solution to the p-median problem. This error arises since, in general, the cost of a given solution is different when evaluated using the ASUs and the BSUs. The total error caused by the aggregation process for a given solution $\bar{X} \subseteq S$ with $|\bar{X}| = p$ is given by:

$$f_A(\bar{X}) - f_U(\bar{X}) \tag{22.4}$$

Hillsman and Rhoda (1978) categorized this error into three different sources with two different causes: error due to incorrect distance estimation (Source A and B) and error caused by misallocating BSUs (Source C). Source A errors arise since the demand weighted distance from an ASU to a candidate facility site is not equal to the demand weighted distances between the corresponding BSUs and the same site. Source B errors are a special case of source A errors and occur when a potential facility site is at the same position as an ASU. For a given solution $\bar{X} \subseteq S$ with $|\bar{X}| = p$ the total source A and B aggregation error is given by:

$$f_A(\bar{X}) - f_{A,U}(\bar{X})$$

Where for $X \subseteq S$,

$$f_{A,U}(X) = \sum_{i \in A} \sum_{j \in U_j} w_j d(X(a_i), u_j)) \tag{22.5}$$

Source B errors result in the cost of a solution, underestimating its actual cost, while source A errors can result in either underestimation or overestimation. Source C errors occur because all demand in an ASU is allocated to a single facility even though some of the corresponding BSUs may be closer to a different facility. For a given solution $\bar{X} \subseteq S$ with $|\bar{X}| = p$ the total source C error can be calculated as:

$$f_{A,U}(\bar{X}) - f_A(\bar{X})$$

Source C errors result in the cost of the solution to the aggregated problem overestimating the actual cost of the solution.

Hillsman and Rhoda (1978) examined aggregation error for uniformly distributed demand in three different configurations and calculated aggregation errors of up to 8%. On different data sets, Current and Schilling (1987) discovered aggregation errors of over 20%.

The discussion so far has concentrated on the total error in the objective function caused by aggregation. However, Goodchild (1979) noted that "aggregation tends to produce much more dramatic effects on facility locations than on the value of the objective function" and Bach (1981) further pointed out that 'the level of aggregation exerts a strong influence on the optimal location patterns as well as on the values of the location criteria. Casillas (1987) clarified this notion by distinguishing two classes of errors that aggregation causes in the solution of p-median problems.

The first is *cost estimate error* defined as the difference between the estimated cost of the solution using the aggregated data and the true objective cost calculated using the unaggregated data. The other is *optimality error* which is the difference between the actual costs of the solution found using the aggregated data and the cost of the solution found using the unaggregated data. If we define:

$$X_A^* = \arg_X \min f_A(X)$$

as the optimal solution to the p-median problem using the ASUs and

$$X_U^* = \arg_X \min f_U(X)$$

As the corresponding optimal solution found using the BSUs, then the corresponding relative cost estimate error is:

$$E_{CE} = [f_A(X_A^*) - f_U(X_A^*)]/f_U(X_A^*) \qquad (22.6)$$

While the corresponding relative optimality error is:

$$E_O = [f_U(X_A^*) - f_U(X_U^*)]/f_U(X_U^*) \qquad (22.7)$$

Note that the cost estimate error $E_{CE} = f_A(X_A^*) - f_U(X_A^*)$ is identical to the total aggregation error defined in (22.4) when $X = X_A^*$ (Bowerman et al. 1999).

22.2.2 Methods for Reducing Aggregation Errors

22.2.2.1 P-Median Models

The effects of aggregation on the solution of facility location models have been recognized by many authors. For example, Rushton (1989) stated that the "optimum locations must be sensitive, to an important degree, at some level of spatial aggregation of data. We do not know how to identify this level in advance for any given application". Goodchild (1979) also identified the importance of aggregation but further noted that the "effects of aggregation are unique to particular solutions, and therefore no general rules of aggregation can be found". In a recent study, Fotheringham et al. (1995) found that solutions to the p-median problem were highly sensitive to both level of aggregation and the definitions of the ASUs and that these "results therefore question the reliability of any locational recommendations from a location-allocation model when aggregate demand data are used". However, in a similar study, Murray and Gottsegen (1997) found that a "certain amount of spatial stability [was] in fact present" in the locational configuration of the p-median solutions and that the error percentage remained relatively low.

Francis and Lowe (1992) also recognized that "too much aggregation can destroy the accuracy of a location model". Furthermore, they validated Goodchild's (1979) claim of there being "no general rules of aggregation" by establishing that the process of determining an aggregation scheme with minimum worst-case error is an NP-hard problem. Nevertheless, Francis and Lowe (1992) proposed a method for determining an aggregation scheme that bounds the level of aggregation error. Their method involves finding a feasible solution to an associated covering problem. These results were further developed as a row–column aggregation scheme for p-median models using rectilinear distances (1996).

Both the effects of aggregation error and the difficulty in finding general aggregation schemes have caused researchers to develop methods for reducing these errors. For example, Mirchandani and Reilly (1986) proposed a method to reduce source A and B errors for zonal or polygon-based problems. The travel distance was decomposed into two components: from a facility to a zone, and the inter-zonal travel distance. These two components were then combined to obtain an improved estimate of the distance from a facility site to a demand zone.

Current and Schilling (1987) introduced a weighting scheme to eliminate source A and source B errors. Their method is based on preventing the loss of locational information during the aggregation process. In their method, the demand weighted distance between ASU aj and a potential facility site $s_k \in S$ is replaced by the demand weighted distance of the BSUs associated with the ASU and the site so that:

$$\omega_j d(s_k, a_j) = \sum_{i \in U_j} w_i d(s_k, u_i) \tag{22.8}$$

where ω_j is defined as in (22.2). Current and Schilling (1987) tested their method on several different data sets, and found that on these data sets their method reduced the magnitude of both the cost estimate error and the optimality error. For these sample problems, their method reduced the average cost estimate error from between -11.8% and -16.4% to between 1.7% and 2.0% and the average optimality error from between 1.3% and 1.7% to between 0.4% and 1.0%. However, their method does not consider source C errors because it adjusts the distances before the problem is solved. Since source C errors depend on the facility locations selected in the solution, these errors cannot be reduced by their method.

Hodgson and Neuman (1993) proposed a method for reducing source C errors in zonal problems, that is, in problems where the demand is distributed over polygons referred to as demand polygons. Their method involves finding *Thiessen* or *Voronoi* polygons with the selected set of facilities as control points. Thiessen polygons have the property that every point in a polygon is closer to that polygon's control point than it is to any other control point (1992). These polygons are then topologically overlaid on the set of demand polygons. Source C error arises wherever any demand polygon spans more than one Thiessen polygon. The area of each demand polygon is partitioned into zero or more *source C error* polygons and a *complementary* polygon where demand is allocated to the correct facility. The Thiessen demand disaggregation method computes the centroid of the error and complementary polygons and assigns them to the nearest facility (Bowerman et al. 1999).

22.2.2.2 The Demand Partitioning Method for Reducing Aggregation Error

None of the currently available methods reported in the literature for reducing aggregation errors consider all three sources of error. In this section, an iterative method for reducing aggregation errors in p-median problems that addresses all three sources of errors by combining Current and Schilling's (1987) method for handling source A and B errors and Hodgson and Neuman's (1993) idea of partitioning the ASUs (or in their case, demand zones) to eliminate source C error is introduced.

The demand partitioning heuristic is an iterative procedure for reducing aggregation error. This procedure is based on applying Current and Schilling's (1987) weighting method and solving the aggregated p-median problem. The ASUs are then partitioned according to the selected facility sites to form a new set of ASUs so that source C error in the original aggregated problem is eliminated. These new ASUs are then used to define a new aggregated p-median problem and the process is repeated until the problem is solved without cost estimate error.

Recall that the weighting method for eliminating source A and B aggregation errors is based on calculating the demand weighted distances between an ASU and a facility as the demand weighted sum of the distances between the BSUs aggregated to that ASU and that facility.

However, this procedure does nothing to eliminate source C errors, which can be significant for some problems.

The source C errors are reduced through a partitioning procedure. In a manner similar to the Hodgson and Neuman's (1993) Thiessen demand disaggregation procedure, the total level of source C errors can be calculated by assigning each BSU to the nearest facility in the current p-median solution. This calculation gives the true cost of the solution and eliminates all cost estimate errors for the original solution. This assignment of BSUs to facilities was then used to partition each existing ASU into one or more new ASUs.

However, the solution found with the original ASUs may not be optimal for the problem defined with the new set of ASUs. The weighting and partitioning steps can be repeated on this new set of ASUs. This suggests an iterative demand partitioning procedure for eliminating all aggregation errors from the solution of an aggregated problem.

Given U, the set of BSUs; A, the set of ASUs; and $U_j \neq \emptyset$, $j \in A$ the indices of BSUs aggregated to ASU_j, the demand partitioning method can be described as follows:

Initialize: Set the iteration count $l = 1$. Set $A^{(1)} = A$ and $U_j^{(1)} = U_j$, $j \in A$

Demand weighting: For each $s_k \in S$ calculate

$$d(s_k, a_j^{(1)}) = \sum_{i \in U_j^{(1)}} w_i d(s_k, u_i) / \sum_{i \in U_j^{(1)}} w_i \quad \text{for all } j \in A^{(1)}$$

Using these distances eliminates source A and source B errors.

Heuristic p-median solution: For $A = A^{(l)}$ find

Defining via the current set of ASUs and the distances calculated in step 2. The corresponding value of the objective function is given by:

$$f_A(X^*) = \sum_{j \in A} \omega_j d(X^*(a_j), a_j) = \sum_{j \in A} \sum_{i \in U_j} w_i d(X^*(a_j), u_i)$$

where $\omega_j = \omega_j^{(l)}$, $U_j = U_j^{(l)}$, and $a_j = a_j^{(l)}$ for all $j \in A$, are defined in terms of the current ASUs. This calculation contains only source C errors and therefore overestimates $f_U(X^*)$.

Set $X_{(l)}^* = X^*$.

Terminate: Stop if $l > 1$ and $X_{(l)}^* = X_{(l-1)}^*$. This step is ignored for the first iteration and otherwise terminates the procedure if the current solution is identical to the solution from the previous iteration. We know that there is no source C error in the value of $f_{A^{(l)}}(X_{(l-1)}^*)$ therefore if $X_{(l)}^* = X_{(l-1)}^*$ then there is no aggregation error in the solution $X_{(l)}^*$.

Repartition: For each $j \in A^{(l)}$ partition $U_j^{(l)}$, a current ASU, into one or more new ASUs as follows:

Assign each BSU in $U_j^{(l)}$ to the facility in the current p-median solution that is closest to it. The BSUs in each nonempty assignment comprise a new and unique ASU. Define $A^{(l+1)}$ to be the index set of the new ASUs.

This step repartitions the BSUs into a new set of ASUs indexed by $A^{(l+1)}$ so as to eliminate source C error. All the BSUs in a new ASU were, in the previously iteration, aggregated to the same ASU and are allocated to the same facility in the current p-median solution. Conversely, any BSUs that were in the same ASU in the previous iteration and that are in different ASUs after repartitioning must be assigned to different facilities in the current p-median solution.

Terminate: Stop if $|A^{(l+1)}| = |A^{(l)}|$. If the number of new ASUs after repartitioning is the same as before repartitioning then the procedure terminates. Since all BSUs in each new ASU were members of a common ASU in the previous iteration, having the same number of ASUs implies that there were no incorrectly allocated BSUs.

Demand weighting: For each $s_k \in S$ calculate the distances between potential facility sites s_k and the new ASUs using:

$$d(s_k, a_j^{(l+1)}) = \sum_{i \in U_j^{(l+1)}} w_i d(s_k, u_i) / \sum_{i \in U_j^{(l+1)}} w_i \quad \text{for all } j \varepsilon A^{(l+1)}$$

Since all BSUs in a new ASU are closest to the same facility in the current p-median solution we know that:

$$f_A(X^*) = \sum_{j \in A} \omega_j D(X^*, a_j) = \sum_{i \in U} w_i D(X^*, u_i) = f_U(X^*)$$

where $A = A^{(l+1)}$, $X_{(l)}^* = X^*$, and $\omega_j = \omega_j^{(l+1)}$ and $a_j = a_j^{(l+1)}$ for all $j \varepsilon A$. Since $f_A(X^*) = f_U(X^*)$ the solution $X_{(l)}^* = X^*$ has no aggregation error for the ASU partitions indexed by $A^{(l+1)}$.

Iterate: Increment l. Go to step 3.

This iterative procedure will always terminate since the maximum possible number of ASUs is equal to the number of BSUs and the procedure terminates if the number of ASUs do not increase over iteration (step 6). Thus the maximum possible number of iterations is $m-q$ where q is the number of initial ASUs. In practice, far less iteration is commonly required.

After the procedure terminates at iteration l^*, the final solution $X_{(l^*)}^* = X^*$ is the solution of the p-median problem defined by $A^* = A^{(l^*)}$ and S with no cost estimate errors, i.e., $f_{A^*}(X^*) = f_U(X^*)$. This procedure electively reduces the cost estimate error to zero for the solution of a particular aggregated p-median problem. There is, of course, no guarantee that the solution to this problem is the same as the solution to the unaggregated p-median problem.

Computational effort in both distances weighting (steps 2 and 7) and partitioning (step 5)

Increases only linearly with the number of BSUs for the following reasons:

(a) *Demand weighting*: Current and Schilling (1987) weighting method requires the calculation of the demand weighted distance between each ASU and each potential facility site. Assuming that the distances between the BSUs and the facility sites are pre-calculated, these distances are calculated as the demand weighted sum of the BSUs aggregated to an ASU and since the ASUs partition the BSUs, it takes $O(mn)$ operations, where n is the number of potential facility sites, to calculate these distances.

(b) *Partitioning*: Since each BSU must be assigned to the nearest of p facility sites this assignment requires $O(mp)$ operations. Identifying the new nonempty ASUs then requires $O(m)$ plus $O(q^{(l)}p)$ operations, where $q^{(l)}$ is the number of ASUs in iteration l. Since $m \geq q^{(l)}$ this partitioning requires $O(mp)$ operations.

Thus both procedures scale well to problems with a large number of BSUs. Consequently, the overall computational effort is dominated by whatever heuristic is used for solving the p-median problem.

An assumption for this algorithm is that there is an initial partitioning of the BSUs into ASUs.

Often, when using real-world data sets, there is a natural partitioning of the BSUs through the use of existing political boundaries such as districts, counties, or areas. This is the approach that is used for the sample data as outlined in the next section. However, other methods have been suggested to partition the BSUs. Casillas (1987) randomly selected BSUs as the reference centers for the ASUs.

Each BSU was then aggregated to its nearest reference center. Current and Schilling (1987) used both visual inspection and solving a p-median problem to select the reference centers. Finally, as mentioned above, Francis and Lowe (1992) proposed finding a feasible solution to a covering problem as a method to determine the reference centers (Bowerman et al. 1999).

22.3 Computational Approach

In this first phase–strategy, our "row–column" DP aggregation procedures involve partitioning the DPs according to a grid imposed over the demand region (Francis et al. 1996; Rayco et al. 1997). The widths of rows and columns in each grid are adjusted by these algorithms to reflect the DP structure. This initial partitioning provides a coarse aggregation structure. In our earlier work, we used a rectilinear l-median or l-center as the aggregate DP for each grid cell. There is no guarantee that this aggregate DP will be on the network. Further, our earlier work was based only on rectilinear distances, not network distances. Therefore, in this paper, to find the aggregate DP in each cell, we carry out a second "fine-tuning" step – tactics – which involves the optimal solution of network location problems on the graph sub networks induced by the grid partitioning. The location found in each sub network, an l-median or l-center, determines the aggregate DP that replaces all DPs in the sub network. Once we place the aggregate DPs on the network, we go through a Monte Carlo sampling phase, to compute network distances and estimate various error values of interest.

Consider the "strategy" step for the p-median model. The grid, with c columns and r rows, is obtained for the p-median problem by solving a c-median problem on the x-axis projection of the DPs, and an r-median problem on the y-axis projection of the DPs; see Francis et al. (1996). Next consider the "tactics" step. Each grid cell induces a sub network whose largest component's optimal l-median is designated as an aggregate DP. Finally, as an optional step, each DP can be "assigned" an aggregate point closest to it; this mapping is given by the Voronoi partition (Hakimi et al. 1992) of the entire network with respect to the DP set.

The aggregate DP set for the p-center model is found in a similar manner, with certain modifications. The grid is constructed by solving a pair of one-dimensional

c- or r-center problems defined with respect to the projections onto the coordinate axes of the images, under a transformation, of the DPs; see Rayco et al. (1997). This transformation results in a 45° rotation of the demand data space. The aggregate DPs for each grid cell, furthermore, are given by the optimal network l-centers of the largest cell-induced subnetwork components.

The projected median problems on the line are solvable in $O((c+r)e)$ time using the Hassin and Tamir (1991) algorithm. The one-dimensional center problems are solvable in $O(e \; log \; e)$ time using a modification of the algorithm by Meggido et al. (1981) for the p-center problem in trees. Let $n = |V|$ and $m = |E|$ be the number of vertices and edges, respectively, of the network. The splitting of the graph into subnetworks requires $O(e \; log \; cr)$ effort, and the optimal solution of the l-median or l-center problems on the subnetworks appears, for typical street networks, to have an average-case complexity of $O(m^2/cr)$ (Andersson and Normark 1995). Finally, the Voronoi partition of a graph may be found, using the algorithm by Hakimi et al. (1992), in $O(e + n \; log \; m)$ time. We use the Voronoi partition to compute nearest network distances between DPs (aggregated or not) and new facility locations when computing $f(X)$ and $f'(X)$

The aggregate set so obtained may define the relevant approximating problem.

Alternatively, it may serve to initialize an iterative location-allocation procedure, which is the adaptation to networks of the well-known planar location approach of Cooper (1963); see also Maranzana (1964). This procedure, however, is computationally intensive, as each iteration requires the solution of network location problems. The location-allocation procedure locates each aggregate DP (Anderson et al. 1998).

References

Andersson G, Normark T (1995) Aggregation methods for large-scale location problems on networks. Master's Thesis, Royal Institute of Technology, Stockholm, Sweden

Andersson G, Francis RL, Normark T, Rayco MB (1998) Aggregation method experimentation for large scale network location problems. Location Sci 6:25–39

Bach L (1981) The problem of aggregation and distance for analyses of accessibility and access opportunity in location-allocation models. Environ Plan 13(9):55–78

Bowerman RL, Calamai PH, Brent HG (1999) The demand partitioning method for reducing aggregation errors in p-median problems. Comput Oper Res 26:1097–1111

Casillas PA (1987) Data aggregation and the p-median problem in continuous space. In: Ghosh A, Rushton G (eds) Spatial analysis and location-allocation models. Van Nostrand Reinhold, NY

Church R, ReVelle C (1974) The maximal covering location problem. Pap Reg Sci Assoc 32:101–118

Cooper L (1963) Location-allocation problems. Oper Res 11:331–344

Current JR, Schilling DA (1987) Elimination of source A and B errors in p-median problems. Geogr Anal 19:95–110

Erkut E, Bozkaya B (1999) Analysis of aggregation errors for the p-median problem. Comput Oper Res 26:1075–1096

Fotheringham AS, Densham PJ, Curtis A (1995) The zone definition problem in location-allocation modeling. Geogr Anal 27:60–77

Francis RL, Lowe TJ (1992) On worst-case aggregation analysis for network location problems. Ann Oper Res 40:229–246

Francis RL, Lowe TJ, Rayco MB (1996) Row–column aggregation for rectilinear distance p-median problems. Transport Sci 30(2):160–174

Francis RL, Lowe TJ, Tamir A, Emir-Farinas H (2002) A framework for demand point and solution space aggregation analysis for location models. Eur J Oper Res 159:574–585

Goodchild MF (1979) The aggregation problem in location allocation. Geogr Anal 11:240–255

Hakimi SL, Labbe M, Schmeichel E (1992) The voronoi partition of a network and its implications in location theory. ORSA J Comp 4:412–417

Hassin R, Tamir A (1991) Improved complexity bounds for location problems on the real line. OR Lett 10:395–402

Hillsman EL, Rhoda R (1978) Errors in measuring distances from populations to service centers. Ann Regional Sci 12:74–88

Hodgson MJ, Neuman S (1993) A GIS approach to eliminating source C aggregation error in p-median models. Location Sci 1:155–170

Maranzana FE (1964) On the location of supply points to minimize transport costs. Oper Res Quart 15:216–270

Meggido N, Tamir A, Zemel E, Chandrasekaran R (1981) An O(n log2 n) algorithm for the kth longest path in a tree with applications to location problems. SIAM J Computing 102:238–337

Mirchandani PB, Reilly JM (1986) Spatial nodes in discrete location problems. Ann Oper Res 6:203–222

Murray AT, Gottsegen JM (1997) The influuence of data aggregation on the stability of p-median location model solutions. Geogr Anal 29:200–213

Plastria F (2001) On the choice of aggregation points for continuous p-median problems: a case for the gravity center. TOP 9:217–242

Rayco MB, Francis RL, Lowe TJ (1997) Error-bound driven demand point aggregation for the rectilinear distance p-center model. Location Sci 4:213–235

Rayco MB, Francis RL, Tamir A (1999) A p-center grid-positioning aggregation procedure. Comput Oper Res 26:1113–1124

Rushton G (1989) Application of location models. Ann Oper Res 18:25–42

Tong D, Murray AT (2006) Geographical information science to enhance location coverage modeling. *UCGIS Summer Assembly*, Vancouver, Washington, USA

Zhao P, Batta R (1999) Analysis of centroid aggregation for the Euclidean distance p-median problem. Eur J Oper Res 113:147–168

Zhao P, Batta R (2000) An aggregation approach to solving the network p-median problem with link demands. Networks 36:233–241

Appendix: Metaheuristic Methods

Zohre Khoban and Saeed Ghadimi

Combinatorial optimization (CO) is the process of finding the optimal solution for problems with a region of feasible solutions. Applications of CO are numerous in fields of industry and economy, such as routing, scheduling, packing, location, transportation, telecommunications, financial services, etc. While much progress has been made in finding exact solutions to some combinatorial optimization problem (COP) such as dynamic programming, many hard COP are still to be solved exactly and require heuristic methods. Moreover, reaching "optimal solutions" is in many cases meaningless, so another aim of heuristic methods is quickly producing good-quality solutions, without necessarily providing any guarantee for reaching the optimal solution (Resende and De Souse 2004). Metaheuristics are high level procedures that coordinate simple heuristics such as local search, to find solutions that are of better quality in comparison to those found by the simple heuristics alone. One of the most important reason of using metaheuristics is to escape from local optimum that heuristics most of the times get trapped in. One of the main goals in any metaheuristic method is to create a balance between intensified and diversified search. Some well-known metaheuristics are: greedy randomized adaptive search procedure (Glover et al. 2003), scatter search (Glover 1999), variable neighbourhood search (Glover et al. 2003), harmony search (Geem et al. 2001), particle swarm optimization (Eberhart and Shi 2001), simulated annealing, genetic algorithms, tabu Search, ant colony optimization and also their hybrids. Hybrids are metaheuristics with one or more additional heuristic modules or combination of two metaheuristics for example TS and GA (Glover et al. 1995) which are more efficient in comparison. In the following sections we describe some of the metaheuristic methods in detail.

Genetic Algorithm

Genetic algorithm (GA) which was first suggested by John Holland (1975) is an evolutionary strategy. The basic mechanism in GA is that of Darwinian evolution: good traits survive and mix to form new while the bad traits are eliminated from the population.

GA is a population based algorithm which starts with an initial population as the first generation which most of the time selected randomly. Each individual solution in the population that is called chromosome is a set of linked features and each feature in one chromosome is named a gene. If one chromosome results in a better result of fitness function which is considered for each problem, it is fit to survive and a new generation is created in every iteration by updating the population, using some genetic operations which make some changes in the survivors.

Fitness function: The fitness of each chromosome is evaluated by a function and a value is assigned to each chromosome. The fitness function is the only component of the algorithm that is generally problem specific. Operators have important roles in GA. The more important ones are:

Selection: The members of the new population are selected based on their fitness. There are many ways of selection varying in complexity. Low selectivity accepts a large number of solutions, high selectivity allows a few or one to be dominated, however a balance needs to be reached in order to prevent the solution from becoming trapped in a local optimum. One simple selection method is roulette wheel selection in which more fit members of the population have a higher chance of being selected.

Crossover: This is the most important reproduction genetic operator. The child of two selected chromosomes in last step gets its features from a random selection of its parents features. Again there are many kinds of crossover, such as one-point crossover which first selects a location to cut the two parents. A new chromosome is then created by copying the first part of the first chromosome, into a bit string, followed by a copy of the last part of the second chromosome into the same bit string. The remaining, un-copied parts of the chromosomes are also copied into a second new chromosome.

Mutation: This would involve making a random change to one of the genes on the string of one chromosome, done randomly by a given probability.

The result of these operations (selection, crossover and mutation) is a new generation of population, the same size we start with. There are various types of chromosome's strings such as bit strings, real numbers, permutations of element, lists of rules, and etc.

The Simple Genetic Algorithm

1. Initialize an initial population mostly in a random way.
2. Select individuals for reproduction.
3. Generate a new generation by the genetic operations.
4. Insert children into population and update the population.
5. If the stopping criteria are satisfied, stop the algorithm, otherwise, return to step 2

Some of GA's applications are parametrization (Al-Duwaish 1999), job-shop scheduling (Cheng et al. 1999), vehicle routing (Tong et al. 2004), time series prediction (Hansen et al. 1999), and chance constrained problem (Poojari and Varghese 2008).

Tabu Search

Tabu search (TS) was first produced by Fred Glover (1986), the basic ideas have also been sketched by Hansen (1986) and additional efforts of formalization are reported by Werra and Hertz (1989). Many good examples and applications of TS with a collection of references could be found in a book by Glover and Languna (1993). The convergence of TS was proved by Hanafi (2000). TS is a neighborhood search with an iterative procedure. In each iteration k, from a current solution i goes to a next solution j which is searched among the solutions in the neighborhood set $N(i, k)$ of current solution i. in addition to $N(i, k)$, there are at least three more components in a simple TS as below:

1. *Evaluation function f(i)*: Evaluation function which is the problem specification, evaluates the value for each solution.
2. *Tabu list*: TS has two kinds of memories, short term and long term, the short term prevents to selecting identical solutions in limited number of consecutive iterations by saving last moves in a selection named tabu list $T(i)$ and forbids moves that might lead to recently visited solutions.
3. *Long term memory*: The value $f(i*)$ of the best solution $i*$ visited so far is saved in the long term memory and updated when a better solution is found, so it prevents to getting trapped in local optimum by jumping to the best current solution when its necessary.

Two Important Concepts

Intensification: Sometimes the search process propend to intensify the search in some region of S, because iteration by iteration the solutions become better in this area, so for giving a high priority to the solutions near the current one, it is possible to introduce an additional term in the evaluation function which will penalize solutions far from this region.

Diversification: Sometimes it is fruitful to diversify the solutions by leaving the current region and exploring another area of S, because continuing the search in this region is not very satisfactory for evaluation function; so for giving a high priority to the solutions far from the current one, it is possible to introduce an additional term in the evaluation function that will penalize solutions which are close to the present one (Hertz et al. 1995).

By using intensification and diversification the evaluation function changes as below:

$f' = f +$ Penalty of Intensification + Penalty of Diversification.

Aspiration criteria A(i): Aspiration criteria is an additional precaution which is taken to avoid missing good solutions. Sometimes a solution in spite of belonging to the tabu list, is better than any solution so far seen; so we would allow the tabu classification of this solution to be overridden and consider the solution admissible to be visited.

A Simple Tabu Search Algorithm

1. Choose an initial solution i in S. Set $i* = i$ and $k = 0$.
2. Set $k = k + 1$ and generate $N(i, k)$ by considering $T(i)$ and $A(i)$.
3. Choose the best j in $N(i, k)$ as a new solution.
4. Set $i = j$
5. If $f(i) < f(i*)$ then set $i* = i$.
6. Update tabu list and aspiration criteria.
7. If a stopping condition is met, then stop. Else go to Step 2.

By using some immediate stopping conditions of TS have been introduced by Hertz et al. (1995). Some of TS's applications are graph coloring (Hertz and Werra 1987), maximum independent set (Friden et al.1990), course scheduling (Hertz 1992), multicommodity location/allocation (Crainic et al. 1993), job shop scheduling (Ponnambalam et al. 2000), quadratic assignment problem (Misevicius 2005).

Ant Colony Optimization

Ant colony optimization (ACO) is a paradigm for designing metaheuristic algorithms for combinatorial optimization problems. The first algorithm which can be classified within this framework was presented in 1991 (Dorigo et al. 1991) and, since then, many diverse variants of the basic principle have been reported in the literature. The inspiring source of ACO is the pheromone trail laying and following behavior of real ants which use pheromones as a communication medium. Analogous to the biological example, ACO is based on the indirect communication of a colony of simple agents, called (artificial) ants, mediated by (artificial) pheromone trails. The pheromone trails in ACO serve as a distributed numerical information which the ants use to probabilistically construct solutions to the problem being solved and which the ants adapt during the algorithm's execution to reflect their search experience. The essential trait of ACO algorithms is the combination of a priori information about the structure of a promising solution with a posteriori information about the structure of previously obtained good solutions.

The ACO metaheuristic: After initialization, the metaheuristic iterates over three phases: at each iteration, a number of solutions are constructed by the ants; these solutions are then improved through a local search (this step is optional), and finally the pheromone is updated. The following is a more detailed description of the three phases (Dorigo et al. 2006).

Construct ant solutions: A set of some artificial ants constructs solutions from elements of a finite set of available solution components. A solution construction starts from an empty partial solution. At each construction step, the partial solution is extended by adding a feasible solution component from the set of its neighborhood.

The choice of a solution component from neighborhood set is guided by a stochastic mechanism, which is biased by the pheromone associated with each of its elements. The rule for the stochastic choice of solution components vary across different ACO algorithms.

Apply local search: Once solutions have been constructed, and before updating the pheromone, it is common to improve the solutions obtained by the ants through a local search. This phase, which is highly problem-specific, is optional although it is usually included in state-of-the-art ACO algorithms.

Update pheromones: The aim of the pheromone update is to increase the pheromone values associated with good or promising solutions, and to decrease those that are associated with bad ones. Usually, this is achieved (a) by decreasing all the pheromone values through pheromone evaporation, and (b) by increasing the pheromone levels associated with a chosen set of good solutions.

Several ACO algorithms have been proposed in the literature. Some of them are the original ant system (Dorigo et al. 1991), MAX-MIN ant system (Stützle and Hoos 2000) and ant colony system (Dorigo and Gambardella 1997). Some of ACO's applications are traveling salesman problem (Stützle and Hoos 1997), Quadratic assignment (Maniezzo et al. 1994) Scheduling problems (Merkle et al. 2002), vehicle routing (Gambardella et al. 1999) and graph coloring (Costa and Hertz 1997).

Simulated Annealing

Simulated annealing (SA) is a random-search technique which exploits an analogy between the way in which a metal cools and freezes into a minimum energy crystalline structure (the annealing process) and the search for a minimum in a more general system; it forms the basis of an optimization technique for combinatorial and other problems. SA was developed in 1983 to deal with highly nonlinear problems. SA approaches the global maximization problem similar to using a bouncing ball that can bounce over mountains from valley to valley. It begins at a high "temperature" which enables the ball to make very high bounces, which enables it to bounce over any mountain to access any valley, given enough bounces. As the temperature declines the ball cannot bounce so high, and it can also settle to become trapped in relatively small ranges of valleys. A generating distribution generates possible valleys or states to be explored. An acceptance distribution is also defined, which depends on the difference between the function value of the present generated valley to be explored and the last saved lowest valley. The acceptance distribution decides probabilistically whether to stay in a new lower valley or to bounce out of it. All the generating and acceptance distributions depend on the temperature. It has been proved that by carefully controlling the rate of cooling of the temperature, SA can find the global optimum. However, this requires infinite time. Fast annealing and very fast simulated reannealing (VFSR) or adaptive simulated annealing (ASA) are each in turn exponentially faster and overcome this problem.

As pointed above (Wang and Zheng 2001), SA is able to converge to the optimum value, but it could be very expensive to get a desired solution in terms of computational time. For that reason, SA has been improved through hybridizing it with other methods such as the genetic algorithms (Huang et al. 2001) or by parallelising the algorithm (Bevilacqua 2002). The evolutionary simulated annealing algorithm was developed to contribute to the progress in this direction. It offers an evolutionary process in which a shorter SA algorithm is substituted for the genetic operators of crossover and mutation to evolve a population of solutions. The SA algorithm is so compact that one can easily use it in any evolutionary process, where SA can manipulate the solutions selected from the population. This makes ESA easily implementable in various environments and together with different methods.

Neural Networks

Neural nets have gone through two major development periods – the early 1960s and the mid 1980s. They were a key development in the field of machine learning. Artificial neural networks were inspired by biological findings relating to the behavior of the brain as a network of units called neurons. The human brain is estimated to have around ten billion neurons each connected on average to 10,000 other neurons. Each neuron receives signals through synapses that control the effects of the signal on the neuron. These synaptic connections are believed to play a key role in the behavior of the brain. Neural networks have emerged as a field of study within artificial intelligence (AI) and engineering via the collaborative efforts of engineers, physicists, mathematicians, computer scientists, and neuroscientists. Although the strands of research are many, there is a basic underlying focus on pattern recognition and pattern generation (Widrow et al. 1988), embedded within an overall focus on network architectures. Many neural network methods can be viewed as generalizations of classical pattern-oriented techniques in statistics and the engineering areas of signal processing, system identification, optimization, and control theory. There are also ties to parallel processing, VLSI design, and numerical analysis. A neural network is first and foremost a graph, with patterns represented in terms of numerical values attached to the nodes of the graph and transformations between patterns achieved via simple message-passing algorithms. Certain nodes in the graph are generally distinguished as being input nodes or output nodes, and the graph as a whole can be viewed as a representation of a multivariate function linking inputs to outputs. Numerical values (weights) are attached to the links of the graph, parameterizing the input/output function and allowing it to be adjusted via a learning algorithm. One of the most applied learning algorithms is the backpropagation algorithm. The backpropagation algorithm cycles through two distinct passes, a forward pass followed by a backward pass through the layers of the network. The algorithm alternates between these passes several times as it scans the training data. Typically, the training data has to be scanned several times before the networks "learns" to make good classifications (Krose and Smagt 1996).

Forward pass: Computation of the outputs of all neurons in the network. The algorithm starts with the first hidden layer using as input values the independent variables of a case (often called an exemplar in the machine learning community) from the training data set. The neuron outputs are computed for all neurons in the first hidden layer by performing the relevant sum and activation function evaluations. These outputs are the inputs for neurons in the second hidden layer. Again the relevant sum and activation function calculations are performed to compute the outputs of second layer neurons. This continues layer by layer until we reach the output layer and compute the outputs for this layer. These output values constitute the neural net's guess at the value of the dependent variable.

Backward pass: Propagation of error and adjustment of weights.

This phase begins with the computation of error at each neuron in the output layer. These errors are used to adjust the weights of the connections between the last-but-one layer of the network and the output layer. The process is repeated for the connections between nodes in the last hidden layer and the last-but-one hidden layer. The backward propagation of weight adjustments along these lines continues until we reach the input layer. At this time we have a new set of weights on which we can make a new forward pass when presented with a training data observation.

References

Al-Duwaish HN (1999) Parameterization and compensation of friction forces using GA. Ind Appl Conf Rec 1999 IEEE :653–655
Bevilacqua A (2002) A methodological approach to parallel simulated annealing on an SMP System. Journal of Parallel and Distributed Computing 62(10):1548–1570
Cheng R, Gen M, Tsujimura Y (1999) A tutorial survey of job-shop scheduling problems using genetic algorithms, part II: hybrid genetic search strategies. Comput Ind Eng 36:343–364
Costa D, Hertz A (1997) Ants can colour graphs. J Oper Res Soc 48:295–305
Crainic TG, Gendreau M, Soriano P, Toulouse M (1993) A tabu search procedure for multicommodity loction/allocation with balancing requirements. Ann Oper Res 41(4):359–383
De Werra D, Hertz A (1989) Tabu search techniques: A tutorial and an application to neural networks OR Spektrum, pp 131–141
Dorigo M, Gambardella LN (1997) Ant colonies for the traveling salesman problem. cBioSystems 43(2):73–81
Dorigo M, Maniezzo M, Colorni A (1991) The ant system: an autocatalytic optimizing process. Technical Report TR91-016, Politecnico di Milano

Dorigo M, Birattari M, Stützle T (2006) Ant colony optimization artificial ants as a computational intelligence technique. IRIDIA–Technical report series: TR/IRIDIA/2006–023

Eberhart RC, Shi Y (2001) Particle swarm optimization developments application and resources. Proc Congress Evol Comput 1:81–86

Friden C, Hertz A, De Werra D (1990) TABARIS: an exact algorithm based on tabu search for finding a maximum independent set in a graph. Comput Oper Res 17:437–445

Gambardella LM, Taillard E, Dorigo M (1999) Ant colonies for the quadratic assignment problem. J Oper Res Soc 50:167–176

Geem Z W, Kim JH, Loganathan GV (2001) A new heuristic optimization algorithm: Harmony Search, Simulation. Soc Model Simul Int 76(2):60–68

Glover F (1986) Future paths for integer programming and links to artificial intelligence. Comput Oper Res 13:533–549

Glover F (1999) Scatter search and path relinking. New ideas in optimization. Wiley, New York

Glover F, Languna M (1993) In: Reeves C (ed) Tabu search modern heuristic techniques for combinatorial problems. Blackwell, Oxford, pp 70–141

Glover F, Taillard E, De Werra D (1993) A users guide to tabu search. Ann Oper Res 41:3–28

Glover F, Kelly JP, Laguna M (1995) Genetic algorithms and tabu search: Hybrids for optimization. Comput Oper Res 22(1):111–134

Glover F, Kochenberger G, Gary A (2003) Handbook of metaheuristics. International Series in Operations Research & Management Science, vol. 57, Kluwer Academic Publishers, Boston

Hanafi S (2000) On the convergence of tabu search. J Heurist 7(1):47–58

Hansen P (1986) The steepest ascent mildest descent heuristic for combinatorial programming, Presented at the Congress on Numerical Methods in Combinatorial Optimization, Capri, Italy

Hansen JV, McDonald JB, Nelson RD (1999) Time series prediction with genetic-algorithm designed neural networks. Computat Intell 15(3):171–184

Hertz A (1992) Finding a feasible course schedule using tabu search. Discrete Appl Math 35:255–270

Hertz A, De Werra D (1987) Using tabu search techniques for graph coloring. Computing 39(4):345–351

Hertz A, Taillard E, de Werra D (1995) A tutorial on tabu search. Proceedings of Giornate di Lavoro AIRO 95:13–24

Holland JH (1975) Adaptation in natural and artificial systems. The University of Michigan Press, The MIT Press, London

Huang HC, Pan JS, Lu ZM, Sun SH, Hang HM (2001) Vector quantization based on genetic simulated annealing. Signal Process 81:1513–1523

Krose B, V-Smagt P (1996) An introduction to neural networks, 8th edn. The University of Amsterdam

Maniezzo V, Colorni A, Dorigo M (1994) The ant system applied to the quadratic assignment problem. Technical report IRIDIA/94–28, IRIDIA, Universite Libre de Bruxelles, Belgium

Merkle D, Middendorf M, Schmeck H (2002) Ant colony optimization for resource-constrained project scheduling. IEEE Trans Evol Comput 6(4):333–346

Misevicius A (2005) A tabu search algorithm for the quadratic assignment problem. Computat Optimiz Appl 30(1):95–111

Ponnambalam SG, Aravindan P, Rajesh SV (2000) A tabu search algorithm for job shop scheduling. Int J Advanced Manuf Technol 16(10):765–771

Poojari CA, Varghese B (2008) GA based technique for solving chance constrained problems. Eur J Oper Res 185:1128–1154

Resende MGC, De Sousa JP, Viana A (2004) Metaheuristics computer decision making. Kluwer, Dordecht

Stützle T, Hoos HH (1997) The max-min ant system and local search for the traveling salesman problem. In: T. Bäck et al. (eds) Proceedings of the 1997 IEEE International Conference on Evolutionary Computation (ICEC'97). IEEE Press, Piscataway, NJ, pp 309–314

Stützle T, Hoos HH (2000) max-min ant system. Fut Gen Comput Syst 16(8):889–914

Tong Z, Ning L, Debao S (2004) Genetic algorithm for vehicle routing problem with time window with uncertain vehicle number. Intelligent Control and Automation. WCICA 2004. Fifth World Congress 4(15–19):2846–2849

Wang L, Zheng DZ (2001) An effective hybrid optimization strategy for job-shop scheduling problems. Comp Oper Res 28(6):585–596

Widrow B, Winter RG, Baxter RA (1988) Layered neural nets for pattern recognition. IEEE Trans Acoust Speech Signal Process 36(7):1109–1117

Index

(Q, r) inventory model, 461

aggregation, 215
Aisle Distance, 8
algorithm
    Weiszfeld, 85
Allocation, 249
    Multiple, 251
    Single, 249
Ant Colony Optimization, 538
    pheromone, 538
Arc Exclusion-Bounding Property, 212

back haul, 397
Big-O notation, 22
binary search, 208, 209
bisection search, 207
Block Distance, 9
bound matrix, 204, 206

Centrum, 195
Class-based dedicated storage location policy, 431
class-based storage location policy, 429, 446
Classification, 505
Classification scheme, 505
Classified on facilities, 94
Classified on the demand, 94
Classified on the physical space, or locations, 94
Combinatorial optimization, 535
Competitive Location Problem, 271
    Attraction Function, 278
    Competition with Foresight, 276
    Decision Space, 279
    Flow Capturing Location Allocation Problem, 288

Game Theories, 274
Gravity Problem, 280
Maximum Capture Problem, 283
Patronizing Behavior, 277
Point vs. Regional Demand, 277
Static Competition, 276
The Maximum Capture Problem with Price, 285
Complexity Classes, 28
    Class NP, 29
    Class NP-Hard, 34
    Class P, 28
    NP-complete, 31
Complexity Theory, 19
Computation models, 19
    Deterministic Turing Machine (DTM), 19
    non-deterministic turing machine (NTM), 19
    Oracle machine models, 19
Computational complexity theory, 19
conflicting objectives, 384
Continuous space models, 94
Contour lines, 74
Cooks theorem, 31
    $P = NP$ Problem, 31
    Satisfiability problem, 25
Covering models, 525
covering problems, 145
    coverage distance, 145
    Partial Covering, 145
    Total Covering, 145
Cube-per-order index, 429
customer has to be covered by only one facility, 96
customers, 93

Decision Problems, 25
Dedicated Storage Location Policy, 423, 446
demand partitioning, 529

545

demand point, 523
　aggregation, 523
　error, 523
Dependency Variable, 348
　Distance-dependent weight, 348
　Time-dependent weight, 348
depot, 396
Designing optimum routes, 328
　MRHT, 330
　OCST, 328
Deterministic change, 348
Discrete space models, 94
distance function, 6, 210
Distance Matrix, 8
distribution cost, 452
distribution network, 451
　customer, 452
　Distribution Centers, 451
　supplier, 452
Duration-of-Stay storage policy, 438
dynamic facility location problem, 347
　Dynamic P-median Model, 350
　Location, 347
　Location–Relocation, 347
　multiperiod location–allocation, 352
　Probabilistic Model, 353
　static location model, 349

Edge covering, 151
ellipses, 74
endogenous, 253, 259
Exogenous, 179, 193, 248, 249, 260

facilities, 93
facility hierarchy, 221
　successively exclusive, 221
　successively inclusive, 221
Facility location problem, 348
　dynamic, 348
　static, 348
facility's opening cost, 97
Family grouping, 446
Fixed Charge Facility Location
　　　Problem, 476
flow discipline, 221
　discriminating, 221
　integrated, 221
flow pattern, 221
　single-flow, 221
Floyd's algorithm, 207
Full Turn-over based storage, 433, 434

Gauges Measures, 10
General LA model, 95
general networks, 148
Genetic algorithm, 266, 535
　Crossover, 536
　Fitness Function, 536
　Mutation, 536
　selection for reproduction, 536
Grasp Algorithm, 173
gravity problem, 73
greedy, 215
　Plus (GrP), 215

Hamming Distance, 12
HAP, 85
Hausdorff Distance, 13
hierarchical, 219
Hilbert Curve, 11
hub, 243, 244
　capacitated, 257
　Center, 258
　Covering, 259
　discount factor, 250, 263
　Maximal Covering, 260
　Median, 251–253
　Set Covering, 259
　single, 247
hyperboloid approximation
　　　procedure, 85

Integrated Decision Making Models, 480
Intersection point, 211
Inventory cost, 298, 452
　lead time, 456
　Order cost, 459
　safety stock, 453

Lagrangian relaxation, 172, 454
less-than-truckload (LTL), 480
Levenshtein Distance, 12
Location-allocation, 93, 261
locations, 93
logistics cost, 451
Lower Bound, 125
　Bounds based on reformulations, 127
　Eigenvalue Related Bounds, 126
　Gilmore and Lawler lower bound, 126
　Semi-definite programming, 127
　Variance reduction bounds, 127
LRP, 399, 401
　Allocation–Routing–Location, 413
　layer diagram, 404

Index   547

    Location–Allocation–Routing, 412
    primary facilities, 404
    secondary facilities, 404

Mahalanobis Distance, 12
maximum covering, 193
maximum covering location problem, 157
maximum covering problem, 216
MCLP, 383
median problem, 177
    CPMP, 182
MFLP, 69
Minimal objective function value
    property, 206
Minimum Lengths Path, 9
minisum, 177
Model with Facility Failures, 493
Model with Multiple Commodities, 490
Model with Unreliable Supply, 491
multi-criteria decision-making, 373
Multi-Objective Combinatorial Optimization, 385
Multifacility location
    Euclidean Distance, 75
    MiniMax, 75
    on sphere, 78
    Rectangular Distance, 72
    Rectangular Multi Product, 77
    Squared Euclidean, 73
    Stochastic, 80
    with Rectangular Regions, 79
Multiple facility
    number of relocating facilities, 349

Network
    general graph, 195, 207
    tree, 195, 199
network, 243
    Access, 262, 263
    Backbone, 262, 263
    completely connected, 243
    connective, 244
    fully connected, 243
    hierarchical, 263
    multi hub, 244
    node, 243
Neural Networks, 540
    backpropagation, 541
    hidden layer, 541
non-hub node, 244
number of relocating facilities, 349
    Single facility, 349

number of relocations, 349
    Multiple relocation, 349
    Single relocation, 349

Obnoxious, 315
    Dispersion problems, 315
    multiobjective model, 337
    OFLR, 331
    Undesirable facilities problems, 315
operational decision, 451
origin-destination pair, 243

p-center problem, 193, 524
    absolute, 194
    Anti, 196
    Asymmetric, 196, 214
    capacitated, 198, 214
    Continuous, 196
    on circular arc graphs, 214
    vertex, 194
    with pos/neg weights, 196, 214
P-Median, 320
    Maxisum, 321
p-median problem, 524
pickup and delivery, 397
Point Single Facilities, 39
    Euclidean distance, 40
    lp-norm distance, 41
    rectilinear distance, 39
    square of the Euclidean distance, 40
Profit Maximizing Model, 488
Pull Objectives, 377
Push Objectives, 377
Push-Pull, 378
    Models, 380
    Objectives, 378

QAP
    Generalized Quadratic Assignment
        Problem, 123
    Multiobjective QAP, 121
    Quadratic semi-assignment problem, 121
    Quadratic Three-Dimensional Assignment
        Problem, 122
    Stochastic QAP, 124
    The biquadratic assignment problem, 120
    The quadratic bottleneck assignment, 120
Quadratic Assignment Problem, 111
quadratic facility location problem, 73
queue, 457

Randomized storage location policy, 444
Reduction, 25
    Linear reduction, 26
    Polynomial reduction, 26
    Polynomial reduction: many-one polynomially reducible, 26
Regional Facilities, 41
Relocation Time, 349
    Continuous, 349
    Discrete, 349
retailer, 473
retrieval
    decision, 440
    operation, 430
    policy, 421
    rate, 448
retrieval location, 428
risks, 324
    risk evaluation, 325
robust optimization, 495
route, 396

service hierarchy, 221
    globally inclusive, 221
    locally inclusive, 221
    successively exclusive, 221
    successively inclusive, 221
service variety, 221
    Nested, 221
    non-nested, 221
SFLP, 69
Shared storage policies, 437, 440
    Adaptive Shared Storage Policies, 441
    Static Shared Storage Policies, 441
Simulated Annealing, 539
    acceptance distribution, 540
    temperature, 539
single facility location problem, 69
Single Sourcing, 477
Software, 513
    S-Distance, 519
    LoLA, 515
    SITATION, 516
spanning tree, 215
Spatial aggregation, 525
spatial configuration, 221
    coherent, 221
spatial pattern, 221
    closest assignment, 221
    path assignment, 221
    single assignment, 221
spoke, 243
Squared Euclidean

Contour lines, 74
Stochastic change, 348
stochastic demands, 98
stochastic programming, 495
storage space, 425, 426
    requirement, 439
storage system layout, 422
    Storage Location Assignment Problem, 419, 422, 423, 436, 444, 448
strategic decision, 451
supplier, 473
supply allocation, 474
supply chain, 473
supply chain configuration, 474
Supply chain management, 473
Supply chain network design, 474
Supply chain operation, 474
Supply chain planning, 474
Supply chain strategy, 474

Tabu search, 537
    Aspiration criteria A(i), 538
    Diversification, 537
    Intensification, 537
    Long term memory, 537
    Tabu list $T(i)$, 537
tactical decision, 451
Taxonomy, 505
The network-based model, 94
three-tiered supply chain, 482
throughput, 421
    requirement, 427
Time Complexity, 24
    Constant Time, 24
    Exponential Time, 25
    Linear Time, 24
    Polynomial Time, 24
Time horizon, 349
    Finite, 349
    Infinite, 349
transportation problem, 297
tree networks, 165
trip, 400
    direct trip, 400
    tour trip, 400
TSP, 263

Uncapacitated, 246
uncertainty, 348
    future condition, 348
    limited knowledge, 348

Index 549

Variance of Distances, 11
Vertex and Intersection Point (VIP) Property, 212
VRP, 395, 398
    CVRP, 398
    DCVRP, 399
    VRPB, 399
    VRPBTW, 399
    VRPPD, 399
    VRPPDTW, 399
    VRPTW, 399

warehouse, 295
    shipment size, 296
warehouse layout, 447
warehouse location problem
    fixed installation cost, 296
    Limited capacity, 296
    Multi period, 296
    multiple product, 296
    Singe Period, 296
    single product, 296
    unlimited capacity, 296
    without fixed installation cost, 296